Cerebral Palsy

A DEVELOPMENTAL DISABILITY

Cerebral Palsy

A DEVELOPMENTAL DISABILITY

Third Revised Edition

William M. Cruickshank, Editor

Syracuse University Press 1976

Third Revised Edition 1976
>Second Printing 1978
>Third Printing 1980

Library of Congress Cataloging in Publication Data
Cruickshank, William M   ed.
>Cerebral palsy.

>Bibliography: p.
>Includes index.
>1. Cerebral palsy.   I. Title. [DNLM: 1. Cerebral
palsy—Rehabilitation. WS340 C412]
RC388.C7 1976   618.9'28'36   75-34275
ISBN 0-8156-2168-X

Manufactured in the United States of America

Preface

THE FIRST EDITION OF THIS BOOK, published in 1955 under the title *Cerebral Palsy: Its Individual and Community Problems,* was the first examination of cerebral palsy that brought together the viewpoints of the medical, psychological, therapeutic, social work, and rehabilitation professions. By placing the discussions of problems and methods of one professional group alongside those of others, we attempted to emphasize the community of understanding and insight which must be held by all who work with the cerebral palsied. This Third Revised Edition has been prepared in an effort to present the latest data on the assessment and treatment of cerebral palsy.

While cerebral palsy continues to be known as a distinct clinical entity, more and more it is being classified, both clinically and legislatively, as a member of a large class of developmental disabilities. The interrelationships between this specific central nervous system problem and others with related characteristics are now recognized.

This Third Revised Edition of *Cerebral Palsy* recognizes the relation of the problem to other developmental disabilities, but because of the uniqueness of the problems of cerebral palsy, the book focuses on this clinical issue alone. In the second edition of the book it was possible to include for the first time a chapter on visual disorders in relation to cerebral palsy. In this Third Revised Edition chapters on the neurophysiology of the problems of cerebral palsy and on dental problems have been added, along with a chapter focusing on the role and problems of interdisciplinary function, an essential concept in cerebral palsy treatment and education, and new material on mental retardation, hearing and communication problems and skills, and family process.

Perhaps no other aspect of the total field of disability has received such marked attention in the past three decades as has cerebral palsy. As a result, many professional schools have developed programs for the preparation of different types of workers in the field. To increase this edition's usefulness as a general textbook in such programs, some materials from the earlier editions of *Cerebral Palsy* have been rearranged for easier access by the student, both within individual chapters and within the book as a whole.

The reader will readily observe that the habilitation or rehabilitation problem for the cerebral palsied is a complicated one. Cerebral palsy presents a problem to professional people quite different from that considered by most other groups of exceptional children. No other single group of children demands the services of so many different professions in the habilitation process. Thus interprofessional understanding of the common problem is essential. Therapists need to understand the educator. Educators must know basic concepts of medical aspects of the problem. The psychologist must be sympathetic to the points of view of the therapists. The dentist, medical specialist, social worker, nurse, and dietician must know the essential features of cerebral palsy as it affects the professional colleagues with whom they work. If this text continues to bring about a better "meeting of the minds" among those concerned with cerebral palsy, its purpose is served.

Since the original edition of this work appeared, many early leaders in the field of cerebral palsy have died. Drs. Winthrop Morgan Phelps, George Deaver, and Temple Fay head a list of medical scientists and practitioners who struggled for years to bring cerebral palsy to the attention of their peers and to have it accepted as a complicated medical and community problem. Much of what is included by the contributing authors in this Third Revised Edition is directly or indirectly related to the broad and continuous stimulation which the problem received from others. Phelps, Deaver, and Fay were also important in the early discussions and actions which led to the formation of the American Academy for Cerebral Palsy, an organization which has moved rapidly to bring the complex problems of cerebral palsy to professional consciousness.

The work of a few has become that of many. Directly or indirectly the efforts of the leaders of the 1940s have resulted in such remarkable organizations as the United Cerebral Palsy Association, Inc., with its state associations and local chapters in many parts of the United States. The American Academy for Cerebral Palsy, bridged by a splendid professional publication to the English Spastics Society Ltd., a powerful professional force, evolved from a gleam in the eyes of Phelps, Fay, Deaver, and their associates. A world-wide interest in and professional attack on cerebral palsy is now the nature of things.

In a book that is a broad survey of the problems related to cerebral palsy, each discussion is necessarily brief. A comprehensive Bibliography, listing all references cited in the text, can be found at the back of the book as a guide to the student.

I wish to express my gratitude to the individual contributing authors for all the vital and painstaking work evident in this Third Revised Edition. Thanks are also due to the members of the Syracuse University Instructional Communications Center for assistance in the preparation of certain illustrative and tabular material for the second edition, some of which is contained herein. Lawrence Lewandowski provided much assistance in readying the manuscript for the publisher. Miss Kirsten Lietz, Librarian, Training Resources Center, and the staff of the Word Processing Center, Institute for the Study of Mental Retardation and Related Disabilities, University of Michigan, have likewise been of remarkable assistance to me. Mrs. Edwena Creason, Miss Joyce Jacobson, Mrs. Christine Ruby, Mrs. Erika Wonn, and Mrs. M. Frances Ingram have assisted in innumerable ways in their capacities as secretaries to the Editor.

William M. Cruickshank

University of Michigan
Ann Arbor, Michigan
Fall, 1975

Contributing Authors

Harry V. Bice, Ph.D., was formerly Clinical Psychologist with the New Jersey State Department of Health, assigned to the Department of Special Education, Jersey City State College, and also formerly Psychologist with the New Jersey Crippled Children's Commission, Trenton, New Jersey.

Julius S. Cohen, Ed.D., is Professor of Education, School of Education, and Deputy Director, Institute for the Study of Mental Retardation and Related Disabilities, University of Michigan, Ann Arbor, Michigan.

William M. Cruickshank, Ph.D., is Professor of Maternal and Child Health, School of Public Health; Professor of Education, School of Education; and Professor of Psychology, Department of Psychology, College of Literature, Science and the Arts; and Director, Institute for the Study of Mental Retardation and Related Disabilities, University of Michigan, Ann Arbor, Michigan.

Richard E. Darnell, Ph.D., is Assistant Professor of Physical Therapy, Department of Physical Medicine and Rehabilitation, Medical School; and Program Director for Physical Therapy, Institute for the Study of Mental Retardation and Related Disabilities, University of Michigan, Ann Arbor, Michigan.

Eric Denhoff, M.D., is Medical Director of the Meeting Street School, Children's Rehabilitation Hospital; Director, Governor Medical Center; Chief of Pediatrics of Miriam Hospital; and Clinical Professor of Pediatrics, Brown University, Providence, Rhode Island.

Edward T. Donlon, Ed.D., is Director of the Clay Learning Center, Ashland, Alabama, and is Visiting Professor of Education, Talladega College, Talladega, Alabama.

Bernard Farber, Ph.D., is Professor of Sociology, Arizona State University, Tempe, Arizona.

Herbert J. Grossman, M.D., is Director, Illinois State Pediatric Institute; Professor of Neurology and Pediatrics, Rush Medical College; Professor of Pediatrics (Neurology), Abraham Lincoln School of Medicine, and Professor of Health Care Services, School of Public Health, University of Illinois; and Professor of Psychology, University of Illinois, Chicago Circle, Illinois.

Daniel P. Hallahan, Ph.D., is Assistant Professor of Special Education, University of Virginia, Charlottesville, Virginia.

Henry L. Kanar, D.D.S., M.S., is Assistant Professor of Pedodontics, School of Dentistry; and Program Director for Dentistry, Institute for the Study of Mental Retardation and Related Disabilities, University of Michigan, Ann Arbor, Michigan.

Rosalia A. Kiss, O.T.R., Ph.D., is Professor Emeritus and former Head of the Occupational Therapy Department, Western Michigan University, Kalamazoo, Michigan.

Ruth M. Lencione, Ph.D., is Professor of Speech Pathology, Division of Special Education and Rehabilitiation, Syracuse University, Syracuse, New York.

Michelle A. Melyn, M.D., is Assistant Professor of Neurology and Pediatrics, Rush Medical College; and Assistant Professor of Pedodontics, University of Illinois College of Dentistry, Chicago, Illinois.

E. Harris Nober, Ph.D., is Professor of Audiology and Chairman of the Department of Communication Disorders, University of Massachusetts, Amherst, Massachusetts.

Robert M. Segal, Ph.D., M.S.W., is Associate Professor of Social Work, School of Social Work, and Program Director for Social Work, Institute for the Study of Mental Retardation and Related Disabilities, University of Michigan, Ann Arbor, Michigan.

Andrew T. Shotick, Ph.D., is Associate Professor, Division for Exceptional Children, College of Education, University of Georgia, Athens, Georgia.

Esther Snell, Ed.D., R.P.R., is Director of the Lubbock Cerebral Palsy and Neuro-Muscular Center, Lubbock, Texas.

Contents

List of Figures

List of Tables

Cerebral Palsy

A DEVELOPMENTAL DISABILITY

1

The Problem and Its Scope

WILLIAM M. CRUICKSHANK

CEREBRAL PALSY PRESENTS a problem or a series of problems far more complicated than those typical of most other types of physical disabilities. This is true not only in terms of the many factors coincident with etiological considerations, but also in terms of the diversity of form and the many degrees of impairment which may be present in any group of cerebral palsied persons. The concept of individual differences nowhere is more meaningful than when one considers the cerebral palsied population. The problem of cerebral palsy in our culture is at one and the same time medical, psychological, sociological, and economic. To discuss cerebral palsy in any one of the above aspects without consideration of the others is to lose sight of the problem as a whole. Similarly, unless the community considers cerebral palsy in its totality as local- or state-supported treatment and rehabilitation centers are established, cerebral palsied individuals are unjustly served.

DEFINITION

The complexity of the problem makes definition difficult, and authorities do not entirely agree on a definition of cerebral palsy. Denhoff (1951) has organized an excellent series of working definitions which he conceives in three parts—a standard definition, a limited definition, and a practical definition. As a *standard definition* he refers to Perlstein (1949), who said that cerebral palsy is generally defined as a "condition, characterized by paralysis, weakness, incoordination, or any other aberration of motor function due to pathology of the motor control centers of the brain." Herein cerebral palsy is defined solely in terms of its physical components. A still more *limited definition* of cerebral palsy is one wherein it is conceived as "a condition in which interferences with the control of the motor system arise as a result of lesions occurring from birth trauma." This definition may be criticized from two points of view: namely, (1) cerebral palsy is more than merely a "motor" problem, and (2) cerebral palsy, etiologically speaking, is not limited to birth trauma alone. Thus, the *practical definition* referred to above warrants serious consideration. From such a point of view cerebral palsy is seen as one component of a broader brain-damage syndrome comprised of neuro-motor dysfunction, psychological dysfunction, convulsions, or behavior disorders of organic origin. In some cerebral palsied individuals only a single factor may appear; other individuals may be characterized by any combination of the factors mentioned. Closely related to the above definition is that of Swartz (1951) and his associates, who believe that cerebral palsy should be defined as an aggregate of handicaps: emotional, neuromuscular, special sensory, and peripheral sensory, caused by damaged or absent brain structures. These latter definitions appear to be more nearly in harmony with the reality of the situation.

Denhoff, in discussing the practical definition, includes mental retardation as a separate charateristic of the syndrome. The present writer has chosen to substitute a reference to *psychological dysfunction* rather than to limit the concept to mental retardation alone. It is true, as will be later discussed, that the incidence of mental retardation is great among the cerebral palsied population. It is also true that numerous psychological problems are to be found coexistent with cerebral palsy in addition to mental retardation. Thus, in the present consideration, problems of mental retardation are included within the reference to more inclusive psychological dysfunction.

It is probably appropriate to make some reference to cerebral palsy defined as a condition (as Perlstein stated) and to cerebral palsy as a disease. If the term "disease" is considered in its strict meaning as a "deviation," as an abnormal state or perversion of function, then cerebral palsy can be correctly defined as a disease. The word *disease* however, has taken on numerous meanings other than that of *deviation,* and thus rarely in current literature is cerebral palsy spoken of as a disease. The later meanings which have been attached to the concept of disease have been culturally negative in their connotations. Parents of cerebral palsied children, the cerebral palsied individuals themselves, and the professional workers engaged in this field have attempted to place cerebral palsy in its best light and thus have avoided the term "disease." They have spoken of cerebral palsy as a "condition." Such is certainly correct, although perhaps misleading. As a disease, cerebral palsy is not progressive; nor is it contagious or epidemic in form. As a neurophysical and neuropsychological *deviation,* however, it is basically a disease. Cerebral palsy has been spoken of as a "long-term, non-fatal, non-curable disease." It is non-curable, but oftentimes amenable to therapy and training. It is nonfatal *per se*. Crothers and Paine (1959) state:

"The term cerebral palsy does not designate a disease in any usual medical sense. It is, however, a useful administrative term which covers individuals who are handicapped by motor disorders which are due to non-progressive abnormalities of the brain."

HISTORICAL BACKGROUND

More than one hundred years ago William Little, Senior Physician to the London Hospital and also founder of the Royal Orthopaedic Hospital, stated that the "foetus in utero was subjected to diseases similar to that which affect the economy at later periods of existence, this being particularly true as regards diformities" (Little 1853). Somewhat later Little presented a paper before the Obstetrical Society of London, a paper of monumental significance entitled, "The Influence of Abnormal Parturition, Difficult Labor, Premature Birth, and Asphyxia in Relation to Diformities" (Little 1862). In that paper he indicated that some babies he had observed were likely to be characterized by a "spastic rigidity" of the limbs. He worried that physicians of his time still appeared unaware that abnormal parturition, in addition to resulting in death or recovery of the infant, might also produce orthopedic disabilities of various degrees. Little had studied approximately two hundred cases, and from these he felt that asphyxia neonatorum could be the cause of what he termed "paralytic contractions of the limbs." He also noticed that in some of his patients, i.e., congenital cases, there was a common accompaniment of contracture which resulted in the inability of the infant or child to use a limb. In a still earlier paper he described a number of traits which he had observed: "An impairment of intellectual powers, which may be slight or great, great irritability, occasional epilepsy, ungovernable temper, cunning and hebetude." In several instances he observed "the intellectual weakeness appears to result less from permanent injury to the brain than from the want of sufficient training and education" (Little 1853).

It is indeed quite remarkable how long-standing are the observations of Little, so clear cut as to make it possible to label his observations as Little's Disease, a term applied to cerebral palsy until the latter term came into general use, particularly in the United States, in the early 1940s. Little, however, established the fundamental approach to the treatment and management of cerebral palsy as we know it today. In this new syndrome Little recognized the most common causes; he saw the need to establish a conservative approach to the establishment of appropriate movement; and he recognized that often such movement could be facilitated by appropriate surgery. Little also recognized the deficiencies which his patients demonstrated in the areas of cognition, appropriate behavior, and learning deficits. The reader will note that with the publication of the present edition of this book many of the topics which Little outlined form the basis of complete chapters. Denhoff has pointed out that there was a long list of physicians who had an influence on Little's thinking and insights. Hippocrates, in the fourth and fifth centuries B.C., established the importance of splints and exercise. Galen, the famous physician of the first century (A.D. 130–201), discovered what we now recognize as neuromuscular physiology, and two centuries later, still fifteen hundred years before Little wrote on these subjects, Antyllus practiced subcutaneous osteotomy. Massage was established as a significant factor in India around A.D. 700. From Hippocrates, medical literature traces the use of braces and splints into Chinese, Hindu, and Egyptian cultures, and they were known to have common application through the Greek and Roman societies.

Other milestones should be mentioned as significant in the development of medical and related types of therapeutic interventions, namely the work of Ambrose Pari with bracing in the fourteenth and sixteenth centuries, the perfection of bracing through the use of metals, leather, and wood by Andry and Venel in the eighteenth century; and the remarkable contributions to this effort by both Von Heine of Wurzburg and Thomas of Liverpool in the nineteenth century. Today the brace-maker and the brace shop are parts of all good orthopedic services.

But others also had their influence on modern-day thinking about cerebral palsy. In the early part of the twentieth century (1910–30) both Lovett and Wright in Boston, MacKenzie in Australia, and Hughling-Jackson in London (Bick 1968) illustrated the values of muscle re-education. While Galen early was concerned with nerve surgery, nerve suture was initially performed by Saliceto during the thirteenth century. By 1880, post-traumatic nerve suture was a relatively common medical practice. Others were important too in pioneering surgical techniques which make possible modern-day surgical practices: Foerster (early 1900s) with the introduction of ramisectomy; Hunter and Royle (1924) with ganglionectomy; Lorenz 1891) with obturator nerve resection to relieve adductor spasm; Stoeffel (1911) with neurectomy; Hacker (1908) and Steindler (1915) with nerve implantation; and Putnam with sectioning of the extrapyramidal tract of the spinal cord (Denhoff and Robinault 1960). Sigmund Freud, in an aspect of his medical career usually unknown to modern-day scholars, was stimulated by Little's work, and wrote several papers on paralytic disorders of children; in 1897, in his text, *Infantile Cerebral Paralysis,* he conclusively stated that the cerebral palsies were not the result of encephalitis alone, but were more often the result of congenital and perinatal complications. Additional neurological data was provided by others which included Cazauvielh (1827), Lallemand, Turch, Cotard, Kundrat, Benedickt, and others, all in the nineteenth century. The foundations were laid for the writings and points of view of William Little as the nineteenth century was concluded. Then such contemporary physicians as Temple Fay, Winthrop Morgan Phelps, George Deaver, and Meyer Perlstein brought the medical knowledge of cerebral palsy to its present level of understanding and also, particularly Phelps, stimulated those in other disciplines to turn their attention on this complicated problem.

THE INTERDISCIPLINARY NATURE OF THE PROBLEM

In a subsequent chapter Darnell will point out the absolute necessity for the interdisciplinary team in the treatment and management of cerebral palsy. This book also emphasizes the necessity of the multivariant dimension of this disease entity. Although because of space limitations it is not discussed in this volume in any extensive manner, pharmacologic therapy and psychopharmacology are necessary adjuncts in a total therapeutic regimen. In similar vein speech and language pathology, occupational therapy, physical therapy, as well as psychology and education are inherent elements in any good program for cerebral palsied children. The nature of this book underscores the multidisciplinary as well as the interdisciplinary nature of the complex human program of cerebral palsy, a concept which Little sensed in his work (see also Cruickshank and Hallahan 1975).

CEREBRAL PALSY AND LEARNING DISABILITIES

Beginning about 1940 professional attention was dramatically focused on the perceptual and learning disabilities of children with diagnosed or suspected neurological problems. Although the antecedents of this development have been traced as far back as Gall (1828), the primary impetus to this thinking was the result of the work of Strauss, a neuropsychiatrist turned special educator, and Heinz Werner, a well-known developmental and comparative psychologist—both emigrants from Nazi Germany to the United States. From their work, first published in the late 1930s and the early 1940s, subsequently came the writings of Kephart (perceptual disorders), Cruickshank (psychopathology of brain injured and hyperactive children), Kirk (language disorders), and Doll (cerebral palsy without mental retardation). In 1963 the term "learning disability" was first utilized widely. This term is hard to define and is so misused that it is practically useless. However, the term does have some meaning if it is seen as the outgrowth of perceptual problems which in turn are, of course, based in the neurological system of the organism. Clements suggested another term, i.e., "minimal cerebral dysfunction," to separate children with perceptual and learning disabilities from those with gross motor problems of cerebral palsy. The value of this latter term is questionable, since when the problems occur in children with or without gross motor problems, the issues are hardly minimal.

However, in 1957 and later in 1965, Cruickshank and Bice and their colleagues demonstrated that most of the problems of perception and perceptual-motor development which Strauss, Werner, and others had seen in exogenous forms of mental retardation were also present in the great majority of cerebral palsy children of the athetoid and spastic subtypes. On the basis of these findings psychoeducational systems of intervention have been developed and can be further refined to meet the needs of the cerebral palsied child.

CEREBRAL PALSY AND DEVELOPMENTAL DISABILITY

Since 1970 the term "developmental disability" has come into common usage. While the term has never been adequately defined, except by listing categories of clinical problems related to it, it nevertheless describes a total group of disabilities generally associated with the neurological system. Defined nationally via federal legislation in the early 1970s on developmental disabilities, the term includes mental retardation and numerous neurological problems such as epilepsy, cerebral palsy, aphasia, and similar clinical entities. The word *developmental* appears to connote long-term if not life-span problems, and does serve to call attention to the fact that the issue has to be faced at all developmental stages in the human. It is just as much a problem of old age and maturity as it is one of infancy and childhood. In our society, however, significant problems of human development are lost to view if they become too amalgamated with other issues, practical as this trend may appear. There are important political, social, scientific, and educational reasons for keeping the concept of cerebral palsy in the forefront of national thought just as there is for mental retardation, epilepsy, and other related disabilities.

Spastic Paralysis

The term "spastic paralysis" has been mistakenly but nevertheless widely used when speaking of cerebral palsy. The literature is filled with references to spastic paralysis wherein the term is applied not only to the spastic monoplegias, paraplegias, hemiplegias, and quadriplegias, but is as well applied to individuals who demonstrate athetoid and ataxic movements. The term is incorrect in many respects. In the first place, as has just been pointed out, *spastic* is inappropriate when considering the other forms of cerebral palsy, i.e., athetoid, ataxic, rigidity, tremor, and mixed forms. Secondly, not all cerebral palsied patients demonstrate actual paralysis. It must be pointed out that in many countries outside the United States, the term "spastic" is widely used to connote the total cerebral palsy problem. In England, for example, The Spastic Society functions in a national leadership role, and the term is widely used there by most professional persons.

INCIDENCE

Completely accurate reports regarding the incidence of cerebral palsy in the total population are not available. There are several reasons for this. Cerebral palsy, while appearing in medical literature as early as 1862, was in large measure ignored as a medical problem. Certainly, until the 1940s, it was ignored as a psychological or a social problem. Winthrop M. Phelps (1950) whose writings and work were largely responsible for an interest in cerebral palsy in the United States, estimated that there would be approximately seven cerebral palsied individuals of all ages per 100,000 population. Despite the work of Phelps and others, cerebral palsy was largely considered to be a stigma by parents, and thus numerous cases remained unreported. Beginning at the close of World War II, parents of cerebral palsied children became exceedingly active in national, state, and local groups, and their children were for the most part no longer hidden. Thus, since 1945 much more accurate studies of the incidence of the problem have been made, but for reasons mentioned above and for others, the results of the studies vary and as yet a truly accurate picture is lacking. It is an even more elusive problem now that cerebral palsy is often included with other developmental disabilities.

Gross Incidence

In 1949, the New York State Departments of Health, Education, Mental Hygiene, and Social Welfare jointly participated in a survey of cerebral palsy in Schenectady County, New York. This survey was one of the earliest and most comprehensive investigations ever undertaken in a limited geographical area for the purpose of ascertaining the prevalence of cerebral palsy and problems related to it. The results of this survey indicated that the incidence of the disease in that county was 5.9 per 1,000 births and that the prevalence was 152 per 100,000 population. On the basis there would be a minimum of 22,000 persons with cerebral palsy in New York State, as noted in Table 1.1.

The Schenectady County Survey further indicated that 9.0 percent of the cerebral palsy patients required no services; 64.1 percent needed services on an ambulatory basis; 8.3 percent required prolonged medical treatment at a hospital-school; and 18.8 percent of the patients needed cus-

TABLE 1.1
NUMBER OF CEREBRAL PALSIED PERSONS IN EACH AGE GROUP ESTIMATED FOR
SCHENECTADY COUNTY AND NEW YORK STATE, 1949

Age Group	Percentage of Cases Schenectady County	Estimated Number New York State
Under 5 years	16	3,250
5-9 years	28	6,160
10-14 years	17	3,740
15-19 years	8	1,760
20-24 years	13	2,860
25-34 years	9	1,980
35 years and above	9	1,980
Total	100	22,000

From Perlstein, "Medical Aspects of Cerebral Palsy," *Nervous Child* **8** (1949).

todial or institutional placement. A later report, however, in referring to the Schenectady survey, states that the number of "known cases of cerebral palsy obtained from every possible source, including the mandatory reporting of cerebral palsied patients in upstate New York which became compulsory January 1, 1950, nowhere near approaches this figure of 22,000. During the reporting years 1950, 1951, and 1952, a total of 3,076 cases of cerebral palsy were reported in upstate New York exclusive of reports received from State institutions."

Many reasons are indicated to account for the discrepancy between the expected number and the actual reported incidence. The report nevertheless states that "the available reports should represent a very large percentage of the cerebral palsied patients in need of service at the present time (1953)." The legislative report further goes on to state, "It is evident that the 22,000 cases of cerebral palsy estimated . . . as a result of the Schenectady County Survey is on the high side." Asher and Schonell (1950) reporting on a school-aged population from four large English communities, report an incidence of 1.0 per 1,000 children. This is considerably below the estimate of Phelps, but it compares favorably with Mackintosh, who estimates 1.2 per 1,000 children of school age in Scotland.

The English and Scottish figures are also considerably below the actual findings and the estimated prevalence of cerebral palsy in the State of Connecticut. This study, completed in 1950, reports the rates per 100,000 population as follows: under five years of age, 148.1; between five and nine years, 274.6; between ten and fourteen years, 291.1; and between fifteen and nineteen years, 198.8. The total incidence under twenty-one years of age in this survey was 228.6 per 100,000. It is difficult under any circumstance to obtain accurate epidemiological or demographic data on cerebral palsy. Hospital records are notoriously inaccurate, and parents often decline to report handicapped children. The problem is apparently worldwide. In 1967, Zivkovic *et al.* reported a Yugoslav study which included 284 children with cerebral palsy. The authors state that "it is of particular interest to mention that around fourteen percent of the total number of subjects had not been reported until the study" was undertaken, "or else had not been diagnosed as suffering from cerebral palsy."

However, with reference to the Connecticut study mentioned above, because the number of children incorrectly diagnosed as cerebral palsied was not known, corrections were made in the statistics on the basis of an arbitrary formula. When this was done, the prevalence for children under twenty-one years of age was revised downward considerably to a rate somewhere between a minimum of 155 and a maximum of 180 per 100,000 population. In the Schenectady County study, a ratio of seven unknown to every ten known cases of cerebral palsy was applied in attempting to ascertain the "true" prevalence rate. If this same procedure is followed in the case of the Connecticut study, a rate of between 265 and 310 per 100,000 population is obtained. The "true" prevalence in the Schenectady County study when this formula was utilized was 350 per 100,000. Thus, one can see the basis of the comment referred to above taken from the 1953 legislative report to the extent that the Schenectady County figures may be considerably higher than actual fact. Reference was made above to Phelps's estimate of seven cases of cerebral palsy born to every 100,000 population. Phelps further stated that of this group one-seventh of the children die within the first six years of life. Since at the time Phelps made this estimate the birth rate in his population was 15 per 1,000, mortality rate would result in a prevalence of four per 1,000 live births. Utilizing Phelps's data as a base, the variability of the English estimates on the one hand and the Connecticut and New York estimates on the other hand is exceedingly great.

Henderson has added some important data regarding the prevalence of cerebral palsy according to chronological age. In a 1955 study of children with cerebral palsy in the eastern region of Scotland, Henderson (1961) found fifty cerebral palsy children between the ages of zero and four years in four counties with a population of 32,400 people (prevalence 1.54); between the ages of five and fourteen years, 133 children in counties with a population of 65,000 persons (prevalence 2.04); and 37 cerebral palsy individuals between the ages of fifteen and eighteen years with a prevalence rate of 1.58 in a population of 23,400. Henderson further summarizes a large number of prevalence studies done in various localities in England, Scotland, and Wales as shown on Table 1.2.

TABLE 1.2
PREVALENCE STUDIES

Study	Date	Percentage Athetoid	Spastic	Incidence Athetoid and Spastic Mixed	Ataxic Rigidity etc.	Total
Brockway (U.S.A.)	1936	8		92		100
McIntire (U.S.A.)	1938	36	36	5	23	100
Phelps (U.S.A.)	1940	40	40	3	17	100
Phelps (U.S.A.)	1942	40	40		20	100
Phelps (U.S.A.)	1942	45	40		15	100
Phelps (U.S.A.)	1945-6	45	40		15	100
Dunsdon (England & Wales)						
a. Special Schools	1952	13.0		81.0	6.0	100
b. Special Inquiry Area	1952	7.8		82.7	9.5	100
c. Average Dunsdon		10.4		81.85	7.75	100

Adapted with permission, Dunsdon, *Educability of Cerebral Palsied Children*, pp. 14-15.

"In this study [the Henderson study] the prevalence was found to be 2.04 per 100 children of school age, the age period at which true prevalence can be most accurately assessed."

Griffiths and Bassett (1967) presented some additional information. Utilizing a population of children in the vicinity of Birmingham, England, they studied 441 cerebral palsied children born between January 1, 1948, and December 31, 1963. They report that the incidence of cerebral palsy is generally stated to be 1.5 per 1000 live births. Their data support this figure, though some year-to-year fluctuation is apparent. Prematurity and low birth weight are seen by these authors as causal factors in approximately 42 percent of the cases studied. Asphyxia was present in over 60 percent of the cases of spastic tetraplegia and athetosis without deafness. "Birth injury was reported almost exclusively in spastic hemiplegia (16 percent) and te-traplegia (36 percent)." Thirteen cases are reported with acquired hydro-cephalus, presumably described as caused by cerebral hemorrhage. Ker-nicterus is reported in all cases of athetosis with deafness in "half the pre-mature infants who developed dystonic athetosis." It is also reported in one-seventh of the cases of premature infants who developed spastic diplegia, but the authors did not consider that it was likely to be an etio-logical factor.

The effects of cerebral palsy of interest to the authors are the in-telligence and educational levels and employment placement. Table 1.3, re-lated to material presented in Chapter 4, gives the intelligence levels of 182 of the Griffiths and Bassett population as tested on the Terman-Merrill

TABLE 1.3
IQs in 182 Patients Tested on the Terman-Merrill Scale

Type of cerebral palsy	Cases	Average or above (80 +)		Educationally subnormal (60–80)		Ineducable (−60)	
		No.	%	No.	%	No.	%
Spastic							
Hemiplegia	46	37	80	7	15	2	5
Simple diplegia	41	32	78	7	17	2	5
Tetraplegia	48	7	16	7	16	34	68
Athetosis	46	23	50	9	20	14	30

From Griffiths and Bassett, "Cerebral Palsy in Birmingham," 41.

Scale. The authors state that if the incidence of cerebral palsy remains constant, "present provision (in England) of school places will remain just adequate." On the other hand, because working life is estimated at three times the length of school life, "it appears that there will be a steadily increasing demand for special facilities for employment over the next thirty years." The authors refute a growing notion that the incidence of cerebral palsy is declining and suggest that "simplification of the nomenclature and classification is a possible method of clarifying the problems of causation."

Incidence by Type

Much more accurate information is available with respect to the incidence of cerebral palsy in the several major types of the disease. Dunsdon (1952) has collected data from which Table 1.2 has been prepared. This table indicates the incidence of cerebral palsy by type in several United States populations and in two populations from England and Wales. Dunsdon reports an average percentage incidence of 10.4 athetoids; 81.85 spastic and mixed; and 7.75 ataxic and others.

Additional information has been supplied by Hopkins, Bice, and Colton (1954), based upon a 1951 survey in the State of New Jersey. Their study of 1,406 cerebral palsied individuals reports 45.1 percent, spastic; 23.6 percent, athetoid; 12.5 percent, rigidity; 10.8 percent, ataxic; 3.4 percent, mixed; 1.9 percent, tremor; and 1.7 percent, rare cases. While direct comparisons cannot be made, the data relative to spastics compare favorably with the later studies of Phelps noted in Table 1.4. Because of category differences, direct comparisons cannot be made. The percentage of athetoids reported by Phelps differs markedly from that of Hopkins and his associates. Comparing these data with that of Dunsdon, one also notes great differences in the percentage of athetoid patients reported. Dunsdon, in Table 1.4, reports 10.4 percent athetoids; the 1951 New Jersey study,

TABLE 1.4
Distribution of Cerebral Palsy by Type

Study	Date	Percentage Athetoid	Spastic	Incidence Athetoid and Spastic Mixed	Ataxic Rigidity etc.	Total
Brockway (U.S.A.)	1936	8		92		100
McIntire (U.S.A.)	1938	36	36	5	23	100
Phelps (U.S.A.)	1940	40	40	3	17	100
Phelps (U.S.A.)	1942	40	40		20	100
Phelps (U.S.A.)	1942	45	40		15	100
Phelps (U.S.A.)	1945–46	45	40		15	100
Dunsdon (England & Wales)						
a. Special Schools	1952	13.0		81.0	6.0	100
b. Special Inquiry Area	1952	7.8		82.7	9.5	100
c. Average Dunsdon		10.4		81.85	7.75	100

Adapted with permission from Dunsdon, *Educability of Cerebral Palsied Children*, pp. 14–15.

23.6 percent. The more recent study by Henderson provides some additional data, more supportive of the Dunsdon study than that of the New Jersey investigators. In the Henderson (1961) study involving 240 cases of cerebral palsy, 188 children were spastic (78.3 percent); 18 were athetoid (7.5 percent).

Incidence by Sex

Dunsdon reports a sex distribution on 575 cerebral palsied children from England and Wales. Within this number she finds 51 percent males; 49 percent females. The more complete report of Hopkins and his associates, which included 1,406 children, indicates 57.0 percent males; 43.0 percent females. Table 1.5 illustrates the incidence of males and females by classification and indicates a marked similarity of distribution for the two groups.

Incidence in Terms of Degree of Involvement

The New Jersey study provides further information which is extremely valuable as a backdrop to the discussions in the later chapters of this volume. Bice, Hopkins, and Colton have provided a breakdown of their data in terms of the extent of the involvement. These data are presented in Table 1.6. Dunsdon presents similar data with regard to the spastic classification only. Among her group of 780 cases of cerebral palsy, 37 percent were spastic quadriplegias; 26 percent spastic paraplegias; and 13 percent spastic

TABLE 1.5
CLASSIFICATION BY SEX AND TYPE OF CEREBRAL PALSY AS REPORTED IN
THE 1951 NEW JERSEY STUDY

Type	Boys		Girls	
	Number	Per Cent	Number	Per Cent
Spastic	374	46.6	271	44.8
Athetoid	192	23.7	141	23.3
Rigidity	96	11.9	81	13.4
Ataxia	95	11.8	57	9.4
Tremor	10	1.2	17	2.8
Mixed Cases	24	2.9	24	3.9
Rare Cases	11	1.3	13	2.1
Total (1,406)	802	100.00	604	100.0

From Hopkins, Bice, and Colton, *Evaluation and Education of the Cerebral Palsied Child*,
p. 1.

hemiplegias. These data cannot be directly compared with the New Jersey
study since the Dunsdon percentages are with reference to the total population of 760 cases, whereas the New Jersey percentages shown in Table 1.5
are with reference to the total number of cases within each category. When
one computes the percentages of the subtypes of spastics in the New Jersey
study and compares then with the England-Wales study of Dunsdon, one is
struck by the marked differences. In the New Jersey study there were 11.3
percent spastic quadriplegias; 21.2 percent spastic hemiplegias; and 8.8 percent spastic paraplegias. The large differences which appear between the
Dunsdon studies on the one hand and the several American studies on the
other hand cannot be accounted for by this writer. Dunsdon herself noted
the differences between her figures and those of other authors but made no
effort to account for them. Differences in diagnostic procedures, in
classification problems, or in general methodological procedures employed
in the studies may account for the disparity in results. The fact of an actual
difference in incidence between the countries involved does not escape the
present writer, although such is seriously questioned by him.

The Henderson study does not assist much in the solution of the
differences which have been noted. Only the data relating to spastic-type cerebral palsy are appropriate here, for a different classification system was
used in reporting the athetoid subjects. Of the 188 spastics, however, 12
were monoplegic (5.0 percent); 89 hemiplegic (37.1 percent); 3 double
hemiplegic (1.3 percent); 29 paraplegic (12.1 percent); 9 triplegic (3.8 percent); and 46 tetraplegic (19.2 percent). Although there is a much smaller
number of subjects in the Henderson study, the abovementioned
percentages vary considerably from those reported by the New Jersey study
and included in Table 1.6.

TABLE 1.6

INCIDENCE BY SUBTYPES IN THE 1951 NEW JERSEY STUDY

	Classification																
	Spastic						Athetoid						Rigidity					
Subtype	B	%	G	%	T	%	B	%	G	%	T	%	B	%	G	%	T	%
Quadriplegia	99	26.4	61	22.5	160	24.8	172	89.5	120	85.1	292	87.6	51	53.1	37	45.6	88	49.7
Triplegia	32	8.8	23	8.1	55	8.5	1	.5	1	.7	2	.6	2	2.0	5	6.1	7	3.9
R. Hemiplegia	94	25.1	63	23.2	157	24.3	8	4.1	12	8.5	20	6.0	26	27.0	17	20.9	43	24.2
L. Hemiplegia	82	21.9	60	22.1	142	21.8	8	4.1	7	4.9	15	4.5	15	15.6	15	18.5	30	16.9
Paraplegia	63	16.8	61	22.1	124	19.2	2	1.0	1	.7	3	.9	2	2.0	7	8.6	9	5.0
Monoplegia	4	.1	3	1.1	7	.5	1	.5			1	.4						
Totals	374		271		645		192		141		333		96		81		177	

Adapted by permission, Council for Exceptional Children from Hopkins, Bice, and Colton, *Evaluation and Education of the Cerebral Palsied Child*, p. 2.

93 boys or 97.8 percent of a total of 95 ataxias were quadriplegic: 57 ataxic girls or 100 percent were quadriplegic. Two boys or 2.1 percent of a total of 95 boys were triplegic ataxias.

TABLE 1.7

INCIDENCE AND ETIOLOGY OF CEREBRAL PALSY IN THE
1951 NEW JERSEY STUDY, N = 1,105

Etiology	Number	Per Cent	Etiology	Number	Per Cent
Birth injury	430	38.9	Hydrocephalic basis	15	1.3
Developmental	315	28.5	Postoperative	9	.8
Postconvulsive	103	9.3	Postnatal toxemia	3	.3
Prematurity	90	8.1	Postembolic	2	.2
Postinfectious	42	3.8	Hyperpyrexia	2	.2
Cerebral anoxia	41	3.7	Petechial hemorrhage	1	.1
Rh Factor	29	2.6	Hemorrhagic disease	1	.1
Postcerebral trauma	21	1.9	Luetic	1	.1

From Hopkins, Bice, and Colton, *Evaluation and Education of the Cerebral Palsied Child,* p. 4.

It will be noted in Table 1.6 that quadriplegia markedly predominates in the athetoid, rigidity, and ataxia classifications, whereas hemiplegia is most characteristic of the spastic classification. Very few paraplegias or triplegias appear among any but the spastic group. The incidence of monoplegias is negligible in all of the types.

ETIOLOGY AND RELATED FACTORS

The New Jersey study provides a relatively complete picture of the factors of incidence and etiology. Etiology is noted in 1,105 of the 1,406 cases reported in the New Jersey study. It can be seen from Table 1.7 that factors related to birth injury and developmental problems of a postnatal nature account for more than 50 percent of the total number of reported cases. Whereas a few years ago prenatal toxemia, the Rh factor, infections, and chronic maternal diseases were believed to be major contributors to the incidence of cerebral palsy, Table 1.8 indicates that in the population therein reported such factors play a relatively minor role. Cerebral palsy following convulsions accounts for 9.3 percent of the reported New Jersey population.

Table 1.8, taken from the New Jersey study, illustrates a further breakdown of the incidence by etiology and type of cerebral palsy. It should be noted that birth injuries and developmental factors account for the highest percentage of cases in each of the four types of cerebral palsy. Since 1862, when Little reported his first case of spastic diplegia, factors related to the birth trauma *per se* have been considered major in the etiology of cerebral palsy. More recent writers, however, have granted less importance to birth injury. The Griffiths and Bassett study, previously cited, supports this

TABLE 1.8
ETIOLOGY OF 1,105 CASES BY RANK ORDER AND PERCENTAGE

Spastic			Athetoid			Rigidity			Ataxia		
Etiology	No.	%	Etiology	No.	%	Etiology	No.	%	Etiology	No.	%
B.I.	255	46.6	Develop.	110	37.8	B.I.	56	39.2	Develop.	84	67.7
Develop.	101	18.5	B.I.	103	35.4	Post-convul.	33	23.1	B.I.	16	12.9
Prema-turity	70	12.8	Rh Factor	25	8.6	Develop.	20	14.0	Post-convul.	7	5.6
Post-convul.	51	9.3	Cer. Anoxia	14	4.8	Cer. Anoxia	14	9.8	Pre-maturity	3	2.4
Post-infect.	21	3.8	Post-convul.	12	4.1	Post-infect.	8	5.6	Post-infect.	3	2.4
Post-cer. Trauma	16	2.9	Pre-maturity	12	4.1	Pre-maturity	5	3.5	Rh Factor	3	2.4
Cer. Anoxia	12	2.2	Post-infect.	10	3.4	Post-cer. Trauma	3	2.1	Post-operative	3	2.4
Hydro-basis	10	1.8	Post-operative	2	.7	Hydro-basis	2	1.4	Hydro-basis	2	1.6
Post-operative	4	.7	Post-cer. Trauma	1	.3	Petechial Hemorr.	1	.7	Cer. Anoxia	1	.8
Prenatal Toxemia	2	.4	Hydro-basis	1	.3	Hemorr.	1	.7	Post-cer. Trauma	1	.8
Post-embolic	2	.4	Pre-natal	1	.3	—	—	—	Hyper-pyrexia	1	.8
Rh Fact.	1	.2	—	—	—	—	—	—	—	—	—
Hyper-pyrexia	1	.2	—	—	—	—	—	—	—	—	—
Luetic	1	.2	—	—	—	—	—	—	—	—	—
TOTAL	547	100.0	TOTAL	291	100.0	TOTAL	143	100.0	TOTAL	124	100.0

From Hopkins, Bice, and Colton, *Evaluation and Education of the Cerebral Palsied Child,* p. 5.

conclusion. The New Jersey study illustrates this to be true in all types of cerebral palsy, although birth injury still remains among the chief etiological factors. Balf (1948) reports that cerebral disorders were found in approximately 6 percent of infants born by spontaneous deliveries, whereas 23 percent of the infants born by forceps deliveries demonstrated cerebral disorders. Nevertheless, factors coincident to the birth process are found to play a less significant role than previously believed.

In the New Jersey study prematurity factors account for 12.8 percent

TABLE 1.9

BIRTH ORDER AND NUMBER OF PREGNANCIES IN THE 1951 NEW JERSEY STUDY

Order of Birth	Number of Pregnancies															Total
	1	2	3	4	5	6	7	8	9	10	11	12	13	14	15	
1st	161	84	27	15	1	0	0	1	0	1	0	0	0	0	0	290
2nd	1*	112	32	16	9	4	1	0	0	0	0	1	0	0	0	176
3rd		5	38	20	6	2	0	1	0	1	0	0	0	0	0	73
4th			1*	26	12	5	4	1	0	0	1	0	0	0	0	50
5th					6	12	2	0	0	0	0	0	0	0	0	20
6th						5	8	3	1	0	0					17
7th							6	4	0	1	1					12
8th								5	2	0	1					8
9th									2	1	0					3
10th										2	1	0				3
11th											1	1	0			2
12th												0	1	0	0	1
13th													1	0	0	1
Total	162	201	98	77	34	28	21	15	5	6	5	2	1	0	1	656

From Hopkins, Bice, and Colton, *Evaluation and Education of the Cerebral Palsied Child*, p. 6.

*Second born of twins.

of the spastics, but for many fewer cases of the other three types, i.e., 4.1 percent of the athetoids, 3.5 percent of the rigidities, and 2.4 percent of the ataxias. The Rh factor, accounting for only .2 percent of the spastics, is the third most important etiological factor for the athetoids, accounting therein for 8.6 percent of the incidence.

Incidence and Birth Order

It has been generally assumed that cerebral palsy was related to the first-born child. This was assumed to be true because of the frequency of difficult labors in connection with first-born children. In this regard, Table 1.9, also taken from the New Jersey study, is very illuminating. In 656 cases complete birth histories were available. Of this number only 161 or 24.5 percent of the cerebral palsied children were the first in order of birth and the result of the first pregnancy. The second pregnancy and second in order of birth accounted for 196 cerebral palsied children or 29.8 percent of the total group. Similarly, an inspection of Table 1.9 indicates that cerebral palsied children may appear coincident with any pregnancy or with any birth. The small number of families with four or more children accounts for the small number of cerebral palsied children at the upper end of the scale in Table 1.9. This fact, however, does not negate the conclusion which must be drawn from the table, that cerebral palsy is a factor related to any or all pregnancies. The fact that more than half of the cases appeared in the first two pregnancies still does not argue against this conclusion. A large number of parents of this group of cerebral palsied children undoubtedly took measures to prevent conception for fear that they might produce additional cerebral palsied offspring.

Related Birth Factors

A further analysis of the 656 cases in the New Jersey study on whom relatively complete birth data are available illustrates further interesting information regarding the complexity of cerebral palsy. Table 1.10, which also presents information by type of cerebral palsy, shows that 134 mothers had experienced miscarriages or stillbirths either before or after the delivery of the cerebral palsied child. The 134 mothers had had a total of 178 miscarriages or stillbirths, 27.2 percent of the total 656 cases herein being considered. Nineteen percent of the miscarriages or stillbirths occurred prior to the birth of the cerebral palsied child; 8 percent afterwards. This may also be evidence to support an earlier statement to the effect that preventative measures are taken by parents to avoid a second cerebral palsied child after the delivery of the first such infant. A total of 143 miscarriages and 35 stillbirths are reported in this study as being related to a cerebral palsied child.

TABLE 1.10
RELATED BIRTH FACTORS BY CEREBRAL PALSY CLASSIFICATIONS IN
1951 NEW JERSEY STUDY

	Total Cases Recorded	Pre Mis- car- riage	Pre Still- births	Post Mis- car- riages	Post Still- births	Total Mis- car- riages	Total Still- births	No. of Cases In- volved	Total Miscar- riages and Still- births
Spastic	337	51	16	25	6	76	22	69	98
Athetoid	158	29	3	8	1	37	4	32	41
Rigidity	84	10	2	3	3	13	5	15	18
Ataxia	77	10	4	7	0	17	4	18	21
Total	656	100	25	43	10	143	35	134	178

From Hopkins, Bice, and Colton, *Evaluation and Education of the Cerebral Palsied Child,*
p. 7.

This writer is hesitant to draw broad conclusions from these data. However, the findings are in general quite similar to those reported in studies by Dixon (1937) and Kallman (1941). The former reported on the genetic background of a group of epileptic children; the latter, on schizophrenic patients. In each instance these authors, together with others writing on related matters, have pointed up the minor-key factors which appear in the immediate family background of the patients on whom they were reporting. The incidence of untoward events in the pregnancy history of the mothers in the present group of cerebral palsied children adds data to the previous studies which have been reported. Certainly evidence is herein presented which warrants further careful consideration of the total health picture of the mother in terms of the eventual production of cerebral palsied offspring. Here there seems to be a factor related to cerebral palsy which is significantly important and which must not be overlooked in future research. The genetic component appears to be another variable in the galaxy of problems related to cerebral palsy.

In Table 1.9 Hopkins, Bice, and Colton draw attention to twins among cerebral palsy children. In 1967, in England, Margaret Griffiths also reported on this problem in greater detail. She examined "78 twin pregnancies which resulted in 58 normal co-twins, 82 cases of cerebral palsy, and 16 neonatal deaths or still births." Incidence is studied according to order of birth. In general "the incidence of cerebral palsy in the first twin was 1.7 to 1 compared to the second twin." Mortality rate of the second twins was 4.3 times that of the first twins. The ratio of first-born normal to second-born normal twins was 1 to 1.5. The incidence of simple spastic diplegia in the first twin was 5.7 times that of the second twin. The propor-

TABLE 1.11
RISK SCORES

| Type of cerebral palsy | Mean Score | | | | | | | | Difference in Score | |
| | Twin | | Total score | | Prem. score | | Score for other insult | | Twin I-II | Affected minus non-affected |
	I	II	CP	Normal	CP	Normal	CP	Normal		
Spastic Diplegia	9.2	11.3	9.2	10.2	5.6	5.7	3.6	4.5	-2.1	-1.0
Spastic Tetraplegia	7.2	9.3	10.2	6.1	3.4	3.3	6.8	2.8	-2.1	+4.1
Athetosis	8.7	11.4	12.7	5.5	2.3	1.9	10.4	3.6	-2.7	+7.2

From Griffiths, "Cerebral Palsy on Multiple Pregnancy," *Developmental Medicine and Child Neurology* 9(1967):723.

tion of second-born twins with spastic tetraplegia was approximately twice that of first-born twins, while the incidence is about equal.

Griffiths examined possible etiological factors according to zygosity, prematurity, intra-pair differences, and abnormalities of pregnancies. "Discordance for all types of cerebral palsy in monozygotic twins" is offered as evidence against an hereditary factor. While this study found 85 percent of the cerebral palsied twins to be premature (see aforementioned Table 1.8), caution is exercised in declaring prematurity a cause of cerebral palsy in these cases. One reason for this is that premature birth is a characteristic of multiple pregnancy. Some intra-pair differences were cited, the most significant being differences in "risks" and in the distributions of spastic diplegia and tetraplegia. A scoring system was devised to determine the risk of first-born to second-born twins. The finding that second-born twins are at greater risk was stated but does not appear to be clearly supported by the author's data as noted in Table 1.11. The much greater frequency of spastic diplegia in Twin I is thought to be due to "cerebral damage in dilating the birth canal," whereas the relatively greater frequency of spastic tetraplegia in Twin II may be due to a "reduction in placental oxygen." This latter assumption is based on the fact that the interval between delay of the first and second deliveries was greater than one hour in 43 percent of the times when the second twin was affected, the average time being 228 minutes. This interval was less than 20 minutes in 81 percent of the times when Twin I was affected. Of the twenty cases of cerebral palsy in both twins, there were sixteen stillbirths or neonatal deaths.

Griffiths minimizes the genetic aspect of cerebral palsy. It is useful to consider this aspect of the problem further. A team of Swedish investigators examined the identical syndromes of cerebral palsy in the same family. Gustavson, Hagberg, and Tanner (1969) made an attempt to distinguish clinical-genetic aspects of cerebral palsy and to study their prevalence and possible modes of inheritance. The authors' classification system is noted in Table 1.12. Forty-three families were surveyed, in thirty of which affected persons were siblings. Of interest to the authors was the group characterized by identical cases of cerebral palsy and normal perinatal history. These families numbered sixteen, with forty-three cases of cerebral palsy in them. Of this group, thirteen families with thirty-seven cases of cerebral palsy showed ataxic syndromes.

Congenital ataxia (ten families, twenty-five cases) is defined as "a pure and non-progressive cerebellar ataxia without pyramidal signs." No definite pattern of inheritance is suggested. Autosomal resessiveness is indicated in three of the families. Autosomal dominat, however, is indicated by the result of Adler's (1961) study. It is thought that genetic factors are most strongly indicated when mental retardation occurs with congenital ataxia.

TABLE 1.12
APPROXIMATE DISTRIBUTION OF DIFFERENT PALSY SYNDROMES IN
CHILDREN ACCORDING TO THE CLASSIFICATION USED IN SWEDEN

Spastic syndromes	%
Hemiplegia	25
Diplegia	30
Tetraplegia	5
Approx. distrib.	50–60
Dyskinetic syndromes	%
Mainly athetotic	5
Mainly dystonic	20–25
Approx. distrib.	25–30
Ataxic syndromes	%
Congenital ataxia	5–7
Ataxic diplegia	5–7
Approx. distrib.	10–15

From Gustavson, Hagberg, and Tanner, "Identical Syndromes of Cerebral Palsy in the Same Family," p. 331.

Ataxic diplegia (three families, twelve cases) means "cerebellar ataxia combined with spastic pareses mainly of the legs." This study suggests dominant inheritance, but neither an autosomal nor an x-linked pattern is specified. Other studies indicate the possibility of a sex-linked recessive in individual families. Spastic diplegia refers to "spastic pareses . . . mainly affecting the legs, but also to a minor degree the upper extremities." Sex-linked recessive is indicated by the one family with two cases observed. Autosomal recessive is indicated elsewhere. (Adler 1961; Blumel et al., 1957; Boök 1953; Gudmondston 1967).

Spastic tetraplegia (one family, two cases) is severe "spastic pareses of all four limbs, the arms being affected to an equal or greater extent than the legs." While perinatal brain damage is the most common cause, genetic factors are obvious in some cases. The authors suspect an autosomal recessive pattern here.

Dystonic tetraplegia (one family, two cases) is characterized by severe affection of all limbs, changing muscle tone, movements "mainly determined by neonatal reflexes," and, sometimes, spastic signs. The cases described under this heading are combined with microcephaly. While genetically determined forms of microcephaly are not usually combined with cerebral palsy, some studies have found this connection. Autosomal recessive inheritance is suggested here.

Cases involving spastic hemiplegia or athetoid syndromes are not reported by these authors.

The authors estimated that 1.5 percent of all cases of cerebral palsy in

Sweden are autosomally recessively inherited, and that sex-linked recessive and dominant forms seem to be much more rare.

In this connection Churchill (1970), in a note apparently based on data from the Collaborative Project in Cerebral Palsy, Mental Retardation, and Other Neurological and Sensory Disorders of Infancy and Childhood (National Institute of Neurological Diseases and Blindness), states that there is "no support for the genetic theory . . . by study of siblings of the spastics," in his population included in a group of 1,364 singleton liveborn infants weighing 2 kg. or less at birth. The genetic influence in cerebral palsy still remains unclear, though some would attribute this factor to the etiology of a small group of children.

CEREBRAL PALSY AND OTHER PHYSICAL DISABILITIES

Because of the intimate relation of cerebral palsy to the central and peripheral nervous systems, it is relatively commonplace to find physical and mental disabilities other than neuromuscular aberrations present in a given individual. Such associated disabilities in some patients may have little or no relationship to the cerebral palsy from an etiological point of view; that is, the two disabilities—cerebral palsy and blindness, for example—may appear in a coincidental relationship. In most patients, however, the same factor—e.g., rubella—coincident to cerebral palsy may also have been basic to the etiology of additional physical disabilities. Associated disabilities take the form of visual impairments, auditory impairments, mental retardation, seizures, disturbances of perceptual-motor function irrespective of mental retardation, or other types of manifestation. Since each of these secondary problems will be treated in detail by other authors in later chapters, the present writer will include only sufficient data to stress the point of complexity in considering cerebral palsy. In this connection reference is again made to the New Jersey study.

The authors of this important study included 1,265 individuals in this phase of their report. Of this number, as noted in Table 1.13, 369, or 29.2 percent, were found to have a history of seizures. The greatest percentage of seizures occurred with the rigidity type, i.e., 41.9 percent; the smallest percentage with the athetoid type, 20.4 percent. Perlstein and Barnett (1952) also comment on the relationship of epilepsy to cerebral palsy. They state that convulsions occur in approximately 0.5 percent of the general population. "In contradistinction, they occur in approximately 40 percent of children with cerebral palsy." They report that the incidence of convulsions is about three times as great in spastics as in athetoids, and in this regard there is considerable difference in comparison to the New Jersey study. Perlstein and Barnett found that in 1,000 consecutive patients with

TABLE 1.13
INCIDENCE OF SEIZURES IN THE 1951 NEW JERSEY STUDY

Type	Number Reported in Seizure Study	Number with Seizure History	Per Cent with Seizures
Spastic	634	179	28.3
Athetoid	313	65	20.4
Rigidity	172	72	41.9
Ataxia	146	53	36.3
Total	1,265	369	29.2

From Hopkins, Bice, and Colton, *Evaluation and Education of the Cerebral Palsied Child,* p. 130.

cerebral palsy 50 percent of all spastics and 15 percent of all athetoids had convulsions.

Dunsdon also reports data concerning the incidence of seizures among her group of cerebral palsied children. Of the 796 cases included in this phase of her study, 14 percent were found to have a history of seizures. The percentage varied according to type of cerebral palsy, i.e., athetoid, 18 percent; ataxic, 19 percent; quadriplegic, 17 percent; hemiplegic, 16 percent; paraplegic, 7 percent. While these figures are lower than those reported by either Perlstein or the New Jersey study, they do indicate that nearly one-fifth of the British population studied was characterized by a multiple problem involving convulsions. Dunsdon found that the incidence of seizures increased as the level of intelligence decreased. In 114 cerebral palsied children distributed according to intelligence quotient range, the relationship to seizures was as follows: under IQ of 70, 72 percent with seizures; 70 to 84, 15 percent; 85 to 99, 8 percent; 100 to 114, 2 percent; 115 to 129, 2 percent; and above 130 IQ, 1 percent. The high incidence of children in the New Jersey study with intelligence quotients below 90 may in part account for the difference in the findings of the two studies.

The New Jersey study also includes nearly 1,300 cases on whom data were available regarding auditory, visual, and speech impairments. Table 1.14 indicates that 21.4 percent of the group had visual impairments; 5.3 percent auditory impairments; and 68.0 percent speech impairments. With respect to vision, data were available on 1,297 individuals. Normal vision was recorded in 79.5 percent of the athetoids; 57.2 percent ataxias. The spastics and the rigidities fell within this range. Defective vision was found in 30.9 percent of the ataxic group; in 17.0 percent of the rigidity group. The athetoids were very similar to the latter. In this instance 17.3 percent were found to have defective vision. Difficulties in completing accurate ophthalmological examinations are indicated in the fact that in from 3 percent to 11.9 percent of the cases questionable results were obtained. Slightly more than 21 percent, or a fifth of the total group, had visual impairments.

TABLE 1.14
ANALYSIS OF VISION, HEARING, AND SPEECH IMPAIRMENTS IN THE 1951 NEW JERSEY STUDY

	Vision						Hearing						Speech		
	Normal		Defective		Question-able		Total	Normal		Defective		Question-able		Total	Normal		Defective		Total
Type	N	%	N	%	N	%	N	N	%	N	%	N	%	N	N	%	N	%	N
Spastic	466	72.7	144	22.4	31	4.8	641	592	92.6	16	2.5	30	4.7	638	291	47.0	315	51.9	606
Athetoid	261	79.5	57	17.3	10	3.0	328	254	77.4	40	12.1	34	10.3	328	35	11.2	275	88.7	310
Rigidity	125	71.0	30	17.0	21	11.9	176	151	86.2	4	2.2	20	11.4	175	44	27.8	114	72.1	158
Ataxia	87	57.2	47	30.9	18	11.9	152	124	81.5	8	5.2	20	13.1	152	22	14.6	128	85.3	150
Total	939	72.4	278	21.4	80	6.2	1,297	1,121	86.7	68	5.3	104	8.0	1,293	392	32.0	832	68.0	1,224

From Hopkins, Bice, and Colton, *Evaluation and Education of the Cerebral Palsied Child*, p. 9.

Eight were classified as being blind. Viewed from a different perspective, Cruickshank and Trippe (1959) found that 205 (7.4 percent) of 2,773 blind children under twenty-one years of age in New York State were also diagnosed as being cerebral palsied.

Twelve hundred and ninety-three New Jersey records contained information regarding hearing impairment. Of this group 5.3 percent had defective hearing; 8.4 percent questionable results; 86.7 percent normal hearing. The athetoid group had the highest percentage of defective hearing, 12.1 percent; the spastic and rigidity groups the lowest percentage, 2.5 percent and 2.2 percent, respectively. The spastic group had the highest percentage of normal hearing, 97.6; the athetoid group the lowest, 77.4 percent.

All groups show a high incidence of speech impairment. The records of 1,224 individuals contained information regarding speech. Sixty-eight percent of this group were found to have impairments of speech; 32.0 percent normal speech. The range among the four types is also quite marked, varying from 47.0 percent normal speech among the spastic type to 11.2 percent normal speech among the athetoid type. The converse is, of course, similar, i.e., 51.9 percent of the spastics were found to have impairments of speech; 88.7 percent athetoids.

The problem of mental retardation in individuals with cerebral palsy will be treated in such detail in later chapters that no discussion will be presented here. Suffice it to say that, as later discussions will demonstrate, the incidence of mental retardation in this clinical group has been found to be considerably higher than earlier believed. Several studies, independently completed, present data to indicate that from 50 to 75 percent of the cerebral palsied populations studied have measured intelligence at or below the dull-normal level. This, of course, presents another exceedingly complicating factor to the total consideration of the problem of cerebral palsy.

In a much more modest study, Love (1970) examined sixty-one elementary school children six to twelve years of age who were diagnosed as physically handicapped. Only thirty-six were classified as cerebral palsied. The purpose was to determine "to what extent physically handicapped children tend to have secondary disabilities requiring specialized remediation." Keeping in mind the small sample as compared to the previously discussed populations, mental retardation was found in 69 percent of all the children. The difference in distribution for cerebral palsied children (80 percent) and "other" (52 percent) is significant at $p < .05$ level. Of the cerebral palsied children, 44 percent were termed "educable"; 31 percent "slow learners"; and 5 percent "trainable."

Twenty-eight percent of all of the children had visual defects with no between-group differences. Eighty-three percent of the cerebral palsied children had speech disorders, compared to 32 percent of the "other" group. Twenty-five percent of the cerebral palsied children required

TABLE 1.15
MAJOR VARIATIONS OF MULTIPLE-HANDICAPPED CEREBRAL PALSIED CHILDREN

Type	Presence of Cerebral Palsy	Presence of Other Physical Defect	Presence of Retarded Mental Development	Presence of Perceptual-Motor Pathology
1	Yes	No	No	No
2	Yes	No	No	Yes
3	Yes	No	Yes	No
4	Yes	Yes	No	No
5	Yes	No	Yes	Yes
6	Yes	Yes	Yes	No
7	Yes	Yes	No	Yes
8	Yes	Yes	Yes	Yes

From Cruickshank, "The Multiply Handicapped Cerebral Palsied Child."

guidance and counseling for emotional problems compared to 40 percent of the "others." Although only thirty-six cerebral palsied children are included in this study, it is interesting to note that the percentages which the author found compare quite favorably with the much more inclusive study of Hopkins, Bice and Colton.

Cruickshank (1953) has presented a theoretical scheme to illustrate the complexity of the problem with which this text deals. While he notes that classification systems do not solve problems, they nevertheless may clarify issues to the point where research problems can be more easily established. Table 1.15 illustrates the issue. Utilizing only three variables—(1) presence of physical disabilities, (2) presence of mental retardation, and (3) presence of perceptual-motor pathology (see Chapter 5 below)—one is able to differentiate seven distinct variations to the cerebral palsy problem. This situation can be compounded many times if one adds specific physical impairments to the list instead of grouping them as has been done in Table 1.15. Visual impairments, auditory impairments, speech impairments, seizures have been shown to play important roles in the total picture of cerebral palsy. Earlier it was stated that the concept of individual differences comes to the fore in considering cerebral palsy. The data presented in this chapter illustrate this fact appropriately. Differences in degree of involvement, differences in degree of hearing or visual impairment, differences in severity and type of seizures, differences in extent of speech involvement, differences in type and degree of perceptual-motor involvement, differences in level of intellectual capacity, differences in emotional development and behavior, differences in the way in which, as the result of any of the above factors, the child responds to his learning environment—all these contribute to the complexity of the problem. The proportions of the problem become staggering insofar as habilitation and education are concerned when one considers the multiplicity of variables possible in cerebral palsied children.

2

Medical Aspects

ERIC DENHOFF

CEREBRAL PALSY is the perfect medical model to demonstrate the spectrum of dysfunctions found in children with developmental disabilities. While its main characteristic is a disorder of movement or posture, the associated perceptual, cognitive, seizure, and behavioral problems are found in many other clinical conditions where developmental progress and learning are impaired. Because cerebral palsy is due to a defect or lesion of the immature brain usually resulting from anoxia and or trauma before, during, or shortly after birth, the clinical findings may change during the long period of brain growth depending upon the location, severity, and extent of the pathology.

CLASSIFICATION

The classification of cerebral palsy is based on both *clinical* and *theoretical* factors. The clinical factors include the neurological findings at examination, the presumed causative factors based on parent history or hospital record, and the associated psychological and social features. The theoretical components include anatomic, pathologic, pneumoencephalographic, and electromyographic findings (Minear 1956).

There are inconclusive correlations between clinical and theoretical features, especially between presumed causative factors and actual clinical outcomes (Josephy 1949). Until there is such clarification, it is prudent to contain classification within a clinical framework based upon neurological evaluation and supportive psychological and educational data.

Clinical Classification

The clinical classification attempts accurately to describe the type, location, degree and tonicity of the primary neuromotor handicap and the associated dysfunctions (Perlstein 1949, 1952).

Clinical

A clinical type is based upon the character of the disordered movement:
1. Spasticity—50–60 percent.
2. Dyskinesia—athetosis, chorea, dystonia, tremor, rigidity—20–25 percent.
3. Ataxia—1–10 percent.
4. Mixed types—15–40 percent.
5. Atonia—rare.

Topographic

A topographic (location) classification is used to complement the clinical designation; the various sites of the neuromotor disability are:
1. Hemiplegia—findings lateralized to one half of the body—35–40 percent.
2. Diplegia—the legs are more involved than the arms—10–20 percent.
3. Quadriplegia—all four extremities are impaired—15–20 percent.
4. Paraplegia—the legs only are implicated—10–20 percent.
5. Monoplegia—one limb is involved—rare.
6. Triplegia—three limbs are involved—rare.
7. Double Hemiplegia—both halves of the body are involved—rare.

Degree

The degree of severity is included as part of the clinical classification; this is rated as:
1. Mild—impairment only of fine precision of movement.
2. Moderate—gross and fine movements and speech clarity is impaired, but performance of usual activities of living is functional.
3. Severe—inability to perform adequately usual activities of daily living such as walking, using hands, or using speech for communication.

Tonus

The state of muscle tonus is classified as part of the clinical picture; muscles at rest may be:
1. Isotonic—normal tonus.
2. Hypertonic—increased tonus.
3. Hypotonic—decreasing tonus.
4. Variable—inconsistent tonus.

Associated Dysfunctions

The associated dysfunctions are:
1. Sensory—vision, hearing, smell, tactile-kinesthetic, proprioceptive.

2. Convulsive—type, degree.

3. Intellectual—type, degree.

4. Perceptual—visual, auditory.

5. Behavioral—hyperkinetic impulse disorder, neurotic, anxiety, withdrawal, acting out, psychosomatic.

6. Learning—specific disabilities, secondary to above disorders (type, degree).

7. Emotional—primary associated with family or biologic factors, secondary to above disorders (type, degree).

Description of Disordered Movement

Spasticity

Spasticity indicates a pathologic state in which motor function is impaired because of disharmony of muscle movements. Clinically, spasticity is manifested by hyperactive deep reflexes, hypertonicity, and abnormal plantar reflexes and clonus. The underlying component of spasticity is the exaggerated contraction of muscles when subjected to elongation or "stretching." When suddenly elongated the muscles being examined contract, providing the examiner with a feeling of brief "catching of the muscle belly." The degree of the "stretch" depends not only upon the extent of the spasticity, but often upon the emotional status of the child at the time of examination. The phenomenon is called the "stretch reflex," and it is used to differentiate spasticity from other types of neuromotor dysfunction. Spasticity interferes with residual motor function.

Hypotonia

Hypotonia (atonia) indicates a pathological state where the muscles fail to respond to volitional stimulation. In cerebral palsy, some infants are hypotonic or "floppy," with absent deep reflexes during the first year or so. Thus, hypotonia is generally classified under the spasticity category. These cases often become spastic quadriplegics or variants.

Dyskinesia

Dyskinesia is characterized by involuntary extraneous motor activity accentuated by emotional stress. *Athetosis* is the most striking of the dyskinetic group. Uncontrollable, jerky, irregular, twisting movements of the extremities, especially the fingers and wrists, are apparent except at rest or sleep. During activity, the disorder of movement may be outstanding.

The other important types classified under dyskinesia are chorea, dystonia, tremor, and rigidity.

Choreiform Movements

Choreiform movements are more continuous, slower in rate, more writhing but less tense in character than athetosis. The movements are often limited to specific muscle groups which display increased resistance to passive movement.

Dystonic Movements

Dystonic movements closely resemble athetosis, but the disorder of movement generally involves the trunk muscles more than the extremities.

Tremor

Tremor is more rhythmic and pendular in character than athetosis. There are several subcategories of tremor, amongst which are intentional, non-intentional, or constant.

Rigidity

Rigidity is a term used to describe increased resistance to passive movement through the entire range of the movement. Rigidity resembles spasticity, but with spasticity there is a feeling of relaxation of the muscle after the stretch reflex is elicited. Rigidity may be described as continuous or "lead pipe" in character, where the feeling of resistance is constant, or as intermittent, where the resistance is interrupted at regular intervals and appears as a jerky movement.

Ataxia

Ataxia is incoordination due to a primary disturbance of balance, sense, posture, and/or kinesthetic feedback. It is characterized by inability or awkwardness in maintaining balance with associated or gross and/or fine motor incoordination.

Mixed

Various combinations of the above types of disordered movement. Athetosis combined with spasticity, or rigidity and ataxia are frequently encountered.

Theoretical Classification

Anatomic

Correlations between anatomic and other theoretical types of classification and the actual clinical situation are often unclear, thus making a theoretical classification in clinical practice impractical. Future studies may some day provide clearer relationships between theoretical and clinical categories.

Lesions involving the pyramidal tracts, the extra-pyramidal tracts, and the cerebellum and/or its connections are presumed to be responsible for disorders of movement. Yet, in cerebral palsy clear-cut correlations between pathologic and clinical findings are the exception. According to dictum, patients with pyramidal tract impairment, either in the cerebral cortex or the subcortical area—especially the internal capsule—or both, should have spasticity. Damage to the basal nuclei and/or their connections should produce dyskinesia, while cerebellar impairment should result in ataxia or atonia. Lesions in the brain stem and upper spinal cord should also produce spasticity (Perlstein 1949). Yet clear-cut relationships have not been found in most neuropathological studies.

The reasons for the poor correlations between neuroanatomy and brain function are emerging. Various neuromotor actions or segments of actions arise from beds of neurons lying within scattered associative zones in the brain. The integrating feature of the information processing of the nervous system depends upon the ability of these neurons to interrelate and to generate specific responses when called upon by the various stimuli to do so. If there are breakdowns between the various systems of neurons—i.e., the cortical sensori-motor analyzers, the limbic-subcortical-brain stem complex, the centrecephalic system, and the cerebellar systems—distortions or alterations in function will result. These may include abnormal neuromotor responses as well as sensory, perceptual, and cognitive inefficiencies. These cellular level inefficiencies are not identifiable with techniques such as the brain scan or the pneumoencephalogram.

Attempts to use the pneumoencephalogram as a basis for classification have been unsatisfactory, as have been electromyographic classifications because of inconsistencies in clinical outcome.

Thus, until new information is forthcoming to clarify the relationships between brain anatomy, muscle function, and clinical ability, the theoretical classification had best be deferred.

Etiologic

Cerebral palsy has been classified according to the presumed time of onset and cause of the cerebral malformation or injury. These are: prenatal-hereditary factors (chromosomal, autosomal, sex-linked, dominant, recessive) and congenital (acquired in utero) (maternal illnesses or disorders affecting the fetus); perinatal (asphyxia and/or trauma) (consequences of "small for date" babies, issoimmunization, hemolytic disorders, and obstetrical complications); postnatal–early infancy (toxic, metabolic infectious, trauma, nutritional); also, mixed factors are frequent.

These classifications will be discussed in depth in the section which follows.

ETIOLOGY

Hereditary (genetic, chromosomal)

Clear-cut cases of cerebral palsy of genetic (chromosomal) abnormality are rare, although many of the patients with chromosomal variances exhibit spasticity or rigidity as part of the clinical syndrome.

Prenatal Disorders

Cerebral palsy has a diversified number of causes, but interference with oxygenation of the brain (anoxia) is the common causative denominator. During the early prenatal period, the embryonic nervous system may suffer from oxygen lack due to a poor intrauterine climate as a result of neurotropic virus infections, X-ray irradiation, or maternal illness of various types.

Amino Aciduria

Investigations in biochemical genetics have brought to light a number of biochemical or enzymatic blocks which result in a variety of syndromes in which delayed development, mental retardation, neuromotor disturbance, epilepsy, and behavior disorder are found. In one group of institutionalized cerebral palsy cases with severe mental deficiency, at least 10 percent were found to be genetically determined (Yannet 1949).

Perinatal Disorders

During the latter part of pregnancy and the delivery period, the interference with fetal and/or maternal respiration and circulation is a most important cause of brain damage. Lack of oxygen supply to the fetus arising from poor maternal blood supply—as would occur from anemia or hemorrhage, placental disturbance, or impairment of fetal circulation from a twisted umbilical cord—is a common cause before the onset of active labor. Once the birth process is initiated, dynamic factors arising from uterine contractures, increased intracranial pressure from respiratory distress, and mechanical obstruction or trauma are responsible.

Neonatal—Infancy Disorders

During the neonatal and infancy periods, respiratory and circulatory difficulties most commonly interfere with oxygen supply, although infections and toxic and metabolic agents are frequent offenders.

Thus cerebral palsy may have its origin in the prenatal, perinatal, or postnatal periods, or in combinations.

Table 2.1 provides an overview of the factors which have been implicated in causing cerebral palsy.

TABLE 2.1
POTENTIAL CAUSES OF CEREBRAL PALSY

I. *Hereditary*
   1. Static—familial athetosis, familial paraplegia, familial tremor
   2. Progressive—demyelinating diseases of viral or undetermined origin (chromosomal breakages are rare in cerebral palsy, as are disorders of metabolism)

II. *Congenital (acquired in utero)*
   1. Infection rubella, toxoplasmosis, cytomegalic inclusions, herpes simplex, and other viral or infectious agents
   2. Maternal anoxia, carbon monoxide poisoning, strangulation, anemia, hypotension associated with spinal anesthesia, placental infarcts, placenta abruptio
   3. Prenatal cerebral hemorrhage, maternal toxemia, direct trauma, maternal bleeding diathesis
   4. Prenatal anoxia, twisting or kinking of the cord
   5. Miscellaneous, toxins, drugs

III. *Perinatal* (obstetrical)
   1. Mechanical anoxia—respiratory obstruction, atalectasis, narcotism due to over-sedation with drugs, placenta praevia or abruptio, hypotension associated with spinal anesthesia, breech delivery with delay of the after-coming head
   2. Trauma—hemorrhage associated with dystocia, disproportions and malpositions, injudicious forceps applications, holding back of head, pituitary extract induction of labor, sudden pressure changes, precipitate delivery, caesarean delivery
   3. Complications of birth—"small for date" babies, prematurity, immaturity, dysmaturity, postmaturity, hyperbilirubinemia and issoimmunization factors (kernicterus due to Rh factor, ABO incompatability), hemolytic disorders, "respiratory distress" disorders, syphilis, meningitis, and other infections, drug addiction reactions, hypoglycemia reactions, hypocalcemic reactions

IV. *Postnatal–Infancy*
   1. Trauma (subdural hematoma, skull fracture, cerebral contusion)
   2. Infections (meningitis, encephalitis, brain abscess)
   3. Vascular accidents (congenital cerebral aneurism, thrombosis, embolic, hypertensive encephalopathy, sudden pressure changes)
   4. Toxins (lead, arsenic, coal tar, derivatives)
   5. Anoxia (carbon monoxide poisoning, strangulation, high altitude and deep pressure anoxia, hypoglycemia)
   6. Neoplastic and late neurodevelopmental defects (tumor, cyst, progressive hydrocephalus).

New Antrospective Data

The Perinatal Collaborative Study, based on antrospective data from more than 31,000 women and their babies, is providing more specific insights into the factors involved in infantile neurological impairment. The study implies that poverty and its sequellae are responsible for the majority of cases of neurological impairment, and that "small for date" babies and their complications are responsible for the bulk of cerebral palsied infants. However, final conclusions must be deferred because the information collected has not yet been fully organized and interpreted.

Maternal characteristics such as age, weight, illnesses, and social and educational status relate both to "small for date" babies and infants with an abnormal neurological classification at one year. The optimal age for child bearing is between eighteen and nineteen years, and mothers less than eighteen years have a 23 percent higher risk for producing a neurologically abnormal child than mothers between twenty and thirty-eight years of age. Mothers who have difficulty in conceiving or holding a baby to term are especially at risk, along with those mothers where the immediate prior pregnancy terminated in fetal or neonatal death or in a low birth weight infant. Short, fat mothers have the highest incidence of neurologically abnormal babies and tall, thin mothers, i.e., those over 67 inches, have the highest rate of "small for date" offsprings. Mothers who gain more than twenty pounds during pregnancy have babies with a fewer number of complications than do mothers who gain less than ten pounds.

Mothers who smoke more than thirty cigarettes a day have smaller ba-

TABLE 2.2
SOCIOLOGIC CHARACTERISTICS OF MOTHERS
CONTRIBUTING TO NEUROLOGICALLY IMPAIRED INFANTS

	White %	Negro %
AGE AT PREGNANCY		
Over 40 years	(6.4)	(0.9)
30–39	(2.4)	(2.0)
15 and under	(3.5)	(0.9)
MARITAL STATUS		
Widowed	(6.4)	(0.9)
Divorced, separated	(3.2)	(3.0)
Unmarried	(2.2)	(2.5)
EDUCATION		
Years in school		
0–4	(3.1)	(5.5)
5–8	(2.0)	(1.4)
CIGARETTE SMOKING		
Number per day		
40 or more	(3.3)	(5.5)
21–30	(1.3)	(4.2)

*Normal rate (1.7)(1.6)

Items omitted were within normal range.

1% = 1 case per 1,000 normal population.

TABLE 2.3

MATERNAL DISORDERS ASSOCIATED WITH NEUROLOGIC ABNORMALITY AT ONE YEAR

Maternal conditions During Pregnancy No. = 31,785	Mothers With Condition %	Conditions	Mothers With Condition %	Conditions	Mothers With Condition %
Heart Disease W	2.5	Diabetes W	4.3	Seizures W	9.2
N	5.7	N	4.8	N	9.3
Rheumatic Fever N	8.3	Hypothyroid N	3.5	Mental retardation W	8.2
				N	8.8
Tuberculosis W	2.0	Hyperthyroid N	7.6	Brain disease W	1.8
				N	3.3
Acute Asthma W	5.5	Nephritis W	7.6	Alcoholism W	2.5
N	3.9	N	4.1		
Status Asthmaticus W	7.1	Other renal W	3.3	Drug habituation W	4.5
N	12.5	infection N	2.3		

(Average incidence of neurologic abnormality at one year in mothers without the above conditions = 1.7% W
                                                                                                        1.5% N)

W = White
N = Negro
1% = 1 case per 1,000 normal population.

From Niswander and Gordon (1972).

bies than mothers who smoke fewer, or not at all. Maternal alcoholism and drug addiction markedly increase the chances for an abnormal infant. A mother with a grade-school education has a much higher opportunity to give birth to a neurologically impaired infant than does one who is a college graduate. Table 2.2 summarizes the sociologic characteristics of mothers who are at risk.

Table 2.3 lists maternal conditions during pregnancy which have adverse effects on the health of the baby. They include asthma, organic heart disease, diabetes, hyperthyroidism, renal disorder, convulsive disor-

TABLE 2.4
PREGNANCY COMPLICATIONS ASSOCIATED WITH
NEUROLOGIC ABNORMALITY AT ONE YEAR

Pregnancy Conditions	Mothers With Condition %	Premature Rupture Membranes	Neurologic Abnormality W %	N %
Placenta praevia		Under 8 hours	1.6	2.0
W	4.3	12–23 hours	2.4	2.7
Hyperemesis gravida		24–48 hours	2.8	3.3
W	4.0	49+ hours	4.7	4.4
Hydramnios				
W	3.8			
Placenta abruptio				
W	3.3			
Prolapse of cord				
W	3.0			
Puerperal infection				
W	2.8			
Vaginal bleeding 2nd trimester				
W	2.5			
Reproductive difficulty with offspring under 2,000 gms.	(3.8)(2.6)			

W = White

N = Negro

1% = 1 case per 1,000 normal population.

(Incompetent cervix and uterine dysfunction are not significant producers of neurological abnormality in this sample).

White women who have difficulty in conceiving over one year have a 2.0% incidence of abnormal infant.

Sample represents between 14,000 and 20,000 pregnancies each, of White and Negro.

Average rate of mothers without conditions = 1.6%.

From Niswander and Gordon (1972).

ders, mental retardation, and neurological disorders. Table 2.4 lists obstetrical conditions which are related to adverse neonatal outcome. These are placental separation, severe vomiting during pregnancy, cord prolapse, puerperal sepsis and vaginal bleeding during mid-pregnancy, breech delivery, difficult forceps delivery, and caesarean delivery.

The Perinatal Collaborative Study data points out that the rate of neurological abnormality in the offspring of a white mother without complicating features in her background is 1.6 percent (16 per 1,000 population) chance and 1.7 percent (17 per 1,000 population) if she is a Negro. Mothers with active disease during pregnancy have a much higher rate of "small for date" babies and neurologically abnormal babies. For instance, the rate in maternal organic heart disease, especially rheumatic fever, is 20 per 1,000, and for active seizures during pregnancy 60 per 1,000. A similar high rate is found with mentally retarded mothers and mothers with cerebral palsy or multiple sclerosis.

Obstetrical Factors

Presentations

Breech delivery, especially frank breech, is associated with the highest abnormal neurological outcome rate for babies. The double-footling breech especially carries the gravest risk for adverse outcome. Face, brow, transverse, and occiput posterior presentations generally have a higher mortality rate than the more common obstetrical presentations.

Labor

A first stage of labor of less than three hours in low birth weight babies carries a higher than normal mortality rate, especially for Negro babies. When the labor is under three hours, the infant neurological abnormality outcome rate is highest in multipara (second or more pregnancies). When the second stage of labor is less than thirty minutes, breech delivery carries the highest abnormality outcome risk. With pitocin induction the risk for a neurologically abnormal baby is slightly increased than with normal, nonmediated induction. Difficult forceps delivery is associated with increased mortality and neurologic morbidity rate, depending upon the weight of the baby and the degree of difficulty encountered (Table 2.5).

Although Negro babies are generally of lower birth weights and have shorter gestation periods than white babies, the neurological abnormality outcome rate at one year is similar.

At this writing the Perinatal Collaborative Study has not been able to establish clearly specific causes for cerebral palsy. However, what the Perinatal Collaborative Study infers is quite clear:

TABLE 2.5
THE RELATIONSHIP OF OBSTETRICAL DELIVERY
AND NEUROLOGIC ABNORMALITY AT ONE YEAR

Type of Delivery	Neurological Abnormality at 1 year %
C-section	2.7 (2.3)
High forceps	1.8
Severe forceps complication	5.3 (3.0)
Breech, spontaneous extract	9.0 (2.2)

1% = 1 case per 1,000 normal population.

The infant who is at risk for cerebral palsy or the related major or minor syndromes of cerebral dysfunction will likely come from poor socioeconomic circumstances, will be "small for date," likely under 2,000 gms. in weight, and will have complications at birth such as asphyxia, respiratory distress, hyperbilirubinemia, or hemolytic disease. If he is not treated promptly and properly he will likely develop signs of central nervous system dysfunction. It will be difficult to pinpoint the neuromotor problems until he is at least one year of age. Such a baby will be the product of a mother with historical features which can clearly point out that there was a risk of abnormal outcome.

NEUROPATHOLOGY

There is no one characteristic pathologic finding in cerebral palsy. Generalized cerebral and/or cortical atrophy is not uncommon, while focal atrophy (which is called microgyria, ulegyria, and hemispheral atrophy) reflects localized blood-vessel changes. Porencephaly and hydrocephaly (generalized lack of cortex) also result from the same process. Primary gliosis, represented by pachygyria, status marmoratus, and status demyelinization, indicates that certain neuraglial cells become condensed. As a result, some gyri seem swollen since adjacent convolutions do not develop properly. Also, certain myelin sheaths become prominent while others degenerate, since the cells of origin have been destroyed in the glial process. These pathologic disturbances have been classified clinically as (1) heredodegenerative disorders, (2) malformations, and (3) residues of destructive processes. They can be correlated with etiological factors, but not always successfully with clinical symptomatology (Josephy 1949).

Autopsies of six hundred Perinatal Collaborative Study cases have been described by Towbin (1971). Four major types of central nervous system pathology which correlate with clinical findings are observed. These are:

1. subdural hemorrhage due to traumatic dural-venous tears;
2. spinal cord and brain stem damage due to mechanical injury;
3. hypoxic damage to the deep cerebral structures occurring predominantly in the premature infant; and
4. hypoxic damage to the cerebral cortex mainly in the mature fetus and newborn infant.

While genetic, metabolic, infectious, and toxic processes also occur, they are uncommon. Mechanical brain trauma, subdural hemorrhage, and severe spinal cord–brain stem damage produce a high mortality rate. The milder forms of cord involvement eventually may be expressed as "body clumsiness." Fetal or neonatal hypoxia, depending upon severity and location, are responsible for most of the clinical disorders grouped within the syndromes of cerebral dysfunction. Severe neonatal hypoxia may lead to total necrosis of cerebral structures resulting in porencephaly or hydrocephaly. A moderate degree of anoxia produces less extensive destruction but varying degrees of severity of scarring and cystic damage to the cerebrum. This is often the basis for cerebral palsy or mental retardation. A mild degree of anoxia results in focal or diffuse neuronal cerebral damage with consequent symptoms of "minimal brain dysfunction."

The hypoxic damage may be deep in the area surrounding the ventricles or may be more superficial in the cortex. Whether deep or superficial, damage to the precentral gyrus produces spasticity; damage to the frontal areas produces defects in mentation; damage to the occipital lobe correlates with blindness or visual perceptual deficits; deep damage to the forebrain relates with athetosis and other forms of dyskinesia. With healing of damaged tissue, a scar may result causing seizures.

The premature baby is less sensitive to anoxia, but the effects of anoxia are usually hemorrhagic deep in the preventricular tissues. These deep lesions may interfer with cortical development in the months to follow. Interference with the venous circulation in the deep cerebral veins may also lead to stagnation of blood flow and tissue necrosis. The degree or extent of pathology depends upon the degree or extent of the hypoxia; the less the hypoxia the more subtle the clinical signs.

There are some correlations between clinical symptoms and pathologic findings. Wide destruction of the motor cortex greatly impairs voluntary movement but never entirely abolishes it. Upper motor neuron (cortical) damage results in uncontrolled spastic contraction of the muscles. Destruction or maldevelopment of the cerebellum causes dysmetria (inability to measure distance) and synergia (poor coordination) and results directly or indirectly in loss of muscle tone. Injury to the nuclei that comprise the extrapyramidal system results in poor coordination, tremor, lack of facial expression, and hemiballismus (violent spasmodic throwing motions of one arm and leg). Decerebrate rigidity, nystagmus, and poorly regulated visceral reflexes (breathing, heart beat, swallowing, and vomiting) result from damage to the vestibular nuclei.

DIAGNOSIS

A pertinent history and neurological examination can often substantiate a diagnosis of cerebral palsy. The younger the child, the more vague the findings and prediction of outcome. Supportive laboratory investigations are often not helpful. The experienced physician develops a diagnostic study plan based on the age of the child.

Newborn Period

Although clinical evidence of anoxia at birth does not guarantee later brain damage, nevertheless, the hyper-irritable or excessively listless infant must be regarded suspiciously for future signs of neurological dysfunction. Hyper-irritability (manifested as seizures, twitching, marked increased Moro or startle reflex) usually reflects cortical instability. The listless infant who is hypotonic, difficult to feed or to awaken, who chokes readily with feedings, or who does not demonstrate a Moro reflex reflects midbrain or brain-stem damage. The prognosis is poorer in listless infants than in hyper-irritable babies. A clue to continuing effects of anoxia is the persistence after birth of head lag when the newborn is lifted by his arms from the supine position. Some healthy newborns, still under the effects of anesthesia, may show this finding for twenty-four hours. The majority of lusty neonates have good head tonus, when lifted by the arms from the supine position, within hours after birth (Denhoff and Holden 1951).

Several reflexes present at birth—such as the tonic neck reflex, the Moro reflex, rooting and sucking reflexes, and the grasp reflex—normally disappear by the third month. These are described in detail by André-Thomas et al. (1960).

Cerebral palsy is infrequently diagnosed at birth because there are few meaningful abnormal neurological signs at this time. The brain damaged neonate may appear normal for several weeks. It is only as the stress of development is placed on the damaged cortex and midbrain that neuromotor difficulties become apparent. The visible signs during the early weeks of life suggesting future neuromotor disturbance may be cyanosis, pallor, stiffening, arching, excessive startle, strabismus, nystagmus, bruises, cephalhematoma, and jaundice. Sudden unexplained fevers are not unusual. Developmental stigmata such as uncleft toes, ear deformities, high-arch palate, hypertelorism, microcephaly, or hydrocephaly, indicating early anoxic insults to the embryo or genetic effects, may suggest the possibility

of associated brain damage. A tiny baby, a thin wrinkled one, or a large ede-
matous infant should be watched carefully. These are the appearances of
premature, dysmature, immature, or postmature babies, or infants of dia-
betic mothers. A rapidly developing jaundice may be associated with kernicterus, while an infant with atelectasis or hyaline membrane disease may
have sternal retractions shortly after birth. It is by no means conclusive
that any infant with the above findings at birth will be revealed as brain
damaged later. For the most part, the story unfolds with growth and development.

Infancy

The study plan includes a detailed pediatric-neurological history. In an early
study of infants suspected of being cerebral palsied, the presenting complaints were convulsions (81 percent), slow development (54 percent), and
feeding difficulties (21 percent). Such findings are most commonly
associated with obstetrical factors (33 percent), prenatal complications (16
percent), and postnatal complications such as head trauma or meningitis
(16 percent). Genetic factors were suspected in 9 percent. Causes were unclear in 39 percent. Physical findings involve delayed motor development
and variances from normal skeletal muscle tonus. Classic reflex changes
were unreliable indicators.

More precise assessment of the newborn and infant has been made
possible by the work of André-Thomas et al. in France and the Bobaths
(1964) in England and Prechtl (1964) in Holland. The French neurologists
depend a good deal on the state of tonus, mainly by observing static postures and the effects of direct and indirect passive movements of the limbs
when the child is alert but not crying. Tonus is evaluated by palpitation of
muscles to detect consistency, by slow passive movements to detect extensi-
bilité (capacity of the muscle to be lengthened), "flapping" the limb at the
joint to detect passivité (resistance to passive movement), and observations
of posture and reflex and recoil to detect tonus d'action (static and phasic
muscular activity of the baby).

The examination is first done with the child lying supine; then in prone;
in sitting posture; in prone and supine suspension; in the vertical position;
and, finally, in the suspended inverted position with the infant grasped by
the legs. Among the signs of importance to be sought are the ocular signs
(ciliary and pupillary reflexes), the cardinal point signs (stroking angles of
the mouth and the center of the upper and lower lip for a "rooting"
response), the Moro response (extension of the arms to startle), the grasp
reflex, and the other postural reflexes. All of these items are present early
and disappear by the sixth month. The persistence of these "brain-stem"

derived activities beyond this time indicates a damaged or dysfunctioning cortex or lower main centers.

In the early months, the infant with spasticity may lie quietly with arms flexed and legs extended. When activity is attempted, movements are jerky and explosive. As the infant grows, the thighs are frequently held in an adducted position because of adductor muscle spasticity, and the tendency toward "scissoring" increases. When the infant is held in a standing position, the hips and knees are held in rigid extension, and the "scissoring" accompanied by ankle equinus and internal rotation at the hip joints becomes more apparent.

During these early months, the deep reflexes may increase and the stretch reflex and ankle clonus may be noted. Increasing periods of hypertonicity, especially when the limbs are moved, are recognized, as is the failure to establish reciprocal leg movements.

Severely damaged infants, especially if mentally retarded, may show "mass movement," in which all of the extremities flex or extend simultaneously. On the other hand, atonia of joints and muscles may be found first. With growth and development, there may be a gradual return to hypertonicity.

In athetosis, arm and leg movement are purposeless in nature if compared to the purposeful repetitious manner of normal infants. When the arms are used, frequently this will initiate extraneous movements of the trunk and legs as well. Tension, in the form of intermittent stiffening spells when reaching for objects, becomes more apparent as the infant grows. Straightening of the arms with clenching of the fists is characteristic.

Spasticity generally appears before six months, whereas athetosis may not be apparent until the end of the first year or later. Spasticity affects the lower extremities more severely, while the head, neck, and upper extremities are often more severely involved in athetosis.

Developmental Diagnosis

The rate of developmental progress is a reliable measure of evaluating both normal and abnormal development. Developmental diagnosis is a practical method to differentiate early the "normal" from the "abnormal" child. In a study of one hundred cerebral palsied children (Denhoff and Holden 1951), the rate of developmental progress was evaluated, and a simple developmental scale was devised.

Head Erection from Prone

The normal infant usually can lift his head upward from the prone position for short periods during the first month of life. It is significant if a baby fails to erect head from the prone after three months of age. Of seventy-four cerebral palsied children studied, 14 percent could hold their heads erect momentarily by one month (normal), 18 percent by three months of age (late normal), while the majority (68 percent) failed to hold their heads erect from the prone within the expected range. The average age of attaining this was 12.4 months.

Reaching

The normal infant usually reaches for nearby objects within from three to five months. In this study, of twenty-eight cerebral palsied children, 3 percent reached for objects before five months (normal), while 86 percent reached for objects later than this. Eleven percent of the cases were reported never to have reached for objects.

Sitting without Support

The normal infant can usually sit without support within from six to eight months. It is abnormal if an infant cannot sit independently by ten months of age. Of seventy-three cerebral palsied children studied, 15 percent could sit without support by eight months (normal), 14 percent by ten months (late normal), while 71 percent did not acquire the ability to sit independently until after ten months. The average age of acquiring this skill was 20.4 months.

Crawling

The normal infant can usually crawl, dragging the body along the floor and drawing his legs after, by seven months, and it is abnormal if this item is delayed beyond eight months. Of fifty-four cerebral palsied children, only 2 percent acquired this skill by eight months. There were 37 percent who crawled after this age, while 61 percent never crawled. The average age of crawling in those who acquired this skill was 26.4 months. Creeping, which utilizes alternating coordination of hands and knees, is ordinarily attained by nine or ten months.

Speech (Single Words)

The normal infant can vocalize single words such as *mama, dada,* or *ball* by eleven months, but lack of this criterion is not abnormal until twelve months. In this study, of sixty-five cerebral palsied children, 11 percent said single words by nine months, 15 percent by ten months, while 74 percent were delayed beyond the twelve-month norm. The average age for the onset of this item was 27.1 months.

Standing Alone

The normal infant can usually stand alone by twelve months, and the late normal limit is thirteen months. In this study, of forty-three cerebral palsied children, 11 percent stood alone by twelve months, 2 percent by thirteen months, and 87 percent did not stand alone until after this period. The average age of standing alone was 27.5 months.

Walking Alone

The normal infant can walk alone between twelve and fifteen months, while not walking alone until after eighteen months must be regarded as abnormal. In this study, of fifty-seven cerebral palsied children, 7 percent walked alone by fifteen months, 16 percent by eighteen months, while 77 percent walked alone only after eighteen months. The average age cerebral palsied children walked by themselves was 32.9 months.

Speech (Two- and Three-Word Sentences)

The normal infant can speak two- and three-word sentences ("want ball," "me go out") by twenty-four months, although speech is not considered seriously delayed until after thirty months. In this study, of thirty-nine cerebral palsied children, 31 percent talked in sentences by twenty-four months, 23 percent by thirty months, while 46 percent did not talk in sentences until after thirty months. The average age for this development was 37.4 months.

Correlations Between Development and Intelligence

The only developmental item which correlated with the intellectual level in the cerebral palsied children studied was age of onset of speaking two- or three-word sentences.

Of the thirty-nine children who were able to speak and about whom reliable speech information was available, thirty-six later had intelligence tests. A significant difference was found between those children who spoke sentences before thirty months and those who spoke after thirty months. Those who did not speak in sentences until after thirty months were later found to be retarded in intelligence at or below the borderline range.

Special Problems

Feeding Difficulties

The persistence through the first six months of feeding difficulties is a suspicious indicator, although many infants present feeding complaints during the earlier months. The complaints usually are excess gas, crying, or indigestion. They may be due to over-vigorous sucking, milk allergy, a tight perianal ring, or even a poor emotional relationship between mother and infant. These symptoms are called "colic," and usually disappear within the first three months.

Cerebral palsied infants have more severe feeding symptoms which grow worse. These symptoms are: refusal to nurse, difficulty in sucking, hyper-irritability, a feeble cry, drowsiness, listlessness, and excessive grunting during feedings.

The feeding difficulty may be due to the persistent forward pushing movements of the tongue, which normally reverse by four to six weeks.

Physical Growth

Cerebral palsied infants, regardless of type, may gain weight poorly from six months of life. After the first year, weight gain slows almost to a standstill, especially in athetoids. Tissue turgor is poor, and anemia is common. Nutritional and vitamin deficiencies are frequent. These, along with excess motility and poor food intake, are probably responsible for slow growth.

Eye Difficulties

Strabismus and nystagmus may be recognized early. Internal strabismus is more common. The nystagmus associated with cerebral palsy is frequently jerky in character, fast, or slow. In athetosis, a paralysis of upward and downward gaze is frequently noted. This may not be recognized until the infant is old enough to start looking around at things.

Preschool and Older Children

As the child grows, the findings of spasticity or athetosis are clearly recognized.

Spasticity

The children with spastic hemiplegia or spastic quadriplegia comprise the largest group. At the nursery or preschool level, hemiplegia is not difficult to recognize. The child usually holds his arm pressed against the body with the forearm bent at right angles to the upper arm and the hand bent against the forearm. The fist may be clenched tightly with the fingers pressed firmly into the palm, in a fixed position. On the other hand, in a milder case, a diagnostic sign is the peculiar overextended appearance of the fingers and rotation of the wrists when the child reaches for items.

The leg may be more involved or less involved than the arm. The hemiplegic youngster may walk on his toe or outer part of the ball of the foot while the leg rotates inwardly and the knee is bent in a limited fashion. At rest, the foot may be held in the equino-varus position with the big toe hyperextended in the "Babinski" position. The deformity results from adductor contraction and weak opposition of the leg muscle groups. The limited knee and forefoot performance is also the result of contracted calf and ankle muscles.

When both legs are involved, the bilateral contractures draw the legs together, rotating them inward at the hips, resulting in a "scissoring" gait when the child attempts any walking activities.

The child with a severe quadriplegia involvement may be unable to sit or walk unsupported and have poor control of his arms. In moderately involved cases, the movements of the child with spasticity are slow and labored, and walking becomes a jerky, unrhythmic mechanism. Balance is poor because of poor weight distribution and contractures from the pelvic muscles to the muscles of the lower extremities.

In a mild case, the only evidence of neuromotor instability may be noticed as the child walks. The gait may be widebased with the arms outstretched, the fingers alternatingly clenched and extended as though reaching for balance. In the mildly handicapped, strabismus and drooling along with hyperactive, destructive, or distractible behavior may be more apparent than the physical handicap.

Athetosis

Children with athetosis or other types of dyskinesia differ from spastic children by their variability of movement. Any or all limbs may be involved. The fingers particularly are overextending and in almost constant activity when not at rest. Their feet may turn inward and the toes tend to be held upward. The head may be drawn back, the neck may be thick and bull-like, the mouth open and tongue protruding, and drooling may be excessive. At times the face may be mask-like, but break into grimaces as the child tries to talk.

The athetoid walks in a writhing, lurching, and stumbling manner with a good deal of incoordination of the arms. The overflow movement is variable, depending on confidence or fear. When he is calm and well rested, he may walk surprisingly well. Athetoid movements may be discussed as tremor, rotary, or shudder, among others.

Ataxia

Ataxia is easily recognized by the high-stepping, stumbling, lurching gait. The child, when walking downhill, may suddenly start to run and then fall flat on his face. He may totter and suddenly stop as he walks uphill. Nystagmus is common, tremor of the head is usual, and overshooting when reaching for a toy is characteristic. Speech may be monotonous and drawling.

There are degrees of ataxia, which depend upon the pathology. The ataxic may be handicapped by severe limited physical and or mental growth. Some ataxic children are bright and alert, but are delayed in speech and coordination. This group makes steady but not dramatic progress.

Mixed Types

There is some disagreement as to whether the incidence of mixed clinical types of cerebral palsy is slight or great. Benda's (1952) observation that the

SUMMARY OF FINDINGS IN CHILDREN WITH CEREBRAL PALSY

Diagnosis	Spastic Hemiplegia	Spastic Paraplegia	Spastic Quadriplegia	Atonic	Athetosis and Tremor	Rigidity	Ataxic
History Family				Consanguinity Genetic Disorder Maternal Illness			Genetic Disorder
Prenatal 1st Trimester			Rubella				
3rd Trimester	Toxemia		Toxemia Pregnancy		Anoxia Placenta Praevia		
Obstetrical	Trauma	Breech	Trauma Precipitate Delivery Caesarean		Placenta Abruptio Breech Anoxia Hemolytic Anemia Kernicterus	Precipitate Delivery Caesarean	Precipitate Delivery Caesarean
Postnatal	Prematurity						
Infancy	Meningitis						
Physical Findings General		Hydrocephaly Average Weight	Microcephaly	Undersized	Underweight		
Cranial Nerves	Strabismus						
Deep Reflexes	Increased Unilateral	Increased Bilateral, both legs	Increased, all extremities especially legs		Normal		Hypotonic
Pathologic Reflexes	Babinski, Stretch, Clonus } Unilateral	Stretch, Babinski, Clonus } both legs	Stretch Babinski Clonus Abdominal		Babinski		
Movement Tonus	Hypertonic, especially upper extremity	Hypertonic, both legs	Hypertonic, especially legs	Hypotonic, all extremities	Abnormal	Pipe stem	Hypotonic
Gait	Spastic	Spastic	Spastic	None	Uncoordinated		Ataxic
Associated Disorders	O Behavior Visual Perceptual/ motor	Mental Retardation Convulsions	Mental Retardation Convulsions	Mental Retardation Convulsions	Hearing Vision Behavior		Variable

mixed type with elements of spasticity, athetosis, and/or ataxia is the most frequently encountered condition in cerebral palsy is sound. These patients as infants appear relatively normal. During the first three years, spasticity of the lower extremities, uncoordinated movements of the upper extremities with poor head control, and the increasing "bullneck" appearance, characteristic of athetosis, become noticeable. Mentality varies, and there is a high incidence of behavior disorders.

   Table 2.6 summarizes the clinical findings in children with various types of cerebral palsy.

Laboratory Studies

Laboratory tests (see Table 2.7) are often not helpful although they are needed to be certain that correctable conditions are not present. Transillumination of the skull in infants can aid immeasurably in detecting early surgically correctable abnormalities, as well as microcephaly with macrocranium, ventricular dilatation, and porencephaly. The method simply consists of applying a flashlight with a special rubber cuff to the skull in a darkened room (Shurtleff 1964). In infancy this test is a prerequisite to attempting pneumoencephalography.

Associated Disorders

Cerebral palsy is not only a problem of physical handicap, but may involve intellectual impairment, behavioral and emotional disturbances, convulsions, hearing, visual, perceptual disorders, and language disorders as well as learning disabilities.

Convulsive Disorders

Between 35 and 60 percent of cerebral palsied children have convulsions at some period during their natural life history. Seizures can be a deterrent to progress as they interfere with information processing. Thus it is important to control them through medication and modification of the environment. Seizures may be classified as either major and/or minor (grand mal or petit mal). They reflect disordered electro-cortical energy from known causes (symptomatogenic) or unknown causes (idiopathic). Some types are familial in origin and are usually referred to as "epilepsy." It is possible that seizures in cerebral palsy may not be the result of brain damage associated with the cerebral palsy, but could instead be of a genetic (familial) nature. Abnormal seizure patterns may arise from various parts of the cortex and/ or deeper in the subcortical areas.

   Spastics have a three times higher incidence of convulsions than athetoids (Perlstein *et al.* 1947). The seizures in the spastics are predominantly a major focal type, but minor (psychomotor) seizures are not uncommon.

TABLE 2.7
LABORATORY TESTS FOR INFANTS WITH DEVELOPMENTAL DISORDERS

Procedure	Purpose	% Abnormal N = 500 Cases
Blood		
Hemoglobin	Anemia	——
White blood count with smear	Infection, lead	——
Urine		
Routine	Renal	——
Bacterial count	Infection	——
Blood Chemistry		
Glucose	Hypo-hyperglycemia	low 0.4/high 1.4
Urea Nitrogen	Renal	4.6
T3/T4	Thyroid	low 11
G. O. Transaminase		2.5
Lactic Dehydroginase		1.0
Creatinine-Phospho-Kinase	Myopathy	——
Aldolase		3.7
Lead	Lead intoxication	
Uric Acid	Lesh-Nyan syndrome	
Ceruloplasmin	Wilson's Disease	0.4
Calcium		
Phosphorus	Dilantin toxicity	0.2
Alkaline Phosphatase		
Spinal Fluid		
Cells	Infection	
Protein	Tumor	1.3
Sugar		1.7
Chloride		
Immunoglobulins	Leucodystrophy	0.05
X-Rays		
Skull	Calcification, erosion	
Extremities/Hips	Dislocation	
Wrists	Bone age; heavy metal	
Other		
Electroencephalogram	Seizures	2.8
Echoencephalogram	Ventricular shift	0.5
Brain Scan	Mass	0.5
Pneumoencephalogram	Cerebral/cortical atrophy	——
Angiography	Mass; Vascular anomaly	——

Major Seizures

Major seizures may be generalized (grand mal) or focal (Jacksonian). In the latter the attack arises from demonstrable abnormal foci within the cerebral cortex, while a generalized seizure has no consistent point of origin.

Focal seizures are common in cerebral palsy. In focal spells the initial phenomenon may be motor, sensory, behavioral, loss of consciousness, or automatism, followed by movements of one part of the body which then spreads to other parts.

Minor Seizures

Minor seizures may be of the petit mal variety, the myoclonic type, or akinetic. The petit mal seizure (a three-per-second wave and spike electroencephalographic pattern) is characterized by brief interruptions in the stream of consciousness. The eyes may stare and often turn upwards while the eyelids blink rapidly. It is not common in cerebral palsy.

Myoclonic seizures consist of sudden involuntary contractions of the muscles of the limbs, trunk, neck, or face without apparent loss of consciousness. Myoclonic seizures may precede a major seizure attack.

Akinetic seizures consist of sudden transient loss of postural tone with a nodding of the head or a sudden fall to the floor. The episodes are brief and consciousness is generally gained promptly.

Psychomatic Seizures (temporal lobe seizures)

The symptoms may involve sensory, mental, or motor complaints characterized by sudden alterations in sensation, behavior, or movement which produce unusual or bizarre reactions in the child.

Mixed Seizures

Mixed seizures, i.e., major and minor types, or psychomotor spells, can occur frequently. Sometimes, treating a minor seizure will precipitate a major seizure previously unknown to exist in the child.

Clinical Observations

The earlier the onset of convulsions the more likely are they related to brain damage. Seizures occurring during infancy, even when associated with high fever, should not be taken lightly. The convulsion is often the first overt sign of brain damage, and the fever only the precipitating factor.

Convulsions in premature infants are different from those in older babies. They may be seen only as fixed posture in an unnatural position, fixed eyeballs, or failure to respond to stimulation.

Seizures—in the form of sudden startles, a flinging of the arm, opisthotonic jerks of the body, throwing the arms backward, turning of the eyes upward—are common in older infants. They are usually mistaken for fear or uncontrolled hypertonicity. It is difficult to tell whether such behavior is a result of minor motor seizures or whether it is a persistence of mass reflexes such as the Moro reflex. Delayed development may be directly related to the inability to maintain posture because of "nodding" or "drop" seizures.

Electroencephalogram

In cerebral palsy the electroencephalogram (EEG) may be completely normal, may show moderately slow activity (generalized or localized), fast activity (generalized or localized), or a combination of fast and slow activity. Abnormal EEG records differ in incidence, depending on whether or not the cerebral palsied child has seizures. Perlstein *et al.* (1947) found that of 212 cases, 75 percent of patients with seizures had normal EEGs. An abnormal EEG in a cerebral palsied patient without seizures may be a warning that seizures may occur.

DIFFERENTIAL DIAGNOSIS

Cerebral palsy can simulate a number of conditions so that often differential diagnosis is a difficult problem.

Babies with nutritional, metabolic, allergic, neurologic, orthopedic, psychiatric, and other related disorders are often referred to cerebral palsy clinics because of their irritability or developmental lag.

An infant with true milk sensitivity can have many symptoms and signs of hyperreactivity, but these will recede promptly when substitute-milk therapy is employed. A scorbutic infant may be very irritable and lay immobile, but when ascorbic acid is given, there will be a rapid improvement.

A baby with phenylketonuria will change from marked irritability to calmness when he is placed on a proper diet. A hypothyroidal infant may be pudgy, pale, and hyporeactive with delayed dentition, pot belly, and an umbilical hernia, but his symptoms and signs will respond fairly promptly to thyroid medication. A baby with a chromosomal defect will often have telltale physical signs, but he may be cute and plump. A baby with amino aciduria will often have a characteristic odor. Most of these infants who will be classified as mentally retarded often have a small head size, congenital or genetic stigmata, hypotonia of the ankles or wrists, and lagging development, especially in speech.

Cerebral palsied children with specific vision, hearing, speech, and language disorders must be differentiated from those who are retarded. For instance, delay or absence of smiling, attention, or speech is often associated with hearing defects.

A good general rule is the "intelligence will out," i.e., those infants and young children with normal intellect but with superimposed deficits on their physical handicap will demonstrate their abilities in one way or another. It is often amazing how a severely handicapped but intelligent child will show his comprehension in some way.

Children with behavior disturbances apparently resulting from cerebral anoxia may have minor deep reflex and superficial reflex abnormality during infancy. Often, they are very active infants with rapid rates of motor development.

Children with environmental emotional disturbances such as anxiety or hysteria may also have aberrant neurologic signs but they are less specific. A history of disturbed family-child relations will help in the differential. Childhood schizophrenia may be confused with some aspects of cerebral palsy in that symptoms may simulate deafness, aphasia, athetosis, or ataxia.

Brain tumor must be considered in every case of cerebral palsy. Subtentorial (cerebellar) tumors are most common. They are insidious in onset and may mask as cerebral palsy, especially spastic hemiplegia, for several months or years. The history of sudden onset or a gradually increasing strabismus, facial paralysis, ataxia, convulsions, or a slowly progressive hemiplegia with gradual weakness of a limb are suspicious indicators of a progressive disturbance.

Brachial paralysis of the newborn, congenital dislocation of the hip, and residuals of unrecognized cases of poliomyelitis are often confused with cerebral palsy. Brachial paralysis is characterized by adduction of the forearm with limpness but with a strong hand grasp. A history of a difficult traction delivery is helpful. A dislocated hip should be suspected when an apparently normal baby does not walk or walks with a limp. X-rays of the pelvic and acetabular region are diagnostic. Poliomyelitis deformities present a rather characteristic appearance of the limb, with atrophy, weakness, and pes cavus deformities of the foot or hand. Since the mass administration of poliomyelitis vaccine, there is a lesser need to consider such a differential.

The muscle disorders (congenital torticollis, amyotonia, dystrophies, atrophies, myotonias, and myasthenia gravis) may simulate cerebral palsy. Congenital torticollis is characterized by head-tilting with the chin rotated to the opposite side. This can be confused with a persistence of the tonic neck reflex.

Amyotonia congenita may at first be misdiagnosed as the atonic type of cerebral palsy. However, reflexes continue to remain absent and the limbs flaccid. Intellect is usually normal, while the atonic diplegic is usually retarded.

Muscular dystrophy is difficult to differentiate early from ataxia or spasticity because of the insidious onset. The syndrome includes a number of different conditions characterized by progressive symmetrical weakness or wasting of muscle groups of the extremities. In the Duchenne type of pseudohypertrophic dystrophy, the muscle groups of the pelvic girdle are involved first and, later, muscles of the upper arm and shoulders. In a child with normal to marginal intelligence, with waddling gait, and large but weak muscles, an abnormal blood value S.G.O.-Transaminase, lactic dehydrogenase, and aldolase may be helpful differential tests. Benign hypotonia in infancy often appears to be like atonic cerebral palsy.

Myasthenia gravis may also occur during infancy and is noted as ptosis of the eyelids, relaxation of the face, and sagging jaws. It may be confused with the dyskinetic types of cerebral palsy. Response to prostigmine bromide may be diagnostic.

PROGNOSIS

Whether or not a child will make an adequate adjustment in later life can be answered by correlating the following factors.

1. *History*—Absence of chromosomal or biochemical abnormality; Absence of *early severe prenatal disturbance.*

2. *Physical examination*—Absence of severe spastic quadriplegia, dyskinesia, or ataxia; absence of profound deafness, blindness, or other sensory deafness.

3. *Laboratory*—absence of severe anatomic defect as measured by the pneumoencephalogram, angiogram, etc.

4. *Psychological testing*—absence of severe depression in cognitive functioning.

5. *Psychosocial*—absence of severe deprivation or family breakdown.

The pneumoencephalogram (see Figure 2.1) can be used as a rough prognostic indicator in cerebral palsy. This statement is based upon studies of thirty-three young children who were observed over a period of five years or more. Using the pneumoencephalogram as a relatively fixed anatomic anchor and correlating the findings with over-all progress in the areas tested above, it appears possible to predict generally those who will make satisfactory progress (Denhoff *et al.* 1956).

The pneumoencephalogram can be classified into seven broad groupings:

1. Generalized (bilateral) cerebral atrophy (normal ventricles).
2. Generalized (bilateral) cortical atrophy (ventricular dilatation).
3. Unilateral cerebral atrophy.
4. Unilateral cortical atrophy.
5. Mixed cerebral and cortical atrophy.
6. Cerebellar atrophy; mild to severe.
7. Normal

As might be expected, the prognosis was poor in those cases with cerebellar atrophy (Group 6) and with severe generalized cerebral and/or

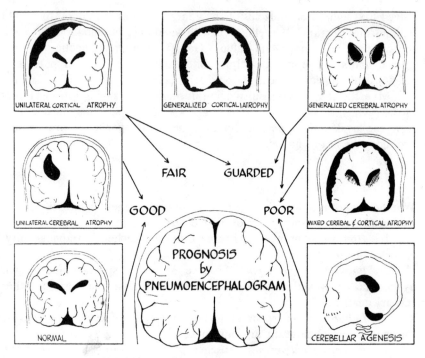

Figure 2.1. Prognosis by pneumoencephalogram.

cortical atrophy (Groups 1, 2, and 5). Clinical progress was good in those cases with unilateral cerebral atrophy (porencephaly) and when the pneumogram was essentially normal (Groups 3, 4, and 7). However, there are some mentally deficient children with normal pneumoencephalograms. The pneumoencephalogram of course does not take into account the multifaceted problem of personality, family, or social factors which contribute to ultimate success.

MANAGEMENT AND GOALS

The management of cerebral palsy demands a comprehensive systematic approach to include general health care, developmental enrichment experiences, remediation of specific neuromotor deficits and/or associated disabilities, and behavioral, emotional, scholastic, and social adjustments. The development of pre-vocational, vocational, and socialization skills is necessary. The goal is normalization to help each child reach optimal functional ability in adulthood. The success of a comprehensive program ultimately depends upon the ability of the family to carry on and carry out both a supportive and a participating role in rehabilitation settings under the guidance of skilled professionals.

General Health Care

Prevention—The Parents

Prevention of cerebral palsy receives high priority. In large measure it involves good medical and obstetrical care for the at-risk mother.

New advances, both in the understanding of the biologic mechanisms of the maternal-fetal-infant relationships and in technological developments, are lessening the number and the severity of the cases of cerebral palsy.

Progress has been so vast in these areas that the readers are referred to specific texts for detailed information (Davis *et al*. 1972; Avery 1972). However, we shall briefly highlight a few specific areas which apply to cerebral palsy.

Amniocentesis

By examining the amniotic fluid obtained by amnioscopy (injecting a needle through the mother's abdomen into the amniotic sac and withdrawing a sample of amniotic fluid), it is possible early in pregnancy to culture the cells for karyotype to confirm the sex and to identify chromosomal abnormalities, to stain cells for chromatin to identify male fetuses for such X-linked recessive diseases as muscular dystrophy, and to try enzyme assay to identify such inherited metabolic diseases as galactosemia. In later pregnancy, information can be obtained about bilirubin for severity of Rh hemolytic disease, about pregnanetriol for the diagnosis of adrenal hyperplasia, about lipid and creatinine content to assess gestational age, and about the lecithin/sphengomyelin ratio to assess potentiality for respiratory distress syndrome.

Maternal Conditions

Malnutrition in the mother, fetus, and the infant has the greatest priority because it is possible to neutralize its adverse effects on the offspring's developing nervous system by application of appropriate dietary measures.

Recent studies (Neye *et al*. 1973) have shown that maternal undernutrition, especially low calorie and protein depletion after the mid trimester, has an adverse impact on fetal body, organ, and cellular growth. These effects will continue if the infant's diet is inappropriate during the next two years. This means that it is of utmost importance to evaluate the nutritional status of the pregnant mother early and correct depletion, especially low calorie, protein, and essential vitamins, before the last trimester. Maternal starvation definitely leads to fewer and smaller neurons in the central nervous system in the offspring. Neuronal depletion is associated with small brain size and mental retardation. Well-nourished babies develop when mothers gain one pound or more per week in the last two trimesters of pregnancy and have extensive prenatal medical visiting (Miller and Hassinein 1973).

In the human brain, like in any other organ, DNA synthesis and hence all cell division stops long before growth stops. Cell division slows down around the time of birth, and by twelve months of age there is very little increase in the total number of brain cells. In contrast, protein synthesis continues throughout the entire growing period, so that with good diet during infancy it is possible to affect the size and function of the cells. However, malnutrition during the first year results in a reduction of brain-cell size as well as curtailment of cell division. The effect is equally severe in the cerebrum and the cerebellum as well as the brain stem.

Malnutrition, especially low protein intake, in late pregnancy and early newborn life adversely affects the orderly sequence of physical, chemical, and functional changes in the brain and leads to inefficiencies in visual, haptic, and kinesthetic sensory integration which leads to inefficiency in learning standard skills (Rosso and Winick 1973). Such children are labeled "mentally retarded."

Maternal Stress Factors

The Perinatal Collaborative Study has focused attention upon a number of maternal factors which are associated with neurological abnormality of the baby. The study has merely opened the door to an area which, when properly dealt with, will lead to a higher prevention rate of cerebral palsy. For instance, while the Perinatal Collaborative Study points out that exposure to certain agents like cytomegalic viruses, herpes simplex, and toxoplasmosis are found in higher incidence in mothers of neurologically impaired babies, other studies (Siege 1973) show that the incidence of congenital malformation in the newborn is no higher than a normal control group when mothers had chicken pox, measles, mumps, or hepatitis during pregnancy. Studies like these narrow the field so that obstetricians and adolescent specialists can concentrate their efforts on lessening the effects of agents known to have adverse effects upon the developing brain.

"Small for Date" Babies

It is generally believed that when the reasons for the "small for date" baby are better understood and their problems eliminated, the incidence of cerebral palsy and related disorders will drop dramatically.

It is now recognized that all small infants are not alike, and that the various terms which have been used to differentiate the normal premature

infant (i.e., delivery weeks before the time because of premature labor) from
the dysmature (undersized and undernourished but full term), the postmature (undernourished because of failure to deliver on time), and the immature (a consequence of fetal malnutrition) are not particularly helpful for
prognosis.

Weight at birth combined with weeks of gestation is a useful index for
prognosis. A term birth includes all infants born between 38 and 42 weeks of
gestation. One-third to one-half of low birth weight babies are term births
with intrauterine growth retardation. Pre-term babies (born before 38
weeks) have a lower mortality rate in relationship to a higher gestational period, so that a 1,000–1,500 gm baby has a better opportunity for survival if
the gestational age is 34 weeks or more, and a 2,000 gm baby's chances for
survival are immeasurably improved if the baby is born at 38 weeks or
more.

The pre-term baby is particularly prone to respiratory distress and hyperbilirubinemia, while the intrauterine growth-retarded newborn is prone
to bouts of hypoglycemia (Bauer 1972).

Complications at Birth

The most common acute causes of premature labor which in turn results in
fetal or neonatal death or morbidity are infections of the amniotic fluid (41
percent), premature separation of the placenta (19 percent), cord accident
(9 percent), and mechanical birth trauma (5 percent). These conditions present themselves in the low birth weight baby as asphyxia, respiratory distress, and hemolytic disease.

Birth Asphyxia

The proper management of birth asphyxia and resuscitation is the key to
the prevention of and lessening the deficits of cerebral palsy. Birth asphyxia
may take the form of failure to breathe, failure to expand the lungs, or both.
The respiratory depression causing failure to breathe may reflect prolonged
intrauterine asphyxia, the effects of analgesic drugs or anesthesia given the
mother, or rarely brain stem injury. Lung expansion deficiencies come from
extreme prematurity or congenital malformations of the respiratory tract
or airway obstruction, usually caused by thick mucous at the level of the
larynx.

Once the airway is cleared, if the baby does not breathe spontaneously,
intermittent positive pressure with bag and mask is applied gently, the baby
is placed in a warm incubator, 40 percent oxygen is given at 2 liters per
minute, and 10 cc. of 7 percent THAM or 8.4 percent bicarbonate solution
followed by $5M^2$ of 20 percent dextrose is injected intravenously, if indicated. All of the various emergencies, such as cardiac arrest, respiratory

obstruction, fetal hemorrhage, and malformations such as choanal atresia must be cared for if they develop. There is definite evidence that proper handling of these situations makes for better outcomes in small for date babies.

Respiratory Distress

Within 24–48 hours, if respiratory distress or jaundice develops, the physician is in an excellent position to treat these conditions properly by intravenous or feedings balanced by proper chemical ingredients, early oral feedings, or prevention of infection. Careful evaluation of the bilirubin level will ascertain whether replacement transfusions are needed, and carefully taken blood sugar and calcium-phosphorus blood specimens correlated with early clinical signs of tremor, or seizures will help decide if glucose or calcium replacement is necessary.

Hemolytic Disease

As stated, this chapter cannot delve into the specifics of the management of hyperbilirubinemia. But it is important to recognize that since the use of the exchange transfusion, kernicterus is now extremely low in incidence and the cases of cerebral palsy due to this factor are lessening. An unpublished seven-year follow-up by the author of Rh infants who received one or more complete exchange transfusions showed that the incidence of neurological disease was the same as in a control population.

Neonatal Complications

Early identification of the presence of subdural hematoma due to birth trauma leads to a normal outcome with repeated aspirations of excess fluid. Correction of neonatal hypoglycemia prevents brain damage and seizure disorders. Biochemical and dietary correction in a host of disorders which interfere with growth and development will improve outcome.

Pediatric Care

Most babies who are later to be identified as cerebral palsied are very irritable or hyperreactive. The outstanding symptoms are excessive crying, feeding difficulty, and constipation.

The treatment of *irritability* rests between the correction of the reasons for the infant's distress and skillful support of the mother. The judicious but limited use of mild antispasmodics such as Bentyl or sedatives such as phenobarbital may be helpful. The *feeding problems* often reflect pathology of the cranial nerves involved in sucking and swallowing, and thickened feedings, special supplies, and techniques which help the baby to swallow better may be required. A well-balanced, moderate-to-high protein diet is helpful. The correction of anemia is important. True milk sensitivity is rare and leucine sensitivity or amino aciduria uncommon. *Constipation* is usually due to poor fluid intake. The addition of fluids such as water or juices and Vitamin B complex and/or a stool softener (Colace) has proved helpful.

As the baby grows attention must be paid to an adequate, well-balanced diet, to early treatment of infection, and to vision and hearing efficiency.

Parent Programming

The Parent Program for Developmental Management is a comprehensive developmental enrichment program designed to meet the total needs of handicapped infants and families during the first three years. The population of atypical and at-risk babies is generally referred from physicians and allied health services. The diagnostic team consists of a pediatrician, a social worker, and physical, occupational, speech, and language therapists. Psychologists, nurses, special educators, and adult educators serve in consultant roles. The actual treatment program is devised and delivered by a "mini-team" consisting of one or more of the diagnostic team.

The parents and baby are first evaluated by the full team, the special and general needs of the baby and his family are outlined, and a program is developed. Within a month the baby and the parents (often the mother) are seen by the "mini-team"—a social worker and the therapist most appropriate for the baby's outstanding deficits.

Specific techniques are demonstrated and directions written on duplicate instruction sheets for home use. If a visiting nurse is involved, she also receives a set of parent programming instructions. Monthly sessions are generally scheduled, but there are a number of options to this plan depending upon the severity of the case and the anxiety of the family.

The goal is to allow the parents to become effective primary programmers for their child. The therapy becomes incorporated into the family's daily routine and includes ordinary materials found at home or which can be made with little expense.

While at first the program is provided on an individualized basis, soon small groups of babies and mothers with common problems are found to meet at weekly intervals. The staffing patterns are changed somewhat to meet the needs of the group. In this group plan, child decision-making, social interactions with peers and adults, development of self-care skills, and independence are encouraged. Of course, the child's individualized requirements are not neglected, whether they be gross or fine motor activities, speech and language, cognitive development, or behavior. At all times, the mother and father are helped to understand and participate in fostering these child-oriented goals through regularly scheduled individual and group sessions with the social worker.

TABLE 2.8
**ORGANIZATION OF PARENT PROGRAM
FOR DEVELOPMENTAL MANAGEMENT**

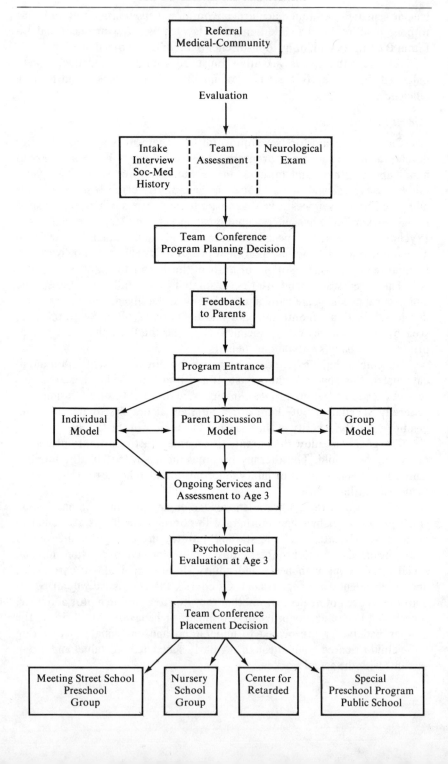

TABLE 2.9
Basic Principles of a Developmental
Management Program for the "At-Risk" Infant

	Early Needs	Instruments
Mother-Infant Interactions	Rocking, Cuddling, Touching, Fondling, Rubbing, Talking, Understanding	Rocking Chair Toweling Self
Sensory Stimulation	Visual Tactile Auditory Eye-hand	"Comfort-Me-Mitt" Mobiles, Lights Sounds, Textures
Feeding/Language Development	Sucking, Chewing, Swallowing, Tasting, Sounding	Primitive Reflex Reinforcement Nipples, Foods
Father-Infant Interactions	Motion through Handling Varied Body Position Changes	Hassock or Barrel Self

Table 2.8 illustrates the general organization of the Parent Program of Developmental Management, while Tables 2.9, 2.10 and 2.11 provide an idea of the techniques involved and how they are implemented in home instruction sheets.

Neuromotor Therapy

There are several approaches to improving the capabilities of the cerebral palsied child. Medical methods include orthopedic, neurosurgical, and pharmocologic.

Orthopedic Treatment

Good orthopedic treatment under the guidance of competent specialists can help the patient achieve overall success in improving both functional mobility and appearance.

Physical therapy and a variety of mechanical aids to help sitting, standing, walking, and functional use of the hands are utilized early.

Bracing helps to overcome limitation of joint motion, with resulting deformities, and to teach ambulatory activities. The type of brace depends upon the disability: (1) adjustable night caliber braces attached to the shoe with toe cap removed are useful for stretching heel cords; (2) abduction splints (Denis Browne) are useful at night to hold hips in abduction and feet in overcorrected position; (3) double upright aluminum braces (short leg) with a right-angle stop or dorsiflexion springs help control equinus or equinovarus; and (4) double upright long-leg braces with knee locks help prevent knee hyperextension. Torsion cable twisters or rigid pelvic band and hinged hip bars can be added to control excessive internal or external hip rotation.

Surgery is utilized only to surmount some definite obstacle to progress. Because of the previous poor success with heel-cord tenotomies and other unphysiologic procedures, there has been a definite tendency in recent years to be exceedingly cautious about surgical intervention. On the other hand, better understanding of neurophysiology has pointed the way to some generally good orthopedic surgical procedures (Denhoff and Robinault 1960).

The principles of orthopedic surgery in cerebral palsy are: (1) careful

TABLE 2.10

EXAMPLE OF INSTRUCTION SHEET FOR
PARENT PROGRAM FOR DEVELOPMENTAL MANAGEMENT

MEMORANDUM FROM MEETING STREET SCHOOL
CHILDREN'S REHABILITATION CENTER

333 Grotto Avenue   JAckson 1-6800   Providence, R. I. 02906

Date __Dec. 2, 1975__

Name __Michael P.__   Next Appointment __Jan. 5, 1976__

Physician's Name __Eric Denhoff, M.D.__   Next Visit __Jan. 14, 1976__

Program recommendations:

Physical Therapy
1. *Standing Activity:* Tie *Time* magazines around Mike's knees with old neckties. Then practice standing him up, holding him between your knees. Rock him from side to side to help him shift his weight.
2. Take Mike through the practice of getting onto his hands and knees; then put his hands up on your knees, then place one foot flat on the floor; then push gently in the fanny and help him to straighten up. (Mother or father to be sitting on a chair while taking him through this.)

Occupational Therapy
1. *Tactile Activities:*
   a. *Sand:* trickle over arms and legs.
   b. *Ice:* rub ice cube in paper towel over his arms, legs, feet, hands, and mouth.
   c. *Handcream:* spread handcream on arms and legs and take Mike's hand and move it over these parts to feel them.

Speech Therapy
1. *Eating*
   a. *Taste:* blend meat and vegetable to consistency he likes. You can also add a little fruit to help him accept it.
   b. *Thickness:* mashed potato or baby cereal to his breakfast; then gradually increase the thickness.

TABLE 2.11

Basic Treatment Principles for Parent Program for Developmental Management

Developmental Stage	Gross Motor Activities	Fine Motor Activities	Speech-Language Activities	Emotional Needs
Unorganized (reflex activity)	Head control Postural reflexes	Eye-hand contact Reaching	Suck-swallowing	Security through sensory gratification
Uncoordinated (conscious contact)	Sitting	Grasping	Babbling Unconditioned tongue reflexes	Security through mother-infant interplay
Poorly coordinated	Standing	Tactile grasp Spontaneous grasp-release	Conditioned tongue and lip control Sound-word association	Exploration of environment
Semi-coordinated	Supported walking	Mature release & transfer Tactile-kinesthetic development	Intersensory Association processing	Awareness of self separate from environment
Body control	Walking Awareness of body in space	Mature bilateral hand grasp	Eating utensil control Control airflow for voluntary speech	Trust in persons outside family
Early skills	Conscious control of all movements	Self-care skills	Readiness for communication	Beginning independence
Maturing skills	Skills sufficient for social participation	Perceptual motor mature Writing established Bilateral hand-eye skills	Mature communication Verbal and written	Independence

evaluation of the total problem must precede any surgical therapy; (2) surgery is merely an adjuvant measure and not a substitution for muscle reeducation; (3) surgery will fail without adequate postoperative therapy; (4) conservative therapy in growing children such as achieved by physical therapy and bracing should always be given an adequate trial before surgery; (5) growing children who are operated on always require postoperative bracing in order to prevent recurrence of the deformity; (6) surgery must be directed against the primary deforming factors and is contraindicated if it retards or impairs functional ability; and (7) contractures due to postural defects should not be corrected surgically unless the patient will be able to use the extremities in the corrected position. Soft-tissue surgery as early as three years of age is often indicated to prevent development of deformities and to minimize the use of braces in establishing ambulation. Many procedures are available for lower-extremity surgery, depending upon specific need:

1.   Adductor myotomy, with obturator neurectomy (Stoffel procedure), for adduction contracture of hips with resulting scissoring.

2.   Souter operation, for flexion contracture of hip.

3.   Stretching under anesthesia with immobilization in long-leg casts in marked external rotation, for mild internal contracture of the hip.

4.   Durham procedure, for persistent internal rotation contraction.

5.   Hamstring tenotomies combined with recession of gastrocnemius muscle head, for flexion contraction of the knee.

6.   Silfverskiold operation (gastrocnemius muscle recession and section of tibial motor nerves to the gastrocnemius), for ankle and foot deformities. This is the most reliable soft-tissue operation in the spastic lower extremities.

7.   Tendon transplant procedures, for flexion and lateral deviation deformities of the wrist (usually, flexor carpi ulnaris transplant to extensor carpi radialis tendons).

8.   Calcaneal osteotomy to stabilize foot support through bony block hindfoot joint structures.

9.   Bone stabilization procedures such as triple arthrodesis with or without tendon transplantation give most satisfactory results in the foot. Operations are recommended upon the foot at nine to ten years, the ankle at thirteen to fourteen years and the hand at twelve to thirteen years.

Neurosurgery

Neurosurgical treatment has not proved reliable in controlling dyskinesia. The removal of one cerebral hemisphere, usually damaged as a result of a porencephalic cyst or similar pathology, is successful in alleviating seizures and hemiplegia. Preventive surgery in craniosynostosis (cranial deformities of congenital origin), in hydrocephalus from congenital malformations in subdural hematoma, arteriovenous malformations, and intractable convulsions of operable nature have been helpful.

Convulsions

The control of convulsions when present is a prerequisite to a successful therapeutic program. Seizures may be easy or difficult, depending upon the type and degree of the seizure and the child's ability to handle medication. Generally, drugs of low toxicity are tried first, and changes to newer medications are made only if seizures remain uncontrollable. Combinations of drugs are frequently needed to keep the seizure incidence to a minimum. Several months may be needed to reach a relatively seizure-free state (Bercel 1952; Lennox 1951). A summary of the indications, dosage, and toxic effects of medications useful against convulsions and currently available is shown in Table 2.12.

Subclinical Seizures

A problem is whether to treat with anticonvulsants a patient with an abnormal electroencephalogram, although he is clinically free of seizures. Authorities are divided on this vexing problem. Generally, if there are atypical behaviorisms or poor memory, Dilantin can be tried on an empirical basis, and if a favorable effect is noted, the medication can be continued for a few months. Then medication should be discontinued and over-all progress reassessed.

Control by Blood Level

The modern management of seizures requires the dosage schedule of medications to be based upon mg/kg/24 hours administration and blood levels to assure proper control.

Muscle Relaxants

Motor reeducation is enhanced when drugs are used that have a relaxing effect on skeletal muscle hypertonia. The drug is especially valuable if it also favorably alters the child's emotional attitude and behavior. Probably no one drug will ever fulfill these criteria. Nevertheless, pharmacologists are continuing the effort to fulfill the requirement.

When a double-blind crossover method is used to evaluate both muscle relaxation and body anxiety reaction in cerebral palsy and related disorders, there often is a higher beneficial placebo effect than drug effect. Eight relaxant drugs were studied between 1949 and 1960. In double-blind controlled studies (Una 1953) beneficial effects on behavior ranged from 8 percent with Mephenesin (Tolserol) to 53 percent with Zoxazolamine (Flexin) with a

TABLE 2.12

Anticonvulsants Useful in Cerebral Palsy

Type Anticonvulsant	Type Seizures	Dosage Mg/K/Day	Blood Level mcg/ML	Remarks
Barbiturates				
Phenobarbital	Major Motor	3–6	10–15	Barbiturates accentuates hyperkinetic behavior. 35 + mcg/ml = oversedation.
Primidone (Mysoline)	Major Motor/focal Minor Motor	5–20	8–12	Prior administration of phenobarbital lessens initial oversedation effects of Mysoline.
Mebaral Demonil		Maximum level—2 weeks		
Hydantoinates				
Diphenylhydantoin (Dilantin)	Major Motor/focal Psychomotor	5–10	10–2	Maintainance of concise blood levels diminishes long term complications.
Mesantoin		Maximum level—7–10 days		15–30 mcg/ML = gingival hyperplasia; nystagmus.
				30 + mcg/ML = ataxia
				40 + mcg/ML = increases seizures
Succinamides				
Ethosuxamide (Zarontin) Celontin Milontin	Petit Mal	20–60 Maximum level—7 days	40	Blood level monitoring of Zarontin necessary to evaluate toxic levels.
Zoxazolidinediones Tridione Paradione				
Others Carbamazepine (Tegretol) Valium Diamox MCT Oil etc.	Mixed	0.3–0.8		

mean of 37 percent. With placebo, improved behavior ratings ranged from 17 percent to 80 percent, and the mean improvement was 46 percent.

Beneficial effects on relaxing abnormal neuromuscular states ranged from 9 percent with reserpine (Serpasil) to 56 percent with Mephenesin (Tolserol); the mean was 33 percent. With placebo, the improvement ranged from 26 to 50 percent and the mean was 39 percent.

When the controlled study results were compared against an uncontrolled office practice study, the results in the office were usually better, occasionally the same, and never worse than in the controlled phase of the study. The conclusion reached for the relaxant drugs was that placebo often had a greater effectiveness than the drug. Of the current muscle relaxants, valium is considered the drug of choice. There was a 36 percent effectiveness against a 48 percent placebo effect. A double-blind controlled study demonstrated a 21 percent less effective reduction of skeletal muscle hypertonia and body anxiety than an uncontrolled office study. This drug, however, was definitely beneficial in six of nine cases of severely disabled nonambulatory cases of cerebral palsy rigidity. The drug was not toxic but had a high incidence of side effects, mainly grogginess and imbalance with excessive dosages (Denhoff and Holden 1961). There is no question that it is a very helpful adjunct when used properly.

Behavioral Medications

Medications which have a favorable effect on hyperkinetic behavior include dextro- and levo-amphetamine sulfate (Dexedrine, Benzedrine) and Ritalin.

Dexedrine (Smith, Kline, French Laboratories, Philadelphia) and Benzedrine (Smith, Kline, French) are effective when used specifically for poor attention span, hyperactivity, mood swings, or variable behavior.

Dexedrine usually is tried first. Adverse effects, if noted within two weeks, are reasons for the substitution of Benzedrine in similar dosage. Adverse effects may be loss of appetite, complete lethargy or withdrawal, excessive crying, or abdominal cramps. However, these drugs are relatively nontoxic and nonhabit-forming. They can also be used beneficially in the treatment of epilepsy, primarily to counteract drowsiness caused by large doses of anticonvulsants. Livingston (1949) and his group found that the drugs favorably control petit mal seizures as well as influence behavior beneficially.

Ritalin (Ciba, Summit, New Jersey) (mephylphenidate) is less potent than Dexedrine. It is valuable in learning disability.

Thorazine (Smith, Kline, French Laboratories, Philadelphia) (chlorpromazine hydrochloride) is a tranquilizer with pronounced beneficial effect because of its unique depressive action on the central nervous system, probably the diencephalon. Agitated, anxious, and rebellious patients be-

TABLE 2.13
Useful Medications in the Management of Cerebral Palsy

	% Drug	Improvement Placebo
Muscle Relaxants		
Zoxozolamine (Flexin)	53	21
Emylcamate (Striatran)	43	55
Tybamate (Solacen)	25	37
Carisoprodal (Soma)	20	75
Mephenesin (Tolserol)	8	80
Diazepam (Valium)	36	48
Dantrolene (Dantrium)	35	58
Behavior Modifiers; Hyperkinesis		
Amphetamine (Dexedrine)	50	17
(Benzedrine)		
Methylphenidate (Ritalin)	Significant differences in behavior	
Pemoline (Cylert)	and learning over placebo	
Anxiety-Depression		
Chloropromazine (Thorazine)	50	17
Thioridazine (Mellaril)	Significant differences in lessened	
Imipramine (Tofranil)	anxiety over placebo	

come quieted when given Thorazine. This is followed by reduced mobility and muscular relaxation (Lehman and Hanrahan 1954). Thorazine is extremely helpful in getting the anxious, querulous child to be quiet enough to accept therapy. Countless hours are saved in the initial stages of the habilitation program by the judicious use of such medication. Table 2.13 summarizes the useful behavior drugs in cerebral palsy.

Special Problems

It is imperative to treat as early as possible associated handicaps such as defective vision, deafness, speech disorders, perceptual disorders, learning disabilities, dental, intellectual, and emotional disturbances. Since each of these topics is fully treated in other chapters in this book, discussion of them will be omitted here.

SUMMARY

It is now apparent to the reader that many diverse problems must be dealt with in the management of cerebral palsy. It is hoped that the reader will be aware of the contributions of many specialists, medical and otherwise, to this complicated field. Although our knowledge has increased, there are still many aspects of cerebral palsy that await answers.

When we consider treatment, other essentials besides the accepted therapies are important. Parents especially must be included in the program if goals are to be reached. Many parents do not altogether accept their handicapped child, either by not facing the extent of his disability or by overprotecting him so that he cannot grow. Society may react adversely with fear or repulsion, though this may be disguised as pity or oversolicitude.

The behavior of the child and the feelings of the parents and the needs of society at large are usually not compatible. Individual and group psychotherapy with parents and child as well as the education of teachers and therapists are as important as motor reeducation. The failure to strengthen the emotional component of the child during the formative years will result in the failure of the habilitation program. The goals for the cerebral palsied cannot be achieved unless these intangible items are treated with proper emphasis during the entire treatments training program.

A vast amount of effort, technical skill, love, and understanding goes into the successful habilitation program. Proper physical growth and development, optimal motivation, and good adjustment are as important as neuromotor improvement.

3

Neurophysiological Correlates

MICHELLE A. MELYN and
HERBERT J. GROSSMAN

CEREBRAL PALSY is a disorder primarily of motor function. Not only is there dysfunction of voluntary movements, but involuntary activity and postural reflexes are often compromised. Although the brain is the site of the pathologic process, because of the numerous connections from descending fiber tracts within the brain, there are secondary or indirect effects on structures within the spinal cord. The basis of motor and postural control resides within the interaction of various facets of the central nervous system, and it is an understanding of this which precedes any discussion of the neurophysiological foundations of cerebral palsy.*

Movement is a series of postures produced by various stimuli. Certain afferent stimuli produce changes in movement through reflex actions, i.e., the avoidance reflex to a noxious stimulus. From the work of Denny-Brown it has been ascertained that each stimulus acts at different levels of the brain and spinal cord and not all stimuli require perception. Certain stimuli modulate other stimuli such that their integration at cortical and subcortical levels usually results in one response or a series of coordinated responses.

It is the equilibrium of input and output within the central nervous system which produces the desired movement or lack of motion. Any disharmony between forces produces an imbalance resulting in an exaggeration of one force, or release of an opposing force, previously silent. Another way of expressing the same thought is that movement is composed in large part of two forces: on the one hand is the force grasping or reaching out toward the external environment, while diametrically opposed to this is

---

*This chapter is intended primarily as an overview of the subject of neurophysiology in cerebral palsy. The reader is referred to standard texts for a more detailed discussion of neuroanatomy, neuropathology, and clinical neurophysiology, especially as they relate to cerebral palsy.

the force avoiding or going away from this external environment. An imbalance between these forces may result in much of the clinical symptomatology expressed as neurologic dysfunction, especially in cerebral palsy.

Analysis of the anatomical substrate responsible for movement demonstrates two primary systems basic to voluntary and involuntary activity: pyramidal and extrapyramidal. Essentially these systems are groups of nerve fibers and nerve cells originating and branching at various separate levels of the brain and both eventually terminating on neurons within the spinal cord.

Within the gray matter of the spinal cord are two types of neurons: the anterior horn cell or alpha motorneuron, and the internuncial cell or motorneuron (sometimes called interneuron) (see Figure 3.1).

Fibers from both of these cells have connections to particular muscles at the same segmental level of the spinal cord, but they also have connections to similar neurons at other segmental levels of the spinal cord, and most importantly with neurons originating within the cerebral cortex and brain stem, the so-called suprasegmental influences. The pyramidal and extrapyramidal systems are part of these suprasegmental influences (above the spinal cord).

The alpha system is the final common pathway for movement, both reflex and volitional. The role played by the gamma system is to influence the state of tonus of muscle, by either inhibiting or facilitating the alpha motorneuron in conjunction with the suprasegmental influences (see Figure 3.2).

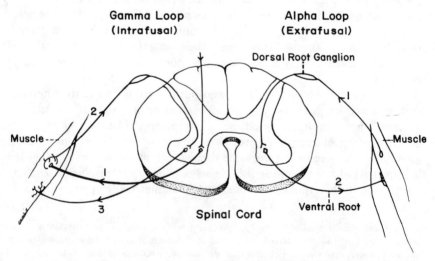

Figure 3.1.   Alpha and gamma systems at the level of the spinal cord.

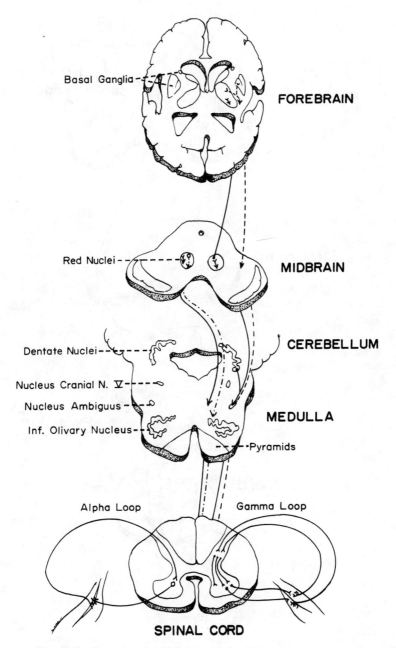

Figure 3.2. Suprasegmental influences on the alpha and gamma systems.

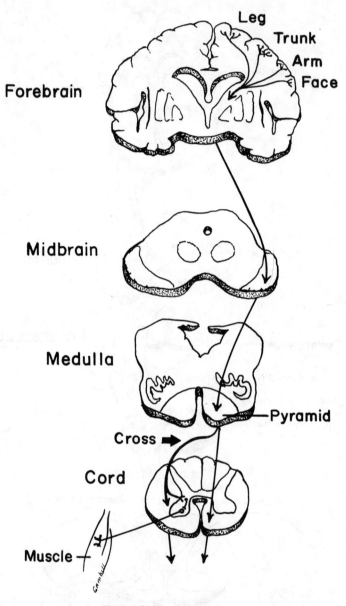

Figure 3.3.   Pyramidal system.

In these diagrams intrafusal fibers refer to those muscle fibers within a given muscle which are innervated by the gamma system, while extrafusal muscle fibers are those which are innervated by the alpha system. Their names are derived because of their relationship to a fusiform swelling within muscle which is the site of a specialized sensory receptor, the muscle spindle. One of the most significant functions of the muscle spindle is to initiate muscular contraction via the stretch reflex which will be further explained below.

The pyramidal system (Figure 3.3) refers to a relatively compact group of nerve fibers originating from cells in the cerebral cortex, particularly from the pre- and postcentral sensorimotor areas, descending into the internal capsule, then through the medullary pyramids to terminate on neurons within the ventral horn of the spinal cord. Fibers from both the motor and sensory systems are arranged somatotopically, and their arrangement is preserved throughout their respective courses. In general the pyramidal tract reflects a "crossed system" in that fibers originating from one side of the cerebral hemisphere terminate on anterior horn cells of the opposite side of the spinal cord.

It can also be seen that fibers from the motor and sensory systems lie in close proximity to one another, and a lesion in one system may very well involve the other system to a varying degree (Figure 3.4).

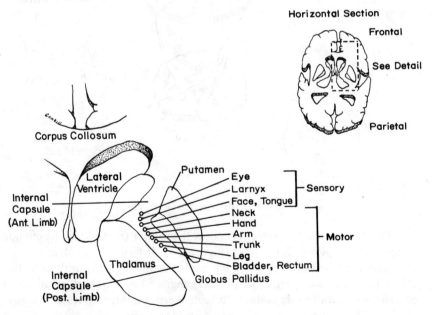

Figure 3.4. Anatomic relationship of motor and sensory systems.

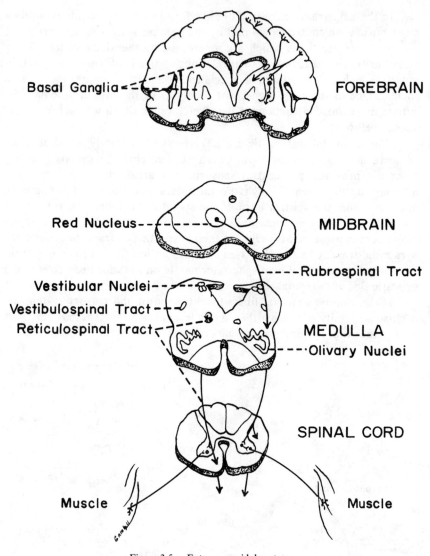

Figure 3.5.   Extrapyramidal system.

The extrapyramidal system denotes those fiber tracts which lie outside the area of the pyramidal system (Figure 3.5). It basically involves vast interconnections between many cranial nuclei, including the rubral, reticular, cerebellar, and those from the basal ganglia. The cerebral cortex also contributes fibers to this system. In fact, there is a large series of extrapyramidal fibers surrounding the sensorimotor cortex of the frontal and parietal lobes in a concentric fashion, yet running in separate paths from the pyramidal tract fibers. Here, again, the ventral horn cells of the spinal cord are the recipients of multiple influences from the extrapyramidal system.

Traditional concepts of the function of the pyramidal system state that these fibers control fine coordinated movement, especially by the activation of one muscle group with inhibition of its antagonist muscles. The extrapyramidal system classically is thought to influence movement by activation of large groups of muscles and suppression of other large groups of muscles. Both the pyramidal and extrapyramidal systems are necessary for the maintenance and suppression of muscle tone, respectively (Gilroy and Meyer 1969; Buchwald 1967).

However, on the basis of some animal studies and human subjects with known neurological lesions, this classic view of the relative dichotomy of the two systems seemed at times inappropriate. Buchwald (1967) has hypothesized another concept of motor control which combines many aspects of the two systems into perhaps a more functional approach. Simply stated, motor control is based on postural maintenance and kinetic energy translated into movement of a limb or other body part. Postural maintenance and tone are dependent on the extrapyramidal system via the vestibulospinal and reticulospinal tracts acting on the trunk and extensor musculature. Limb movement is a reflection of the workings of the pyramidal system via the corticospinal and rubrospinal tracts acting on the distal and flexor musculature. All of these pathways exert their actions through the interneurons and motorneurons of the spinal cord.

Such conceptualization allows a more tenable explanation of clinical deficits observed following a lesion of one or the other motor system. For example, a lesion within the extrapyramidal system results in a disorder of postural control. This can be interpreted as a conflict between certain reflex actions necessary for postural control, such as grasping and avoiding. Dysfunction is seen clinically as an instability of posture reflected in manifestations such as athetosis, tremor. The nature of these signs depends on the site of the lesion as a variety of different clinical syndromes may arise from different distinctive lesions within the extrapyramidal system. Additionally the same manifestation may be observed with lesions in several different areas, i.e., tremor from a lesion in the substantia nigra, while chorea from a lesion in the thalamus and/or globus pallidus.

Another effect of a lesion in the extrapyramidal system is the adoption by the subject of a hemiplegic posture: flexion of the arm with some extension of the leg (Langworthy 1970). Subsequent to a lesion of the corticospinal tract flaccidity of the contralateral limb results.

Spasticity or increased tone in those muscles later becomes evident and prominent because it is difficult to have a "pure" lesion of the pyramidal tract alone; the extrapyramidal tract is almost always involved as well.

Although suprasegmental influences through the pyramidal and extra-

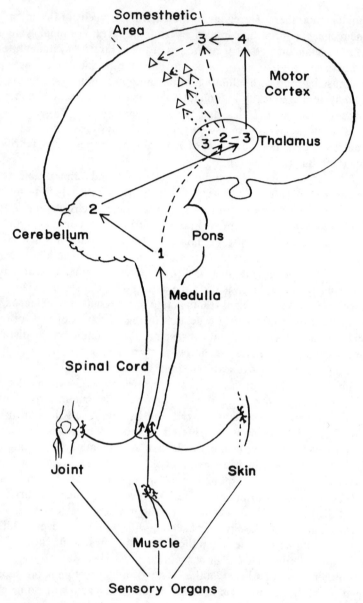

Figure 3.6.   Schematic representation of the sensory control of movement and posture via peripheral and central mechanisms.

pyramidal systems allow expression of an action, the sensory control of movement and posture at both a peripheral and central level is also very important. Through the sensory organs in the skin, whether for tactile, kinesthetic, pain, or temperature sense, afferent stimuli are transmitted to the thalamus, and some onwards to the cortex for perception (Figure 3.6). Such sensory information acts at a subcortical or cortical level relaying impulses via the cerebellum and reticular formation to the pyramidal and extrapyramidal systems, modulating activity. For example, a lesion in the sensory cortex may affect kinesthetic sensation such that there may be incoordination of limbs and further difficulty in limb movement. In other words, consolidation of kinesthetic cues from certain muscles may be dysfunctional because of a central lesion. Certain selected movements based on these stimuli may be inaccurate. The cumulative result is defective proprioception and equilibrium.

It is the integration of specific stimuli through the central nervous system, particularly in the brain stem, which is responsible for a series of patterned responses or reflexes. Many of these reflexes are necessary for the maintenance of posture and muscle tone and subsequently allow for coordinated movement. These reflexes are easily demonstrable in animals and in the human neonate. As myelination of the fiber tracts proceeds in the

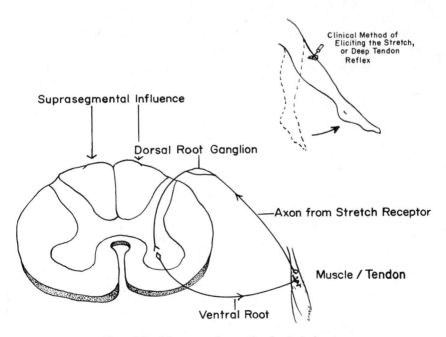

Figure 3.7. Monosynaptic stretch reflex (apha loop).

human nervous system, these primitive early reflex patterns become increasingly subservient to higher cortical centers. When this occurs, the "pure" reflex can no longer be elicited, and the resulting movement or posture now, with an appropriate stimulus, is a composite of the earlier reflex activity modified by suprasegmental and intersegmental influences. There are some reflexes whose presence is never normal while other reflexes fail to appear when they normally would because of a lesion anatomically near their primary site of integration within the brain or spinal cord. However, much of the dysfunction in cerebral palsy relates to the persistence or exaggeration of these subcortical reflexes beyond the expected age of disappearance, due to lesions within the cerebral cortex and its connections with the pyramidal and extrapyramidal systems. The presence of these primitive postural reflexes interferes with movement, both gross and fine. Because these reflexes require more than one muscle group for their execution, spread of this aberrant or exaggerated activity may adversely influence the performance of many other related movements.

Elemental to an understanding of postural reflex activity is the stretch reflex (Figure 3.7). Here afferent stimuli are carried to the dorsal root ganglia (group of neurons for sensory reception located just outside the spinal cord yet connected to it through fiber tracts) and then synapse at the motorneuron of the spinal cord within that same segment resulting in a response. Clinically interpreted, a tap on a muscle tendon results in stretching of that tendon. Stretching sets up a small shower of impulses to the anterior horn cell of that segment of the spinal cord, resulting in contraction of the muscle, really extension. Spread of impulses to the other

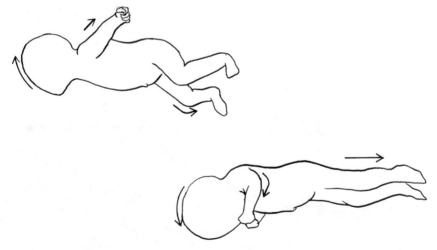

Figure 3.8a.   Symmetrical tonic neck reflex.

extremity may also produce more extension, the crossed-extension reflex, and aid in maintaining posture. Alpha and gamma systems with their suprasegmental influences are the anatomic substrates of this reflex.

In addition to the basic stretch reflex the following are some of those primitive postural reflexes normally elicited in infancy.

TONIC NECK REFLEX

1.   Symmetrical: If an infant is placed in the prone position, ventral flexion of the head produces flexion of the arms and extension of the legs. When the head is extended, the infant assuming the same prone position, there is extension of the arms and flexion of the legs. This response is normally present to the age of six months (Figure 3.8a).

2.   Asymmetrical: With the infant supine rotation of the head to one side results in extension of the arm and leg on the face side and flexion of the

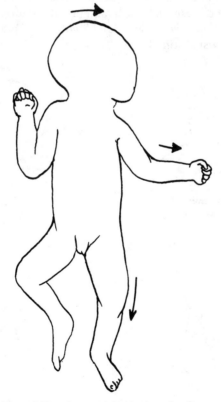

Figure 3.8b.   Asymmetrical tonic neck reflex.

contralateral limbs. Usually this response disappears by the age of seven months (Paine *et al.* 1964). Persistence of this response beyond 30 seconds at any age is abnormal and is referred to as an obligatory tonic neck reflex (Hagberg *et al.* 1972, Taft 1973). Typically infants retain the asymmetric tonic neck attitude for only a few seconds until the position is interrupted by the infant's crying or other movements (Figure 3.8b).

Both of these reflexes appear to be integrated in the upper cervical cord and brain stem.

RIGHTING REFLEX

In infancy this can be elicited when the child lies supine. Following rotation of the head to one side, there is corresponding rotation of the shoulders, trunk, and pelvis to the same side. When the head is rotated to the other side, the rest of the body follows accordingly. Maturation of this response in the older child and adult allows for correct orientation of the head and neck relative to the body, especially with an upright posture. Integration of this reflex appears to involve several levels within the brain stem, especially those relating to visual stimuli.

Figure 3.9a.   Stepping reaction.   Figure 3.9b.   Placing reaction.

POSITIVE SUPPORTING REACTION

When an infant is suspended vertically, head up, the infant's feet will make automatic stepping movements (see Figures 3.9a and b). Should the top of the foot touch the underside of a table, the infant normally will place that foot off the table top; subsequently the other foot will follow. This response is fairly easily elicited in infancy, as primarily a reflex. In the older child this becomes a more voluntary activity. Tactile stimulation initiates this reflex which is integrated at lower brain stem levels.

From this type of reflex the ability to stand is evolved. When there is an exaggeration of the positive supporting reaction (extensor thrust) (Figure 3.10) combined with tonic rigidity of trunk muscles, reflex standing can be seen and is evident in certain lesions of the brain stem, particularly in conditions of decorticate and decerebrate rigidity. Decorticate subjects are those with lesions high in the brain stem, especially at the level of the dienceph-

Figure 3.10.   Exaggeration of positive supporting reaction.

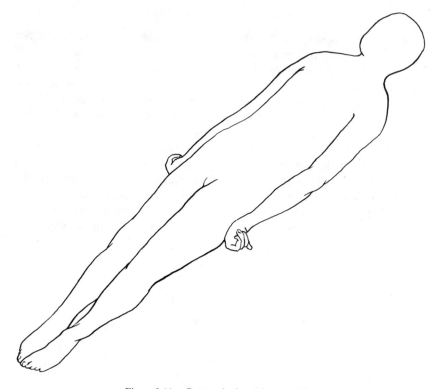

Figure 3.11.   Posture in decerebrate rigidity.

alon, whereas decerebrate subjects possess lesions in the midbrain or pons. In decerebrate rigidity there is increased tone in the extensor musculature and release of active tonic neck reflexes. Vestibular and cerebellar connections are important in achieving this posture (Figure 3.11). Decorticate rigidity consists of flexion of the upper extremities and extension of the lower extremities (Figure 3.12). The performance of any voluntary activity is rendered exceedingly difficult if either type of rigidity is present. Both of these forms of increased muscular tonus may be seen in cerebral palsied subjects.

LENGTHENING REACTION

When a muscle is stretched there is a gradual increase in muscle tone and some resistance to continued stretching. Beyond a certain point, however, there is a sudden "give" or release to the muscle and it continues the remainder of the motion under decreased tension. This is said to be a protective reflex preventing damage to the muscle from excessive or prolonged

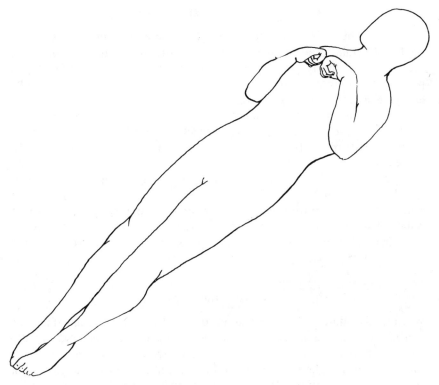

Figure 3.12. Posture in decorticate rigidity.

tension. Infants may demonstrate this reaction to a variable degree, but because of their normally increased state of muscle tonus and flexion, it is more difficult to assess at that age. In an older child or adult the response is easily elicited. However, the response is very prominent in lesions of the pyramidal tract.

PARACHUTE REACTION

This response is present from the age of nine to eleven months and persists throughout life (Paine *et al.* 1964). It refers to the extension of the subject's arms with fingers spread apart when he is held prone and suddenly lowered to a table top or other surface. Integration of this response probably occurs at both cortical and subcortical levels. Asymmetric or absent responses at a time when the response could normally be elicited are always important and may be seen in cerebral palsy.

Several other reflexes are significant in infancy, although they do not specifically reflect postural mechanisms.

PLANTAR REFLEX

When a noxious stimulus is applied along the lateral border of the sole of the foot, certain responses may be elicited. Normally there is flexion of the toes and foot, the response being symmetrical. However, in infancy and perhaps to approximately fifteen months of age the response is usually extensor in nature (the sign of Babinski) with dorsiflexion of the great toe, fanning of the other toes and occasionally withdrawal of the foot. The extensor plantar response at this age reflects the presence of partially myelinated corticospinal tracts. As these tracts become progressively myelinated within the first year of life, the response is no longer elicitable and eventually becomes flexor in nature. Should damage occur to the corticospinal tract perinatally, the Babinski sign may linger indefinitely as a reminder of the compromised nervous system. Also, if the pyramidal tract is damaged after infancy, at a time when the plantar reflex had already become flexor, it is possible that a Babinski sign may be elicited replacing the usual flexor response.

GRASP REFLEX

When tactile stimuli are applied either to the soles or palms of an infant, the immediate response is flexion of the toes or fingers respectively. Initially this is a purely reflex activity but within a few months cortical influences become evident and the response is more discriminating being supplanted in part by volitional activity. It is seen when a subject wants to grasp an object implying coordinated movements of thumb and fingers. Frontal and parietal cortex are necessary for the development of this response (Gilroy and Meyer 1969, Langworthy 1970). Persistence of the tactile grasp response in reflex fashion suggests lack of maturation of dysfunction within the cerebral cortex, especially within the cingulate gyrus or frontal lobe, permitting expression of a predominantly subcortical activity. When the grasp reflex is present under these circumstances it serves no purposeful activity and may interfere with the performance of other motions. Another type of grasp reflex is that which requires visual stimuli for its completion. The temporal lobe, as well as the frontal and parietal cortices, are necessary for this reflex. This response is seen in the intact individual when reaching for an object using visual cues. A lesion in the temporal lobe causes an abnormal response in that the subject may reach indiscriminately for objects in his or her visual fields.

There is yet another response which has components of both reflex and voluntary activity: the avoiding reaction. At the level primarily of the spinal cord this is seen as a flexion response of an extremity to a noxious stimulus. However, from studies of Denny-Brown (Langworthy 1970), avoiding responses can be observed with lesions of the parietal and frontal lobes. Whether this is a "positive" effect due to the dysfunction of higher influences acting on subcortical centers, or a "negative" effect due to release of subcortical structures from higher control, cannot always be determined.

MORO REFLEX

This has also been called the "startle" reflex and is another infantile automatism. It consists of sudden abduction then adduction of the arms in response to a variety of stimuli. This response is normally elicitable until about the age of six months and is probably integrated at the level of the brain stem.

SUCKING REFLEX

This response is simply as its name implies. In infancy it is only a reflex mediated through cranial nerves at a subcortical level. After several months the reflex is abolished but the ability to suck is retained on a more volitional basis.

Allied with the sucking reflex is the rooting response making its appearance at the same age and disappearing at about the same time. When an infant's cheek or corner of the mouth is lightly stroked, he or she will turn the head toward the side of the stimulus and bring the lips closer to the stimulus, as if preparatory to sucking. In subjects with cortical lesions these reflexes may persist and interfere with movements of the facial musculature, especially phonation.

Cerebral palsy is characterized primarily by a delay in motor development. Contributing to this retardation in the acquisition of motor skills is a variety of factors: dysfunction of postural mechanisms, involuntary movement patterns, and what Hagberg et al. (1972) term dysequilibrium. Although the ability or strength within individual muscle groups to execute a volitional act may be compromised by specific pathology associated with the anterior horn cell, the seeming weakness of an extremity is more often due to the presence of abnormal postural reflexes interfering with movement rather than any inherent weakness of the muscle itself.

Dysfunction of postural mechanisms often takes the form of persistence of infantile postural reflexes long after their expected age of disappearance; exaggeration of these same reflexes during the period of time they are usually elicited; or failure of an expected reflex to appear during the prescribed age range. The presence of one or more postural reflexes at a time when they should have been abolished, or the finding of any of the other abnormal responses mentioned above, is not distinctive of cerebral palsy alone but certainly suggests this as a consideration. Also no one grouping of abnormal reflexes denotes a particular type of cerebral palsy. Disorders of posture and tone may be found in the spastic type of cerebral palsy as well as in the athetoid or ataxic types. However, within each type of cerebral palsy there are fairly distinctive features which permit its differentiation from the other types.

In the following paragraphs an attempt will be made to correlate many of the clinical aspects of several forms of cerebral palsy with disturbances in posture and movement.

Spastic cerebral palsy implies dysfunction of the pyramidal tracts. Because of the proximity of the extrapyramidal system anatomically, subjects with this type of deficit usually reflect dysfunction within this system as well, but to varying degrees. The hallmark of this form of cerebral palsy is increased muscle tone with hyperactivity of the stretch reflexes and extensor plantar response (Babinski reflex). The "clasp-knife" phenomenon or an exaggerated lengthening reaction is often demonstrable in the involved muscles. Many subjects with this deficit retain some primitive reflexes, such as Moro, tonic neck, or grasp. The positive supporting reaction is often so prominent that many other sequential activities are precluded because of the severely increased muscular tonus. It is a characteristic of spastic cerebral palsy that the distal portions of an extremity are more affected than the proximal, making fine skilled movements of the hands or walking difficult or impossible. Initially infants so affected may demonstrate normal or decreased muscular tone reflecting damage primarily to the pyramidal system. But with time, a matter of months to years the relatively normal tone or hypotonia becomes transformed into classical spasticity which is then a reflection of the combined lesions in both the pyramidal and extrapyramidal systems.

Of the various forms of spastic cerebral palsy the hemiplegic or hemiparetic type is the most common. It is characterized by unilateral paralysis or weakness, the upper extremity usually being affected more than the lower extremity, particularly in the act of extension. With the increased muscular tone on the involved side, a hemiplegic posture is frequently adopted when standing or walking. Deep tendon or stretch reflexes are increased and occasionally pathologic reflexes are present on the affected side. Subcortically the pyramidal tracts lie adjacent to the fibers from the sensory tracts. A lesion in the pyramidal system is often associated with one in the sensory system. The nature of the sensory deficit is usually one of proprioception although there may be neglect or impaired awareness of the affected limbs as a manifestation of parietal lobe dysfunction. Thus hemisensory deficits may contribute to disorders of movement. Another poorly understood result of parietal lobe lesions is the trophic influence exerted in some patients on the hemiparetic side. This usually takes the form of diminution of growth of the affected limbs.

Next in order of frequency of the different types of spastic cerebral palsy is spastic quadriplegia or quadriparesis. This entity is characterized by paralysis or weakness in all limbs with increased muscular tone. The decorticate attitude may be seen in some subjects. In its most severe form a position of decerebrate rigidity is seen. This posture may be observed irregularly and to varying degrees but is usually heightened during emotional tension or even tactile stimulation. With this form there is dysfunction of the pyramidal tracts bilaterally, although one side may be more involved than the other. With extreme muscular hypertonus the patient may appear to stand or walk, if supported, but in reality these patterns are more a reflection of excessive positive supporting reactions and infantile stepping responses. The scissoring posture seen when these subjects stand or attempt to walk can be explained again by hypertonicity and spread of excessive postural reflex activity from one leg to another. Since both cerebral hemispheres are involved here, the acts of swallowing, chewing, and even talking may be compromised as well.

In spastic diplegia there is weakness or paralysis associated with hypertonicity primarily in the lower limbs. Although such children may have little or no difficulty with skilled movements in the hands, their main deficit revolves about such activities as sitting, walking, climbing. In mild forms there may be only "toe-walking" due to increased muscular tone at the ankle in addition to weak dorsiflexion of the foot.

Other forms of spastic cerebral palsy can be distinguished: monoplegia, the weakness or paralysis involving one extremity; and triplegia with the paresis or paralysis primarily involving three extremities. However, on further inspection they may be more closely allied with one of the previously named categories. The same neurophysiological principles enumerated above are also operant for these forms.

Lesions within the extrapyramidal system encompass not only disorders of tone and posture but include disorders related to involuntary movement. When there is involuntary motion the lesion lies deep within the brain stem, the basal ganglia being particularly prone to causing such disturbance.

Clinically involuntary movement may assume one of several forms: *athetosis,* slow writhing movements of the extremities, trunk, and/or face; *chorea,* quicker, more jerky movements in the same distribution as athetosis; *dystonia,* excessive retention of an athetotic posture; *tremor,* rhythmic oscillation of an extremity, trunk, or head. Chorea, athetosis, and dystonic posturing are often found in the same individual and it may be difficult to distinguish one from another. Because of this the term "dyskinesia" is more appropriate referring to all involuntary movement disorders when a particular type cannot be adequately ascertained.

In this form of cerebral palsy as in the others many primitive postural reflexes are retained far into childhood. Especially prominent in this type is the obligate tonic neck reflex (Taft 1973). Distal portions of the extremities are usually more involved, probably because of the added association of pyramidal tract involvement, but the reverse can also be found. Walking and feeding can be very difficult activities to perform. It has been said that walking may be almost impossible or certainly difficult to achieve if much of an obligatory tonic neck reflex is present (Crothers and Paine 1959).

The motions in an athetotic patient often are initially purposeful, but because of the imbalance between the grasping and avoiding reflexes the action may be negated or seemingly reversed. Emotional tension and a variety of other stimuli may aggravate the involuntary movements as well as the postural reflexes, thus contributing further to the neuromuscular deficit.

The extrapyramidal system also has connections to cerebral centers for mastication and phonation. Compromise of these centers through lesions in the basal ganglia may result in much incoordination in activities necessary for maintenance of life. Speech may be delayed or imperfect because of this. It should be mentioned that the typical involuntary movements seen in classical athetoid cerebral palsy usually are not seen until eighteen–twenty-four months of age. This is due no doubt to the prominence of infantile reflexes as well as other disturbances in muscle tone.

When the ataxic type of cerebral palsy is considered less is known concerning its etiology and pathology than the preceding types. The term "dysequilibrium," given by Hagberg et al. (1972), which refers to difficulties in maintaining posture and equilibrium secondary to dysfunction of the postural reflexes, seems more appropriate. This form implies the problem is more one of proprioceptive integration rather than one of tonicity or involuntary movement, although these too may be present.

Lesions in the cerebellum, vestibular apparatus, or various interconnections have been said to be the anatomic correlate of ataxic cerebral palsy, but it is difficult to establish these associations accurately.

Subjects with this type of cerebral palsy are often hypotonic as infants with decreased activity. Righting responses may be slow to develop. Reciprocal crawling is very difficult for these patients. Although hypotonia persists, it gradually decreases. However, at the stage when standing becomes possible, it is initially hampered by hypertonia of the legs due to exaggerated positive supporting reactions. With such responses the child may fall backward with stiff legs. When the subject overcomes these responses, standing and walking are often achieved on a broad base with much incoordination.

Perceptual deficits are also seen with this form, reflected in poor orientation of the body in space. This can be expressed by semiperfect or no coordination of arm movements in walking or right-left disorientation. Misjudgment in speed and in visuo-spatial tasks are other types of perceptual dysfunction, all seemingly on a cortical level. Speech may also be affected, resulting in a delay of language or irregularities in phonation.

Included in the ataxic variety of cerebral palsy may be "hemi" syndromes, implying that the deficit in coordination is only on one side, or on one side more than another. Associated with this may be tremor or an unevenness of skilled movement with one extremity.

Little is written about the atonic or hypotonic types of cerebral palsy, and some doubt their existence. It is rare to find an individual with only a disturbance in tone and only minimal to no deficit in postural reflexes or other dysfunction. Although hypotonia is often the initial presentation of most of the other types of cerebral palsy, it is usually transient and becomes replaced by spasticity or athetosis.

Cerebral palsy of the rigid type is quite similar in character to that of the spastic form. However, in the lengthening reaction muscular resistance is intense through the entire range of motion and does not result in a sudden release. Rigidity may be integrated more at the brain stem level. Subjects with such deficits will have much difficulty in performing simple voluntary activities because of the overriding stiffness within the muscles.

Although relatively pure types of cerebral palsy have been described above, it is not unusual to find mixed forms, the severity of deficit always correlated with the degree of compromise of postural reflexes.

There are many etiologies for cerebral palsy but only a few pathologic mechanisms. Anoxia or hypoxia is one of the prime physiologic consequences resulting from the varied influences known to cause cerebral palsy. Cerebral blood flow may be reduced because of untoward influences, but decreased oxygenation may further contribute to diminution of cerebral blood flow. Such a sequence of events will eventually lead to destruction of brain tissue; hence the lesions seen in cerebral palsy. If the insult is diffuse, the neuromotor deficit will be great and perhaps bilateral. It may also involve other portions of the nervous system, resulting in mental retardation and/or seizures. If the insult is very circumscribed, a focal deficit may be observed, as, for example, in lesions of the basal ganglia resulting in dyskinesias or in a hemiplegic syndrome. The latter results from dysfunction of cerebral tissue within an area subserved by a specific blood vessel. When the lesion is more localized, the incidence of associated disabilities is less and the movement disorder is more easily recognized. There is no correlation between focality and severity of the clinical deficit.

Although cerebral palsy may assume many clinical disguises, the pathophysiologic mechanisms which are compromised are very similar among each of them, resulting in a common denominator of dysequilibrium in posture and tone, eventually translated into a disorder of movement.

4

The Evaluation of Intelligence

WILLIAM M. CRUICKSHANK and
DANIEL P. HALLAHAN
with HARRY V. BICE

THE TESTS AND EXAMINATIONS with which most people are acquainted have been part of their school experience. As a rule they are a review of past work designed to determine how much has been learned. Though all pupils may have had the same instruction, not all are found to have learned equally well. It is more desirable to know in advance which children can learn certain material and which cannot, than to let all attempt it when some are sure to fail. Tests having some measure of predictive value are therefore needed in any school system. When there is a physical or mental condition or a combination of the two which may interfere with learning, it is even more important to know a child's potentialities as early as possible. The research of Haskell and Anderson (1970) and Bull (1966) for example, emphasizes the importance of considering the influence of extraneous variables on the test performance of cerebral palsied children. Assessing cerebral palsied children for selection to Uganda's first special school, Haskell and Anderson found a preponderance of non-responding. They speculated that the personality characteristics of passivity, docility, and submissiveness may explain the inability of these children to respond in testing situations. Likewise, Bull found parents of cerebral palsied children in a county in Ontario, Canada, to exaggerate the level of functioning of their children. Cerebral palsy is a condition which does interpose special problems for education and psychology.

The professional worker needs more than a generalization if the child is to be understood. It is important to know how much a child has learned from the experiences to which he has been exposed. Closely allied to that is some determination regarding his rate of learning. Is his mental de-

The authors gratefully acknowledge the assistance of Bette Heins, Graduate Student at the University of Virginia, and Walter Kwik, Research Assistant, and Lawrence Lewandowski, Research Assistant, at the University of Michigan, for their assistance in the preparation of this chapter.

velopment well rounded and even, comparable to that of most children, or are there areas in which he is more or less proficient than in others? Are there unusual conditions which may affect learning such as emotional instability, inadequacies of perception, association, or conceptual thinking?

Parents often seek a psychological evaluation of their child long before he is ready to attend school. Some have realized that the infant did not smile, hold up his head, or give evidence of some other accomplishment indicative of maturation at the expected time. They have consequently become greatly concerned. Others have heard that certain children whose physical condition is similar to that of their own have failed to develop normal mentality. They want to know as early as possible what they can expect as their child grows older and what they can do to bring about the best possible development for him. Without professional help in this regard, the parents are left to decide themselves what the severity of their child's impairment is. Research, however, indicates that parents of cerebral palsied children are not very accurate predictors of their children's ability. Unfortunately, the research suggests that parents, if left to their own opinions, may not fully realize the potential problems their child will have. Keith and Markie (1969) found that parents tended to overestimate the functional level of their cerebral palsied children in comaprison to the ratings of professionals.

The family physician or specialist should also want to know about the psychological maturation of a child. With such knowledge available, they can advise parents more realistically. In some cases physicians feel they can prescribe more accurately the therapies which are suitable at a given stage of the child's development.

An important historical development has occurred with regard to mental measurement. It has become popular to posit that intelligence is not a global phenomenon. Intelligence now is generally regarded to be composed of different abilities. Also, in this regard, the concept of scatter and pattern analysis introduced by Wechsler along with his first adult scale was an important contribution to clinical psychology. His ideas served to direct the psychologist's attention toward a qualitative analysis of the behavior of the child during the test situation and toward the relation between different levels of performance on the subitems of the test rather than toward the quantitative results alone. This has been an exceedingly important development, particularly in terms of the evaluation and assessment of the capacities of disabled children, for with this group of children the standard tests frequently have serious limitations (Newland 1971). Several other psychological tests have been developed for the assessment of exceptional children, particularly the physically handicapped. Among these are the

Raven's Progressive Matrices, the Ammons Full-Range Picture Vocabulary Test, the Columbia Test of Mental Maturity, the Peabody Picture Vocabulary Test, and the Illinois Test of Psycholinguistic Ability. The tests most widely used with children are the Wechsler Intelligence Scale for Children and the Stanford-Binet Intelligence Scale; Form L-M of the latter is presently coming to be preferred. These two tests are basic to the discussion in this chapter, but, since they also have some limitations in their use with handicapped children, certain uses of other tests will be included.

TEST ADMINISTRATION

The method used in examining a child varies according to his or her physical condition (Ruszcynska *et al.* 1972). There is, in many cases, no need to modify test administration. A large percentage of children with cerebral palsy are able to talk well enough to be understood easily. Thus, administering verbal tests is a comparatively simple matter, assuming the pertinent sensory modalities are intact. Many cerebral palsied children also have at least one good hand and so are able to manage the blocks, cards, and other material of which performance tests are composed. If some minor adjustment in procedure is necessary, it will be along the lines adopted for the child with a more extensive handicap.

When physical limitations are more serious, it often becomes necessary to make adaptations or adjustments. At the outset, the examiner chooses the type of test which can be administered with the least modification. If the subject has good hands and poor speech, performance tests are appropriate. If the opposite is true, verbal tests may have priority. In the majority of cases, the examiner will be able to give at least part of both these types of tests. At times it is necessary to omit tests. A child who can neither walk nor use a wheel chair cannot be asked to go to a chair to place a pencil or to go to a door and open it. Scores can be prorated as necessary.

On occasion a child can tell the examiner what to do, although the child cannot do it himself. This could occur on the maze items in the Binet scale or on other mazes if they are not too complicated. A child who cannot move a pencil may be able to tell an examiner the directions in which to move and when to stop. Caution is advised lest this method be extended too far. Certain values could easily be lost if the examiner assisted in completing the picture of the man in the Binet scale, for example. The child should tell not only what to draw but where to draw it. Even though the examiner exercises the greatest care, evidence of the child's inability to comprehend spatial concepts may be missed. The child who, when doing the drawing himself, located the nose and the mouth outside the outline of the face and who further placed both ears and the limbs on remote parts of the page is illustrative of one who probably has poorly developed spatial concepts (and, if one carries the drawing of a person into the realm of self-concept and body image, is a child whose body-image concepts are either immature or poorly developed because of emotional or perceptual problems). Even less can the examiner permit the child to direct him in the drawing of a geometric figure; children are seldom so adept at description that the drawing would represent what the child means.

A response given in pantomime may be accepted if there can be no doubt about the answer. It is not too difficult for some to make it clear in what way certain objects are the same and in what way different, even though the child does not speak. Many of the Binet absurdities items can be answered in the same way.

Some tests can be used as though they were multiple choice in nature. Arithmetic problems, for example, frequently can be administered in this way. Many general-information questions are also amenable to this procedure. Naming objects from memory is another possibility. Almost any examiner would have a number of appropriate objects from old Binet sets to reveal to the child after the test item is hidden. Thus, if speech is lacking, choice can be made by pointing.

Test materials can be modified. A child who cannot pick up small blocks may be able to handle large ones. Even a piece of wood as small as a match stick glued to movable material may make it possible for a child to solve a form board problem, although without the additional piece he could not lift any part. The examiner will be aware that, by attaching the match stick, he changes the configuration and conceivably increases the difficulty level of the problem.

These methods of modifying test materials or situations are merely suggestive. The alert examiner will use many more. *He will not, however, make the mistake of thinking that the modified test is the same as when administered in standard fashion.* An intelligence quotient based on change situations is not the same as one derived from standard administration. Evidence is to be presented which will indicate that an intelligence quotient seldom means the same in the case of a child with cerebral palsy as it does in a child without it.

It hardly needs be stated that any test worth administering yields more than a numerical score. The examiner will constantly be observing more details than are ever required in order to conclude that a response is right or wrong. Does the child give a superficial, though correct, or a mature type of response? Terman and Merrill (1937) have observed that there is a difference in quality of definitions and that, when this is taken into account, the vocabulary test score correlates more highly with the mental age. The time involved in such scoring and the subjective factors that are difficult to avoid in grading led these authors to adopt the simpler system. Wechsler decided in favor of higher numerical credit for better responses. Regardless of the test used, the examiner will observe many differences in quality.

It is important to know whether the child attempts to guess or bluff when he does not know an answer. Some children quickly indicate that they do not know; others remain silent. Still others name a word which sounds like the one they should define, if, for example, the vocabulary test is the one under consideration.

In some tests a child is expected to make a choice of several possible answers. Some do not hesitate at all, or do not even take time to look at the several items which are involved in the choice. They point to the one they chance to be looking at when the question is asked.

In like manner the examiner will be constantly on the alert to learn whether the level of conceptual thinking is adequate or not; if self-critical ability is present and, if so, if it is of a high order. Is memory adequate or superior; is it equally apparent in all types of tasks where it is involved? Does any sort of problem particularly disturb the subject?

It should be noted that the foregoing discussion on the alteration of testing materials is concerned with assessment of the cerebral palsied child's "true" intellectual level or potential. The modification of the testing materials is for the purpose of enabling the cerebral palsied child to respond on an equal footing with his normal peers. In other words, this use of testing is designed to determine the child's intellectual capacities when the child is not held back by physical handicaps. There are times, however, when it may be desirable to find out how a cerebral palsied child, given his physical problems, responds relative to his peers. In this assessment situation, the examiner may wish to know what the specific behavioral responses of the child are, and, in this case, the test would not be altered at all. The difference between this latter testing use and the former one can perhaps be clarified by considering the distinction drawn by psychologists between *competency* and *performance* in language (McNeill 1970). In determining competency, psychologists are concerned with an individual's true capacity, whereas in performance, they are measuring the child's overt responses which can be influenced by a host of variables such as distractors or fatigue. With regard to testing the cerebral palsied, we may wish to discover an individual's intellectual *competence* and thus might modify the test to eliminate the extraneous variable of physical handicaps. On the other hand, we may be concerned with the child's *performance*.

QUANTITATIVE STUDIES OF INTELLIGENCE IN CEREBRAL PALSIED

New Jersey Study

The results of the psychological evaluation of 1,000 children are presented in Table 4.1. Some factors of selection should be noted. All cases in the files of the New Jersey State Crippled Children's Commission at the time of the study were inspected. In approximately 15 percent of the total group it had not been possible to obtain an intelligence quotient. These were not included in the table. There were twenty-four tremor cases, with a median intelligence quotient of 75.8, and thirty-five children who had been diagnosed as "mixed." The median intelligence quotient for the latter was 66.2. These two groups were omitted from the group of 1,000 cases because the numbers were so small. In none of the major medical classifications in the table was the number less than 100. In only one instance, spastic triplegia, was there a subgroup with fewer than 100 subjects. Data included in Table 4.1 consist of test results on 1,000 children with cerebral palsy to whom examinations could be administered and completed.

TABLE 4.1

MENTAL LEVELS OF CHILDREN WITH CEREBRAL PALSY N = 1000

I.Q. Range	Quadri-plegia			Tri-plegia			Hemiplegia Right			Hemiplegia Left			Para-plegia			Total Spastics		
	M	F	T	M	F	T	M	F	T	M	F	T	M	F	T	M	F	T
150-159	1	0	1	0	1	1	0	0	0	0	0	0	0	0	0	1	1	2
140-149	0	0	0	0	0	0	0	0	0	1	1	2	1	0	1	2	1	3
130-139	0	0	0	0	2	2	0	1	1	1	1	2	1	0	1	2	4	6
120-129	2	1	3	0	0	0	0	1	1	2	3	5	2	1	3	6	6	12
110-119	2	0	2	1	0	1	2	1	3	7	1	8	4	1	5	16	3	19
100-109	3	0	3	2	1	3	8	10	18	9	7	16	7	5	12	30	22	52
90-99	5	4	9	2	4	6	9	3	12	13	7	20	12	7	19	41	25	66
80-89	5	3	8	3	2	5	12	10	22	5	1	6	11	12	23	36	28	64
70-79	8	3	11	4	2	6	18	9	27	7	5	12	7	5	12	44	24	68
60-69	7	4	11	1	0	1	9	4	13	12	5	17	3	6	9	32	19	51
50-59	9	1	10	8	1	9	10	4	14	7	6	13	5	5	10	39	17	56
40-49	6	7	13	2	2	4	2	4	6	5	5	10	2	4	6	17	22	39
30-39	12	2	14	2	0	2	3	2	5	2	4	6	3	1	4	22	9	31
20-29	8	4	12	3	4	7	6	1	7	0	1	1	3	2	5	20	12	32
10-19	4	3	7	3	0	3	1	0	1	1	1	2	2	2	4	11	6	17
0-9	2	1	3	0	0	0	0	0	0	0	0	0	1	0	1	3	1	4
Total	74	33	107	31	19	50	80	50	130	72	48	120	64	51	115	322	200	522

TABLE 4.1 (*Continued*)

Athetoids			Ataxics			Rigidities			Cumulative Frequency	Grand Total			Cumulative Frequency	I.Q. Range
M	F	T	M	F	T	M	F	T		M	F	T		
0	0	0	0	0	0	0	0	0	1,000	1	1	2	2	150-159
0	0	0	0	0	0	0	0	0	998	2	1	3	5	140-149
1	2	3	1	0	1	0	1	1	995	4	7	11	16	130-139
1	0	1	0	1	1	0	0	0	984	7	7	14	30	120-129
9	7	16	0	1	1	2	1	3	970	27	12	39	69	110-119
17	9	26	2	4	6	3	1	4	931	52	36	88	157	100-109
24	19	43	5	1	6	9	4	13	843	79	49	128	285	90-99
20	15	35	7	2	9	2	4	6	715	65	49	114	399	80-89
12	9	21	11	3	14	4	6	10	601	71	42	113	512	70-79
14	18	32	10	3	13	6	4	10	488	62	44	106	618	60-69
7	6	13	13	8	21	7	1	8	382	66	32	98	716	50-59
12	6	18	10	5	15	7	7	14	284	46	40	86	802	40-49
5	5	10	9	7	16	5	7	12	198	41	28	69	871	30-39
7	5	12	11	4	15	3	5	8	129	41	26	67	938	20-29
7	5	12	4	6	10	4	4	8	62	26	21	47	985	10-10
4	3	7	0	1	1	3	0	3	15	10	5	15	1,000	0-9
140	109	249	83	46	129	55	45	100		600	400	1,000		

It is probable that there were other, less easily discoverable, selective factors than those noted above. Some afflicted children are probably private patients whose names are not in the state files, although legally physicians are required to report all cases. Some very mild cases may never have been reported. This might mean that, were these included, the average intelligence quotient would be higher. There is, however, a balancing condition. Many cerebral palsied children are referred for institutional placement. As soon as they enter a state school, their folders are removed from the files of the commission. Institutionalized children are not represented in the table at all. In general, the inclusion of this latter group would lower the mean scores for the population quite markedly.

*Statistical Analysis**

In the total group, 600 males and 400 females, there were no differences between the sexes insofar as intelligence quotient is concerned. The mean quotient and standard deviation for the males is 68.51 and 30.0, respec-

*Appreciation is expressed to Dr. Norman E. Wallen, who made the statistical analysis of these data and whose comments on them are included here.

tively; for the females, 68.6 and 30.8. The remaining data on sex comparisons reveal no statistically significant differences between the sexes with respect to means or variances within any diagnostic category. The means and standard deviations for the sexes are very close within each major diagnostic category.

Within the spastic category, there is a suggestion of possible difference between the sexes of certain subtypes. The difference in means of the sexes for triplegia approaches significance, the probability being .08. The difference in means of the sexes for right hemiplegias approaches significance; the p value is .08. Larger samples might lead to significant

TABLE 4.2
SEX COMPARISONS OF PROPORTIONS BELOW IQ 70

Group	Sex	No. of Cases	Proportion	Critical Ratio
All Spastic	Male	322	.447	1.0
	Female	200	.430	
Athetoid	Male	140	.400	1.0
	Female	109	.440	
Ataxic	Male	83	.687	1.0
	Female	46	.739	
Rigidity	Male	55	.636	1.0
	Female	45	.622	
SPASTIC Quadriplegia	Male	74	.649	1.0
	Female	33	.667	
Triplegia	Male	31	.613	1.70
	Female	19	.368	
Rt. Hemi.	Male	80	.387	1.0
	Female	50	.340	
Lt. Hemi.	Male	72	.375	1.0
	Female	48	.458	
Paraplegia	Male	64	.296	1.07
	Female	51	.392	

None significant at .05 level

TABLE 4.3
PROPORTION OF DIAGNOSTIC GROUPS SCORING BELOW IQ 70

Spastic	Athetoid	Ataxic	Rigidity	Quad.	Tri.	R.H.	L.H.	Para
.44	.42	.71	.63	.65	.52	.35	.41	.34

differences. This is most probable in the case of the triplegia group (Bice and Cruickshank 1966).

Since no significant differences were found, the sexes were combined and the diagnostic categories compared. There were again no statistically significant differences between the spastics and the athetoids or between the ataxias and the rigidities. Each of the former groups was clearly superior to each of the latter in mean performance. No differences in variability were found (Bice and Cruickshank 1966).

Quadriplegias were significantly inferior to the right and left hemiplegias and paraplegias. It may also be said that triplegias were inferior to left hemiplegias and paraplegias.

The proportion of each sex scoring below 70 was obtained for each group and the sexes compared (Tables 4.2 and 4.3). There were no

TABLE 4.4
SIGNIFICANCE OF DIFFERENCES IN PROPORTIONS OF GROUPS HAVING IQ BELOW 70

Groups Compared	Difference	Critical Ratio	Probability of Occurrence
Spastic-Athetoid	.023	1	.32
Spastic-Ataxic	.264	5.42	.001
Spastic-Rigidity	.189	3.47	.001
Athetoid-Ataxic	.287	5.31	.001
Athetoid-Rigidity	.212	3.61	.001
Ataxic-Rigidity	.075	1.21	.22
Quad-Tri	.134	1.61	.11
Quad-R.H.	.300	4.62	.001
Quad-L.H.	.246	3.78	.001
Quad-Para	.316	4.65	.001
Tri-R.H.	.166	2.02	.04
Tri-L.H.	.112	1.35	.18
Tri-Para	.181	2.18	.03
R.H.-L.H.	.054	1	.32
R.H.-Para	.015	1	.32
L.H.-Para	.069	1.11	.27

significant differences except for triplegias, where the superiority of females as suggested by the mean differences again occurred.

The sexes were then combined and group comparisons were made (Table 4.4). The pattern for major categories was the same as for mean values. The ataxic and rigidity groups had significantly greater proportions below 70 IQ than the spastic and athetoid. In the intraspastic categories, the quadriplegias again had a significantly greater proportion below 70. There was also the suggestion that the triplegias were inferior to left hemiplegias and paraplegias (Bice and Cruickshank 1966).

In general, there was no evidence of sex differential in any groups, with the possible exception of the triplegias. Athetoids and spastics were about equal and superior to ataxias and rigidities. Quadriplegias were inferior to the general group of spastics, and triplegias may also have been.

In summary form, Figure 4.1 graphically illustrates the data discussed above. From this figure it can be seen that some variations occur in the shape of the curves produced. The curves which have been inset in the figure are rough approximations of the data detailed below and are included to give the reader a more graphic picture of variations which are produced.

Item Difficulty

In an earlier report (Hopkins *et al.* 1954) a discussion of item difficulty with cerebral palsied children on the Revised Stanford-Binet Intelligence Scale,

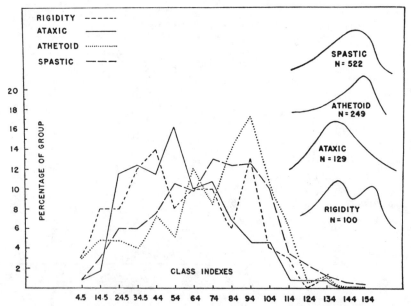

Figure 4.1. Comparison of IQ distribution in major medical classifications.

TABLE 4.5
ORDER IN WHICH TESTS ARE PASSED

II		Percentages Passed
3	Identifying parts of the body	84.2
4	Block building, tower	81.2
1	Three hole form board	78.3
6	Word combinations	78.3
2	Identifying objects by name	75
5	Picture vocabulary	74.2
II :6		
2	Identifying parts of the body	87.6
1	Identifying objects by use	83
3	Naming objects	81.5
4	Picture vocabulary	74.5
5	Repeating two digits	74.5
6	Three hole form board	68.3
III		
2	Picture vocabulary	68.6
4	Picture memories	68
6	Repeating three digits	60
3	Block building, bridge	56.9
5	Copying circle	40.3
1	Stringing beads	36.3
III :6		
1	Obey simple commands	84.6
5	Identifying objects by use	77
6	Comprehension	74.3
4	Response to pictures	65
2	Picture vocabulary	48
3	Comparison of sticks	44.7
IV		
2	Naming objects from memory	75.4
4	Pictorial identification	68
6	Comprehension	65.8
3	Picture completion: man	61.4
1	Picture vocabulary	52.7
5	Discrimination of forms	46.4
IV :6		
1	Aesthetic comparison	61.7
3	Pictorial likenesses and differences	60.8
6	Opposite analogies	58.5
2	Repeating four digits	58.2
4	Materials	44.7
5	Three commissions	43.6

TABLE 4.5 (*Continued*)

V		Percentages Passed
3	Definitions	90.1
1	Picture completion, man	53
5	Memory for sentences	44.9
6	Counting four objects	44.9
4	Copying a square	42
2	Paper folding, triangle	35
VI		
1	Vocabulary	83
3	Mutilated pictures	72
5	Pictorial likenesses and differences	58.3
4	Number concepts	55
6	Maze tracing	54
2	Copying a bead chain	40
VII		
6	Repeating five digits	50.4
1	Picture absurdities	49.6
5	Opposite analogies	45.3
4	Comprehension	44.9
2	Similarities	40
3	Copying a diamond	26.5
VIII		
2	Memory for stories	75.1
1	Vocabulary	61.5
6	Memory for sentences	46.3
3	Verbal absurdities	44.0
5	Comprehension	37.3
4	Similarities	33.9
IX		
4	Rhymes	54.6
5	Making change	54.6
6	Repeating four digits reversed	52.6
2	Verbal absurdities	40.2
3	Memory for designs	36
1	Paper cutting	24.7
X		
1	Vocabulary	51.3
2	Picture absurdities II	50
5	Word naming	48.7
4	Finding reasons	38.75
6	Repeating six digits	38.75
3	Reading and report	21.25

Form L, was presented. In this earlier report results of tests with 190 cerebral palsied children were included. Table 4.5 presents data derived from the examinations of 743 cerebral palsied children. The trend remains much the same as when the original 190 children were reported. The addition of 553 more cases influences the data very little. Among the 345 children are those who were able to complete all the items of at least one-year level. If an individual were unable to complete any considerable number of items because of physical disability, the results were not included herein. Some of the children had to omit such an item as Three Commissions. If these omissions were not figured into the percentage noted in Table 4.5, there would be a slight change in the rank order given. Ninety-eight children could not complete item IV-6, 5. If this group were deleted from the percentages noted, the percentage would be 61, and the item, Materials, would then be the most difficult item in that level. There are few instances of this kind.

At Year II, the percentage of pass and failure is approximately the same for all items. A similar situation is true for Year II-6 with the exception of item 6. This latter item, involving the three-figure form board, was the most difficult one for this age group, 31 percent failing it. Much variation in pass and failure percentages was noted at and above the level of Year III. While the items failed in these higher levels varied, in general they involved psychological abilities of judgment, discrimination, memory, visuomotor abilities, and locomotion. The items which received the largest percentages of passes involved language development in eight of the eleven higher levels of the test (Bice and Cruickshank 1966).

RETEST DATA

The records of 153 children were available reporting first and second examinations administered by Dr. Harry V. Bice. The average chronological age at the time of the first examination was six years and three months; at the time of the second, exactly nine years. The average IQ for the first examination was 68; for the second, 65.

From the above group all cases were selected in which there had been either a gain or loss of ten points in IQ. There were sixteen children who had gained. On the basis of test behavior and accomplishment when they were first examined, eleven were considered to have greater ability than the intelligence quotient indicated. The rise in intelligence quotient did not change the diagnosis in any of these. A change resulted in five cases. Four of the five children represented one or more of the following experiences during the three years between examinations: intensive education, control of seizures, or development of emotional stability. In the remaining case, nothing was discovered to account for the change. The most pronounced change was from borderline deficiency to dull.

TABLE 4.6
COMPARISON OF IQ LEVELS OF ENGLISH AND AMERICAN
CEREBRAL PALSIED CHILDREN, REPORTED IN PERCENTAGES

Intelligence Quotient Levels	English		American	
	Entire Group N-916	Selected Areas N-448	Washington, D. C. N-119	New Jersey N-1,000
100 and above	8.7	11.1	12.6	15.7
Under 100	91.3	88.8	87.3	84.3
Under 70	53.6	51.5	54.6	48.8

There were thirty-three children whose intelligence quotients decreased ten or more points. In twenty-four of these, the examiner entered in the record at the time of the first examination a comment to the effect that the history and present status of the case suggested that a later examination would probably reveal a lower score. In three other cases, the examiner noted that the diagnosis was evidence of leniency on his part. In two cases, serious seizures developed and continued; two others became emotionally unstable. One child, who had been examined by use of the Wechsler scale on the second occasion but the Binet on the first, gained two points in verbal quotient but had a very low performance score. In one case no condition could be discovered that would account for the loss. The diagnosis was changed in three cases from borderline deficiency to unqualified mental deficiency; in four instances, the change was only to a more severe degree of deficiency.

Comparison of the New Jersey Data with Other Studies

It is appropriate to examine the data just reported in the light of the findings of studies previously mentioned. Dunsdon (1952) reported the results of the examinations of 916 children, approximately one-half of whom were from selected geographical areas in England; the remainder were from special school candidates. Unpublished records of psychological evaluations completed in Washington, D.C., were made available for use in this study.* In Table 4.6 a comparison is made between these two populations and the New Jersey population reported above. The similarities are striking. Both American groups have a slightly higher percentage of children above 100 intelligence quotient. The English selected areas, which probably represent random selection better than the special school candidates, are more nearly

*Appreciation is extended to W. P. Argy, M.D., of Washington, D.C., who made these data available and permitted their inclusion here.

TABLE 4.7
COMPARISON OF IQ LEVELS OF CHILDREN IN BUFFALO AND NEW JERSEY

Intelligence Quotient Levels	Buffalo, N-330		New Jersey, N-1,000	
	Number	Per Cent	Number	Per Cent
110 and above	15	4.5	69	6.9
90-109	77	23.0	216	21.6
80-89	36	11.0	114	11.4
70-79	38	11.5	113	11.3
60-69	39	12.0	106	10.6
40-59	51	15.5	184	18.4
Under 40	74	22.5	198	19.8

equivalent to the American groups. On the whole, the Washington group more closely resembles the English population than does the New Jersey group of children.

Differences in the method of presenting data indicate a need for comparisons to be made with the work of Asher and Schonell (1950) (Birmingham, England) and Miller and Rosenfeld (1952) (Buffalo). Hereinafter each of these studies will be designated by the location of the work. Tables 4.7 through 4.10 present much of these data. Miller and Rosenfeld found 33 percent of ataxics below 70 in IQ. In the New Jersey study, there were 70.5 percent of ataxics below 70. This means that ataxics in the Buffalo group will vary considerably in all intelligence quotient ranges from the New Jersey ataxics.

The most probable significance of this finding is that there is a great difference in the point of view of the physicians who diagnose ataxia. If the inconsistency were in the psychological evaluation, it would appear in the other medical classifications as well.

The percentage of children whose IQs were under 70 was from 48.8 to

TABLE 4.8
COMPARISON OF IQ LEVELS OF CHILDREN IN BIRMINGHAM AND NEW JERSEY

Intelligence Quotient Levels	Birmingham, N-354		New Jersey, N-1,000	
	Number	Per Cent	Number	Per Cent
130 and above	2	0.6	16	1.6
110-129	12	3.4	53	5.3
90-109	71	20.1	216	21.6
70-89	95	26.8	227	22.7
50-69	81	22.9	204	20.4
0-49	79	22.3	284	28.4
Not yet assessable	14	3.9		

TABLE 4.9

COMPARISON OF MEAN IQS AND STANDARD DEVIATIONS IN SUBCLASSIFICATIONS OF
SPASTICITY, BIRMINGHAM AND NEW JERSEY GROUPS

	Quadriplegia		Right Hemi.		Left Hemi.		Paraplegia	
	Bir-mingham	New Jersey	Bir-mingham	New Jersey	Bir-mingham	New Jersey	Bir-mingham	New Jersey
Mean I.Q.	50.2	57.39	76.8	74.73	77.9	79.73	74.3	76.76
S.D.	27.6	30.86	26.0	24.47	20.1	28.46	23.6	28.38
N	80	107	57	130	41	120	85	115
Not yet assessable	4		2		1		2	

54.6, with the New Jersey group having the fewest at that level. The percentage with quotients under 90 ranged from 71.5 to 78.1; again New Jersey has the lowest percentage, but its figure is in substantial agreement with the others except the Washington group which is high.

In a more recent study conducted in India, Bharucha, Patel, Bharucha, and Mulla-Frioze (1968) found a similar proportion of lowered intelligence in the cerebral palsied. The found that 56 percent of their 64 subjects had IQs below 90. Thirty-three percent had IQs below 70, and 20 percent had IQs below 50. While not as great a proportion of these Indian children were retarded as in the Washington and New Jersey studies, the results are generally comparable. In addition, Bharucha et al. replicated the general finding that spastics and athetoids have higher intelligence than ataxics.

Since the most frequently quoted earlier studies have not stood up under examination and there is remarkable agreement in the major independent studies to which reference has been made here, it appears appropriate to plan education for these children accordingly. These reports are not wholly pessimistic. It was not so long ago that all cerebral palsies were considered to be in the lower group, whereas now only approximately 50

TABLE 4.10

COMPARISON OF MEAN IQS AND STANDARD DEVIATIONS, BIRMINGHAM AND
NEW JERSEY GROUPS; BIRMINGHAM MIXED CASES OMITTED

	Spastic		Athetoid		Ataxic	
	Bir-mingham	New Jersey	Bir-mingham	New Jersey	Bir-mingham	New Jersey
Mean	67.9	71.94	67.6	72.60	63.3	54.96
S.D.	27.7	29.73	25.5	30.41	19.3	27.06
N	277	522	41	249	4	129
Not yet assessable	9	0	4	0	0	0

percent are so diagnosed. In addition, much evidence has been brought together to confirm the already fairly well-established fact that there is no essential difference in the measurable intelligence of spastic and athetoid children.

OTHER TESTS

Compiling a mass of statistical data has value, but it can also result in an emphasis which the authors do not fully intend. In making the evaluation, the psychologist may have employed a test which seemed for this examination to be the single most valuable instrument—one which may have been in use many years. For supplementary data, he may have chosen a test which was quite new. With the next child the relative importance of the tests could be reversed. In order to help place the *individual* in proper focus, brief references will be made to values of certain other tests. The contributions which some of them can make to the understanding of the individual are illustrated in the case history included later in this chapter.

Three decades ago, both parents and professional people helped give impetus to a movement to develop new tests to be used in the evaluation of the handicapped. One frequently heard a parent expressing this point of view: "Psychologists are using tests that were standardized on normal children. How could they be fair to the handicapped?" Often they were overlooking the fact that the one thing they wanted most was for their child to develop so that he would be as nearly normal as possible. The tests parents criticized had the definite value of pointing out to psychologists and educators something of what the areas of weakness were in the expression of mental capacity. Psychologists were impressed and were disturbed by the frequency with which they entered in their reports statements to the effect that one child or another had capacities for understanding which could not be made explicit in the use of the tests which were available. Tests are still appearing to which children can respond adequately merely by pointing, looking, or employing some very inconspicuous signal.

The tests under consideration often do provide objective scores, a fact that will be of greater significance to some psychologists, of lesser to others according to the individual point of view or depending on the use which is to be made of the results. One must keep in mind that these tests may not tap multiple facets of the intellectual life (as, for example, a Binet does), and some measure of expressive disability is frequently involved. For both these reasons the meaning of the mental age or the intelligence quotient to educators and to many parents may require some explanation.

Any test provides an examiner with an opportunity to observe samples of a child's behavior. This opportunity may be greatly extended by the use of supplementary tests. Sometimes data will be revealed at levels well above that at which a child could function on some other scale. Assume, for example, that a seven-year-old child's only means of response is to point. In order to find something which he can do, the examiner may start at the II-Year level of the Binet. By the time he has reached the V-Year level, there would have been approximately a dozen tasks to which the child could respond by pointing. He would find no other basis within that range which would normally prompt an examiner to continue the test. With even one of the more limited of the supplementary tests, e.g., the Ammons, which require only the physical ability that this seven-year-old has, the number of responses would be more than doubled. Half of these could easily be of a degree of difficulty which would show capacity within normal range for this child.

Even the test which requires the minimum response from the child can show his method of working. An examiner will quickly note that the child studies every possibility and makes a choice, or that he has a finger ready to point before the stimulus word is given and quickly jabs his finger in any direction. One child has the insight which leads him to indicate that he does not know an answer; another keeps guessing as long as material is placed before him.

Failure on the part of the child to respond to one of the multiple-choice tests should serve only as a challenge for the psychologist to find out why. The failure may represent a general lack of mental competence, inability to understand the directions because of an auditory perceptual disability, or inability to respond to the kind of abstraction of which the test material is composed. A *pie* in the Ammons scale, a *chair* in the Peabody test are merely symbols, outline sketches which do not necessarily have meaning to the child. How very often, in response to a question, does a psychologist hear from a mother, "He never colored pictures when he was smaller. He did not like to, so I did not make him do it." Is the coloring of sketches one step in learning their meaning? Ability to define *envelope* in the Binet vocabulary test together with the inability to select a sketch of it when presented with three other drawings may point to a specific disability or at least provide a clue which should be followed by the penetrating clinician.

A requirement in many different tests is that the subject being examined must discover a principle and then apply it in increasingly difficult situations. This is true in the Columbia Test of Mental Maturity. In general, the complex problem of abstraction and generalization is involved; at first, with multiple clues of color, form, and size. As the test progresses clues may be limited to color, or size, or form, and proceed to utilize quantity, biologic category, or some other category or classification.

The Vineland Social Maturity Scale is brought to the attention of the reader in this context, although it is not and was not intended or designed to be an intelligence test. Scores on the scale, however, are affected by many factors such as physical disability, lack of education, training, changing social customs, or other experiences. It can give the psychologist an insight which might not be available from other sources. The following combination of circumstances is found: the child's handicap is mild; he responds reasonably well on verbal and performance tests; his social age is a year or more inferior to his mental age. On this basis the psychologist finds it valuable to question the parents as to whether or not they are doing all they can to promote all aspects of the child's development. Almost uniformly, parents admit that their child could do more if it were required of him; but the parents do not agree on discipline, because they are trying to make life easier in view of his disability, or for some other reason discipline is relaxed. At least the psychologist now knows the child a little better; at most, parents may be motivated to attend to their responsibilities more diligently. If, on the other hand, the social age is well above the mental age, the child may have resources which were not apparent in tests directed primarily at the investigation of intelligence.

Although the factors discussed in the preceding paragraphs are essentially clinical and qualitative in nature, the quantitative aspects of the supplementary tests are significant as well. It is essential that the clinician understand the statistical framework of the supplementary test being employed in order to avoid the creation of absurd situations. No two psychological tests currently in use have a correlation coefficient of 1.0, nor rarely do they approach this desirable relationship level. Most tests when compared with another have much lower correlation coefficients. Usually it is a form of the Binet test or one of the Wechsler scales with which other supplementary tests are used and against which they are compared. Unless the clinician is thoroughly aware that the test he is using with a child produces results that are statistically *expected* to be higher or lower than the basic instrument being used, misleading assumptions and conclusions about the child may result. One often hears it stated that Test A, for example, produces results which are uniformly higher than Test B, the basic test, in spite of the fact that Test A was intended for use with the physically handicapped. For this reason Test A can be no good, or at best, invalid. If the complaining psychologist were aware of the statistical base underlying the development of Test A and understood that close qualitative similarities could not be expected from the two tests, but that each test in its own right provided both qualitative and quantitative insights of significance, then more realistic and helpful planning could be undertaken for the child. It is essential that clinical introspection and qualitative analysis of a given instrument be premised on sound conceptualization of the quantitative elements inherent in the test, as well as on a thorough understanding of the impact of physical disability on normative growth and development. Together these factors render almost any psychological test a significant asset in understanding the intellectual characteristics of children with cerebral palsy.

That one should be careful to note which particular intelligence test was used in a testing situation with cerebral palsied is suggested by the results of three studies (Ando 1968; Irwin and Korst 1967 and; Nicholson 1970). For example, all three studies generally found that the Peabody Picture Vocabulary Test (PPVT) correlates relatively highly with other IQ tests, but that there are large differences in the mean IQ obtained with this test and others. It is possible for two tests to correlate highly but for one to give consistently higher scores than the other. Ando found the PPVT to correlate .79 with the Verbal Scale of the WISC. Irwin and Korst found the same two tests to correlate .94. Nicholson found a correlation of .65 between the PPVT and the Columbia Mental Maturity Scale and a correlation of .41 between the PPVT and the Raven Coloured Progressive Matrices. However, Nicholson found these cerebral palsied subjects to score about 20 points higher on the PPVT than each of the other two tests, while all three tests provided similar IQs for normals. Ando's results indicated that for the children with the most severe speech and physical impairments the scores were generally lower on the WISC Verbal Scale than the PPVT.

In using intelligence tests with cerebral palsied children, another consideration the examiner should be aware of is the possible instability of the IQ score obtained. Research results are varied on this subject but generally support the notion that the stability of the IQ is quite good for the majority of cerebral palsied individuals but that some can change dramatically.

Tabary and Folliot (1965) retested sixty-six subjects on the WISC, Columbia Mental Maturity Scale, or Raven after a mean test-retest period of five years. They found that 27 percent of the subjects changed more than 2.5 points, most of them declining. Their results are difficult to interpret, however, since they reported that most of these declines were due to a technical error in the standardization of the Columbia on the French population.

Nielsen (1971) found that after a mean interval of four years 55 percent of the subjects changed less than 10 points and 78 percent changed less than 15 points. This does mean, however, that more than two out of every ten individuals tested changed more than 15 points. Nielsen also presented test-retest correlations by subgroups: hemiplegics, .68; paraplegics, .79; tetraplegics, .82; diplegics, .44; athetoids, .77; ataxics, .87; epileptics, .67.

Klapper and Birch (1967) found much less stability in their study. This could be due to the fact that their follow-up was conducted over a period of fourteen years. They found the scores were stable only for the most severely retarded and normal subjects. The mildly and borderline retarded subjects, on the other hand, had quite variable IQs.

The results of the above studies taken as a whole indicate that even more than with normal children the IQ score of a cerebral palsied child should never be assumed to be the absolute, final indication of the child's potential. While for the majority of cases the IQ will remain relatively stable, there are enough who change to make it imperative to consider each individual case separately. While the degree to which one can rely upon the predictive value of an IQ score will depend on the competence of the examiner, it is inappropriate for one to consider one IQ test to be the final answer.

Progressive Matrices

The Raven's Progressive Matrices have been used with cerebral palsied populations. The matrices are an extended version of the nonverbal analogies test originally devised by Raven as a supplementary test for dull and backward school children. In its current form the test is used as an intelligence test for children above six years of age. It is nonverbal in nature and consists of sixty items, i.e., analogies, which are intended to be graded in terms of level of difficulty. The analogies consist of multiple-choice items involving the selection of the proper element to complete a design.

To date the scale has been used with very limited populations. Conclusions are difficult to make because of this fact. In the case of Taibl's (1951) work, the cerebral palsied population of 115 subjects includes subjects from six years of age to adulthood. Grade groups included the first through the eighth, but the fifth grade had no subjects. No high school students were included, but two college graduates were. The results which Taibl presents are not questioned. The age-grade spread of his subjects and the very small number of subjects at any one level makes it impossible to generalize from the matrices to the total cerebral palsied population.

The idea basic to the matrices appears to be a valid one. Much further intensive and extensive work is needed with populations of disabled children. Obvious, too, is the need for careful statistical reevaluation of the test itself in the light of additional standardization data. Banks and Sinha (1951) who completed an item analysis of the Raven's Progressive Matrices, indicate many limitations with respect to reliability and validity in the present form of the test. Item difficulty and item placement within the scale need further consideration. These authors conclude that "although the test appears unquestionably promising, it would be premature to accept it in its present form."

Columbia Test of Mental Maturity

A second test that has been published is the Columbia Test of Mental Maturity, designed to provide insight into the intellectual ability of children in the mental age group of from three to twelve years. "It differs from other individual intelligence measures in that it calls for no verbal response and for a minimum of motor response on the subject's part. These characteristics make the test particularly suitable for use with subjects having serious verbal or motor impairment" (Burgemeister et al. 1954). The scale includes 100 multiple choice items, each item placed on a card 6-by-19 inches. The test is individually administered and scored with easy translation of mental age and IQ scores. IQ correlations of between .66 at the 8–0 to 8–11 age level to .88 at the 11–0 to 11–11 age level between the Columbia and the Stanford-Binet scale are noted by the authors. Reliability of scores on the Columbia was investigated by the authors by comparing the odd and even items. Spearman-Brown coefficients using this method range from .89 at the 4-year level to .92 at the 10-year level. Further extensive research with populations of physically disabled children will demonstrate the applied value of this instrument. From a theoretical point of view, the scale offers much since it permits great adaptation to the individual handicapped child. The minimum of verbal and motor performance required of the child means that, insofar as the testing situation is concerned, nearly optimum arrangements are provided.

Illinois Test of Psycholinguistic Abilities

The Illinois Test of Psycholinguistic Abilities (ITPA) was developed at the Institute for Research on Exceptional Children at the University of Illinois. The first report on the present test appeared in 1961. A revised edition of the ITPA was published in 1968. The ITPA is a battery of tests which has been developed into a comprehensive instrument for the assessment of language development in exceptional children, especially at the preschool level. The test provides cues for the remediation of deficits in differential psycholinguistic functions which are often found among cerebral palsied, brain injured, and certain emotionally disturbed children. The ITPA seems to be a useful instrument for precise and deliberate work on linguistic deficiencies.

The psychodiagnostic profile derived from the battery outlines the child's strengths and weaknesses with the assumption that the strengths will be used as a base in a remedial program to ameliorate functioning in the weaker areas. Six psycholinguistic abilities related to the meaningful use of language and three related to automatic usage are assessed. The authors recognize that the model from which the test was derived may be incomplete and that more than nine functions may exist and need to be evaluated. The model is behavioral rather than neurological and, thus, as Kirk and

McCarthy (1961) state, no assumption of neurological or neurophysiological correlates of behavior is made. The emphasis is on assessing behavior related to psycholinguistic phenomena.

The clinical model for the ITPA resembles the theoretical communication model of Osgood (1957) and the more clinical language model of Wepman *et al.* (1960). The model for the ITPA includes three dimensions: (1) channels of communication or modes of input and output; (2) levels of organization, i.e., automatic-sequential and representational; and (3) psycholinguistic processes, i.e., receptive (understanding), association (making relationships), and expressive. The twelve subtests in the ITPA battery are designed to measure functioning in the various areas represented by the model. For example, at the representational level, six subtests are constructed to measure receptive, association, and expressive processes. Six subtests measure processes at the automatic-sequential level.

Like the Binet, the Kephart Perceptual Rating Scale, and the Wechsler Intelligence Scale for Children, the ITPA provides broad coverage and is frequently administered first in a battery to determine appropriate tests for more specific evaluations. Items in the ITPA are designed, as much as possible, to accommodate the limitations of handicapped children taking the tests. The test battery, after several revisions, was standardized in 1959 and 1960 on seven hundred normal children between the ages of two and a half and nine years, providing language age and standard score norms. The validity characteristics of the ITPA are summarized by McCarthy. He points out the need for auxiliary tests to supplement the ITPA data in diagnosing children with linguistic defects, particularly dyslexia. The test still is being developed and refined. For a complete report on how the test was constructed and the exact statistical data the reader may refer to Kirk and McCarthy (1961).

Hallahan and Cruickshank (1973) have more recently reviewed the validity studies of the ITPA. They conclude that one should be careful, particularly at the younger age levels, in relying upon the idea that the test is tapping separate abilities. In addition, the particular names of the subtests do not always correspond with the ability apparently being assessed.

There is considerable interest in the ITPA because of its applicability to the problems of remedial education. Hart (in Bateman 1962) investigated the effects of language programs on cerebral palsy children at a School for Spastic Children in Queensland, Australia. The ITPA was administered before and after a seven-week period of instruction for forty-five minutes each day. The experimental and control groups were made up of nine matched pairs of children. The children, all second-graders, had grossly retarded language ability. The mean IQ for both groups was 80. The experimental group gained 12.3 months (mean total language age) and the control group 1.1

months during the seven-week period, with the implication that a short-term language program can significantly increase the total language age of cerebral palsy children as measured by the ITPA. Bateman points out that, although further investigation is necessary to determine retention of gain, the implications for identifying and successfully remediating certain language deficiencies in cerebral palsy children seen clear.

Meyer (1963) used the ITPA to study language disabilities of spastic and athetoid types of cerebral palsy children (ages 4-0 to 9-0, approximately 80). The author concluded that the ITPA can be used to discriminate between athetoid and spastic children. Bateman (1962) found that the test was useful with children who have severe visual defects, but who are not legally blind. On the basis of her findings, Bateman suggested that the test measures central psychological processes which appear relatively independent of sensory processes or acuity. Olson et al. (1965) did a case study of the effects of a short-term program which utilized curriculum with mentally retarded children based on linguistic strengths and weaknesses. The ITPA was used as one index to measure gain. They raised a question as to the effectiveness of the ITPA in measuring linguistic ability of children who are extremely low in intelligence.

Peabody Picture Vocabulary Test

The Peabody Picture Vocabulary Test (PPVT) provides an estimate of a subject's verbal intelligence by measuring his hearing vocabulary. The test consists of a series of pictures grouped in sets of four. For each set the examiner provides a word (orally) that is more nearly related to one of the four pictures. The subject's task is to select the appropriate picture in each set in a series of increasing difficulty, until a ceiling is established. Alternate forms are provided to facilitate retesting.

The test has certain obvious advantages for use with exceptional children. It does not require that the subjects read, point, or necessarily make oral responses. It is only essential that the subject indicate yes or no in some manner that the examiner can understand. The pictures do not include fine detail, thus minimizing figure-ground reversal problems. These physical features of the test, of course, commend its use with nonreaders or poor readers, or speech-handicapped and motor-involved youngsters.

The PPVT can be used with youngsters between the ages 2-6 and 18. The test is untimed and usually takes ten to fifteen minutes to administer and one or two minutes to score. No special training is required to administer it.

Olson (1965) points out the greater lingusitic sensitivity of the PPVT as compared to the more global Binet and raises the question as to whether the PPVT may be more effective in measuring gains made in areas of language ability.

The test was standardized on 4,012 subjects, and studies have indicated the PPVT is reasonably stable for average, mentally retarded, and cerebral palsied subjects.

Dunn and Harley (1959) studied the comparability of four individual tests of intelligence, one of shich was the PPVT, with twenty cerebral palsy children, ages 7-1 through 16-2 years. They also studied the correlation of test measures with reading and arithmetic achievement. It was concluded from the study that all four tests could predict school success with cerebral palsy children. Further, the correlations of teacher ratings on arithmetic and reading achievement with the PPVT mental age scores were .90 (.91 on Form B) and .87, respectively. Dunn and Harley found the alternate form reliability coefficient for the PPVT to be .97. Dunn notes that the weakest point in validity is probably at the superior adult level. A further weakness appears to be at years six and thirteen.

In two other independent studies—Ando (1968) and Nicholson (1970)—however, as was pointed out previously, the IQ scores on the PPVT were substantially higher than on other intelligence tests. Thus, while the correlations are high, there appears to be a tendency for cerebral palsied subjects to score higher on the PPVT than on other measures.

CASE STUDY

A method of studying a case may be illustrated by the first two sessions with Sara. She was ten years, two months of age. She was in the fourth grade of a private school. She was considered at the request of the parents who at first vaguely referred to inadequacies in school and the child's emotional life. There was no medical diagnosis available, though some workers thought of her as a mild athetoid. During the first visit the Binet and Ammons tests were administered; during the second, the Columbia Test of Mental Maturity, the Bender-Gestalt, and a projective sentence completion test.

The Binet yielded a double basal at Year VI and Year VIII. The only failure at Year VII was the Diamond, which on no trial could she produce an adequate result. At the Year IX level she failed Verbal Absurdities and Rhymes; at Year X, the Picture Absurdity, Reading, and Memory for Digits. She required all the permissible time for the reading, recalled details just well enough to be acceptable, and made three errors in the reading. Only the Memory for Sentences was adequate at the Year XI level.

Her work on the Ammons test was consistent and adequate for her age. At times she appeared to be somewhat superficial in making selections and made several corrections on her own initiative.

Sara was not reasonably cooperative at any time during the first session. At first, she said she did not want to do the work, then insisted she would not but did. Finally, she reached the point of absolute refusal, crying so much that the session was ended. Obviously, any scores obtained under such conditions would be minimal. There were some brief periods in which she really seemed to try.

Sara was wholly cooperative during the second session. She gave no explanation of the reason for the changed attitude and appeared to enjoy the work. There was not the slightest indication that she was unhappy in the test situation. The Columbia scale was given in part to evaluate it as an instrument to use with the cerebral palsied and in part to observe the child's method of work. She had previously earned an IQ of 90 on the Binet and 105 on the Ammons; she now earned an IQ of 99 on the Columbia.

There were four adequate drawings on the Bender. Of the remainder, two were scored *Concrete* on the basis of repeated counting, two involved marked difficulty in making angles, and in one figure the parts were disproportionate. When reproducing Figure 2, the subject did an excessive amount of counting and seemed interested only in having the correct number of loops, following the method of approach to Figure 1. Figure 5 which is also made of small units was handled differently. Here Sara started to count, stopped and said, "I'm not counting them; I don't feel like it." She produced a somewhat unbalanced figure but with the liberal scoring adopted, it was considered adequate. The projective sentence completion test was especially revealing. She may have been telling the truth when she indicated that she would rather play than anything else. (Without knowing of this remark, Sara's mother stated that the child wanted her school schedule changed so there would be more time for play.) It is doubtful that she completed all, or even most of the sentences as accurately. Two of the partial statements refer to faculty members, principal, and teacher. In each case the child gave the appropriate person's name and added, "This time I'm telling the truth."

Each sentence in which reference was made to physical disability brought the same generalized completing words; the blind, deaf, stutterer, and those who use crutches are "in a fix." It is possible that the words indicate her failure to adapt to and assimilate her own mild handicap. Further investigation should be made into her thinking on the point. Is the child unable to adjust because she is "in a fix" and does not know what to do about it?

References to the child's mother are generally favorable; to her father, unfavorable. Her mother's only failures as Sara sees it, or as she reported it, is that she does not provide homemade cake. The introductory words, "My mother hardly ever—" and "If my mother would only—" were completed by "bakes cake" and "bake cake," respectively. Sentence completions that refer to her father are at times factual as, "My father—*works in a market*"; others reflect feeling. "I am worried about—*daddy.*" "My father hardly ever—*brings me anything.*" "If my father would only—*bring me something.*" Judging by the child's own remarks and statements from other members of the family, Sara has far more possessions than the average child her age. The family has attempted to solve all problems with gifts. If Sara has temper tantrums, she can expect a bribe to stop; it appears to be the same with every self-centered thing she does.

Additional statements indicate that she is troubled if people look at her. Teachers are too strict, and relationships with boys are coming to have some importance. "When I am with boys—*I think I go nuts.*"

Before the psychologist continues to work with Sara, there will have to be an adequate medical examination. There may be a handedness problem which still causes difficulty. Her mother said that when Sara was a baby, her right hand was bound to her side for rather long periods to encourage development of the left. The child wanted to be right handed. Sara has scarcely yet overcome the need to refer to her hands as "Mr. Left" and "Mr. Right." It is clear that she was faced early with frustration over hand use. At ten years of age she still makes reversals, a fact which appears to be related. Whether the temper tantrums are to be considered epileptic equivalents or not is a matter for the doctor to determine.

The next step will be to find out whether her ability as measured correlates well with school achievement as measured by standard tests. Any marked inequality will lead to efforts to effect adjustment between ability and school requirements.

The final aspect of the problem to which attention will be directed is the emotional life. It is necessary to know in more detail what the child is like emotionally and how it is affecting her total adjustment. Investigation should be directed toward finding out what factors brought about the present maladjustment and in what way it can be modified.

SUMMARY

The evaluation of the intelligence of children with cerebral palsy is a difficult process at best. There is no single test of intelligence which is specific to this group of children or adults, and the best tests in the opinion of these authors all contain items which are inappropriate to cerebral palsied individuals or are in fact beyond their accomplishment at all due to their physical impairment. If the psychologist fails to take the physical limitations of the person into consideration, gross mislabeling of cerebral palsied persons can ensue. Although the litigation which has appeared in both federal and state courts since 1965 regarding the inappropriate use of intelligence tests has been directed more specifically at populations of educable mentally retarded children and those with perceptual and learning disabilities, it does not take much to see that the plaintifs' complaints would apply equally well to those individuals who have cerebral palsy. The evaluation of intelligence of cerebral palsy children is an arduous process which requires the highest skills and perceptions of the diagnostician.

These writers are of the opinion that, except for legal necessities, the total use of any single intelligence test is inappropriate with cerebral palsied individuals. At the childhood levels, the goal of testing is to ascertain the intellectual (learning) strengths and weaknesses of the individual. The specific intelligence quotient does not provide the educator with very much meaningful information at best. The mental age provides a bit more guidance to the educator, but this information is often ignored in the educational process! More significant to the teacher and to the learning process is information which will make possible an appropriate matching between the qualitative observations of the psychologists and the day-to-day educational planning for the child. Cruickshank (1975) has referred to this as the *psychoeducational match,* while Kephart (1975) earlier referred to somewhat the same concept as the perceptual-motor match. The concepts of prescriptive teaching and task analysis depend almost wholly on the psychoeducational match. Quantitative results of intelligence evaluations are helpful if done accurately, but are at best limited in their usefulness with cerebral palsied children and youth; qualitative assessments which bridge psychology and education are significant and can lead to realistic educational planning for these handicapped persons.

5

Personality and Behavioral Characteristics

WILLIAM M. CRUICKSHANK and
DANIEL P. HALLAHAN
with HARRY V. BICE

A REVIEW OF THE LITERATURE on cerebral palsy illustrates growth in understanding of these children. Since 1945, a remarkable and sizable quantity of writing and a most interesting modification in professional point of view regarding the personality of children with cerebral palsy have occurred. Winthrop Morgan Phelps must be credited with having sensitized the professions to the magnitude and diversity of problems related to cerebral palsy. His contribution cannot be minimized, and professional history must always note with great respect the continuing force which he directed to bring the problem of cerebral palsy to the attention of his own medical colleagues and personnel in related professions. Phelps, as an orthopedic surgeon, found it necessary to write in many fields outside his own. In doing so he was often required to utilize the data of others, data which were not always conclusive or reliable. Research in the field of psychology insofar as cerebral palsy was concerned was noticeably lacking, yet Phelps found it essential to stimulate psychologists and to record his comments and observation concerning the emotional development of children with cerebral palsy. Not to his discredit, it is understandable that points of view not currently held sometimes appeared in the literature. One of these statements, which clearly represents a point of view no longer valid in the light of later studies, is interesting to the student of psychology and is important in the historical consideration of cerebral palsy. Phelps stated:

> . . . There are a few fundamental psychological attributes which are observed in these children in their respective groups. Thus, for example, the athetoid child is found to be almost universally lacking in an over-development of fear, whereas the spastic child is filled with

The authors gratefully acknowledge the assistance of Bette Heins, Graduate Student at the University of Virginia; Walter Kwik and Lawrence Lewandowski, Research Assistants at the University of Michigan, for their assistance is the preparation of this chapter.

fears of all types, and is considerably limited in his activities by the presence of fear. The ataxic child does not show very much change from the normal with regard to fear.

The emotion of affection is found to be very highly developed in the athetoid, whereas in the spastic affection is only shown in connection with protective measures. The athetoid is extraverted and makes friends easily and widely and is not particularly concerned about his handicap. The spastic, on the other hand, is intraverted and is fearful of strangers and takes considerable time to make friends.

With regard to anger and rage it can be said that the athetoid shows a great deal of rage or anger and is likely to be much more the victim of his dislikes, whereas the spastic on the other hand is much slower to anger and when he is angry it is usually a very short lived emotion. These differences are simply brought out as fundamental differences which are usually found and which are often helpful in setting up the teaching program for the particular type of child which is being studied.

These interesting observations of Phelps are historical but have never been supported in psychological research. Specific emotional reactions are not typical of specific medical classifications. Dichotomies such as Phelps early described do not exist insofar as group characteristics are concerned. Personality characteristics involving specific emotions such as fear, affection, or rage, which in and of themselves are difficult to identify as single psychological traits, are not found to be generic in nature. Emotions are the product of learning, not of medical classification.

Freeman has concluded that, while the cerebral palsied adolescent may frequently have emotional disorders, the behavioral deviancies are not necessarily *directly* related to the brain injury itself. In addition, he states that there is no typical psychiatric syndrome associated specifically with cerebral palsy.

It is generally accepted that the causes of behavior lie within the phenomenal field of the behaver. A truism applicable to all individuals, it has special meaning in understanding the adjustment problems and subsequent personality characteristics of cerebral palsied persons as well as certain other groups of disabled individuals. The physically normal individual, although faced with barriers to the accomplishment of a goal, is uniquely different from the handicapped in two ways: (1) he is able to communicate or freely move around in his environment and, thus, can effect changes in barriers to this adjustment, and (2) for the normal person the barrier itself is rarely the same in all situations.

The cerebral palsied individual, on the other hand, is frequently unable to communicate adequately or to move within his environment; he cannot direct or effect changes in his environment with ease; and thus, often he must continue to effect adjustments within a situation which is completely negative to him. The cerebral palsied individual, if the disability is a barrier to adjustment at all, is faced with the same barrier (the disability) in all aspects of his adjustment. The physically normal individual from time to time may experience wealth, social position, education, religious differences, political differences, or lack of certain skills or comforts of living as, individually or collectively, barriers to the attainment of a new goal situation. These barriers change from time to time in the face of one different adjustment situation after the other. The elements listed above are, of course, pertinent to the cerebral palsied individual also, but in addition to all of these there is the physical presence of cerebral palsy per se. If the physical condition is an actual barrier or is conceived of as such, it is always a barrier. It can never be removed completely. The same barrier, in combination with others which are more transitory, is basic to all forms of life adjustment to the cerebral palsied individual, i.e., school learning, selection of friends, marital adjustment, vocation, self-help skills. The cerebral palsied individual's self-concept regarding the presence of the physical disability appears to be basic to the potential for satisfactory personal adjustment. The dilemma presented to the cerebral palsied child may be considered from two points of view: (1) from the point of view of the social situation in which the cerebral palsied child lives and is observed by parents, the community, teachers, and friends, and (2) from the point of view of his self-concept.

We have stated that causes of behavior lie within the phenomenal field of the behaver. In patients with central nervous system impairment a second factor in conditioning behavior is also inherent. Data are available to demonstrate that in varying degrees such impairment may affect the perceptual-motor abilities of the individual. The adjustment problems of the cerebral palsied must then be considered from a third point of view, namely, from the point of view of the extent to which the lesion or other type of brain damage affects adjustment.

EXTERNAL EVALUATIONS

Twin Studies

The value of twin studies in practically any aspect of human development is well known. In such studies variables which psychologists seek to control are just about as stable as it is possible to obtain. The environments in which the twins are placed, theoretically, are identical. Even in this type of situation there are, of course, great environmental variations for each twin. On the other hand, many of the variables which are difficult to control in studies of siblings or in studies of children unrelated by birth or minimized in the case of twins. Few psychological studies of twins are to be found in the literature of cerebral palsy. Shere (1954) has completed such a study involving thirty pairs of twins, one of whom in each pair was a cerebral palsied child. The Thirty pairs included five pairs of identical boys, five pairs of identical girls, eight pairs of fraternal girls, one pair of fraternal boys, and eleven pairs of boy-girl twins. The twins ranged in age from eighteen months to sixteen years. Shere was interested in ascertaining the impact of the interpersonal relationship of parents and child on social and emotional adjustment of the cerebral palsied twin. The present writers view this relationship as an external factor or stress upon the adjustment of the cerebral palsied child. Utilizing several rating devices, Shere reaches four conclusions:

1. The behavior of the parents toward the twins differed only in certain areas. They tended to be more understanding of the potentialities of the cerebral palsied twin and to get along with them with less friction. They tended to expect the non-cerebral palsied twin to assume more responsibilities and to act in a more mature manner than age or capabilities would warrant. Moreover, the parents appeared to be aware of the problems of the cerebral palsied child but to be oblivious to those of his twin. They did not seem to realize that the latter was regarding himself as being unfairly treated. It is believed that the lack of conformity exhibited by the non-cerebral palsied twin, and the consequent disciplinary friction with the parents, was part of the behavior pattern of the rejected child.

In other areas the behavior of the parents was actually more desirable toward the non-cerebral palsied child than it was toward his twin. He was accepted in an objective matter-of-fact way, accorded a place in all family activities, given help when such was necessary, protected from real dangers, encouraged to participate in new activities and allowed to govern his own activities as much as possible without too many suggestions from the parents. On the other hand, the parents tended to over-protect the cerebral palsied twin; to prevent—consciously or unconsciously—his growing up; to give him little or no active part in forming family policies; to direct his activities in a loving, but usually arbitrary manner. In general, it might well appear that their behavior was governed by emotion rather than by reason.

2. The behavior of the twins differed. The non-cerebral palsied child was more curious, more ready to explore than was his cerebral palsied twin. However, the latter was more cheerful and less stubborn and resistant to authority. He was less easily excited and less

prone to violent emotional outbursts. He was more willing to wait his turn without becoming impatient. He was not as sensitive to either flattery or disparagement as his twin and was not unduly jealous.

3. There appeared to be no statistically significant difference in either parent or child behavior between the three age groups.

4. This study appears to indicate that while the behavior of parents may be equally desirable toward both twins or actually to be more so toward the non-cerebral palsied twin, if the latter contrasts their objective behavior toward him with the emotional behavior which they exhibit in certain areas toward the cerebral palsied twin, he will exhibit behavior indicative of a rejected child.

The personality differences which Shere observed appeared to emanate from a relationship with parents rather than from intrinsic factors which were inherent within cerebral palsy itself. The factor of cerebral palsy, however, was the element which apparently disturbed the parent-child relationship and which motivated the parent to assume different attitudes and permit different behavior toward the twin with cerebral palsy.

Klapper and Werner (1950) studied three pairs of identical twins, one of whom in each pair was a cerebral palsied child. In each of the three cerebral palsied children studied, certain specific things were done to them early in their lives which were markedly different from the provisions made for the normal twin in each pair. Retarded physical development required additional parental attention or placement in special nursery school or clinical facilities, and other similar differences in approach resulted in reported differences in personality characteristics. It is interesting to note that these differences were less apparent in the set of twins wherein the cerebral palsied child had a very mild physical impairment. In the other two pairs of twins, the cerebral palsied child "is less tolerant of frustration and failure," is "more anxious and irritable," "is more easily distressed by difficult tasks," "is less careful, precise, and persistent in her efforts." These differences are the result of environmental interaction and learning and are not the specific characteristics of cerebral palsy *per se*. In part they are the result of attitudes of the normal twin toward the cerebral palsied sibling, i.e., "the normal twin is quite protective of his brother." It should be pointed out that the findings of these studies are not limited solely to cerebral palsy. In general, whenever a physical disability is inserted into the family constellation, the learning situation and the potential for healthy growth and development are seriously altered. The development of what might be termed negative personality characteristics in the cerebral palsied children included in the twin studies cited is merely corroboration of this fact. Basically different attitudes are expressed toward the cerebral palsied child by the members of the society of which he is a part from those expressed toward physically normal peers.

THE CEREBRAL PALSIED CHILD IN HIS SOCIAL MILIEU

Klapper and Werner hypothesize that as the degree of severity of brain injury increases, the level of endowment and level of performance decrease. Lagergren (1970), too, has found that associated handicaps are more frequent among cerebral palsied children than among children having other locomotor disabilities such as muscular dystrophy, special muscular atrophy, spinal bifida cystica, or thalidomide malformation. Mental retardation and speech problems were the most frequent of the associated handicaps. The present writers would hypothesize that, as the degree of severity of visible physical disability increases, the scope of personality characteristics and their degree of psychological severity increase. It is the nature of the visible physical disability to which society reacts and which tends to set the cerebral palsied child apart. Research is available to demonstrate that cardiac children, with a non-visible physical disability, function as physically normal children do in several different types of personal-social situations involving self-appraisal. In contradistinction to this situation, children with visible physical handicaps, including a group of cerebral palsied, were observed to be very different in personality characteristics to physically normal peers with whom the former had been matched by sex and chronological age.

Researchers interested in the problems of cerebral palsy are seeking more exact information regarding the area of damage to the brain and its relation to the location and severity of muscular involvement. Knowledge of the relationship of emotional patterns to brain damage is even less complete. In the clinical experience of these authors, the situation in which the child lives is always an extremely important contributing factor to the child's emotional development. Parental attitudes, attitudes of society, and attitudes of peers are in effect the only things which can be drastically altered. Cerebral palsy and its physical and psychological components can be changed only slightly, and such change is effected only over a long period of time. Although Farber discusses parenting of cerebral palsied children later in this book, emphasis will be made here of this problem since the impact of parents on the personality development of the cerebral palsied child is so significant.

Parents commonly attribute anything unusual in the life of the child to the brain damage itself. In one case a child was afraid of anything purple. No clothing with that color in it was worn in the home. According to the mother's opinion, nothing but cerebral palsy caused this reaction. Investigation revealed that actually the child's reaction was a rather simple matter of conditioning. The child had been treated for Vincent's Angina with gentian violet. He found it an unpleasant experience. The change in the color of his saliva frightened him, and he was scolded because he soiled his pillow with it. The relation of this series of experiences to the color purple accounted for the child's negative reaction to things containing that color. Cerebral palsy had no relationship to the situation whatsoever.

There are many indirect ways in which cerebral palsy contributes to emotional involvement. Frustration is the experience of all people, but not all experience it in just the way the cerebral palsied do. One who said that as a group they "are known for what they cannot do" pointed to the major frustrations. Very early in life the child learns that he cannot keep up with others and so is not wanted as a playmate. He seldom is able to compete in sports as he grows older, and he thus loses an opportunity to gain status. Therapies require so much time that the child is seldom as advanced in school as other children of his age. Later, the desire to be profitably employed and establish a home reemphasizes the significance of the handicap.

Learning starts very early, and the handicapped child has an opportunity to see others do things he does not do. He may be urged to do them, and he cannot. When therapies begin, he is exposed to a routine which few other children have to face. Some parents have expressed the opinion that temper displays really begin when therapy starts. This may be the result not only of the fact that the therapy program is physically tiring, but also that during therapy the child is "forced" to perform in ways which are basically distasteful to him. In addition, if the cerebral palsied child has been overprotected by his parents, the institution of a structured therapeutic regimen may cause conflict between the parents and the child. Even though he sees other children walking, he is not impressed with the importance of his going through endless specified movements of a leg or legs. He views the physical-therapy manipulations as separate and apart from the actual walking experience. One cerebral palsied child had neither walked nor talked when he was old enough to enter school. His parents had repeatedly been advised to place him in an institution for the retarded. In his late twenties (when by now he had been graduated from college and was working), in trying to recall earlier experiences, he said, "I cannot remember feeling any need to walk or talk; I was getting everything I wanted without it."

The child's interpretation of the therapy requires further consideration, probably more than the fact that he faces a more or less tiring regime. The child with a mild handicap observed, when he first saw more severely handicapped children having physical therapy, "they are naughty children." The conclusion seemed obvious to him. Naughty children are those who do not do as they are told. The children he saw were not all doing the things they were told to do. Some of them cried. Nothing was more logical to the observing child than to assume that the others had been punished.

There is a wealth of clinical data and some research evidence to indicate that parents of cerebral palsied children, as a group, tend to overprotect their handicapped children. Shere and Kastenbaum (1966) studied the interaction of mothers and their severely involved cerebral palsied children by interviewing them and observing their behavior. In general, they found that the mothers kept their children in a stimulus-deprived environment. They did not make objects readily available for their children to play with. This behavior may have been due to their fear that their children would hurt themselves. In any event, the mothers did not seem to be aware of the importance of attempting to improve their children's cognitive development.

In terms of expectations for adjustment, there is some evidence that even when the cerebral palsied child reaches adolescence, the mother does not predict the child's performance very accurately. Nussbaum (1966) found the following correlations between the mother's expectations and the child's performance: on vocational tasks (.20), social development (.26), vocational potential (.53), and intelligence (.37). Even though these correlations were higher, i.e., more realistic, than the cerebral palsied adolescents' own predictions, the generally low nature of the correlations suggests that mothers are relatively unaware of the level of functioning of their cerebral palsied children.

Clinical experience shows that siblings of the handicapped can also be affected by the particular social milieu of the family with a handicapped child. Not only the cerebral palsied child, but also the child's siblings, can be affected by the attitudes of the mother. There are greater discrepancies in attitudes of mothers toward their two children if one was cerebral palsied than if both were normal. The siblings of the cerebral palsied children are more anxious, hostile, and fearful than the siblings of normal children. Furthermore, emotional maladjustment is related to the degree of discrepancy of the attitudes toward normal and handicapped siblings.

There is undoubtedly a need for early professional guidance for parents and their cerebral palsied children. Many mothers think that the personnel they contacted during the first few months do not provide emotional support or practical suggestions. Those professionals contacted tend to neglect to inform the mother of the possible psychological problems the child might eventually have. Instead, physical symptoms are usually the major focus of professional concern.

Many parents of the cerebral palsied acknowledge that they overprotect and pamper their handicapped children. In group or individual counseling this is a most common admission to the present authors: "He misses so much in life that I try to make it up to him." By the time the parents have realized that by doing everything for the child they have prevented him from doing what he could, he has learned to enjoy his dependence on others and will not willingly relinquish this status.

After the first three or four sessions of group counseling with parents, someone usually brings up the subject of guilt. Only a minority of parents deny that they have felt guilty because of the condition of the child. Parents whose children acquired cerebral palsy after birth usually make that fact clear when the others discuss guilt. Some of the parents assume they are responsible, others blame their husbands or wives. When a husband thinks it is his wife's fault the child is crippled ("She didn't take care of herself when she was pregnant") or a wife blames her husband ("He probably had a bad disease one time"), the child has little chance of growing up in a calm atmosphere.

In response to this latter attitude by parents, the cerebral palsied children often find that they are a nuisance to their parents. in this connection, the word *nuisance* in a vocabulary test often embarrasses cerebral palsied children. Some hesitate, then smile, and give a definition; others glance at a parent, and respond: "It means me; that's what I am." One child remarked that she knew her parents had to spend so much money for braces that they could not have a vacation. Another, just entering adolescence, asked her parents: "Is it so hard to take care of a child with cerebral palsy?" The handicap in this case was mild and the mental level better than average. It is not known whether the question was based on attitudes of the parents which the child had observed or whether she had overheard them discussing the possible outcome of her recent illness.

In a counseling situation one of the authors had been seeing the parents of a ten-year-old cerebral palsied child. The daughter is a very large girl; the mother a very small woman. The child is a quadriplegic athetoid who must be lifted from place to place and cannot move of her own accord to any extent. As the child has grown older and has become heavier she has presented a real problem to the mother, for during long periods of the day there is no one in the home to move the daughter except the mother. The mother has a very objective attitude toward the situation and has what the therapist feels is a wholesome and genuine love for her daughter. Partly to be humorous, partly to make conversation, and partly in truth, the mother would say to the child as she lifted her from place to place: "My, you're getting heavy." Or on another occasion her spontaneous comment on lifting the child might be: "Oh what a big girl you are getting to be." The child, on the other hand, interpreted these comments as being expressions of dislike on the part of the mother, and on one occasion commented to her mother: "You don't like me any more, because it hurts you to lift me."

Parents may be very frank in their discussions regarding the possibility of the extreme in rejection, or they may attempt to hide what they are thinking in statements which outwardly indicate great affection. Much may be said in a moment of despair. A certain amount of bravado may appear during counseling, but enough is said to make it clear that the thinking of parents does not always provide the best emotional climate for the child. It can be the unqualified: "Euthanasia is all that is left to us." It may be the more guarded: "I do not believe that mercy killing is bad." Few parents can think in that manner and keep their feelings entirely from their children. A mother expressed the effect of her attitude in the statement: "When I am feeling bitter, he recognizes my frame of mind and reacts against it."

There is much in the attitudes the cerebral palsied meet in their community that helps develop feelings of inferiority even if the home atmosphere has been of the best. Furthermore, Kreiger (1967) found a significant relationship between the accepting attitude of significant others and the proclivity of cerebral palsied individuals to accept social responsibility.

CEREBRAL PALSY AND THE SELF-CONCEPT

Group Discussion

The observations of young adults with cerebral palsy are pertinent to the understanding of their emotional lives. The discussions in many group counseling sessions could be briefly summarized in four statements: (1) "We may be different because of the brain damage itself." (2) "We could be emotionally unlike others because our experiences are not the same." (3) "We may intensify our emotions because there is some value in it for us." (4) "Whatever the cause of our emotions, we can do something to modify our expressions of them."

The cerebral palsied child's resentment grows, and he is more likely to make it known as he grows older. Young people are understandably displeased when others in the home make plans for them without inquiring into their wishes, answer questions directed to them without allowing time for the handicapped to answer, fail to assign responsibilities that are suitable, or otherwise appear not to include then in the family group. The thinking of one group of young adults was reported to include at least five ways in which parents could be more helpful in the growth and development of their children. (1) "Parents must admit the child's condition to themselves." (2) "They should talk about it calmly, unemotionally, when there is occasion to do so in the child's presence." (3) "They should make it clear to the child at appropriate times that his physical condition prevents him from engaging in certain activities." (4) "They should provide suitable substitute occupations," (5) "They should face frankly any aspect of the problem, since evasion tends to intensify the child's concern."

Expressions of Early Adolescence

Sixteen children who were having intensive treatment were asked to write or dictate anything they cared to about cerebral palsy. A few likes and dislikes were expressed by children under twelve, which was the median age. Beginning at that age, almost every child did express attitudes.

There was very little criticism of therapies, but some indicated dislike for certain details: "I go to speech therapy twice a day. The teacher pushes her finger, in a rubber glove, against my jaw and I push against her. I also do it with my lips and tongue. I don't like this."

Most of the older children were impressed by either their own disabilities or those of others they knew. Some wrote about what the others "won't do," some about what they "don't do," and still others about what they "can't do." Reference is commonly made to difficulties with seeing, hearing, walking, and the need of appliances or protection such as one might get by wearing a helmet. Others wrote of personal habits: "I am learning to control my drooling; it is very hard." A blind ten-year-old wrote of the difficulty of dressing, they stressed what she could do: "I can sing very well; I am walking the best of all in the whole school."

Some of those who were above the median age wrote of the effects of their condition on their emotions: "Sometimes I have to repeat myself and I get embarrassed." "If you see another child walking on crutches, make sure your boy or girl doesn't make fun of them. Your child could have been like them." The boy who made that statement was, like the others, free to write anything he wished about cerebral palsy. With the exception of the above one sentence, he devoted his time to telling what he thought people should know in order to prevent cerebral palsy.

Some of the children wrote only of attitudes—including self-pity, a tendency to be satisfied with less than one's best, anxiety about slow progress, or the need to find happiness in case walking and talking are unattainable. Others told of the satisfaction derived from helping some who were more afflicted than they. A thirteen-year-old, after telling of the routines in education, therapy, and self-care, ended with the paragraph: "Now I am going to tell you how CPs feel. They feel like you, but they can't walk like you. If they aren't CPs, they grow up like nothing but if they are CPs, they have to work like mad. I am a CP and I like being a CP."

As a rule the young person who has found that it is possible to modify expressions of emotion has had the advantage of good parental guidance. The conclusion that was most satisfying to the group, though not the most easily attainable, included a rationalization that few people fully understand the condition of the cerebral palsied. It included the assumption that most people do not want to be rude in attitude or remark. It expressed the hope that they as cerebral palsied young people could attempt to treat the incident which might arouse emotion as a commonplace one or turn it into a joke directed at one's self.

The statements presented above illustrate practically the day-to-day frustrations and tensions which both cerebral palsied children and their parents face. Out of these tensions, which more often than not remain unrationalized or unaccepted, grow personality maladjustments that are deepseated and dynamic. It is part of the psychologist's responsibility to recognize when the service that can be offered is not suitable for the condition of the child or parent. Recommendations for psychiatric or other medical care should then be made.

Self-Expressions of Individual Children

The psychologist has a number of methods through which the cerebral palsied child can project his self-concepts. Frequently these may be much less threatening than the cerebral palsied child's actual discussion of his feelings in a face-to-face counseling situation with a therapist. The Bender-Gestalt test, to be discussed below, is an important instrument in this connection. Another projective device, closely associated with the Bender, is the Draw-a-Person Test.

Subject No. 1

Subject No. 1 had a chronological age of 7-8 years, a mental age of 7-0 years. On the Wechsler Intelligence Scale for Children (WISC), he obtained a verbal intelligence quotient of 86 a performance quotient of 82, and a full-scale quotient of 83. Figure 5.1 is the drawing of a person which he made at the examiner's request. After the child had made the head and body on this drawing, he began to describe what he was doing. He drew the left arm first, then he began to make the small marks beginning near the hand. He said: "I'll put a finger here, and one here," and continued with the same words until he had made all the small marks on the left side of the individual he was drawing. He then put his pencil on the other side and looked at the examiner asking, "How can I give him an arm here? I'll give him just a little one and I won't give him any fingers." This child had represented himself in the drawing. On one side he had no use of his arm while on the other he was very inaccurate because of his athetosis.

Subject No. 2

Subject No. 2 is an eighteen-year-old boy. He has a mild athetosis involving primarily the upper extremities. He is able to walk and drive a car, although he still retains considerable involvement in his lower extremities. He was silent throughout his drawing, but upon completion, as he handed the paper (Figure 5.2) to the psychologist, he said: "I stuck his hands in his pocket. I can't draw hands. Anyway, his probably aren't any better than mine, and mine certainly are a hurdle to me." This session was held the day after he had been told by a college advisor that his disability would prevent him from moving into the field of meteorology because his hands were not adequate for fine muscle movement. The awareness of the body image is important in a consideration of cerebral palsy, since through the drawing the

(5.1)   (5.2)

Figure 5.1.   Drawing of a man by a cerebral palsied boy, chronological age 7–8 years.
Figure 5.2.   Drawing of a man by a cerebral palsied adolescent, chronological age 18–0 years.

psychologist may obtain an understanding of the way in which the body appears to the individual, and thus understand personality dynamics in terms of this physique. Perceptual disturbances, equilibrium problems, integrative disturbances of an emotional nature, and feelings of social inadequacy, among other things, may affect the body image of the cerebral palsied child and may be reflected in the child's drawings.

There is evidence, however, which should caution one from indiscriminantly using such an instrument as the Draw-a-Man to determine a child's body image. Particularly with cerebral palsied children, who already have poor visual-motor coordination, bizarre drawings may merely indicate a child's poor drawing abilities. Abercrombie and Tyson (1966) found that they could predict the mental ages of cerebral palsied children as well by having them copy simple geometric figures as by using the Goodenough Draw-a-Man Test. Thus, poor drawing ability could account for the diagnosis of body-image disorder. Abercrombie and Tyson point out that normal children, too, sometimes make errors which could be interpreted as indicative of body-image problems. The clinician must therefore be aware of the frequency with which the particular child makes errors indicating a body-image problem.

Nondirective Individual Counseling

In the experience of two of the present writers, counseling sessions following the premises of nondirective therapy have proven of real value to cerebral palsied young people. Not only have these experiences proven beneficial to the client in assisting him to gain insight into his problems and to effect a more satisfactory life adjustment, but they have given the therapists an insight into the magnitude of the adjustment problem which faces some cerebral palsied persons. It is not the intention of the authors to discuss the pros and cons of nondirective counseling. Suffice it to say that both nondirective counseling and information-giving counseling are used effectively with cerebral palsied adolescents and adults. The technique is described here merely as another way to demonstrate the variety of personality characteristics and the magnitude of the problems of the cerebral palsied youth.

Subject No. 3

A counseling protocol of a sixteen-year-old quadriplegic athetoid has been reported elsewhere, but is repeated here as being pertinent to the subject under discussion:

> Subject: I just don't know why the doctors let me live when I was born. I'm no use to any one the way I am.

Counselor: You feel that you are of no value to society and that discourages you.

Subject: Yes, I know what I want to do and I can talk O.K., but every time I try to do anything I'm stymied. I can't walk or even eat without some help.

Counselor: You feel, because of your physical condition that you can't do many of the things you want to do and you feel frustrated when this happens.

Subject: It's worse than that. When I can't succeed in something and when I know I could succeed if I weren't a C.P., I get more than discouraged because I'm so helpless. You're stuck and you hate yourself for being stuck.

Subject No. 4

The problems of adolescence and the frustrations at being unable to meet them are typified in the counseling protocol of a seventeen-year-old mild right hemiplegic spastic girl:

Subject: Last time we were talking about dancing. I'd like to start with this again, because I'm really pretty mad about it today.

Counselor: You feel upset because of something which happened at a dance recently.

Subject: Yes, last night. Now I know I am a C.P. I know that the other girls have a head start when it comes to looks and dancing ability. But last night I had a new dress and I had a date. I never can tell, though, whether the boy really calls me because he wants to or if my mother arranges it and doesn't tell me. Anyhow the party was a flop for me, because when we got there, Miss Martin, she was the chaperon, right away came up to me and invited me to sit with her because she was alone. This left my date to play the field. He did come and ask me to dance several times, but each time Miss Martin would assure him that "we were enjoying ourselves" talking. I am certain that this was all prearranged between my mother and Miss Martin, and I don't know what to do.

The permissiveness of the nondirective counseling situation permits feelings to come to the surface, to be reflected or interpreted by the therapist, and insights to be formed or re-formed by the client. The depth of the problems and their seriousness are clearly depicted in the portions of the two protocols just quoted. The value of the nondirective approach is found in that the individual himself ultimately comes to his own formulation and acceptance of the problem. The role of the counselor is thus to provide an atmosphere in which freedom of expression can be effected and in that setting to reflect appropriately the emotions which are expressed. Many of the problems faced by the cerebral palsied individual are physically not possible to change. The inevitability of the physical condition would make directive counseling a frustration rather than a therapeutic experience. Counseling with the cerebral palsied has as its goal the development of new insights and acceptance of a difficult and unremediable personal situation at a level which will at the same time permit the individual to deal positively with people and social situations.

PERCEPTUAL CHARACTERISTICS OF CEREBRAL PALSIED CHILDREN

Much information about the personality characteristics of cerebral palsied children can be ascertained through the use of tests which involve different types of perceptual or conceptual abilities.

The Bender-Gestalt Test

The Bender-Gestalt test, developed by Lauretta Bender, was utilized initially with adults. It is frequently utilized by psychologists in evaluating both personality characteristics and perceptual characteristics of children with cerebral palsy.

A great deal of caution should be exercised by those who interpret Bender drawings of children with cerebral palsy in terms of personality problems or characteristics. A part of a psychologist's report following an examination of twelve-year-old John, a spastic child, designated him as "a predelinquent child." When asked the basis ʻfor this judgment, the psychologist had nothing to offer but his interpretation of *Figure 7* from the Bender-Gestalt test. The two parts of the figure, as drawn by John, were separated, and angles at the base were poorly formed; one of them was inverted so that the acute angle, instead of pointing away from the center of the hexagon, pointed toward it. The explanation given by the psychologist follows: "When John saw *Figure 7,* it symbolized to him closed jail doors [although John did not state this]. Since he was contemplating delinquency, he could not stand to have them closed. That accounts for the separation. The way he drew the angles is indicative of probable sex delinquency."

The authors are aware of the place of symbolism in the expression of one's thinking, and of the possible importance of psychoanalytical theory in assessing the dynamics of individual behavior. It does make a difference whether the interpreter, on the one hand, assumes that he knows the significance of the symbol or, on the other, that he believes it is his responsibility to determine what the symbol means to the individual who produced it. What may be a sex symbol to one individual may in another be evidence of malfunctioning in visuomotor activity. Actually, John had incorporated into his drawing of this one figure the two types of errors made by the greatest number of cerebral palsied children when they produce the Bender-Gestalt figures. As will be noted below, of the 216 children reported in this chapter, thirty-six children separated the parts of figures and forty-one had problems in making angles. No other type of error was made by as many children. If their drawings are to be interpreted as John's was, the "predelinquency" rate among the cerebral palsied must be a serious problem indeed.

Mike was not doing very well in school. The Bender-Gestalt was one of the tests used in a psychoeducational evaluation of the boy. After it was completed, the psychologist asked him, as he looked at each picture: "What did you draw there?" Mike said of Bender *Figure 4:* "A pirate being hit on the head with a block;" of Bender *Figure 5:* "A tank gun;" of Bender *Figure 7:* "A boat crashing into a boat." One seldom sees more frank symbolism or expression of aggression in the production of the nine drawings.

As stated above, the Bender-Gestalt test was administered to 216 children with cerebral palsy to determine if this method could contribute to an understanding of their personalities and their adjustment problems. About half the tests were given as a part of a regular testing program; the remainder were given children whose psychological evaluation had been made previously. The results of the studies of intellectual capacities were available for the entire group of children.*

Experimental Procedures

Each child was asked to write his name on paper that he placed as he chose. Throughout the test, the paper was kept in that position, although there was a strong desire on the part of many to change it. It is not uncommon for a child who is drawing a four-sided figure to attempt to rotate the paper so that the line he is drawing at any one time is drawn in the same plane as every other with respect to body position. The test card was placed flat on the desk with the longer side parallel to the top of the paper. The child was told: "Here is a card with something drawn on it. I want you to make a drawing just like it." Any question about procedure was answered: "You are to draw it just the way you see it on the card." The manner of the approach to the task and any remarks were recorded.

Bender's summary chart was used as a basis for comparison of the test results whenever the maturation level of a drawing was under consideration. Figure 5.3 presents the original models from the Bender-Gestalt test while Figure 5.4 illustrates sample drawings made by cerebral palsied children.

*The authors wish to express their appreciation to Elsa Miller, then of Buffalo, New York, and to Ethel Jackson Evans, of Philadelphia, Pennsylvania, for the opportunity to procure some of the drawings.

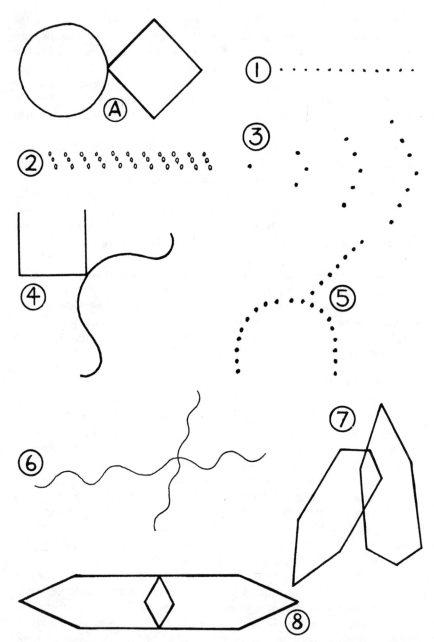

Figure 5.3.　Bender-Gestalt test figures. *By permission of the American Orthopsychiatric Association and Dr. Lauretta Bender.* References to *Figure A* and to *Figures 1* through *8* are to traditional Bender drawing numbers and not to independent figures in this book.

Figure 3

Restrictive Concreteness

Athetosis

Chronological Age 16.6
Mental Age 11.6
Intelligence Quotient 77

"It's a Christmas tree and these are the legs on the tree."

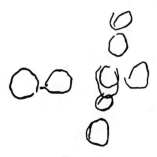

U S

Figure 4

Restrictive Concreteness

Left Spastic Hemiplegia

Chronological Age 8.1
Mental Age 5.6
Intelligence Quotient 65

"I'll make a *U.S.*"

Figure 5

Restrictive Concreteness

Spastic Quadriplegia

Chronological Age 10.2
Mental Age 8.2
Intelligence Quotient 80

"It's a house and a chimney."

Figure 6

Incorrect Elements

Left Spastic Hemiplegia

Chronological Age 5.10
Mental Age 6.0
Intelligence Quotient 103

Figure 8

Inverted Angles; Rotation

Spastic Quadriplegia

Chronological Age 12.5
Mental Age 9.4
Intelligence Quotient 75

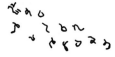

Figure 3

Rotation; Disproportion

Spastic Quadriplegia

Chronological Age 18.0
Verbal Intelligence Quotient 103
Performance Quotient 47
Full-Scale Quotient 73

Much of the distortion resulted from emotional disturbance over first effort to make the drawing.

Figure 5.4. Bender-Gestalt test drawings by cerebral palsied children. (See Figure 5.3 for original Bender Figures *A* and *1–8*.)

Figure A

Incompleteness

Athetosis

Chronological Age	11.5
Mental Age	9.2
Intelligence Quotient	80

Figures 6 and 8

Result of Visual Defect

Right Spastic Hemiplegia

Chronological Age	9.11
Mental Age	10.2
Intelligence Quotient	103

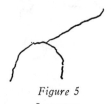

Figure 5

Immature

Spastic Quadriplegia

Chronological Age	8.4
Mental Age	8.4
Intelligence Quotient	100

Figure 5

Concrete

Spastic Quadriplegia

Chronological Age	16.6
Verbal Intelligence Quotient	96
Performance Quotient	56
Full-Scale Quotient	75

The subject's only concern was that he make the right number of dots. When the two parts did not join, he said, "It didn't go down far enough; I started too low" (with the horizontal line).

Figure 2

Perseveration

Ataxia

Chronological Age	8.0
Mental Age	8.0
Intelligence Quotient	100

Figure 5.4. (*Continued*)

Figure 5
Closure

Left Spastic Hemiplegia

Chronological Age	11.10
Mental Age	10.9
Intelligence Quotient	91

Figure 5
Rotation; Added Elements;
Enlargement

Right Spastic Hemiplegia

Chronological Age	7.5
Mental Age	5.9
Intelligence Quotient	78

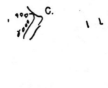

Figure 3
Immature; Incorrect Elements

Spastic Quadriplegia

Chronological Age	10.6
Mental Age	9.0
Intelligence Quotient	117

C was the most satisfactory effort; A and B represent trials 1 and 2. Only those acquainted with the test would know what the subject was trying to draw.

Figure 7
Distorted Angles

Ataxia

Chronological Age	15.0
Verbal Intelligence Quotient	69
Performance Quotient	49
Full-Scale Quotient	55

A superior child before removal of brain tumor. The drawing was done 3 years after operation. The acute angle is the angle that would be formed by the two sides that are separated.

Figure 7
Unrecognizable

Athetosis

Chronological Age	6.11
Mental Age	9.0
Intelligence Quotient	130

Figure 5.4. (*Continued*)

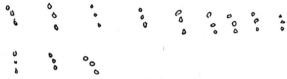

Figure 2
Meticulosity

Rigidity

Chronological Age   13.4
Mental Age   12.7
Intelligence Quotient   95

Subject counted and recounted the loops; it was important to her to have the right number, regardless of the figure.

Figure 6
Restrictive Concreteness
Right Spastic Hemiplegia

Chronological Age   10.9
Mental Age   7.9
Intelligence Quotient   72

"This is *S*."

Bender found a 60-year-old mild right hemiparetic who tended to interpret dots as letters.

Figure 3
Restrictive Concreteness

Rigidity

Chronological Age   9.11
Mental Age   5.0
Intelligence Quotient   50

"I believe that looks like a Christmas tree."

Figure 5
Incorrect Elements

Rigidity

Chronological Age   7.1
Mental Age   8.0
Intelligence Quotient   113

Figure 8
Distorted Angles
Right Spastic Hemiplegia

Chronological Age   10.6
Verbal Intelligence Quotient   76
Performance Quotient   68
Full-Scale Quotient   68

Figure 5.4.   (*Continued*)

Figure A
Distorted Angles: Separation
Right Spastic Hemiplegia

Chronological Age	11.2
Verbal Intelligence Quotient	104
Performance Quotient	83
Full-Scale Quotient	86

Figure A
Distorted Angles; Displaced Part
Spastic Quadriplegia

Chronological Age	12.2
Mental Age	9.5
Intelligence Quotient	77

Figure 6
Separation or Fragmentation
Athetosis

Chronological Age	8.9
Mental Age	5.2
Intelligence Quotient	59

Figure 3
Compression
Right Spastic Hemiplegia

Chronological Age	10.6
Mental Age	11.6
Intelligence Quotient	110

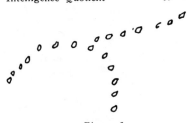

Figure 5
Enlargement; Incorrect Elements
Spastic Quadriplegia

Chronological Age	12.5
Mental Age	10.4
Intelligence Quotient	83

Could be considered Perseveration of *Figure 2*.

Comparable to drawing by a 27-year-old man with multiple fractures of the skull, right-sided convulsions, and right-sided paralysis.

Figure A
Disproportion
Rigidity Hemiplegia

Chronological Age	14.1
Mental Age	14.1
Intelligence Quotient	100

Figure 5.4. (*Continued*)

Figure 2

Erratic Approach

Figure 8

Inverted Angle

Right Spastic Hemiplegia

Chronological Age	13.4
Mental Age	11.11
Intelligence Quotient	90

Athetosis

Chronological Age	9.5
Mental Age	9.2
Intelligence Quotient	97

Numbers indicate order in which child worked.

Figure A

Separation

Left Spastic Hemiplegia

Chronological Age	11.5
Mental Age	11.6
Intelligence Quotient	101

Figure 4

Displacement

Athetosis

Chronological Age	7.1
Mental Age	6.8
Intelligence Quotient	92

Figure A

Miscellaneous Distortion of Angles;
Right Angles

Figure 7

Failure to Overlap

Left Spastic Hemiplegia

Chronological Age	12.2
Mental Age	10.4
Intelligence Quotient	85

Right Spastic Hemiplegia

Chronological Age	5.0
Mental Age	5.8
Intelligence Quotient	111

Subject's signature:

HoLEFoDoLYT

Figure 5.4. (*Continued*)

Figure 8

Miscellaneous Distortion of Angles;
Modification of Drawing to Avoid
the Problem; Rotation

Figure 4

Rotation: Displacement of a Part;
Disproportion and Separation

Athetosis

Chronological Age	8.6
Verbal Intelligence Quotient	91
Performance Quotient	96
Full-Scale Quotient	93

Spastic Quadriplegia

Chronological Age	8.10
Mental Age	8.10
Intelligence Quotient	100

Figure 5.4. (*Continued*)

(The reader should note that references in the following sections to *Figure A* and *Figures 1* through *8* are to traditional Bender drawing numbers and not to independent figures in this book.) With this exception, the tabulation of results was made without reference to any previous study either for classification or explanation. The authors, having a considerable amount of pertinent material, wished to study it without permitting preconceived notions to influence their findings. The important considerations were: *What did the child do?* and *What did he say about it?* Such data could be correlated with other available material for a fuller understanding of children with cerebral palsy.

Definition of Categories

The results have been categorized as *adequate* or *inadequate,* with the inadequate performances further divided with respect to method of work and the resulting distortions. Additional possible classifications may occur to the reader. They were found in such small numbers that they were not included. Frequent attempts to rotate the paper while working could be included in method. "Flight," drawing such a figure as No. 2 with horizontal rows of loops instead of slanting groups of three, was encountered, but it was rare.

Immature—Seriously inferior for the mental age of the child. This category could be used for either method or results but was limited to the former. The term indicates that the work represented two or more years' inferiority to the examples in Bender's table. In this classification, the mental age of the child was used for comparison. A child of eight years with a mental age of six drew *Figure A* (Bender) as 75 percent of six-year-old children do, with the two parts separated. This was not considered inadequate in method or result. To avoid overlapping of scoring errors, a drawing that fell in this category was not included in any other. Dissociation is sometimes evidence of immaturity; therefore, no drawing was considered to represent both dissociation and immaturity.

Concrete, or restrictive concreteness—Marked, obvious dependence on previous experience. Ability to deal with the abstract figure is limited or absent. There is a pronounced and continuing need for and dependence on the substantive and the literal. A drawing was placed in this category when a subject (1) hesitated before making it until he had given it a name; (2) demanded a name instead of assigning one himself; (3) made a common concrete interpretation of the figure, though he did not name it; (4) mentioned a use for the "object," a name being implied; or (5) copied one element of a figure at a time with little or no concern about the pattern. The first three procedures can be illustrated by productions of *Figure 4* which the child with cerebral palsy may interpret as "U.S." Reference to use of the item is less frequent; it is illustrated by *Figure 5* which is "to cook in." Care must be exercised with the last-mentioned procedure. A child may count dots or loops in a figure because he has been subjected to much pressure when parent and teacher insist on his work being done perfectly. It is when the figure as such has no apparent significance for the child and he is compulsive only about getting the right number of dots or other elements that the result has been scored as representative of concreteness.

As in other categories, overlapping classifications have been avoided. A comparatively mature subject was baffled by *Figure A* until he found something in his experience which it could represent. He commented, "Oh, it's a ball and window." He then proceeded to draw the two figures he had named but with some distance between them. In his experience, ball and window do not belong together. Regardless of the distance separating the two elements of the figure, it was not classified as dissociation.

Only in rare instances was a drawing considered to represent this category if it was not named. There could be no doubt in the case of the child who said when looking at *Figure 2*, "It's candy; and this is the way I make candy." She did not name *Figure 3* but did produce the rather common "Christmas tree." This could be scored *concrete* on the basis of the type of drawing she made and frequency of this interpretation. *Figure 7* as "two boats" is rare. Regardless of the fact that a child made two separated figures which might appear to be outlines of boats, the classification would not be used unless the name was applied.

Perseveration—Continuing according to an established set without regard for the limitations indicated in the figure. The subject continues to add elements to a figure that is already completed or uses the elements of one figure inappropriately in one drawn later. *Figure 1* is correctly made with dots. If then *Figure 2* is made with dots instead of loops, it is recorded as a perseverative response. *Figure 3* made of loops, following *Figure 2* which should be so made, need not be perseveration. It could be an adequate drawing depending on the age and ability of the child. The majority of six-year-old children make some loops instead of dots.

Erratic approach—No discernible pattern in the work. This occurs most often when a figure is composed of dots or loops. A few children make a point of letting the examiner know there is something unusual about their method. One remarked: "I don't do this like other people would, but when I finish it will look right."

Dissociation—Detachment, displacement, discontinuity, incompleteness. Figures composed of two parts that should join are drawn so that they are *separate*. A clear-cut error is indicated, never an accidental result of incoordination. Some children separate parts by as much as 30 millimeters. When a minimum of 3 millimeters was chosen as a lower limit, the average separation was 11 millimeters. Displacement of a part designates an inadequacy in which some parts of a figure that should touch are actually in contact, but at the wrong point. *Failure to overlap* may be found in *Figure 7;* the parts are drawn so that there is no apparent intent to make them overlap; in fact, at times there appears to be much effort to draw the sides so that they just touch. *Incompleteness* is just what the word implies, i.e., some important part of the figure is omitted. Some subjects, when asked if the figure is complete, say that it is.

Closure—Addition of parts, making an enclosed figure, though in the pattern it is not. This is found in *Figure 4* and *Figure 5*. It may be that concreteness is illustrated in some of these instances, but there is not sufficient information given by the subject to justify placing his work in that category.

Incorrect elements—Inappropriate parts. *Figure 6* made of dots or loops represents this error. The possibility of perseveration has to be considered in this connection.

Unrecognizable—Little or no discernible similarity to the pattern. The drawing in this category must be numbered at the time it is made if the examiner wishes to know at a later time what it is supposed to be. It should be emphasized that it does not represent either lack of muscular control or regression. *Figure 8* made as a circle within a circle would be recognized as the figure in its most primitive form by those who work with the test.

Distorted angles—Any pronounced inadequacy in the formation of angles. The most easily defined type is the inverted in which the apex of an angle is directed toward rather than away from the center of the figure. If there is an angle at the top and bottom of the figure as in *Figure 7*, the one at the top is more frequently correct than the one at the bottom. Some drawings that have been placed in the miscellaneous group are illustrated.

Rotation—Turned as on an axis out of normal position. No figure was placed in this category unless it was rotated at least 45 degrees. It is possible that, if the children were permitted to rotate the paper, the resulting figure would be in the proper position. It would be of interest to determine whether any considerable group of the children who rotate their figures also have difficulty with angles.

Compression—Reduced in size. All distortion of size is easily measured. Liberal scoring rules were adopted. Figures less than the size of the pattern by 50 percent or more are entered in this category.

Enlargement—The entire figure or some major dimension increased in size. A figure is placed in this category if the increase in size is 50 percent of the pattern or more.

Disproportion—Out of balance. The proper relationship between parts of a figure is not maintained. A variation of 50 percent or more in a major dimension is the basis of this score.

Evaluation of Drawings

Since the subjects in this part of the study are intellectually superior to cerebral palsied children as a whole, it cannot be assumed that the results show how serious the problem is. In order to make a comparison of those above and below 80 IQ, it would be necessary to include more than one medical classification. Important factors could easily be overlooked in the process.

The Chi square was employed for the statistical analysis of these data.* Since the data, as collated, were broadly dichotomized into (1) number of children who made particular types of errors and (2) number of errors made by these children, this plan was followed in the statistical analysis. Before the findings are discussed, a limitation in the extensiveness of the analysis should be first mentioned.

The minimum expected (theoretical) frequency accepted for permitting the application of the Chi square test here was five, since it was felt that to use a smaller number would violate one of the basic conditions, i.e., the normal distribution of the observed frequencies about a given expected frequency. An examination of the data discloses that certain errors were made relatively infrequently and the number of children making such errors was also relatively small. Since these, at times, were less than five, it was found

*Appreciation is extended to Dr. Howard Norris, then Research Assistant, Education of Exceptional Children, Syracuse University, for his help in completing the statistical analysis discussed here.

necessary to omit the use of any statistical analysis, i.e., Chi square, in eight cases out of a possible seventeen when comparing errors (Perseveration, Erratic Approach, Displacement of Parts, Failure to Overlap, Incompleteness, Closure, Incorrect Elements, and Unrecognizable). In addition and for the same reason, four cases were not used when comparing errors between the spastic classifications (Preservation, Erratic Approach, Failure to Overlap, and Closure). Three were not used when comparing errors between IQ groups (Erratic Approach, Failure to Overlap, and Closure). To increase the extensiveness of the analysis, it would be necessary to increase the size of the sample.

Number of children who made errors—The first analysis was concerned with a comparison of types of errors made by the children in the four major medical classifications: athetoid, ataxic, rigidity, and spastic. The null hypothesis tested here may be stated as follows: There is no relationship between the major cerebral palsy medical classifications and the number of children making each type of error. An examination of the results reveals that this hypothesis can be rejected at somewhat better than the 1 percent level in one case out of a possible eight, i.e., Immature. Thus, there seems to be a relationship between medical classification and number of children making Immature errors in the Bender-Gestalt test. Further inspection indicates that the highest proportion of children making Immature errors may be expected from the ataxic group, while the lowest proportion may be found among spastics. The remaining error types analyzed are not significant at .05. There is, therefore, no evidence of a relationship between the number of children making Concrete, Separation, Inverted, Miscellaneous, Compression Enlargement, Disproportionate, and Rotation errors and the medical classifications.

The second analysis was concerned with a comparison between the various spastic classifications, i.e., quadriplegia, right hemiplegia, left hemiplegia, and parplegia, and the number of children making each type of error. In this analysis, it was found that in no case could the null hypothesis be rejected at .05. Here again there is no evidence of a relationship between number of children making errors and the four spastic classifications.

The next analysis was concerned with a comparison of the several IQ groupings and the number of children making each type of error, regardless of medical classification. It was found that the null hypothesis of no relationship could be rejected in the Incomplete error type at somewhat better than the .01 level and the Unrecognizable type at .05. Although not significant at .05. Although not significant at .05, several other measures approached significance. These were Displaced, Separation, Incorrect Elements, and Rotation which had p values of .06, .07, .08, and .09, respectively.

TABLE 5.1
CLASSIFICATION OF ERRORS MADE BY CHILDREN WITH CEREBRAL PALSY
ON THE BENDER-GESTALT TEST

Medical Classification	I.Q. Range	No. of Cases	Errors of Procedure								Errors of Configuration			
			Immaturity		Concreteness		Perseveration		Erratic performance		Separation		Displaced part	
SPASTIC			a	b	a	b	a	b	a	b	a	b	a	b
Quad.	90-	22	7	3	13	6	1	1	1	1	11	5	2	2
	80-89	9	6	4	6	5	2	1	2	2	13	8	2	2
	70-79	9	5	4	7	3	0	0	1	1	6	4	6	5
	50-69	5	5	3	2	1	2	1	0	0	4	2	2	2
Subtotal		45	23	14	28	15	5	3	4	4	34	19	12	11
Right Hemi.	90-	8	5	2	3	2	0	0	0	0	9	4	1	1
	80-89	4	3	2	0	0	0	0	0	0	6	3	1	1
	70-79	13	5	2	10	5	4	3	1	1	6	4	5	4
	50-69	6	3	2	0	0	2	1	1	1	15	6	1	1
Subtotal		31	16	8	13	7	6	4	2	2	36	17	8	7
Left Hemi.	90-	9	3	1	1	1	0	0	0	0	8	5	2	1
	80-89	1	0	0	0	0	0	0	1	1	1	1	0	0
	70-79	4	0	0	0	0	2	2	0	0	9	3	0	0
	50-69	9	6	2	1	1	2	1	2	1	13	8	2	2
Subtotal		23	9	3	2	2	4	3	3	2	31	17	4	3
Para.	90-	14	8	3	4	2	2	2	1	1	12	8	1	1
	80-89	7	0	0	3	2	4	3	1	1	15	6	0	0
	70-79	7	3	1	3	1	3	2	2	1	7	4	2	2
	50-69	5	0	0	7	3	2	2	0	0	5	4	0	0
Subtotal		33	11	4	17	8	11	9	4	3	39	22	3	3
TOTAL SPASTICS		132	59	29	60	32	26	19	13	11	140	75	27	24

NOTE: Columns a indicate the number of errors of each type that were made.
Columns b indicate the number of children who made those errors.

With permission, H. V. Bice, *Visual-Motor Performance of Children with Cerebral Palsy* (Trenton: New Jersey State Department of Health, 1960).

Thus, it is seen that there is some evidence of one score (Immature) being related to major medical classification and two (Incomplete and Unrecognizable) being related to IQ. Further discussion of these results is necessary. In all, thirty-five Chi squares were computed. One would then

TABLE 5.1 (*Continued*)

																Errors of Position			
Failure to overlap		Incomplete		Closure		Incorrect elements		Distorted angles		Compressed		Enlarged		Disproportion		Unrecognizable		Rotated	
a	b	a	b	a	b	a	b	a	b	a	b	a	b	a	b	a	b	a	b
1	1	1	1	1	1	6	5	16	13	22	10	4	3	7	5	4	4	5	4
0	0	3	3	1	1	5	5	14	9	8	4	2	2	13	7	12	2	8	4
0	0	3	3	0	0	10	5	15	9	6	5	3	2	9	5	1	1	13	6
0	0	2	2	0	0	0	0	2	2	3	2	3	1	1	1	15	4	4	2
1	1	9	9	2	2	21	15	47	33	39	21	12	8	30	18	32	11	30	16
1	1	2	1	0	0	0	0	10	7	11	4	6	4	5	5	4	3	9	5
1	1	2	2	0	0	0	0	8	4	7	2	1	1	1	1	0	0	9	2
3	3	3	3	1	1	4	3	12	10	10	6	6	4	5	4	2	2	26	9
1	1	2	2	0	0	0	0	8	5	2	1	3	3	3	3	2	2	7	5
6	6	9	8	1	1	4	3	38	26	30	13	16	12	14	13	8	7	51	21
2	2	1	1	0	0	2	1	7	5	5	3	7	4	6	4	3	2	9	4
1	1	0	0	0	0	0	0	0	0	4	1	0	0	1	1	0	0	5	1
0	0	1	1	1	1	1	1	3	2	8	2	4	3	2	2	0	0	4	3
0	0	1	1	0	0	1	1	6	5	9	4	1	1	4	4	9	5	10	7
3	3	3	3	1	1	4	3	16	12	26	10	12	8	13	11	12	7	28	15
1	1	0	0	1	1	7	5	5	5	9	4	2	1	5	4	1	1	7	3
1	1	1	1	2	2	3	1	17	12	9	4	4	2	10	6	0	0	8	6
0	0	2	2	0	0	3	2	11	6	9	6	1	1	2	2	4	1	14	6
0	0	1	1	0	0	1	1	6	4	11	3	4	2	4	2	1	1	1	1
2	2	4	4	3	3	14	9	39	27	38	17	11	6	21	14	6	3	30	16
12	12	25	24	7	7	43	30	140	98	133	61	51	34	78	56	58	28	139	68

NOTE: Columns *a* indicate the number of errors of each type that were made.
Columns *b* indicate the number of children who made those errors.

*

expect two to be significant at the .05 level or below, and three are found. Since the difference is so small, it is expected that these three may have occurred by chance. For all practical purposes, none would be expected to be significant at the .01, and two are obtained. The probability of this occurring by chance is approximately .044 and, therefore, one would suspect that something other than chance may be operating.

TABLE 5.1 (*Continued*)

Medical Classification	I.Q. Range	No. of Cases	Errors of Procedure								Errors of Configuration			
			Immaturity		Concreteness		Perseveration		Erratic performance		Separation		Displaced part	
			a	b	a	b	a	b	a	b	a	b	a	b
ATHETOID	90-	19	8	5	8	4	1	1	2	1	14	10	4	4
	80-89	7	4	3	2	2	0	0	1	1	5	3	0	0
	70-79	11	10	5	7	2	0	0	0	0	12	7	1	1
	50-69	7	3	1	2	2	1	1	0	0	11	5	1	1
Subtotal		44	25	14	19	10	2	2	3	2	42	25	6	6
ATAXIC	90-	7	8	6	3	3	1	1	0	0	6	4	0	0
	80-89	3	3	2	0	0	1	1	0	0	5	3	0	0
	70-79	3	8	2	4	1	0	0	0	0	3	1	1	1
	50-69	8	8	4	5	1	1	1	0	0	13	6	1	1
Subtotal		21	27	14	12	5	3	3	0	0	27	14	2	2
RIGIDITY	90-	9	3	3	2	2	1	1	0	0	7	4	0	0
	80-89	4	3	2	2	1	0	0	0	0	7	4	1	1
	70-79	1	0	0	0	0	0	0	0	0	2	1	1	1
	50-69	5	4	3	8	4	1	1	1	1	13	5	1	1
Subtotal		19	10	8	12	7	2	2	1	1	29	14	3	3
GRAND TOTAL		216	121	65	103	54	33	26	17	14	238	128	38	35

NOTE: Columns *a* indicate the number of errors of each type that were made. Columns *b* indicate the number of children who made those errors.

The probability of finding one out of nine error types within the major medical classification group significant at the .01 level is within the realm of chance as is the probability of finding two out of fourteen significant at .05 within IQ groups. It is noted, however, that six out of fourteen were significant at .10 in the IQ breakdown. The probability of this occurring by chance is approximately .001.

In summation, then, there is no evidence for believing that a relationship exists between spastic breakdown and any measure. There is some evidence for believing a relationship exists between major categories and one measure (Immature error). There is good evidence for believing that there is a relationship between IQ and several of the measures; the data, however,

TABLE 5.1 (*Continued*)

															Errors of Position				
Failure to overlap		Incomplete		Closure		Incorrect elements		Distorted angles		Compressed		Enlarged		Disproportion		Unrecognizable		Rotated	
a	b	a	b	a	b	a	b	a	b	a	b	a	b	a	b	a	b	a	b
1	1	2	2	0	0	2	2	21	16	15	9	16	10	19	12	2	2	17	9
0	0	2	1	0	0	1	1	6	5	18	4	4	2	3	3	1	1	1	1
4	4	5	4	0	0	3	3	21	13	8	4	5	3	10	6	9	4	9	5
0	0	2	2	0	0	0	0	9	6	1	1	4	3	1	1	5	2	6	2
5	5	11	9	0	0	6	6	57	40	42	18	29	18	33	22	17	9	33	17
0	0	0	0	1	1	1	1	8	5	6	3	4	3	1	1	1	1	5	3
1	1	0	0	0	0	0	0	3	2	3	1	4	2	1	1	2	2	3	1
1	1	0	0	2	2	0	0	2	2	0	0	6	3	5	2	3	1	2	1
2	2	4	4	2	2	0	0	8	5	7	4	4	3	3	3	8	2	13	5
4	4	4	4	5	5	1	1	21	14	16	8	18	11	10	7	14	6	23	10
2	2	0	0	0	0	1	1	7	4	16	6	6	4	9	5	1	1	2	2
0	0	1	1	0	0	3	1	4	3	6	2	2	2	3	2	0	0	2	2
0	0	0	0	0	0	0	0	2	2	2	1	0	0	0	0	1	1	2	1
0	0	0	0	0	0	2	1	7	5	6	4	2	2	1	1	6	1	3	2
2	2	1	1	0	0	6	3	20	14	30	13	10	8	13	8	8	3	9	7
23	23	41	38	12	12	56	40	238	166	221	100	108	71	134	93	97	46	204	102

NOTE: Columns *a* indicate the number of errors of each type that were made.
Columns *b* indicate the number of children who made those errors.

do not enable one to determine specifically which of these measures. One would have most confidence in predicting those related to IQ at the .01 and the .05 levels or the Incomplete and the Unrecognizable error types, respectively.

Number of Errors Made—The following information deals with the number of errors made by these children. The statistical procedure employed here, as in the former case, was Chi square, and the same minimum expected (theoretical) frequency of five was permitted for its application. However, since five is considered a bare minimum, it was felt that greater confidence could be placed in findings which had higher frequencies. As was mentioned above, the data under consideration here are concerned with number of errors, which can be regarded as scores. Since it is permissible to combine scores, such was done herein wherever possible; frequencies were thus increased. In the previous analysis such summing was not possible because children rather than scores were then being considered.

The following are the error types which were combined: Immature, Concrete, Perseveration, and Erratic were combined under *Inadequate Method;* Separation, Displacement of Parts, Failure to Overlap, and Incompleteness were combined under *Distortion of Configuration,* i.e. Form Dissociation; Inverted and Miscellaneous were combined under *Distorted Angles;* Compression, Enlargement, and Disproportionate were combined under *Size.* All other error categories have remained the same except for Rotation, which is now entitled Position.

The results of combining now permit a maximum of seven analyses. In no case, however, as previously, was it necessary to omit any analysis because of failure to meet the assumption of minimum theoretical frequency. While an expected frequency of only 4.93 was obtained for the rigidity group making the Incorrect Elements type of errors when comparing major cerebral palsy classifications, it was noted that this deviated merely .07 from the criterion of 5. Nevertheless, a further analysis was carried out for this type of error which excluded the rigidity group, and it was found that the obtained difference of Chi squares was negligible.

The first analysis is concerned with a comparison of the major medical classifications in terms of number of errors made within each error type. The null hypothesis may be stated in a somewhat different manner: There is no relationship between the major medical classifications and the number of errors made within each type of error. An examination of the results reveals that this hypothesis can be rejected at at least the 4 percent level of confidence three times out of a possible seven. These three are the errors labeled Inadequate Method, Incorrect Elements, and Position. The former has a p value of approximately .02; the remaining two have p values of approximately .04. Considering Inadequate Method, it was observed that proportionately fewer errors, in terms of quantity of observed as compared with expected errors, were made by the ataxics, while the athetoids and spastics made somewhat fewer. Those in the rigidity classification made about the proportionate number of errors which were expected, close to the theoretical frequency. The ataxics also made proportionately the greatest number of Position errors, but, in this case, there was about an equal percentage of spastics who did the same. These were followed, on a gradually declining scale, by athetoids and rigidities. When considering Incorrect Elements, the largest number of errors related to the spastic category. This group was followed, thereafter, by athetoid and ataxic.

The next analysis was concerned with testing the hypothesis of no relationship between the various spastic classifications—i.e. quadriplegia, right hemiplegia, left hemiplegia, and paraplegia—and the number of specific types of errors. Again it was found possible to reject the null hypothesis in three cases out of a possible seven. Incorrect Elements had a p value of approximately 0.3, and Position and Unrecognizable errors had probability levels of approximately. 0.2 and .003, respectively. Quadriplegics and paraplegics committed proportionately the largest number of Incorrect Elements errors, with right and left hemiplegics committing somewhat less. Quadriplegics also made proportionately the greatest share of Unrecognizable errors, followed by a slightly lesser share by the left hemiplegics. The smallest number accounted for was by the right hemiplegics and the paraplegics. Examining the Position errors, the right hemiplegics made proportionately the greatest number of these, followed by gradually and progressively lesser percentages by the left hemiplegics, paraplegics, and quadriplegics.

The final analysis was devised in an attempt to test the hypothesis of no relationship between the IQ groups and number of errors of each particular type. Rejection was possible in six cases, all of which had p values of at least approximately .008. The single exception was that of Size. Both Inadequate and Incorrect Elements types of errors received confidence levels of approximately .008; Angles, a confidence level of approximately .006. The other three—Dissociation, Unrecognizable, and Position—had probabilities of less than .001. As might be expected, the proportionately smallest number of observed as compared to expected type were made by those falling at IQ 90 and over. The one exception to this occurred within the Incorrect Elements type of error, in which case it was next to the smallest, the smallest being IQ 50 to 69. Beyond this, the results were scattered. The highest proportionate number of errors of the Inadequate type was split between IQs of 70 to 79 and 50 to 69. IQ 80 to 89 remained at about the expected level. The Dissociation type error was made approximately an equal number of times between IQ 80 to 89, 70 to 79, and 50 to 69. Within Incorrect Elements and Position, the proportionately greatest share of errors fell in the IQ range of 70 to 79. There was a gradual decline, then, in the former group to the 80 to 89 range and thence to that of 50 to 69. In the latter group, a somewhat smaller proportion could be seen to have occurred almost equally between IQs of 80 to 89 and 50 to 69. The largest percentage of errors scored on the basis of faulty Angles, still referring to observed compared to theoretical frequencies within each category, fell almost evenly between IQs 80 to 89 and 70 to 79. A slightly smaller percentage occurred in the 50 to 59 range. On the other hand, the 50 to 69 range had proportionately the greatest share of errors of the Unrecognizable type. Both IQ groups of 80 to 89 and 70 to 79 within this error category produced approximately the expected number of errors.

At this point in the discussion, it should be emphasized that statements referring to proportionately greater or lesser numbers of errors have been made primarily to inform the reader of the internal makeup of the various Chi squares. Whereas the errors of other similar groups of cerebral palsied children might fall in the same manner, little confidence can be placed in the prediction of such an occurrence.

An important aspect of the previous report was the possibility of obtaining significant Chi squares through the operation of chance alone. Such a consideration need not concern us here, however, because of the relatively high ratios of significant results observed, i.e., twelve out of a total of twenty-one. Within each of the three analysis categories, the proportions were also comparatively high, namely three of seven in the second and six of seven in the third.

Summary—In conclusion, there is fairly good evidence for believing a relationship exists between major medical classifications and those types of errors labeled Inadequate Method, Incorrect Elements, and Position when number of errors are used as the score. There is good evidence for believing a relationship is present between the various spastic groups and Incorrect Elements, Position, and Unrecognizable errors. Finally, there is strong evidence for believing a relationship exists between the several IQ groups and Inadequate, Incorrect Elements, Angles, Dissociation, Unrecognizable, and Position errors. Thus, within each breakdown the number of certain types of errors seems to be related to diagnostic categories and intellectual levels. This is especially evident in the latter case where almost every type of error is significantly related to variations in intelligence. Of interest is the fact that in almost all instances, the highest IQ group tested, those with 90 and above, committed proportionately the smallest number of errors.

It is generally felt that the results obtained on the number of errors, as presented here, have less meaning than those found on number of children, even though much greater significance was found in the former case. Such a thesis is based upon the assumption that it is probably more important, or at least more meaningful, to determine if a relationship exists between number of children and medical classification or intelligence level than similar categories and number of errors, since dealing with errors *per se* rather than which child made them does not offer much of predictive value.

Comparison with Other Populations

Limited reference is made to similarities between drawings by children with cerebral palsy and some of the subjects reported by Bender. A much more extensive study would be rewarding. The cases under consideration are not generally comparable. Bender's subjects were older, had suffered some type of organic brain disease, or were hospitalized following some traumatic experience. The precise terms used for both groups would not always be the same, even though the appearance of the drawings was similar. Regression to more simple or more primitive forms was found with the older subjects. The counterpart of *regression* would be the *immaturity* shown by the cerebral palsied children. In addition, both groups showed the tendency to perseveration, concreteness, rotation, compression, use of substitute forms, incompleteness, or other forms of dissociation.

Bender pointed out that the degree of disturbance in production of the forms was not closely correlated with the extent of brain damage when this was known. This is common to cerebral palsy also. The most severe cerebral palsy case may produce the figures well, while some of the milder cases will scarcely be able to make one adequate drawing.

The similarity between the productions of the cerebral palsied and those of normal and superior subjects who are reacting to tachistoscopic presentation is also of interest. Various distortions of form, size, and position are found in both cases.

The manner in which many of the cerebral palsied children react to the task of making the drawings should give some clues of value to education. Much further investigation is needed before the full significance is known. Some children will cooperate to the limit of their abilities in any verbal type of test, but will refuse to attempt the drawings. Others assert that they are willing, but cannot do the task: "I'm no good at this." You picked the wrong one to make drawings." They are critical of their work when it is done: "I've drawn the circles [*Figure 2*], but it does not look like the card." "I think I have no concept of space as others seem to have." A somewhat dull child whose mental age was eleven years, six months, finished *Figure 1* looked at *Figure 2*, and said: "More dots." The drawing seemed to mean no more than that, and he made dots at random over the paper. The examiner asked him to look at the card carefully and try again. He then made a single line of loops. Another child looking at the card before him commented: "It just don't make sense." Some who want the task to "make sense" produce the concrete drawings. This can be done with any of the nine figures. The following are a selection of children's comments regarding such drawings: *Figure 2*: "It's just a lot of little holes, but I can't make them." *Figure 3*: "A Christmas tree." The child proceeded not only to make the tree, but to put ornaments on it. *Figure 4*: "It's U.S." *Figure 5*: "A house with a chimney." *Figure 6*: "Two worms." *Figure 7*: "Two boats." *Figure 8*: "A rocket; and how is a man going to ride in a rocket without a seat?" The child placed a "seat" in it instead of the diamond.

Parents who have observed the test have likewise made pertinent observations: "If you knew the trouble we had trying to teach him to put a stamp in the right place on a letter, you wouldn't ask him to make anything." The father of a boy doing good work in the eighth grade said to the examiner: "Sometimes I think he is dumb even if he does get good school grades. I sent him twice to post a letter and he brought it back. He would not try to mail it because he could 'see that it would not fit the opening in the box.' " Such comments appear to be extreme, but even if they were rare, they suggest that the disability revealed by the test goes far beyond the abstract task set before the child.

Some children including older ones become very emotional when trying to make the drawings. An eighteen-year-old boy with normal verbal ability was disturbed because when he first tried *Figure 3* he rotated his work 90 degrees, working from the top toward the bottom of the paper. He wanted to try again and was encouraged to do so; once more he rotated the drawing. He completed it, but he was so disturbed that he could no longer make a simple dot. He regressed to primitive loops so poorly formed that one might think they were done by an athetoid, though he was a spastic. Others have become so disturbed that the last few drawings were unrecognizable.

A rare comment, but a pertinent one, was made by a mentally superior child who was failing the task badly. He laid his pencil aside and asked the examiner: "Why can't I make my hand do what my eyes see?"

Examples and comments such as these suggest more caution when interpreting the results. Much has been said about disabilities in space perception. The child who becomes emotional over what he interprets as failure and the one who asks such pertinent questions as that just cited imply that the problem may be less one of perception and more of association and execution.

It should be noted that, in general, a type of error that is made by children in one medical classification is made by those in others. The only exception is the rare tendency to close a figure that should have one open side. Only twelve children made this error; all were in the spastic or ataxic group. The sixty-three athetoid and rigidity cases cannot be assumed to be representative of all with those diagnoses.

Other Studies Using the Bender-Gestalt Test

Patel and Bharucha (1972) have also used the Bender-Gestalt to look at the visual-motor copying ability of cerebral palsied and normal children at different age levels. Both cerebral palsied and normal subjects had fewer errors at the older compared to the younger age levels. At each age (five, six, seven, eight, nine, and ten years) the cerebral palsied had more errors; the difference was significant at ages five, nine, and ten years.

Simpson (1967) studied the visuo-motor behavior of athetoid and spastic children between the ages of $7\frac{1}{2}$ and $10\frac{1}{2}$ years. He found that the spastic subjects tended to perform better than athetoid subjects on the

Bender-Gestalt. He also found no relationship between perceptual-motor performance and IQ as assessed by the Peabody Picture Vocabulary Test.

PERCEPTUAL-MOTOR BEHAVIOR

Reference has been made above to the similarities of performance between the cerebral palsied group and other groups of individuals with central nervous system involvement. A considerable amount of data is accruing that demonstrate common characteristics of perceptual-motor behavior between many different clinical groups, including cerebral palsied individuals. Cerebral palsied children frequently show impairments in tasks which require spatial judgment. Basic to such an impairment is the development of visuo-motor capacities, the ability to attend, or, the opposite, the ability to refrain from reacting to stimuli which are not pertinent to the task at hand. There are certain similar basic psychopathological characteristics. In large measure the same characteristics are typical of the idiopathic epileptic children when they were matched and compared with endogenous mentally retarded or normal children.

A general psychological syndrome involving several specific aspects of perceptual-motor behavior is typical of children with cerebral palsy (and is likely also to be typical of children in all classifications involving central nervous system disorders). Such being the case, two types of diagnosis are required with every brain injured child: (1) medical diagnosis to ascertain the type and extent of brain injury and the medical treatment which may be required, and (2) psychological diagnosis for the purpose of determining intellectual level of function and the presence and extent of the psychopathological component. Such is not characteristic of all brain injured children, as has been stated elsewhere in this chapter. It does not appear to be related to the degree of motor involvement or the extent of brain damage: It is a problem which can most adequately be assessed through the careful administration and interpretation of both quantitative and qualitative psychological tests which are geared to provide clinical insight into the characteristics of cerebral palsied children, as discussed in the following section.

The Figure-Background Relationship

In normal individuals the figure-background relationship involves a general characteristic of perception wherein the isolation of the total field endows different parts of the field with different degrees of shape and articulation. The *figure* consists of those parts which are emphasized through color, form, or scope; the *ground* is the less shaped, generally more indistinct, parts of the field. Typically in perception, the figure is derived as a group of impressions from a single sense, and these are perceived as a *gestalt* or an independent unit. The ground, being unattended or possibly the result of negative adaptation, plays a less important psychological role in the formation of the total percept.

A pathology in this normal figure-background relationship has been demonstrated many times in individuals of different clinical classifications with central nervous system disorders. Such a pathological situation involves not only a reversal of field phenomena, but may also result in confusion and vagueness in the isolation of ground from figure or in the apparent equal value of both ground and figure to the perceiver. Klapper and Werner (1950) have reported on the pathology of the figure-background relationship in the three sets of twins mentioned earlier in this chapter. In this connection the authors tachistoscopically presented a series of cards to the children, who were asked to report what they saw. Clinical differences were marked. Perceptual accuracy appeared to have no relation to the severity of the brain damage, but only to the fact that a brain damage existed. In Twin Pair A the normal twin responded correctly, i.e., with figure in nine out of the nine cards presented. The cerebral palsied twin gave figure responses to three cards, background responses only to four cards, and two vague responses. With Twin Pair B, the normal child gave six figure responses and three background responses. The cerebral palsied child gave one figure response, one background response, and seven diffuse and perseverative responses. The final pair of twins, Pair C, illustrates similar differences. The normal twin responded with figure to ten out of the eleven cards presented; one response was background only. The cerebral palsied child gave three figure responses, seven background with "something in the middle," and one background only. Differences which are demonstrated in these three sets of twins have rather consistently been found by other researchers with somewhat larger groups.

Dolphin and Cruickshank (1951) obtained statistically significant differences between the responses of two groups of children, the first consisting of thirty cerebral palsied children, the second, thirty physically normal children who had been carefully matched with the former group individually by pairs. Nine cards were used in this study, each of which was presented in a given order to the child by the use of a tachistoscope. Exposures were for one-fifth of a second, twice in succession. The preponderance of responses from the cerebral palsied group are those involving background. Background alone and background with incorrect figure account for 191 or 70.7 percent of the 270 total responses. On the other hand, the normal children produce 130 (48 percent) figure responses; the cerebral palsied children 24 (.08 percent) such responses.

The same groups of children were given another task of a somewhat

TABLE 5.2
COMPARISON OF FREQUENCY SCORES OF CEREBRAL PALSY AND
NORMAL GROUPS FOR THE PICTURE TEST

Picture Test Type of Response	Cerebral Palsy Group Frequency Scores	Normal Group Frequency Scores	Chi Squares	Level of Significance
Correct figure	16	74	44.86	.001
Incorrect figure	8	56	40.84	.001
Background with correct figure	55	53	.0378	.90
Background with incorrect figure	97	60	12.36	.001
Background only	94	27	47.8126	.001

similar nature. A stimulus card with an abstract design was presented to the children. Three other cards were likewise presented from which the child was to select the one which was most similar to the original card. One of the cards contained the background pattern only of the original card, a second, the original background with a different figure, and the third, a different background with the original figure. Of the thirty responses possible in each group the following distribution was obtained: cerebral palsy group, ten background, eighteen original background with different figure, and two different background with original figure. Normal children gave five background, fifteen original background with different figure, and ten different background with original figure. The inability of the cerebral palsied children to select the original figure regardless of the background is apparent in the better than 1 percent level of significance between the two groups (Chi square, 6.6640; level of significance, .01).

Cruickshank, Bice, and Wallen (1957) undertook a major study of the figure-background relationship in cerebral palsied children. A sample consisting of 325 cerebral palsy children and 110 nonhandicapped children between the ages of six and sixteen years was obtained. The cerebral palsied children consisted of 211 who were diagnosed as spastic, 114 as athetoid. All had intelligence quotients above 75 and a minimum mental age of six years. The cerebral palsy subjects all had one usable upper extremity and intelligible speech. The authors recognized that, in establishing a minimum mental age and intelligence quotient, an atypical population of cerebral palsy children would be obtained. However, the nature of the testing that was planned required that the child possess sufficient intelligence to be able to participate fully and with understanding. Figure 5.5 illustrates the

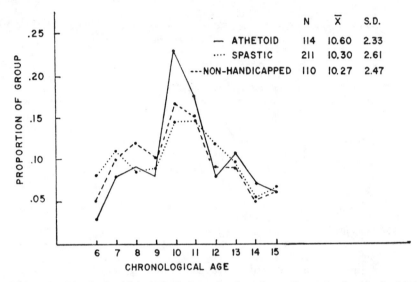

Figure 5.5.   Distribution of chronological ages for three diagnostic groups of cerebral palsied and normal children.

chronological age distribution for the three groups of children; Table 5.4 shows the cumulative proportions at each age level for each group.

Among the several tests that were administered to the three groups of children was the Syracuse Visual Figure-Background Test (SVFB), which consisted of sixteen slides produced with an airbrush which resulted in a three-dimensional effect. These slides, some easy, some difficult; some with meaningful backgrounds, some with nonsensical backgrounds, were administered at different speeds from .50 second to .04 second by the use of

TABLE 5.3
CUMULATIVE PROPORTIONS AT EACH AGE LEVEL FOR EACH DIAGNOSTIC GROUP

Age	Athetoid	Spastic	Nonhandicapped
15	1.000	1.000	1.000
14	.930	.930	.915
13	.870	.875	.865
12	.765	.780	.775
11	.685	.660	.685
10	.510	.515	.535
9	.280	.370	.370
8	.200	.275	.270
7	.110	.190	.150
6	.030	.080	.050

With permission, Cruickshank et al., Perception and Cerebral Palsy, 2nd ed., p. 59.

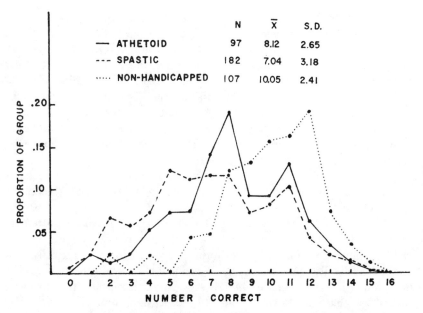

Figure 5.6. Distribution of SVFB test number correct score for each of the diagnostic groups.

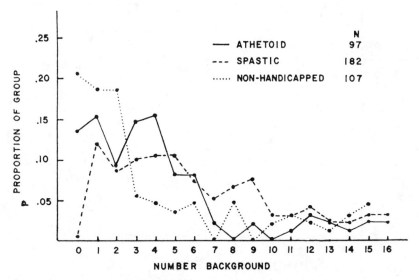

Figure 5.7. Distribution of SVFB test number background scores for each of the diagnostic groups. Ordinate values denote proportion of group.

a tachistoscope mounted on a standard projector. Figure 5.6 indicates the number of "correct" responses which were produced by the subjects in each of the three groups; Figure 5.7 shows the number of "background" responses. No sex differences were observed in this or in any other of the tests employed in this study. Low, but significant, relationships were obtained between chronological age and the "number correct" score. The spastic group of children made a significantly greater mean number of responses which included reference to background than did either the athetoid or the nonhandicapped groups, and as noted in Figure 5.8, the spastic children did not demonstrate any appreciable modification in their performance with increased chronological age. Maturity appears to be of greater benefit to the athetoid and to the normal children in this instance than to the spastic children.

Cruickshank, Bice, Wallen, and Lynch (1965) extended the aforementioned study with a different group of 401 spastic type cerebral palsied children each of whom met the criteria described earlier. A specially constructed tachistoscopic test was developed and individually administered to this group. This test consists of 128 slides arranged in quartets involving several variables: black-white, color, two dimension, three dimensions, size of figure, and size of background. The slides were administered at exposures of from .5 second to 5 seconds; the latter was considered infinity. The study resulted in four major generalizations:

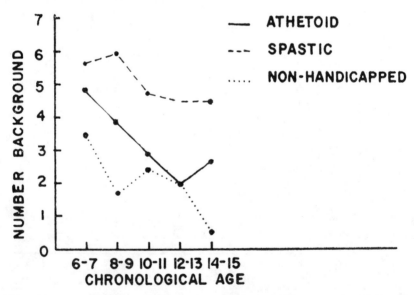

Figure 5.8.   Age trends for each diagnostic group on the SVFB test number background score.

First . . . , as time increases the ability of the cerebral palsy child to perceive figure also increases. It should be pointed out that as time increases the child also tends to perceive more detail. This may well be a negative factor if what the child is seeing includes details unessential to the learning situation. Second, the child perceives more figure when the materials being presented are in color. This finding tends to support previous statements to the effect that with children who demonstrate a visual perceptual problem, the stimulus value of the thing to which the child's attention is desired should be increased while at the same time the stimuli in the environment should be decreased insofar as possible. . . .

Third, there was a slight advantage to the child in the perception of figure when the material was presented to him in a three-dimensional manner as opposed to two-dimensional materials. . . .

Fourth, the structure of the visual material is also important. More figure was perceived by the spastic cerebral children when the presentation included large figure on large background than with any of the other three combinations [of figure and background]. . . .

Throughout the study the great amount of variation in perception among the subjects at all chronological age levels was very apparent. Marked individual differences exist corroborating other studies wherein this same observation was apparent. It is also apparent that a genuine visual perception pathology exists in many spastic cerebral palsy children. The relation of this dysfunction to learning is recognized.

Distractibility

It has been indicated above that basic to the phenomenon of figure-background disturbance is the factor of hyperdistractibility which has been commented upon by numerous authors as being a significant perceptual-motor corollary to brain damage. The children are highly distracted by any stimuli in the environment—i.e., noises, moving objects, or colors. The attention span is limited in duration. As a result of reaction to multiple stimuli, physical hyperactivity, motor disinhibition, as well as psychological distractibility is often observed. These children are frequently restless; at times they engage in seemingly purposeless random activity, and are erratic and unpredictable in their behavior. Such behavior apparently stems from the inability of the child to refrain from reacting to isolated stimuli or groups of stimuli whether or not such stimuli or such reactions are related to the specific task at hand. The effect of such behavior, psychologically, is to be seen in the performance of many cerebral palsied children on tasks which involve visuomotor abilities.

In comparing two groups of children on two marble board tests, one a group of thirty cerebral palsied children, Dolphin and Cruickshank (1951) observed distinct differences in the performance. While certain similarities of method and approach were found for both groups, the cerebral palsied children tended to be more incoherent in their productions and to be less capable of perceiving the pattern which they were to reproduce in a *gestalt*. Cruickshank, Bice, Wallen, and Lynch also used the marble board test in their battery with the large groups of spastic and athetoid cerebral palsy subjects. Of the four marble board designs employed, 25 percent of the spastic children, 9 percent of the athetoid, and 9 percent of the nonhandicapped children were unable to complete the designs. The high percentage of the spastic children who were unable to perform satisfactorily is related to the higher percentage of this same group of children who responded to background rather than to figure as discussed in the preceding section. The high incidence of extraneous stimuli in the background of the marble boards distracts the spastic child from an adequate perception of the figure which is to be completed. The proportion of each group finishing who achieved perfect performances declined from the nonhandicapped to the athetoid to the spastic. These proportions were respectively: .45, .23, and .15.

It is hypothesized that the performance of the children and the end result of their attempts is due to two factors: (1) dissociation, which will be commented upon below, and (2) the presence in the testing situation and in the test item itself of a multiplicity of extraneous stimuli only slightly related to the specific task. The construction of the marble boards themselves needs to be examined. These boards, approximately 15 inches square, consisted of ten rows of ten holes each on which were arranged abstract geometrical designs made out of black marbles. The child was asked to make a design on his marble board, a design which appeared in front of him on a second marble board. On the two boards then there was a total of two hundred holes, each of which is considered a stimulus to which the child potentially could react. In addition, there were the marbles themselves, which were added stimuli involving motor activity. To a child unable to withstand the impact of extraneous stimuli, the test situation could evoke much random, purposeless reaction. Such random psychological activity would interfere with production and the final product. The incoherent behavior noted by the investigators in some of the cerebral palsied children may very well have resulted from this situation.

Several of the cerebral palsied children compressed their productions into an unrecognizable mass of marbles. Others utilized the edge of the marble board itself as a base of operation, apparently being unable to cope with the problem of space when working in the center of the marble board. In many instances the children on this visuo-motor task functioned similarly to the cerebral palsied children reported earlier in sections of this chapter on the Bender-Gestalt test. The intimate relationship between distractibility and forced responsiveness to irrelevant stimuli warrants much further psychological investigation.

It has been hypothesized that the factor of distractibility also accounts for differences noted in the behavior of several groups of children in tasks requiring tactual-motor performance. Shaw found significant differences between his groups of epileptic and nonepileptic children in the perception of tactual stimuli when these were embedded in distracting backgrounds and when background influence was kept at a minimum. Dolphin and Cruickshank also obtained statistically significant differences between their groups of cerebral palsied and normal children in tasks involving tactual motor perception. The cerebral palsied children were much more often disturbed by the background containing multiple stimuli (Chi square 29.72. p less than .001). The normal children, on the other hand, produced almost three times as many figure responses as did the cerebral palsied subjects (Chi square, 16.52; p less than .1). The relationship between this factor of distractibility and achievement level in school learning is immediately apparent. Whether or not the effect of distractibility on adjustment in a broader sense is direct or indirect needs further research. It is assumed, however, that an indirect or secondary relationship exists between the two.

Hallahan and Cruickshank (1973) have brought together the literature dealing with problems of attention, memory, cognition, and perceptual-motor characteristics in children with central nervous system disorders. These data essentially corroborate the preceding discussion, and the reader is referred to that work for a fuller development of this topic than can be included here.

Hallahan and his colleagues have found some evidence to suggest that not all cerebral palsied subjects have selective attention deficits or that attentional problems are only evident on certain kinds of tasks. Hallahan, Stainback, Ball, and Kauffman (1973) used a central-incidental task originally used by Hagen (1967). Hagen and Huntsman (1971) have found evidence that institutionalized mentally retarded children, but not community-reared retardates, have attentional deficits in comparison to normal peers equated on mental age. In addition, Hallahan, Kauffman, and Ball (1973) have found learning disabled children to be poor selective attenders. The results of Hallahan, Stainback, Ball, and Kauffman found educable retarded, spastic, cerebral palsied children not to differ from normals equated on mental age in selective attention performance. For both normals and cerebral palsied subjects there was an increase in selective attention ability with age. Hallahan *et al.* (1973) provide the following possible explanations for these results:

The evidence of no attention deficit associated with spastic cerebral palsy is also in opposition to the findings of Cruickshank and his colleagues tachistoscopic presentations of figure-background slides. Again, the two tasks differ considerably. The Hagen task demands sustained attention over time while Cruickshank's Syracuse Visual Figure-Background Test requires S to orient himself to a screen after a "ready" signal. Performance on the latter task is highly susceptible to momentary inattention or distractibility. Thus, it appears that spastic cerebral palsy affects attention differentially.

An alternative interpretation also presents itself. Since the Ss of Cruickshank and his colleagues were of normal intelligence, it could be that attention is impaired in cerebral palsied Ss of normal intelligence but not in retarded cerebral palsied Ss.

It should be added that Hallahan (1975) has more recently summarized his and his colleagues' research and tentatively speculated that selective attention problems may be more evident in nonlearners who are of higher intelligence than retardates.

Some investigators have held the viewpoint that if cerebral palsied children are distractible, then they might be able to benefit from reduced environmental stimulation. Logue (1965) found that the recitation time of athetoid cerebral palsied subjects was decreased with lower levels of illumination. Fassler compared cerebral palsied and normal children's performance on a number of tasks under normal and reduced auditory input. The latter condition required the children to wear earphones to muffle environmental sounds. The reduced auditory input condition did not affect normal subjects, but cerebral palsied children benefited significantly in terms of a number of memory and attention measures.

Dissociation

It is again doubtful that dissociation as a characteristic of the behavior of brain-injured persons is independent of other characteristics which have been discussed. It is probably more nearly correct to say that, from the factor of distractibility, which can be related to neurological and psychological dysfunction, dissociative tendencies result. In this situation the individual has difficulty in relating parts to the total configuration. The greater tendency is toward segmentation of the whole with the ultimate possibility that the whole or the *gestalt* is never perceived by the subject. Several illustrations of dissociation have been depicted in Figure 5.4. In these there is seen the difficulty the child has in relating two or more parts of a total figure. The problem is a commonplace observance by psychologists in the administration of such tests as the Kohs Block Designs in the Grace Arthur Performance Scale or in many other tests where it is used. Dissociation likewise is frequently observed in the Goldstein-Scheerer Block Design Test or in the Stick Test of the same series. Here the brain-injured child often has difficulty in correctly relating the colored blocks into the configuration which as a model is placed before him.

Dissociation, as revealed in a test, may indicate a relationship to a particular sense modality. One child can make any phoneme in the language but cannot synthesize sounds to make a word; another, a blind cerebral palsied child, can tactually discern the number of braille elements, but cannot discern the pattern: "They are just separate dots." Julie's problem was reading. She was excellent in her studies until, in her first high-school year, a hemispherectomy resulted in right spastic hemiplegia. Nearly four years later she had no difficulty in making an average score on the Binet; much of her work was accomplished at a superior level. The following conversation took place between Julie and the psychologist:

> Psychologist: "How is your reading?"
> Julie: "Oh, I don't read any more."
> Psychologist: "Why?"
> Julie: "When I look at a page, I know every word on it. I can tell you what they mean if you ask me. But I cannot put any two words together in reading so that they mean anything."
> She could define words very well. She added the following explanation: "If I keep trying to read, I shall have to admit that something pretty bad happened to me. I am not yet ready to admit that."

Julie's report is indicative of dissociation, but it also emphasizes the interrelationship between the several characteristics of psychopathology herein described. Dissociation, true, but it is also a fact that each word on the page for which she knows the individual meaning is *figure* as she attends to it. All the rest of the words on the page are *background* and, in terms of the specific figure (word), are *extraneous stimuli.* Dissociation may come about because of the distraction to extraneous stimuli to the point where a meaningful whole or, in this instance, a concept in reading cannot take place. Or conversely, because of dissociation, figure and ground reversal takes place.

Perseveration

Perseveration is a factor frequently observed in the behavior of brain-injured children in psychological tests. The behavior of the brain injured child is not necessarily the result of lack of attention (mentioned in connection with forced responsiveness), but the opposite behavior may actually be observed in many such children—namely, overattention or the perseverative characteristic about which we now speak. Clinically, the observation of perseverative tendencies is to be noted often in the performance of brain injured children on such tests as the Goldstein-Scheerer Color-Form Sorting Test, the Hanfmann-Kasanin, and in the responses of cerebral palsied and other types of brain injured children and adults to the Rorschach cards. The various thematic apperception tests or the Despart Fables may elicit perseveration on an ideational level in the themes which are produced. Several Bender drawings are included in Figure 5.4 wherein perseverative tendencies are suspected.

Other Aspects of Perceptual-Motor Behavior

Several other behavioral and personality characteristics have been mentioned by writers in this field. Dolphin and Cruickshank working with cerebral palsied children and Strauss and Werner evaluating exogenous mentally retarded children have commented on such characteristics of performance as *meticulosity* and *formalistic behavior*. In a grouping test similar in nature to those used by the aforementioned authors, Shaw observed that his epileptic children were significantly different (1 percent level of confidence) from the nonepileptic children in the reporting of *logical function* of objects, in making *illogical relationships* between objects, and in the frequency with which the epileptic children employed *imaginary situations*. This latter relates to the *dynamic-concrete grasp of relationship* reported by Dolphin, Cruickshank, Strauss, and Werner.

Motor disinhibition, which is probably closely related to hyperactivity and reaction to extraneous stimuli, is reported. The *catastrophic reaction* is oftentimes a clinical observation of psychologists and is frequently reported in the literature pertaining to brain injury.

Another important area of perceptual-motor functioning which has been the subject of some investigation is that of intersensory integration. Intersensory integration has been measured by assessing how well subjects are able to match stimulus information from two modalities. For example, subjects are presented with a pattern of auditory tones over earphones and are then asked to match the pattern with the correct visual representation made with dots. Assuming phylogenetic and ontogenetic development evidences an increase in intersensory integration, research has been conducted to indicate that brain damaged individuals are deficient in intersensory relative to intrasensory functioning. Deutsch and Schumer (1967) found brain injured children of normal or near-normal IQ to perform similarly to normals on unimodal tasks but to be deficient compared to normals on cross-modal performance. Cravioto and his colleagues (1966) have found poor intersensory integration in undernourished children. Birch and Belmont (1964) found poor readers to have problems in auditory-visual integration, which might be expected if one considers that the act of reading is composed of translating visual into auditory information.

Specifically with regard to the intersensory functioning of the cerebral palsied, Birch and Belmont (1965) found evidence for a deficit but Jones and Alexander (1974) did not. Definitive conclusions are, thus, unwarranted. It should be pointed out that previous work in the area of cross-modal integration has met with considerable methodological criticism (e.g., Sterritt and Rudnic 1966). For example, some of the first studies presented the auditory stimuli by having the experimenter tap with a pencil which the subject could see.

COGNITIVE ABILITIES OF THE CEREBRAL PALSIED

There is a relative paucity of research on the cognitive development of cerebral palsied children. This is particularly surprising when one considers that cerebral palsied individuals, being motorically and sometimes perceptually handicapped, would make the ideal subjects for a testing of some of the primary theoretical notions of psychologists such as Piaget and Werner. Many cognitive psychologists posit that later conceptual development is built upon early perceptual-motor development. One of the most direct tests of this hypothesis was conducted in a study by Melcer (1966). He found evidence that there is a relationship between perceptual-motor and conceptual development. He found that compared to normals, cerebral palsied children had a deficit in "action" concepts. Also, cerebral palsied children used non-motoric rather than motoric methods of dealing with means-ends situations.

Cronholm and Schalling (1968) found only partial support for a cognitive deficit in cerebral palsied teenagers and young adults. Cerebral palsied subjects did poorly on abstraction ability but not on sorting tests.

Birch and Bortner (1967) found cerebral palsied subjects to be more stimulus-bound than normals. The following is a summary of their study:

> The hypothesis that defective conceptual functioning in brain damaged children is due to the domination of behavior by immediately present stimulus properties and not by the child's failure to possess concepts of a higher order was tested. Object matching behavior in 104 cerebral palsied (aged 5–21) years) and of 188 normal children (aged 3–10 years) was studied under two conditions. In the first condition the key object could be matched on the basis of stimulus similarity, common function, or common class membership. In the second condition the competitive presence of stimulus similarities was markedly reduced. Cerebral palsied children who could not express concepts of function and class membership under conditions of stimulus competition did so when such competition was systematically eliminated.

The results of this study thus suggest that perhaps the cerebral palsied child's distractibility to irrelevant stimulus details may inhibit his conceptual processing. This finding corroborates that of Strauss and Werner,[49] who found mentally retarded children suspected of being brain injured to perform poorly on a concept task due to attention to stimulus details.

SUMMARY

At best the emotional and personality development of an individual is a complex progression. When the normal processes of the development of this aspect of human behavior are complicated by neurophysiological problems as complex and diverse as those observed in cerebral palsy, the potential for healthy achievement of positive personality characteristics is indeed limited. It can be seen from these pages that much research is yet needed before a full understanding of the matter of personality development in cerebral palsied children and youth is obtained. Chapters 4 and 5 of this book are closely interwoven, for much of the control on personality in an individual is exercised by the native intelligence of the person. One can hardly undertake research in one area without accounting fully for the other. This complicates the problems of the research, yet at the same time provides a challenge to be overcome. There is little question but that the impact of a disability is great insofar as the adjustment of the individual is concerned. How to alleviate this impact, both on the life of the child or youth as well as on the adjustment and attitudes of adults and other family members who surround the child, is the problem which researchers and clinicians must study and solve.

6

The Development of Communications Skills

RUTH M. LENCIONE

INTRODUCTION

THE ROLE OF THE SPEECH PATHOLOGIST and speech/language clinician has changed substantially in the past ten years. This change has occurred in most areas of communication disorders, but perhaps none more so than in the philosophy and theoretical constructs dealing with at-risk and neurologically impaired infants and young children. There are a number of reasons for this changing perspective. One has to do with the growing body of evidence from normal infant research demonstrating the newborns capacity to learn from the moment of birth. Other factors which have influenced this change has to do with the kinds of health-care services available in both the private and public sector. The provisions of the Maternal and Infant-Care Programs for the diagnosis and management of high risk mothers and their infants has provided an opportunity for early identification of these children. The passage of the Handicapped Children's Early Education Act of 1968 mandated special education for children beginning at three years of age. All of these developments have led to the implementation of early interventive programs for cerebral palsied and developmentally delayed infants and their families as early as two to three months of age. It is anticipated that current legislation, in progress, will make provision for special services to handicapped children beginning at birth. All of these factors have led to significant changes in the training, role, orientation, and management procedures of the speech/language clinician. In addition, the contributions of psychologists, linguists and psycholinguists has brought about pertinent changes in the study of language acquisition with concomitant effects on diagnostic and management procedures.

What has become apparent, empirically at least, is that the optimal time for the development of cognitive-symbolic processes and skills for all children, and particularly for the child with cerebral palsy, is during the period from birth to three years. Furthermore, there is a concerted effort in education toward the concept of helping all children to discover generative principles, and of mainstreaming the handicapped child into the normal flow of daily living and schooling. Because of these evolving developments there is a change in emphasis in this chapter over its counterpart in an earlier edition. This chapter includes some of the concepts dealing with the philosophy of infant intervention; the results of recent research in selected area of cognitive and symbolic development in the normal and cerebral palsied infant; and an overview of infant language intervention programs in cerebral palsy. The first section includes a summary review of speech and language disorders reported over the past twenty-five years. The second section deals with the rationale of early intervention; models of prenursery and nursery school programs in cerebral palsy; infant language intervention procedures; infant language programming in a transdisciplinary model; and communication aids.

SPEECH AND LANGUAGE DISORDERS

During the past twenty-five years a variety of kinds and types of speech and language disorders associated with cerebral palsy have been evaluated and reported in the literature. The major focus of most of these studies has dealt with breathing, respiratory, phonatory and laryngeal disturbances; articulatory disorders; language delay; and the differences in the communicative competency of individuals classified as predominantly spastic and athetoid types. For the purpose of providing a setting for discussion on current language intervention and management strategies, the following section will present a summary review of these earlier studies.

Breathing and Respiratory Disorders

Cerebral palsy may not only affect the muscles concerned with pharyngeal, laryngeal, and respiratory function, but may also involve the brain centers of respiratory regulation. In the speech act respiration is an important component because it produces the air currents for phonation, speech-sound production, and speech phrasing. Blumberg (1955 a, b) has indicated that the hypothalamus, because of its contiguity to the basal ganglia, may be affected in individuals with a predominantly athetoid type of cerebral palsy. Conversely, in the predominantly spastic type there is less likely to be damage to the central respiratory regulating mechanism. In order to evaluate atypical breathing patterns found in children with cerebral palsy it is necessary to understand the chronology of normal maturational patterns. Peiper (1963) has summarized the stages of respiratory maturation in breaths per minute (BPM) from birth to fifteen years of age. For the first seven days of life, the rate is from 22 to 72 (BPM); 21 to 58 (BPM) for the first six months; 19 to 45 (BPM) for the period from six to twelve months; 15 to 31 (BPM) for the fifth through the tenth years; and 14 to 31 (BPM) for the tenth through the fifteenth year. Mysak (1971) reports that the infant at rest uses nasal respiration. After the sixth month the previously predominantly diaphragmatic pattern is replaced by a mixed diaphragmatic and thoracic pattern; and that thoracic breathing becomes established by the seventh year of life.

Almost every known type of respiratory disorder has been reported for individuals with cerebral palsy. One of the earliest studies which investigated and quantified respiratory deviations was conducted by Hull in 1940. Breathing records were obtained for children described as spastics to determine whether there were any consistent breathing patterns during silent and speech breathing. He reported that this population exhibited thoracic and abdominal opposition during both silent and speech breathing, speech activity increased the breathing anomalies, and that there was an unusual amount of thoracic expansion during speech. In 1946, Perlstein and Shere were among the first to report the phenomenon of "reversed breathing" in spastics and tension athetoids. Wolfe (1950) compared respiratory involvements, during speech, of athetoids, ataxics, and spastics. He found that 50 percent of the athetoids and ataxics had severe respiratory speech dysfunction; whereas 60 percent of the spastic group had no involvement, 10 percent had severe and 30 percent had moderate problems. Cypreanson (1953) studied the breathing and speech coordination of cerebral palsied and normal children to determine the relationship of breathing movements to speech intelligibility. Her results indicated that for silent breathing the cerebral palsy group had a greater number of cycles per minute than the controls. During speaking the cerebral palsy group employed a significantly greater amount of time, number of phases, and abdominal amplitude than the control group.

Hardy and Rembolt (1959), in a study of lung volume of children with cerebral palsy, demonstrated that inspiratory capacities and expiratory reserves are, in general, reduced as compared to normal children; expiratory reserve is by far the most reduced lung function in the cerebral palsied; and many of these children have no expiratory reserve. Westlake and Rutherford (1961) were among the first to delineate the effects of infantile breathing patterns and reversed breathing on speech production. They reported that many cerebral palsied children retained infantile patterns of breathing beyond the normal period and that this type of disability occurs more frequently in the athetoid. McDonald and Chance (1964) classified five types of breathing anomalies in cerebral palsy which interfere with speech production: too rapid breathing rate which may cause lack of vocalization in infants; difficulty in ability to take deep inspiratory breaths which may be associated with inability to produce more than one or two syllables on exhalation; difficulty in controlling prolonged exhalation which may cause noticeable escape of air before initiation of vocalization of speech sounds; antagonistic diaphragmatic abdominal movement which may produce difficulty in sustained vocalization and involuntary movements in respiratory musculature causing interruptions and unintentional and atypical loudness of voice.

Laryngeal and Pharyngeal Disorders

In addition to the involvement of the muscles of respiration, cerebral palsy may also involve those muscles concerned with pharyngeal and laryngeal functions. The laryngeal blocks which occur are usually a part of the more generalized neuromuscular dysfunction and may be related to atypical speech breathing patterns. When the child attempts to produce controlled exhalation for speech, the increased tension which occurs may spread to the laryngeal musculature causing various types of laryngeal spasms. McDonald and Chance (1964) classified these dysfunctions as adductor spasms in which the vocal cords are held together and phonation is initiated with difficulty; abductor spasms, in which there is breathiness and an aspirate vocal quality; and varying tension in laryngeal muscles, in which there may be corresponding variations and atypical pitch, intensity, and quality. Mysak (1971) cites several other types of anomalies which may possibly reflect infantile respiratory-laryngeal behaviors. These include delay in the initiation of voicing due to a delay in shifting from vegetative breathing patterns during speech attempts; an abnormally high rate of breaths per minute (BPM); and weak phonation due to shallow breathing.

The literature has indicated the effects of neuromuscular incoordination associated with respiration and articulation as causative agents in the speech problems of children with cerebral palsy. Hardy (1961) postulated that inability to produce sufficient intraoral breath pressure and palatal dysfunction may be related significantly to the total speech problem. To test this hypothesis, Hardy conducted a study to explore velopharyngeal competency through the use of lateral head x-rays; cinefluorography; oral versus nasal air-flow measurements; and intraoral breath pressure measurements. The results of the study suggest that the palate may be partially or wholly paralyzed allowing air to escape into the nasal passage during speech, precluding the possibility of a pressure build-up in the mouth; inability to generate adequate oral pressure may be due to paretic involvement or weakness of the respiratory mechanism; and paretic or weak articulators (lips, tongue, jaws) may impede the oral air stream to the extent necessary to build up air pressure behind the lips and tongue for adequate speech production. Netzell (1969 *a, b*) used simultaneous recordings of intraoral air pressure, rate of nasal airflow, and a speech sample to evaluate velopharyngeal function in cerebral palsied children. The results indicated that this type of assessment was an efficient diagnostic tool in delineating different patterns of velopharyngeal dysfunction; and that the pressure-flow technique facilitates the work of the prosthodontist in developing the optimal size of a palatal life or obturator.

Netzell delineated five different patterns of velopharyngeal dysfunctions using the intraoral air pressure rate of nasal air-flow (pressure-flow) technique in diagnosis. One subject repeated the speech sample /t∧/ at rates of four and five per second. Velopharyngeal closure was achieved during the initial segments, but at about the seventh segment nasal airflow began to appear and intraoral air pressure dropped to zero. In effect, the velopharynx gradually opened as the syllable train progressed, and it opened earlier at the faster rate of repetition. This kind of atypical pattern was defined as "gradual opening." The pattern of "gradual closing" of the velopharynx was exhibited by a subject who had previously had a pharyngeal flap. Closure on syllable repetition was maintained at the rate of two per second; however, when syllable repetition was attempted at five per second the velopharynx gradually closed. A third type of atypical closure, "anticipatory opening" of the velopharynx was found in one subject while repeating the syllable train /∧ t∧n∧/. With each repetition of these syllables there were two bursts of nasal flow; one with the /t/ and one with the /n/ indicating that in anticipation of the /n/ the velopharynx opened early with resultant inappropriate nasal airflow. Another subject was found to have "retentive opening" of the velopharynx on repeated production of the syllables /∧ n∧t∧/. Two bursts of nasal airflow were emmitted with each utterance, although the nasal airflow was not acoustically perceptible. The second burst of airflow is not characteristic of pressure-flow patterns in normal speakers. In what is described as an apparently rare abnormality, one of the subjects exhibited a "premature opening" of the velopharynx. Upon repetition of /∧ d∧t∧/ two inappropriate burst of nasal airflow occurred. The first burst occurred simultaneously with the increase in intraoral air pressure during /d/ formation. In the presence of the continued increase in intraoral air pressure, oscillographic recordings indicated an apparent initial opening and closure of the velopharynx during the stop-phase of the /d/. This would appear to indicate that the velopharyngeal seal was broken at the point in time when closure was most necessary.

Farmer (1972) in a study of the speech sound status of adults, ₍diagnosed as predominant spastic and athetoid types, discovered the presence of a prevocalization (PV) verified both spectrographically and phonetically. Spectrographically, the PV consisted of a combination of regular and irregular striations indicative of glottal pulsing prior to the plosive line for initial stops. The phonetic nature of the PV appeared to indicate that these speakers were demonstrating a type of delayed velopharyngeal closure. However, the stop production subsequent to the PV indicated that velopharyngeal closure occurred after the time-delay involved in the PV production. Farmer reports that in her sample population the PV occurs significantly more often in the speech of adult athetoid than spastic speakers. Subsequent pilot studies by Farmer have indicated that the PV also occurs in the speech of young cerebral palsied children and that the occurrence is more prevalent in athetoids than in spastics (unpublished data).

Articulatory Disorders

The articulatory status of the cerebral palsied child has received a great deal of investigation, particularly in the areas of speech sound testing and therapy. Irwin (1972) in a ten-year study has probably contributed the most detailed body of information. Using quantitative procedures, Irwin constructed a battery of standardized tests of articulation designed to assess vowel and consonant proficiency according to manner, place, voicing, and types of errors. The results of these pioneer studies include the following. When the manner of articulation is considered the labial sounds are easier to produce and the dental and glottals are the most difficult; for the place of articulation the nasals are least difficult in the initial and final positions; fricatives and glides are most difficult in all three positions; stops appear to be least difficult in the medial position; and semivowels, in combinations, vary somewhat among the initial, medial, and final positions. When test scores were evaluated in terms of the order of difficulty with voiced and voiceless consonants, the data indicated that there was a tendency for the voiced consonants to be less difficult than the voiceless cognates. In studies to determine the relationship of substitution and omission errors in cerebral palsied children and a normal control group Irwin found that omissions significantly exceeded substitutions in the cerebral palsied, whereas in the normal group substitution errors greatly exceeded omissions.

In a study of the speech sound ability of children ranging in age from eight to fourteen years, diagnosed as predominantly spastic and athetoid types, Lencione (1953) found that when the position of the sound was considered, the rank order of correct production progressed from initial to medial to final position. For place of articulation consonantal proficiency was highest for the tongue-tip simple, lip, and back of tongue sounds; and that the tongue-tip complex sounds were significantly more difficult than the sounds in the other three categories. There was a marked relationship between age and consonantal proficiency. At eight years the percentages of correct consonant production in the initial, medial, and final positions were

75, 73, and 71; at fourteen years they were 93, 90, and 92. When errors were considered the incidence of substitutions and omissions was essentially equal, but there was a larger percentage of omissions in the medial and final positions. Analysis of the order of difficulty with voiced and voiceless cognates indicated that the voiceless sounds were considerably more difficult to produce correctly.

Byrne (1959) evaluated the speech sound status of children ranging in age from two through seven years, diagnosed as spastic and athetoid types. She found that the greatest accuracy for correct responses was in the initial position, followed by the medial position. Few sounds in the final position reached the 72 percent level of proficiency for her age group. Consonantal proficiency was highest for the bilabial sounds, followed by the tongue-tip complex sounds. In general, voiceless sounds were more frequently misarticulated than the voiced cognates.

In an investigation of the hypothesis that the athetoid child does not achieve the same efficiency in speech sound production as that of children diagnosed as spastic, Irwin evaluated the phonetic status of children from one to twelve years of age. The findings indicated that there was no statistical evidence that differences exist among spastics and athetoids. Lencione (1953) compared the speech sound proficiency of spastic and athetoid groups ranging in age from eight to fourteen years. The spastic group was found to be consistently more proficient than the athetoid group in ability to produce both voiced and voiceless consonants, and this proficiency was considerably more marked with the voiceless sounds. The spastic group had significantly fewer omission and substitution errors, and in general, the pattern of performance resembled that of seven year old children; the athetoid group tended to resemble the articulatory behavior of normal children below six years of age. Byrne (1959), in a comparison of spastics and athetoids ranging in age two through seven years, found that the overall scores for tests of speech sound proficiency were not significant, but that in all of the subtests the spastics had higher percentages or mean scores.

Haphazard, extraneous, meaningless or nonstandard speech behaviors have been clinically observed in the cerebral palsied (Berry and Eisenson 1956, Van Riper 1954, West et al. 1957). Probably because of the nature of articulatory testing, dealing solely with the phonetic transcription of specific target sounds, experimental descriptions of these extraneous behaviors have not been reported. Recently, one of these nonstandard speech behaviors, prevocalizations (PV), has been analyzed by Farmer (1972). The PV, a nasalized, neutral vowel, was found to occur with or without a nasal consonant. The most frequent occurrence of the PV was found to take place in the transition from silence to speech rather than between interspeech word transitions. When sentence production was evaluated the PV occurrence steadily decreased from the first through the third word. Prevocalizations occurred in descending order of frequency before voiced obstruents, voiceless obstruents, and sonorants. The results of this study demonstrated the presence of PV's which results in the addition of nonstandard syllables interferring with intelligibility from segmental distortion. This distortion, which does not carry semantic information, may account for one aspect of the lack of intelligibility found in many athetotic speakers.

Language Delay

The kinds of language delay in children with cerebral palsy has been variously investigated. Among the early studies Dunsdon (1952) found an average retardation of vocabulary and verbal recall of from three to four years as compared to normal children; Achilles (1955–56) found that 66 percent had either no speech or no more than one year of oral language development; 20 percent were rated as having a fair means of communication in that they were able to make their primitive wants known; and 14 percent had good communicative ability but intelligibility was characterized by articulatory lapses and irregularities in rhythm and rate. Hood and Perlstein (1956) studied the case history records of children with spastic hemiplegia ranging in age from one to twenty years. They found that there was a delay of nine months in the use of first words and six months in the use of sentences. When seizures were present the mean age of the use of first words was twenty-seven months, when seizures were absent the mean age was eighteen months. Byrne (1959) found that her experimental group was three months delayed in the appearance of first words; twelve months delayed in the use of two-word sentences; and forty-eight months in the use of three-word sentences. Denhoff (1966), in a study of the rate of language development, found that 11 percent of his sample population used single words by nine months, 15 percent by ten months, while 74 percent were delayed beyond the twelve month norm. The average age for the onset of single words for this group was 27.1 months.

Most of the early studies reflected broad, gross estimates of language development reported in case histories and/or clinical observations. In 1964, Love was among the first to detail specific language abilities in a test situation using a battery of six language tests. Three tests required the subjects to formulate oral language to express concepts implied in matching, sorting, and describing the themes of picture stories. The experimental population consisted of children diagnosed as spastic and athetoid types ranging in age from ten to fifteen years. The control group consisted of physically handicapped children with no obvious speech and hearing problems. The results indicated significant differences between the experimental and control groups in the number of words available on an expressive naming vocabulary test, but no differences on a receptive vocabulary test. The cerebral palsied group showed no greater discrepancy between the items correct on the receptive and the expressive vocabulary tests, which suggests the absence of a clinical naming disorder. No gross differences were apparent in the language used to describe performance on an object matching test or in language used in describing sorting, pictorial themes, or in defining words. On the basis of these findings, Love concluded that disorders of comprehension and formulation of oral symbols, often attributed to the cerebral palsied, were not present in the group studied. Myers (1965) evaluated the language abilities of a group of cerebral palsied children ranging in age from four to nine years with the Illinois Test of Psycholinguistic Abilities. The results indicated that the spastic group was significantly superior to the athetoid group on the Automatic-Sequential Level factor; on the Auditory-Vocal, Automatic, and Auditory-Vocal Sequential. The athetoid group was superior to the spastic group on the Representational Level factor, Motor Encoding, and Auditory-Vocal Association. These findings indicated that spastic children can be expected to be inferior to athetoid children on language tasks at the representational level, but superior on tasks involving the automatic-sequential level.

A retrospective interpretation of these earlier studies demonstrate that while the degree of competence in producing speech sounds was, in most instances, delayed or severely distorted, the acquisition of the phonological system followed essentially the same course of progression as that of the normal child. Most of the reports on language were based on retroactive case histories and clinical observations. It was not until the late 1950s and early 60s when language tests suitable for evaluating the language processes of cerebral palsied children became available. In those studies that systematically explore language there were strong indications that for those children who had acquired expressive language, syntactical and semantic behaviors were similar to those of normal speakers. In 1964, Love was one of the first to present this kind of evidence. What appears to be emerging from recent research is that the degree of the speech and language problem in cerebral palsy may be more closely related to "intelligibility" or motor skills rather than to disorders of language processing. For many years it has been assumed that associated disorders more adversely influenced the final habilitative outcome than did the neuromotor disability. There is a small but growing body of evidence that indicates that it may indeed be the lack of early sensory intervention that is the critical agent in language disorders. The following sections will present some of the emerging concepts and procedures designed to provide early and appropriate intervention programs.

RATIONALE FOR EARLY INTERVENTION

One of the most significant developments in recent years has been the evidence from normal infant research concerning the neonate's capacity to learn. A considerable body of information has accrued that indicates that the newborn has the capacity and ability to learn from the moment of birth. The overall picture of cognitive and perceptual development that is emerging is very different from traditional ones. It has long been assumed that perception is a process of construction; that is, that at birth and for the first few years of life infants receive fragmentary sensory information that is elaborated and built on to produce the ordered perceptual world of the adult. In the past most observers of infants and toddlers have tended to regard this period of life as a projected gestation outside the womb. Although the exact mechanisms of many learning processes are still unclear, research findings are beginning to document that perceptual, cognitive, social, and communicative capabilities in the normal infant are far more acute than has been previously recognized. These capabilities increase rapidly, especially if appropriate and structured stimulation is provided. For the child born at risk or with known neurological dysfunction the early months and first three years of life are a crucial period. As a consequence, intervention, to be effective, needs to be implemented during this time rather than at age three or later. In order to provide a background for early intervention programs for children with cerebral palsy a brief overview of a selected number of studies in infant research are presented in the following section.

Normal Infant Development

Recent studies have shown that the newborn can hear, see, and interact with the world around him within the first few hours and weeks of life. Eisenberg (1969, 1970), and Eisenberg *et al.* (1964) report that differential sensitivity from simple constant tones to patterned auditory stimuli are present at birth, including infants with known CNS abnormality; Birns *et al.* (1965) found that newborns from 36 to 96 hours of age respond to low-frequency tone rather than high-frequency tone in terms of reflective inhibition of behavior; and Papousek (1967) has shown that infants respond to auditory stimulus by appropriate turning of the head to right or left. Siqueland (1970) and Lipsitt (1967) demonstrated that the newborn can discriminate complex visual patterns within the first two days; Lewis and Spaulding (1967) report that there is a differential cardiac response to visual and auditory stimuli by six months; Webster *et al.* (1972) found that seven-month-old infants show a significant change in the fundamental frequency of their vocalizations from baseline to high pitch stimulus periods, but not from low pitch stimulus.

Studies by Eimas *et al.* (1971) indicate that infants as young as one month of age are responsive to speech sounds, are able to make fine discriminations, and are capable of perceiving speech sounds along the voicing continuum in the same categorical manner that adult English speakers discriminate such sounds; and Moffitt (1971) found that infants twenty to twenty-four weeks of age could discriminate between synthetic speech syllables of *bah* and *gah*. Friedlander (1968, 1970, 1971), in a comprehensive series of experiments, assessed auditory discrimination of normal infants using the "Playtest" system. This equipment consists of recordings of preprogrammed tapes controlled by two switches which are mounted on each side of the crib. The procedure enables the infant to select, at his choice, the kind and amount of stimulation preferred. The frequency and duration of these self-selected listening choices are automatically recorded. Friedlander's findings indicate that infants as young as eight months of age show a marked preference for speech over other types of auditory stimulation. Infants between eleven and fourteen months made complex auditory linguistic discriminations and responded to language differences concerning who was speaking; flat and bright intonation; degrees of redundancy; speech and non-speech sounds; and could discriminate the voice of their mother from that of a stranger. What these findings are beginning to demonstrate is that very young infants are able to sort acoustic variations of adult phonemes into categories with limited exposure to speech, with essentially no experience in producing these sounds, with little, if any, differential reinforcement for this form of behavior, and that they can make judgments of similarity between their own utterance and those of other persons in their environment. The implication of these findings for intervention with cerebral palsied infants assumes great importance because of the suggestion that perception, in a linguistic mode, is operative at an unusually early age.

Other reports dealing with a variety of infant learning abilities in the first year of life include Kagan's (1972) study which indicates that three-month-old infants become consistently reactive to discrepancy; and White's (1971) finding that four-month-old infants can coordinate two sense systems, i.e., looking and reaching. Kagan (1972) has shown that by eight or nine months the infant is capable of generating hypotheses; and Peiper (1963) reports responsiveness to olfactory, tactual, and proprioceptive stimuli. Kessen and Nelson (1974) have characterized perceptual cognitive changes during the first six months of life as the time in which the infant is constructing figure from ground; and the time from six months to twelve months as the period in which information that the infant has learned about objects begins to be put into the context of his environment.

Another area of research that is producing a number of changes in perspective is the significant influence of maternal behavior on the infant's perceptual-cognitive and symbolic development. Physical handling that is frequent, firm and gentle, particularly in the first months and year of life, has been shown to have a direct correlation on the infants early cognitive and motor development (Ainsworth *et al.* 1971). Frequent and reciprocal verbal stimulation from the mother, by talking, touching, and playing with the infant, has been related to cognitive development as measured by more frequent vocalization and greater language ability (Irwin 1967, Goldberg and Lewis 1969, Kagan 1971–72). In a study by Yarrow *et al.* (1972) the authors found that five-month-old infants whose environment included a wide variety of inanimate objects were advanced in a number of areas of cognitive development that differed from those of infants who had rich, warm, and varied social stimulation. Earlier vocalization and language development was found to be more closely related to the environment that provided social and verbal reinforcement.

Research on perceptual-cognitive variables indicates that the mother's response to the infant's behavior has a significant effect on the later occurrence of the behavior. If the mother's response and stimulation is appropriate for her infant according to his physical state, individual capacities, and developmental level, she will tend to be more affectionate, accepting, and nonrestrictive (Clarke-Stewart 1973). Furthermore, the degree of eye contact between the mother and the infant has been reported to lead not only to a stronger tie with the mother, development of responsiveness, and attachment, but also to more advanced social and cognitive progress. The combination of verbal and visual stimulation appears to accelerate development, particularly if it occurs during play rather than caretaking activities.

Studies on maternal influence have indicated that the mother not only serves as a direct source of stimulation herself, but is also the "mediator" of stimulation from the environment (Clarke-Stewart 1973). If the mother mediates the child's interaction with toys and play opportunities by offering appropriate materials and by talking to the child, there is evidence that cognitive and symbolic development is enhanced. These skills do not emerge in the same manner in children who are merely exposed to a stimulating physical environment (Collard 1971, Yarrow *et al.* 1972).

Another significant dimension of information stemming from studies of maternal influence is the increasing evidence that the mother's behavior is "contingent" on the infant and what the infant does. The physical state of the infant greatly influences both the effectiveness of the mother's behavior and the form and pattern of that behavior. Harper (1971) has reviewed evidence which demonstrates that certain infant behaviors can either facilitate or inhibit the responses of their caretakers. For example, the mother will smile when the baby smiles, and she will talk and fondle the child more frequently when the baby coos and babbles. Beckwith (1971), Bell (1971), and Reingold *et al.* (1959) have shown that social responses from the mother are directly related to the infant's smiling and vocalizing. The study of reciprocal mother-infant interaction is beginning to demonstrate that behavioral sequences are more frequently initiated and/or terminated by the infant than by the mother. Moreover, these studies are providing evidence that the infant has a sustained effect on maternal behavior. Over time, the baby's pattern of response, eye contact, smiling, and verbal and non-verbal communication can produce long-term positive or negative effects on the mother's attitudes and behaviors (Kogan 1974).

Atypical Development

More than twenty years ago Phelps (1948, 1949) and Crothers and Paine (1959) described the sensory and perceptual defects in children with cerebral palsy. However, it was not until 1963, when Birch and Lefford published their monograph on "Intersensory Development in Children," that adequate data on the chronology of the maturation of these functions became available for normal children. Birch and Lefford's study indicated that there is a relatively slow maturation of intersensory integration and organization. They presented evidence that these functions do not reach maturity until the normal child is at least ten years of age. In other words, sensory and perceptual deficits were described in children with cerebral palsy before sufficient data was available on when these functions develop and integrate in normal children (Swinyard 1967). During this same period a number of investigators reported on the types and kinds of sensorimotor and perceptual disturbances, and many reports appeared dealing with therapeutic and management procedures designed to lessen these defects.

That associated sensory and perceptual disorders are present clinically is clearly apparent. There are, however, several mitigating factors which need to be considered concerning the inevitability of the disrupting impact of associated disorders on behavioral development. One of these factors is that there is relatively little or no data to indicate the learning capabilities of infants born with known neurological dysfunction. A second and equally important factor is that the earlier research findings were based on studies of cerebral palsied children who had not received early intervention, that is, before age three, and in a majority of cases before five years of age. What is becoming increasing apparent is that the perceptual, sensory, cognitive, and communicative capacities of the infant born with cerebral palsy has not yet been scientifically documented as has been done in normal child development. Whether the degree and severity of associated disorders are inherent and irreversible awaits the outcome of further research, not only in assessment, but also in the results of early intervention procedures. This does not mean to imply that all handicaps can be overcome. A child with severe spastic/athetoid involvement will probably never become a physically normal child. Nonetheless, appropriate and early stimulation of the environment in the first three years, and more importantly, in the first year, may help to significantly avoid many social-emotional and communicative problems in later years.

The clinical changes that are observed in some cerebral palsied children demonstrate the inherent capacity of neural tissue to repair and adapt to local or general brain damage. Postnatal brain maturation extends for a period of ten years, during which time both structural and functional changes occur in the brain. There is a modest and growing amount of research evidence to indicate that early intervention may accelerate the learning processes of the child born with cerebral palsy. The following section will present an overview of the results of current studies on the sensory-perceptual-cognitive abilities of cerebral palsied infants and children.

Visual Perceptual Disorders

Children with cerebral palsy often have difficulty on tasks involving visual perception, although motor control is adequate for the task and the level of general intelligence is such that a better performance is expected. In 1966, Nielsen was among the first to indicate that the relationship between the motor handicap and perceptual-motor performance in cerebral palsy was slight. In order to explore this hypothesis Wedell et al. (1972) investigated "size constancy," which they define as a lower-level function of perceptual-motor integration. Size constancy is the individual's tendency to judge the size of an object to be the same at different distances, in spite of the variations in the size of the object's projected image on the retina. Bower (1966) reported evidence of size constancy in normal infants between six and eight weeks of age; and Wohlwill (1960) has shown that size constancy increases with age during the period of childhood.

The purpose of the study by Wedell and his associates was to investigate the relationship between experience in independent walking and size constancy in cerebral palsied children. The experimental group was composed of twenty-four cerebral palsied children who had independent walking, ranging in age between six and eight years. A normal group of children in the same age groupings were given the same tests, although the authors stress that this group was in no sense a control group. For purposes of analysis the cerebral palsied children and the reference group of normals were divided into three chronological age groups of six, seven, and eight years. The test procedure consisted of a technique which required the child to match the height of an adjustable rod at two feet with four standard rods all subtending the same visual angle of 5°. The standard rods were placed at 2, 7, 12, and 17 feet from the child. Judgments of height in terms of physical equality were required.

The results of the study indicated that (1) the cerebral palsied children showed a lower degree of size constancy at distances over 7 feet in comparisons with the reference group; (2) for distances below 7 feet the scores for both groups were comparable; and (3) that cerebral palsied children with the longest history of independent walking achieved higher scores at greater distances than those who had not had as long a history of walking. What these findings tend to suggest is that visual disturbances, in some cerebral palsied children, may not be the direct result of the brain damage *per se*, but rather the effect of the degree of environmental deprivation in walking due to the motor handicap.

Conceptual Disturbances

The literature on associated disorders has indicated that children with cerebral palsy usually perform poorly on a variety of tests designed to measure conceptual ability (Strauss and Werner 1943; Dolphin and Cruickshank 1951; Birch 1964). These deficiencies have included a tendency to be attracted by details, difficulty in changing set, and making insufficient use of function in definitions. In 1966 Birch and Bortner tested the hypothesis that preferential responsiveness to "stimulus factors," and not the lack of possession of concepts of class and function, underlies the failure in "normal" children to use class function in making categorical choices. To test this hypothesis, object-matching behavior of normal children was studied using two test conditions. In the first test, results indicated that when object choices permitted the child to use stimulus similarity as well as class membership and function, younger children preferentially matched for "stimulus" properties rather than for "functional" relations. In the second test, where the stimulus competition was eliminated, many of the younger children exhibited the capacity to use concepts of class and functional relatedness in matching.

To determine how cerebral palsied children would respond in the same test conditions, Birch and Bortner (1967) analyzed the effects of stimulus competition and its systematic elimination on object matching behavior. The cerebral palsied population consisted of children between the ages of five and twenty-one years; the normal group was made up of children from three to ten years. The two tests contained identical index objects. In Test A the "index object" was presented with three "stimulus competitive" objects from which a matching choice had to be made. For example, the child received a "metal bell" as the index object, and was asked to choose the object that goes best with it from a group which included a thimble, a toy church, and a silver button. In Test B, the three choice objects were "non-stimulus competitive," i.e., they contained no obvious stimulus properties such as color or form. For the index object of the "metal bell" the choice objects were a cigar, pliers, and a toy church. In each test the toy church was the correct categorical choice.

A comparison of performance by the two groups showed that when chronological and mental age were held constant, the normal children matched on the basis of class and function more frequently than did the cerebral palsied. However, all of the cerebral palsied children performed significantly better on Test B than on Test A. With the elimination of the stimulus competition of form and color the cerebral palsied children showed an increased tendency to make matching choices according to class and function characteristics rather than on the basis of stimulus similarity. The findings of this experiment tend to support the hypothesis that cerebral palsied children possess higher-order concepts of functional relationships and class membership. When the stimulus competition is reduced they perform similarly to normal children at comparable chronological and mental ages. These findings provide significant guidelines for systematic clinical management procedures, but probably equally critical evidence that appropriate interventive manipulation of the learning environment may enable some cerebral palsied children to more normally develop conceptual skills.

Auditory Perceptual Disorders

Another chapter in this book will deal with auditory problems in greater detail. It is noteworthy at this point to include several studies on auditory perceptual abilities in infants and young children with cerebral palsy. The experiment by Cyrulik-Jacobs et al. (1975) may, in time, be a significant forerunner of studies documenting the auditory perceptual capabilities of infants with cerebral palsy. The study was designed to explore the effectiveness of the "Playtest" system to evaluate the auditory perception and processing capabilities of cerebral palsied infants ranging in age from ten to twenty-seven months. The infants had been medically diagnosed as mixed spastic/athetoid, spastic quadriplexia, and hypotonia. Each infant had a "Playtest" unit attached to his crib at home for a minimum of six days. The audio stimuli prerecorded selection tapes included (1) a five-minute selection of "Sesame Street" songs, and (2) a monotone hum.

The performance data of the cerebral palsied infants and normal infants were compared on two measures: (1) mean daily listening (MDL), and (2) average single response (ASR). The MDL of the cerebral palsied infants was, on average, twice as long as that of normal infants (Friedlander and Cyrulik-Jacobs 1970). Variability of individual ASR ranged from 1:8 to 16:0

seconds in the cerebral palsied group and 1:1 to 7:5 seconds in the normal group. The similarity of the normal and experimental infant's ASR indicated that the two groups operated the apparatus with comparable facility. The significant preferential listening to music over hum by the cerebral palsied infants showed that they made highly selective responses which paralleled those of normal infants. Additionally, this study also demonstrated improved motor control in reach and grasp by the cerebral palsied infants as measured by pre- and post-video tapes, and an improvement in environmental interaction recorded by clinical observation of therapists and parent reports (Shapira *et al.* 1973). The significance of the results of this study may have far-reaching effects on at least several aspects of early intervention. The "Playtest" system may be a signpost for more accurate assessment of auditory perception in the hard to test infant with neurological deficits and may provide guidance for more appropriate perceptual-language programming during the first year of life.

A study of the auditory perceptual abilities of older cerebral palsied children between the ages of eight and eleven years was conducted by Griffin (1971) to determine whether their abilities differed from those of a matched normal group. She administered eight linguistic tests of auditory perception in the areas of (1) auditory verbal memory, (2) auditory verbal sequencing, and (3) auditory verbal discrimination in three acoustic conditions—in quiet, in a background noise at a signal-to-noise ratio of 30 dB, and in a background noise of 5 dB.

Griffin's data indicated that (1) the cerebral palsied children as a group did not differ significantly from the matched control group in performance of auditory perceptual tasks; (2) a significant difference as a function of age level was found in the performances of both the cerebral palsied children and the control group collectively in that the performance of the eleven-year-olds was superior to the performance of children at the three younger age levels; (3) the cerebral palsied children and the controls performed in a similar manner at all four age levels, and (4) the cerebral palsied children did not differ significantly from the normal children in performances on the auditory perceptual tasks as a function of any of the acoustic backgrounds. She concluded that a general deficit in auditory perception did not exist in the experimental group of cerebral palsied children, although certain subgroups of cerebral palsied children, such as those with low intelligence levels, hearing impairments, or linguistic deficits may have auditory perceptual problems.

In an experiment designed to determine the amount of learning which would take place under conditions of a normal speaking rate of 175 words per minute (WPM) and a rapid rate of 275 WPM de Hoop (1965) compared the performance of groups of cerebral palsied and physically handicapped children. The cerebral palsied group had a mean age of 15.4, the control group had a mean age of 13.7 years.

The results indicated that the scores for the cerebral palsied group were significantly below those of the control group for the normal listening rate of 175 WPM. There were, however, essentially no differences between the two groups on the scores for the 275 WPM test. The author indicated that he had expected the cerebral palsied group to do less well on the rapid 275 WPM task because of the documented evidence concerning auditory perceptual disturbances usually ascribed to this group. The 275 WPM test rate is an unusual stimulation condition, yet for this group of children the accelerated feedback time apparently proved to be a compensatory aid rather than a deterrent.

Sensory and Perceptual-Motor Disturbances

Disturbances of sensory and perceptual-motor functions, when they exist, are usually of the corticosensory type. Tizard *et al.* (1954) were among the first to assess the disturbance of sensation in children with hemiplegia. They reported that there was impairment of sensation in about 50 percent of the cases. The single ability most often impaired was stereognosis (ability to recognize objects by the sense of feeling); followed by two-point discrimination; diminished sensation in the handicapped hand; and a visual field defect commonly coexisted with the hand impairment. The authors noted that it was striking that the severity of sensory involvement was not correlated with the severity of the motor disability, the degree of muscular underdevelopment on the affected side, or mental status. Similarly, Tachdjian and Minear (1958) found that the most common sensory defects in the hands of children with spastic hemiplegia were astereognosis, impaired two-point discrimination, and position sense. In a study designed to explore the difference in sensory disturbances of children classified as athetoids and spastics Kenney (1963) found that, in general, the children with athetosis had very few disturbances of sensation, whereas the spastic children revealed multiple disturbances.

In 1967, Barrett and Jones undertook a study to determine the effect of repetition of a structured multisensory experience on motor function of the affected hand in hemiplegic infants and young children. The subjects were children between the ages of nineteen and sixty months: four were right and two were left hemiplegics. At the beginning of the study, use of the hemiplegic hand ranged from very poor to fair plus. The technique used was the "Sensory Story" for a period of three to five months. The authors reported that this procedure resulted in a significant increase in the spontaneous use of the affected hand during the training sessions and that there appeared to be a carryover into play activities at other times. A subsequent study by Jones *et al.* (1969) with hemiplegic infants aged eighteen to thirty six months, with an adaptation of a three-dimensional turntable "Sensory Story," demonstrated similar results. The results of these two experiments are beginning to offer some significant projections concerning the way in which sensorimotor disturbances in hemiplegics may be inhibited by appropriate early intervention.

MODELS OF INFANT AND TODDLER INTERVENTION PROGRAMS IN CEREBRAL PALSY

Some of the earliest reports concerning educational intervention with the cerebral palsied were made by Berenberg *et al.* (1952); Denhoff and Holden (1954); Thelander (1954); and Thelander and Phelps (1961). These authors emphasized the need for "nursery schools" as a means of altering the social environment of the child in order to foster emotional and intellectual development, to provide increased sensorimotor experiences, and to offer support and guidance to the parents. In the past twenty-five years a variety of models and programs have been developed. The following section presents a summary review of a number of representative models.

Medical-Educational Nursery School Model

In 1949, Jones was one of the first to develop a nursery school model for cerebral palsied children. Initially the children in this program had been treated in traditional one-half hour therapy sessions in an outpatient hospital center. They had not adjusted well to this schedule and to the variety of therapists. At the request of the parents, an experimental nursery school which met for several hours each day was initiated. The staff included a pediatrician, a physical, occupational, and speech therapist. During the five years of the pilot program the staff and parents agreed that the school provided better integration of training than had been possible on the previous outpatient basis. Emphasis on therapy leads both parents and children to the conclusion that the most important factor relating to success in later years in physical competence. According to Jones *et al.* (1962), experience with this facility indicated that early intervention should emphasize teaching and personality development, and that the treatment of the physical aspects of the disability should be carefully integrated with all of the other activities of the child's life during the early years.

Medical-Educational Prenursery Model

In 1954, Jones initiated a "prenursery school" for cerebral palsied toddlers eighteen to thirty-six months of age. The staff consisted of a pediatrician; a director/teacher; an assistant teacher; physical, occupational and speech therapists; a consulting psychologist; a social worker; a variety of medical specialists which included an orthopedist and a psychiatrist; and volunteer aids. The prenursery school offers an educational program which integrates therapy with a planned learning environment. The program provides for individualized instruction and procedures in order to care for the variabilities of the children in terms of their particular physical, sensorimotor, cognitive, communicative, emotional, and social needs. The children attend three to five mornings a week, for three to four hours per day, depending upon their readiness for an extended program.

The school curriculum is based on child development principles providing experiences in daily living in a social group. The teacher is the pivotal person whose direction provides a setting in which the child's daily activities become more than a succession of individual therapies. Ancillary activities, treatment, special examinations, and training procedures are all integrated into the nursery day. For example, the teacher keeps a daily record of each child's behavior in the areas of response to materials, peers, adults, and self-related skills. The therapists record the child's response to therapy sessions and classroom behaviors. Often the therapists are in the classroom, working with the children or observing the teachers as they interact with the children. The staff meets weekly to exchange ideas based on the daily records. This type of ongoing interchange between teachers and therapists provides the setting for a flexible program that enables the staff to meet each child's changing needs and interests.

At regularly scheduled intervals, parent participation in the classroom is required as well as in the therapy sessions. A close relationship to the school program keeps parents in touch with the school's objective for their children and provides knowledge of ways of meeting these goals. It also enables each parent to view the child in proper perspective as he/she sees and works with other children and their parents. The social worker, in addition to in-take interviews, is also available for individual parent counseling. The child psychiatrist meets with the parent group twice monthly to explore various aspects of child development, parental feelings about handling a handicapped child, and other related topics of concern or interest. The school staff also participates in these meetings (Rogers 1972).

In a follow-up study made forty-four months after fifty-four of the children had left the program, Jones et al. (1962) reported: (1) the diagnosis of cerebral palsy made at a mean age of 2 years 5 months was consistent with re-examination at mean age of 6 years 11 months; (2) of the total group, 63 percent were educable, i.e., 13 percent were in regular school and 50 percent were in schools for the handicapped; (3) 34 percent of the total group were not educable, and (4) progressive increases in IQ from 60–70 to 95–100 were reported in four of the nine children for whom ratings during and after prenursery school were available. What this type of prenursery school program and learning experience demonstrated was the value of early intervention in subsequent achievement, and that timing and involvement of human relationships are essential to children's learning, in addition to sensorimotor stimulation and treatment. The Jones prenursery school model has continued to make programming changes. A description of the model will be published in 1976 by United Cerebral Palsy Associations, Inc., as part of their report on "Programming for Atypical Infants and Their Families."

Neurodevelopmental Model

Another type of infant program, based on the Bobath neurodevelopmental method (1955, 1967) was developed by Kong in 1956. The rationale underlying this program was that prognosis in cerebral palsy can be improved by early physiotherapy. Early treatment emphasizes the inhibition of tonic reflex activity, combined with facilitation of normal automatic movements. The theoretical model for this approach is that intervention within the first six to twelve months, or before abnormal movement patterns have become fixed, will provide an opportunity to more easily inhibit atypical patterns so that normal sensorimotor patterns may be acquired.

The program provides for daily treatment, with the active participation of the mother. In order to establish the desired sensorimotor patterns frequent repetition is necessary and must be incorporated into the child's daily life and everyday handling by the mother. While the physiotherapist treats the infant, the mother is shown how to use the various movement patterns under supervision.

Kong indicates that ten years ago a large proportion of the cerebral palsied children in the Bern Center were severely involved. At present the majority have slight or minimal neuromotor involvement which she attributes, in part, to intervention within the first six to twelve months of life, and the use of the neurodevelopmental approach. Reporting on the age range of the center's population, Vasella (1966) indicates that the number of infants enrolled under one year progressed from four in 1956 to 203 in 1964.

Kong has reported on a follow-up of sixty-nine children that entered the program under one year of age. Of this group 75 percent (fifty-three cases) had normal gait and showed only minimal neurological signs under stress; and only sixteen were still under treatment. Kong also noted that there were fewer mentally retarded children among the cases of cerebral palsy treated early. It was her impression that "normal motor experience has given these children a chance to develop their normal potentials. Children treated later lack this experience and do not have the same chance to develop normally, so that, unless they are of superior intelligence, they are likely to attain only a subnormal performance." Readers are also referred to Bobath (1967), Crickmay (1966), and Finnie (1970) for a more detailed description of the neurodevelopmental/neurophysiological method.

Meeting Street School Home Development Guidance Program

A third type of program was developed by Denhoff *et al.* (1970). This program is a planned approach to fulfill the total needs of infants and toddlers during the early developmental period. Designed over a fifteen-year period, the management program is based on the principle that nurturance in the early years "significantly helps lagging maturational processes to unfold cognitive related potentialities, especially when advantage is taken of genetically directed critical emergence periods." The procedures emphasize the value of exercise at the time of a critical emergence period; the stimulation of developmental sequences; and the use of early sensorimotor stimulation to provide for later cognitive development. The basic assumption underlying the program is that "input" is necessary before "output" can be expected.

The Home Development Guidance Program concentrates on providing developmental stimulation to babies through an individualized family-oriented program. To achieve these goals, a developmental stimulation team is used in interchangeable roles. The idea, Denhoff states, "is to catch a developmental set of behavior attitudes at a critical period and to exercise it from a prereadiness state through skillfulness. The challenge is to anticipate the emergence of the next set and prepare for it" (Denhoff *et al.* 1970).

The theoretical framework includes the "Information Processing Model" based on Osgood's psycholinguistic model. With this method the three basic modalities considered to contribute to early learning and cognitive development are: (1) body awareness (sensory) and body control (motor); (2) visual-perceptual-motor skills; and (3) language efficiency. The speech and language therapists make on going evaluations of each child to determine the extent and degree of disorders of intake (understanding), integration (meshing thoughts into ideas), and output (verbal expression), awareness to sounds and verbal cues, and consistency in following directions and responding to spoken language.

Following the speech/language evaluation a treatment plan is developed around each child's functional language level. Parents are instructed in ways to make speech fun so that speech failures are minimized; and they are shown how to provide successful communication through other modalities. Readers are referred to Denhoff *et al.* (1968) and Hainsworth and Siqueland (1969) for a description of the Meeting Street School Screening Test.

Infant and Toddler Programs for Children with
Developmental Disabilities

Another type of early infant program was initiated by Frances Berko (1974) and her staff at the Ithaca Special Children's Center. Beginning in 1970 the center (for which the writer served as language consultant for ten years) began developing additional approaches to the care and education of developmentally disabled children under the age of thirty months, including those with cerebral palsy, and their families. The rationale of these program services is founded on the following premises: (1) the concept of developmental disabilities, rather than individual diagnostic categories, is the only viable approach to designating the population who receives services; (2) the label of developmental disabilities is not an indication of the type of program services needed by the given disabled infant and his family. Program services include a complete evaluation as an on going process involving a broad spectrum of specialists, interchanging perceptions on common service planning with each other and with the family members. The transdisciplinary team approach is used in which each specialist shares expertise with colleagues in such a manner that they are capable of assuming some of each other's responsibilities, but not accountability, for the individual family and child; (3) many children who later experience language-learning-behavioral failures are not diagnosed as disabled in infancy, nor perhaps should they be. However, they seem to emerge from the population of infants diagnosed "at risk." Later failures may be prevented if early intervention could occur without imputing any diagnosis of disability; (4) in child development, infancy does not extend to thirty months of age, or even twenty-four months. In the first two years of life, the child seems to go through two gross stages of development, the dividing line of which seems to occur when the child begins to move around the environment by him or herself, verbally establishes a primitive communication with the world around him or her, and cognitively manipulates the environment. The Special Children's Center differentiates between these developmental periods, that is, the infant and toddler periods, rationalizing that the basic interventions between the two should vary.

The "Infant Program" for the education of the child below twelve months of age centers about the home and the interpersonal relationships between the family members, particularly the mother or the parent substitute, and the infant. At this level of programming, intervention occurs mainly within the home environment. The primary professional intervenor for the infant educational phase of the program is the Home Service Director, whose responsibility is to go into the home and teach the parent how to fulfill her role as a mother of a deviant infant, as opposed to the role of therapist, teacher, or caretaker. However, experience has shown that, as this home intervention continues with the more markedly or severely developmentally disabled child, some parents develop a feeling of isolation. Procedures to overcome these feelings include: (1) scheduling the parent for individual counseling with one of the center's social workers; (2) scheduling periodic parent-child programs with the center's trained professional staff; (3) scheduling workshops for parents of developmentally disabled and multiply handicapped children under the age of five in which the parents of the infants participate; (4) facilitating the organization of parent groups, independent of The Special Children's Center and within the home community, so that parents can share information and experience without organizational structure or supervision but with the expertise of the center's staff available to them upon request; and (5) making available to both the parents and the Home Service Director specialists of a variety of orientations, particularly speech pathologists, to train them in specific procedures to enhance development within the framework of normalized parent-child interactions.

Believing that language development is the foundation for cognitive and social development, all of the center's programs are founded upon strategies for speech and language development. Integrated in the Home Service intervention is the establishment of a good relationship between the parent and child by instructing the parents so that they do not "turn off" when the child does not speak to them, but rather that they continue to talk to their child in such a manner that the child is exposed to a normal speaking environment. Specific instructions are given in how to talk to the child, as well as what to expect by way of response from the child, so that the parents feel less tension and understand more about the appropriate ways of dealing with the child.

The "Toddler Program" is an educational program for multiply handicapped children between the ages of thirteen and thirty months, based upon parent-child-staff interaction. Within the toddler group, there are a number of subgroups as part of the overall continuum of services in early childhood education. Each subgroup consists of three to six pairs of parent-child, meeting at various frequencies within the week, and for varying lengths of time. Since this program is conceived as something different than individual medical rehabilitation therapy, which the child may also receive, the primary purpose of the toddler program is to establish a normal parent-child relationship. Whatever gains are made by way of infant stimulation, language, learning behavior, gross-motor improvement, parental understanding, and acceptance of the fact of the child's disability, are considered simultaneously as processes, by-products, and dividends of the primary purpose.

As part of each toddler educational session activity stations are set up with the activities chosen by the parents. The parent-child pair moves freely from one activity to another; staff members (two or more professionals) intervene where, in their judgment, intervention is needed, for as short as possible a time. Parents, being the primary intervenors, help plan the curriculum on a weekly basis, as co-equals with staff. On a rotating basis they serve as recorders in the ongoing observations of the program. Other center staff specialists—such as physical, occupational, and speech therapists, psychologists, social workers and medical specialists—serve as consultants to the toddler program.

Conductive Education System

A number of the infant/toddler programs reviewed here stress the importance of a team approach in which the roles of each discipline are interchangeable in a prenursery, nursery, or preschool setting. The Peto method, or Conductive Education System, provides for a unified approach in the education and management of cerebral palsied children by "one" teacher/therapist. The system was designed by A. Peto a number of years ago in Budapest, Hungary (Cotton 1965, Cotton and Parnwell 1967–68). The distinctive features of this system include training experiences for the teacher/therapist in education, physical, occupational, and speech therapy; and a technique called "rhythmical intention." In this model, cerebral palsied children are placed in groups in a preschool or school setting under the supervision of a teacher/therapist. He or she manages all of the activities during the regular school day which include teaching as well as the modalities of physical, occupational, and speech therapy. Throughout the day some of the activities are carried out by the technique of rhythmical intention, in which the child "speaks" his intention while carrying out the movement pattern. During this activity the children may either be seated on stools or lie on elevated slatted wooden boards. The teacher/therapist begins by providing a verbal and motor model. He or she may say, "I put my right hand up" and then orally count from one to five. The children then imitate the motor and verbal model. In some instances, instead of counting, the teacher selects one of the operative words of the movement and the children repeat this word five times. For example, operative words in the above sample might be *right, hand,* and *up.*

An experimental unit based on the Peto system was implemented at the Wernher Centre in England in 1966 under the direction of E. Cotton. In observing the unit in 1968, this writer was favorably impressed with the concept of a teacher/therapist trained to provide guidance in four of the primary disciplines usually required in the management of the cerebral palsied child. The unit consisted of a team of two teacher/therapists and a group of children ranging in age from three to twelve years. In all of their activities the children were interacting with each other and with the team of teacher/therapists in a natural manner, interchanging ideas and wishes both verbally and nonverbally. For a more detailed description of the rhythmical intention technique as applied to speech and language programming, the reader is referred to Miller (1972).

Programming for Atypical Infants and Their Families

In late 1967, United Cerebral Palsy Association, Inc., initiated a nationally organized collaborative project to delineate methods and procedures for the delivery of comprehensive services to atypical infants and their families. Beginning in 1971, the project received partial funding from the Bureau for Education of the Handicapped in the U.S. Office of Education. The five original centers, comprising the consortium, include the University Hospital School, Iowa City, Iowa; the Program for Infants and Young Children with Developmental Disabilities, University of California Medical Center, Los Angeles; the Atypical Infant Development Program, Marin County, California; United Cerebral Palsy of Greater New Orleans, Inc.; and the Meeting Street School, Providence, Rhode Island Home Development Guidance Program. Beginning in 1972, a number of "Ripple Centers" were added to the consortium.

The goals of the project included six broad objectives: (1) to pool the knowledge, skills, and experience of five centers (the consortium) providing services for handicapped infants under two years of age and their families for the purpose of mutually enriching and expanding these services and making them more comprehensive; (2) to focus on the cognitive as well as the physical development of atypical infants through strengthening the role of the educator on the staff team; (3) to emphasize the "transdisciplinary" approach to work with atypical infants. This approach requires that individual team members share their skills with one another so that any one member of the team may serve as the primary contact with a child and the child's family; (4) to strengthen the role of family members as the primary programmers for the child (including emphasis on training of parents by staff) while at the same time avoiding deleterious effects on the life style of the family; (5) to delineate a curriculum and develop a method for team training in the transdisciplinary concept of delivery of service to infants and their families; and (6) to develop a model which encompasses those elements which are judged most effective in terms of the progress of the infant with a strong focus on cognition, the promotion of the family's nurturing role, and the efficient use of personnel.

One of the primary objectives of the project had been the development of a prototype model which might, in general form, serve as a master guide for centers and clinics dealing in comprehensive services for atypical infants and their families. Preliminary reports have been disseminated in the literature (Hensley and Patterson 1970), and by papers presented at national and regional meetings of most of the major professional organizations dealing with atypical infants. These reports are beginning to give clear indications that a single model cannot be specified. The delivery of services in the various units of the Consortium and Ripples indicate that although objectives are the same, procedures differ. Nonetheless, these organizational procedures and theoretical constructs are equally viable for the populations for which they have been developed. As a consequence of this changing perspective dealing with the development of a single model, emphasis has been placed on an analysis of the other major goals.

The distinctive and significant programming concepts which have emerged from the preliminary reports of the collaborative project have included the new emphasis, and in many centers, the implementation of the importance of cognitive development in the growth of the atypical infant through the augmentation of the role of the special education teacher on the management team. Another development arising from the project is the strengthening of family involvement, and particularly the mother, as the primary programmer for the infant during the first three years of life. Perhaps the most critical contribution has been the emphasis to bring new awareness to the clinical application of the "transdisciplinary" approach in the management of atypical infants and their families. The multi- and interdisciplinary approach has a long history in the field of multiple handicaps. The transdisciplinary approach is difficult to achieve, however, because of the usual training and experience in the specialty disciplines which includes the areas of physical, occupational, and speech/language therapy. The move toward early parent-child interaction requires that the members of the team are capable of functioning in a variety of interchangable roles. Home management programs for the infant under twelve to eighteen months of age frequently use a "single facilitator." Depending on the organizational structure and theoretical orientation of the team, the facilitator may be any member of the team—physical, occupational, speech/language therapist, social worker, psychologist, or teacher. For readers interested in this type of programming, it is anticipated that the UCPA Five Year Collaborative Project Report, edited by Frances Connor, will be published in 1976.

INFANT LANGUAGE INTERVENTION PROCEDURES

ALTHOUGH EARLY LANGUAGE INTERVENTION PROGRAMS with cerebral palsied infants and toddlers has gained wide acceptance, the theoretical models for the types and kinds of programs are widely divergent. This may be accounted for, in part, by the significant changes in the study of language acquisition which have occurred in recent years. The learning theory approach represented by Mowrer (1960), Osgood and Sebeok (1965), and Skinner (1957) placed primary emphasis on the environment as the key factor in shaping linguistic performance. This approach centers attention on the immediate antecedents and consequences of behavior rather than on the interaction between the infant's cognitive structure and the environment. The modification of behavior requires that the behavior the infant is to develop is defined, and that eliciting and reinforcing stimuli are brought under control. If these conditions are met, it is assumed that the development of the child's behavior can be arbitrarily determined (Strother 1970).

The Piagetian construct contends that there is a necessary sequence of stages through which behavior develops and that development can be facilitated by arranging the environment so that the infant can engage in the next step necessary in the sequence. The period of infancy is considered to be a succession of stages of sensorimotor development in which the growth of intelligence and symbolic processes begins after the sensorimotor period ends at about eighteen months. Chomsky's (1957, 1966) contribution to the development of the theory of transformational grammar proposes that the ability to decode and organize grammatical structures is an innate function, and Lenneberg's (1967) biological theory of language present significantly different points of view. Inherent in the theory of the innateness of language is the concept of maturation, linguistic universals, and critical periods of learning.

Another factor which contributes to language programming procedures has to do with the concept of "critical periods" of learning. The way in which the infant's learning capacity develops with age is by no means fully understood. The critical period concept has been used in two distinct ways: a period "beyond" which a given phenomenon will not appear; and a period or time "during" which the infant is especially sensitive to various developmental modifiers, which if introduced at a different point in the life cycle, may have little or no effect. In the case of language acquisition this means that at a certain developmental stage linguistic signals will be optimally received and used for prelinguistic activities; and that linguistic input must be experienced at a certain stage, or it becomes decreasingly effective for use in emergent language skills (Northern and Downs 1974). Other viewpoints contend that to speak of critical periods of learning is, in essence, to describe certain temporal characteristics of the phenomenon. Connolly (1972) suggests that more emphasis should be placed on critical "events" which occur in the infant's experiences.

What is presently known about the infant's learning capacity is that sensory deprivation differs markedly depending on the age at which deprivation occurs. If it begins at or near birth the results may be devastating. In infants with cerebral palsy there is, as a consequence of the brain damage, a delayed and imperfect maturation of the brain. What is now known about intervention procedures is that the variety of stimuli which the newborn with cerebral palsy receives from the mother and total interaction with the environment is critical for the development of behavioral and language acquisition. Translated into management strategies the evidence points to the role of the speech/language clinician and other members of the team in early interaction with the mother and infant. The method of interaction is less clear. There are significant implications in these various theories for the development of programs in early language intervention. At this time there is relatively little scientific verification of the results produced by these various approaches with the cerebral palsied infant.

Based on current knowledge about language acquisition we know that there is a lawfulness and chronology in the normal child. All children begin to vocalize shortly after birth; begin to babble at about six months; use the "first word" at about ten to twelve months; combine words at about eighteen to twenty-four months; and acquire syntax almost completely by forty-eight to sixty months. All children, except those impaired by brain damage, deafness, and the severely socially deprived, learn the language of their environment. They acquire language in almost the same form, at nearly the same age, and after exposure to random language and fragmented phrases and sentences. Once they have acquired the skeleton of a complex grammar, normal children can then invent a great number of grammatically correct sentences which they have never heard before or which no one has spoken before. All of the theories acknowledge the role of linguistic input although the manner in which the infant receives the input varies from one theory to another. What can be said at this time is that both learning and maturation are necessary conditions for the development of language, but neither is sufficient (McNeill 1970).

That there is a significant correlation with cognition and psycho-social development, and that expressive language is part of the total function has been demonstrated in the recent literature. There is also an increasing body of evidence that the prosodic features of intonation, rhythm, stress, and vocal quality are being processed by the central nervous system during the first three months of life and may account for vocalization and babbling (Weir 1966, Crystal 1972–73). The role of vocalization on subsequent speech development and of babbling on the acquisition of language is, however, described differentially by learning theorists and linguists (Cruttenden 1970, de Hirsch 1970, Sedlackova 1967, and Winitz 1969). Although theories of normal language and speech acquisition vary, current knowledge of these processes indicate a maturational sequence of development. Although the infant is able to differentiate various speech sounds in the first few months of life, production does not develop at the same rate. By one month cooing sounds are made and by three months true babbling begins. That the infant begins to use these sounds in a repetitive manner probably indicates the time at which the auditory feedback loop has become effective. From about two to four months presumably the sequence of these vowel-like sounds appears to be from middle, the "shwa," to front and back vowel types. At about five or six months the repetitive production of consonant-vowel (CV) sequences begin. According to Menyuk (1972), consonant sounds used at the beginning of the babbling period, for American-English speaking children, have the features of either + voice, + grave, and + nasal and occur more frequently than those having + diffuse, + strident, and + continuant features. If the usage of the types of sounds is considered in relationship to the effort of the vocal mechanism, then sounds produced by the lips (p, b, m) are easier to produce than either alvealores (t, d, n) or velars (k, g, n) because the tongue is in a resting position for lip sounds and has to be moved purposefully for the other sounds. It has been reported that up to five or six months the sounds made by the infant do not seem to be related to the speech sounds heard. To date the relationship between production and perception at this stage of development is not clear. Menyuk (1972) indicates that it may be due to the fact that the infant is producing certain sounds because of the nature of the developing vocal mechanism while observing distinctions between other and different speech sounds because of the nature of the developing auditory mechanism.

Despite these kinds of theoretical implications the phenomenon of increased vocalization is usually considered to be predicative of eventual expressive communicative skills, and that elementary babbling sounds have a significant prelinguistic function. Babbling can be considered to be one of the earliest functions in the preprogrammed schedule of linguistic activities that Lenneberg (1967) has described as being innate processes. Its importance in the prelinguistic sequence may be that it reinforces vocalizations by means of rewards. But more than the discrimination of speech sounds is necessary to language learning. Temporal patterns of speech may be more significant than frequency formants in perceiving language (Northern and Downs 1974).

Although babbling appears to be a precursor of expressive language we know that receptive language, in the hearing child, precedes expressive language. We know that children learn from hearing things named at the time that an object is present or has their interest. The storage of recall and memory are considered to be necessary before verbalization occurs. Viewed from this point of view, perception is the process of the integration of all types of sensory stimuli, of which language is a particular type.

The effect of the kind of language environment the child receives during these early years also appears to have a critical effect on subsequent cognitive-symbolic behavior. To date, only a few manipulative learning experiments have been reported. One such by Cazden (1968) was conducted on the acquisition of grammar. Cazden (1968) indicates that the acquisition of grammar and of vocabulary require different kinds of environmental assistance. She contends that learning the meaning of words, that is the relations among ideas, seems to benefit from active instruction which comes from the conversations between the child and an interested adult.

Based on earlier studies Cazden found that mothers tend to ignore immaturities in their child's speech except errors in meaning and errors of omission. In errors of omission, or telegraphic speech, mothers usually try to expand the phrase to the nearest complete sentence. She cites the example of the child saying, "dog bark" to which the mother responds "Yes, the dog is barking." This form of response is called expansion. In expatiation the mother will respond to the same remark by saying "Yes, he's mad at the kitty." In this procedure the child is offered alternative structures, synonyms, and more complex language. In a study to determine the effects of expansion and expatiation with toddlers twenty-eight to thirty-eight months Cazden found that the group that received expatiation showed marked gains in six measures of language development, a sentence imitation test, and five measures of spontaneous speech. Cazden indicates that the evidence that expatiation aids in the acquisition of grammar suggests that richness of verbal environment, more than just good language environment, may be the critical feature in language acquisition. For additional references on the verbal environment of the child, and for systems of language programs the reader is referred to Bloom (1973), Broen (1972), Gray and Ryan (1973), Monsees (1972), and Hatten et al. (1973).

To date, there is very little scientific data concerning the development of linguistic processes in children with cerebral palsy. Two important issues arise: (1) the "manner" in which symbolic skills emerge, and (2) the kind of language "programming" approach which will best serve the individual needs of these infants. With this background, an attempt will be made to state some tentative implications concerning current methodologies in clinical use in early language intervention programs with infants and toddlers with cerebral palsy. Language strategies may be said to fall into three broad categories: (1) the learning theory approach, (2) the maturational approach, and (3) a judicious combination of both methods. The evidence for the procedurial techniques for the first two methods stem from research findings in the fields of speech and language pathology and psychology.

Learning Theory Approach

The extent to which adult vocal stimulation modifies spontaneous prelinguistic vocalization in terms of frequency of emission, length, and phoneme range of utterance in young infants has been variously investigated. Webster (1969) demonstrated that during the presentation of vocal stimuli, vocalization was suppressed. He suggested that immediately following stimulation, infants engaging in vocal play would increase the frequency of vowel or consonant types that had been presented. He hypothesized that a perceptual distinctiveness is forced upon sounds heard during stimulation. As a result they become temporarily more reinforcing when they are approximated in vocal play during the period immediately following stimulation.

To test Webster's hypothesis and to clarify some of the stimulus factors involved, Dodd (1972) measured the effects of three types of stimulation on the spontaneous vocalizations of infants nine to twelve months of age during the first fifteen minutes following stimulation. This age range was selected because imitative behavior is reported to occur after the ninth month and to reach its peak at the end of the first year (Luchsinger and Arnold 1965). Each experimental group was exposed to one of three types of stimulation for approximately fifteen minutes. Condition 1 presented prerecorded stimuli which consisted of consonant-vowel phonemes and non-speech sounds babbled in a sequence unit; condition 2 consisted of social-vocal stimulation in which the experimenter babbled the sounds in the same way as in condition 1; condition 3 consisted of social-only stimulation in which the infants were engaged in play but speech was used normally and no babbling sounds were made by the experimenter.

The results indicated that for the experimental group which received social-vocal stimulation there was an increase in the number and length of utterances. Although there was not a significant increase in the total time spent in vocalizing after stimulation, there was a strong trend in this direction. For the groups of infants who received prerecorded-vocal stimulation (condition 1), and social-only stimulation (condition 3), there was no increase in the number and length of utterances. For the three experimental groups there was no increase in the range of consonant or vowel phonemes. The findings of this experiment suggest that there is an increase in the frequency of emission of sounds after stimulation, but the increase occurs only if the vocal stimulation is accomplished by both social and vocal cues. From these data it appears that non-social stimuli, and adult speech in a play situation had no effect on the number and length of vocalization. Further, this study indicates that imitation does not play a significant role in the infant's acquisition of consonant-vowel production at the 9–12 month age.

Other studies have investigated the effects of increasing the infant's verbal output through learning procedures using conditioning techniques over a period of time. Rheingold *et al.* (1959) studies two groups of three-month-old infants over a period of six days. During the first two days a baseline was taken during which an adult looked at the infant with an expressionless face; during the two-day condition phase, the adult maintained the same behavior except that immediately after the child vocalized the adult smiled broadly, lightly touched the child, and said *tsk*. During the two-day extinction phase, the adult reverted to the baseline procedure. The results for the two groups of infants were similar: the number of vocalizations increased during the two days of conditioning and decreased during extinction. On the basis of these findings the authors conclude that: (1) the social stimulus was a positive reinforcement which produced an increase in verbal output, and (2) the presence of the social stimulus alone may have been responsible for initiating the vocalization and may have no correlation with the conditioning response made by the adult "after" the behavior occurred.

In another type of study Routh (1967) conducted an experiment using contingent social reinforcement and selective reinforcement with infants between the ages of two and seven months. One group of infants received a stimulus contingent on each consonant sound; the second group received the stimulus for each vowel; in the third group consonants and vowels were not differentiated and the reinforcement was given for any vocalization that occurred. All the groups demonstrated an overall increase in vocalization during conditioning. For the groups of children given consonant and vowel reinforcement, both groups showed appropriate selective increases in the respective categories. During extinction the curves deflected but the decrease in vocalizations was not significant. The results of this study indicate that vocalizations of infants can be increased by contingent social reinforcement and that selective reinforcement can increase the frequency of consonant and vowel production.

In a study with infants between the ages of 75 to 100 days, Todd and Palmer (1968) studied the effects of social reinforcement on vocalization. The results indicated that both groups of infants showed significant increases during conditioning, but the overall effects were greater for the group which was conditioned in the presence of an adult. For more detailed descriptions of operant verbal behavior techniques the reader is referred to Girardeau and Spradlin (1970) and Siegel (1969).

In a series of experiments, Kagan (1972) has demonstrated that toward the end of the second month of life the infant begins paying more attention to stimuli that differ markedly from those usually encountered. The relation between the duration of attention and the nature of the external event is termed the "discrepancy principle." The evidence for this type of behavior comes from studies of heart-rate changes in response to discrepant events. In a study of normal infants ranging in age from 5½ to 11½ months, Kagan administered 8 to 12 repetitions of a meaningful phrase of speech followed by a discrepant speech phrase. The older the infant the more the heart rate increased in response to the discrepant stimulus. According to Kagan, this type of response suggests active mental work in the form of selection of hypotheses. Moreover, there was an increased tendency, with age, for the infants to vocalize more 'after' the discrepant speech phrase than during its presentation.

In a long-term study of 180 infants whose reactions to a set of visual and auditory stimuli were assessed, Kagan (1972) reports that moderate attentiveness and vocalization stability occurred between thirteen to twenty-seven months. In addition, this study indicated that up to six months of age differences among normal infants in motor and cognitive development were fairly independent of the child's social class and some aspects of environment conditions. By the second half of the first year, however, differences in environmental experiences seriously affected cognitive functioning.

In another type of experimental model, Irwin (1967) designed a structured speech and language-stimulation program. He conducted a twelve-month experiment with normal young children between the ages of thirteen and thirty months to determine the effect of systematic reading of stories on phonetic production. During this period the mothers of the infants in the experimental group were instructed to spend fifteen to twenty minutes each day reading stories to their children from illustrated books. They were told to point to the pictures, and in general to furnish information supplemental to the text so that the speech sound environment impinging upon the children would be enriched. Books and reading instructions were not furnished to the parents in the control group. The children in both groups were regularly visited at two month intervals and their spontaneous speech was recorded in the International Phonetic Alphabet. The data revealed that there was little difference between the experimental and control groups in mean phoneme frequency scores from the thirteenth until about the seventeenth month. After the seventeenth month the scores for the two groups changed with the experimental group having consistently higher phoneme frequency scores.

With the advent of early home intervention for cerebral palsied infants under twelve to eighteen months a number of speech/language clinicians, in conjunction with other members of the home guidance team, are using contingent social reinforcement and selective reinforcement techniques with these infants in order to help initiate vocalization and babbling. The rationale for this type of approach is based on the concept that the building of language recognition and response, which takes place during this age period, cannot occur unless proper circumstances and experiences are programmed to help facilitate these behaviors. The purpose of these procedures is to help initiate prespeech and prelinguistic skills in order to strengthen the auditory feedback loop and the acoustic signals generated by vocal tract movement. Tangentially, these procedures help the mother or caretaker in learning how to cope with the child's lack of verbal responsiveness. The mother-child relationship is probably significantly enhanced when she acquires techniques which aid her in initiating and promoting an active communicative interplay between herself and the child.

Maturational Approach

Most prenursery and nursery programs incorporate the modalities of the maturational approach in the total programming of activities. Only two studies in the current literature have reported on the effects of a systematic evaluation of this approach in cognitive-symbolic behavior with infants and toddlers. Both of these experiments were conducted by Jones and her associates at the UCLA prenursery school for cerebral palsied children.

Sensory Story

The child with cerebral palsy often has a number of sensory deficits in varying degrees and combinations. Some of the problems of older cerebral palsied children may be the result of deprivation of stimulus experiences needed at certain optimal periods of learning. Barrett and Jones (1967) state that if there are, in the human infant as in animals, critical periods in learning, the timing of sensory training especially during the first three years, is of crucial importance. Schermann (1966) reports that visual, tactile, kinesthetic, auditory, and olfactory sensations are the child's raw materials for thinking and learning; and the Bobaths (1967) emphasize the need for early stimulation of prioprioception, tactile sensations, and stereognosis. Birch and Lefford (1967) report that "intersensory integration is dependent upon the kind of intrasensory information that is made available by the separate sense systems as the raw materials for integration."

In the very young child, only gross methods for determining corticosensory function are currently available. However, if the development of communicative skills are dependent on a variety of input stimuli, defects in the sensory mechanisms from birth and/or deprivation of sensory experiences in the infant require early intervention. One such technique developed to provide multi-sensory training is the "Sensory Story" designed by Barrett and Jones (1967). The story was originally developed to measure the effect of repetition of a structured experience on motor function of the affected hand in young hemiplegic children. Barrett and Jones (1969) used the Sensory Story with two groups of cerebral palsied infants and toddlers between the ages of eighteen and thirty-eight months. Results of the experiments indicated: (1) during the story all the children were observed to communicate verbally or nonverbally in direct response to the situation or object; (2) the children who had achieved some expressive speech responded with single words and two- and three-word sentences; (3) the children com-

TABLE 6.1

SENSORY STORY

Nancy* was sound asleep.
"Hi, Nancy. It's time to get up."
A *soft* red blanket covered Nancy.
Nancy rubbed her hand on the *soft* blanket. The blanket felt *soft* and *smooth*.
On the floor was a rug. The rug was *soft* and *bumpy*.
Nancy rubbed her hand on the *soft, bumpy* rug.
Mummy† gave Nancy her pink brush. The brush was *stiff* and *hard*.
Nancy brushed her hair with the *stiff, hard* brush.
After breakfast Nancy played outside.
Nancy played with the ball.
Nancy rolled the ball on the ground.
She found another ball.
The ball was *round* and *sharp*.
Nancy played in the sand. The sand was *dry*.
Nancy wanted to make a sand cake.
Nancy poured water into the sand.
Splash, splash went the water in the sand. The sand was *wet*.
Nancy took the *wet* sand in her hand.
She made a *wet* sand cake.
Mummy called, "Nancy come help me get dinner ready for Daddy."†
Mummy helped Nancy wash her hands.
The wash cloth was *wet* and *hot*.
Mummy gave Nancy a *cold* ice cube. Nancy put the *cold* ice cube in Daddy's glass.
The ice cube was *wet* and *cold*.
Nancy heard something outside.
What did Nancy hear?
Nancy ran to the door.
Nancy opened the door.
She saw Daddy in his car.
Daddy honked his horn to Nancy.
"Hi, Daddy. Dinner's ready."

Contrasting stimuli are printed in italic.
*Child's own name. †Other appropriate person in family.

Barrett and Jones (1967), p. 450.

municated attitudes toward the story; (4) identified objects; (5) expressed ideas which were familiar by association, and ideas which suggested identification with the story; and (6) a few of the children showed indications of growing comprehension in concepts of association.

The story is set up purposefully as a simple, uncomplicated presentation of "contrasting stimuli." It provides a vehicle for a natural and simple mode of language interaction. The mother and/or clinician can develop an infinite variety of stories with appropriate objects to meet the child's growing environmental interests. It enables parents, teachers, and clinicians with a special time to talk to the child and also an opportunity to take time to listen to his or her way of communication whether by language or behavior. The story technique provides a setting and time for sharing familiar experiences in a one-to-one relationship by means of disparate sensory stimuli. When the technique is used by a teacher/therapist during prenursery sessions, a separate, small quiet story room should be used with a cutout table and chair for the child. Throughout the story, one object at a time is placed on the child's table. The responses are recorded in direct relation to each object used. This type of record keeping provides a method for longitudinal analysis and also helps guide the teacher/clinician in making on going changes of materials. The total time for telling the Story may vary with each child but should usually involve only a few minutes per day. The rationale, philosophy, and organization of the Sensory Story provides an excellent approach to language stimulation and for this reason is suggested as one type of specific technique in language intervention with cerebral palsied infants and toddlers. A sample of one type of Sensory Story is shown on Table 6.1.

Confined Space

Children with cerebral palsy are usually immobile in infancy and experience limited opportunities to build concepts of body and space relationships through proprioceptive and exteroceptive sensory feedback. The Piagetian theory contends that it is only through gradually increasing sensorimotor experience acquired during the first eighteen months of life that the child acquires spatial links. A child who cannot look and touch at the same time or turn his head to locate the source of sound has little chance of integrating different sense perceptions (Ram 1963). To determine the effects of an early structured sensory approach, Barrett et al. (1967) explored the use of group experience in a "confined space" on the verbal, motor, and social behavior of cerebral palsied infants and toddlers twenty-three to forty months of age. The purpose of the study was to determine whether experience in a confined space would heighten perceptual awareness and lead to more interpersonal reactions, and an increase in communication and purposeful activity.

The confined space, termed the "little playhouse," consists of a space surrounded by a four-foot high partition providing 2½ square feet per occupant, i.e., about 6 × 5 feet for 11 individuals. A small chair is provided for the adult recorder, and except for watching to prevent children from hurting one another, the recorder is instructed to allow the children complete freedom. For this experiment, the total time in the confined space ranged from approximately 10 to 24 minutes, for a period of approximately 4½ months.

The results of the study indicated that the confined space heightened the verbal response of all children equally during the experience. The effect on movement was to stimulate the least active children and calm the more lively ones. Confining the space affected the social responses of all of the children in a like manner while in the playhouse. Also a delayed reaction of greater social activity occurred with the less social children when they were returned to the nursery school area. The authors indicate that while each child appeared to gain in overall development as a result of the confined experience, the extent of verbal, social, and motor growth was more closely related to the child's individual need, and therefore not equal.

An analysis of the data also indicated that only during the confined space were the verbal, motor, and social responses significantly related. The mean verbal responses were highest during the period in the confined space. In this situation, the children responded holistically with attempted words and sounds, bodily movement, and interpersonal actions. Before the confined space experience when a child moved he tended to verbalize; after the playhouse experience, when he verbalized he was social. The awareness of other children in the confined space, and each one's identification with others, seemingly fused verbalization to social activity after the children returned to the nursery play area. This observation lead Barrett et al. (1967) to speculate about the role of proprioceptive feedback from fine movements in integrating perception and mediating verbal responses. On the basis of these findings the authors raised the following questions: Did the confined space experience assist in overall perceptual integration? Were the concepts of space, body image, and human identity advanced to the extent that increased movement was possible and higher level symbolic verbal and social responses were facilitated?

A second experiment, conducted by Jones et al. (1969), explored behavior and communication both verbal and nonverbal with children aged twenty-eight to thirty-nine months. Two sets of recordings were made: one during the time within the confined space, and the second immediately following in the outside nursery area. The total time in the confined space ranged from 10 to 24 minutes during which two to three one-minute recordings were made for each child. Four behaviors were recorded: (1) state of the child on entry to the confined space and at each minute of observation; (2) verbal communication; (3) nonverbal communication; and (4) social interaction.

Analysis of the recordings indicate great individual differences in the children during the six-week experimental period. Jones *et al.* (1969) state that while gains are difficult to summate for the total group certain trends were noted. Nonverbal communication and social interaction were increased during periods in the confined space as compared to periods outside. For some children this technique resulted in an increased ability to relate to other children, and in a desire to initiate and/or imitate play. Seven of the eight children were rated quite high in nonverbal communication during the first session; all increased nonverbal responses during succeeding sessions, indicating a response to a situation of closeness of peers. Five of the eight children initiated language patterns or used language in the first session, and one child showed more verbal communication in the confined space than at any time outside. When the children left the confined space the majority again became passive observers or isolates.

What these two procedures have demonstrated in repeated use with younger-aged children at the UCLA Prenursery School is that opportunities to experience a variety of sensory experiences, in a natural and play situation, encourage the development of vocalizations and attempted speech, and promote the establishment of peer relationships, an awareness of environmental objects, and the effects of purposeful activity.

INFANT LANGUAGE PROGRAMMING IN A TRANSDISCIPLINARY MODEL

One of the most significant developments in recent years has been the awareness of the potentialities of the crucial period that occurs immediately after birth and during the first few years of life for the infant born with neurological impairment. What is presently known about perceptual-cognitive-symbolic development clearly suggests that the pattern of the child's ultimate behavioral development may be set during the early months and first three years of life. It is equally clear that the effect of variations in the environment may serve to either facilitate or inhibit optimal development; that the mother or caretaker's behaviors significantly mediate the infant's interaction with the environment; and that the mother's behaviors are contingent upon the infant and his or her responses. Of equal importance is the development of intervention programs for atypical infants and their families as young as two months of age, and of prenursery and nursery schools. As part of these programs the development and clinical application of the "transdisciplinary approach," stemming from the UCPA National

Collaborative Study, may prove to be one of the hallmarks of early intervention. All of these developments are beginning to provide extremely optimistic implications that some aspects of perceptual-cognitive-symbolic
handicaps may be significantly modified by appropriate and manipulative
early intervention strategies. While it is too early to know the degree of
effectiveness of this kind of intervention there are some preliminary indications that transdisciplinary programming may have important consequences on earlier and more normal language acquisition.

In the transdisciplinary approach each member of the team assumes
interchangeable roles in management procedures. For example, the speech/
language clinician is responsible not only for the basic theories and skills of
his or her discipline but must also have a basic knowledge of the skills of the
other team members. This involves the sharing of knowledge in such a way
that each member of the team is able to help guide the mother in her total
interaction with the infant. The move away from the interdisciplinary approach, in which a number of therapists and specialists interact with the
family and infant, to a "single facilitator," at least during the first year, is
another distinctive feature of this method. If the speech/language clinician
is the single facilitator she is responsible not only for fostering language behaviors but also needs to be skilled in helping the mother in all types of
activities which include proper feeding, handling, motor positioning, etc. If
another member of the team assumes the role of primary facilitator, the
speech/language clinician, while releasing individual involvement, is still
responsible and accountable for the infant's progress.

Transdisciplinary Approach in Language Intervention

Although no one specific model of infant language programming appears
now to take precedence, the philosophical and clinical application of the
transdisciplinary approach more closely incorporates emerging information
concerning child development. No attempt will be made to describe specific
techniques and procedures for this type of approach. Rather, a flow-pattern
of sequences will be offered to serve as guidelines by teams to be included
with their own distinctive methods of the delivery of total services to the infant and toddler with cerebral palsy and the family. The delineation of the
infant period, birth through twelve to eighteen months, and the toddler period from eighteen to thirty-six months is made primarily for purposes of
description, although there are some procedural strategies which lend
themselves to these two age groups.

Infant Period

Almost all of the activities of the team members, or facilitator, are carried
out in the home during this period. The infant born with cerebral palsy is

usually destined to experience a variety of psycho-social, cognitive, and communicative deprivations in varying degrees of severity. During the first few months, or as soon as the disability becomes apparent, the parents, and particularly the mother, find themselves in a crisis situation. The physical and medical management of the child becomes the primary priority. The mother-child interaction and the variety of stimuli which the infant receives become stilted and modified. Yet it is this very variety of stimuli and the quality of maternal handling that is so vital and essential to normal behavioral development.

Although there is very little scientific documentation concerning how much time the mother spends talking to the child with cerebral palsy, there is an abundance of clinical evidence that mothers talk less to their handicapped children. Case history reports compiled by the writer over a three-year period demonstrate that the reasons most mothers give for this lack of communication falls into two broad categories: because of the complexity of the physical management, especially during the first year, almost all of the mother's time is spent in overall physical care and relatively little time can be spared to talk and play with the child; and when attempts at vocal play are made the child often does not respond, or responds inappropriately so that in time the mother gradually decreases her talking. An observation made by a much smaller group of mothers is that they have found that when they play with their children they notice that the baby's attempted vocalization often triggers a number of violent "spasms" (i.e., extensor spasms). Assuming that these spasms may be painful, or may cause additional damage, these mothers report that they try to minimize their talking and try to keep the child as quiet as possible.

Perhaps the most important feature of intervention begins at this time and may serve to shape the ultimate development of the child. The facilitator needs to show the mother in the home how to become the mother of a deviant child. This includes helping her to learn how to bathe, feed, dress, and play with the child; how to work through her own feelings of depression and in some cases guilt concerning her handicapped baby; how to cope with her child's often bizarre responses, or lack of response; how to learn to talk to her child, and to pick up cues which will help her recognize the baby's vocalizations and gurglings, even though they are infrequent or different from those of other children of the same age.

Perhaps the most significant link in initiating expressive language in infants with cerebral palsy is vocalization and babbling. Clinical experience has clearly demonstrated that these children are much more quiet than normal infants. It is possible that controlled manipulation of the distance receptors, namely vision and hearing, may provide an avenue of stable information for the cerebral palsied infant. These two systems are readily modifiable and are the basic ingredients of symbolic responses (Robinson 1970, Connolly 1969). One way of providing this stable information may be by the implementation of augmented auditory feedback. Research by Yeni-Komshian et al. (1968) has demonstrated that children with less practice in generating speech motor activity, were also less vulnerable to delayed auditory feedback (DAF). These findings would appear to indicate that the amount of change in speech is less closely related to the amount of experience a child has had in practicing the motor organization of speech than it is to the "non-motor" aspects of the organization of speech. A procedure using an auditory feedback mechanism (AFM) is currently being field tested by the writer with cerebral palsied infants and toddlers. There are some preliminary indications that this type of intervention may serve as an adjunctive aid in facilitating both motor and non-motor aspects of speech.

Another procedure which sometimes helps to focus attention on the infant's vocalizations is to have the mother keep weekly or monthly tape recordings. As a rule, most mothers will state that their child does not make enough vocalization to record. It is interesting to note, for the mothers who pursue this procedure, that they soon begin to recognize the time at which these babblings usually occur and are often surprised at the amount of "cooing" that their child does. Some report that her child does this kind of "talking" in the morning after awakening; others find it occurs more frequently after bathing or feeding. Even minimal amounts of vocalization by the baby spur most mothers, without any training on the part of the facilitator, to begin to respond to their baby's babblings by more frequent eye contact and play activities. The tape recording also serves a second function. It provides the speech/language clinician with an opportunity to evaluate the child's emerging expressive language on a longitudinal basis and to offer the facilitator suggestions for the mother.

Other activities in the home management program include helping the mother to learn how to position her child for head and sitting control during feeding, which also facilitates more frequent vocalizations; and how to use toys and other common objects in the home in meaningful play activities. Feeding procedures frequently used are those developed by Mueller (1972, 1975).

Toddler Period

Most large communities, in conjunction with special service clinics and centers and some public schools, offer prenursery school programs for children between eighteen and thirty-six months. Increasingly, many of the prenursery schools include a teacher as part of the team. The primary goal of the educational model is to provide experiences of daily living in a social group. In the transdisciplinary model the activities usually include opportunities for learning in a natural play environment with toys, games, and other common household objects adapted to meet the child's physical needs, and socialization activities with peers. In this type of model the members of the team participate in most of the classroom activities in interchangeable roles. The goals of this approach are to promote psycho-social interaction in as normal a setting as possible and to include therapeutic management as the need arises. The parents are encouraged to become part of the prenursery activities so that they can continue the same kind of experiences and attitudes in the home.

COMMUNICATION AIDS

Many different types of aphonic communication aids have been developed over the past two decades for severely involved cerebral palsied individuals who cannot speak (La Voy 1957; Feallock 1958; Evans 1960; M. V. Jones 1961; Goldberg and Fenton 1961; Miller and Carpenter 1964; Jenkin 1967). Most of these devices were designed for older children and young adults who had failed to develop expressive language after many years of traditional speech therapy. Some of these earlier aids consisted of word/picture language boards; some incorporated electronic features for pointing devices; and some were adaptations of electric typewriters. In general, the rationale underlying the use of aphonic aids was predicated upon a choice of last resort.

More recently, the "early" use of language boards has been implemented with severely involved cerebral palsied children. Clinical evidence is beginning to emerge which indicates that many young children under five years of age are capable of using this type of equipment, and in some instances it markedly facilitates vocalization and attempted expressive language. A number of selected types of communication aids will be reviewed in this section. For a more detailed review of the various kinds of aids the reader is referred to Luster and Vanderheiden (1974), Vicker (1974), and Kafafian (1970–71).

Non-Mechanical Language Boards

For young children who are educable and aware of their environment the frustrations encountered by their inability to make themselves understood often causes serious intellectual and social-emotional problems, as well as delays in language development. Quite often parents and other individuals in their environment react to the lack of intelligibility by a decrease in talking and in time the child may discontinue speech attempts and remain silent. For children who fall into this category the early use of a language board may serve as an excellent facilitator in the development of language skills. McDonald and Schultz (1973) have developed and used a variety of language boards and signalling systems. One type of language board designed by these authors provides for the display of letters, words, pictures, and sentences. An adaption of the Fitzgerald Key is used as the system for teaching language structure. This method divides language into the structures of "who," "what," "when" words and verbs. For the cerebral palsied child, sentence structure can be facilitated by adding one column for articles, conjunctions, and prepositions, and a second column for adjectives and adverbs. A replication of the typewriter keyboard can be used for spelling out words and as a way of preparing the child for typing; and a number column can be added to facilitate expression of numerical concepts. The board can be constructed for use on a wheelchair tray, or as a hinged board, which can be worn by the ambulatory child. McDonald and Schultz indicate that each language board must be individually developed and its characteristics based on a careful evaluation of each child's physical, intellectual, and educational status. This type of board is relatively inexpensive and is functionally practical in that the specific language materials required by the child can be adapted to his developmental needs. Vicker (1974) presents a description of a similar language board developed at the Iowa University Hospital School.

Mechanical Language Boards

An electronic language board, the Auto-Monitoring Communication Board (Auto-Com), has been developed by the Cerebral Palsy Communication Group (CPCG), an interdisciplinary team at the University of Wisconsin–Madison. This device incorporates a matrix of proximity detectors which are coupled with a delayed activation mechanism. This mechanism provides a monitoring system which is sensitive to the "lack" of motion rather than discrete motion as in normal switch or keyboard arrangements. The Auto-Com is completely contained within a 1½" lapboard and is wheelchair mountable using standard Everst and Jenning wheelchair brackets. The surface of the board is a hard, unbroken sheet of formica which can be used for eating or other work when not being used for communication, but is always available in front of the child.

To operate the Auto-Com the user need only have limited pointing skill. The individual activates the mechanism by positioning the magnet near the character he wants printed and holds it in the area for a short time. Because the monitoring system is able to track even erratic pointing or momentary loss of control incorrect letters will not be printed. In addition to the monitoring feature the Auto-Com has the capacity to "print-out" characters. In this manner the child is able to communicate independently and on his own time, without the full-time attendance of a second person. With the Auto-Com the teacher/clinician need only take the time necessary to read the message. In addition to printing out letters, an accessory component called the "Wordmaster" provides for the print-out of words, phrases, sentences, and multi-sentences.

To help meet the various types of communication requirements of the handicapped, a variety of output forms are available for use with the Auto-Com. The most significant for educational purposes is the Television Read-out. This system provides the user with clear visual feedback while at the same time enabling him complete correctability. If hard copy is desired, the Auto-Com can directly control a teletypewriter or any other standard printer which uses American Standard Code for Information Interchange. Recently, the Auto-Com has been interfaced with an IBM Correctable Selectric Typewriter. This allows the user to produce hard copy while still retaining the ability to correct. It can also be directly interfaced with most computers. This feature offers potential employment opportunities in the computer field for the severely handicapped, and may also be used for computer-aided instruction. Experiments, in progress, are being conducted involving the use of the Auto-Com in controlling a voice synthesizer. It is anticipated that this procedure may ultimately make it possible for the non-vocal to "speak" through the use of synthesized speech (Luster and Vanderheiden 1974).

Second Language Systems

The two language boards described above use English syntactical patterns and alphabet. Two language boards have been designed which use a nonoral second language system (Bliss Symbols 1972–73), and the Initial Teaching Alphabet (Shane 1972).

The "Ontario Crippled Children's Center Symbol Communication Research Project" (1972–73) developed an electronic device using visual symbols developed by Charles Bliss. The system contains 340 Bliss Symbols which are described as a universal expression system based upon symbolic logic. In this format, the meaning of the word is conveyed by a symbol. For example, x means (more); + means (of, belongs to); and ·l means (before). The symbols are placed in trays and the child points to the selected symbols to convey his or her thoughts (McNaughton 1974).

A technique using the Initial Teaching Alphabet (i/t/a) was designed by Shane (1972) to be used in conjunction with a specially constructed electronic conversation board called the "Expressor." The device contains a circular electronically controlled light display. Templates with the language materials are placed within the circumference of the circle. When the user activates the control switch the light can be moved to the section of the template which contains the desired orthographic symbol.

The i/t/a system was selected for the language system because it provides a one-to-one sound to symbol correspondence. With this method one symbol (grapheme) represents one sound (phoneme), and all of the symbols are represented in lower case form. In the Roman alphabet more than two thousand combinations of the twenty-six alphabet characters are required to represent English words in writing. In contrast, by correct sequencing of the forty-four i/t/a symbols, a nonverbal communicator using the Expressor is capable of producing graphemically all the words of the English language.

Shane conducted a sixteen week experimental training program with two nonverbal mentally retarded, cerebral palsied teenaged children. During this period both children learned to use sixteen of the symbols. In a follow-up evaluation of visual tests of symbols recognition, auditory tests of sound discrimination and auditory sequential memory, and word recognition and spelling both subjects were able to use the symbols in nonverbal expressive tasks.

Sound Signalling Aids

For the severely mentally retarded cerebral palsied child who is bedfast Hagen *et al.* (1973) designed an audio-signalling system called the "Electromechanical Device." This device consists of a battery operated audio-oscillator which emits a clear, crisp tone through a loudspeaker. The level which the individual presses to activate the sound is attached to a splint which can be tailor-made to fit each person's most easily controlled muscle group. The mechanism is 3" by 6" and weighs two pounds.

In general, nonverbal patients in a hospital environment most frequently need to communicate three basic needs: "I need help," "Yes," and "No." The type of information which these patients want to communicate usually falls into four main categories—wants, feeling, people, and places. Using these four categories, the items that each patient most frequently wanted to communicate were listed on his individual code card.

The children in the experiment with the Electromechanical Device ranged in age from ten to twelve years. They were taught a simple code which consisted of four signals; a continuous sound stood for "I need help"; one short sound for "Yes"; two sounds for "No"; and three short sounds for "see the list." Three of the four patients learned how to use the code system in six weeks. During this period, the authors conducted inservice training sessions with the staff associated with the patients. For the three children who were able to use the sound system the clinical staff reported that they appeared to be more relaxed physically, and therefore easier to take care of and treat. There was a fairly wide range in level of usage of the device by the three patients. They would frequently make random sounds with the device, either when they were alone or with each other. The authors interpreted this type of behavior to be a form of vocal play similar to that of a young child developing speech. Some of the patients used the device to indicate their basic needs as taught in the code. Others expanded the code beyond the basic system. The degree to which the children continued to use the communication system depended upon the reaction of the responding persons in their environment. When members of the staff did not respond to the sound signal some of the children stopped attempting to communicate. Conversely, when staff members responded to the signal the amount of communication by means of the device increased.

Prosthetic Devices

The National Institute for Rehabilitation Engineering (NIRE) has developed a family of electronic speaking aids which can be used as prosthetic devices with some cerebral palsied individuals. Some models use a voice sensor attached to a headband, or eyeglass temple bar, which is connected to an electronic processing network. Another type employs a special contact sensor which can be placed on the neck. The speech aid amplifies and filters frequency content and reproduces the improved speech through a loudspeaker built into the speech aid.

The "Electronic Speaking Aid" is especially constructed to meet each individual's speech needs. Donald Selwyn, Director of NIRE (1974) indicates that a person's speech is tested with laboratory equipment against approximately eighteen different speech processing networks. A panel of listeners determines which combination yields the best speech. The selected parameters are then built into the speech aid. Although miniaturized models have been used clinically with cerebral palsied children and adults, the NIRE engineers emphasize that the device will not work for all cerebral palsied individuals (Medical World News 1973).

In 1965, Berko reported on an "Auditory Feedback Mechanism" (AFM) developed for him by electrical engineers at Cornell University. The laboratory model of the AFM consisted of a microphone which was fed into a preamplifier which boosted the output through a variable band filter, and the output of the bank filter was fed into a audio-amplifier to the binoural headphones worn by the speaker.

Berko's experiment with the AFM was conducted with athetoid adults to determine whether preselected amplified band pass frequencies would aid in speech intelligibility. In a series of experimental feedback conditions the subject read a fifty three-word test passage. A prerecording was made of each subject's "unaided" speech to establish a baseline. A series of experiments were carried out with three experimental conditions: (1) accelerated, amplified feedback without band pass filtering; (2) accelerated, amplified feedback with high band pass filtering; and (3) accelerated, amplified low band pass filtering. Tape recordings of the three conditions were evaluated by a panel of judges to determine "intelligibility" scores. The results indicated that amplified high band filtering resulted in speech which was globally judged (against the baseline condition) to be smoother, better paced, and easier to understand with the experimental population of athetoids.

Subsequently, a portable transistorized model was used with athetoid and spastic children. Berko (1967) reports that 70 percent of the athetoids showed significant increases in intelligibility with amplified high band pass filtering; and that about 40 percent of the spastics showed some measure of improvement. There was little consistency in the type of band pass filtering that produced the best results for the spastic subjects. A trend was noted that for the spastic individuals, the condition of feedback with low band pass filtering appeared to provide the best results.

The AFM and the "Electronic Speaking Aid" are prosthetic devices designed to be worn by the individual to produce changes in speech intelligibility. Ongoing pilot research by Lencione (1974) is being conducted to determine whether the AFM can be used as an early interventive technique to facilitate phonation and vocalization in infants with known or suspected neurological deficits. Lencione has modified the AFM mechanism to provide for more discrete input and output signals and controls, and adapted the headphones for use with infants. Preliminary findings with fifty cerebral palsied infants is beginning to give some indications that the AFM may function as a facilitator in initiating expressive language behaviors in some of these children.

7

Auditory Processing

E. HARRIS NOBER

INTRODUCTION

Incidence and Etiology of Auditory Impairments in Cerebral Palsy

CEREBRAL PALSY (CP) does not necessarily produce any pathognomonic aberration of the auditory mechanism. Although some types of auditory impairments are frequently associated with it, it is doubtful that any specific hearing impairment is unique to cerebral palsy. As most of the etiologic agents of cerebral palsy can concommitantly cause destruction to the auditory mechanism, there is a significantly greater incidence of auditory impairments in this population. In addition, cerebral palsy children are also more susceptible to the adventitious childhood diseases that also produce hearing loss.

Table 7.1 lists twenty-two etiological agents of cerebral palsy and shows whether they can cause peripheral and/or central auditory disorders. Note that all of the agents listed can cause central auditory disorders, while about 73 percent cause peripheral disorders as well; clearly, it is understandable that the incidence of hearing loss would be higher.

Estimates of hearing loss in a cerebral palsy population show a wide range, from 6 to 41 percent. There are several reasons for the wide incidence variations. One reason concerns the criteria to determine whether a hearing loss actually exists. Some studies consider only the critical pure tone range for speech (e.g., 500, 1000, 2000 Hz) while others consider the entire testing spectrum from 250 Hz to 8000 Hz. Since, characteristically the cerebral palsy population shows an affinity for a high tone loss and in many instances the loss is beyond the upper limit of the critical speech range, these subjects may or may not be included as part of hearing loss statistics.

A second criterion relates to the upper threshold level for normalcy with a criterion that has ranged from 10 to 30 decibels (dB). One study

TABLE 7.1
ETIOLOGIC AGENTS OF CEREBRAL PALSY AND AUDITORY DISORDERS

Pathology		Cerebral Palsy	Auditory Disorders	
			Peripheral	Central
Prenatal	Genetic-heredity	X	X	X
	Rubella	X	X	X
	Radiation	X		X
	Toxemias	X	X	X
	Structural deformities	X	X	X
	Erythroblastosis fetalis	X	X	X
Paranatal	Jaundice	X	X	X
	Abnormal labor-delivery	X		X
	Prematurity	X		X
	Anoxia	X	X	X
	Trauma	X	X	X
	Cerebral vascular accident	X		X
Postnatal	Meningo-encephitic	X	X	X
	Trauma	X	X	X
	Tumors	X	X	X
	Neurological diseases	X	X	X
	Toxemias	X	X	X
	Vascular-hemalytic	X	X	X
	Convulsions	X		X
	Endocrine	X		X
	Allergies	X	X	X

reported a CP hearing loss incidence of 18 percent with a 20 dB loss criterion but an 85 percent incidence with a 10 dB loss criterion.

A third reason for incidence variation relates to grouping according to cerebral palsy types. Athetoids have the highest incidence of hearing loss, so general cerebral palsy statistics vary with the percentage of athetoids in the group. Hopkins *et al.* (1954) provided a specific breakdown: spastics, 7.2 percent; rigidity, 13.7 percent; ataxic, 18.4 percent; athetoid, 18.4 percent; but these may vary widely. For example, Nakano (1966) reported spastic, 38.8 percent; athetoid, 33.3 percent; spastic-athetoid, 16.7 percent. Other variables affecting the incidence relate to age of the subjects, the kinds of tests employed, the ability to condition the subjects, and the success in eliciting appropriate responses.

When the various estimates of incidence are collated without regard to cerebral palsy type, the mean incidence is approximately 22 percent and the median 17 percent. In general, it can be said that the incidence of hearing loss in the cerebral palsy population is about 20 percent.

ANATOMY AND PHYSIOLOGY OF THE AUDITORY PROCESSING MECHANISM

The following discussion will provide a basic foundation for lay students not acquainted with this area.

External Ear (Outer Ear)

This consists of the auricle (pinna) and a 2.5 cm. canal called the *external auditory meatus* which terminates at the *tympanic membrane* or *eardrum*. The framework of the canal is composed of a yellow elastic cartilage. The cartilage of the outer half is covered by an epithelial tissue which contains the *cerumen (wax) glands* and hair follicles. There are also nine *auricular muscles* that serve no functional purpose for hearing. In fact, the entire outer ear serves only to direct the sound to the middle ear and provide some protection against physical trauma. The blood supply to the outer ear emanates from branches of the superficial temporal arteries and veins and the posterior auricular arteries and veins. The nerve supply is fed from the auricular nerve and the auricular branches of the facial, glossopharyngeal, and vagus nerves.

Middle Ear

This is located between the outer and inner ear divisions (Figure 7.1). It is separated from the outer ear by the tympanic membrane (eardrum) and

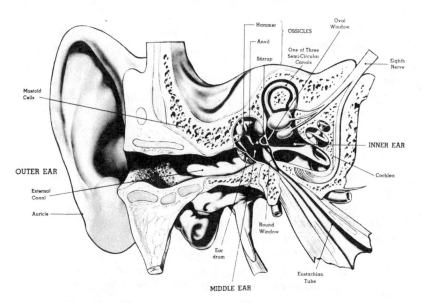

Figure 7.1.   The human ear. *Courtesy of the Sonotone Corporation*

from the inner ear by the oval and round windows. The middle ear cavity or the *tympanum* is an irregular space, approximately one to two centimeters in length which normally contains air supplied from the nasopharynx via the eustachian (auditory) tube. The *tympanic membrane* is a thin, semi-transparent, pearl-gray structure that is inclined at an oblique 50° angle. Its conical shape facilitates a broader frequency output with minimal distortion. The eardrum is attached to the bony wall of the canal by an incomplete ring of fibrous tissue; the incomplete section is located above and called the *pars flaccida* or *Shrapnell's membrane*. This area represents approximately one-eighth of the tympanic membrane; the remaining seven-eighths is the *pars tensa*. A perforation in the pars flaccida will not result in any appreciable hearing loss, but a perforation in the pars tensa area can produce a demonstrable hearing loss. The degree of hearing loss depends on the location and size of the perforation. Functionally, the maximum loss associated with pathologies of the eardrum is about 30 decibels. The vibration of low frequencies differs at the central, peripheral, and intermediate zones of the eardrum. The central portion around the umbo pumps like a piston.

The *middle ear cavity (tympanum)* is bounded by six walls: (1) the lateral wall is the tympanic membrane; (2) the medial wall has the oval and round windows; (3) the anterior wall contains the superior opening of the eustachian tube; (4) the posterior wall leads to the mastoid antrum; (5) the floor; and (6) the upper wall that separates the middle ear cavity from the cranial cavity.

Within the tympanum is the *ossicular chain*, a leverage system, indeed a mechanical transducer, composed of the three smallest bones (ossicles) of the body. It is designed to transmit sound energy to the cochlea: (1) the *malleus* (hammer) (2) the *incus* (anvil) and (3) the *stapes* (stirrup). The malleus has three parts: the *manubrium* or handle, the *neck*, and the *head*. The manubrium attaches to the apex (umbo) of the eardrum in a manner that keeps the tympanic membrane taut. This tension is maintained by the aid of the *tensor tympani muscle* which pulls the eardrum upward and inward. The head of the malleus articulates with a second ossicle, the incus; this malleo-incudal (incudomaleolar) articulation is covered by a thin capsular ligament. The joint rocks as a unit until the sounds become intense, then the coupling loosens dissipating some of the energy and at the same time adding some distortion. The incus has a short process and a long process. The short process projects into a space below the horizontal semicircular canal, and the long process articulates with the stapes in a ball and socket joint. The stirrup shaped stapes has three parts: a *footplate*, an *anterior crus*, and a *posterior crus*. The footplate is fitted into the oval window and held there by the *annular ligament*. The anterior and posterior crura unite at the head of the stapes, which subsequently articulates with the incus to form the *incustapedial joint*. Another small muscle, the *stapedius*, attaches to the neck of the stapes and serves as an antagonistic to the tensor tympani, thus exerting an outward and downward pull. The stapes vibration for moderate sound is a piston-type back-and-forth rocking motion around the more rigidly fixed posterior border. High intensity sound yields a side-to-side rocking motion. As a result of the total mechanical ossicular system, there is a 20–35 dB increase in force. Hearing loss associated with disarticulation of the ossicular chain is about 28 dB.

Below the oval window is the *round window*, which leads to the scala tympani. It is covered by an elastic membrane which provides flexibility for a reciprocal movement with the oval window. Thus, as the stapes pushes the oval window inward, the round window bulges outward and vice-versa. Resistance in either of these windows lowers the efficiency of the inner ear by reducing the compressibility of the cochlear mechanism. If the ossicular chain is defective and sound goes directly to the round window, there is a cancel effect of about 12 dB.

The *eustachian tube* connects the middle ear cavity to the nasopharnyx. Its superior opening is midway between the floor and roof of the anterior wall. Inferiorly, it communicates with the lateral wall of the nasopharynx. In infants, this tube is almost horizontal and can be a source of middle ear infections, especially when the child sucks the bottle in a prone position. But as the child's head elongates, the middle ear opening is raised about 2 cm. above the nasopharyngeal opening so fluids are less likely to be trapped and subsequently infected. Because of its elastic tissue composition, the pharyngeal orifice of the tube is normally closed but opens from increased pressure during yawning, sneezing, yelling, shouting, and swallowing from the contraction of the tensor veli palantini, the levator palantium, and the salpingopharyngeous muscle; the tensor is the major muscle. The open eustachian tube permits outside air to enter the tympanum to ventilate and equalize the pressure that exists between the middle ear cavity and atmospheric air pressure peripheral to the body. It also permits effusion of fluids from the tympanum to the nasopharynx by a ciliary movement outward. Ventilation replenishes the absorbed oxygen in the air trapped in the tympanum.

Thus, the normal middle ear mechanism serves to conduct sound through the ossicular chain to the oval window. This is called the *ossicular route*. The overall mechanical leverage of the ossicular chain provides the significant 20–35 dB increase in pressure that is needed at the oval window to push the cochlear fluids which have an impedance of about 20–35 dB. The ossicular chain also serves as a protective mechanism against outside trauma. Intense sounds will loosen the usual tight coupling of the malleus and incus so that they no longer move as one functional unit, allowing the energy to dissipate.

The intrinsic *intra-aural middle ear* muscles involuntarily contract at about 70–90 dB (250–4000 Hz) to increase the tension and ultimately attenuate the sound. The tensor tympani is larger and stronger than the stapedius. Contraction ultimately is a function of the intensity and frequency of the sound stimulus. Tensor contraction pulls the eardrum inward, while the antagonist stapedius contraction forces it posteriorly, resulting in a collective force that is at a right angle to the ossicular movement. As a result, amplitudes are damped or reduced, but the force from the eardrum to the stapes is increased. Thus, there is a low frequency attenuation of about 10 dB which serves as a frequency selective protection for the cochlea against loud sounds.

In addition to the ossicular route to the cochlea, sound can travel by two other routes. A second route, the *aerotympanic,* occurs when the stimulus travels directly from the eardrum to the round window because of a break in the ossicular chain. This can amount to a 30 dB threshold shift. The third route, the *osseous* or bone conduction route, occurs when the sound bypasses the middle ear and is transmitted directly to the cochlea via the cranial and facial bones. There is a qualitative and perceptual difference from the sound conducted via the osseous route relative to the ossicular route. This is part of the reason a speaker's voice appears qualitatively different when he hears a recording of himself via the air conduction route as compared to the combination of osseous and ossicular when he speaks.

An impairment of the middle ear mechanism reduces the efficiency of the conduction impedance matching; hence hearing impairment is a *conductive* or *transmission* type because of the reduction in sensitivity from mechanical mismatching. The middle ear matches low impedance air vibration to high impedance fluid activity. Both have different elastic density resistance values. Occasionally, these hearing losses are called "impedance" losses because sound energy is lost due to mass, stiffness, and functional changes; hence "impedance audiometry." The degree of hearing loss is related to the degree of the middle ear pathology or impedance mismatching. With increased mass, resonance tends to favor the low frequencies so the high-frequency thresholds are increased. Likewise, with increased stiffness, high-frequency resonance is favored so low-frequency thresholds are raised. Thus, fluid loading from otitis media can raise high-frequency thresholds. Stiffness increases from eardrum retraction, otosclerosis, and stenosis of the eustachian tube, and adhesions can raise the low tone thresholds.

Inner Ear

Within the petrous portion of the temporal bone is the complex series of sacs and ducts known as the labyrinth. It has two parts: (1) the *osseous labyrinth,* which is the excavated canals, and (2) the *membranous labyrinth,* the sacs and ducts within the canals. The osseous labyrinth contains a fluid called *perilymph* that runs through its three parts, i.e., the *cochlea,* the *vestibule,* and the *semicircular canals.* It also communicates with the subarachnoid space of the brain through a *perilymphatic duct.* The vestibule and semicircular canals are the organs for balance and crude vibration while the cochlea is the end organ for the analysis of sound (see Figure 7.2).

The *cochlea* is a small, snail-shaped mechanism that spirals 2½ to 2¾ turns around its central axis, a hollow bony post called the *modiolus.* Uncoiled, the cochlea measures about 5 cm. from its base to the apex. Part of the basal portion forms a bulge, the *promontory,* which projects into the middle ear between the oval and round windows. The cochlea is divided into

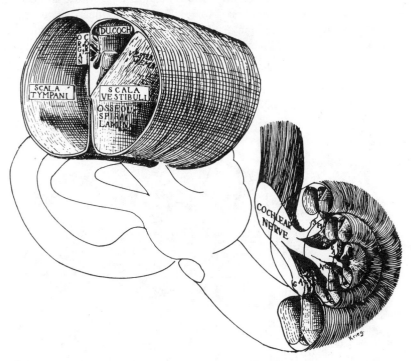

Figure 7.2. A section of the chochlea through the modiolus. *Courtesy of the Aurex Corp.; from W. J. S. Krieg,* Visualization of the Functional Anatomy of the Ear *(Chicago: Aurex, 1945)*

an upper chamber, the *scala vestibuli,* and a lower chamber, the *scala tympani,* by a thin shelf of bone, the *osseous spiral lamina* that projects from the modiolus. Both scali contain a fluid called *perilymph.* Contiguous to the edge of the spiral lamina is a tough but flexible basilar membrane that stretches to the outer wall of the cochlea completing the separation of the two chambers. At the apical end of the cochlea is a small opening (1–2 mm.) called the *helicotrema.* The purpose of the opening is not fully understood, but physiologists suggest that it enables the release of excessive pressure between the scala vestibuli and scala tympani chambers. The basal ends of the scala vestibuli and tympani lead to the oval and round windows, respectively. Any interference in the normal reciprocal movement of these two windows will attenuate the displacement amplitude of basilar membrane vibration—and subsequently reduce cochlear sensitivity.

There is a third duct within the cochlea, the *cochlear duct* or the *scala media.* It is a triangular shaped canal that runs the length of the cochlea between the scala vestibuli and scala tympani, containing a fluid called *endolymph.* Its base is the *basilar membrane* while its hypotenuse is the vestibular membrane or *Reissner's membrane.* This membrane originates near the junction of the spiral lamina and basilar membrane and projects to the outer wall of the cochlea. The third leg of the cochlear duct is the *spiral ligament.* The inner surface of this ligament has the *stria vascularis*—the site

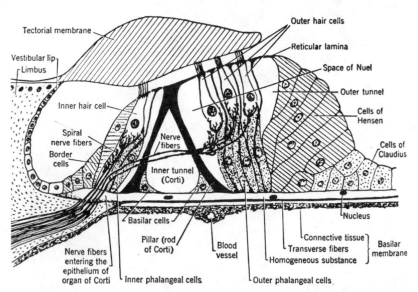

Figure 7.3.   A cross-section of the organ of Corti. *From A. T. Rasmussen,* Outlines of Neuro-Anatomy *(Dubuque, Iowa: William C. Brown, 1943)*

for producing endolymphatic fluid and oxygen for hair cells. Endolymph differs from the perilymph as the former has a high potassium content.

On the inner vestibular surface of the basilar membrane is the *organ of Corti*. See Figure 7.3. It consists of two heavy pillars or rods of Corti that unite at the apex and form a triangle. Part of the basilar membrane forms its base. The space between the rods of Corti is the *tunnel of Corti* which divides the organ of Corti into an inner and outer portion. On the inner portion is a single row of approximately 3,500 sensory cells called inner or *internal hair cells*. On the outer portion are three or four additional rows of approximately 20,000 outer or *external hair cells*. The inferior ends of the internal and external hair cells are imbedded into a structure called the *reticular lamina* while the superior ends make contact with the *tectorial membrane* that hovers above it. The tectorial membrane runs somewhat parallel to the basilar membrane and is suspended from the *limbus* that projects off the modiolus.

The inner ear contains two types of fluids, *endolymph* and the *perilymph*. The cochlear duct (scala media) contains endolymph and the scala vestibuli and the scala tympani contain perilymph. These fluids provide the nutrients to the inner ear structures, remove the catabolic products, regulate systemic pressure, aid in vibration, and establish the electrolytic chemical environment for energy transformation. The fluids flow around the membranes creating the electrolytic and protein variances needed for the delicate vital balance between the organ of Corti and the tissues. Most likely, the fluid flow is from the perilymph through Reissner's membrane into the endolymph but filtered by the stria vascularis.

Functionally, a loose contact between the hair cell cilia and the tectorial membrane enables a shearing action to occur when the basilar membrane is activated. This subsequently produces a bioelectric discharge from the hair cells called the *cochlear microphonic,* an alternating current that is synchronous and proportional in intensity and frequency to the auditory signal transmitted to the cochlea. The hair cells transmit the discharge to terminal branches of the auditory nerve located just below the basilar membrane.

The synapses of hair cells and nerve fibers form an interlacing network; each hair cell connects with several nerve fibers and each nerve fiber connects with several hair cells. This complex matrix of neurological redundancy prevents Wallerian degeneration if a hair cell or nerve fiber expires. There are about 24,000 to 30,000 of these nerve fibers. They pass into the modiolus where they synapse and form the *spiral ganglion*. As the spiral ganglion is the origin of the auditory nerve, it is considered a *first-order neuron* and its electrochemical neural discharge is called an *action potential*. Action potentials are *all-or-none* impulses with the "absolute" and "relative" refractory characteristics that nerve fibers exhibit. The discharge magnitude is independent of the stimulus intensity and linear in frequency to the signal up until 2000 Hz but not beyond this point because of the refractory characteristics. Ultimately, the intensity and frequency properties of the signal are preserved through a neurological coding system that programs the signal with temporal and spatial patterns as it ascends to the auditory cortex.

Ascending Pathways to the Higher Auditory Centers

The auditory nerve fibers of the spiral ganglion leave the modiolus and enter the dorso-lateral border of the pons where the fibers bifurcate and synapse into masses of gray matter called the *dorsal cochlear nucleus* and the *ventral cochlear nucleus.* These are the points of origin for the second-order-neurons. Here, most fibers cross to the contraleteral *superior olivary nucleus* although some ascend along the ipsilateral side. The ascending fibers form a distinct auditory tract, the *lateral lemniscus* which extends to the inferior colliculus of the midbrain—the center for auditory reflexes. Here, another synapse originates the third-order neurons. These pathways continue upward and have their fourth synapse in the *medial geniculate body.* From the medial geniculate emanate the *auditory radiations* that ultimately terminate in Heschl's gyrus (Brodman area 42) of the temporal cortex. See Figure 7.4.

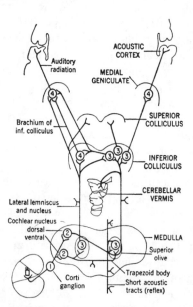

Figure 7.4.   Ascending auditory pathways. *From A. T. Rasmussen,* Outlines of Neuro-Anatomy *(Dubuque, Iowa: William C. Brown, 1943)*

The synapse relays described above do not necessarily apply to all pathways. Some pathways assume more direct routes with longer collaterals that bypass some synapse stations. The final projections of the auditory radiations into Heschl's gyrus assume an orderly topographical spatial arrangement relevant to frequency. The nature of frequency analysis in the cortex is still not fully understood. Some of the auditory analysis is even attributed to the subcortical or medial geniculate area. Intensity analysis is also not fully understood. The most commonly accepted theories of hearing are the *place theory* (Davis 1957) and the *volley theory* (Weaver and Lawrence 1954).

Descending Olivocochlear Pathways

Although sensory pathways are inherently afferent, there are some efferent recurrent pathways in the auditory system. A bundle of fibers, now called *Rasmussen's bundle* or the *olivocochlear pathways,* originate from the superior olivary nucleus. The olivocochlear recurrent pathways provide a servo-feedback mechanism for the modulation of incoming auditory signals. Physiologically, they can reduce the amplitude of a nerve impulse by exuding a chemical inhibitor. Anatomically, the descending pathways are intertwined with the ascending pathways, but the two still manage to maintain an orderly positional relationship.

Reticular Mechanism and Programming

Auditory processing is further complicated by the integration and programming of input and output activities that affect both cortical and subcortical areas. While it is contended that cortical areas are more responsible for cognitive and informational storage, it is ostensibly the subcortical reticular mechanism that serves as the gateway for all sensory input to be programmed and subsequently integrated into meaningful new and past experiences. Anatomically, the corticothalamic and thalamocortical pathways are located in this reticular formation area. Physiologically, the reticular mechanism provides for the delivery of neuronal relays relative to stimulus-integrated responses, indeed an operational arc. Thus, it is an internuncial pool which serves as a biological reservoir to program the temporal-spatial coded auditory and nonauditory impulses to appropriate neuronal relays. It also serves as the feedback facilitator for afferent-efferent homeostatic monitoring. Thus, at this subcortical retricular level—sometimes designated as the "centrencephalic" system—the input and output is probably sorted and programmed.

PSYCHOACOUSTICS

Psychoacoustics denotes the human or psychological sensations and perceptions from physical acoustic stimulation. It also connotes the individual's relations to the sound stimulus, voluntary and involuntary. There are a number of physical parameters to sound which have physiologic counterparts.

Intensity

Intensity denotes the physical magnitude parameter of energy. In acoustics, intensity is expressed as a decibel in either power or pressure units. A decibel is a logarithmic ratio of two intensity levels. It can be expressed in pressure or power since pressure is equal to power squared.

The psychological (psychoacoustic) counterpart of intensity is *loudness*—the individual's perception of the intensity. The two are related but not identical. Thus, equal incremental intensity changes may or may not precipitate equal perceptual loudness impressions. Clinically, a significant discrepancy between loudness and intensity has pertinent diagnostic implications about disorders of the auditory mechanism.

Human sensitivity to intensity is so acute that under controlled laboratory conditions, a normal young adult can perceive sound when the displacement of the eardrum is equivalent to one-tenth the diameter of a hydrogen molecule. Actually, human sensitivity for intensity compares favorably with the most sensitive animal ears. The well-known superiority of animal hearing is due to their extended frequency range rather than superior intensity sensitivity.

The remarkable sensitivity of the human ear for intensity is a ratio of 1:100,000,000,000,000 from when the sound is first detected to the point of physical insult to the ear. Because of this cumbersome ratio, the convenience of the logarithmic scale was chosen as the unit of measure. Hence, this value can be expressed logarithmically to a base of ten with an exponent of 14. The unit would be 14 bels (after Alexander Graham Bell), but since this value was too large it was decimated into smaller units, the decibel, e.g., one bel equals 10 decibels.

The loudness unit is the *sone*. One sone equals the loudness perception of a 1000 Hz tone at 40 dB. There is also the unit of *loudness level, the phon*, which is equated for each frequency relative to the 1000 Hz tone at any given level. Hence, there are equal loudness contours extending from threshold to 140 decibels. The zero scale on the audiometer is actually a loudness contour relative to absolute threshold levels at different frequencies. This scale suggests the ear is not equally sensitive at all frequencies, but indeed some frequencies are more sensitive than others. Actually, audition simulates other bodily functions following a U-shaped curve, e.g., sensitivity is greater in the mid range and poorer at the extremes of the spectrum. In human audition, sensitivity is most acute in the frequency range of human speech. Audiometer calibration is based on the equal loudness contour scales. The U-curve becomes a straight-line configuration at high intensity levels.

Frequency

The frequency parameter of sound is the number of oscillations or vibratory activity. It was once expressed as the number of cycles-per-second (cps) that the particles vibrated back and forth, but the current unit is designated the Hertz (Hz) after the physicist Heindrick Hertz. The psychological counterpart of frequency is *pitch,* i.e., the high tone or low tone dimension of the sound. The unit for pitch is the *mel* (after *mel*ody). One mel equals the pitch of a 1000 Hz tone at 40 dB, the complement of the sone.

Frequency sensitivity refers to the range of tones that the ear can perceive. In humans, 20 Hz to 20,000 Hz is the extreme of the "best" ears under ideal laboratory conditions. The speech range is more constrained to about 100 Hz to 10,000 Hz. A deep male voice fundamental would be in the lower range while the consonants extend to the upper range. The critical range for speech communication is 500 Hz to 2000 Hz inclusive, hence, a hearing loss in this area is proportionally more detrimental to aural communication. Loss of hearing at the extremes of this range affect the quality of the sound more than the intelligibility. The extent of the breakdown in auditory perception is relative mostly to the degree of the hearing loss in this critical speech range. Variations depend on age of onset, type of loss, intelligence, social factors, etc.

Auditory Sensitivity Threshold Measurements

Auditory sensitivity refers to the ability of the ear to detect vibratory sensations relative to a threshold. In audiometry, several kinds of thresholds are used, but for assessing sensitivity, the concept of absolute threshold is employed. This is the level where 50 percent of the pure tone stimulations are perceived. If a series of ten tones is given to a CP child, at several intensities, the absolute threshold is the level where five of the ten tones are detected.

The 50 percent criterion is also used with speech material to yield the *speech reception threshold* (SRT) where the correct recognition of 50 percent of the words represents threshold. Still another type of threshold used in audiometry is the *threshold of discomfort.* There is no 50 percent criterion in this instance but only the indication that an auditory stimulation causes discomfort. In still another type of differential threshold, the person's ability to perceive minute changes in tone intensity is referred to as the *difference-limen (differential-sensitivity) threshold.*

TYPES OF HEARING IMPAIRMENTS

Hearing impairments are anatomically dichotomized into peripheral and central disorders. Peripheral disorders include impairments of the conductive and sensory-neuural auditory mechanisms, while central disorders denote impairments in the higher brain centers. The latter are disorders of interpretation and integration, e.g., agnosia and aphasia language disorders. Peripheral auditory impairments produce the problems associated with a reduction in sensitivity and speech discrimination.

Peripheral Disorders

Conductive Impairments

These are caused by any blockage or "impedance" of the sound in the external and middle ear divisions. The hearing loss is due to a mechanical resistance to efficient sound transmission. Audiograms (hearing charts) typically show a flat air conduction loss or one with poorer hearing (raised thresholds) in the low frequencies and gradual improvement in the higher frequencies. Bone conduction thresholds are within normal limits since bone conduction reflects inner ear sensitivity. Speech reception threshold scores tend to agree with the air conduction threshold average for 500, 1000, and 2000 Hz. Because of purely mechanical constraints, the discrimination scores are high, tolerance for loud sounds is greater relative to the attenuation provided by the mechanical amplitude reduction. The voice may be soft since the individual hears his own voice more efficiently by bone conduction. Since most of these problems are due to ear infections, hereditary disorders, and trauma, they occur in cerebral palsy persons as in any other person.

Sensory-Neural Impairments

These are caused by damage to the cochlea, the auditory nerve, the retrocochlear pathways, or any combinations. Because irreversible cellular and nerve tissue damage occurs, the receptive and perceptual implications are more complex than for the conductive lesions. Most "typical" cerebral palsy hearing problems fall in this category. There are vast numbers of air conduction configurations associated with sensory-neural pathology. Almost any audiogram shape is possible: flat, ogive, U, and various degrees of high-tone slopes. Perhaps the most common and typical configuration is the progressive slope from the low to the high frequencies—the well-documented high-tone hearing loss. Bone thresholds are either intertwined with the air thresholds or are absent altogether in the more severe loss.

The SRT may be slightly poorer than the pure tone average (500–2000 Hz) because of the concommitant discrimination difficulty. In fact, closer agreement is often obtained by averaging the two best frequencies to estimate the SRT. The discrimination scores can vary from 0 to 100 percent, depending on the slope of the curve and the degree of the loss. In general, the flatter the AC loss, the better the discrimination, and the greater the high-tone loss, the poorer the discrimination. Discrimination also deteriorates as the magnitude of the loss increases.

Mixed Hearing Impairment

This signifies the combination of conductive and sensory-neural pathology. Varying combinations can occur so the symptoms of both impairments are combined. These are commonly seen in cerebral palsy children.

Central Hearing Impairment

Synonymous with the term *central dysacusis* is central hearing impairment. Both of these terms are nearly outmoded and replaced by the more extensive term *central auditory disorder*. In true central impairment, "hearing loss" as reflected in the air conduction audiogram may be mimimal and misleading, as the classical audiogram usually shows normal or near-normal threshold sensitivity. The problem is not in the ability to receive sound but rather in the ability to perceive and integrate the sound. Indeed, the problem is auditory processing at the higher perceptual and cognitive levels. Since the cerebral palsied have primary brain pathology, there is a greater incidence of central auditory disorders in this population.

CLASSIFICATIONS OF HEARING LOSS

Hearing Loss (hypacusis)

This refers to a reduction of auditory sensitivity as reflected in a threshold raised beyond the normal limit. The medical term *hypacusis* is preferable as the term *hearing loss* has been used for thresholds that range from within normal hearing limits to total deafness. The term *hearing threshold level* (HTL) is currently used wherever a numerical or quantitative value is needed, while "hearing loss" is more general.

Hard of Hearing

In a child this term designates sufficient residual hearing that does not require a school for the deaf, but the child can develop adequate language and speech with amplification, aural rehabilitation, and speech therapy. The hard of hearing adult also has sufficient residual hearing to compensate for the hearing loss and function relatively well. "Hard of hearing" is a relative term connoting magnitude of loss in an elusive noncommittal frame of reference. Considering human difference, the term is operationally meaningless.

Deafness (anacusis)

The term "deafness" is reserved for a profound or complete loss of hearing. While technically deafness starts at about 82 dB (the mean PTA value of 500, 1000, and 2000 Hz in the better ear), operationally a congenitally deaf child with thresholds as low as 60 dB may require special placement in a school for the deaf. Most schools for the deaf accept students with hearing thresholds that are considerably better than 82 dB, so it is not uncommon to find students with 60–70 dB hearing levels at schools for the deaf (Nober 1963). For "deaf" children, the supplement of amplification, speech therapy, etc., is not sufficient to provide the language development necessary for this child to attend a normal hearing school and compete scholastically with the other children.

Many cerebral palsied children labeled deaf are not actually deaf. The term "deaf athetoid," for example, is a cliché frequently used with technically hard of hearing athetoids. The confounding of multiple handicaps confuses the behavioral picture. Since this child requires extensive speech and language rehabilitation, he or she is occasionally inappropriately placed in a school for the deaf.

In recent years there has been a trend to use functional designations of the hearing handicaps and to avoid stereotyped labels such as "hard of hearing" or "deaf." Rather, the degree of the hearing threshold levels are designated into six classes based on air conduction pure-tone average (PTA) at 500, 1000, and 2000 Hz in the better ear. An additional 5 dB is added to this amount when the poorer PTA equals or exceeds 25 dB.

A class A designation includes all PTA thresholds up to 25 dB; it is essentially within the normal hearing range so faint speech is heard without difficulty. Class B thresholds range from 26 to 40 dB, but difficulty does arise for faint speech. In class C, 41–55 dB, frequent problems arise with normal speech. Class D, 56–70 dB, poses marked problems even with loud speech. Class E, 70–90 dB, is considered severe, and amplification is mandatory in many instances. Finally, class F, 90 dB or more, is a profound hearing loss and even amplification does not assure functional discrimination of speech. Audiograms in classes E and F where the responses are at excessive intensity output may not even reflect true or valid hearing but rather *cutaneous-tactile (cutile)* exteroception (Nober 1963, 1964, 1967, 1970). Thus, it is entirely possible that the audiogram is not designating true auditory reserve but vibrotactile sensation that is not immediately apparent to the examiner or to the client. Implications for rehabilitation are important, particularly for hearing aid selection and auditory training.

SYMPTOMS ASSOCIATED WITH HEARING IMPAIRMENT

Dysacusis

This term refers to the complications that accompany the basic loss of auditory acuity. There are two major classifications of dysacusis: *central dysacusis,* i.e., the auditory agnosis and receptive aphasias and *peripheral dysacusis* which includes phenomena such as diplacusis, recruitment, phonemic regression, and reduced discrimination. Since the latter comprise the symptoms that often accompany a hearing loss, they will be reviewed briefly.

Diplacusis

This term means double hearing. It occurs monaurally and binaurally; in the former, a single tone is perceived as two or more tones, while in the latter, one tone is perceived as two different tones in the two ears. Diplacusis occurs in both middle and inner ear pathologies. Middle ear diplacusis can often be treated medically, but neural diplacusis problems are usually irreversible.

Recruitment

Recruitment is pathognomonic to cochlear pathology. Some investigators have attempted to show that it can occur in retrocochlear lesions, but these cases represent isolated instances. Furthermore, these studies never convincingly rule out concommitant cochlear pathology. Recruitment is a nonlinear or disproportionate increase in the loudness sensation of intensity increments once the threshold is exceeded. In other words, when recruitment is present, the loudness and intensity parameters do not parallel each other. The hearing loss seems to disappear or regress at suprathreshold levels. Recruitment is also associated with poor discrimination and hypersensitivity to small increment changes in intensity or frequency, although no direct causal-effect relationship has been demonstrated.

Classification includes partial recruitment, complete recruitment, hyperrecruitment and de-recruitment. Partial occurs in moderate cochlear involvement, while hyper and complete occur in severe cases. De-recruitment occurs in acoustic neuroma where loudness grows slower than usual because of auditory summation problems.

Several procedures have been employed to identify recruiting ears; these fall into two categories, i.e., direct or indirect. In the former, the loudness perception of a normal ear is directly compared to that of a defective ear. In the latter, some related function like differential sensitivity to incremental intensity, e.g., the difference-limen, is ascertained.

One direct recruitment test is called the *loudness balance test*. It can be given either monaurally or binaurally. The alternate binaural loudness balance test (ABLB) requires a normal ear to be compared to the defective ear or vice versa. The test is relatively simple to administer. Assume a person has a normal right ear and a 0 dB threshold at 1000 Hz. Also assume the left ear threshold is 40 dB at 1000 Hz. The difference between the two threshold levels is 40 dB (e.g., 0 vs 40 dB). Then, the alternate binaural loudness balance test is begun. The tone in the normal right ear is increased to 20 dB as the reference ear and the tone in the left ear is increased until the patient indicates the tone in his left ear is equally loud to the 20 dB tone in the right ear. Suppose this level is 50 dB in the left ear. Now the difference between the ears is only 30 dB compared to the 40 dB difference at threshold. If still another 20 dB increment is added to the normal right ear, e.g., 40 and the match is made to the left ear, they may seem equally loud with the left ear intensity at 60 dB; now the loudness balance difference is only 20 dB between the right 40 dB and left 60 dB. Perhaps at 60 dB in the right ear and 60 dB in the left ear, both will seem equally loud. Thus, a 60 dB 1000 Hz tone in the right and left ears seem equally loud, and the decibel levels are equal compared to threshold when the difference was 40 dB. These values traced on an audiogram constitute a "laddergram." Clearly, the left ear is recruiting. In a nonrecruiting ear, the systematic 20 dB increments in the normal right ear would be matched in loudness with comparable 20 dB increments in the left ear so the threshold and suprathreshold 40 dB difference is maintained. As the relationship between intensity and loudness remains linear and constant even at suprathreshold levels, recruitment is not present.

A *monaural loudness balance* laddergram is administered in a similar principle except that only one ear is tested, but two different frequencies are employed. This is given when one ear is not normal, but when one frequency is near normal, usually a low frequency. Thus, a 500 Hz tone will be tested against a 4000 Hz tone. The same 20 dB incremental changes in the better reference frequency are used. Equal 20 dB increments at 500 Hz, if matched by less than 20 dB increments at 4000 Hz, indicates recruitment; if not, recruitment may be absent.

Recruitment can be quite debilitating in extreme cases. Cochlear distortion may be extreme; subsequently, discrimination is poor. Sounds may be inaudible at one level and painful only a few decibels above this level. Hence, the *dynamic operating range (DOR)* from distortion to discomfort is restricted. Fortunately, most cases of recruitment are not severe, and hearing aids can be successfully fitted.

Phonemic Regression

This term refers to a discrimination loss that is excessive and out of proportion to the air conduction thresholds. It originally denoted hearing problems associated with old age (presbycusis) but is occasionally used to designate other populations with hearing problems. In advanced cases the air thresholds may be close to a normal limit yet not be possible to obtain a speech reception threshold at high-intensity levels. Discrimination loss may be 100 percent. This individual would complain that the speech was loud enough but unclear and distorted.

Phonemic regression suggests retrocochlear degeneration of neuroauditory pathways and higher auditory centers. Thus, a hearing aid may be useless as sensitivity is within normal limits, and amplification cannot improve intelligibility. Often the aid aggravates matters since these people are distressed by loud sounds. Rapid speech is also difficult for them to process because the neurological mechanism can no longer integrate and program the more accelerated temporal patterns of the neural impulses. The only real salvation lies in slower speech through deliberate or accentuated enunciation.

Discrimination Loss

This should not be confused with phonemic regression which is reserved for presbycusis subjects where the discrimination loss is disproportionate to the air conduction thresholds due to retrocochlear degeneration. Reduced discrimination refers to difficulty in discerning the finer differences among phonetic elements due to cochlear or retrocochlear pathogenesis. It is often related to the magnitude of the hearing loss.

Tinnitus

This word literally means *to jingle.* It refers to any subjective head noises of otologic origin. These noises have been described as roaring, buzzing, tingling, ringing, and hissing sounds. It can be classified as *central,* which is diffuse, or *peripheral,* unilateral or bilateral. The noise may be continuous or intermittent. Sometimes the tinnitus is specific to an ear or even to a particular frequency. In some instances the tinnitus is so loud that it keeps the subject awake at night. Some actually use radio music to mask the tinnitus so they can sleep. The etiology may be vascular, muscular, or neural. It is commonly associated with degenerating cochlear hair cells, but is often found in subjects with normal hearing. Children may have it after a viral episode, after ototoxity, acoustic noise trauma, otosclerosis, Menieres disease, or sudden deafness. Tensions from psychological and physical stress also can cause the tinnitus. There is no specific treatment that works in all cases.

Paracusis Willisi(ana)

This symptom is pathognomonic to a conductive loss. The person understands better in noisy places—strange as it may seem. This happens because the person talking increases his intensity output in an effort to overcome the noise interference. The resultant effect is an improvement in the ratio of the level of speech to the level of noise, i.e., S/N ratio. This improvement in the S/N ratio enables these people to ostensibly hear better in noisy places.

Speech Articulation Defects

Articulation denotes the molding of sounds into phonetic units. The development and production of normal articulation is directly dependent on normal hearing. Articulation defects due to inadequate hearing can be so specific that a skillful speech therapist or audiologist can estimate the type and degree of hearing loss from an analysis of the speech pattern. The type of articulation defects, i.e., distortion, substitution or omission also depends on the degree of hearing loss and the frequencies affected. A low-frequency hearing loss is more likely to affect the articulation and resonance of the vowel sounds while a high-frequency loss affects mainly the consonants. The onset of the hearing loss is pertinent. If the loss occurred after the development of good speech, then an intensive conservation program may help maintain and establish speech patterns and prevent gradual deterioration.

ETIOLOGIES OF AUDITORY IMPAIRMENTS

Hereditary Deafness

The forms of deafness from genetic inheritance can be dominant, recessive, and/or sex-linked. The incidence from inheritance varies, with estimates from 46 to 60 percent. A general estimate is that approximately 50 percent are of genetic origin. Several hereditary deafness classification systems have been used: (1) congenital and delayed, (2) by the system involved, and (3) dominant vs. recessive transmissions. Recessive genes can produce deafness when they are homozygous. About forty-five recessive genes account for 90 percent of the cases of hereditary deafness; the remaining 10 percent are attributed to the dominant autosomal genes. Furthermore, genotype and environmental agents can interact to produce deafness. Sex-linked deafness is transmitted through the X-chromosome. Deafness from environmental and genotype interactions are commonly found in cerebral palsy patients. If hemolytic diseases that cause kernicterus are considered hereditary, then heredity accounts for 10 percent of deafness in the audiometric patterns associated with kernicterus. Deafness from the other hereditary disorders assumes almost any degree of audiometric patterns. Most of the cases of total deafness are due to hereditary etiology. Several middle ear conductive impairments may occur from hereditary etiology.

Erythroblastosis

This is a congenital hemolytic disease that produces destruction of the red blood cells and causes hyperdevelopment of erythroporetic tissue. It is the result of an isoimmunization of the child against the mother. When an Rh negative mother receives Rh positive substance, her blood produces anti-Rh agglutinin that may be passed back to the fetus. Subsequently, there is destruction of the fetal red blood cells. Recent advances in immunization medicine have minimized this problem.

Kernicterus

This is a pathological condition caused mainly by erythroblastosis but which can also be associated with other conditions. It is the jaundiced or yellow-bile staining of the basal ganglia due to an excess of bilirubin—a chemical that is released into the blood when the red blood cells are hemolyzed. Because bilirubin has an affinity for the basal ganglia, it is the major cause of athetosis. While some 5 percent of all pregnancies involve a hemolytic disease, the percentage of deafness is small. Incidence studies range from 0.3 to 2.5 percent.

The specific site of the lesion in the athetoid whose hearing impairment was caused by kernicterus is still unresolved. Some authorities claim that the pathology occurs in the cochlear nuclei. Later studies were unable to demonstrate this involvement and contended that spiral ganglion destruction was secondary to the destruction of the cranial nuclei. Other authorities contended that the site of the pathology was the cochlea, as they were able to demonstrate recruitment in their subjects. Lesions also occur in the higher auditory areas producing aphasoid sequela rather than a reduction in auditory sensitivity. When both the peripheral and central auditory areas are impaired, multiple handicaps become manifest.

Anoxia

Approximately one-third to one-half of cerebral palsy cases experienced anoxia at birth. Anoxia can damage the cortex, thalamus, spinal cord, basal ganglia, and the cerebellum. It may cause hearing impairment, but this is still speculative. Functionally, oxygen deprivation reduces the generation of cochlear microphonics and action potentials.

Viral

Viral agents are a common cause of brain damage and subsequently cerebral palsy. They can cause hearing loss directly or indirectly. Indirectly, they cause meningitis, otitis media, and encephalitis. Tubercular meningitis, a common postnatal cause of cerebral palsy, is also responsible for cases of sudden deafness. Purulent meningitis has a direct effect by destroying the cochlea and auditory nerve. The hearing loss can assume any degree or auditory configuration since conductive, sensory-neural, or mixed losses are possible. Central dysacusis is also a common impairment. Other viral infections that directly cause deafness are mumps, influenza, and measles, although these are not etiologically associated with cerebral palsy.

Toxemia

A number of toxic substances that cause cerebral palsy are also ototoxic. Since 5–10 percent of cerebral palsy is caused by toxic agents, the magnitude of hearing loss and brain damage depends on the total absorbed quantity of toxic poison. Arsenic, lead, quinine, and salicylate are common toxemic agents responsible for severe hearing loss or total deafness. The latter two have effects that are often reversible, although ototoxic damage from antibiotics is usually irreversible. Streptomycin shows an affinity for destroying the vestibular mechanism but can also affect the cochlea; dihydrostreptomycin and viomycin are primarily ototoxic to the cochlea and the vestibular mechanism secondarily. Neomycin and kanomycin are ototoxic to the cochlea primarily and vestibular mechanism secondarily.

Cerebral Vascular Accident

This is rare as an etiology of cerebral palsy. When it occurs, it is in early life—usually in the form of a thrombosis to the mid-cerebral artery or to the internal carotid artery. Deafness due to a vascular accident is exceedingly difficult to diagnose, so the etiology is inferred from a presence of the same condition in other areas of the body. The audiometric picture varies from mild to total deafness. In some instances, the cochlea is able to survive temporary interruptions in the blood supply with only a mild loss, while in other instances, a greater loss ensues. The size of the thrombosis and the amount of blood deprivation determines the magnitude of the loss. Recruitment, poor discrimination, and tinnitus are the otologic symptoms.

Acoustic Neuroma

This is a tumor of the eighth cranial nerve. A fully grown tumor can occupy the entire cerebellopontine angle and prevail upon structures in the cerebellum, pons, or medulla causing secondary symptoms (diaschisis). The symptoms are the same as with other cranial tumors but with added hearing loss and tinnitus. The typical audiologic picture shows a high-frequency loss, the absence of recruitment, excessive auditory adaptation, and a discrimination loss that is disproportionate to the amount of threshold shift. Treatment is surgical removal.

Temporal Bone Fracture

This is often associated with concommitant cranial fractures that can cause brain damage and cerebral palsy. The temporal bone fracture can be longitudinal, transverse, or both. The former is more commonly associated with middle ear damage to the ossicles and eardrum, but damage can occur to the cochlea. Transverse fractures cause severe sensory-neural deafness by injuring the cochlea and auditory nerve. Any varieties of audiometric configurations are possible.

Acoustic Trauma

This refers to a hearing loss from exposure to intense noise. It may be a violent explosion or a percussion blast that damages the tympanic membrane, the ossicular mechanism, or the cochlea. As a result, the hearing loss can be conductive, sensory-neural, and mixed. Consequently, any degree of loss or audiometric configuration is possible. Trauma from physical accidents are not included in this category.

Noise Induced Hearing Loss (NIHL)

This is a specific case of acoustic trauma and classified as a separate entity. NIHL usually denote a gradual or incipient loss of hearing from noise exposure over a prolonged, protracted period of time. Hearing loss incurred in this fashion is exclusively sensory-neural due to cochlear damage. The most notable site is the hair cells. It often starts with a high frequency (e.g., 4000 Hz) notch and spreads toward the low and high frequencies. Usually the maximum notch on the audiogram is at 4000 Hz, since the 4000 Hz receptors (10 mm. from the oval window) are most vulnerable. An abundance of research regarding the effects of noise on the ear has resulted in the *damage-risk criterion*. These are complex charts on available intensity levels relative to frequency bands that impose a damage risk to hearing. These charts are intricate, but it is safe to generalize that any noise 85 dB or more can potentially cause hearing loss. Noise below this level does not usually damage hearing.

The issue of whether the cerebral palsied may incur noise induced hearing loss because of paresis of the protective middle ear muscles against intense sound is still unresolved. Some contend that the similarity in the audiogram configuration of the athetoid and that of a typical noise induced audiogram pattern is only circumstantial. Since there is no definite evidence that the middle ear muscles of the athetoid are nonfunctional or any different from the spastics who do not have this particular audiogram configuration, the issue is still under exploration. Furthermore, studies involving subjects with known stapedial paralysis from Bell's palsy failed to show any threshold shift.

Meniere's Disease (endolymphatic hydrops)

This is caused by a hypersecretion of endolymphatic fluid into the cochlear duct. The disorder is in the mechanism that regulates the production and disposal of the endolymphatic fluid. Etiology is speculative and still unknown. There is a classical triad of symptoms—deafness, vertigo, and tinnitus, but there are other commonly associated symptoms, i.e., vomiting, nausea, dizziness, and diplacusis. It typically is unilateral (80–90 percent) and occurs primarily in adults between 30 and 60 years of age.

Hearing loss is sensory-neural with damage often inflicted on the vestibular membrane, the hair cells, and the stria vascularis. In the early stage, the audiogram is rising, i.e., the low frequencies showing greater loss than the high frequencies due to increased stiffness of the basilar membrane from excessive endolymphatic distention. As the condition progresses, the audiogram flattens due to increased destruction of the organ of Corti; eventually the typical downward sloping audiogram of cochlear impairments emerges. Recruitment, tinnitus, and discrimination loss are present and vary in severity with the degree of cochlear damage.

The symptoms of Meniere's can remit as suddenly as they appear, to recur several weeks later. Attacks can last from a half hour to twenty-four hours, following a cyclical pattern. Even though the hearing loss eventually becomes permanent and irreversible, there may be a partial threshold and discrimination improvement during the remission periods. Treatment is symptomatic therapy, since the etiology is unknown. It usually runs its course, builds up in frequency over the years, and after the inner ear is destroyed, it declines. There is no specific data relevant to Meniere's disease and cerebral palsy. The incidence is probably the same as in the non-cerebral palsy populations.

Presbycusis

This is a progressive hearing loss due to old age. The pathogenesis is epithelial and neural atrophy; the former refers to cochlear deterioration, and the latter to destruction of the spiral ganglion and neurons of the auditory pathways. The audiometric pattern typically shows normal thresholds up to 1000 Hz, and then a gradual decline toward the high frequencies. Eventually, the low frequencies also become depressed, and in some instances, there may even be a concomitant conductive involvement. Discrimination loss is often so disproportionate to the pure tone thresholds that this symptom has been called "phonemic regression" as indicated earlier. It is expected that about half the cerebral palsied subjects will develop prebycusis since this is the incidence in a normal population.

Otitis Media

This is the most common cause of middle ear hearing loss in children. A cardinal cause of otitis media is dysfunction of the eustachian tube precluding normal intratympanic pressure and ventilation in the middle ear cavity. As a result, a pressure drop or vacuum forms within the cavity (relative to the external atmosphere pressure) causing the effusion of fluids from surrounding tissues into the cavity. When fluid appears, the condition is called *suppurative otitis*. If the fluid becomes infected, it is then *purulent*. Excessive fluid in the middle ear can distend the tympanic membrane until it ruptures to relieve the pressure. If the otitis lasts a short period of time, it is an *acute* otitis, but as it lingers it becomes *chronic* otitis. Acute otitis usually produces a conductive hearing loss with a flat configuration or one with greater loss for the low tones. Tinnitus may be present. As the condition becomes more chronic, fibric changes occur and the hearing loss gets worse. A characteristic chronic otitis audiogram will depict a 10–15 dB bone-conduction shift in the high frequencies, i.e., 2000 Hz and above while the low-frequency bone-conduction thresholds may be 5 to 10 dB better than normal.

Otosclerosis

This is a progressive disease that attacks the otic capsule. The spongy embryonic cells of the early stages are eventually replaced with sclerotic bone. The most prominent site of lesion is the oval window, although other parts of the middle ear are affected. Recent evidence has suggested that pathology can occur to the cochlea as well. Etiology of otosclerosis is still unknown, but the prime suspect is heredity. Hearing loss and other clinical symptoms become noticeable at puberty with evidence histological onset may start at birth. In the early stage, the audiogram shows a conductive loss with a progressive depressed bone conduction configuration that reaches a maximum at 2000 Hz and then abates. This *Carhart notch* (Carhart 1950), as it is called, is due to the lack of normal reciprocal movement between the oval and round windows. Functionally, the cochlear fluids are immobilized, yielding a mechanical inner-ear block. In the advanced stage the bone thresholds are shifted beyond the Carhart notch, indicating cellular cochlear impairment.

Atresia

This refers to any congenital malformation of the ear. It is more typically found in the outer and middle part of the ear. Anomalies can be osseous, vascular, neural, muscular, or any combination.

Cholesteatoma

This is a tumor of the temporal bone. It, too, can affect any part of the ear. As it impinges on adjacent areas, various diaschises or secondary symptoms such as facial paralysis occur.

Mastoiditis

This is an infection of the mastoid bone usually caused by an otitis. It can produce conductive losses as great as 60 dB. Modern developments in antibiotic therapy have practically eliminated this condition.

Sudden Deafness

This is a sensory-neural hearing loss that spontaneously appears within hours or days. The loss may be temporary or irreversible, unilateral or bilateral, and of varying magnitude for mild to profound hearing loss.

Classifications are based on the degree of loss and auditory configurations. Since several etiologies have been cited—noise, rabies, pressure changes, mumps, measles, mononucleosis, vascular—treatment varies.

AUDIOMETRY

This term generally denotes the quantitative assessment of hearing. A more restrictive connotation has evolved so that it is currently used to indicate the measurement of hearing with an audiometer.

Crude Tests of Hearing

Hearing tests trace back to the Bible and perhaps earlier. The oldest hearing test known and one that is still in current use as a crude estimate of sensitivity is the *whispered voice test* which basically tests the higher speech frequencies. Other crude tests are the *watch tick* and the *coin click* tests which screen hearing acuity in the lower frequencies.

Tuning Fork Tests

Tuning fork tests provided the foundation for basic air and bone au-diometry. Each tuning fork generates one specific frequency called a *pure tone.* By using a series of tuning forks of different frequencies, the hearing spectrum can be tested. Extremely pertinent qualitative information is elicited, but one imposing limitation is the lack of substantive qualification. Three major tuning fork tests have been developed that are still used routinely by otologists:

1.   The *Rinne* test is a comparative measure of the efficiency of the bone conduction mechanism to air conduction mechanism. The tuning fork is activated and placed near the external auditory meatus; then it is moved to the mastoid process to determine whether the subject hears it louder in front of the ear (the first position) by aid conduction or "behind" the ear (the second position) by bone conduction. Normally, people hear better by air conduction (positive Rinne), but with a conductive impairment, the sub-ject hears better by bone conduction (a negative Rinne).

2.   The *Weber* test is also a bone conduction test. The bone oscillator is placed on the forehead, and the person is required to localize the tone in his head. Normally, the tone is localized to the center of the head, but if one ear has a conductive loss, the bone will lateralize to that ear; in bilateral conductive loss, the tone usually lateralizes to the poorer ear. Quite often the subject is surprised to hear in the poorer ear and may even be reluctant to indicate this. The test is very tenuous as the responses are contingent on the type and degree of affliction in the two ears.

3.   The *Schwabach* test is a bone conduction test that originally com-

pared the bone conduction acuity of the client to that of the doctor. It has also been used to compare air conduction acuity. The test is administered simply by comparing the length of time the tone is audible to the doctor vs. the patient. It presumptuously assumes that the doctor has eternally normal hearing acuity.

Audiometer

An audiometer is an electronically calibrated instrument for testing hearing. It has an audio-oscillator that generates pure tones (a pure tone by definition has a fundamental that always exceeds any harmonic, if present, by at least 25 dB); more elaborate units have a speech circuit for speech audiometry. There is an intensity attenuator with decibel increments (some are continuous) and a series of pure tones, 125, 250, 500, 1000, 1500, 2000, 4000, 6000, and 8000 Hz. Air conduction pure tone audiometry is generally given at these frequencies (some omit 125, 1500) while bone conduction is tested at 500, 1000, 2000, and 4000 Hz. While most of the manual audiometers have discrete step intensity and frequency output units, there are automated audiometers that use continuous intensity and frequency output with no audible incremental changes. Other features can include an interrupter switch, VU meter, microphone, phonograph and tape inputs, channel mixers, masking frequency and intensity modulations and so on. The output signals can be presented through earphones, the bone oscillator, or loudspeakers.

Specifications of Audiometers

Audiometric instruments require professional maintainence to insure close adherence to standards, i.e., calibration. An audiometer is vulnerable to fluctuations, and the more complex the unit, the more that can go wrong. Normal use affects the instrument's calibration and minor abuse like dropping the earphones or the bone oscillator, excessive heat, etc. can alter calibration. Audiometers should be checked prior to use so field adjustments can be implemented. Factory calibration should be done at least once a year. One survey revealed that 98 percent of the audiometers were out of calibration in some way. Audiometers are also standardized for quiet listening conditions so the specifications are only valid in an environment with minimal environmental noise. For this reason, commercially available sound suites are in widespread use for audiometric testing. In 1969 and 1970, the *American National Standards Institute (ANSI)* made the most recent revision for audiometer specifications relative to intensity, frequency, attenuation, loudspeaker, and earphones.

Calibration of the audiometer is based on the sensitivity of the human ear; hence, the zero designation of the intensity attenuator dial is related to the minimal energy output that is needed by the typical or average normal young ear (devoid of any hearing impairment) to detect the presence of the sound at any given frequency. For example, the ANSI 1969 values at zero hearing threshold level for air conduction are 45 dB at 125 Hz; 25.5 dB at 250 Hz; 11.5 dB at 500 Hz; 7.0 dB at 1000 Hz; 9.0 dB at 2000 Hz; 9.5 dB at 4000 Hz; and 13.0 dB at 8000 Hz. Bone conduction values are 40 dB above these values to compensate for the energy dissipation through relatively heavy bone structure. The speech calibration value for zero is not frequency locked but 20 dB above the 1000 Hz value through the TDH 39 earphone. Thus, zero on the audiometer intensity dial does not designate that there is zero or no energy present, but indicates that the same (no more or no less) amount of sound energy is required as for the average ear to detect threshold at that particular frequency. Calibration values differ for mode of output, i.e., between earphones and loudspeaker; the latter values are about 6 to 7.5 dB less than for earphones. This occurs because of the difference between coupled and uncoupled resonance patterns of the ear. Responses through earphones are called *minimal audible pressure (MAP)* values, and the loudspeaker responses are called *minimal audible field (MAF)* values.

Pure Tone Audiometry

Pure tone audiometry provides considerable information about the auditory mechanism as a total unit including the ability of the person to attend, condition, and respond to an auditory stimulus. The basic air and bone thresholds ascertain auditory sensitivity for the hearing spectrum, but there are also several supra-threshold pure tone measures that are used to test differential sensitivity, recruitment, auditory fatigue (tone decay), diplacusis, etc. The data contrasts hearing levels relative to normal hearing, threshold shifts, site of lesion, type of loss, tolerance, operating range— indeed, the integrity of the auditory mechanism.

Air Conduction Thresholds

This basic test is usually given with earphones so each ear can be tested separately. In special instances, particularly with young children, the tones may be delivered through loudspeakers into a sound field for the child to look toward the source of the sound. Tones, given in a sound field, have to be "frequency modulated" to break up standing wave patterns. The psychophysical procedure used in the basic air conduction test is a *method of limits* procedure where the different tones are given until the lowest level or absolute threshold is determined. The response can be anything from a verbal "yes," raising the finger, to an eyeblink or eyeshift for the cerebral palsied child with motor limitations. Assuming the responses are reliable and valid, they are plotted on a graphic chart called the audiogram that serves as a record for future reference. The audiogram depicts the hearing threshold configuration; it has significant diagnostic and rehabilitative implications.

Bone Conduction Thresholds

Bone conduction testing is usually implemented by placing a bone oscillator on the mastoid process located just behind the auricle. Normally, the ear canal is unoccluded to provide *relative bone conduction thresholds,* but there are special techniques of occluding the canal and eliciting absolute bone conduction thresholds using a masking procedure.

The mechanism that conducts bone vibration is quite complex. Briefly, the sound bypasses the outer and middle ear going directly to the inner ear; hence it subsequently measures cochlear reserve. Physiologically, bone conduction involves a total process since the conductive mechanism is coupled to the sensory-neural mechanism. Hence, bone thresholds are influenced by participation of sound radiated into the external auditory meatus, the impedance of the middle ear ossicles, inertia of the inner ear fluids, as well as the compressional activity of inner ear space. But clinically bone thresholds are used to ascertain the integrity of the sensory-neural mechanism.

The mode of bone conduction per se is complicated by the interaction of two modes of bone vibration, *inertial bone conduction* associated with the low frequencies (800 Hz and below) where the cochlea is shaken back and forth and *compressional bone conduction* (e.g., 1600 Hz and above) which is characterized by alternate or distortional compressions of the cochlea shell. Hence, while bone conduction audiometry basically reflects cochlea reserve, bone thresholds can be altered with air pressure changes in the ear canal, eardrum loading, and external canal occlusion.

Conditioning procedures for eliciting the audiometric response can vary from a simple hand gesture to a complex electrophysiologic reaction. Thresholds can be obtained by a serial intensity presentation of the tone in an ascending sequence, in a descending sequence, usually both. In the ascending technique, intensity is increased from an inaudible level until a response is elicited; with the descending technique, the tone is first given at an audible or supra-threshold level and then decreased until the tone is no longer audible. The descending technique yields a 5 to 10 decibels lower threshold because of the stimulus trace effect. In both techniques, the absolute threshold is the lowest level where the tone is heard. Most audiologists combine the ascending and descending into a "bracket" procedure.

Audiogram

An audiogram contains a considerable amount of diagnostic information relative to the hearing levels at different frequencies in the auditory spectrum, the site and type of impairment, even etiology. Air conduction thresholds measure the entire auditory mechanism from the outer and middle ear conductive mechanism as the sound travels to the cochlea and then to the brain. Since bone conduction measures essentially the same, but ostensibly without the conductive component of the outer and middle ear, the difference between the air and the bone threshold, the *air-bone gap,* indicates the amount of conductive impairment. In common parlance, the bone threshold designates sensory-neural acuity. Suppose at 1000 Hz there is a 60 dB AC threshold and a 25 dB bone threshold. This would indicate a mixed loss with a 25 dB sensory-neural component and a 35 dB conductive component (60–25 dB). A truly conductive loss would yield bone thresholds at 0 dB, and a purely sensory-neural loss would yield AC & BC thresholds at 60 dB in this example. Below is a simplified pedogogical formula to exemplify this analysis: AC = air conduction; BC = bone conduction; CM = conductive mechanism; SnM = sensory-neural mechanism:

			Mixed	Conductive	Sensory-Neural
AC	CM + SnM	=	60 dB	60 dB	60 dB
BC	SnM	=	25 dB	0 dB	60 dB
AC − BC	CM		= 35 dB	60 dB	0 dB

Hearing threshold levels are always given in decibel units; these units in no way represent "percentage" values as is commonly misconstrued. Decibel values can be converted to percentages with a special formula which assigns different speech weighted values at each frequency and intensity level. The weighted values indicate that all frequencies and intensity levels do not carry equal importance for speech intelligibility. Furthermore, the better ear is weighted more heavily than the poorer ear for a binaural percentage loss. Thus, a normal ear and a totally deaf ear would yield a binaural loss of approximately 6–7 percent.

In addition to the information gleaned from the relationship between the air and bone thresholds, there is significant diagnostic information from the configuration of the thresholds. A progressive downward sloping line signifies poorer high tone acuity and is usually symptomatic of a sensory-neural loss. On the other hand, a flat configuration or one that slopes upward (i.e., better high tone acuity) is more indicative of a conductive impairment. There are many exceptions to these configurations, but these two generalizations usually prevail.

Speech Audiometry

Information gleaned from the pure tone thresholds is crucial to assess the magnitude and type of hearing loss and the site of lesion, but it fails to evaluate the ability to recognize and discern speech stimuli. For example, a moderate sensory-neural hearing loss will impose a greater speech discrimination deprivation than a comparable conductive loss. In fact, it is atypical for conductive losses to have any speech discrimination deprivation. But sensory-neural impairments do, and the persons with similar sensory-neural impairments may differ markedly in perceiving speech. Speech tests, then, have been developed to test this function, but they also provide significant diagnostic information. Special speech audiometers are available for this purpose. There are several varieties of speech tests, but two in particular are in standard use, the *speech reception threshold* and the *discrimination* score.

Speech Reception Threshold (SRT)

This is the minimum intensity level for the subject to identify 50 percent of the words correctly. Special bisyllabic words are used where there is equal stress on each syllable, i.e., mailman, baseball, railroad, etc. Because of the spondaic pattern, the words are called *spondee words*. These words are especially well suited for threshold measurement because they yield a narrow (5–10 dB) range between the threshold of detectibility (where the subject just hears the words) and the threshold of intelligibility (where the subject recognizes the word). There are thirty-six spondee words to the list that can be given through earphones or a loudspeaker. The words are grouped into clusters of six, and the SRT is the decibel level where three are missed and three are correct.

Presentation can be live voice with intensity monitoring through a VU meter or from commercially prepared phonograph discs. Discs are standardized with a 1000 Hz reference tone for the VU calibration adjustment and a carrier phrase (say the word . . . mailman) preceding each word. While standardization and consistency of presentation is the major advantage of commercially available records, they may not be practical for young children or cerebral palsied children who cannot respond at the predetermined pace. Thus, live voice allows for vocabulary flexibility and presentation at a slower pace. This procedure allows for a child to point to a picture or an object that corresponds to the word. Whenever possible, the better ear is tested first with words initially presented about 20 dB above the 1000 Hz threshold. As most speech audiometers have 2 dB intensity increments, the SRT is the level where half of the words are correctly recognized.

SRT and air conduction thresholds differ somewhat as the former is a recognition threshold, and the latter is a detection threshold. Nevertheless, the differences are minimal operationally, and the two can be equated clinically. Thus, the mean of the pure tone (air conduction) threshold average (PTA) for 500, 1000, and 2000 Hz should approximate the obtained SRT. In instances of a sharply sloping audiogram, the two better AC thresholds are often averaged in lieu of the three frequency formula. This indirect procedure for estimating the SRT is used with children who have insufficient language for a direct SRT assessment. It is especially valuable with cerebral palsied children.

Speech Discrimination Hearing Tests

Speech discrimination is the ability to discern phonetic differences among sounds. Unlike the other hearing tests discussed so far, this is a suprathreshold test given at approximately 40 dB above the speech reception threshold or at some "most comfortable listening level" (MCL). Furthermore, the discrimination score is a percentage value relative to 100 percent rather than a decibel unit. Hence, a perfect score is 100 percent although 90–100 percent is within normal limits. When the scores are between 75 to 89 percent, slight communication difficulty is expected, and moderate difficulty occurs with scores between 60 to 74 percent. Scores from 50 to 59 percent are associated with marked difficulty with conversational speech, and below 50 percent results in excessively poor communication. These assessments are based on adults listening to adults, but the results are markedly different for adults listening to children (Nober 1974a, 1974b), particularly in noise.

Discrimination tests are usually given in a sound treated room where extraneous noise is under control. A number of speech testing materials have been developed and used through the years, e.g., monosyllabic words, sentences, multiple choice procedures, rhyme tests, nonsense syllables, competing message tests, etc. Clinically, the most prevalent in use is the *phonetically balanced* word list as modified by Hirsh *et al.* (1952) from an original list of words developed at the Harvard Psychoacoustics Laboratories. Phonetic balance connotes that each list of fifty words contains a sampling of the English sounds in the same proportion used during conversation. Since each word is weighted 2 percent, a perfect score is 100 percent. Several research clinicians have studied list reduction to twenty-five words; hence the value for each word doubles and the phonetic balance is altered somewhat. In subsequent years, several phonetically balanced lists were developed and improved. Irwin *et al.* (1963a, 1963b, 1964, 1965) devised speech discrimination tests specifically designed for the cerebral palsied child.

Word discrimination testing offers pertinent diagnostic and, indeed, rehabilitative information when combined with other audiologic and otologic data. For example, conductive impairments do not usually affect the discrimination score, but sensory-neural impairments reduce the scores to an amount that depends somewhat on the severity and locus of the impairment. In cochlear damage (sensory component) there is some relationship between the hearing threshold levels, the frequencies affected, the amount of recruitment, and the subsequent discrimination loss. While the relationship is not linear or predictable, it is safe to generalize that the greater the threshold shift due to cochlear damage, the poorer the discrimination score. This relationship does not occur in neural impairments, e.g., retrocochlear damage. Indeed, marked discrimination losses can accompany relatively normal looking audiogram configurations. This is also the case in central impairments.

Discrimination testing provides some measure of predictability for rehabilitation, and subsequently, it is an integral part of hearing aid evaluations. It is also useful in differentiating among hearing aids when they vary in acoustic specifications, particularly when noise is used to make the test more critical. But the variances need to be marked as the progressive engineering improvements in printed circuitry and transducer (microphone and receiver) stability has minimized differences among hearing aids.

Normally, discrimination or intelligibility scores remain at 100 percent beyond a given maximum level, but not always, particularly with cochlea impairments. Hence, in diagnostic audiometry, discrimination testing is conducted at several levels with 40 dB re: SRT serving as the general point of reference. In this instance, the objective is to determine the maximum score and trace for roll-off or reduction in discrimination as intensity is increased. This information has diagnostic and rehabilitative implications. Diagnostically, a roll-off suggests a sensory-neural impairment and physiologic overloading as normal ears and conductively impaired ears do not exhibit this pattern. Rehabilitation prognosis is diminished when this occurs, as amplification is limited in compensatory value. Thus, loud speech may be bothersome and unclear, or distorted, while soft speech is unintelligible. The magnitude of this difficulty may be confounded by recruitment and other dysacusic problems.

Masking

Masking is used almost routinely in pure tone and speech audiometry. It occurs when the threshold for one signal is elevated or increased by the presence of another. While most sounds can serve as maskers, some are more efficient than others. Noise masks pure tone well and a number of noise stimuli are in clinical use, e.g., *white* noise (all frequencies in spectrum included, amplitudes about equal), *complex* noise (low frequency fundamental plus harmonies), and *narrow band* white noise. Narrow band noise is filtered white noise where the center frequency represents the pure tone under test. It is based on the *critical-band concept,* i.e., only a restricted part of the noise band equal to the acoustic energy of the test tone is necessary to mask it. Anything more or less is not necessary from a clinical perspective. Narrow band masking is in wide clinical use by audiologists because of its efficiency in raising the threshold or diminishing the participation of the ear not under test.

Masking is used in pure tone audiometry to preempt or eliminate the participation of the contralateral ear; i.e., the ear *not* being tested. In bone conduction, masking is almost a standard procedure because of the tendency of the tone in the test ear (ipsilateral ear) to cross over to the other ear. In bone conduction, transcranial attentuation from one side to the other is only about 5 to 10 dB.

But the situation is markedly different in air conduction audiometry since the head mass provides an interaural attentuation of approximately 40–60 dB. Thus, unless there is a difference in threshold sensitivity between the two ears of at least this amount, the ear under test (ipsilateral ear) will receive the tones; if the difference exceeds this amount, there is the possibility that the sound will lateralize to the ear not being tested (contralateral ear).

Masking is also used in speech audiometry to selectively interfere or reduce the redundancy of the speech signal under controlled conditions. In this fashion, programmed signal-to-noise (S/N) ratios can be ascertained in speech discrimination testing. Masking in speech audiometry has pertinent diagnostic and rehabilitative implications (Nober 1975).

SPECIAL TESTS TO ASSESS THE AUDITORY PROCESSING MECHANISM

A vast number of research investigations have been conducted in the last two decades to develop special diagnostic assessment procedures for children and adults. These tests attempt to assess the hearing levels for pure tone and speech, the integrity of the auditory mechanism in dealing with auditory stimuli, the site of lesion, the type of hearing loss, and the implications for auditory rehabilitation and educational management. Some of the tests attempt to identify hearing problems in newborn high-risk infants, assess the hearing of difficult-to-test (DTT) populations, such as the retarded and cerebral palsied; the latter employ techniques that use responses associated with behavioral or systematic physiologic changes. Some of the elicited responses are unconditioned, while others are conditioned to the auditory stimulus. Still other tests measure the mechanical alterations of the conductive and vestibular mechanisms. A number of the tests are well documented for validity and reliability, while others are still in the exploratory stages. The following classifications are generally used to categorize these tests:

Pediatric Audiometry

There are no techniques to assess hearing sensitivity that will work effectively with all children, or for that matter, all adults. Through the years a number of techniques have been adapted, but the goals are similar in trying to determine: (1) does the child hear; (2) how much does the child hear; (3) what type of hearing loss; (4) where is the site of auditory impairment; (5) what is the etiology; and (6) auditory rehabilitation and educational prognoses and management. If these data can be obtained accurately, they also provide some pertinent information about speech and language potential. When audiological information is combined with psychometric, educational, medical, and sociologic data, then structured coordinated plans for therapeutic and educational management are possible. This is crucial since the early formative years are fundamental to language acquisition and development.

While it is difficult to ascertain specific thresholds in the neonate, relatively reliable hearing estimates can be made. For the cooperative child, three years or older, voluntary behavioral responses can be elicited, so test procedures for this age group often parallel those used with adults. From two to three years, the conditioning techniques are largely operant, i.e., *play audiometry,* where the response is moving a block or pushing a button when the tone is just audible. Some cooperative bright children can be tested at two years accurately with simple conditioning procedures. Generally, with children below the age of two, it is not possible to secure the "subjective" participation of the child; and, consequently, "objective" audiometry using a motor reflex, auditory localization (conditioned or unconditioned), or some electrophysiologic measure is utilized.

Subjective audiometry, by definition, requires a voluntary, purposeful response from the subject to indicate he or she heard the tone or recognized the word. *Objective* audiometry usually involves an involuntary, physical response, e.g., an overt startle reaction, a cessation of activity, an orienting glance toward the sound, or perhaps a covert physiologic reaction that is recorded electronically. Reliability and validity of all audiometric procedures varies with age, the integrity of the child's nervous system, the test procedures, the skill of the audiologist, the test environment, instrumentation, etc.

A considerable amount of research in testing infants, e.g., *neonatal audiometry,* focuses on identifying high-risk children within a few hours of birth or before they are discharged from the hospital. The screening procedures in neonatal audiometry use meticulous, systematic observation of the infant's behavior relative to a controlled sound output. Methods of rating the observations have received considerable attention in the past decade.

Observations in neonatal audiometry include the Moro reflex, the auropalpebral reflex, sucking or non-nutritive inhibition, localization of the sound, and general arousal. Responses can be quantified on a five point scale from (1) no response to (5) paroxysmal response. A special sound generator that warbles a 3000 Hz tone at an output of 70–90 dB is used as the sound stimulus in most instances. The procedure has the major limitation of observer reliability. As a result, the interpretation can have false negative or false positive responses, seriously questioning the validity. Some reserve the procedure only for high-risk babies.

Reflex Audiometry

In this group of tests, the involuntary overt reflex constitutes the response. It does not include electrophysiologic reactions. Skeletal or motor reflexes to a sound stimulus may be diffuse or specific, learned (conditioned) or unlearned (unconditioned). Sometimes results only provide a crude index of sensitivity and at other times yield thresholds of uncanny accuracy. Since reflexes are present at birth, neonatal reflex testing is possible within hours of birth.

    1.   The *Moro startle reflex* is a diffuse, unconditioned reaction to intense stimulation. When it occurs to sound, it indicates that some hearing is present, but its absence does not necessarily confirm hearing loss. Some designate the response as an "arousal" to auditory stimuli. Intense percussion sounds are very effective for eliciting the Moro startle in early childhood, but the abruptness can produce a violent stretch reflex in the spastic child or trigger excessive motor activity in the athetoid. Hence, for the cerebral palsied, there is no direct relation between the magnitude of the reflex and the perceptual loudness of the sound.

    2.   The *auropalpebral reflex (APR)*, i.e., the eyeblink, is the sudden closing of the eyes if they are open or a tightening of the closure if they are already closed; it is an unconditioned reaction. The APR has been elicited within a half hour of birth. It has been used on normal infants ranging in age from one to seven days old.

    3.   The *orienting reflex* refers to the nonspecific reflex that is initiated when there is a change in stimulus. There are two forms of the orienting reflex to sound, the generalized which is the response that occurs initially to the stimulus, and the localized which is the response that occurs only after repeated stimulations.

    4.   The *conditioned orientation response* is a conditioning procedure (not to be confused with the above) where the child is taught to look toward one of two loudspeakers while sitting midway between the two in a soundfield. It is based on the natural tendency to localize a sound source in space.

    5.   *Respiratory audiometry* deals with changes in the breathing or respiratory patterns. While a number of mechanical devices have been developed, the latest uses a photoelectric unit. The technique has been used with varying success in neonates.

Behavioral Audiometry

This refers to any overt subjective reactions given as the response to an auditory stimulus. It is usually voluntary but can be involuntary such as the localization toward the source of a sound. Some authorities include startle and auropalpebral reflexes under this category, but this author prefers to list the latter as a separate reflex category.

Play Audiometry

Pure tone tests form the core of any total audiometric evaluation, and all efforts are directed at eliciting air and bone thresholds to assess the sensitivity of the auditory processing mechanism. The ultimate goal is to obtain a sharp conditioned response as soon as the tone is perceived, i.e., the absolute threshold. The child may simply be required to raise the hand or move a block as the response. This basic procedure can be successful with children as young as two years. A cerebral palsy child with extensive upper extremity involvement cannot always negotiate sustained voluntary control, and the audiometrist may have to improvise a more practical response. Some audiologists have cerebral palsied children conditioned to shift their eyes to the side or perhaps close them as the response to the tone. An effective technique with hyperactive children is to require them to stand up quickly when they hear the tone and sit down when the tone is inaudible. This also helps to dissipate their excessive energy toward a useful purpose.

In audiometry there is little or no relationship between the complexity of the testing apparatus and the recurrent success of the technique. In fact, if any generalization is professionally tolerable, it is that the simpler procedures seem to be more reliable. Success depends heavily on the technical skill and resourcefulness of the audiologist.

For the age group from two to four, testing techniques are based on games. Play audiometry was introduced with a "peepshow" where the child's appropriate response to a tone presentation is rewarded by an intriguing scene. Subsequently, dozens of innovative devices have been developed to motivate a reluctant child to participate in the hearing test. In recent years, a number of modifications have been contrived that use visual reinforcement.

One prevailing problem in audiometry concerns the conditioning process per se, as conditioning cannot occur if the tone is inaudible to the subject during the reinforcement trials. Children with a mild or moderate hearing loss do not present a major problem in this respect, but children with severe or profound hearing loss create the following dilemma: Does the absence of a behavioral response to a tone reflect a lack of hearing or lack of conditioning? One solution is to determine whether the child can be conditioned with another type of stimulus such as a vibratory stimulus. Thus, the bone oscillator is placed in the child's hand and the child is conditioned to give a response when he feels the vibratory sensation in his hand. Nober (1964) has provided quantitative data for the vibratory thresholds with the bone oscillator for frequencies 250 and 500 Hz in the hand and on the mastoid bone. At 250 Hz the tactile threshold is about 25 dB on the mastoid bone and approximately 15 dB in the hand; for 500 Hz the mastoid vibratory threshold is 50 dB and approximately 35 dB in the hand. The accuracy of the conditioning toward threshold can then be gleaned by comparing the tactile thresholds obtained by the therapist with the expected thresholds provided by Nober (1964). It is also preferable (Nober, 1963) to use a 500 Hz tone during the conditioning process (reinforcement trails) as it is a reliable frequency and audible to about 95 percent of deaf children.

Speech tests are used with children who have developed language. Various types of speech play techniques have been devised to obtain speech reception thresholds and discrimination scores. Spondee words and a Phonetically Balanced Kindergarten (PBK) word list have been adapted for children.

Acoustic Impedance Audiometry

Acoustic impedance measures the resistance or oppositional force of the conductive mechanism to a flow of energy. It has emerged as one of the most formidable new otological assessments, particularly since it is a sensitive and reliable objective procedure. It does not actually measure hearing levels, but rather the mechanical efficiency of the conductive mechanism. The reflex component has neurological significance.

In the normal ear, the outer and middle ear conductive mechanism with its low impedance (415 ohms/cm²) is well matched by the ossicular chain to the high impedance (1900 ohms/cm²) of the inner ear. The acoustic energy impinging on the relatively large area of the tympanic membrane (eardrum) is transduced to mechanical energy with concentrated force on the relatively small areal surface of the oval window. This impedance match depends on the pressure relationship between the middle ear cavity (the tympanum) and external ambient environmental pressure on the external auditory meatal side of the tympanic membrane. Hence, acoustic impedance is measured at the lateral surface of the tympanic membrane in the external auditory canal. Thus, in the normal ear with optimal ossicular, eardrum, and eustachian tube performance, the acoustic impedance is predetermined by the structures and relationship of the internal and external air pressures. Any alteration of this balance, up or down, designates a malfunction somewhere in this complex mechanical system.

Clearly, acoustic impedance assessment, when combined with other otologic and audiologic data, provides considerable information. Three acoustic impedance tests are in general clinical use, i.e., *tympanometry, static impedance,* and *stapedial reflex* assessment. These provide ways to assess eustachian tube potency, eardrum potency and scarring, otitis media, otosclerosis, ossicular disarticulation, fluid effusion, stapedial and tensor tympani intergrity, trigeminal, acoustic and cranial nerve integrity, brain stem impairment, sensory-neural impairment, etc. Most tests are based on two types of acoustic impedance measures: static (absolute) and dynamic. The former designates, in absolute values, the acoustic impedance associated with the mobility of the ossicular system as determined by ambient atmospheric pressure in the external auditory canal and the middle ear mechanism. Static acoustic impedance measurements are used for the differential diagnosis of conductive impairments often associated with otitis media, otosclerosis, and ossicular discontinuity. Otitis media and otosclerosis yield a high impedance, and ossicular discontinuity yields a low impedance.

In dynamic measurements, pressure changes are systematically induced in the external auditory meatus for tympanometry measures which can be traced on a permanent graph called the *tympanogram.* Changes are usually consistent and predictable because of their mechanical nature. Normally, acoustic impedance increases at the eardrum when the air pressure in the external auditory canal differs (either higher or lower) from the atmospheric pressure, but abnormal structural and functional conditions of the middle ear mechanism will yield results different from a normal conductive mechanism. The information has extensive diagnostic value. Thus, a retracted drum would add stiffness to the middle ear system, reduce efficiency, and raise impedance on the tympanogram differently than would scars on the eardrum, ankylosis of the stapes, malleolar fixation, or a chronic otitis. Otitis lowers static compliance and often abolishes the stapedial reflex.

Measurements have been done on the eardrum relative to: scarring, perforations, fluid effusion, tympanum air pressure, ossicular discontinuity, otosclerosis, otitis media, eustachian tube integrity, stapedial reflex. Measurement more specific to sensory-neural and peripheral nervous system (cranial nerve) disorders include tests of recruitment, abnormal adaptation, brain stem disorders, intercranial pressure, tests of the integrity of the trigeminal, facial, and acoustic cranial nerves. Hence, acoustic impedance audiometry is particularly pertinent to cerebral palsy as they do not require rapid motor reactions, test cranial nerve integrity, and reflex activity of the intra-aural musculature.

Short Increment Sensitivity Index (SISI)

This test is based on differential sensitivity, i.e., the smallest increment necessary to perceptually detect that a change in the stimulus intensity has occurred. In clinical audiology, the intensity *difference-limen (DL)* is a standard procedure although some earlier research investigated frequency difference-limen. A term once used synonymously with difference-limen is the just-noticeable-difference (JND).

Normally, the intensity difference-limen is larger at the threshold level, where the ear is less sensitive and becomes smaller as the intensity is increased to where the ear is more sensitive. Thus, DL provides a quantitative assessment of differential sensitivity of the ear. In normal ears, the DL is approximately 3 dB at threshold (depending on the frequency) and about 0.3 dB at 40 dB above threshold. Since recruiting ears symptomatically exhibit an accelerated buildup of loudness sensation beyond the detection threshold, recruitment is exhibited by smaller DL's just above threshold. Indeed, the comparative DL intensity magnitudes above threshold and at 40 dB above threshold would show less difference for recruiting ears than for normal ears.

The DL procedure used in the short increment sensitivity index (SISI) (Jerger, et. al., 1959) is currently the most widely used test. In this relatively simple test to administer; a steady pure tone is presented 20 dB above the threshold level (for any given frequency) with a 1 dB intensity increment increase superimposed on the steady 20 dB tone every five seconds. The pattern is randomized to avoid establishing a rhythm. Twenty 1 dB increments are given, and the subject signals when he perceives an increment. The score is expressed as the percentage of correct identifications to the 20 increments. The range for normal and conductive ears is 0 to 25 percent, while ears with cochlear involvement may have scores from 70 to 100 percent; the midrange from 25 to 65 percent requires interpretation.

Bekesy Audiometry

If for some reason it was only possible to use one audiologic technique to provide maximum diagnostic information, Bekesy audiometry would be the choice. It has been used on adults, on children as young as $2\frac{1}{2}$ to $3\frac{1}{2}$ years, auditory adaptation, difference-limen, tone decay, recruitment, and group testing. It has been used for diagnosing specific etiologies such as psychogenic problems, acoustic neurinoma, sudden deafness, ototoxic damage, cerebral meningioma, otosclerosis, cholestleatoma, Meniere's disease and cerebellopontine angle tumor.

Bekesy audiometry basically uses a different psychological technique as compared to behavioral audiometry which employs a *method-of-limits* psychophysical procedure. Here an examiner manipulates the intensity and frequency parameters to find the subjects' threshold limits. Bekesy audiometry uses a *method-of-adjustment* procedure where the patient controls and manipulates the intensity attenuator himself, continuously tracing threshold as the frequency sweeps automatically from 100 Hz to 10,000 Hz. For a tone decay test, the audiometer can be locked into one fixed frequency. Operationally, the subject pushes a button to diminish the intensity and releases the button to allow the intensity to increase. Intensity is attenuated at 2.5 or 5 dB/second speeds, with a total range of 120 dB. By manipulating the intensity attenuator, the subject brackets his own threshold from audible to inaudible. While the intensity rise seems continuous perceptually, the actual intensity changes are 0.25 dB steps.

The tone stimulus is presented either in a continuous sweep mode or as a pulsating interrupted sweep with 2.5 interruptions per second, of equal on-off duration. The audiogram relationship between the two modes is of diagnostic significance. All Bekesy audiograms are automatically traced by a marking stylus on a moving drum that serves as a permanent record. Thus, the designation "automatic audiometry" has become synonymous with Bekesy testing.

Bekesy audiograms depict up and down "tracking" envelope tracings that resemble the teeth of a rip saw. The peaks at the upper decibel levels ostensibly designate where the tone just becomes audible, and the lower intensity peaks where the tone becomes just inaudible; the midpoint between the two upper and lower parts correlates well with the conventional audiogram. In the normal ear, the excursions are relatively equal throughout the audiogram tracking, e.g., 5-15 dB, but in instances of recruitment, the amplitude excursions diminish to 3 dB or less because of the small difference-limen just above threshold. In effect, the subject is tracking his difference-limen for intensity.

Both the continuous and interrupted trackings are depicted on the same audiogram for comparison. While an extensive number of patterns converge, five major "types" have been evolved (Jerger 1960). In the *Type I* Bekesy audiogram, the continuous and interrupted tracings are intertwined, amplitudes are about 10 dB, and the trackings are relatively flat. Normal ears and ears with conductive involvements fall into this category; on some occasions, cochlea ears give this pattern. *Type II* Bekesy audiograms have intertwined, continuous and interrupted tracings until approximately 1000 Hz, but then the continuous tracings drop about 10-15 dB below the interrupted and run parallel to it for the remainder of the range. Most cochlear impairments are in this category. *Type III* continuous tracking shows an early marked decline in auditory threshold sensitivity, often to the limits of the audiometer; but the interrupted does not follow this pattern. Acoustic neurinoma and other retrocochlear involvements often yield this pattern.

Type IV patterns also show an immediate drop of the continuous tracking, but the amplitudes of the continuous are often the same magnitude as that of the interrupted. *Type V* reverses the total pattern, where the interrupted falls below the continuous; this often occurs in psychogenic disorders. The drop in continuous trackings in Type II, III, and IV are precipitated by a perstimulatory fatigue that does not occur in the interrupted tone presentation, where the auditory neural mechanism has sufficient resting time to rejuvenate during the short intervals.

Tone Decay Test

The tone decay test quantifies perstimulatory decrease in threshold sensitivity; it is related to auditory fatigue. If tone decay shows perstimulatory threshold increases, there is evidence of retrocochlear lesion. A number of techniques for administering the tone decay test have been used through the years, but basically, the subject acknowledges the presence of a continuous tone, either at threshold or just above threshold for a predetermined time duration (e.g., a minute or less) depending on the choice of the technique. If more intensity is needed because tone audibility disappeared or "decayed," the intensity is increased until the patient continues to hear the tone for one full minute. The additional amount of intensity needed is quantified. Classification systems vary, but generally 0–5 dB increase is normal, 10–15 dB is mild tone decay, 20–25 dB is moderate, and 30 dB is considered severe. Mild to moderate tone decay may be associated with impairment of the cochlear origin while any increase in excess of 30 dB is suggestive of retrocochlear impairment. Furthermore, the more severe the pathology, the greater number of frequencies involved.

Electrophysiologic Audiometry

Electrophysiologic audiometry employs electronic apparatus to record the covert physiologic responses to an acoustic stimulus. An impressive number of electrophysiologic tests have been developed through the years.

Electrodermal Audiometry (EDA)

This is one of the forerunners of this group. Initially it was designated the *psychogalvanic reflex (PGSR)*, then shortened to *galvanic skin reflex (GSR)*, and currently is the *electrodermal reflex (EDR)*. The reflex is the physiologic reduction in skin resistance caused by a precipitous stress; initially it was the unconditioned shock. While the EDA can be elicited to a tone, it quickly extinguishes after a few trials so a complete hearing test is not possible. Thus, a process of conditioning is necessary. This is done through a conditioning process of pairing the tone and shock in a predetermined temporal sequence, i.e., reinforcement trials. After a series of reinforcement trials, the shock is removed with the expectation that the tone will produce a stronger and more enduring EDR—more resistant to extinction. Auditory thresholds for various frequencies are determined by the intensity level at which the EDR ceases (Nober, 1958). The reliability and validity of this procedure has been established with older children, but is still of questionable validity with very young infants, the brain damaged and emotionally disturbed. It is especially dubious with cerebral palsied children because of the motor activity that comfounds the tracings.

Electroencephalographic Audiometry (EEA)

This is the electronic recording of the changes in the neural-wave activity of the brain to pure tones. It requires elaborate and expensive apparatus, is difficult to administer, and interpretation of the data is extremely complex—indeed, far from "objective" as the category connotes. Nevertheless, a trained audiologist can estimate auditory thresholds on children with surprising accuracy, i.e., to within 10 dB of the actual behavioral threshold. Responses occur at all ages, but vary according to age, brain damage, etc. EEA has met with little diagnostic success for differentiating among various types of central auditory impairments, but Goldstein and Kendall (1963) were able to identify slight EEG differences between children with central auditory impairments and those with peripheral auditory impairments. Foley (1968) found the EEG deteriorates in cerebral palsied children.

A major procedural breakthrough occurred when an electronic averaging computer was added to the EEG system. The computer stored and added successive repitions of tone impulses with the cortical responses to the tone in a time-locked program. The cumulative response is then built up in magnitude into an *averaged evoked (electroencephalographic) response* (*AER*). The AER diminishes the random (extraneous) background response by using an electronic cancellation process. Since extraneous responses are inadvertent, i.e., not time-locked to a stimulus, the cumulative additive effects can be electronically averaged.

AER consists of three components, i.e., *early, slow,* and *late.* The ranges are 18–50 msec., 80–300 msec., and 275 msec. and beyond, respectively. Each component reflects different activities, but the relative importance is still not fully determined. Basically, the late component is used to determine the auditory response; it has a wave form with two positive peaks (P1, P2) and two negative peaks (N1, N2). These peak relationships are variable depending on age, physiological state, drug use, sleep stage, acoustic intensity, and frequency.

Electrocardiographic (Heart Rate) Audiometry

The procedure of identifying heart rate changes—i.e., acceleration or deceleration—on newborn infants, even premature infants, retarded children, is in an exploratory stage of development.

Attempts to establish pure tone threshold measures show responses around 35 dB. Relationships are being investigated between response magnitude, rate, and stimulus magnitude. Some neonates show habituation to repeated tone stimulation so responses decrease over a period of time. A change to a different tone (implying frequency discrimination) reinforces the response magnitude. Apparently, the response is mediated through the sympathetic nervous system with noticeable increases in response magnitude during the first five days of life.

There is another cardiovascular technique called *peripheral vascular response* (*PVR*) audiometry which also holds some promise for screening infants. It measures pulse volume at the periphery, e.g., finger pulse, but requires intense sound.

Electro-oculogyric Audiometry

This records eye muscle impulse changes as the response to sound. Widely scattered responses have been reported, but the technique holds promise. Other general indices of muscle contraction changes to sound have been explored under the generic designation of *electromyographic audiometry.*

Electronystagmography (ENG)

While ENG is not an electrophysiologic "hearing test" that assesses hearing, it is a pertinent diagnostic otologic test of vestibular function used in the total medical battery. By ascertaining the integrity of the vestibular mechanism (body orientation and equilibrium) and the auditory mechanism, the otologist may determine the site of lesion. Organic disorders are suggested when there are cochlear and peripheral vestibular impairments; conversely, a normal ENG suggests that the vestibular system is normal.

Nystagmus is a symptom (not a disease) commonly associated with brain pathology, often seen in the cerebral palsied. It reflects the vestibulo-occular reflex, an involuntary eye movement of vestibular origin, caused by an imbalance of bilateral neural synchronization. Nystagmus is spontaneous and can be induced by upsetting the vestibular function with a stimulus that is disruptive to reciprocal right and left coordinated activity. It is characterized as an abnormal eye movement, exhibiting a slow component in one direction and a rapid movement in the opposite direction. The movement (or drift) which can be horizontal, vertical, or rotational, extends to a given point and then the reflex mechanism rapidly reverses the motion.

Electronic nystagmography is a recent improvisation to perform a caloric test of vestibular functioning. Changes in fluid temperature (some are air) induce a biological potential known as the "corneorentinal potential."

Hence, any positional change of the cornea relative to the retina is recorded on an electric graphic that serves as a permanent record. Electronic nystagmography has the added advantage of quantifying the magnitude of the nystagmus, the velocity of the slow movement, and the degree of the eye movement.

Electrocochleo Audiometry

This is the electrocochleogram recording of electric potential from the cochlea. While recording cochlear potentials is not new, its application to clinical audiology and humans is exploratory since it requires a surgical procedure. Extratympanic recordings are being investigated.

Central Auditory Tests (CAT)

Disorders of the central auditory nervous system include all auditory impairments proximal to the first and second order neuron of the dorsal and ventral cochlear nuclei. Hence, these tests include retrocochlear processes. Anatomically, the central auditory nervous system consists of the brainstem pathways of the lateral lemniscus and Heschl's gyrus (primary auditory projection area) of the temporal lobe. In contrast, the peripheral auditory system includes the conductive mechanism, comprising the external auditory canal and the middle ear, the cochlea, and the eighth cranial nerve. These are located distal to the first and second dorsal and ventral cochlear nuclei.

Perhaps the most characteristic audiometric difference between peripheral and central auditory disturbances lies in the relationship between the pure tone results and speech discrimination. Peripheral disturbances are reflected in pure tone threshold shifts which may have concommitant auditory distortion, abnormal adaptation (tone decay), recruitment, and other dysacuses. Typically, the greater the peripheral disturbance, the greater the threshold shift which has a frequency-bound relationship. This pattern does not prevail in central auditory disorders where pure tone hearing threshold levels may be well within normal limits, but discrimination loss is excessive. Thus, the marked deficit in auditory discrimination for coherent speech is notable as it is for non-coherent signals of a binaural nature. The general expectation for the relationship between pure tone auditory sensitivity and speech discrimination becomes progressively less predictable as the locus of the impairment ascends from the cochlea to the superior temporal convolution of the brain.

A major difference between the peripheral hearing test battery and the central hearing test battery is that the former is basically monotic with ipsilateral implications, while central tests are basically dichotic with contralateral implications. Contralateral implications occur in central disorders because the auditory pathways cross from the ipsilateral first and second order neurons in the cochlear nuclei to the opposite side through the superior olivary nucleus or directly at the brain stem level. The crossed pathways may also interconnect with some ipsilateral pathways at several levels. Hence, audiometric tests of the peripheral mechanism reflect the integrity of the same or ipsilateral side tested while central auditory tests reflect the integrity of the opposite or contralateral side of the central auditory nervous system.

Most auditory level listening is binaural involving binaural integration. This complex integration of normal binaural auditory processing, coupled with the inherent linquistic redundancy of most speech stimuli, makes it difficult to identify a central hearing problem unless special listening procedures are employed. Indeed, one hemisphere tends to assist the other. Thus, it is axiomatic in central auditory testing that the tests involve: (1) diotic listening (both ears simultaneously receive the same signal), (2) dichotic (each receives a different signal), and (3) that redundancy of speech signal is reduced. Under these conditions, listening is more critical and accurate responses will require cortical binaural integration.

The bilateral nature of the central auditory pathways does not imply equality of both sides in processing various types of auditory signals. Brain damage and laterality complicate the processing. Generally in a right handed person with left lobe dominance, the right ear has functional advantage for word tests, nonsense syllables, backward or reversed speech, consonant sounds, spatial components of the signals; the reverse usually holds for a left handed person with dominance in the right side of the brain. The nondominant hemisphere apparently has functional superiority for melodic patterns, nonspeech sounds, vowels, and the temporal components of the auditory signals.

To demonstrate ear advantage for these parameters, dichotic stimulation that fosters contralateral inhibition of ipsilateral signals is used. Signals sent up toward the brain will proceed unilaterally or cross to the appropriate hemisphere. Hemisperic lesions become manifest during dichotic listening because each ear simultaneously receives a different signal or a fraction of the same signal, but the signal components are not fused cortically into a meaningful unit. Hence, central auditory integration is needed to unify different parts of the signal or to localize a pure tone in time and space.

Some central auditory tests, called *competing message tests,* use a dichotic signal where the dominant hemisphere is activated by the speech signal while the other side receives a competing signal. This procedure "strains" the limits of the auditory processing system, as binaural fusion is needed to yield good perception with interference from competing messages. Unlike peripheral hearing tests with standardized levels of difficulty, central hearing tests are individualized to match the disorder and precipitate a breakdown in auditory processing efficiency; indeed, different people have different tolerance levels before breakdown of communication occurs.

Central auditory tests, like peripheral test, are primarily composed of pure tone and speech timuli. Both peripheral and central tests are based on duration, rise-time, phase, repetition rate, onset, and sequence. Responses can be ascertained for auditory reaction time, difference-limen, post-stimulatory fatigue, binaural fusion, lateralization, click preference, etc. The speech battery includes tests based on distortion, accelerated speech, interrupted speech, competing messages, masking, time compression, time expansion, low pass filtering, split signals, and discrimination rollover. An all-inclusive designation, "sensitized speech tests" (SST), is commonly used to describe tests that reduce normal speech redundancy. Jerger (1973) outlines a primary battery:

1. *Performance-intensity function for phonetically balanced words (PI-PB).*
   PB words are tested as intensity is increased. A progressive drop in one ear which has normal pure tone thresholds indicates damage to the contralateral side of the brain.
2. *Synthetic sentence identification (SSI-ICM).*
   Artificial sentences are given repeatedly in different random orders of competing continuous discourse in the same earphone with varying levels between the two messages. This test is especially sensitive to brain stem lesions.
3. *Synthetic sentence identification with contralateral competing messages (SSI-CCM).*
   Similar to the above, but with competing messages in the ear opposite that receiving the sentences. Normals have little or no trouble, but temporal lobe lesions precipitate trouble when levels are unfavorable. The relative score between SSI-ICM and the SSI-CCM differentiates between a brain stem and temporal lobe pathology. A greater ICM deficit suggests brain stem lesion, while a greater CM deficit suggests temporal lobe lesion.

One dichotic competing message test has been used directly on cerebral palsied children. This is the Staggered Spondaic Word Test (Katz 1962, 1968). In this test, two spondee bisyllabic words are recorded so that the first part of one word goes to one ear (noncompeting) while the second part of the second bisyllabic word (noncompeting) goes to the other ear with overlapping competition between the second part of the first word and the first part of the second word. Katz, Myrick, and Winn (1966) tested ten normal and 26 cerebral palsied and found that the cerebral palsied subjects did poorer. Older cerebral palsied subjects did significantly better than the young cerebral palsied patients so an analysis was done with the older and younger cerebral palsied and normal children with a cutoff age of thirteen years. In their refined analysis, only the younger cerebral palsied children yielded abnormal scores. The authors questioned whether the young cerebral palsied auditory mechanism was not still premature in auditory integration, as Birch and Belmont (1965) found in comparing auditory visual integration of normal and cerebral palsied children.

AUDITORY REHABILITATION

The prevalence of hearing disorders vascilates with the criteria used to define an impairment, i.e., the degree of loss, its social and educational impact, whether it is unilateral or bilateral, etc. When a criterion of educational, social, or vocational deprivation is employed, approximately 6,000,-000 Americans have handicapping hearing problems, and some 236,000 are classified as deaf. Approximately 700,000 have multiple visual and auditory handicaps. The cerebral palsied have a much higher percentage of hearing and multiple sensory handicaps.

There are many facets to the auditory rehabilitation of a hearing defective cerebral palsied or noncerebral palsied child. These include auditory training, language training, speech and reading therapy. Psychological, vocational, and social counselling must also be interwoven with the various therapies. Progress and procedure will depend on the resultant interactions of the therapy and psychoeducational programs, as well as variables such as age of onset, type or degree of hearing impairment, overall intelligence, innate language aptitude, home and social support and personality traits. Management of a hearing defective child is a total process of enormous dimensions. Below are discussions of the implications and influences these variables contribute to the prognosis.

Variables

Age of Onset

Adults with normal speech and language who develop partial or total hearing loss require a very different remedial and therapeutic approach than a child who never acquired these basic skills. Existing neuronal speech and language sets in the adult need to be maintained through a speech conservation program. On the other hand, a child with congenital hearing deficiency may not really attain normal linguistic development, but the degree of language retardation will depend on the other factors listed. Even his or her basic cognitive processes may differ as the deaf child is arrested in the language concepts that are needed to abstract and integrate his experiences meaningfully.

Auditory stimuli may be received by the ear, but if the deafness is excessive, the hearing signals are distorted and auditory processing is impaired. This adds considerable confusion if the child is not trained to interpret distorted material to maximum proficiency. Language training is essential as early as possible as the capacity to develop language is greatest in the younger child and decreases with age. There are all sorts of programs relative to age, e.g., infant, preschool, school, adult, geriatric. With the infant the mother becomes the initial therapist (parent-centered) who bombards the child with auditory and visual stimulation on a continuous on-going basis.

Therapy for the congenitally deaf or hard-of-hearing child begins with the very *awareness* of sound. The child is taught to attend to sound and lip movements. This is natural for the young infant who is naturally face oriented and loves to pick at people's faces. The symbolism of acoustic and visual stimuli must be taught, so the child learns the lip movements and speech sounds are purposeful. Only then will concrete and abstract concepts be interpreted with meaningful language experiences.

Type of Loss

Generalizations are much more prevalent in regard to the type of loss. It is worthy of repetition that conductive impairments do not impose the restrictions on language and speech development that sensory-neural impairments incur. Also central hearing impairments have different speech and language repercussions than peripheral impairments.

A conductive loss is not usually associated with any prevailing dysacusis. Consequently, a child with a conductive loss is more successful with a hearing aid and may require little or no additional auditory rehabilitation except for a period of supplemental work with amplification.

Children and adults with sensory-neural hearing losses have difficulty recognizing the information bearing phonetic elements, especially for the finer differences among the high frequency consonants. Consonants are notoriously difficult for the deaf child because they are relatively weak in power (compared to vowels), are inherently less audible to people with high frequency loss, and more adversely affected by low-frequency noise interference. Unfortunately, consonants contain a considerable amount of the information hearing elements. Vowels may be more difficult for the person with a conductive impairment because of their low frequency components.

The presence of recruitment, discrimination loss, tinnitus, or any dysacusic component complicates the effectiveness of a hearing aid. Amplification is not a panacea; it is only a hearing "aid," not a hearing cure.

In some instances, amplification can be a deterrent as the sound can physiologically overload the neuroauditory hearing mechanism and precipitate internal distortion.

Degree of Loss

It is safe to generalize that as the peripheral sensory-neural hearing loss increases so does the magnitude of the language and speech problems. In instances of retrocochlear and central lesions, the rule does not apply as the language difficulties may involve agnosic and aphasic components. As indicated earlier, the relationship between air conduction thresholds and auditory discrimination becomes progressively more unrelated as the auditory pathways are ascended toward the higher auditory centers.

Classifications of children into categories of deaf and hard-of-hearing serves a functional purpose. Usually the criteria are based on the degree of loss, but considerable flexibility is maintained for individual differences. Educational management places heavy demands on auditory processing, whereas vocational or social settings are less stressful to a comparable loss.

Davis (1965) classifies hearing deficient children into six levels or classes according to the average hearing loss at frequencies 500, 1,000, and 2,000 Hz in the better ear:

Class	Degree of Handicap	More Than	Not More Than	Ability to Understand Speech
A	Not significant		25 dB ISO	No significant difficulty with faint speech
B	Slight handicap	26 dB ISO	40 dB	Difficulty only with faint speech
C	Mild handicap	41 dB	55 dB	Frequent difficulty with normal speech
D	Marked handicap	56 dB	70 dB	Frequent difficulty with loud speech
E	Severe handicap	70 dB	90 dB	Can understand only shouted or amplified speech
F	Extreme handicap	91 dB		Usually cannot understand even amplified speech

Silverman and Davis (1970) group the educational needs of children with different amounts of hearing loss. In group 1, where the hearing loss is 40 dB or less, special seating arrangements and speechreading are advised. Group 2 includes losses between 41 and 55 dB where speechreading, amplification, speech correction, speech conservation and favorable seating are advised. Group 3, 56 to 70 dB loss, is similar to group 2, but with special language training. Group 4, 71 to 90 dB, also includes the above, but with special educational management. Group 5, 90 dB to total deafness, requires intensive total educational management and placement.

Intelligence

This is so closely related to language development that they are operationally inseparable. Most intelligence tests rely so heavily on vocabulary and language structure that the former can be predicted from the latter. Even the so called nonverbal performance tests require abstract activities that are based on deductive and inductive language-related reasoning. As a result, the deaf child with reduced language development will score lower on any intelligence test that is standardized on a normal hearing population and relies on language measures. Special tests with norms based on a deaf population have been developed for a more valid estimate of basic intelligence of deaf subjects.

Pragmatically, the deaf child in a hearing environment may be at a disadvantage and probably will never achieve a comparable degree of success regardless of potential. The cerebral palsy child with the added handicap of deafness invariably alludes to a child with less intelligence than he or she may actually have. As a consequence, this child is often mistaken for mentally retarded.

Personality

This is a term that is used freely. In this section, the emotional stability and perceptual aspects of personality of the deaf will be reviewed. Studies in this area suggest that deaf children were less stable emotionally and less adjusted than hearing children. Since the perceptual processes of the deaf child are derived from different psychic experiences, Levine (1963) questioned whether the differences she found actually reflected maladjustment or simply a different type of "psychic integration." Myklebust (1964) contended that deafness modifies the perceptual processes causing the psychological equilibrium of the deaf to have a different foundation. Even psychomotor tasks like lateralization, locomotor coordination, and motor speed are inferior to the hearing child. The cerebral palsied child has the added motor paralysis and is impossible to evaluate in psychomotor areas.

Home and School Influences

The history of education of the deaf provides us with a measure of the complexity of the problems of appropriate educational and familial philosophy of children with special needs. The goals of education of the hearing impaired child are to guide the student into a self-adjusted, well-integrated, happy and fulfilling life. Education begins the moment the child's hearing impairment is diagnosed. Therapy and rehabilitation are usually instituted at home as these children require intensive and continuous special help. Early fundamental training in speech, speechreading, auditory training, manual communication skills (if necessary), and behavior patterns enables the hearing impaired child to make the fullest use of his/her capacities. Programs vary from total oral to total manual to the combination of *total communication*. The national trend toward mainstreaming the hearing impaired child into regular public schools following the Cascade Model is generating major interest in developing in-service training programs for regular classroom teachers, speech educators, and school administrators.

Hearing Impaired Rehabilitation Programs

The prevaling trend to establish speech and language "models" has helped to formulate a perspective of totality which views the individual from a variety of inter-connecting inputs and outputs and connecting parodigms. The model approach permits theoretical constructs to be synthesized with pragmatic knowledge. In most models speech and language processes are basically depicted as a unit that have an *input channel,* an *integrating channel,* and an *output channel.* Any breakdown in one channel affects the other processes as they all interrelate. Functions are self-monitoring through servofeedback loops, as well as through external sources that can yield imposing influences. The more elaborate models have internal and external circuits.

Pioneers of auditory rehabilitation dealt basically with the auditory input channel, such as Max Goldstein's *acoustic method.* He emphasized auditory stimulation, quite a departure in the 1930s from the visually oriented lip reading input emphasis, or the manual (fingerspelling and signing) input systems. Since the early work of Goldstein, a number of systems have evolved, the most recent the "total" approach that is more eclectic using the best of all worlds:

Unisensory Approach

This auditory rehabilitation paradigm uses only the auditory channel of input at any given period in the lesson. The rationale contends that concentration on auditory alone enables the person to focus and make maximum use of all the cues in the auditory signal. Ostensibly, this reduces interference or reliance on other sensory modalities, such as the kinesthetic and visual (Wedenberg 1970). Training in the latter two modalities are separated from the auditory during training with the expectation that perceptual synthesis will occur later. The term "acoupedics" has been used to signify the unisensory approach. Apparently, good success has been reported. Fry (1966) asserts he can obtain normal speech and language if he starts deaf children early enough. With intensive auditory training, he claims to improve the audiograms through increased perception.

Multisensory Approach

From the outset the multisensory paradigm seemed like the logical approach since speech and language are indeed a total process. Thus, the visual and tactile modalities are employed to supplement and augment the auditory input, but all are taught and practiced simultaneously. Investigators have demonstrated that while the visual modality alone and the auditory modality alone are poor, the combined integrated approach yields superior results. Thus, the lessons are structured in such a fashion that all three sensory input modalities are used concurrently. Programs using both informal and formal lessons are used.

For the speech output training which is combined with the auditory input, the reinforcement of visual, kinesthetic, and auditory are used quite a bit. In a relatively new technique, the *verbotonal* (Guberina 1969), an extensive amount of gross bodily patterning and movement is stressed. In this procedure, gross body positioning, or "macromatricity" accompanies the sounds. For the input channel, the speech signal is transduced into a low frequency range as an indirect way of training to the high frequency components of the speech signal.

A formidable issue of whether all deaf people can benefit from auditory input has prevailed for years. Some investigators who contend that total deafness is a rare occurrence demonstrate that audiograms can be elicited on most deaf subjects. Nober (1963, 1964, 1966, 1967) seriously questioned the validity of these audiograms and demonstrated that the so-called auditory thresholds obtained at high intensity levels were not always auditory but rather represented vibrotactile exteroception, mediated through the cutaneous tactile receptors. He subsequently designated these thresholds as *cutile,* after *cu*taneous-tac*tile,* so they could be identified appropriately since they were "real" thresholds but not auditory. Nober showed that comparable threshold levels can be elicited from the palm of the hand nearly identical to those obtained from the ear. Thus, he concluded that more people are totally deaf than assumed, and for these people more attention should be directed to the use of tactile input.

Auditory Training

An auditory training program attempts to obtain the maximum use of residual hearing by taking full advantage of all sounds and other clues. It involves the reception, perception, identification, interpretation, and integration of sounds that are part of our daily lives. One goal is to make listening an enjoyable and meaningful experience. Auditory training can be delineated into three parts: (1) orientation, (2) hearing aid training, and (3) sound discrimination training.

Orientation

Discussions focus on the nature and meaning of deafness and the ramifications for the present and future. Differentiation between the functional terms deaf and hard-of-hearing should be specific enough so the individual appreciates where he fits into the hearing impaired continuum, from mild hearing to total deafness. The type and degree of loss should be understood and clarified. Elementary psychophysics may help the individual appreciate what sound is, how it is used by the auditory mechanism, and why his problems exist. Some of the social and psychological implications should be reviewed. Hence, the individual or parent learns to understand his handicap so goals and strategies become more meaningful.

Much of the material that goes into a basic audiology course would help the hearing impaired to gain insight into his problems, anatomy and physiology of the ear, hearing testing and interpretation of audiogram charts, medical problems, hygiene of the ear and hearing conservation. Lists and discussions of social and vocational agencies are always welcomed, especially with the geriatric population. The level of sophistication for the orientation is strictly a relative matter and must be geared to the management and experiential background of the individual. A new manual designed for these purposes called Hi-Fi (Hearing Impaired Formal Inservice Manual) has been designed by L. Nober (1974).

Hearing Aids

Both professional and lay people have significant difficulty in understanding hearing aids from mechanical, psychophysical, and rehabilitative objectives. One cannot realistically initiate an auditory training program unless one understands the purposes, functions, and limitations of amplification in general, and the hearing aid in particular.

1. *Components of a hearing aid.* A modern hearing aid is an electroacoustic device that amplifies acoustic energy through its transistors and battery energy source. Hence, each hearing aid has a microphone, an amplifier, a volume control, and a receiver. The major purpose of a hearing aid is to provide "compensation" for the loss in auditory sensitivity so the

person can communicate with optimal proficiency. Amplification does not correct a hearing loss in the sense that eye glasses correct visual aberrations. Furthermore, glasses do not generate additional energy or convert one form of energy into another. The hearing aid is complex and has to transduce acoustic energy into electrical energy, and then back to acoustic energy again. Each time energy is coded and decoded from one form to another, the original signal is modified and some fidelity is lost.

A transistor hearing aid consists of three major components: the microphone, the amplifier, and the receiver. Sound impinges on the diaphragm of a magnetic microphone which subsequently vibrates in patterns that correspond to the signal. This activates an electrical current to create the electrical pattern. Hearing aid microphones generally do not transmit well below 250 Hz.

A modern transistor *amplifier* intensifies the sound with energy provided by its transistors and batteries. A transistor is a combination of pure and impure semi-conductor materials arranged in a sandwich pattern. Only one-millionth of an impurity such as arsenic will precipitate electrical voltage when connected to a pure substance such as germanium.

The *receiver* converts the electrical energy from the amplifier to acoustic sound. Air-conduction receivers are fitted into the external auditory meatus through an earmold. The physical properties of the hearing aid receiver generally limits the high-frequency range to a maximum of about 4000 Hz. The overall fidelity of the hearing aid is determined by the characteristics of the hearing aid as a total operation unit so distortion in any one part affects the entire mechanism.

There are usually three tone-control positions on an aid—flat, low-tone suppression, and high-tone suppression. The flat response is preferred for a hearing loss configuration with relatively even reduction in sensitivity throughout the range. Low-tone suppression limits low-frequency amplification, thereby yielding proportionally greater amplification of the higher frequencies. This is preferred in noisy environments or by people with good low frequency acuity. Likewise, the high-tone suppressor circuit permits for low tone emphasis; this is preferred by people with good high frequency acuity. The gradient of suppression for the low, high tone circuits generally follows a 6 dB or 12 dB per octave tilt. These three frequency responses are usually sufficient to assist most types of hearing loss that will benefit from an aid. Rarely is an attempt made to compensate for the threshold shift at each frequency by mirroring the audiogram loss exactly. Complications such as recruitment make this undesireable.

Recruitment complicates hearing aid fitting. The raised SRT and the reduced tolerance level constricts the *dynamic operating range*. Protection against discomfort is built into hearing aids by means of an *automatic gain control (AGC)* such as a compression amplification circuit which monitors the input. AGC automatically reduces the higher amplitudes, but preserves the wave pattern of the sound. In less elaborate hearing aid circuits, the amplitudes may simply be clipped off. *Peak clipping* also monitors amplitude output but is less desireable as it violates the wave pattern or the fidelity by introducing harmonic distortion. Fortunately, harmonic distortion only distorts quality and has minimal adverse effects on auditory discrimination.

2. *Characteristics of hearing aids.* The maximum output level of an aid generally does not exceed 135–140 dB SPL. Anything beyond this point is painful to people regardless of the amount of hearing loss.

Gain is the amount of power the aid provides, e.g., the decibel difference between input and output. This generally does not exceed 70–75 dB, even in the most powerful instruments. Output is the cumulative result of the gain and the signal power. Maximum gain is ascertained as the mean value at 500, 1000, and 2000 Hz at full volume. Maximum output is the upper limit that the aid can amplify; beyond this level peak clipping occurs.

The frequency range of a good hearing aid extends from approximately 250 Hz to 4000 Hz. Considering that the normal hearing range, at best, is from 20 to 20,000 Hz, the marked constriction of an aid is startling. Actually most daily hearing occurs in a range of 100 Hz to 10,000 Hz. But hearing aids do transmit in the *critical speech range* (500–2000 Hz) effectively where apparently 90% of the information bearing elements are clustered. It is not crucial that the complete frequency range be heard because the auditory mechanism phenomenologically fills in the missing elements of the original pattern. For example, a series of pure tones 2000, 3000, and 4000 Hz presented simultaneously to the ear will be perceived as a 1000 Hz tone pitch. In essence, the 2000, 3000, and 4000 Hz tones are the second, third, and fourth harmonics of a 1000 Hz fundamental, but the ear perceives the difference tone of the harmonics. This auditory illusion is called the "case of the missing fundamental." Specification charts that plot the gain relative to frequency should be provided with each hearing aid to estimate its performance characteristics. The average gain can be calculated from this chart by assessing the mean of 500, 1000, and 2000 Hz while the bandwidth is calculated by drawing a horizontal line 15 dB below the mean gain with the lower and upper frequencies intersections representing the bandwidth range.

3. *Types of hearing aids.* Hearing aids have been classified as individual aids, desk aids, and group aids. Until now the discussion was focused to individual aids. Desk and group aids are larger, more expensive, but have greater fidelity. The desk aid usually has its own amplifier and is worn by the individual. A group aid has outlets for several people and the receivers feed off one large amplifier. In both types the wearer controls intensity independently. One highly debated question regards the pragmatic advantage of

the different units during speech and language training. In recent years auditory training units using earphones are in widespread use in special classes. The original units used an electronic induction loop which in essence wired the room and eliminated the need to be connected to a table. More recently, frequency-modulated (FM) trainers have been developed which use a restricted short-wave band. The teacher wears a mike, the student the receiving unit with a mike too. In this instance, there are no wires as a short-wave circuit is provided. Most teachers prefer the better quality and freedom to move about these units provide during training. Auditory training units provide the acoustic patterns for more refined speech development. Many teachers still caution against someone becoming dependent on a superior group aid for communication and then having trouble with the smaller individual unit because of its limited fidelity.

Individual aids can be worn on the body or at ear level, i.e., behind the ear, or in eyeglasses. While ear level aids eliminate body or clothing noise, reduce the body baffle, and place the microphone in its natural location, the body aids are more elaborate, more powerful, and have better fidelity. About 80 percent of the hearing aids sold currently are ear level types; the latter are adequate up to about 60 dB hearing threshold levels and of some value for hearing levels up to 80 dB levels. Maximum output with an ear level aid is limited by the acoustic squeal, due to the proximity of the microphone to the receiver. The closer the mike to the receiver, the greater the chance of squeal. Acoustic or electrical "squeal" is the tone that is produced when the amplified energy emanating from the receiver is inadvertently fed back into the microphone. Acoustic squeal is eliminated by reducing the gain, placing the microphone and receiver farther apart, and tightening the earpiece that couples the receiver to the ear.

The earmold that couples the receiver to the external auditory meatus (ear canal) can sufficiently alter the performance characteristics of the amplification system depending on the material, the system, the tubing, venting, and attachment. Most earmolds are now of a soft material that molds with the ear. Low frequencies can be affected by leaks or vents due to loose fitting. The primary resonance peak region is affected by the hole size in ear molds and the damping mass. When the hole is lengthened, the high frequency cutoff is lowered and is extended when the hole is shortened. The vent connects the ear cavity in the canal with the outside. By equalizing pressure, the aid feels more comfortable and may damp very low frequencies, possibly even increase the mid and low frequencies. An open-canal mold, used in special cases, sometimes can enhance auditory discrimination for high frequency losses.

4. *Monaural fitting versus binaural fitting.* It has become fashionable to fit aids binaurally with two completely independent units. In the past, pseudobinaural fittings were used with a bifurcation in a Y-cord to feed each

ear, but the signal came from one amplifier. Since the advent of the miniature ear level and eyeglass models, it became practical to wear two separate aids at ear level. Theoretically, there are advantages to binaural or "stereophonic hearing." It doubles the loudness effect without adding energy so that the sound seems twice as loud or as if it were amplified about 6 decibels. (A 6 dB intensity increase is perceived as "double" the loudness.) Hence, with binaural hearing summation, the person benefits by a 6 dB perceptual gain, assuming the two ears are approximately equal. This is helpful to people with recruitment who cannot tolerate any more intensity but benefit from additional loudness. Indeed, binaural aids do require less gain. Other advantages of binaural hearing are: the ability to localize sound or improve directional ability; interference from masking noise is reduced, due to foreground-background differentiation; sensitivity may even be improved. Selective listening through spatial separation is also enhanced, and a neurological suppression also occurs. Most hearing aid wearers subjectively favor binaural fitting, particularly because the wearer can listen on either side without "head shadow" interference. Audiometric tests cannot always demonstrate any quantitative superiority in discrimination with binaural aids unless "competing messages" are used.

In order to provide directional hearing to people who wear aids, but have a unilateral loss, an aid fitting was developed with "contralateral routing of the signal" (CROS) from the poor side to the good ear (Harford and Dodds 1966). Even though all sound is directed to the good ear, the difference in quality of the amplified sound serves as a clue and provides a sense of binaural hearing. A modification of this type uses two instruments with open ear molds. Still another modification is BICROS, where one ear receives the sound from two microphones fed through one amplifier.

5. *Selection of a hearing aid.* The selection and fitting of a hearing aid is another area of major controversy among audiologists. Formerly, audiologists did not recommend an aid in instances of unilateral hearing loss, only as specific request, e.g., for the purposes of directionality and localization was an aid fitted; there is now evidence it enhances discrimination in noise. Actually, the criteria for fitting an aid has been greatly modified.

Generally an aid is advisable wherever the threshold in the better ear exceeds 30 dB. The choice of which ear to fit, or whether to fit both ears, is based on audiometric and medical data, the clinical wisdom of the audiologist, and the needs of the consumer. There are no definitive rules, only guidelines. If the two ears show significant differences in discrimination ability, then the ear with the better discrimination score is selected; here the threshold levels are of secondary importance. If both ears are audiometrically comparable and binaural fitting is not advisable, the flatter audiogram is fitted; or it may be sensible to make ear molds for both ears so the aid can be alternated routinely. Considering the above, the ear with the wider dynamic operating range (from SRT to threshold of discomfort) is also a criterion. Binaural fitting is complicated when the thresholds of the ears differ appreciably, or if the thresholds are similar but have different types of impairments, e.g., sensory-neural in one ear and conductive in the other. Auxillary deterrents such as cost and cosmetic sensitivity or availability of dealerships may also play an important role when considering binaural fitting.

Conductive hearing impairments receive the most benefit from amplification. Sensory-neural losses benefit in varying degrees depending on the amount of the dysacusis. Central deafness problems are rarely fitted with an aid, since the impairment is with auditory processing and not basic auditory sensitivity. In instances of childhood aphasia, therapists may employ amplification as a training ploy to focus the sound during a therapy session and compel the child to attend. When using an aid on subjects with normal thresholds, caution must be exercised to avoid excessive amplification. There are considerable nonauditory effects associated with exposure to loud sound stimuli (Nober 1974) which should be considered. All sound above 85 dB is potentially hazardous from a psychological and physiological perspective.

Children should be fitted as early as possible. Some fit aids in the crib at two months, hence the focus on high-risk infant hearing screening. Amplification fosters an awareness of sound and, subsequently, symbolic concepts. Since the most propitious years for language acquisition are the early formative years when children are neurologically geared to develop language, they need the most natural input that can be provided on a continuing basis.

6. *Hearing aid evaluation.* The purposes of a hearing aid evaluation are to determine whether an aid should be fitted, which ear to fit, the type of aid to recommend, the output, gain, and frequency characteristics, and to ascertain the problems that will accompany the use of an aid. An evaluation can be formal or informal. An informal evaluation is usually not conducted in a controlled acoustic environment but rather a home, at work on a trial basis. This procedure is often used by hearing aid salesmen who have the customer try several aids then select one to use for a few days. Not infrequently, it works well. Informal procedures may also be used to evaluate the infant or young child. In this instance, an aid is selected on the basis of the pure tone audiogram and whatever audiologic and otologic data can be accrued.

In a formal hearing evaluation, controlled stimuli are used in a controlled environment. For the very young child, aided pure tone thresholds and tolerance tests may be used. Above three years, simple speech tests

(SRT and discrimination scores) can be used with the aid on, i.e., the "aided" condition. With adults, the aided SRT is ascertained, aided discrimination scores and signal-to-noise ratio discrimination tests are given with the hearing aid on. These are basic along with tolerance levels. Additional procedures include how gain affects discrimination, the effects of selective amplification on auditory discrimination, different earmolds in quiet and noise. Additional discrimination tests may be conducted at several hearing threshold levels in both quiet and noise. Some audiologists use a competing message test, an intermodulation test, and an electroacoustic evaluation of the aid's actual technical specifications.

The two or three hearing aids which give the "best" scores are selected as the choices; the final selection also considers quality, service availability, cost, size, freedom from internal noise. The policy in most audiology centers is to avoid choosing one particular aid, but to advise the person to select from a choice of two or three tested under a number of conditions.

Auditory Discrimination

This is the ability to distinguish among sounds correctly. This basic, indeed innate, ability varies among hearing handicapped individuals, but it is directly influenced by the type and degree of hearing loss and other variables as indicated earlier. The purposes of auditory discrimination training is to enhance the ability to perceive and recognize phonetic elements rapidly and accurately so the subject can obtain maximum use of residual hearing. With a child, the first step is "awareness" of sound, and then training to cultivate good listening habits. It is essential that the training concentrate on the recognition and analysis of sound elements so they can be instantaneously perceived and recognized. This requires intensive concentration and attention. It is a process that must be continued at home and throughout the day. Formal training starts with the recognition of gross environmental sounds and progresses to differentiation among environmental sounds that are similar in their acoustic patterns. After training with gross sounds, simple speech patterns such as vowel recognition is used, and subsequently, the consonant speech patterns. Environmental and speech sounds are practiced first under favorable or quiet listening conditions then under adverse or noisy listening conditions. Therapy is given with the hearing aid on, or perhaps through an auditory training unit for better fidelity. Music is used extensively to foster rhythm patterns. Even recordings on one's own voice, the speech of others, and musical comedies have been used for auditory discrimination training. Success is judged in degrees, i.e., prescriptive teaching with behavioral objectives individually set. It is essential to start this therapy as early as possible as the ability to discriminate depreciates with age.

Speechreading

1. *Definitions.* The now defunct term *lip reading* was used to designate the interpretation of lip movements and some concommitant facial cues. It was abandoned because it was too constrained as it didn't include the essential elements of facial expressions, bodily movements, contextual cues. It failed to connote the "totality" of the situation. In lieu, *speechreading* is used which is operationally more inclusive of ancillary cues and facial expressions.

2. *Analytic vs. synthetic.* When the basic core of the speechreading technique is syllable drill, it is called *analytic.* The goal is to develop rapid and precise identification of the speech units, usually by its rhythmic patterns. In the *synthetic* approach, the thought is stressed, and the training pursues the idea rather than a precise interpretation of the signal. In a restricted sense, the analytic system is more closely related to the term lip reading, while the synthetic approach is better described by speechreading. Detailed examinations of these two methods reveal more similarities than dissimilarities; their cardinal difference lies in the degree of importance assigned to the syllable and word drills, as well as the sentence, phrase, and paragraph practice.

3. *Technique.*

a. The *Bruhn method* is an analytic approach that she learned in Germany from Müller-Walle. The system is based on rapid, rhythmic, syllable drill; it is designed to train the eye and mind to be more alert. She accepted that perception of the "whole" was needed, but felt that grasping the details of lip movements was more important. The lessons consist of defining movements of the sounds, contrasting these with other sources and practice at various angles. Voice is used to preserve the natural lip movements of the sounds and the rhythm as exaggerated and distorted mouth movements are a deterrent to interpretation. The technique was originally designed for adults but has been adopted for use with children.

b. *Nitchie method* was first published in 1912 by Edward Nitchie. He died young so his wife Elizabeth continued his work and revised his material in 1940. The Nitchie technique is a synthetic approach with the focus on getting the thought. Nitchie felt that the understanding of words came from the thought rather than the reverse. Training is concerned with the idea. Eye and mind training are stressed to enhance speech alertness. Words and sentences are practiced for proficiency in speed and accuracy. Mirror practice is used with homophonous words. These words look alike, such as *pat, mat, bat,* etc. The teacher is encouraged to be natural, thorough, and interesting. This technique originated for adults but has been adapted for children.

c. *Kinzie method* was originated by Cora Kinzie who became deaf in her second year of medical school. She studied with Bruhn and later Nitchie, so her system is actually an integrated combination of the two (analytic and synthetic) with the major stress synthetic. Eventually, her sister, Rose, a school teacher, joined her, and the system was expanded to include children. In fact, their major contribution was the grading of material for children and for adults. They stressed intuition, synthesis, and rhythm. Voice and mirror practice were used during the practice sessions.

d. *Jena method.* Anna Bunger studied with Brauchmann of Jena, Germany and modified it for use in this country. Kinesthetic awareness is stressed to compensate for the lack of auditory awareness. Bunger's cardinal objective was to instill an awareness of sound and a sensitivity to the feel of the movements. As this is basically an analytic method, syllable drill is stressed. Multi-sensory reinforcement is stressed so speech is approached from the visible, audible, mimetic, movement, and gesture aspects. Rhythm is practiced by clapping, tapping, bouncing a ball, and dancing.

4. *Preschool deaf children.* In a preschool speech reading program, the language training, speech training, and auditory training are all integrated. These aspects of the communication process cannot be taught as independent units efficiently. Consequently, early training stresses an informal approach. Programs are geared to suit the individual needs of the children so experiences must be made meaningful. Since the understanding of language precedes its use, the receptive aspect is emphasized. Hence, the child must be made aware of oral language and through speechreading develop the basic language concepts.

Speechreading is a basic process. Most infants innately attend to human faces and naturally imitate the lip movements of the mother. When the visual perceptions are reinforced by the concommitant auditory stimulation, the infant soon learns to associate language signals with lip movements. The hearing child naturally depends on the auditory stimulus but the deaf child deprived of the concommitant auditory reinforcement cannot automatically associate lip movements with meaningful language. It is imperative that the deaf infant maintain interest in the face and constantly observe it for meaning.

Obviously, speechreading and language training are launched as one integrated process in early life by the mother. Training is an ongoing process that permeates every aspect of the infant's life. The mother must make maximum use of the natural and meaningful glances of the infant to the face so they will become more frequent, purposeful, and of longer duration. Eventually the movement becomes meaningful language.

Parents are vital elements for effective early speech and language training with the infant. They must create a language atmosphere by talking continuously to the infant. The mother must take her time and use a natural and clear manner. Voice quality and articulation must not be exaggerated or the natural rhythmic movements will be disturbed. The mother must use simple language and frequent reinforcement. Manual actions only distract attention from the face. Three feet is the optimal distance between the infant and the mother, and the mother's face must be adequately lighted. The light should come from behind the baby so it does not obstruct vision. Facial animation should be encouraged as the infant becomes sensitive to the subtle language cues.

Care must be taken to make speechreading or language training a meaningful and pleasurable experience. The parents must train other members of the family and close friends to talk appropriately to the infant. The infant must be trained and expected to interpret the lip movements meaningfully the *first time* the statement is made. Repetition is given during training, but this can become dangerous, as in normal communication statements are said only once. Rapid, instantaneous, and accurate interpretation are stressed and fostered. By the time a congenitally deaf child approaches the school environment, he should be a proficient lip reader. The formal speechreading program enlarges his sphere of language development.

5. *Elementary and secondary school years.* Habilitation and educational concerns of parents, teachers, and educators of hearing impaired children become manifest during the school years. Language arts skills become the emphasis of the curriculum for hearing impaired children. Multihandicapped children are provided with additional stress on language arts since written-receptive communication is the major avenue for future acquisition of information. Special techniques and methodology comprise the curriculum in special schools and classes. The Fitzgerald Key, the language experienced based program, the use of mediated language environments, etc. are currently being used with varying degrees of success (Schlesinger and Meadow 1972). Some specific considerations in educational programming for hearing impaired children are: stress on written language, development of idiomatic language, emphasis on pre-vocational training, increased use of media in classrooms, frequent experiences with integrated educational settings, counseling, and improvement in opportunities for higher education. These trends are based on the cumulative needs which have been identified by the varied professionals and parent groups which have worked with hearing impaired children.

8

Visual Disorders

EDWARD T. DONLON

THE SENSORY AREA OF VISION is one of the most important in learning. It is also of inestimable importance for the development of personal identity and the maintenance of perspective in physical and psychological space. The importance of eye contact is well known in circles that stress effective communication. The relationship of visual feedback to communication is also well known. Mimicry of movements and expressions is fostered by identity and can only be developed when vision is used. The positive and negative conditioning value of this process is noted in many books. Mimicry of behavior patterns is one important means of identity by a child with his adult model. Lowenfeld (1963) considers several aspects of this: "The problem of facial expression and of its development in the blind is of practical as well as theoretical importance. The questions of the innateness of certain expressions and of the cultural determination of expressive mimicry have received considerable attention. The social value of "normal" facial expression for blind children and adults has been stressed by many educators."

It takes only a short observation of a speech-therapy session to be convinced of the animated part vision plays in treatment of speech disorders. The same situation exists in general education and is perhaps most acutely recognized in education of the deaf. The deaf-blind child is probably the most challenging problem of communication today. In more than one hundred "deaf-blind" children seen at Syracuse University there has never been one child who had the combination of no measurable hearing and no measurable sight. Of this group of children, however, it is quite obvious to the clinic staff that those with some sight and no hearing are much more communicative than those who are totally blind with some degree of hearing. It is almost as if with a lack of sight there is a lack of knowledge about the environment and a lack of desire to find out more. Other sensory areas in such handicapped children frequently function for stimulation value alone and not for the more appropriate use of analyzing and modifying the environment.

The orientation in this chapter is toward the contribution made by those who specialize in the problems of the visually handicapped. There is no such person as a vision therapist to correspond with the speech therapist in the treatment center. Such a person is not necessarily recommended, but the reason for this is based less on need than it is on a realization of a maximum number of specialists who can work with a given child and a limitation of cases and treatment funds to support such people. It is important to be aware of new and useful techniques and to have these applied at opportune times to appropriate cases. Provision should be made for this to be done wherever it is needed in the treatment process. A special educator trained in the area of visual problems is recommended as a consultant to identify areas of concern and demonstrate techniques of treatment. This person may also be used as a teacher at certain selected times when knowledge of special technique is important. The use of these techniques and their integration in the treatment program must usually be carried out through the permanent staff. The special educator in this area has unique knowledge of the part sight plays in school achievement and peer adjustment. This person is also well acquainted with methods useful for making maximum use of residual vision and for developing other senses in a compensatory manner.

The special teacher may at times function in a classroom, but more often he or she either fills a consultative role, or evaluates pupil progress. Concern is frequently with the development of special skills in the visually handicapped child. Timing is important in the development of many skills and sometimes the special teacher only needs to support the regular teacher. At these times the main part of programming may be to suggest that no modifications are needed. Although some visual disorders may appear bad, the effect on learning may be only minor and of little consequence. The opposite is, of course, possible when a minor visual disorder results in a major educational problem. The special educator's familiarity with these conditions allows for completeness and accuracy in treating this handicap in the cerebral palsied child.

In outlining possible procedures for this area it has been necessary to rely rather heavily on the limited findings of those who have worked with visually handicapped children with no other obvious problems. This practice is difficult to justify as completely valid with cerebral palsied children. There is little experimental proof that the methods advocated are useful with this group of multiple-handicapped children. Most of the procedures noted here, however, are based on conservative practices in the field. All of them have been tried and are applicable to at least one type of visual disorder. In this respect they may be said to have at least face validity. It is hypothesized that the use of these methods for specific and selected persons will be valuable. If not, then, careful analysis of their deficiency should lead to better and more useful techniques with the cerebral palsied population.

Most programs for the multiply handicapped blind are concerned with children who have multiple sensory disorders. With the exception of one, the author knows of no school for the visually handicapped which serves a group also afflicted with cerebral palsy. Many of the children served have symptoms of brain injury. Some obviously have a mild to moderate degree of cerebral palsy, but there is seldom recognition of the fact in those curricular modifications necessary to improve learning ability. Beyond recognizing the need for research, though, it is important to develop systems whereby data can be stored and research results retrieved and applied.

Several programs have been developed for this purpose. The ERIC project administered by the Council for Exceptional Children is one phase of a larger project to search and retrieve information and especially written material about any disability. Subscribers may request searches and can obtain microfilm copies of reference materials as they are located. One problem with this and many similar series is cost. While it is not high for the results obtained, it can be considerable for the parent or teacher who could use the materials. The research center or university would generally not suffer this problem but it can be most frustrating to know that a quantity of professional materials could be available but is not.

The American Printing House for the Blind also has a project more specific and devoted to materials used by the visually handicapped (Lappin 1972). This may also be useful as both a screening technique for inappropriate materials and a device for selecting those which have been useful to others. Communication is the key. If systems can be developed where information can be found and disseminated and programs implemented in a useful manner, then new techniques will be adopted. The data available can be overwhelming and their application can be even more so.

The *Research Bulletin* published by the American Foundation for the Blind is still one of the most important documents in the field today. The purpose of this publication is "to inform the research-minded and also to stimulate further inquiries into a vast and largely untracked field." Appropriate issues of the *Review of Educational Research* have reviewed research in this specific area for the periods involved. As these summaries and reviews are read it is difficult to deny the fact that the disability of a visual handicap is devastating in many ways and that treatment for the condition and the disability must be energetically pursued.

It would be beneficial if there were an exact way to describe the nature and effect of a visual disorder. In fact there are several. The most widely used method, for children is by an expression of acuity and recording of any evident restrictions of the visual fields. This is not the most useful method, and the trend seems to be toward other considerations which include functional ability and different types of physiological measurement.

The purpose for which measurement is made is always a factor in deciding the method used and information to be collected. Legal blindness for most requirements is defined as a visual acuity of 20/200 or a field restriction of 20 degrees recorded with a maximum correction. This was also adopted as a criterion for establishing eligibility of children to receive aids for the blind. It is still maintained as such and many legal benefits and educational materials are obtained for persons who come under this category. The above definition varied throughout the world and even within the United States; therefore, if it is important to define legal blindness, consideration must be given to geographical area.

Most professionals today consider it important to view visual disability as a total spectrum of disorder. Visual acuity loss is represented as a continuum from normal sight to total blindness. Field deficits, muscle imbalance, corneal and lens distortions are described by severity and the effect they have upon the functioning individual. Some are recommending more emphasis on behavioral measurement, especially for the purpose of educational planning. Nolan applies a nine-point scale in a longitudinal study of reading medium preferred by the blind (Nolan 1971). This system, however, still relies on a refractory examination, and though more specific, it does not necessarily separate discrete groups for educational planning.

It is important to recognize specific problems as they relate to each visual disorder. These are discussed in more detail later in this chapter. Perhaps the most important definition for establishing need is still that of Jones (1963). He states that the term "visually handicapped" should be applied to "children who either have no vision of whose visual limitations after correction result in educational handicaps unless special provisions are made."

This is a logical approach and one that reveals more common factors than divisions as previously expounded by those who separate "blind" from "partially seeing." It is important for the person not acquainted with writing in this area to recognize the fact that a dichotomy exists in research as well as practice especially in the United States. The reader could easily become confused over seemingly conflicting research results unless careful consideration is given to the description of the population.

Various forms have been available for reporting visual condition; they are useful for describing groups and etiology when known. The etiology is valuable for those informed persons dealing with specific disorders if treatment modifications are in order as a result of interpretation of the conditions (i.e., implications for educational modifications of children who have retinitis pigmentosis as opposed to macular scarring). Indications of prognosis are also of value, but seldom can be stated with clarity on a report form. Personal contact with the ophthalmologist is usually needed for this, as it is for developing appropriate recommendations for treatment.

It is important to recognize that while many techniques have been developed to measure visual acuity, much research is needed before definitive judgment can be made regarding its correlation with visual problems. One factor which should be made clear is that the technician, whether medical doctor or optical expert, is limited in scope of treatment. He or she can correct the physical factors but it is usually beyond his or her training to continue treatment and work with the psychological and educational aspects. This task is left primarily to the supervision of the professional educator. On the other hand, the educator cannot possibly know the implications that certain behavioral symptoms connote to the medical and optical experts. Unless there is meaningful, consistent, and long-term communication between these persons, many children's progress will be reduced to a minimum change from the specific treatment received.

Much consideration should be given to attitudes of and about the visually handicapped. One must be constantly aware of the multiplicity of factors influencing the person with a handicap. These are difficult to recognize when the handicap is physical and are even less evident when accompanied by psychological, social and educational concomitants. The term "handicap" is used here in Riviere's (1970) rationale in which the handicap is the result of a disability and implies a loss of function. The differentiation of definitions developed by Rehabilitations Codes, Inc., is appropriate:

Impairment: any deviation from the normal which results in defective function, structure, organization or development of the whole, or of any of its facilities, senses, systems, organs, members, or any part thereof.

Disability: any limitation experienced by the impaired individual, as compared with the activities of unimpaired individuals of similar age, sex, and culture.

Handicap: the disadvantage imposed by impairment of or disability upon a specific individual in his cultural pattern or psychosocial, physical, vocational, and community activities.

An impaired individual is not necessarily disabled or handicapped by the impairment but he may be either disabled or handicapped, or both.

PHYSIOLOGICAL ASPECTS

It is comparatively easy to secure a diagram of the eye with accompanying illustrations of the visual pathways and their function. These are important to study for reference purposes when reading any material on visual function. At first glance one is impressed with the simplicity of the diagram. The camera analogy is obvious in the construction of the eye as is the similarity to electrical circuitry leading from the optic disc to the occipital area of the cerebral cortex. There is even a certain simplicity about the description of cranial nerve function and its relationship to various parts of the visual system. There comes a time, however, when the student refers to the diagram more frequently, then to the medical dictionary, the textbook of neurology, and perhaps to other references books in physiological psychology.

The goal of the present section is to outline the nature of several conditions found in cerebral palsy and their contribution to the total disability of the handicapped individual. Vision is accomplished through the summation of several processes: The general refractory system allows for proper focus of the image on the retina. The retina is appropriately stimulated and the information received is then transmitted via the optic pathways to the brain and especially to the area of the occipital lobe where final analysis takes place and use is found for the information. Reflexes, i.e., eye blink and pupil response, may be considered to be most basic and lowest in order for brain function. The range continues through voluntary motor responses and into the higher intellectual process of abstract thinking. If there is malfunction in any of these parts, then the total visual process may be modified or even completely destroyed. Both fine and gross muscle movements exist for proper positioning of the image on the retina. This also allows for stereoscopic vision which is important in many ways. Muscle imbalance can result in double vision or in amblyopia.

A review of the nature of eye disorders in cerebral palsied children leaves no room for question that this group has a high incidence of these conditions. Samples of children screened yield incidences of abnormalities consistently above 25 percent; some identify as many as 75 percent of the population who have at least one abnormality which is known to need correction. Unfortunately, there is no generally recognized system of reporting, and some investigators were searching for only one type of disorder, such as muscle imbalance, so that direct comparison is difficult. It is the writer's opinion that specific descriptions should be reported more frequently in the literature and that there is presently ample evidence to indicate a need for intensive evaluation and treatment of visual disorders in this population. Evaluation techniques and reporting systems should be standardized as much as possible. The need for completeness in reporting and consistency over a long period of time cannot be overemphasized. The normal physical and neurological development of a child is enough to warrant considerable change in visual ability. When one is physically handicapped, frequently from birth, with injury in the central nervous system, there is even more cause for concern and even less security can be placed in the nature and condition of the visual system.

Of all types of cerebral palsy the spastic population has the highest frequency of visual disorders. Muscle imbalance is reported by many to be particularly evident in this group. Many have found that 25 percent or more children with spasticity have such a condition. This is compared with a rate of .16 percent in the nonhandicapped population.

The athetoid group seems to have a greater degree of hyperopia. Several authors refer to the high incidence of visual defects in unselected groups of cerebral palsied children. They consistently find a higher incidence of almost every eye defect in this population. Smith (1963) presents a selective summary of findings with his comment: "Probably the most reliable work in the United Kingdom is Douglas' series, because of its size; moreover, its very nature reduced the possibility of unfair selection. Douglas found squint to be present in 37 percent of cases of cerebral palsy; Jameson Evans reported an incidence of 31 percent, Asher and Schonell gave 25 percent and Ellis 17 percent. Figures from the United States tended to be higher. Guibor gave 60 percent from a series of 142 cases, Breakey gave 48 percent and Schachat 43 percent." The monograph edited by Smith is one of the most complete reviews of the information on visual disorders and their occurrence. With this as evidence, there should be no question that every child should have ophthalmological evaluations at regular intervals. These should begin at the time the brain injury is recognized. It is also important to be aware of the necessity for close communication about implications of any disorder for those involved in the day-to-day treatment. When this is done the information can then be used to serve the dual role of the prevention of secondary eye disorders and the appropriate modification of treatment.

There should be even less excuse for such disorders as amblyopia exanopsia in the child with cerebral palsy than there is with the normal individual. It is important to realize that neither diagnosis nor treatment can usually be accomplished exclusively by any one professional working with the child and family. There are too many chances for breakdown in communications with the family and/or a lack of verbal reporting ability in the child to yield sufficient evidence for treatment to be started. It is common knowledge that children seldom report abnormalities in vision even if they recognize them. Since this is the case the role of recognition must be delegated to medical persons with the educator and paramedical professional being responsible for supplying sufficient evidence to make this recognition as reliable and accurate as possible.

Basic corrective procedures are usually applicable to children with cerebral palsy. Acuity deviations and muscle imbalance are corrected with appropriate modifications for the brain injury. Safety lenses should be standard for all children. The cerebral palsied child who has extraneous head movements to any degree or who has problems in hand coordination may benefit by special frames or by adaptations which maintain the position of the glasses on the head. Low-vision aids may also present problems for the severely involved child unless the lens can be maintained in a stable position to the user. There should be recognition of the fact that only a very small portion of the lens is correct for the prescription. This is a small portion in the center. If the glasses are not positioned so that the child looks through this area then distortions and lack of proper correction will result, which is usually accompanied by rejection of the glasses.

Field defects should be recognized, but correction for this problem is not a possibility for prescription by lens modification unless prismatic correction is advised. These defects should dictate a flexibility, however, which encourages experimentation by the child to make maximum functional use of the intact area on his retina. If there is a coloboma or other type of retinal lesion this is especially important to recognize. Definite areas of the retina are destroyed, but it is frequently possible to stimulate other areas to such an extent that a satisfactory result can be obtained with an increase in functional vision.

Strabismus if left uncorrected is nearly always accompanied by amblyopia and by loss of stereoscopy. Many recommend surgery for this at a younger age today than was practiced in the past. This is frequently advised even if there is a good chance for recurrence. The feeling seems to be that in the child with cerebral palsy there is an even greater need for stereoscopic vision than in the normal child who has a more complete system of alternatives to accommodate for the resultant monocular vision. This condition in normal children is not generally considered as handicapping. When combined with the multiple handicaps of cerebral palsy, however, the problem may be complicated beyond our present estimates. Smith (1963) considers this and summarizes the situation quite adequately:

> A child with a squint will have one and possibly two associated lesions of function. Firstly, stereopsis is difficult or impossible. Secondly, some degree of amblyopia commonly develops in one eye. Guibor regarded 25 percent of all children with cerebral palsy as amblyopic compared with 2 percent . . . for the normal population. Can these factors influence general development of the child? Douglas . . . felt that the absence of stereopsis was not a retarding

factor in otherwise normal children. Both these abnormal conditions are well compensated by the other special senses and by monocular mechanisms such as parallax.

In cerebral palsy, however, the other special senses are often abnormal. Quite apart from other visual lesions such as hemianopia . . . defects of hearing and sensation are common. . . . Under these circumstances the child afflicted may be found to rely on vision to a greater extent than the normal child. If stereoscopic vision is never present, and worse still, if the child is functionally uniocular, the complex knowledge of his immediate surroundings that depends so much on accurate visuospatial assessment may be late and imperfect in development. Terman and Merrill . . . noted that normal children under 3½ years of age were more interested in form than in colour. This very phase of development is commonly retarded in cerebral palsied children, as it is associated with reading difficulties later on.

Medical treatment of eye disorders has been rapidly developing in many areas. Some recent developments worthy of special consideration to those working with cerebral palsy will be highlighted here. It is important to be aware of the fact that significant advances are being made in many areas related to vision. Theory, methodology, and technology are all developing in an accelerated fashion. It is not possible for one person to be aware of all the implications. One may only note some of the indicators and plan accordingly.

Problems associated with nystagmus are not easy to identify or treat. Theoretically, children with this condition should have considerable difficulty in functioning. Actually, however, many seem to make adjustments and develop their abilities far beyond predictions. This is apparently possible by several identifiable techniques developed by the children. There are, undoubtedly, others not so evident but just as effective. If given freedom to move the object, many children are able to control the nystagmus by fixating at various angles from the normal vertical plane. Others rely on the high accommodative power of the lens and hold the object as close as possible. This may cut down the material observed by one cycle of the eye and allow for something akin to after-image to complete the process of analysis. These practices on the child's part are frequently cause of concern to the teacher who cannot tolerate bizarre positions by students. Usually the child's ego and drive to see help him or her to persevere, but the situation can be considerably improved by words of encouragement from the special teacher. There is also the interesting condition of latent nystagmus in which there is normal fixation with both eyes until one eye is covered at which time the uncovered eye has considerable nystagmus. This condition is frequently seen by persons doing vision screening and is confirmed by testing with no occlusion. It is of minor consequence as a disorder unless damage is incurred to one eye, but consideration of this and similar conditions by those experienced in working with cerebral palsied children is especially important to be sure of its significance for each individual child.

The importance of stereoscopic vision for depth perception should be emphasized again as part of a larger group associated with perceptual problems. These disorders are covered elsewhere in this book, but the importance of visual examination in determination of extent and in prognosis must be stressed. The lack of well-defined concepts of space and distance is of concern to those working with these disorders. This is especially the case when such concepts are needed as referents for further development.

Surgical and optical treatment for strabismus is still relatively new in methodology. Original attempts date back to early times, but modern techniques of measurement and precise correction are still being perfected. When these are combined with new developments in materials, such as plastic lenses, the wearer is made more comfortable and chances for acceptance of the nonsurgical procedure are enhanced. Since strabismus has such a high incidence in cerebral palsy, these procedures should receive special consideration in all cases. It is also important to recognize the time factor involved and the implications for vision when treatment is developed. It is easy to neglect eye conditions in staff conferences when there is obviously so much to do with arms, legs, speech, and their appropriate functioning. The resultant blindness which can occur in one eye and loss of some spheres of visual perception should be considered for each child and corrective or preventive measures pursued diligently. (See also Pigassou-Albouy and Fleming 1975.)

Cataracts are treated by needling procedures which do not have such complete results as more drastic surgery but can be performed on young children and can be repeated when necessary. The safety factor involved in this operation makes it especially beneficial. The aspiration technique is another example of a technical development which has made possible more satisfactory and predictable results. This is especially true when accompanied by the use of sub-zero freezing of the tissue by cryosurgical procedures. Early recognition of disorders and diseases is especially important. Treatment by drugs is useful and effective for an increasing list of conditions. Congenital glaucoma is responsive to several forms of chemotherapy, and vision can be maintained in a more satisfactory manner than ever before. Keratitis, optic neuritis, iritis, and choroidoretinitis also benefit from treatment by this means.

Developments in the area of keratoplasty are of increasing effectiveness in the treatment of corneal anomalies. The gradual solution of problems related to tissue intolerance will also lead to more exact predictability of treatment for many disorders. Artificial materials for both lens and cornea are in experimental stages of development with varying degrees of success claimed for each. More universal use of these techniques is still directed toward some future date, but there is no question that use is within the foreseeable future.

New developments related to cortical stimulation through physical sensors, such as miniature television cameras lead the optimistic to believe that some day the diseased eye might actually be bypassed. Other efforts involving chemical treatment to improve tissue regeneration and especially those drugs acting on nervous tissue lead to other possibilities and dreams of treatment which could be revolutionary in aiding physical and mental processes of the handicapped to develop more normally. These are in the future and one not today available to the practitioner as part of the treatment process.

FUNCTIONAL EVALUATION OF VISUAL DISORDERS

The specialist in the education of the visually handicapped is not a therapist. He or she is first an educator with preparation in general education, including emphasis on child growth and development and the development of techniques and methods for stimulating and maintaining this growth. The preparation also demands that a sound and consistent philosophical framework be developed to support the methodology that is accepted.

The concept of optimum growth rate is important. The non-handicapped child has a rate which has been studied rather exhaustively and can be predicted with a high degree of accuracy. This is not so easily done with the handicapped child. Varying handicaps and degrees of severity dictate different predictions of growth. The type and degree of visual disorder is no exception. One role of the special educator in this area is to estimate the effect a visual disorder has an optimum development. The recognition that visual disorders contribute to the handicap leads to appropriate modification of methodology and the development of techniques to aid the child in overcoming his disability. Basic at this point is the presence of a teacher acquainted with those visual disorders which may be handicapping. Next in priority is that he be aware through records and referral when such conditions are recognized. It is also important to observe children for determination of effect and to note any possibility that unrecognized conditions may be present.

The three prerequisites may be considered further. Records of visual examinations including diagnoses or suspected conditions must be interpreted and brought to the teacher's attention. The child is thus automatically referred for further consideration. Some conditions appear to be especially severe "on paper," but when the child is observed functioning in his or her own life space, the child may be considered to have adequacy in the area at the time.

Referral beyond notation of records requires more consideration. Other staff personnel must be educated to the fact that visual disorders are handicapping. They must also recognize some signs which should make them suspicious. Rapport and trust must not be minimized. If a specialist is not trusted in all respects another teacher will not seek advice and certainly will not place a student in his care. The specialist must have something to offer in knowledge and must be able to demonstrate this clinically.

Skill in observation is the most valuable tool for anyone to possess. For accuracy, this skill must be highly developed. The special educator working with the visually handicapped is usually in an integrated classroom setting. Most of the child's academic and social needs are met by another teacher. The effects of the visual abnormality are pertinent and the special educator's task is to minimize so that the child can overcome these effects as early as possible.

For several years the author and W. Scott Curtis have been working on a structured program for observing children's behavior and classifying the results of their observations in a meaningful manner. This project began with an analysis of terms by specialists in team evaluations of the multiply handicapped. Results of this analysis indicated that there were few descriptive terms related to the child's behavior which were meaningful and specific to the child. In other words, specialists in each discipline used the same terms in describing the child and each of these descriptions could be used for many other children. They were much too general and did not contribute to the reader's knowledge of the child or what to do with the child.

These findings led to development of a behavioral observation protocol which could be used to sample a child's behavior during an average day in his life (Donlon and Curtis 1972). Video tapes have been used to record these observations. This has made it possible for other judges to observe and rate the same behavioral segments and thus to analyze better the effectiveness of such a procedure. Data collected from this project are interesting and supportive of this technique for evaluating severely multiply handicapped children. It is suggested here as a useful technique for working with the multiply handicapped cerebral palsied child.

Diagnosis of a disorder should indicate a course of treatment. Whether the condition is static or progressive is certainly important knowledge in outlining immediate and long-term treatment plans. The part of the visual system affected is also of consequence. The diagnosis of congenital glaucoma, for example, leads to different educational treatment than congenital cataracts, and conditions affecting the peripheral retina lead to different modifications than those which affect the macula. These conditions do not always entail disability. This can only be concluded by evaluating the effect the condition has on functional ability.

Progressive disorders or the possibility of recurrence should be considered. It is important, however, to be careful in assessing this and to be sure of the time limit involved, the degree of progression, and the possibility for treatment either now or in the future. Cataract formation is a case in point; the prognosis of several years ago would certainly be more pessimistic than that of today. The time span for glaucoma to become severe with and without modern treatment is another example.

Some discussion may now be directed to syndromes which indicate types of visual disorders. These may be useful as guidelines or markers of a sort to be tested by further techniques and observation in order to describe visually handicapped children better. The range in disorders may be from total lack of sight to a mild acuity loss. They may also vary in type of disorder and site of damage. With nonverbal or nonmobile children the problem is complicated by lack of feedback to the examiner about questions or situations presented. Techniques and considerations which follow are primarily clinical in nature and are not intended as useful in diagnosis of specific disease. Their value is to allow for some evaluation of the functional capacity a child may have in using one or more of his senses. Primary, of course, in this section is the visual modality, but it is sometimes impossible to separate this from other senses as they interact in learning and adjustment.

The most frequent referral of an untrained person is made to see if a nonverbal child has any sight. The concern usually arises because the child is not looking at the person or does not look at objects. Diagnosis of the presence or absence of sight is usually not difficult and can be accomplished through observation alone. Most children in this group are quite young, probably within the first two years of life. They exhibit a fixed stare, lack of interest in objects and people, and are usually immobile. The problem here usually becomes one of differentiating the symptoms of autism from severe retardation. With the cerebral palsied child it is also possible to have similar symptoms with cases of rigidity or athetosis. Extreme myopia may also lead to a general lack of interest in surroundings.

If no visual interest can be detected in toys or objects of any sort which are silent and not touched by the child, it may be possible for one familiar with him to indicate objects he favors. Touch and hearing can then be used to obtain a response as a reference line. If this response can be elicited consistently, then one or more senses can be eliminated in the testing procedure and signs of anticipation can be observed which are triggered by vision alone.

An eye blink is a reflex act and can usually be noted. It is difficult to evaluate the significance, however, since the eye is sensitive to air currents and a reflex eye blink may be demonstrated with loud sounds. Consistent turning of the head away from a moving object which is accompanied by an eye blink is a more certain sign of vision. When a child is mobile or has any type of hand movement it is easier to note the presence of some degree of vision. A child who consistently moves toward a light source has some sight. One who has no bruises on his legs and is active is seldom blind. If a child moves around many large objects, it can be assumed that the child has vision related to object perception. Recognition of a person in the room by visually following the person when quiet is, of course, another sign.

If a child is severely involved with cerebral palsy, then eye-hand movements must be discarded as indicators since it is frequently difficult to decide which are random and which directed. Since there is also seldom any consistent and well-defined facial expression, this sign also must be eliminated. The child who is not brain injured will sometimes not respond to slow movements. The reverse may be true with a child who has cerebral palsy. It may be possible for the child to respond visually to a slow-moving object while the one of higher velocity is just too much for the child's visuomotor system. Care should be taken in this case to decrease the possibility of excitation by secondary stimuli. It is easy to create overflow movements or facial changes by other means and thereby bias the results. Repetitions when this happens will usually allow for more adequate evaluation. The cerebral palsied child will become conditioned and tend to enjoy the "game" while the severely retarded child will see it as a new experience and the disturbed child may develop a selective inattention. When categorizing responses it is important to be aware of consistently negative as well as consistently positive ones. Either tells whether or not the child is reacting to a situation. Constant rejection of a toy or food which is presented only in the visual sphere is an important diagnostic sign and usually indicates discriminative ability of a higher order.

If controlled lighting is available and near darkness can be attained, the observation of a child in this environment is often important. If he has been using vision as a means of gaining information there will usually be a change in activity. Increased vocalization and gross motor activity are frequently noted. When small light sources can be alternated and localization observed a child can be tested in a manner similar to freefield testing in audiometry.

Children with some types of visual disorder leave the impression that there is good functional vision in all areas when in reality there is not. Disorders in the macular area may give this impression since good mobility is maintained but fine discrimination is absent. The child in these cases will frequently avoid exposure to situations which might exhibit his incompetence. If there are many opportunities for this exposure, the child may generalize his fears to other areas of activity until, in its extreme, a character disorder will develop. Some children with macular destruction may form a pseudomacula. This is adjacent to the one destroyed and is another reason for odd positioning of material in the visual plane when fine discrimination is desired. A child may have complete bilateral loss in the area of central vision (macular area) and still appear in general life to be having no problem. To be sure, the child's vision will be reduced to 20/200, but the child's awareness of the environment may be close to normal. The child is in fact seeing what most people see when they do not "focus" on an object. This child is probably also using as many clues as possible both visually and in other sensory areas. Such behavior indicates good adjustment and probably good visual efficiency at certain developmental levels. It is comparatively easy for the child to "look normal" and avoid frustrating situations. There comes a time, however, when lack of concept development in areas which rely on finer visual discrimination becomes a more important part of the child's educational life and the true handicapping condition is evident.

As one observes the child with peripheral field defect different behaviors will be evident. If the restriction is complete and is more than that required for legal blindness (20 degrees), there is usually a marked restriction of mobility. The resulting "tunnel vision" makes it impossible for the child to see objects, and unless extreme care is taken the child will suffer continuous bumps on furniture, open doors, and from moving objects. It is easy to see why this person will move haltingly and if not trained properly will startle at quick movements and loud sounds. If the child's central vision is good, he or she may gain much reinforcement from reading and other sedentary activities. Concept development may suffer here also in those areas which rely on visual ability. This will not be because of lack of clarity, as in the previous case. If present, the deficiency will occur because of lack of experience by the child. Bilateral hemianopia is a similar problem and may be quite restricting, depending on the quadrants affected. This condition has been recognized as occurring more frequently in cerebral palsied children. When field restrictions are incomplete or are not bilateral it is probable that little restriction in activity will be experienced. Overlapping visual fields and compensating eye movements will overcome the effect of "blind areas."

Optic pathway and retinal deficiencies may result in a lack of discriminative ability. The degree in this case is important, and it is difficult to predict the effect this will have on vision. In such losses the rest of the eye is probably normal with the deficiency occurring after the image has fallen on the retina and is in focus. This condition may be highly restricting or it may not, depending on the child's own structure and motivation. Magnification frequently helps and it is often possible to "teach" better discrimination to these children. Increased light intensity by several means is also useful. The "healthy looking eye" in these cases presents a better appearance to the public, but vision is no less damaged. This type of loss may be considered central and may be compared with nerve loss in auditory disorders. Other perceptual deviations may exist from injuries in areas which include the cerebral cortex, but these difficulties are not generally associated with visual disorders.

Extreme myopia when not corrected can definitely limit a child's functioning. If the child does not know he or she can see better, the child probably will not complain. This severely limits any clear knowledge of the world more than a short distance away. Sounds can be heard and impressions gained from this, but no supportive information from vision can be used unless the child gets up and moves toward the object. There has to be an end to the constant energy and exposure to failure this method requires, so withdrawal to "close work" results, and the child becomes content to make a few errors and avoid many which impinge on his life from "out there." In extreme myopia there may be a lack of recognition that vision is useful and the child may consider him or herself as blind. Children in this category are remarkably successful cases when corrective lenses are used and they begin to see how much they have missed. It should be realized here that normal focal distances for some children are very near the eye and posture looks awkward to most adults. This does not damage the eye and when noted is usually a sign that maximum vision is being used.

Similar problems and results exist with extreme hyperopia. Sometimes this is not readily evident in children because of their ability to accommodate. The child can see but tends to reject reading materials and those which need fine discrimination at close distance. Lenses of high magnification allow for good correction. Children who have had cataract surgery (aphakic) need such lenses and adapt very well. No accommodation is possible by usual means of lens change within the eye, but some do experience change in focus by squinting. The squinting process which is closing the eyelid and narrowing the palpebral fissure, should not be confused with squint, which is a medical term used as a synonym for strabismus. The former is a process for gaining depth of focus similar to the condition resulting from decreasing the lens aperture on a camera. Children are almost never seen doing this unless they have visual discrimination of objects. Squinting may also be a sign of photophobia as is found in albinism or aniridia but these conditions would not be long undiagnosed in any setting. There are other signs of phobic reaction to light such as moving out of sunlight and turning away from windows. Other conditions can cause squinting, such as infections, and should be investigated immediately when occurring in the child with cerebral palsy.

Aberrations in the refractory system are hard to note functionally since the brain has power to modify images toward consistency with other sensory modalities and concepts already formed; the child then behaves as he identifies with peers or as he perceives others perceiving him. Any condition leading to aberrations of form on the retina necessitates extra effort by intra- and extraocular muscles and produces fatigue with accompanying muscle spasm and pain.

Defects of this extraocular muscle system or the innervation centers controlling these muscles usually should be identified as early as possible. Incidence figures have already been cited of amblyopia accompanying strabismus. Less is known of the effects and incidence when stereoscopic vision occurs. More is known of the mechanism by which double vision is merged and of the techniques for corrections. It is still difficult to determine this without patient cooperation and reporting. Still, in light of what has been said, it would seem important that every effort should be made to correct muscle malfunction leading to these conditions.

Nystagmus is easy to see, but its effect is difficult to interpret. Observation of the condition makes the untrained observer wonder how anyone can see while the eyeballs are in such motion. It must be remembered that eye motion must be stopped, if only for an instant, and that, theoretically, is when one sees. The trained observer notes first what a child can see, then where the child is looking when seeing it. This child may need to hold print 60 degrees from the usual vertical plane of vision, but at that point the eye movement is stopped and the image falls on the fovea. If such flexibility is allowed and in fact encouraged, maximum vision may be obtained. If correction is needed, this presents a problem since most lenses are constructed so that the prescribed correction is in the center of the lens where the pupil is looking directly forward. Technical problems may need to be solved in frames and lens grinding, but the principles of correction should be the same. Further problems are encountered when various head-stabilization techniques are used to control unintentional motor movements in the cerebral palsied child and these are contrary to the position needed for optimum vision. When this occurs, as it does all too frequently, it taxes the ingenuity of all persons involved to devise satisfactory solutions.

It is frequently difficult to be definite in the assessment of useful vision. Many disorders are changeable in nature so that time becomes a factor. Many children are poor reporters, so the aspects of the examination which rely upon reporting of what is seen frequently cannot be accurately measured by one examination. With modern ophthalmological techniques refractory examination is possible without the patient's verbal cooperation. In fact, many such examinations are given to children under general anesthesia. It is after lenses have been prescribed and accepted that the predictive factor seems to break down. Some children with almost no measurable vision function more adequately than their peers who have fared better by the ophthalmologist's reckoning.

Motivation must be considered when determining visual efficiency. Many children can be observed who are using all the powers at their command to increase their ability. Others seem content to be able to accomplish certain standard practices and then stop. Some would rather use compensatory senses, such as touch and hearing, and rely on sight as little as possible. The self-concept of a child must also enter into the functional ability. If a child thinks of him or herself as "blind" and has always been treated as such, then it is quite possible the child will not try to use this modality to its utmost.

The phenomenon of attending must also enter the efficiency picture in some respect. This area will be covered in other parts of this book, but the teacher should be continually aware of evidence for inter- and intrasensory interference from extraneous stimuli. The brain-injured child is especially subject to problems in this area. Breakdown in the child's ability to attend visually or awareness of conflicting stimulus in other sensory areas would certainly alter the child's functional ability. If the input signal through the visual modality is not of sufficient strength to overcome distracting auditory or tactual material, then the intended information will not be received. This now borders on the more classic problems encountered with perceptually involved brain-injured children. These are usually labeled as symptoms of distractibility or figure-ground disturbance and are considered elsewhere in this book.

A final point should be suggested under the consideration of visual efficiency. It is difficult to state definitely the relative contributions of the various sensory modalities. This differs with time, the environment, the situation, and previous experience. While it is not possible to measure total contribution, it may be more within the realm of speculation to measure change in emphasis of one modality to another during varying conditions. In this manner one could estimate the primary and secondary sensory areas involved for information reception and could conclude, through many variations in conditions, which area is used and when it profits by extra help from another modality.

The basic theoretical model applies as a description of input stimulus, cortical integration, and behavior of some sort, either vocal or motor, to demonstrate completion of the thought process. When the areas of higher abstract ability are assessed, it is necessary to work in different theoretical systems and other models become appropriate. The levels of brain function involved in this technique are useful for hypotheses and in developing designs for further study. Of perhaps more importance is the stress on the intersensory areas of involvement, especially in the input phase. There is clinical evidence to justify the existence of inhibition by one modality over another when receiving concurrent stimuli. Confusion in many brain-injured children can be attributed to this as well as the more traditional intrasensory basis for pathology, and this should be considered in any sensory evaluation of a cerebral palsied child.

More specific examples of intersensory inhibition can be seen when evaluating children if both the visual and auditory modalities are stimulated with similar commands. A pantomimed and a verbal command to "pick up the block" would be one level of such stimulation. When the response is compared to that received for similar commands given in one modality, inferences may be drawn on the basis of differences in performance. Theoretically, the child responding to stimulation in more than one area should perform better than if he were reacting to either alone. When this is not the case, as frequently happens in brain-injured children, one can suspect a condition of intersensory inhibition. It is known that functional ability varies with any visual disability. Several factors contribute to this variance and should be analyzed over a period of time so that maximum conditions for learning can be created.

It is tempting to suggest a further development of the tests devised to evaluate the effect of intersensory contribution or inhibition. This would allow for presentation of stimuli in a discrete manner to the sensory areas as is presently done. The addition would be a multisensory presentation of comparable material for the purpose of evaluating changes in both input and encoding ability. There are several important variables operating in this basic sequence of presenting a stimulus to one or more modalities and receiving a response in others. The areas of vision, hearing, touch, taste, and smell can all be used for receiving certain types of commands. Responses are usually given either through speaking or a motor movement. It is possible for a stimulus to be enhanced by the addition of a sensory area. The person who just barely hears a whispered message usually receives it clearer when he watches the speakers lips. As mentioned, with some types of brain injury such an act inhibits rather than enhances reception of the message. If this could be incorporated into a testing procedure the results obtained could add a new dimension to the assessment process.

The phenomena of intersensory summation and inhibition have been noted for their particular contribution to the learning process. Consideration should now be given to the related area of sensory preference. This is particularly evident in visually handicapped children who are known to have a measurable degree of residual vision. Some have a definite preference for the tactile or auditory modalities over the visual. Their reliance on one area over another is sometimes so striking that they will not accept stimuli in other modalities unless the preferred one is also excited.

There are definite and important educational implications of the phenomenon of sensory preference. Barraga (1964) described a procedure for developing residual vision and produced positive results by her method. It has also been noted that children with some sight treated in a fashion similar to the treatment of totally blind braille-readers tend to read braille rather than print. Lowenfeld (1963) points to one bit of evidence when he compares the print-reading ability of public school and residential school children: "However, the fact that, among children with a visual acuity of 20/200, 92 percent read print in local schools and only 50 percent did so in residential schools indicated that residential schools tended toward teaching braille while day schools preferred to use print as reading media for their pupils."

More consideration will be given these possibilities as evaluation techniques and methodology advance. At present the advance is significant especially in the light of the fact that not long ago it was not considered necessary to report visual acuity of less than 20/200 and visually handicapped children were segregated to sight-saving classes on the grounds that to be placed in an integrated setting might make them lose what little residual vision they had.

As was noted earlier in this section, the above points are only beginnings in the consideration of visual abnormality. All have various degrees of defect and each child presents some new problem or unique solution. Perhaps the first rule of any treatment procedure is to wait and see what the child does to solve his own problems, then, through a cooperative process with the child as a contributing partner, attempt several experiments to improve on this solution. It can be extremely rewarding and can satisfy a primary goal for the teacher of the visually handicapped, which is to promote optimum visual efficiency.

Differential evaluation and treatment of children with a variety of visual disorders is probably the most technical and highly refined task the teacher of the visually handicapped is prepared to perform. The other major problem is knowing the techniques and methodology involved in working with the learning process as modified by a visual disorder. This is a task which also relies upon satisfactory conditions of learning, such as developing motivation, establishing rapport, and creating an interest in learning through recognition of future needs and development of satisfactory goals. The special techniques and methodology of education are emphasized here. Visually handicapped children do have differences in their reactions to the areas of motivation, goal-setting, etc., but the recognition of these is possible for the experienced teacher and is part of the basic personal skills which make a master teacher indispensable and a true practicing professional.

PHYSICAL ENVIRONMENT

There is a variety of basic organizational patterns of special programs for visually handicapped children. Recognition that these children need modifications has led to several types of programs from complete segregation in a residential setting to almost no special treatment in a totally integrated public school class. It is important to assess a child's total abilities and problems accurately, so as to match them as closely as possible to the appropriate program. If cerebral palsy is the primary condition in need of treatment, there would probably not be segregated programs for this group in a residential school for the blind. Many are concerned that the specialist in visual handicap should assume responsibility for this group. There are many reasons why careful consideration must be given before this is adopted. Cruickshank (1964) outlines these reasons and presents several conditions which should be met before a program can be adequately developed. The conditions he presents seem imposing, but to follow any other path would lead to compromises which would be intolerable to most professionals. It could be possible for present segregated programs serving the blind to work with the visually handicapped cerebral palsied child. Several schools in fact have developed programs for the multiply handicapped child with visual disorders as one of the conditions. Children with cerebral palsy are usually evident in these programs. Certainly space and staff could be made available since most schools for the blind have experienced decreased enrollments in the past several years. This has made it possible for the schools to become more involved in programs for multiply handicapped children. This is not to say, however, that these programs could begin meeting the needs of a group with as complex problems as the cerebral palsied. It is quite probable that most could not. There is a need for careful consideration of programs and methods for working with the multiply handicapped. Several problem areas must be delineated and direction given for their solutions. In recognition of these factors Donlon and Burton (1975) have offered an approach which could well be applied to the cerebral palsied child with other handicapping conditions.

Educational situations in residential programs are for the blind and usually only for those who are braille-readers. The child attends a school as a residential student and with few exceptions attends segregated classes for his or her educational experience. Other segregated situations exist in local school programs, with the difference coming about when the child goes home after school hours.

The cooperative-class and resource-room systems are modifications of segregation. The child enrolled in the former uses the special class as homeroom and, whenever appropriate, attends integrated classes. The latter program allows for an integrated homeroom situation with children attending the resource room for special learning tasks related to the visual handicap. In both of these situations a teacher is usually on full-time duty in the school.

Itinerant teachers move from one school to another on a scheduled basis. They visit children who go to the school nearest their home and are enrolled in the regular class. The itinerant teacher consults with the child and his teacher. Modifications to program are suggested and special skills are taught the child as needed. It may be that the "special needs" of the visually handicapped are becoming even more accepted by the local school systems. The trend in school programs is toward larger school systems or at least cooperative arrangements to provide services to the handicapped on a broader basis. This allows for children to be served and have a better chance of remaining in their local school system. Busing is more generally accepted, and is no longer reserved for the handicapped. So when necessary a child can be moved to a school providing special services without the stigma of being moved because he or she is different.

The following techniques and modifications should not be considered universally valid, but are only suggestions which have been useful with some visually handicapped children. They should not be used without careful consideration, introduction, and follow-up evaluation to determine results. Their purpose in this chapter is to emphasize possible modifications and to suggest cautions. The latter is especially important since some have been emphasized in the past but have generally been discarded as impractical for teaching. The methods described are modifications used with visually handicapped children as they experience the basic curriculum of a nonsegregated educational program. Many also apply to other populations and are useful with cerebral palsied children. The general categories are formed by those areas in which extra time and energy are known to be necessary in order for the visually handicapped child to become adequate.

The abnormalities presented by the handicapped as symptoms of maladjustment to life, school, self-help, orientation, socialization, or whatever the problem should be the basis for modifying methodology. Many categories could be suggested for the visually handicapped, but there seems to be a logical division into two general groups. One emphasizes physical changes in the environment by the use of mechanical aids. The purpose of these is usually to enhance the use of remaining senses. The other group is more a development of the person than modification. The child must learn to do certain things in order to be as self-sufficient as possible, or the child must accept the fact that because of the nature of his or her handicap these particular things are impossible. Modifications in this group are toward development of residual senses and to the use of other senses in a compensatory manner. Both groups are only used when necessary and must provide a more acceptable and efficient method for accomplishing a task than was previously devised by the child. There are other considerations which have both positive and negative influences and which come from the outside. They may influence the person without his or her knowledge, or in ways on which the person can exercise no control.

When a person is observed functioning in society certain aspects are prominent; general affect is one. If there is a degree of poise and ease about the person's behavior, if the person is appropriately groomed and has adequate social habits, the person is usually thought to be well adjusted. Many skills are needed to present this appearance and must be considered by the person working in the educational setting. Self-help skills and activities of daily living are stressed. The nature of the child and his or her handicap determine the percentage of time and effort which must be spent to promote adequacy.

Some gross symptoms typical of maldevelopment may be useful as examples, but it should be recognized that there is a continuum presented and that an infrequent sign of any one does not place a label of maladjustment based on that one sign. In addition, much attention to any behavior can increase intensity and cause a problem where one did not exist in the past. Lack of visual feedback can cause many extraneous movements. Abnormal positioning may be the result of a long history of neglect, by those who have sight, to inform the visually handicapped person of his difference. There is a degree of motor release behavior that may be pleasant. This is usually repetitive in nature and is certainly distracting to any observer. Other acts are self-stimulating in specific sensory areas; most common with blind children is a pressure on the eye which in turn apparently stimulates the optic nerve producing a visual sensation. These manifestations are generally classed as mannerisms. They commonly occur with those who have less than light perception but this is not always the case. Mention is made here because similar symptoms are also related to other disorders such as emotional disturbance and mental retardation. Children with cerebral palsy who commonly have many gross motor behavior patterns could also demonstrate these signs from a similar etiological basis.

Proper rapport with consistent appropriate auditory feedback can alter these symptoms in time. It is important to recognize these factors in their treatment here because children with cerebral palsy may show similar mannerisms which may be connected with a central nervous system disorder rather than the visual disturbance. Treatment of these cases in a similar manner could yield negative results.

The goals of personal and social adequacy were suggested as major tasks of the educator. This is appropriate and especially so with the teacher of the visually handicapped. The present system of education frequently stresses academic achievement over all other areas. In the long-term plan any deemphasis of the other important areas will lead to an inadequate product.

Treatment and correction of abnormal appearance whenever possible is an important aid to the handicapped person. If it is not possible, or if the correction inhibits functional behavior or learning capacity, then it is usually preferable to promote acceptance of the abnormal appearance. This condition frequently applies to modifications necessary for a person to use his residual vision maximally or to adjust in other areas of development. The mechanical and physical modifications available for these purposes are numerous and varied. Many are useful for specialized purposes and are quite complex, such as electronic testing equipment for the blind. Others serve more general purposes and are useful to nearly everyone with a visual handicap. Braille watches and measuring devices modified for tactile use are examples of this group. Other activities in this field have led to more concerted efforts at classifying and organizing materials. This is important work and inevitably some findings will be transferred to other populations who will benefit from new aids and materials and their use.

Apparatus for physical modification may be categorized in several ways. One useful system is by the sensory area served and its function. This allows for analysis of results in a more structured way than when classification is based on either one alone or by supplier and academic or other specific area of use. No further consideration is given here of supplier or cost; both of these are variable. Again, it has been recognized by many, that cost frequently is inversely related to usefulness. In other words, the more the cost, the less value the item frequently has for the visually handicapped. Often minor adaptations to standard equipment are more useful than a specially made, nationally advertised gadget. The motivation and need of the individual are always crucial in acceptance of any device.

Subnormal visual aids were described previously. Their sole purpose is to modify the image as it is projected onto the retina. When this is necessary the aid can be tried and various combinations used depending upon requirements.

Print size and type has long been a topic of discussion. There is presently no resolution of its value and the decision as to when it can be used and by whom is largely left to the individual case. Modifications of print size and other structural aspects of books have many disadvantages. These frequently outweigh the positive gains to be had even though large-print materials are becoming more readily available through new processes of reproduction. In addition, they are only useful for a very select group of the visually handicapped and the possibility for variety of reading material is still limited by production. Other problems include the psychological factor when a handicapped person needs this extra modification. The very real physical problem of handling and storing materials which have approximately twice as much volume as standard texts and are too long and too wide for storage is always present. Added to this is the optical principle that magnification can be accomplished by other means, as discussed above, and magnification is the only value that can be ascribed to the large print. A person so visually handicapped as to need large print in the upper elementary grades will probably be a very slow reader and will need to rely on other means for obtaining information. The primary-grade child is reading enlarged print normally in his basic reading series.

Some children need special consideration in placement within the classroom and need special provisions for modifying the work space. Close approximation to instructional areas such as chalkboards and screens for audiovisual materials is helpful to some while others may need to be away from strong light sources if they are photophobic. Newly developed high-intensity lights appear promising as an aid to children who need this. Desks which tilt and reading stands for holding books in a vertical plane are also available. They decrease the fatigue factor and allow for more comfortable body position while working.

Modifications in the other sensory areas dealing with input are concerned with the tactual and auditory modalities. The development of tactual abilities in form perception is aided by three-dimensional models. In addition, some raised-line material such as maps and diagrams are used, but their value is difficult to assess. When braille is the primary mode of reading, the tactual area is used for gaining a large proportion of information. The use of braille is considerably limited when cerebral palsy is also present. Learning this medium takes considerable sensitivity and discriminative ability as well as coordination of the hands and arms. The population of totally blind cerebral palsied children is limited in number. Problems surrounding the use of braille with these children will probably be limited to a tutorial situation. For this reason it is largely discounted in the present chapter. A considerable quantity of material is available on the theory and method of teaching and using braille. This, in fact, has been one of the most discussed areas in education of the visually handicapped.

The auditory area holds promise for development as a medium of information input with the visually handicapped. Talking books are full length recordings on both record and audio tape. Their use was at one time restricted to the blind. They are now available to any handicapped person who needs them. Recorded materials sample the entire field of literature but are weighted most heavily in the area of fiction. Other groups record materials both academic and scientific. Many volunteers are also pressed into service for satisfying immediate needs of students and professionals.

Technical developments of variable speed playback and indexing have yet to be perfected, but this method holds promise for study and leisure-reading by the visually handicapped. It also could be of considerable use with others who for one reason or another cannot gain concepts from reading. Many cerebral palsied children fall into this group. Other technical developments make equipment more usable and available. Light-weight battery-operated recording and playback machines are more portable and useful in a variety of environments with a minimum of extra adaptations. Some attempts have been made to increase playback speed by various processes of compressing speech. The value of this is to increase the reading speed without essentially changing pitch of the recorded material. There has been some indication that speech compression devices will be commercially produced and available to individuals. If this comes about, then many more persons will benefit and will be able to apply compressed speech recording to their own individual needs.

The area of listening and of mentally arranging materials for maximum efficiency in this process is certainly important. There is a wide variation of capabilities for those who need to listen as a primary means of gathering information. Scientific study of this area will need to be continued. The teaching of this skill is a primary goal for the special teacher of the cerebral palsied and the visually handicapped. Efficiency is important for the reception of information required for learning in the formal academic environment of lectures. Adequate availability of recorded materials can entirely supplant vision for the use of the student in obtaining the data usually obtained through reading print.

The final area of consideration for development as a compensation for visual loss is in the output phase of communication. Increased performance by well-developed self-help skills and the process of orientation and mobility have been discussed and may be considered as the other observable processes by which adequacy is noted in the functioning visually handicapped person. Adaptations in these areas are necessary but generally not academic. The communication process does need attention. Visual loss is handicapping to the communicator in two general ways. It does not allow the person to use visual cues as feedback to discern acceptance or rejection of information by the listener. This is usually important and is especially so when discussion is contingent upon development of points and of interchange by several persons toward agreement. In general, the process of group dynamics applies in this area and is particularly important as a consideration for adjustment to visual handicaps.

The second area relies on the ability of the visually handicapped person to communicate through other media. Writing is most important here, and a recognition that the person will be restricted in this is important. Positive modification comes from increased skill in written expression and in typing skills. Dictation ability and outlining of material for presentation is also necessary. This in effect is promoting adequacy in areas of high value to society. The person's strength is in his ability to communicate and to reduce tensions of those who are nonhandicapped and sometimes ignorant of the problems of a handicapped communicator. His success in this may be significant in determining capacity in many other areas.

The presence of a visual disorder can stand alone as a severely handicapping condition. Its nature reduces capacity in a variety of areas basic to personal, social, and intellectual development. The addition of this condition in its many forms to other disorders leads to a multiplicative rather than an additive factor of necessary treatment ramifications. The resultant conditions have not been adequately defined or studied. Their existence and effect have been noted as has the need for further evaluation and experimentation.

It must be recognized that treatment is not simple. It cannot be considered as primarily medical, educational, or rehabilitative in nature. The various disciplines represented in treatment can be described in isolation but can never be considered as such. A total approach is necessary during any instant of time and throughout life. There may be stabilization of any disability and maximum efficiency may be reached for the individual in any area of development, but this does not always mean a termination of professional responsibility. Perspective must be maintained toward the contribution a visual disorder makes to the total handicap, and decisions are needed as to which professional shall maintain directive responsibility. Modification of the person's visual system is made in many ways. Several disciplines are engaged in this and in the total treatment process. Professional preparation and competency should be considered before determination is made of each person's role in treatment. This still leaves many undefined areas to be developed in the total needs of the visually handicapped. More research and program development is needed to clarify these areas and the appropriate techniques for treatment. Respect for the individual must be maintained above all. Any negation of this integrity will lead to diminution of results. When this is recognized, the individual's role as partner and participant in the process of growth toward adequacy will be evident to all. At this time the contribution of each handicap to the disability will be minimized and effective treatment obtained.

9

Physical Therapy

ESTHER E. SNELL

THE TREATMENT OF THE PATIENT with cerebral palsy presents an interesting challenge to the physical therapist. Although there may be similarities in the extent and type of involvement, no two cases are alike. The homes in which they live differ; or, in cases from the same home, the reaction of the siblings and parents is not identical. Each person with cerebral palsy is an individual with his or her own likes and dislikes; the person's capabilities and limitations and reaction to the handicap differs from every other person who has cerebral palsy. The person's reaction to the handicap is not static but may change from time to time. Since much is yet to be learned about cerebral palsy, by alert observation the physical therapist can contribute to the understanding of this disability. Not only does the physical therapist have an opportunity to observe and treat the patient, but also to promote understanding of cerebral palsy on the part of the members of the family and the community. If the parents' interest in the child is physical perfection, they can make the child's life and those around him or her most unpleasant, since the cerebral palsied do not achieve physical perfection. If, however, the parents can accept the limitations of the child and recognize the child's capabilities, the child's outlook for a pleasant and, in many instances, a profitable life is far greater. Just as the therapist has a responsibility to the members of the family of the individual with cerebral palsy, so also does the therapist have a responsibility to the community. The physical therapist can do much to determine the climate of opinion regarding the worth of the individual with cerebral palsy in the community.

In treating the cerebral palsied patient, the responsibility of the physical therapist will be determined in part by the other specialists who also treat the child. Regardless of how isolated the area in which the therapist works, he or she never works alone. There is always the physician who cares for the general health problems of the child, the specialist who is primarily concerned with the disability resulting from cerebral palsy and who prescribes care to be given, and the parents of the child. Treating the patient there are ideally the many specialists of the medical profession such as the orthopedist, pediatrician, and neuropsychiatrist, the speech and occupational therapist, psychologist, dentist, social worker, public health nurse, nutritionist, teacher, vocational counselor, and many others. It is the coordinated effort of all these specialists that makes for the most effective program of habilitation of the cerebral palsied. However, with the present limited number of specialists in each field it is not possible to have a complete staff in each center treating the cerebral palsied. For this reason it is even more important that the physical therapist be constantly aware of the many ramifications of cerebral palsy and that he or she keep well informed of new developments in the field.

THE CEREBRAL PALSIED PATIENT

The Changing Concept in the Treatment of Cerebral Palsy

Emphasis in treating the child with cerebral palsy has changed from waiting until the child has reached the first or second birthday to treating the child as soon as the disability is recognized. The therapist may help prevent poor patterns of use from being established if the child is treated during the early months of life. The infant will move in any way he or she is able to move and the therapist has an excellent opportunity to help the child develop more nearly normal patterns of use of muscles groups with early treatment. Parents should be instructed regarding an exercise program to carry out at home but should not be expected to assume full responsibility for the child's exercise program with only occasional contact with the therapist.

If the child has the ability to learn motor skills, early treatment has a marked advantage. The child may be able to roll over, sit, stand, and walk at an age more nearly comparable with the nonhandicapped child. The child with cerebral palsy at birth who receives no treatment until three or four years of age may develop contractures and poor patterns of use of muscle groups and may accept having things done for him or her, so that the child loses much of the motivation he or she had during the early years of life, regardless of the child's mentality. The child who is markedly mentally retarded also profits from treatment early in life in that less severe contractures may develop, such as marked scissoring of legs and fingers tightly closed over the thumb, thus making the child's care easier for the parents or attendants.

There are many advantages of early treatment of children with cerebral palsy. In observing hemiplegias at six or seven months of age grasp and release objects such as rattles or blocks, one realizes that many seem not to know when an object is in the involved hand. Tizard *et al.* (1954) reported a disturbance in sensation of involved hands in hemiplegia acquired at birth in about half of the 106 cases studied in followup. These authors noted sensory disturbance as the major reason for lack of use of the arm, in some instances. In this writer's experience, in children under a year of age, after a period of intensive treatment of exercises and use of the hand, sensation in the involved hand apparently improves and the child responds in a comparable manner when using the involved hand or the uninvolved hand when handling objects, so far as sensation is concerned.

Paine (1962) reported, in the spastic whose treatment was started before the age of two years, the eventual walking pattern was improved, contractures were less, and there was a slight decrease in the need for orthopedic surgery later in the individual's life. In the Lubbock Cerebral Palsy and Neuromuscular Center there are fewer children with feeding problems, fewer children with difficulty in chewing and swallowing, and fewer children with speech handicaps when treatment is started early in the child's life. With early treatment the child learns to sit, stand, and walk within more nearly normal limits and seems to be a much happier child. The latter could result in part from less tension on the part of parents and greater acceptance of the child by the parents. It should be stressed that results obtained from treatment are dependent on the child's capacity to learn. On the other hand, potential may be lost if treatment is not started early. A good mind is of limited value if the individual lacks muscular control to talk, walk, use the hands, and participate in a competitive society.

Evidences of Cerebral Palsy in the Young Child

Since full-term babies are now referred for therapy within the first months of life, the therapist may have the responsibility of assessing the infant's motor control. It should be noted that a single observation is of little value since the infant does not always respond in the same way at different times. Functions of the developing nervous system are complex and easily modified by hunger, sleepiness, discontent, and changes in environment. Sherrington (1947) noted that reflexes of posture are easily interrupted by other reflexes. The infant with evidences of cerebral palsy during the early months of life will continue to have very poor motor control, if untreated. Therapy should be started early, preferably as soon as the disability is recognized.

Reflexes which may be observed in healthy infants are much more evident in the involved child with cerebral palsy. Among these reflexes are the Moro reflex, Galant's reflex, asymmetrical tonic neck reflex, Landau reflex, and tonic labyrinthine reflexes. The Moro reflex is present at birth and may be much more evident in the involved cerebral palsied child than in the normal child. Parents are aware of this reflex and will describe the child as being "very nervous" or state that the infant "jumps at every noise." The Moro reflex can be elicited by letting the baby's head fall back a few degrees onto the therapist's hand when the child is raised from a supine position, or by a sudden noise or a sudden motion of the supporting surface. The infant's arms will abduct and extend with wrists extended and fingers fanning out. In normal infants this reflex becomes progressively less complete and may not be present after six months of age. It may persist much longer in the untreated child with a diagnosis of cerebral palsy.

Galant's reflex is checked with the infant in the prone position. The area between the 12th rib and the crest of the ilium in the lumbar region is stimulated, resulting in incurving of the stimulated side. It may be present in the normal infant for two or three months but may persist longer in the athetoid type of cerebral palsy and is thought to interfere with the child's ability to learn motor control sufficient for symmetrical stabilization of the trunk.

The asymmetrical tonic neck reflex can be checked with the child back lying with the head in the midline. When the head is turned to one side actively or passively, the arm and leg on the face side will extend and the opposite arm and leg will flex. In older, involved, untreated children with cerebral palsy, this reflex can be demonstrated with the patient in a sitting position and either a change of position of the arms or head results in the reflex. If it is present in the normal child, it should disappear by six months of age. Vassella and Karlsson (1963) reported in a study of 108 healthy children between the first and sixth day of life, only 8 percent had a true asymmetrical tonic neck reflex and it was not present in any of the infants at seven months. However, when present in a normal child, it is not as evident as in the involved child who has cerebral palsy. The therapist is probably as aware of an asymmetrical tonic neck reflex as any persistent reflex the child exhibits. It precludes self-feeding and hand use and is most disabling to the child. It is impossible for the older child who has an asymmetrical tonic neck reflex to look at material in his hand because the head is turned away from the flexed elbow, and the strength exerted by the neck muscles, extensor muscles of the face arm, and the flexor muscles of the opposite arm, is very great.

To test for the Landau reflex, the child is held in the prone position with support under the chest. When the child lifts the head when held in this position, there is an increase in tone in the extensor muscles of the legs and back. With passive flexion of the child's head, the legs will flex. It is reported to appear from the third month of life and persists as long as two and a half years. Schaltenbrand (1928) found it to be a combination of the labyrinth righting reflex and neck reflexes.

The tonic labyrinthine reflexes are normal until four months of age. These reflexes produce tone in the flexor muscles when the infant is in the prone position. Lying supine, the tonic labyrinthine reflexes produce tone in the extensor muscles. These abnormally strong reflexes are not seen to that degree in the healthy infant and are very disabling to the child with cerebral palsy. Extension of the spine is very great; the shoulders are pulled back; and the upper arms are abducted. The involved infant is unable to bring his hands to the midline or to take his hands to his mouth. The tonic labyrinthine reflexes are frequently seen in the spastic type of cerebral palsy.

During the neonatal period, the normal infant will turn the head to one side and flex the arm in front of the face. The rooting reaction is present— that is a response to stimulation of the peribuccal area which results in the infant turning the head in the direction of the stimulated area. Either absence of motion or excessive motion is significant at this age. Excessive crying in a high-pitched tone or excessive sleeping may be significant.

By three months of age the child should have a meaningful gaze, coo, respond to individuals in the environment, and play with the hands which he or she brings to the midline. Many normal children roll from prone to supine and supine to prone by this age. Fisting of one or both hands is significant. Reciprocal kicking is evident, and, although the child may kick with one leg or the other part of the time, kicking with one leg only may be evidence of hemiplegia. Scissoring of legs may be in evidence, and, although the tightness in the adductor muscles of the legs will not feel great to the person evaluating the infant during the early months of life, it may be evidence of cerebral palsy. An internally rotated arm, when the elbow is extended, is significant.

By six months of age, the less involved child shows evidence of cerebral palsy. Placed in a weight-bearing position, the child may cross his or her legs in a scissored position. It may not be possible for the child to take steps when supported in an upright position, or the child may not take weight on the feet as the normal child does. The child may lack the head control expected of a child of this age and may be unable to turn from a back-lying position to face lying. The hemiplegic may use only one hand to hold toys and the opposite hand may be fisted.

The child who has cerebral palsy may support weight on his or her feet by nine months of age, but there may be an increase in tone in the extensor muscles of the legs and back. The normal child can sit alone by this age, but the child who has cerebral palsy may not be able to do so because he or she cannot flex the hips and knees.

The guidelines of normal development are only guidelines, and siblings do not follow stages of development at the exact time. It is a composite of a number of abnormal responses and reflexes that is significant.

Name _____ Birth date _____

Key: N Normal   P Poor
       G Good   O Zero
       F Fair   X Functions with resistance
                        given another muscle group

	DATE	DATE	DATE	DATE
NECK				
Forward flexion				
Flexion to right				
Flexion to left				
Extension				
TRUNK				
Flexion				
Extension				

	R	L	R	L	R	L	R	L
SHOULDER								
Flexion								
Extension								
Internal rotation								
External rotation								
Abduction								
Adduction								
ELBOW								
Flexion								
Extension								
Pronation								
Supination								
WRIST								
Flexion								
Extension								
FINGER								
Flexion								
Extension								

Figure 9.1.   Evaluation of range of motion.

	DATE		DATE		DATE		DATE	
THUMB	**R**	**L**	**R**	**L**	**R**	**L**	**R**	**L**
Flexion								
Extension								
Abduction								
Adduction								
Opposition								
HIP								
Flexion								
Extension								
Adduction								
Abduction								
Internal rotation								
External rotation								
KNEE								
Flexion								
Extension								
ANKLE								
Plantar flexion								
Dorsiflexion								
Inversion								
Eversion								
TOE								
Flexion								
Extension								

Figure 9.1.   (Continued)

THE PHYSICAL THERAPIST AND THE CEREBRAL PALSIED PATIENT

Patient Evaluation

On the initial visit of the child and parents to the physical therapy department, information regarding the child's development may be obtained from the parents. Already present on the record may be data regarding the responses of the child during the first few weeks of life such as the child's ability to suck and swallow and whether the child's color and crying seemed normal. If the child has exceeded the age of two weeks when first seen by the

Name _____ Birth date _____

	DATE	DATE	DATE

ROLLING
    Back to stomach (to right)
    Back to stomach (to left)
    Stomach to back (to right)
    Stomach to back (to left)

SITTING
    Tailor fashion with hands on supporting surface (length of time)
    Tailor fashion with hands off supporting surface (length of time)
    Unsupported in straight chair
    Unsupported on stool

CRAWLING
    Moves using arms only
    Can support weight on arms and legs
    Normal crawling pattern

STANDING
    Stands holding to object
    Stands with back against supporting surface (length of time)
    Stands without support (length of time)
    Can come to standing position holding to object
    Can come to standing position without assistance

WALKING
    Walks holding to furniture
    Walks in parallel bars
    Walks with crutches
    Walks with canes
    Walks without assistance (number of steps)
    Walks with heel-toe motion

Figure 9.2.   Evaluation of coordination.

DATE   DATE   DATE

ARM USE
   Can grasp object with right hand
   Can release object with right hand
   Can grasp object with left hand
   Can release object with left hand
   Can take right hand to mouth
   Can take left hand to mouth
   Can get right hand behind back
   Can get left hand behind back
   Can get right hand back of head
   Can get left hand back of head

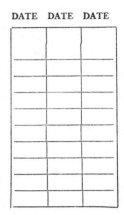

Figure 9.2.   (Continued)

physical therapist, the therapist will be interested in the child's movements and positions assumed.

To obtain as accurate a picture of the child's physical condition on admission or as soon after as possible, the therapist should have forms for recording ranges of motion and skills achieved. If, on admission, the child is old enough to recognize strangers it may not be possible to learn motions the child is capable of achieving because of apprehension on the part of the child. After a few visits and the child feels at ease with the therapist, a more accurate record may be obtained. Findings should be recorded on forms that can be kept and further evaluations recorded at intervals.

Figure 9.1 illustrates a form for recording results of evaluating range of motion. For example, if a child is twelve months of age on admission and it is not possible to bring the right leg to 90° in straight leg raising with the opposite leg held in extension on the table as the child is back lying, it would be record "L-P," indicating limited motion passively; preferably the degree of motion would be recorded.

The skill with which the patient can use muscle strength that is present should also be evaluated. Figure 9.2 illustrates a chart which has been found useful in evaluating coordination.

A third method of recording the child's muscular control on admission and at intervals during the treatment program is the use of movies. Movies may be made at approximately six-month intervals and have been found to be of considerable value in studying the child's progress.

Prescription for Care

It is the responsibility of the orthopedist or physiatrist to prescribe care to be given by the physical therapist. If the therapist has had an opportunity to

Name_____ Birth date_____
Key: N Normal   A Active
      L Limited   P Passive

Name_____ Birth date_____ Date_____

Diagnosis_____

Involvement:

	R. Arm	L. Arm	R. Leg	L. Leg	Face	Trunk
Athetosis						
Spasticity						
Ataxia						
Rigidity						
Tremor						

Prognosis:

Area of body to be treated:_____

_____

Treatment:

Exercise program_____

_____

Functional training:

Rolling_____ Sitting_____ Standing_____

Walking: with crutches_____ without crutches_____

Other_____

_____

_____

_____

_____ _____

Signature of physician

Figure 9.3.   Prescription for treatment.

observe the patient, a report of the therapist's evaluation should be made available to the physician. However, the organization of the treatment center may be such that new patients come to the therapist after the initial prescription has been made. The physician will be interested in the results of the therapist's findings each time the child is reexamined. The therapist should not assume the responsibility of long periods of treatment without a re-evaluation by the physician, but rather the patient should be reexamined no less frequently than once each six months. Figure 9.3 shows a prescription for physical therapy care.

Treatment Techniques

Perhaps the earliest system of therapy was established by Colby and later carried out by Mary Trainor at Children's Hospital, Boston, Massachusetts. Conditioned reflex training is the basis of this system of therapy. A rhyme is used with each motion and motions follow a sequence with exercises starting at the joint nearest the body and moving out to the farthest joint from the body. The patient learns the motion expected from the hold taken on the extremity and the rhyme sung by the therapist. Depending upon the age of the patient, the child learns to participate in the movement expected.

The entire series is not necessary for each child; each exercise is used on a selective basis as determined by the needs of the child. Recordings of songs are of no value. When the child capable of assisting with exercises fails to work with the therapist, the exercise is stopped and the child's attention is directed again toward the participation expected. Exercises are given both in prone and supine positions, and the parents of each patient can be taught to carry out these exercises at home.

Exercises developed by Colby and Trainor (presented here by permission of Mary Trainor) and adapted for use in the Lubbock Cerebral Palsy and Neuromuscular Center are as follows:

I. *Position of Patient:* Back, lying—legs extended on table.
   Motion: Hip flexion and extension.
   Precautions: Keep knees straight. Opposite leg should remain on table—full range of motion to right angle may not be possible when exercises are started.
   Rhyme: Shoot the rocket, shoot the rocket,
   Shoot, Shoot, Shoot.

II. *Position of Patient:* Back, lying—legs extended on table.
   Motion: Abduction and adduction of legs. Abduct both legs and return to midline.
   Precautions: Keep knees straight. Do not roll legs in or out.

Rhyme: One, two, buckle my shoe,
Three, four, open the door,
Five, six, pick up sticks,
Seven, eight, lay them straight,
Nine, ten, a big fat hen.

III. *Position of Patient:* Back, lying—legs extended on table.
Motion: Internal and external rotation of legs.
Precaution: Do not bend knees.
Rhyme: Roll over, roll over, so merry and free,
My playfellows dear, come join in my glee.

IV. *Position of Patient:* Back, lying—legs extended.
Motion: Knee and hip flexion. Flex right knee, slide right foot along table to buttocks, straighten right leg. Flex left knee as right leg is being straightened.
Precaution: Do not roll legs in or out.
Rhyme: Gallopy, gallopy, gallopy trot,
Gallopy trot to the blacksmith shop.
Shoe the horse, shoe the mare,
And let the baby colt go bare.

V. *Position of Patient:* Back, lying—legs extended.
Motion: Flexion and extension of ankles.
Precautions: Motion should be in ankle. In pulling foot up, discourage use of toe extensors.
Rhyme: Up, down, up down,
This is the way we go to town.
What to buy, to buy a fat pig,
Home again, home again, jig-a-jig, jig.

VI. *Position of Patient:* Back, lying—legs extended.
Motion: Inversion and eversion of feet. Both feet move in at same time and out at same time.
Rhyme: This way, that way, blows the weather vane.
This way, that way, blows and blows again.
Ever pointing, every showing
How the merry wind is blowing.

VII. *Position of Patient:* Back, lying—legs extended.
Motion: Toe flexion and extension.
Rhyme: Little birdies in the nest
Go hop, hop, hop, hop.
They try to do their very best
And hop, hop, hop, hop.

VIII.   *Position of Patient:* Face, lying—legs extended.
Motion: Hip extension. Alternately raise legs from table keeping knees straight.
Precaution: Do not raise leg more than 10 to 15 degrees from the table.
Rhyme: Shoot the rocket, shoot the rocket,
Shoot, shoot, shoot.

IX.   *Position of Patient:* Face, lying—legs extended.
Motion: Knee flexion. Alternately bend knees bringing heel to buttocks.
Precautions: Pelvis should not change position as heel is brought toward buttocks. Full range of motion may not be possible when exercises are started.
Rhyme: Up, down, up, down
This is the way we go to town.
What to buy, to buy a fat pig.
Home again, home again, jig-a-jig, jig.

X.   *Position of Patient:* Back, lying—arms at side, palms down.
Motion: Shoulder flexion and extension. Alternately bring arms from position at side of body forward and up to extended position over head.
Precaution: Do not bend elbow or rotate arm.
Rhyme: Shoot the rocket, shoot the rocket,
Shoot, shoot, shoot.

XI.   *Position of Patient:* Back, lying—arms at side, palms down.
Motion: Shoulder abduction and adduction. Bring both arms out to shoulder level and return to sides.
Precaution: Do not bend elbows or elevate shoulders.
Rhyme: Sunbeams rise and sunbeams fall,
Rise and fall, rise and fall.

XII.   *Position of Patient:* Back, lying—arms at shoulder level, palms down.
Motion: Internal and external rotation of shoulders. Roll arms in and out, bringing back of hand to table as arms externally rotate, and palm to table as arms internally rotate.
Precautions: If there is any tightness in shoulder do not force this motion. Upper arm should be kept at right angle to body—range of motion may be very limited when starting exercise.
Rhyme: Pump the water, pump the water,
Pump, pump, pump.

XIII.   *Position of Patient:* Back, lying—arms extended at side, palms up.

Motion: Bend and straighten elbow.

Precautions: Keep palm in same position throughout exercises. Discourage child pulling with wrist muscles. Wrist should be kept in neutral position.

Rhyme: Up, down, up, down,
This is the way we go to town.
What to buy, to buy a fat pig
Home again, home again, jig-a-jig, jig.

XIV.   *Position of Patient:* Back, lying—upper arms at side, elbows bent.

Motion: Pronation and supination of elbow.

Precaution: Keep wrist in line with forearm.

Rhyme: Roll over and over, so merry and free,
My playfellows dear, come join in my glee.

XV.   *Position of Patient:* Back, lying—forearm at right angle to upper arm.

Motion: Flexion and extension of wrist.

Precaution: Motion should be in wrist—not in fingers.

Rhyme: This way, that way, blows the weather vane.
This way, that way, blows and blows again.
Ever turning, ever showing
How the merry wind is blowing.

XVI.   *Position of Patient:* Back, lying—forearm at right angle to upper arm.

Motion: Flexion and extension of fingers.

Precaution: Motion should be in all joints of each finger.

Rhyme: Little birdies in the nest
Go hop, hop, hop, hop.
They try to do their very best
And hop, hop, hop, hop.

XVII.   *Position of Patient:* Back, lying.

Motion: Tip of thumb is brought to tip of each finger in succession.

Rhyme: Thumbkins and pointer say "How do you do?
How do you do? How do you do?"

Thumbkins and tall man say "How do you do?
How do you do? How do you do?"

Thumbkins and ring man say "How do you do?
How do you do? How do you do?"

Thumbkins and wee man say "How do you do?
How do you do? How do you do?"

Dr. Temple Fay described a method of treatment based on primitive
patterns of movement. An outgrowth of this method was that developed by
Doman-Delacato (Freeman 1967), who established a rigidly structured
system of treatment. Four exercise periods daily of five minutes each are included. Each exercise period requires the participation of five people. Fluid
intake is limited. The child is not permitted to progress from one skill to
another without perfection in the previous skill. The child is required to
rebreathe air by use of a face mask to improve cerebral function. Music is
eliminated from the child's environment. No distinction is made as to the
type of cerebral palsy or to the intellectual capacity to learn skills. Because
of the time involved, the large number of people required to treat the child,
and failure to permit the child to progress from one skill to another until
perfection is achieved, it has been found that this technique compounds the
problem already present for the cerebral palsied child and increases the
burden on parents and siblings.

A technique of treatment described by Margaret Knott and Dorothy
Voss (1956) is based on three components of motion: (1) "flexion and extension"; (2) "motion toward and across the midline and across and away from
the midline"; and (3) "rotation."

Mass movements, spiral and diagonal in direction, may be carried out
passively, actively, or against resistance in a full range of motion from the
pivotal point or through a partial range of motion. Timing is emphasized
and is a goal of treatment. Holds taken by the therapist are purposeful and
should not produce pain. Verbal commands describing the motion to be
achieved are also used as stimulation through the tone of the therapist's
voice. This technique of treatment can be used with the patient in prone and
supine positions.

A technique of treatment is described by Rood (Gillette 1969) which
activates muscles through sensory receptors. Icing, heat, brushing, and
pressure are used to create an awareness of normal patterns of muscle use.

Dr. and Mrs. Karl Bobath (Pearson and Williams 1972) have developed a system of therapy based on inhibition of abnormal reflexes. This
technique of treatment consists of inhibiting tonic reflex activity through
positioning the patient and of introducing "normal qualities of postural
tone." The abnormal tonic reflex activity originates in proximal parts of the
body—head, neck, shoulder girdle, etc. These areas are referred to as "key
points." By changing the child's position at these "key points," abnormal
tone in the extremities is inhibited. "Key points" are adapted to the needs of
the child and are changed as indicated by hypertonus in extremities. Motor
function of "higher organization," such as righting and equilibrium reac-

tions, is introduced to replace abnormal tonic reflex activity. They recognize that the results of therapy are determined by the child's intellectual capacity.

The therapist is fortunate if he or she works in a facility where part or all of a specific technique can be used which best meets the needs of a specific child and is not limited to one system of therapy. Cerebral palsy is a complex disability and no two cases are identical. The therapist should have a number of techniques at his or her disposal and use the technique or parts of several techniques to obtain the most effective results with a given case.

Functional Training

Functional training means training in skills which are part of daily living. This begins with the earliest age of admission of the child for therapy. If the child exhibits an abnormal asymmetrical tonic neck reflex on admission, the child probably cannot bring the hands to the mouth; if the child has an abnormal Moro, Landau, and/or tonic labyrinthine reflex, the child may seem "stiff" to the parents and thrust his or her head back. It may be difficult to dress or bathe the infant because of hypertonicity.

Positioning of the child is important, and parents should be taught to place the child in a flexed position when holding him or her, keeping the head forward and in the midline with the knees flexed. Often parents will carry children, letting them to push their heads back and extend the legs which only encourages poor patterns of use. Feeding, bathing, and dressing are accomplished much more easily if the child is supported in a position with the head in the midline and knees flexed rather than allowing the child to assume a position of total extension. Dressing may be more easily accomplished with the child in a sitting position with hips flexed and trunk forward and the mother working from back of the child.

Frequently parents of infants will report that the child cries when placed in the prone position. A recent case referred to this Center was a girl twelve years of age whom the parents reported could not lie in a prone position. Since the family were migrant workers who changed locations continuously, the child had received no previous therapy. The parents were given an exercise program and taught how to help their child learn skills she had not acquired. Within two weeks, the child was comfortable in the prone position. Infants soon become comfortable in a prone position and parents should be encouraged to place them in a face-lying position, first at short intervals and then increasing the time.

If the full-term infant is not sitting by nine months of age, the child should be taught to do so. Sitting tailor fashion, with hands on the supporting suface, is frequently used. During the early training periods the child may be able to maintain this position only a few seconds. The child gradually increases the time he or she can keep the hands on the supporting surface. There is little value in passively raising the child's head, if the child lets it fall forward. Many children will raise their heads if the therapist strokes the cervical-thorasic area of the spine. Use of a toy which the child wishes to see can serve as motivation for the child to raise the head.

Early gait training may be started in a number of ways depending upon the response of the child. It may be started in parallel bars if the child is able to grasp bars; if not, it may be given with the therapist giving the child support at the hands with the child's elbows extended and at the sides. Walking training may also be started with the child standing against a supporting surface, pulling out from the supporting surface and taking a step or two to a person in front of him or her. This method of training allays fear the child may have of falling, and the child gradually learns to take more steps alone and gains confidence in his or her ability to walk. Since many cerebral palsied children flex their elbows and hold their arms away from their bodies, it is well to work with the arms at the sides using as normal a pattern as possible from an early age. Lines for foot placement may be of value in creating a consciousness of foot placement. So-called foot-placement ladders are of less value, since the child is expected to place the feet in a specific location, and this increases tension on the part of the patient.

A heel-toe motion is not learned by the average child until about two years of age; the beginning walking pattern is one of a wide base of support and placing the entire sole of the foot on the supporting surface. As the child's balance improves, the base of support becomes more narrow and the child learns to use a heel-toe motion. In training the cerebral palsied child, the normal pattern of learning should be followed. When the child has acquired a pattern of walking in which the gait is secure and the child has reached the age at which a heel-toe motion should be learned, training should be begun. Many of these children will not learn to push off with the weight-bearing foot and place the heel of the advancing foot on the supporting surface first, unless they are taught to do so. Many hours of practice over a considerable period of time may be required to achieve this skill. The spastic hemiplegic may need to be taught to use this pattern with the involved leg, and it may be necessary to teach the child to bend the knee. One of the aids in teaching knee-bending is stair-climbing, in which one foot and then the other is used in ascending and descending stairs. Gait-training before a mirror is valuable to the child who is old enough to evaluate his or her pattern of walking.

Crutch-walking may be prescribed for the cerebral palsied child, and the pattern of walking does not differ from that for any other handicapping condition in which crutches are prescribed. The cerebral palsied child may have the added problems of poor hand control and of poor coordination of arms and legs. It has been found helpful to weight the base of the crutches for some children and thus permit more accurate placement of the crutches. In initiating the use of crutches, the child may stand with his or her back to the supporting surface; the crutches are handed to the child to place under the arms, or they may be placed under the child's arms until he or she learns to do so. The child is then taught to pull the body forward from the supporting surface and maintain balance with the crutches. To learn this skill may require training during several treatment periods. Standing against the supporting surface, the child is also taught to lift one crutch and place it, then the opposite foot, the second crutch, and the foot opposite that crutch, if the child is to learn four-point crutch-walking. This procedure is then used with the patient away from the supporting surface but with the surface close enough to give the child confidence. After this skill is achieved, the child is ready to begin crutch-walking. The therapist should remain close enough to prevent falling and allay the child's fear. After acquiring some skill in using crutches, the child is taught to fall and to come to a standing position using the crutches.

Records

A record of patient progress is essential in any program treating the cerebral palsied. The therapist may feel progress is slow and that it is not necessary to record care given the child or the response of the patient to care at each treatment. But it is most important to know how the patient responds to care given and the length of time necessary to achieve skills. Equally important is that the system of recording results not be so detailed that much of the therapist's time is spent recording.

Daily narrative reports including attitude of the patient and response to treatment are most valuable in accurately recording the patient's progress. In addition, at approximately six-month intervals, range of motion and skills achieved should be recorded.

Bracing

Although the prescription for braces falls entirely into the field of the physician, braces are of very real concern to the physical therapist. In cerebral palsy, braces are used for support, correction of deformity, and control of extra motion, as, for example, with the athetoid.

The materials from which braces are made are steel, aluminum, and plastics. Surgical steel or high-carbon steel may be used. Braces may be custom-made or prefabricated. The latter facilitates more rapid assembly by the brace fitter and reduces the cost over custom-made braces. Stainless steel is also used. Aluminum, which is available for prefabricated or for custom-made braces, is brought into use. However, another metal such as brass or steel is needed at the joints since aluminum wears through rapidly.

Plastics such as plexiglas, celastic, and others are used primarily for wrist, hand, and thumb splints and feeding and writing splints.

Parts of the braces may be classified under these headings: uprights, crossbands, joints, stops, cuffs, pelvic bands, gluteal pads, knee caps, and knee pads. Uprights are self-explanatory and need no further clarification. Crossbands are made from metal covered with leather and are used to prevent buckling and torsion of the uprights. Joints may be classified into four groups: (1) simple joints, that is, two pieces of metal attached with a rivet; (2) box joints, in which two pieces of metal meet; (3) ball-bearing joints; and (4) spring joints, such as ankle joints used in overcoming plantar flexion of the foot. Stops are used to stop motion, as the name implies. These may be used to prevent plantar or dorsiflexion of the foot or to limit motion at the hips. Cuffs are made from leather and are secured with lacing, straps, or zippers as indicated for each case. Pelvic bands are made from metal covered with leather and extend from one anterior superior iliac spine around the back to the opposite anterior iliac spine. They may be made in two pieces attached by a strap in the center back, thus allowing for adjustment, or from a solid piece of metal. Gluteal pads are used to support the trunk. Knee pads are circular discs attached to the inner aspect of the knee joint on the metal upright and serve to prevent or correct a knock knee deformity. Knee caps are used to prevent knee flexion and are attached to the medial and lateral uprights. Recurvatum straps are used to prevent hyperextension of knees. T-straps are attached to the shoe and fasten by means of a strap and buckle to the medial or lateral upright to maintain the foot in as normal a weight-bearing position as possible.

Braces may be attached to the shoes in several ways. Permanent attachment may be used, which necessitates putting on the shoes and brace at the same time. Since, with the cerebral palsied child, it may be difficult to get the foot into the shoe, braces that are permanently attached to the shoe add further to the difficulty. Many braces can be removed from the shoe. Whenever possible, the shoe should be removed from the brace and put on the child; the heel of the foot must be well into the heel of the shoe. The types of attachments of braces on shoes are (1) a caliper attachment and (2) a stirrup attachment. The round caliper fits into a metal attachment inserted into the heel of the shoe. Stops may be used to limit plantar and dorsiflexion. One disadvantage of this type of attachment is that the joint is at the heel rather than at the natural ankle joint. The stirrup-type attachment may or may not be removable from the shoe. This attachment allows no motion at the site of attachment and an ankle joint is provided in the brace in line with the natural axis of the ankle.

For the cerebral palsied, short leg braces, long leg braces, long leg braces with pelvic band, or long leg braces with pelvic band and back support may be prescribed. One need only visit cerebral palsy centers to realize the many variations in braces used with the cerebral palsied. There are, however, basic principles in the care of braces important to the physical therapist. Each time the therapist treats the child, braces should be checked, both on and off the child. In inspecting braces off the child, all joints should be examined to determine if they are easily movable; if the brace is a bilateral long leg brace with pelvic band, alignment should be checked. Leather should be checked to be certain it is receiving proper care. It can be cleaned with saddle soap, and many brace-fitters believe that the leather which comes in contact with the skin should be powdered each time the brace is worn. Ball-bearing joints are packed with a lubricant and need no further lubrication. All other joints should be oiled once a week; this is a responsibility parents can assume if the child is not institutionalized. The caliper box should be cleaned once a week and a few drops of oil put into it after it has been cleaned.

In applying braces, parents should be instructed to put the child's shoes on first, having removed the braces if they are removable from the shoes. The child is laid on the treatment table or a firm surface when braces are applied. The braces should be placed into the shoe and the T-strap then fastened. If the brace is a bilateral long leg brace, and is to be worn with knees locked, it is this writer's experience that the most satisfactory procedure is to fasten the knee lock next. The knee cap is then fastened. Following this the lower and upper cuffs are fastened and the pelvic band.

The brace is then checked with the child in a standing position. The ankle joint should be at the level of the lateral malleolus; the calf band should fit over the upper part of the calf; the thigh band should include the upper and middle thirds of the thigh; the pelvic band is usually fitted just below the crest of the ilium. The knee joint of the brace should be parallel to the medial aspect of the anatomical joint.

Children's braces should have provision for extension both in lower and upper leg. The therapist should check skin along the uprights for areas of pressure. The pelvic band should produce no pressure, either in sitting or standing positions.

Shoes

As soon as the child begins weight bearing, he or she should be fitted with shoes which have a firm sole and offer support. The physical therapist may be responsible for checking shoes to be certain they fit properly if this is not done by the orthopedist. A corrective shoe which comes from the manufacturer with an inner heel and sole wedge may be prescribed for the child who pronates. In some instances, additional correction is indicated and, although it is not the responsibility of the physical therapist to determine the correction needed, the therapist should observe the child's foot and leg position in weight bearing and bring the findings to the attention of the orthopedist. Shoe size should be checked at frequent intervals.

An aid to balance and gait training are so-called square heels. These are heels in which the layer of the heel touching the supporting surface extends beyond the sides and back of the heel. The increase in size depends upon the size of the heel of the shoe—varying from one-eighth of an inch for the child of two years of age to one-fourth of an inch for the child of four or more years. This gives the child a larger base of support and is most useful to the athetoid or ataxic in learning standing balance and walking.

Equipment

Today considerable equipment appears on the market for use with the cerebral palsied patient. Equipment should be evaluated according to the function it serves and use made of it. For example, a walker may serve a purpose if the patient, in using it, maintains good body alignment and does not become dependent on it. However, every therapist with experience working with the cerebral palsied has admitted to the case load children who have used walkers improperly in the home, and the therapist knows the difficulty of re-educating the patient to develop a more nearly normal walking pattern. The therapist also knows the hours involved in training the child to become independent of the walker after dependence has been established.

Criteria for evaluating equipment may be listed as follows:
1. Is the equipment designed to require that good body alignment be maintained?
2. In all probability, will the child maintain good body alignment while using the equipment?
3. Will the child become dependent upon the equipment?
4. Will the equipment speed or retard the patient's rehabilitation program?

Basic equipment essential for work with the cerebral palsied includes (1) treatment table, (2) mat, (3) mirrors, (4) parallel bars, (5) tricycle, (6) rubber matting for gait training, (7) stairs and ramps, (8) standing table, and (9) chairs.

The treatment table should be sturdy and of a height comfortable for use by the physical therapist. It may be padded with foam rubber and covered with a material easy to clean, or a sponge rubber mattress may be used on the table top. It should be at least thirty inches wide and seventy-two inches long if the case load includes patients from a wide age range. If the case load is limited to preschool children, a smaller table may be used. Steps to permit the older child to climb onto the table should be provided. Two steps built as a unit are usually adequate and should be of heavy enough construction that they will not tip or move with the patient. A mirror attached to the ceiling or suspended from the ceiling over the treatment table is a valuable aid.

A mirror approximately sixty inches high and twenty-four inches wide placed on a movable standard is useful in gait-training. Placed in front of the mirror may be rubber matting on which lines are painted to serve as a guide to the child for approximate location of foot placement. Highly polished floors or waxed asphalt tile floors are slippery and do not allow the child to get adequate traction.

Stairs with steps of varying heights on either side and with hand rails adjustable in height are essential equipment. The stairs should be covered with rubber matting. Parallel bars should also have adjustable hand rails if the case load includes patients varying in age.

Tricycles may be used by the cerebral palsied child as a means of locomotion before the child has acquired skill in functional walking. A back may be attached to the tricycle—the wheel base widened several inches on either side so the tricycle does not turn over easily—and straps may be attached to the pedals to hold the child's feet on the pedals.

Standing tables are useful for the child for whom weight-bearing has been prescribed and who is unable to maintain balance without this aid. Mats approximately forty-eight inches by seventy-two inches in size covered with a washable material are useful in teaching the child rolling or sitting if the child is apprehensive when these skills are attempted on the treatment table. Adjustable chairs are essential equipment. It is desirable to have a chair with as many adjustments as possible for use in the physical therapy department if cases from a wide range of ages are included in the patient load.

Additional equipment which may be useful in the physical therapy department includes sand bags, weighted doll buggies, and large plastic balls. Weighted doll buggies may be used for balance for the child in early walking. The handle of the buggy should be high enough so the child maintains good posture. Foot placement should be checked and the child should not be permitted to lean forward and walk on the toes while pushing the buggy.

Large plastic balls are used in some instances with the child lying across the ball prone or supine and the ball being moved. The child finds it necessary to make postural adjustments. However, some children are most apprehensive when moved unexpectedly, and there is no value in adding to the child's apprehension. The use of this equipment should be on a very selective basis.

The amount of equipment essential for a successful physical therapy department for treating the cerebral palsied is not great. With treatment started during the early months of the child's life, the child learns to come to a standing position and walk without as many aids as were needed when therapy was begun at a later age. Less adaptation of equipment is needed, and the child is able to use a tricycle, for example, without a widened wheel base or back. A few cases will be referred later in their lives, and the therapist should have this equipment available for use if it is indicated. In using each piece of equipment the therapist should evaluate that equipment from the standpoint of whether the patient can maintain good body alignment while using the equipment and whether the child will become dependent upon that piece of equipment.

Nutrition

Because of difficulty in chewing and swallowing experienced by some patients with cerebral palsy, they may not be able to eat foods served other members of the family. Although the physical therapist may not be qualified to offer a counseling service regarding the methods of meeting the dietary needs of the patient, the therapist should be aware that a problem may exist in this area. It is her responsibility to know what constitutes a balanced diet. The food intake should be adequate in quality and quantity to maintain body processes, supply energy, repair tissues, and, in the case of children, to build tissue because of increasing height and weight.

If the child has difficulty chewing, parents may continue to serve the child commercially prepared baby food beyond the age this would normally be used. We have found a blender to be most useful. Foods prepared for other members of the family can be changed to a useful consistency by putting them through a blender. Parents should be advised to add broth to meat and liquid in which vegetables have been cooked to the vegetables when these foods are put in the blender. Without the addition of liquid, the consistency of foods will be undesirable for blending and consumption.

The physical therapist, working with the child and parent, has an excellent opportunity to learn the food likes and eating habits of the child and, in staff conference, to bring this to the attention of the person qualified to counsel with parents.

Motivation

Methods of establishing and maintaining interest on the part of the cerebral palsied individual in improving his or her muscular control present an interesting challenge to the physical therapist. Many centers treating the cerebral palsied admit cases covering a wide age range, cases with widely different interests, and probably no two cases with identical involvement.

Perhaps the most important consideration is to help the child develop a desire to achieve skills which he or she is capable of learning. Because of lack of understanding on the part of the people with whom the child has been associated, the child's every need may have been anticipated and it may not have been necessary to do anything for him or herself. Learning muscular control is similar to other learning, and the child should have realistic goals toward which he or she works. For the young child these goals should be realized in a short time, but for the older child they may be further removed. For the child just learning to take steps, the goal may be to reach a toy of interest; for the older child, gait training may be carried out so that the child can attend school with other children in the neighborhood. The patient should derive satisfaction from skills achieved, and from this satisfaction the therapist should be able to encourage the child to learn more difficult tasks.

Devices used to maintain interest in the skill to be achieved will depend upon the initiative and imagination of the therapist. If the child receives attention for a skill well done, the child will work for this attention. If attention is obtained only for work done poorly, the therapist may expect less good work from the child because all children, handicapped or non-handicapped, want attention and learn behavior that is attention-getting.

Perhaps it is well for the therapist to remember that every practice period will not meet with equal success. If the patient is emotionally upset, the reason should be understood and time allocated to physical therapy may be spent discussing with the patient the particular problem at the moment. The therapist should be an understanding person, a friend, and a person to whom the child can look for guidance. Although the therapist cannot supply the motivation necessary for learning, he or she can set the stage so the child will want to achieve the task at hand.

Acceptance of the Handicap

The extent to which the person with cerebral palsy who is educable succeeds or fails in a competitive society will depend to a large extent upon his or her attitude toward the handicap. As soon as the child is old enough to ask about the handicap, questions should be answered in as much detail as the child is capable of understanding. The child must learn to live within the limits of the disability and get along with other people.

It is important that the child develop a sense of responsibility; tasks should be assigned that the child is capable of doing and the child should be expected to do them. If the child is to exist in a competitive society, he or she must be able to form judgments and should be trained to make decisions comparable with his or her age level rather than expect someone to make decisions for him or her. It is necessary that the child develop an appreciation of time, quality, and quantity, and, in these also, training should be started early. Because of the handicap the child should not expect that every effort will meet with success, but the child must learn that he or she may fail and learn to try again.

The physical therapist is one of the people who begins work with the child early, perhaps earlier than any of the other therapists, if the pediatricians are referring cases as soon as they are found to have some disability. The therapist may be one of the people to whom the family looks for guidance. Through discussions of cases in staff meetings, the staff's efforts will be coordinated and the therapist will be acquainted with the outlook for the child as determined by the psychologist and, as the child grows older, the teacher and vocational counselor. The therapist in no way replaces these people but is one more person helping the family understand the child's limitations and capabilities.

If the therapist is a member of a staff which does not employ a vocational counselor, the services of the vocational counselor employed by the state vocational rehabilitation department will probably be available to cases being treated in the center. The vocational counselor will be interested in having cases referred while the child is in junior high school so that the counselor may become acquainted with the child and start vocational planning with the child. With increased understanding of cerebral palsy by the public should come an increase in vocational opportunities for the person with cerebral palsy, and with better training for the handicapped person should come more adequately qualified people to fill positions.

THE PHYSICAL THERAPIST, PARENT, AND CEREBRAL PALSIED PATIENT

Few cerebral palsied children are institutionalized for a long period of treatment in a hospital, rehabilitation center, or residence school, if at all. Therefore, parents play an important part in the habilitation program. The physical therapist should work closely with the parents of the child, since care of these children is not limited to a period of exercises once a day or once a week.

In the first interview, the therapist should establish good rapport with parents and patient. The therapist has an important role in helping parents realize that all members of the staff are available to work with them, to help them understand the nature of the child's handicap, establish realistic goals for the child, and understand and accept the child. As parental tension is relieved, parents become better able to work with their children in the total habilitation program.

Understanding the child's handicap is an important step in the parent's acceptance of the child's handicap. Every therapist working with parents has seen the look of relief on the faces of parents when they learned the causes of cerebral palsy. Some parents apparently have feelings of guilt, and, through understanding, these guilt feelings are removed. The child should feel wanted and loved by members of the family and have a feeling of security and belonging in the home. If the parents are expected to work with their cerebral palsied children, they should know as much about cerebral palsy as they can comprehend. The majority of parents are not well acquainted with the structure of the brain, attachment of muscles, or specific muscle functions, but damage to the brain and muscle function can be explained to them on a level they can understand. With understanding comes acceptance of the cerebral palsied child by the family and this is important to the child's adjustment to life.

The therapist can further the understanding of cerebral palsy on the part of parents in many ways. Taking time to answer parents' questions and supplying literature which may be of interest to them are two methods most frequently used. Parents' clubs are used in many centers. Newsletters, in which articles regarding various aspects of cerebral palsy are reviewed, are useful. The method or methods of supplying information to parents will vary with the needs of the particular locality the center serves, but it is an aspect which the physical therapist cannot overlook.

The therapist is offering a real service to the family when teaching parents an exercise program to carry out at home. The therapist may not want the parents present when the child is in therapy. If the parents can be present during therapy and participate in the exercise program, they have an advantage in learning methods of working with the child. If the parents are brought into the treatment room only occasionally, the child will probably be concerned with showing the parents what he or she can and cannot do. If the parent is present from the first treatment period, his or her presence is accepted. Life may be much more pleasant for the parents if they have a part in the habilitation of the child.

It may be the responsibility of the physical therapist to teach parents principles of good posture both from the standpoint of weight-lifting and as it applies to the child with cerebral palsy. In standing, good posture is that of head up, chin in, chest up and forward, abdomen flat, feet parallel. In sitting, the head and trunk are held erect as in standing, hips are flexed at right angles to the trunk, and knees flexed with the feet supported. Parents can build a chair for the cerebral palsied child if the child needs more support than regular furniture provides. The principles of good body alignment should be carried out. A tray can be attached across the arms of the supportive chair at a level that the forearms rest easily on it, and it will serve as a place for the child's toys. The chair may have casters attached which facilitate moving it and make it possible for the child to be moved easily without being lifted. In lifting the child from a low surface or from the floor, parents should be taught to stoop down to pick up the child rather than bending over to do so. A kitchen table covered with a pad can be used when giving the child exercises in the home.

The physical therapist should constantly encourage parents to teach their children independence. Cerebral palsied children are seen who have reached the ages of eighteen months or two years who are capable of sitting alone and are not sitting except to be propped in the corner of a heavily upholstered chair or divan. Parents complain that their children do not like to sit in a high chair or they slide down in the chair, and after a few attempts on the part of the parents, the high chair is discarded. Adjustments can be made in high chairs, such as reducing the length of the back legs slightly, so the front of the chair is higher than the back. A piece of wood two inches wide and four inches high may be attached to the center front rim of the seat of the high chair; this may be padded and covered with a plastic material so that it can be easily cleaned. The child is placed in the chair with a leg on either side of the bar so that it is not possible for the child to slide out of the chair. If trunk and neck control is poor, it may be necessary to use straps across the child's chest and shoulders. These are attached to the back of the chair and extend across both shoulders on either side, crossing the chest, and are attached to the chair at about waist level. Tight bands around the child's rib cage interfere with breathing and are undesirable. The child's position should be changed at intervals, and the child should not be permitted to sit for long periods of time in the same position. The handicapped child should not be permitted to sit with the legs under him or her but rather should be taught to sit tailor fashion. The nonhandicapped child will transfer from a crawling position to sitting with the knees flexed and legs under him or her, thus sitting back on the heels. However, the child changes position frequently. The cerebral palsied child may transfer from crawling to this position and remain there for considerable periods of time, and deformities may result. For young children, jumper swings are less desirable than chairs with firm surfaces where better body alignment can be maintained.

THE PHYSICAL THERAPIST AND THE COMMUNITY

Cerebral palsy cannot, for the most part, be prevented and cannot as yet be cured, and it is a part of every community. The physical therapist has a responsibility, along with other members of the staff, to help the community understand the nature of the handicap. Acceptance of the handicapped person is a goal of any center treating the cerebral palsied. It is the responsibility of the physical therapist to speak before clubs and organizations and to appear on radio and television when asked to do so. Cooperation with other agencies in the community is indicated.

The physical therapist's role is that of working with the other members of the staff toward the maximum recovery possible to obtain from the handicap, toward an acceptance of the remaining handicap on the part of the patient and family, and toward an understanding and informed community, so that the cerebral palsied child may enjoy the same rights and privileges enjoyed by the nonhandicapped in the community.

10

Dental Characteristics

HENRY L. KANAR

"One morning about eight years ago, a young dentist passing through the waiting room of an out-patient dental clinic in New York City noticed a woman with tears rolling profusely down her cheeks, sitting on one of the benches with a child in her arms. Realizing that the woman must be in great distress, he stopped to inquire if he might be of any assistance to her. The story that she unfolded seemed to him incredible.

"Her child was badly in need of dental treatment, but because he had cerebral palsy, she had been turned away by every dentist who had seen the boy with the explanation that it was impossible to treat him. She had come to this clinic as a last resort, hoping that here he would be accepted, but to no avail. She further related that parents of many children who have cerebral palsy were finding themselves in the same predicament." Edward Kilbane (1972)

IT MUST BE TAKEN AS GIVEN that the person with cerebral palsy is entitled to receive all of the benefits of this society as is any other member. Proper dental care is one of these benefits. There have been efforts on the part of the dental profession to include the handicapped in their practice. The specialty of pedodontics has assumed leadership in these efforts. Nevertheless, the cerebral palsied individual or those with other handicapping conditions cannot always have their dental needs met in the offices in their communities.

The purpose of this chapter is to discuss the orofacial and related needs of the cerebral palsied and to provide some information useful in meeting these needs. There is no need to go into great detail on technical procedures. These are well covered in the dental literature. Conversely, sufficient information specific to the dental needs of the cerebral palsied must be pre-

TABLE 10.1
Orofacial Conditions Associated with Cerebral Palsy

Author	Oral Hygiene	Caries	Periodontal Disease	Malocclusion	Enamel Hypoplasia	Bruxism
Swallow (1968)	+	N	± varies with age	N		+
Miller and Taylor (1970)	−	+	+	N		+
Harrison (1964)	−	+	+	+	+	+
Koster				+		+
Fishman et al. (1967)	N	N	+			+
Herman and McDonald (1963)					+	
Massler and Perlstein (1958)		N	N	N	+	+
Watson (1955)					+	

+ = increased over normal
− = decreased over normal
N = normal

sented if what is written is to have any real meaning and application. Therefore, the effort will be made to achieve a balance.

THE OROFACIAL PROBLEMS ASSOCIATED WITH CEREBRAL PALSY

Anyone attempting to provide dental services for any significant number of the cerebral palsied soon realizes that there is a tremendous amount of remedial treatment needed. This is particularly true if the overall degree of involvement is great or there is an additional associated handicap, such as mental retardation. The reason for this backlog of unmet dental needs could be attributed to several factors, such as nonacceptance of the cerebral palsied by the dental community or perhaps real differences in problems between the cerebral palsied and the general population. It is this latter possibility that will be discussed first.

The literature contains conflicting evidence on the incidence of several orofacial abnormalities in the cerebral palsied as compared to the normal (see Table 10.1). The most common chronic disease of children and young adults is dental caries. The prevalence of dental caries is indicated commonly by the DMF rate, the number of decayed, missing, and filled teeth per individual. In the younger age groups, missing teeth, other than those which could be lost through normal exfoliation, are generally assumed to have been lost due to caries attack. The literature presents conflicting opinions on the greater or lesser incidence and prevalence of dental caries in the cerebral palsied as compared to the normal. Swallow (1968), Fishman et al. (1967), and Massler and Perlstein (1950) found no difference between the cerebral palsied and the control populations with regard to the prevalence of dental caries. Miller and Taylor (1970) found that the cerebral palsied had increased DMF rates. It is probable that the cerebral palsied population experiences caries at a normal rate.

Generally, it is agreed that the cerebral palsied will show increased periodontal disease. Three factors are related to this increase. These are the drug diphenylhydantoin, bruxisim, and poor oral hygiene. These factors may be found alone, but are frequently found in combinations with each other. One of the chief contributors to the increased periodontal disturbances in the cerebral palsied is the anticonvulsant drug, Diphenylhydantoin (Dilantin). Harrison (1964) lists this drug as a contributing factor in the production of periodontal disturbances. Kapur, Girgis, and Little (1973) reported that 67 percent of the subjects studied who were on Dilantin showed gingival overgrowth or hyperplasia. They also felt that the severity of the hyperplasia was proportional to the dose and serum levels of the drug.

Another factor felt to contribute to the production of periodontal

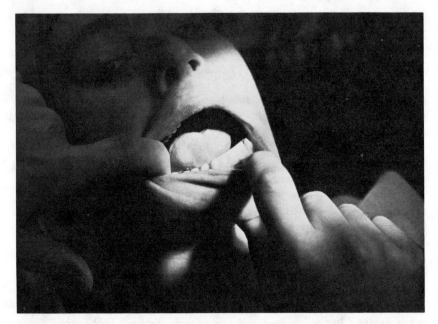

Figure 10.1.   The patient is a young adult woman. Note the flat occlusal and incisal edges of
the teeth associated with bruxism.

disease is bruxism or chronic grinding of the teeth (see Figure 10.1). This
condition is almost universally accepted as being increased in the cerebral
palsied, and mostly in those individuals showing primarily the athetoid
form.

Periodontal disease can also be related to poor oral hygiene. Some
authors, such as Swallow (1968)[28] and Fishman *et al.* (1967),[29] found the
oral hygiene of the cerebral palsied individuals studied improved or the
same as the control populations. The degree of oral cleanliness present is
subject to several variables, such as the degree of physical disabilities in the
individuals being studied as well as their age and mental ability.

The occlusion of the cerebral palsied has been studied with considerable interest. Abnormal muscle functioning is thought to be one of the
major causes of malocclusion. The expectation would be that the cerebral
palsied would show a greater prevalence of malocclusion than the general
population. Harrison (1964), Swallow (1968), and Koster (1956) noted abnormal muscle functioning, such as facial grimacing, abnormal chewing and
swallowing patterns, and tongue thrusting. Despite general agreement that
abnormal orofacial muscle function exists in the cerebral palsied, there is
less agreement on the prevalence of malocclusion. Massler and Perlstein

(1958), Miller and Taylor (1970), and Swallow (1968), found no differences in the distribution of occlusal types between the cerebral palsied and the normal populations studied. Koster (1956), on the other hand, found that 75 percent of the spastics and 90 percent of the athetoids studied had some form of malocclusion. The explanations for these diverse findings may lie in the differences in the criteria for malocclusion utilized by the various authors. This author's clinical impressions would be that, if there are not major differences in occlusal relationships in the cerebral palsied, there are frequent minor tooth irregularities, including open bites associated with abnormal tongue movements. Protruding maxillary teeth, accompanied by narrow constricted maxillary arches and incompletely covering upper lips are often seen in severely involved spastics. Splayed maxillary teeth, wide and relatively low maxillary arches are more frequently associated with the athetoid.

There are other dental conditions related to cerebral palsy which have received attention. These would include an increased number of fractured anterior teeth due to trauma resulting from falls, mouthbreathing and enamel hypoplasia. Because of its diagnostic significance, this last condition requires further explanation.

THE RELATIONSHIP BETWEEN CEREBRAL PALSY AND DENTAL DEVELOPMENT

Calcification, the deposition of highly mineralized salts into the developing crowns of teeth, begins around the fourth month *in utero* or somewhat earlier for the primary teeth. This same time is also eventful in the development of other structures such as the heart and brain. It is reasonable to see how some pathologic agent, acting in this critical formative period, could affect many developing structures. The teeth can serve as indicators of such an event. The crowns of teeth calcify in a sequential manner from incisal edge or cusp tip toward the cervix of the crown. The average degree or stage of calcification of crowns in utero and postnatally is known. If some pathologic agent marks the crown, the location of the defect gives a fair indication of the approximate time of occurrence. The transition from intrauterine to extrauterine life itself is so marked a change that it leaves an indication on the crowns of the primary teeth called the neonatal line. Defects located above the neonatal line toward the root of the tooth occur after birth. Those located below the line toward the incisal or cusp tip occur prenatally. Those occurring around birth are neonatal.

Several investigators have noted that the teeth of cerebral palsied children exhibited altered crown morphology. This alteration, termed a hypoplasia, can range from a chalky appearing area with an irregular surface through deep pinpoint defects in the enamel to crowns showing considerable loss of their enamel covering. Cohen and Diner's study (1970) showed a positive relationship (60 percent) between subjects with "hard" neurological signs and enamel hypoplasia. There was also an increased relationship between hypoplasia and subjects with "soft" signs (48 percent), and negative neurological signs (28.6 percent) of children attending a clinic for students with suspected neurological, intellectual, or other developmental disturbances. The studies of Massler and Perlstein (1958) and those of Forester and Miller (1955), Watson (1955), and others support the clinical impression that cerebral palsied children have a higher incidence of hypoplastic defects. Furthermore, hypoplastic defects were more common in those individuals with athetosis and specifically those with athetosis related to kernicterus due to erythroblastosis fetalis. The location of the hypoplastic defect was frequent (42 percent) in the early prenatal period, while the spastic children in the study showed hypoplastic defects in the neonatal area (16 percent), according to Massler and Perlstein's study. The indication of early prenatal injury is remarkable. Most of the damage

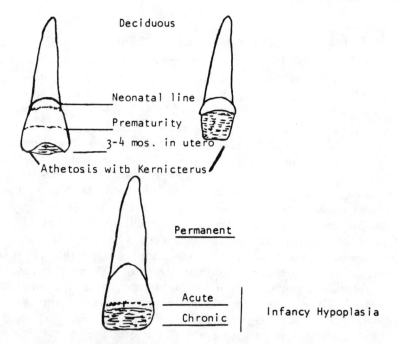

Figure 10.2.   Varieties and chronologic levels of enamel hypoplasia in deciduous and permanent incisors. *Modified from Massler and Perlstein.* Permission of the author (M.M.)

associated with blood incompatibilities is generally thought to take place at birth and shortly after. Evidently, the placenta does not provide a complete barrier to antibody passage. Recent medical advances should reduce the amount of enamel hypoplasias associated with blood incompatibilities.

Herman and McDonald (1963) could not identify factors which consistently produced hypoplasia, although 36 percent of the cerebral palsied individuals in their study showed hypoplastic defects as opposed to 6 percent for their control group. Seventy percent of the cerebral palsied cases having a defect showed a correlation between the location of the defect on the tooth and the time the insult occurred. The evidence indicates that although the etiologic agent may not be specific, except possibly for erythroblastosis fetalis, enamel hypoplasia occurs frequently in the cerebral palsied population. The location of the enamel defect is useful in determining the time of insult to the fetus or child (see Figure 10.2).

The supposition that staining of the teeth might occur during calcification due to circulating products of hemolytic disease was investigated by Massler and Perlstein in 1958. Five cases of intrinsic staining were found in 19 cases (26 percent) of children with kernicterus. Green staining can be caused by jaundice other than that caused by kernicterus, as indicated by Watson (1955).

The teeth can serve as recorders of physical developmental history. The primary and permanent dentitions develop during critical times for the overall development of the individual. Because their development spans both intra- and extrauterine life and because of their openness to inspection, they present the investigator and clinician with the opportunity to understand with greater specificity the nature of altered development in the cerebral palsied.

THE RELATIONSHIP BETWEEN THE DENTAL TEAM AND THE CEREBRAL PALSIED

Dentistry has much to offer the cerebral palsied. In this society, with its emphasis on physical beauty and its tendency to isolate the exceptional, it is important that the cerebral palsied person not be subjected to displaying obvious dental neglect, thus marking that individual as even more outside of the ordinary. Yet, even though the best preventive and therapeutic measures are carried out, treatment should not be considered complete until a comfortable relationship between practitioner and patient has been reached. Despite a considerable amount of popular opinion to the contrary, a visit to the dental office need not be uncomfortable; indeed, it can be pleasantly eventful. Although there are differences in techniques, in general terms it is proper to speak of dental care for the cerebral palsied as being included in the overall picture of dental care for the handicapped. The terms "handicapped" and "cerebral palsied" will be used interchangeably at times in this and in other sections.

The key to reaching a comfortable relationship is experience. This statement is based on several years of experience by the author in training pedodontic graduate students, dental interns, and hygienists to work with the handicapped. Once the practitioner learns that the patient with cerebral palsy or with other handicapping conditions is neither threatening nor made of eggshells, real progress can be made. The dental team members cannot allow themselves to be bogged down with undue sentiment; neither can they be strictly production minded. There are very strong human needs to be met for both patient and professional. What the patient needs is competent care delivered by understanding practitioners. People in general tend to prefer working with the less severely handicapped. However, as individuals work with and become more knowledgeable about the handicapped, more acceptance is gained.

There is no better way to provide the community with dentists, hygienists, and assistants skilled in treating the handicapped and readily accepting them into their practice than by providing these members of the dental team with a controlled and guided course of clinical instruction. The majority of patients with cerebral palsy or other handicaps can be treated in the usual dental office if the practitioner is well prepared. This means that experienced instructors select patients suitable to the student's level and provide close supervision until the student demonstrates proficiency. Unfortunately, the curricula of the dental schools have not been sufficiently infused with such instructors or courses. McConnell reported in 1967 that of the fifty-four dental schools contacted, thirty-eight provided one to three hours of lecture or clinical observation in dental care for the handicapped in either the junior or senior years. Sixteen schools had no time allotted for the subject. He estimated that 4,000 dentists are graduated each year ill-prepared to provide adequate treatment. A few dental schools traditionally offer three or four-day continuing education courses on the dental care of the handicapped. Others occasionally offer such courses.

The dental schools of the United States produce graduates who are competent in producing services of a highly technical nature. This is praiseworthy. The dental curriculum stresses attention to technical mastery and detail. There is less emphasis on such subjects as the dental care of the handicapped. Unfamiliarity with this aspect of dentistry leads to a stressful situation when a dentist is asked to treat a handicapped person. The practitioner finds his self-image as a doctor shaken.

Many authors point out the benefits of knowing as much as possible about the nature of handicapping conditions as a means of reducing stress in the practitioner and gaining greater acceptance of the patient in the community dental offices. However, an individual cannot be expected to know all about each handicapping condition nor to solve all of the associated problems. There are individuals who cannot be treated using ordinary means. This does not mean failure. It means that alternatives to the ordinary must be found. These cases are a minority. In general, the dentist who has developed competency through experience focuses attention on the needs of the patient rather than on the handicap and becomes less concerned about failure. Having made the decision to accept the handicapped, with sufficient background to feel confident in his or her abilities to successfully provide treatment, freed of the need for excessive ego protection and less tense, the practitioner can approach any patient, regardless of handicap, with a positive feeling. Productive experiences can develop this desirable attitude in the mind of the dentist, assistant, and hygienist.

The patient profits from this positive approach. It is important that the dentist or hygienist convey their attitude of assurance and understanding to the patient. There are several ways to do this. The most obvious is by verbal communication. Not only must the dentist or hygienist explain what they intend to do, but they should also explain as much as possible, their understanding of the patient's difficulties. For example, the dentist should tell a patient with athetosis the type of treatment to be performed. The dentist should also provide the assurance that the patient's uncontrolled movements are anticipated. Commanding the patient to relax would have the opposite effect from that desired. Too forceful a verbal command places additional stress on a person who is already in a stressful situation. But, if the patient knows that the dental team members expect some movement and that these present no insurmountable problems, then anxieties can become reduced, less movement encountered and better service rendered.

Communications should be carried out within the patient's abilities to understand. The communication between dentist, hygienist, assistant, and patient, is a network of verbal, visual, emotional, and tactile messages which have both direct and indirect channels and feedback mechanisms. The dentist should be aware of these and use whatever channels seem most appropriate to communicate the message of assurance and the desire to help. A smile and a firm but gentle touch are essential means of communication.

Dentistry for the handicapped must reach a state in the minds of the graduating dentists or hygienists where it is accepted in the same manner as carrying for children or any other segment of the population.

THE RELATIONSHIP BETWEEN THE DENTAL TEAM AND THE FAMILY

The cerebral palsied person, like the non-cerebral palsied person, ordinarily has a family. This family may consist of the parents or guardians, husband, or wife—someone who is concerned for their welfare. The way in which this concern is made manifest can be either beneficial or, at times, detrimental to the rendering of dental services. Some parental problems are the result of previous experience in which the parents were turned away from a dental office because of having a handicapped child and are unwilling to run further risk.

The problems caused by overly fearful and protective parents are well known. There has been more or less general agreement that the parents should not be present in the operatory when the child is receiving treatment. It might be assumed that the parents of the cerebral palsied should be treated in the same way. Actually, the presence of the parents of either cerebral palsied or the parents of the non-handicapped during treatment should not be subject to rules, but rather to judgment. While some parents would definitely hinder treatment either by directly distracting the dental team or because of their child's pleading responses to their presence, others can be a source of positive reinforcement to their child's appropriate behavior. The parents or the concerned persons must have information regarding the nature of the dental procedures to be carried out. The dental team too needs to know certain information such as the medical and dental history of the patient. Depending on the functional abilities of the patient, they or the concerned persons can be the informant. A technique that this writer has found successful has been to meet the family and the patient in the reception room. This is essentially a neutral setting, free of the dental equipment and surroundings. It is also an indication of the dentist's willingness to be outgoing. Generally, the family of the patient does not mind this history-taking discussion, even if others are present in the waiting room. It is always better to ask in advance. If there are objections, the history taking can be carried on in a more secluded area. In this manner, the necessary information can be gathered and the dentist, family and patient have a chance to form a relationship in an atmosphere of normality and helpfulness. Now if the choice is made to have the patient treated unaccompanied by the parent or guardian, separation can be more easily and gracefully accomplished. It is important for the dentist to have some time to meet with the caring person, not only for history-taking, but also to determine their concerns, expectations, possible misconceptions, and to outline the treatment program.

The help of the parent, concerned person, or caretaker, the latter term being used in its best sense, must be enlisted to aid in the all important home and school oral hygiene program, including the proper selection of foods and the reduction of cariogenic food consumption. Furthermore, this cooperative concept must be periodically reinforced. The parent also helps to prepare the patient for the subsequent treatment visits. Since children are influenced by modeling behavior, parental attitudes and conduct are important both at home and when they themselves are being treated.

It is well to keep in mind when taking histories and discussing proposed treatment plans with parents, or others, in the presence of the cerebral palsied person who is to be the recipient of treatment, to include that person in the process as much as possible. This is important to strengthen the idea of a mutually cooperative effort in the minds of all of those involved (see Figure 10.3).

No treatment program for the cerebral palsied who depend on others for their oral hygiene needs will be successful if the valuable contributions that can be made by those involved people are neglected.

THE INTERDISCIPLINARY APPROACH

The need for cooperative effort between the various disciplines concerned with helping the cerebral palsied is self-evident. Some specific dental considerations should be mentioned. The patient's physical status must be known if the dentist is to provide optimum service. This is essential if congenital heart disease, rheumatic heart conditions, convulsions or other conditions which might be compromised by dental treatment exist. Consul-

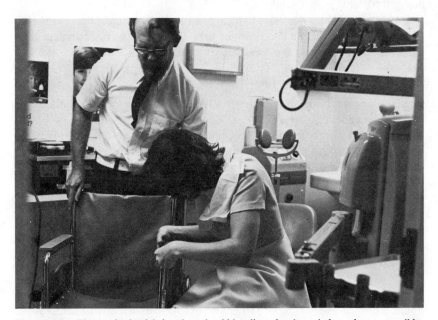

Figure 10.3. The cerebral palsied patient should be allowed to be as independent as possible. Here, the patient transfers herself from the dental chair to the wheelchair.

tation with the physician is also necessary if premedication for behavioral management or general anesthesia is contemplated.

Speech problems, common in the cerebral palsied population, generally cannot be solved by correcting the occlusion or placing appliances to thwart aberrant tongue movements. Consultation with a speech and language pathologist is necessary before such attempts are made. The speech pathologists, for their part, should not build unwarranted expectations in the minds of patients or parents regarding the beneficial results for speech to be obtained from orthodontic therapy or other dental interventions.

The dentist should be aware that the sound of a high-speed dental turbine amplified and transmitted through a hearing aid might produce adverse behavioral responses in patients using such devices. An audiologist can provide the dentist with a personal experience in the use of hearing aids and with other considerations to keep in mind when treating individuals with severe hearing loss.

The need for the dentist or hygienist to consult with and otherwise learn from other disciplines generally centers around patients having problems bearing on dental treatment but outside of the training provided by the dental schools. The dental team, in turn, has an obligation to make known to other disciplines the benefits modern dentistry can contribute to the well-being of patients with disabilities.

It is only when dentistry and every other discipline concerned with meeting the needs of the handicapped take their place as full partners that these needs receive the full attention that is due to them.

TREATMENT CONSIDERATIONS

Dental treatment for the cerebral palsied can be conveniently discussed under two general categories—one dealing with management considerations, the other with technical procedures. In actual practice, the two are combined. How well they are combined determines the level of treatment the patient receives. It has been argued that dental procedures may have to be compromised in the cerebral palsied in deference to overall patient needs. Others feel that standards for treatment need not be lowered. Unquestionably, the cerebral palsied should receive treatment that is of the same quality as the rest of the public, if at all possible. The principal factor that has prevented this has been the practitioner's inability to cope with some of the behaviors of the cerebral palsied. The uncontrolled spasms and movements of the body limbs, head, and jaws of the patient accentuated by the apprehensions of the patient and dentist, have contributed to the history of nonacceptance and rejection. Other factors have also contributed to some degree: the extra time generally required to treat the handicapped patient and the possible loss of income, the tendency to avoid dealing with the unusual, the fear that handicapped patients will cause some of the regular patients to leave a practice, a feeling of frustration and loss of self-image due to an inability to provide treatment, parental lack of interest or appreciation of good oral health, or the inability to cover the cost of treatment. Good management techniques can successfully reduce some of these negative factors. The necessary and most important aspect of providing treatment, the positive attitude on the part of the professional, has been discussed earlier.

Patient Management

"Tie me up." Perhaps inelegant, but to the point, this was the manner in which one cerebral palsied boy expressed his preference for treatment procedures. He had been given the choice of having the assistant use her hands to restrain him, a sedative drug, or a full restraint jacket, all of which he had previously experienced. He chose the last. An adult with cerebral palsy was heard to tell a group of dentists his choice was to be given a sedative drug to the point of relaxation. Then, he hoped that the dentist would hold on to him with sufficient control to accomplish the necessary procedures.

Physical restraint and the use of sedative drugs both have their proper place in the treatment of the cerebral palsied. While they and other appropriate management techniques should never be used indiscriminately, when indicated, they should be used unblushingly. It is essential that the patient does not think of the use of physical restraint as a punitive measure. It is much better to explain the use of restraint measures beforehand and in a friendly and open manner, thereby reducing the chances for misinterpretation. Physical restraint can be applied in many ways. The assistant can use hand restraint, or conventional rubber bite blocks, a variety of mouth props (see Figure 10.4), rubber bottle stoppers equipped with finger loops, padded tongue blades, seatbelts, body straps and wristlets with velcro fasteners, sandbags, sheets, commercial and individually constructed full restraint jackets can be employed. The use of mouth props or bite blocks should not preclude the use of the rubber dam. The rubber dam itself should be thought of as a means of physical restraint. Its use is highly recommended in treating the cerebral palsied because of the frequent difficulties in swallowing and the potential danger of aspirating the debris associated with operative procedures. A length of dental floss should be tied around the rubber dam clamp to facilitate retrieval if it should be accidentally lost in the patient's mouth. Individuals who have extremely powerful tongues or who have ground the clinical crowns off to a great degree present the operator with problems of application and maintenance.

Proper positioning of the patient in the chair is essential to control un-

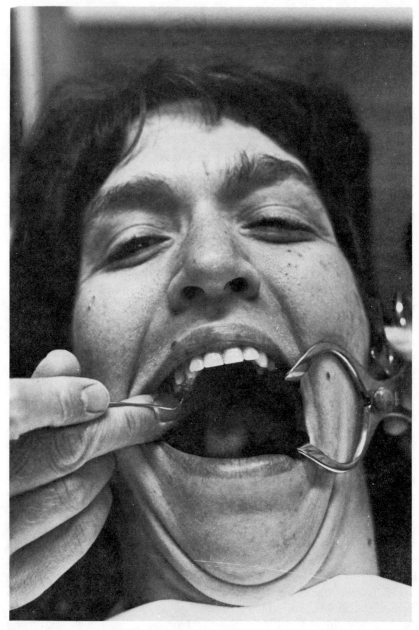

Figure 10.4. Mouth props are useful in controlling involuntary jaw movements. The adult size shown here is generally the most useful.

wanted bodily movements. The contoured dental chair with its extended leg support can be tilted backward, dropping the patient's head near the lap of the seated operator and assistant. Gravity favors the maintenance of this position and limits the patient's ability to sit up, pull away, or slide down and out of the chair. This position also allows the operator to cradle the head of the patient in the arm and hand which is not holding the handpiece. With a little experience, the cradling arm and hand can also hold or stabilize the mouth prop or bite block and the mouth mirror. This arm also "telegraphs" the movements of the patient and allows for compensatory movements on the part of the operator.

The dental chair can be temporarily made to accommodate limbs bent to awkward positions or unusual body contours by the use of pillows, pads, foam blocks, or plastic bead-filled bags which can be formed to support the patient's body. These bags, used in radiographic positioning, when evacuated of air remain formed to the body part, thereby providing continual support and restraint.

The role of the dental assistant, well trained in basic techniques and accepting of the need to treat the handicapped, is extremely important. The assistant and the dentist or hygienist should consult with each other before the start of treatment so that there will be a minimum of time spent in making adjustments once treatment has begun. Time spent in this manner is as much a part of the treatment as any other phase. The concept of four-handed dentistry is applicable in the treatment of the cerebral palsied (see Figure 10.5). The assistant can maintain the mouth prop or bite block, if one is used, while providing for the suctioning of the operative site. The assistant also helps in applying restraint devices. In this, she may even be assisted by the parents. Her rapport with the patient is essential in creating the helpful atmosphere which, in great measure, determines the success or failure of treatment. The need for a qualified and experienced dental assistant is as important in treating a patient under general anesthesia as in more conventional settings. The well-trained, experienced, and concerned assistant can do much to facilitate treatment and reduce stress to the point where the need for sedation is lessened or omitted for some patients.

In addition to behavior modification techniques, verbal control, and physical restraint, there are other means of modifying the behavior of cerebral palsied patients which are available to the dentist. These would include the use of sedative drugs, nitrous oxide analgesia, and general anesthesia. Each has its place. Their use must be based on a knowledge of the drug's action and side effects coupled with the prescriber's ability to cope with unexpected complications. Indiscriminant use must be discouraged.

What constitutes acceptable patient behavior is highly subjective. Behavior on the part of a patient which allows one person to provide treatment

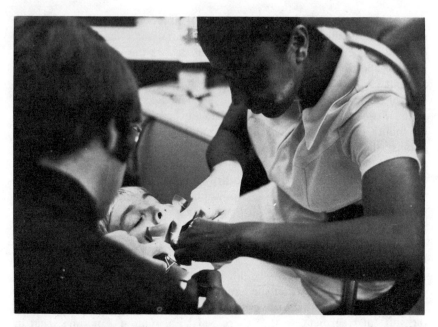

Figure 10.5.   A well-trained dental assistant is an essential member of the dental team. Here the dentist and assistant apply the rubber dam to the patient.

may be unacceptable to another. The effects of premedication may vary from a slightly altered sense of consciousness to a patient who is asleep. The prescriber should have in mind which effect is to be achieved and prescribe accordingly.

There is a variety of agents available. Some may be used alone or in combination with others. Posology, the art and science of prescribing drugs, is not an exact science. Patients respond differently to different drugs and to different dosages of the same drug. These factors illustrate a complex situation with regard to arriving at a suitable dosage of a suitable drug to produce a desired response.

Among the drugs prescribed to modify patient behavior are the moderately fast acting barbiturates, meperidine (demerol), belladona derivatives, promethazine, chlorpromazine, chloral hydrate, diazepam, and hydroxizine. Kroll (1969), in his study on the effects of premedication on handicapped children, found a strikingly inconsistent effect on individual patients. He felt further studies to clarify the effects of dosage were needed.

Two drugs this writer has found useful are chloral hydrate and hydroxizine. They can be used alone or in combination. If used alone, the effects are somewhat different. Hydroxizine's chief effect is to reduce anxiety. Chloral hydrate is a depressant and can produce effects from drowsiness to deep sleep. One result of combining the two drugs is to prolong the effects of the chloral hydrate. The combination also reduces the amount of chloral hydrate needed to produce sedation. The combination works best with individuals under 80 pounds, although it can be effective with larger individuals. The dosage varies with the weight of the individual, plus other factors such as the behavior of the recipient. If a patient is hyperactive or has a high anxiety level, the dosage will generally have to be increased over that given to an individual who is quite placid except during dental treatment.

If used alone, hydroxizine can be prescribed on a one milligram per pound basis as a maximum dosage. Chloral hydrate alone can be prescribed on the basis of 500 milligrams per ten pounds of body weight for any patient 20 pounds or over up to a maximum of 2,000 milligrams, or two grams. Thus, a 40-pound patient could receive the maximum dosage which the physician's desk reference lists as the maximum adult dose. Obviously, one does not start out with this maximum dosage, particularly for smaller patients. Generally, the dosage is one half of the maximum or less, either alone or in combination. The dosage is then increased incrementally at subsequent appointments until the desired results are achieved or until the maximum dose is reached. Absorption and effects are more predictable if given on an empty stomach. However, since chloral hydrate is irritating to the gut, it should be given with a small amount of milk or water. Chlorbetaine can be substituted for chloral hydrate on an equivalent basis. It is less irritating to the gut, but is not available in liquid form.

An important fact to remember is that a dental treatment can be a learning experience for the patient. Premedication with sedative drugs can enhance the climate for learning by reducing anxieties, but a completely unconscious patient learns nothing. An interesting phenomenon takes place when practitioners use premedication for any period of time. They find, as their experience increases, there is less need to premedicate, despite being more familiar with sedative drugs and their usage.

General anesthesia has been advocated as a means of providing treatment for difficult patients who could not be treated by other means. It need not be thought of as a last resort. Under certain circumstances, such as a patient requiring a large amount of treatment with a considerable distance to travel to receive it, general anesthesia may be the treatment of choice. The rubber dam can be used in treatment under general anesthesia in conjunction with the customary moistened throat pack and mouth prop. Amalgam and tooth debris from operative procedures are thereby kept out of the pharynx. The quality of dental care delivered to a patient under general anesthesia should be as high as that given under routine conditions.

Obtaining adequate radiographs from a cerebral palsied individual can be difficult. A number of techniques have been suggested. Steinberg and Bramer (1964) have described combination intra- and extra-oral procedures. Commercial pariapical filmholders and film cassettes can be useful. Occlusal films can be used in place of five by seven inch cassettes in obtaining lateral jaw views. Another technique involves using needle holders or similar forceps to hold the films intra-orally. The person holding the films for the patient should wear protective lead apron and gloves. Furthermore, the person taking a radiographs should not be in the direct beam and should have the benefit of a radiation monitoring device. This last procedure has been deemed acceptable by the radiation section of the author's State Department of Health. It is wise to seek consultation regarding such procedures from the various state health departments regarding safety precautions to be observed.

Technical Procedures

Ultimately, the most important procedures are those that are preventive in nature. The Manual for Children's Dental Care Programs (1974) ranks preventive programs, the relief of pain, and the removal of sources of infection as three basic and equal needs. Dentistry in the past has perhaps overemphasized corrective measures. Recently, the emphasis has been on prevention. This is the first and most important step toward the elimination of any disease. Techniques may change and improve, but these are futile if acceptance and utilization by the profession and the public are not present.

The public has been made aware of the term "dental plaque." Plaque is a complex of bacteria, bacterial byproducts, food substances, and salivary constituents which adhere to the surface of teeth. It is felt to be necessary if dental caries and periodontal disease are to develop. The longer plaque is allowed to accumulate on tooth surfaces, the greater the chances of developing caries and periodontal disease. The benefits from the mechanical process of toothbrushing, flossing, and gingival cleansing are chiefly derived from the removal of dental plaque. Some dental plaque becomes highly mineralized and forms hard depositions on teeth, called calculus. Plaque may be visible if stained with special preparations for disclosing its presence. Calculus deposits, on the other hand, often reach considerable size to the point of obscuring much of the clinical crowns of teeth and are quite visible. The presence of dental plaque on tooth surfaces can lead to the development of dental caries. These, in turn, can progress to the point where the pulpal tissues of the tooth become infected, necrose, and form abcesses. Generally, this is a painful process and can have systemic as well as local consequences. Plaque can also lead to the development of periodontal disease which can range from mild inflammation of the gingiva to the destruction of the supporting bone and associated structures. Eventual tooth movement and tooth loss result. It has become axiomatic that more teeth are lost due to periodontal disease after age 35 than to dental caries. The person having cerebral palsy is evidently as susceptible to the formation of plaque and its sequela as the non-afflicted.

If the person having severe abcess formation due to caries or severe periodontal disease has a congenital heart condition, the situation can be life threatening. Therefore, the consequences of poor oral hygiene and accumulation of plaque can be considerable.

Nowhere is preventive dentistry more important than in the handicapped. The prevention of the two most common dental ills—caries and periodontal disease—depends to a large extent on the prevention or removal of dental plaque. This can be accomplished in a number of ways: toothbrushing, the use of dental floss, topical and systemic fluorides, oral irrigation, and the reduction of a cariogenic diet. All of these can be applied to the cerebral palsied (see Figures 10.6 and 10.7).

There are necessary factors which must be present if a disease process is to develop. So it is with plaque production. There must be: (1) plaque-producing bacteria; (2) they must have a source of food; (3) there must be a susceptible host; and (4) there must be the absence of environmental an-

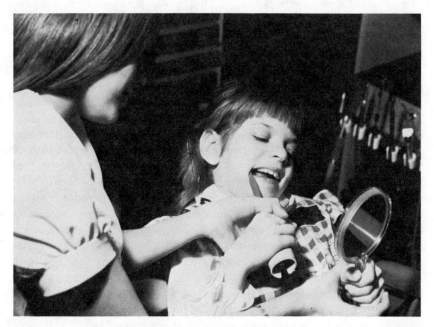

Figure 10.6.   A young cerebral palsied child being instructed in self-care by a dental hygienist. Note the adaptation of the toothbrush handle.

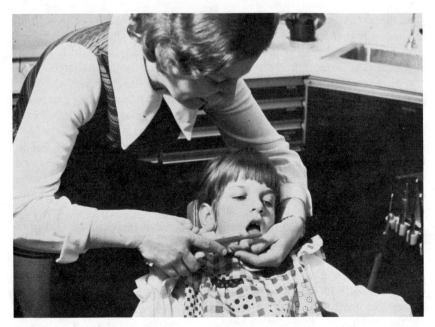

Figure 10.7.   The mother of the child in Figure 10.6 repeats the oral hygiene instructions.

tagonists whose presence would inhibit the growth of the bacteria. Unfortunately, most of the population qualifies as susceptible hosts. Therefore, our efforts are best directed toward reducing the amount of bacteria by making the oral environment less suitable and by reducing the amount and frequency of the cariogenic foods consumed.

The patient's oral environment can be made less suitable in the production of disease by removing plaque through toothbrushing and flossing. Flossing can be carried out by the individual or by others, in the case of those who cannot care for themselves. For those providing their own care, the floss can be applied either by the use of their own hands or through the use of some of the devices available commercially for the purpose. The use of a floss holding device is preferable when working with those individuals who cannot perform flossing by themselves. In either method, the objective is to remove plaque accumulations and food debris in the interproximal areas between the teeth which cannot be reached by brushing. The floss should be held against the side of one of the teeth, maintaining as much lateral pressure as downward pressure to avoid an abrupt snap beyond the contact area, thus lacerating the papilla. The floss should then be manipulated so that the surfaces of the adjacent teeth are cleaned from the level of the tissue attachments through the contact area.

Toothbrushing should follow flossing. The use of a soft-bristled multitufted brush is advocated. The size of the brush will vary according to the size of the patient. Ideally, brushing should be done immediately after eating, particularly after the ingestion of readily fermentable carbohydrates rich in sucrose. Fox (1973) describes the sulcular method of brushing. A somewhat similar method is the circular scrub. In this method, the brush head rests partly on the occlusal surfaces of the teeth with most of the rows of bristles touching the labial, buccal or lingual surfaces. Then the brush is rotated in a small circle allowing the bristles to sweep down to and below the gingival margins. This method is readily taught and readily acquired by institutional staffs. Brushing must be carried out in a systematic manner so that all surfaces are reached. For example, brushing can proceed from the buccal, occlusal surfaces of the teeth in the posterior of the upper right quadrant around though the labial and on through the upper left quadrant. Then, the occlusal and lingual surfaces of the upper arch can be brushed in a similar manner. Once this is completed, systematic brushing can be carried out in the lower arch repeating the sequence. Care must be exercised so that the tissues are not traumatized. Thorough toothbrushing initiated in an individual whose oral hygiene has previously not been good and who exhibits some degree of gingivitis can produce bleeding initially. This generally ceases within a week or two of continuous and thorough brushing. Parents and attendent staffs need assurances that the bleeding is temporary so that they will persist in their efforts. The dentists, of course, must be alert to the possibilities of other conditions being responsible for gingival bleeding.

The choice of either manual or electric toothbrushes is a matter of personal preference. Both can accomplish the stated objective if correctly used. The electric toothbrush is especially suited for individuals whose dexterity does not allow adequate cleaning through the use of manual brushes.

The use of toothpaste is optional. A small amount of toothpaste should be used with young children since the essential oils used as flavoring agents can be irritating to their oral mucosa. Fluoride containing toothpaste can add an additional amount of protection to a preventive program. Disclosing tablets or solution which stain plaque can be used to check the effectiveness of the brushing and flossing procedures.

The uncontrolled movements associated with cerebral palsy present problems in providing acceptable levels of oral cleanliness. Occasionally, individuals who must receive oral care from others, will not open their mouths and will purse their lips tightly together. Flossing cannot be accomplished in these individuals. It is difficult to introduce the toothbrush into the oral cavity. With practice, the brush can be introduced through the lips into the space between the buccal surfaces of the posterior teeth and the cheek. Here there is room to maneuver the brush head and cleanse these ac-

Patient's Name_____   Birthdate_____

Address_____   Sex_____

_____   Medications_____

Parent/Guardian_____   _____

Brief description of the child's handicapping condition:_____

ORAL HYGIENE ASSESSMENT: Yes   No

   1. child can identify

      a. sink   _____   _____

      b. cup   _____   _____

      c. toothbrush   _____   _____

      d. toothpaste   _____   _____

      e. teeth   _____   _____

      f. tongue   _____   _____

      g. gums   _____   _____

   2. gets own toothbrush   _____   _____

   3. turns on cold water   _____   _____

   4. wets toothbrush   _____   _____

   5. unscrews toothpaste cap   _____   _____

   6. puts toothpaste on brush   _____   _____

   7. can hold brush adequately   _____   _____

   8. can place brush on some teeth   _____   _____

   9. can place brush on all teeth   _____   _____

  10. can produce brushing motion in mouth

      a. with assistance   _____   _____

      b. without assistance   _____   _____

  11. fills cup with water   _____   _____

  12. rinses mouth and

      a. swallows water   _____   _____

      b. spits out water   _____   _____

  13. rinses brush   _____   _____

  14. turns off water   _____   _____

  15. screws on toothpaste cap   _____   _____

  16. returns brush and cup to proper place   _____   _____

  17. wipes mouth and hands   _____   _____

COMMENTS:

REACTIONS TO DENTISTRY:

Figure 10.8.   An oral hygiene checklist. *Courtesy of Beverly Entwistle, R.D.H.*

cessible areas. Often the introduction of the brush to this extent results in further opening so that additional tooth surfaces can be reached. Mouth propping to achieve access to all areas of the mouth can also be useful for some patients.

There are variations in positioning of the individuals receiving oral care and the person providing it which can aid in performing these functions. For those individuals who stand to have their teeth brushed, the person providing the brushing may find it advantageous to stand behind and brace the head while parting the lips with the nonbrushing hand. In this position, the body of the person brushing braces and supports the head. Brushing can also be accomplished for those in chairs in similar fashion. Any number of approaches to patient positioning can be adopted. The one selected should be based on the recipient's physical status and ability to receiving care.

It is important that oral hygiene procedures be carried out not only at home, but in other locations as well. The cerebral palsied child in school, particularly those in special classrooms, day care centers, or community agencies, is likely to encounter carbohydrates in the form of cookies or candy used as rewards or snacks. Many behavior modification programs employ candy as a reinforcer. The dentist and the dental hygienist should provide inservice education to the staffs of the agencies and instruct the students or residents in oral care. It is advantageous to evaluate each individual in a program noting the need for dental care, oral hygiene skills, and dietary habits. A checklist which is helpful in noting progress is shown in Figure 10.8. As the individual progresses as a result of instruction, advancement should be checked periodically. The parents should be informed of the program and encouraged to carry out and record a similar home care program.

One essential element of any good oral hygiene program is dietary counseling. It is unrealistic to attempt to remove all of the readily fermentable carbohydrates from the average diet. The parents and teachers should be made aware of the dangers of frequent consumption of these substances. They should also be made aware of which foods are to be avoided and which foods can be used as substitutes (see Table 10.2).

Sweets can be consumed, but it is important to limit the frequency of consumption. If the sweets are eaten after meals, followed by brushing, or by rinsing the oral cavity with water within a short time after eating, the effects are less deleterious than the frequent between meals ingestion of these substances. Particularly to be avoided are sweet foods that have a sticky consistency, such as caramels, or those that maintain a high sugar level in the mouth over a long period of time, such as candy lozenges.

Fluorides should be supplied to the cerebral palsied as part of a comprehensive preventive program. Fluoride can be supplied systemically

TABLE 10.2
DIETARY CONTROL OF DENTAL DECAY

The following are examples of foods containing larger quantities of sugar. This is by no means a complete list. Therefore, when food shopping, become label conscious. Read the label to see that it does not contain sugar. If you buy foods such as soft drinks, candy, gum, wheat wafers, or cereals, be sure the label reads: no sugar, sweetened with sugar substitute.

TRY TO AVOID EATING OR DRINKING THE FOLLOWING (WHERE POSSIBLE):

Apple juice	Frozen fruits	Ice Cream
Chocolate drinks	(sweetened with	Sherbet
Cocoa or Ovaltine	sugar syrups)	Jello
Hi-C Drink	Custard	Cake
Kool-Aid	Pudding	Cookies
Malted milk	Marshmallows	Donuts
Milkshake	Peanut butter	Pastries
Soft drinks	(containing sugar)	Pies
Sweetened juices	Jams and jellies	Graham crackers
Applesauce	Sugar coated and	Soda crackers
Canned fruit	most non-sugar	Ritz crackers
Dried fruit (dates, figs,	coated cereals	Honey
raisins, prunes)	Candy	Molasses
	Gum	Syrup
		Sugar

YOU MAY EAT OR DRINK THE FOLLOWING:

*Nuts	Popsicles (from	Triscuit wafers
*Popcorn (not	unsweetened juice)	Cooked cereal
sugar coated)	Fresh fruits	Shredded Wheat
Potato chips	Fresh vegetables	Puffed Rice
Corn chips	Milk	Puffed Wheat
Fritos	Cheese	Rye bread
Sugarless candy	Hard-boiled eggs	Whole grain bread
Sugarless gum	Meat strips	Sugarless peanut butter
Unsweetened juices	Bologna	Macaroni
Sugarless soft drinks	Salami	Spaghetti
	Whole wheat wafers	
	without sugar	

*These items are not suggested for children under three years of age.

Table taken from Lawrence A. Fox, "Preventive Dentistry for the Handicapped Child," *Pediatric Clinics of North America* 20(1) (1973): 254.

or applied topically. Systemic fluorides are supplied in tablet and liquid form. Lozenges are available which supply a topical effect when disolved in the mouth and a systemic effect when swallowed. Topical fluoride can be applied in liquid or jell form, in commercial or in individually constructed trays or applied by cotton tipped applicators. These procedures can be carried on in the dental office and at home. The choice should be determined according to which method is best suited to the individual situation.

The efficacy of employing sealants to reduce the incidence of caries has not been adequately established for the cerebral palsied. Sealants may be of use in coping with an extremely deleterious habit found occasionally in the cerebral palsied and other handicapped populations. This habit, which has been called rumination, is the ability of certain individuals to bring up stomach contents into the oral cavity at will. The regurgitation of the stomach contents of partly digested food, digestive enzymes and hydrochloric acid leads to the dissolution of the enamel covering of the teeth and makes them more susceptible to secondary bacterial invasion. Sealants may prove advantageous here, although there is no indication from the literature to support this contention. Unfortunately, little else can be offered to correct the situation. Stainless steel crowns properly applied so that the margins are below the gingival edges can be resistant to the effects of the habit. The time and cost factors involved generally make covering all of the teeth in this manner a prohibited procedure. Sealant and composite restorations can be useful in restoring good aesthetics to hypopolastic teeth.

Mouth guards, similar to those worn by athletes, can be constructed to reduce the wear on teeth caused by bruxism. Mouth guards can also be used to protect the teeth of children who are in crutch or brace training. These individuals are subject to frequent falls and are often unable to protect themselves adequately from trauma. The anterior maxillary teeth are one of the first areas to strike the floor after a fall, resulting in fracture or, at times, evulsion. The success of these devices for these purposes is largely dependent upon the ability of the patient to accept them.

Operative techniques for the cerebral palsied should be the same as for other patients. The use of local anesthetics combined with a rubber dam and appropriate management techniques as necessary are advocated so that the cerebral palsied patient receives the same level of treatment as the nonaffected individual. Some modifications in technique may be necessary to accommodate the special problems of the cerebral palsied. For individuals who have worn away most of the natural anatomy, restoration of these teeth with amalgam does not call for the replacement of the anatomy. Where large restorations are needed to restore carious lesions in the mouth of individuals who brux severely, stainless steel crowns may be the treatment of choice.

WHERE TO OBTAIN HELP

The cerebral palsied individual should not wait until an emergency situation is present before seeking assistance. Part of any good preventive program is the provision for regular professional visits and checkups. A cerebral palsied person or those who provide for their care have several routes to take in seeking professional attention. The family dentist who generally provides care may also have the desire and ability to treat the cerebral palsied. A family dentist may prefer not to treat the cerebral palsied directly, but to refer to practitioners who do. If the cerebral palsied individual has no family dentist, the local dental society should be contacted. The society, whose phone number is generally listed in the classified section of the phone directory, should be able to provide the name or names of the nearest dentist or agencies providing care for the handicapped. Dental schools can be helpful to the cerebral palsied individual, either by providing direct services through their many departments or by referral elsewhere. Many large metropolitan hospitals and university hospitals have dental departments or visiting dental staffs which can provide services for the handicapped. The state cerebral palsy association and the state health department are other referral services to contact when seeking assistance.

Three national professional organizations have memberships whose interests include dental care for the handicapped. These are the American Society of Dentistry for Children, the American Academy of Pedodontics, and the Academy of Dentistry for the Handicapped. The membership of these organizations, especially the Academy of Dentistry for the Handicapped, provides direct care or referral services. The national secretaries of these organizations can be contacted to obtain membership rosters. The executive secretary of the Academy of Dentistry for the Handicapped can be reached through the central offices: 1240 East Main Street, Springfield, Ohio 45503. The American Academy of Pedodontics and the American Society of Dentistry for Children can be reached by writing to them at: 211 East Chicago Avenue, Chicago, Illinois 60611.

11

Occupational Therapy

ROSALIA A. KISS

THE PURPOSE OF THIS CHAPTER is to provide an overview of the contribution of occupational therapy to the habilitation and rehabilitation of the individual with cerebral palsy. The objectives and the means by which the occupational therapist deals with the complex ways cerebral palsy interferes with performance and the developmental process are discussed. Emphasis is placed upon the interdependence of the client, the parents, the physician, the occupational therapist, the physical therapist, the speech therapist, educators, and representatives of community agencies for successful therapeutic effort.

In order to understand the role of occupational therapy in any rehabilitative endeavor, it is necessary to know how the profession defines itself and what it educates its practitioners to do. The current statement from the American Occupational Therapy Association (1972) describes occupational therapy as directing

> participation in selected tasks to restore, reinforce and enhance performance, facilitate learning those skills and functions essential for adaptation and productivity, diminish or correct pathology, and to promote and maintain health. Its fundamental concern is the development and maintenance of capacity throughout the life span, to perform with satisfaction of self and others those tasks and roles essential to productive living and the mastery of self in the invironment.
>
> Since the primary focus of occupational therapy is the development of adaptive skills and performance capacity, its concern is with factors which serve as barriers or impediments to the individual's ability to function, as well as those factors which promote, influence or enhance performace.

Accordingly, the occupational therapist approaches the individual with cerebral palsy at many points of time during his life span with a multiplicity of purposes related principally to prevention, intervention, facilitation of daily life tasks and occupational adjustment. These purposes are achieved through service functions familiar to the rehabilitative professions, including the evaluation of performance capacities of the individual, the establishment of treatment objectives appropriate to the results of evaluation, and the selection of tasks or activities to meet these objectives and facilitate client participation in the achievement of the treatment goals.

The underlying principle of occupational therapy with a disabled child requires consideration of all parameters of behavior simultaneously, rather than from the limited perspective of specific problems. Llorens (1970) has stressed "that although emphasis may be placed on the facilitation of growth in one parameter, simultaneous though perhaps less attention must be given to all of the other areas of growth as well in order for an integrating growth experience to take place." Banus (1971) has identified the role of occupational therapy with children as being developmental stimulation and developmental therapy:

> The multiply handicapped child shows more developmental problems than a normal child because of reciprocal relationships. . . . Handicapped children, particularly, need more developmental guidance so that maturation and learning will occur, for these children may not be able to cope physically or emotionally with their environment, and may, therefore withdraw from it. . . . The therapist must assist in the analysis of the child's total developmental process in order to provide the stimuli which are meaningful and developmentally appropriate.

Formulations of an approach to the disabled adult are tending to a similar direction. However, in practice there remains a persistence on the part of therapists to limit attention to areas of specialization. Mosey (1968) views the occupational therapist's objectives to be facilitating the client to learn those things the client had not learned in the normal developmental process. She proposes, as a basis for evaluation and treatment planning, a sequential development of learned patterns she calls "adaptive skills" which reflect increasing interaction between the biological or physical components of behavior and the environment.

THE ROLE OF OCCUPATIONAL THERAPY IN ASSESSMENT

The occupational therapist brings to the interdisciplinary team working with cerebral palsy a perspective of neuromotor, psychosocial, and perceptual-motor development and dysfunction that complements and confirms the contributions of other disciplines. The occupational therapist will recognize potential gaps in the developmental cycle and contribute to the prevention of maladapation in the various parameters of behavior. The evaluation may be initiated on an informal basis, or standardized tests or parts of tests may be used as they appear to be indicated by the status of the child under treatment.

Assessment of Perceptual-Motor Development

Areas of assessment well defined and managed by occupational therapists are related to sensory integration and motor function. Research and leadership has been provided by A. Jean Ayres (1972a), who developed a series of tests designed to determine the nature of sensory integrative dysfunction. The information is fundamental to understanding the quality of sensory input upon which a child with cerebral palsy must base functional skills. From a developmental standpoint, reflex and postural responses and subsequent motor patterns are dependent upon the utilization of sensory information received by the central nervous system. Sensory information about the environment through visual, tactile, proprioceptive, and vestibular modalities results in the development of motor behavior which enables the child to accommodate to the environment. It provides the basis for awareness of the child's body, its position and balance, for motor planning, and the development of form and space perception.

The pediatric occupational therapist will present activities designed to elicit discriminatory responses or samples of perceptual organization in order to assess a child's perceptual motor performance. In general, the pediatric occupational therapist will not choose to administer standardized tests to children with moderate to severe handicaps. The evaluative tasks will be planned with consideration for other parameters of function which are influenced by neurological deficits. Verbal and motor responses, for example, will be minimized in order to observe the critical elements of perceptual performance (Miller 1955). Performance will be assessed only after varied and repeated opportunities for the child to respond to the stimulus task (Hayes and Komick 1971).

For children with lesser involvement, standardized tests, whole or in part, will assist in identifying which perceptual modalities may be interfering with function. Most widely used among occupational therapists are Ayres's *Southern California Sensory Integration Tests* (1972a) designed to measure performance in tactile, proprioceptive, vestibular, and visual motor integration. Other tests in use are the *Meeting Street School Screening Test* (Denhoff *et al.* 1969), the *Purdue Perceptual-Motor Survey* (Roach and Kephart 1966), *Beery's Developmental Test of Visual-Motor*

Integration (1967), and Frostig's *Developmental Test of Visual Perception* (1964).

Early testing for sensory impairment is essential for children with cerebral palsy because of the close relationship of the sensory and neuromotor systems. Tizard *et al.* (1954) attributed the lack of use of the upper extremities to sensory disturbances in the hands of hemiplegic children. This type of impairment includes difficulties in discriminating points touched on the body, hot and cold, or in identifying common objects or shapes placed in the hand when vision is occluded.

Daily Living Performance

A practical approach to the assessment of motor performance and social interaction of the individual with cerebral palsy is through activities of daily living. These are skills essential to everyday life that range from personal care to the ability to participate in family and community activities. Check lists are commonly used to inventory the degree of independence and provide a basis for treatment planning for both children and adults.

Prevocational Evaluation

Prevocational evaluation is an important effort to assess what skills, capacities, and tolerances for work in today's world are possessed by the handicapped individual. It contributes information necessary for realistic occupational planning by the client and the rehabilitation team. Tests may include sampling tasks critical to a given occupation or simulated job requirements. The degree of independence in moving about in the community is considered to be a facet of some job requirements, and as such it becomes a component of assessment.

TREATMENT PLANNING

Knowledge of the status of a child is of little value if the information gathered is not reflected in the management of the child and the environment to facilitate the child's best performance. The process by which this is achieved is treatment planning. Like the evaluative process, treatment planning is an interdisciplinary effort by the professional representatives and must involve the child and his or her parents. From the outset, the ultimate or long-range goals must be identified and frequently reconfirmed in terms of the individual's life role. They will encompass more than institutional or agency objectives. The goals of occupational therapy in an educational setting may focus on adaptations suitable to his needs in the classrooms, but they will, in addition, support performance of the child within the family circle and in the community. "Therapists realize that brain-damaged children need a place to go in life. They deserve a chance to become competent, to achieve a sense of mastery, to have a feeling of dignity about their lives" (Johnson 1971).

After treatment goals are identified, priorities are established. Considerations include both maintenance and the preservation of competencies available to the individual, and the reduction or circumvention of barriers to the performance of essential tasks. The goals must be within the range of realistic achievement, although at times they will be attained at considerable effort and time of all involved: the client, parents, physicians, therapists, and educators.

Short-term goals are steps toward long-term goals. They are not, at best, ends in themselves. Short-term goals for children should be viewed in relationship to the tasks of adolescence and adulthood. They define the nature and the sequence of skills needed to facilitate the developmental process and daily living performance of the individual (Bailey 1971).

OCCUPATIONAL THERAPY

Having established the goals, the therapist must indicate those which can best be facilitated, then plan ways of implementing them in the process of treatment and for measuring the degree of success in meeting them. One of the major factors for successful implementation is the therapeutic setting, or milieu, in which a child is to be mobilized to deal with his or her own problems of adaptation and to organize his or her own resources. Ayres (1972b) has described the situation as one which "attempts to modify both the child's capacity and environmental demands to make it possible for the child to succeed in organizing a response. If dysfunction makes it difficult to do so alone, the therapist must intervene, assisting the child to achieve that which he cannot do independently. The program is focused not only on physical function but allows for socialization and fosters a feeling of accomplishment."

Another factor critical to the implementation of occupational therapy is the selection of purposeful activities which will permit the child to respond at an increasingly higher level of function. The program should provide for the acquisition of life skills through developmental stages and will range, variably, from the elicitation of basic motor developmental responses of infancy, the development of feeding, dressing, or other self-care skills, to social skills and play as indicated by the child's capacity.

In choosing an approach to treatment, the occupational therapist tends to be eclectic. Under most circumstances, the therapist adheres to principles of developmental theorists and views children as autogenetic and achievement oriented, but at other times it may be necessary to rely upon behavioristic formulas to encourage the development of function and independence. Developmental orientations are likely to relate to Gesell's (1940, 1947) processes of development, White's (1959, 1971) competency motivation, Piaget's (1952) stages of cognition, Erikson's (1963) psychosocial stages, and Havighurst's (1967) life tasks. Reilly (1974) and her students have provided a rationale for the consideration of play and work activities in the developmental framework as significant for the nurture of adaptive behavior. Work and play activities have always been used by occupational therapists to engage patients in meeting specific treatment goals. The principal purposes for the selection of work and play activities have been to improve motor performance, interpersonal relationships, or self-identity. However, the recent reexamination of the work-play phenomena, apart from the treatment of symptomatology, has been as an integral life experience, "one of identifying the nature of adaptations or the acquisition of new skills, and examining socialization patterns to support daily living performance of patients in their life role" (Matsutsuyu 1971). Reilly (1970) has said: "Play, in a chronological or longitudinal sense, we believe, is the antecedent preparation area for work. In a cross-sectional sense we have found it clinically useful to see an adult social-recreation pattern as a sublatent support to a work pattern. The entire developmental continuum of play and work we designate as occupational behavior."

To render treatment most effective, it is believed that occupational therapists must take action beyond the single activity and fragment of time in occupational therapy, extending their influence regarding work and play throughout the days, evenings, and weekends. It is in this context that involvement of the client and the family in programming is seen necessary.

The primary objective of treatment of the child with cerebral palsy is the development of functional skills which the normal child achieves through play and exploratory activities. The child who cannot move or adjust without assistance from the mother or another person is deprived of essential sensorimotor experiences on which further development is based. Finnie (1968) has many practical suggestions for structuring the environment that the child with cerebral palsy may comfortably explore the surroundings and engage in play. She suggests that a child who is severely restricted in movement may be placed on a bolster or sloping board in order that he or she can adapt to lying on the stomach with the head up and to bring the arms forward in a position for functional use of the hands. The child will need continued help and encouragement from members of the family to touch, hold, and manipulate toys.

The moderately involved child or the child who is beginning to play should have opportunities for self-initiated activities. Finnie emphasized introducing simple play: "If the slightest accidental movement on his part makes an object move or even makes a noise, he will have made something happen himself and this will stimulate him to try again." The occupational therapist will assist parents to discover how to position their child for best use of the hands and arms and will make recommendations for facilitating play.

Parents need assistance and guidance in home management of the moderately involved child that will develop habits of attention and work anticipatory to adult independence and productivity. Maurer (1971) stresses the importance of making a transition from play to work during childhood and adolescence. She points out the need for developing a self-concept and identifying with a worker, getting along with peers, developing habits of industry, and learning to work with and adjust to authority. In the earliest stages of this development, occupational therapists can help with the selection of simple household tasks which are within the capabilities of the child with cerebral palsy and which will provide the child with satisfying opportunities to share responsibilities with other members of the family.

Neuromuscular Function

A principal concern in the treatment of a child with cerebral palsy is the child's ability to interact with the environment and to respond to it adaptively. The nature of treatment is dependent upon the apparent maturation of the child's nervous system as reflected by the level and quality of sensorimotor performance, the status of postural reflexes, and muscle tone. Treatment consists of making more adaptive and effective responses available to the child as he or she progresses through developmental sequences of sensorimotor behavior.

The two aspects of adaptive responses are integrally related. If the sensations of vision, sound, movement, touch, or gravitational pull have no meaning to a child's nervous system, the child's movements, or motor output, will be meaningless. For example, if the child cannot recognize the qualities of the sensation of gravitational force received through the vestibular system and relate them to his or her own position in space, the child will undoubtedly have difficulty in making appropriate postural adjustments necessary for raising the head or for sitting and, eventually, standing.

Treatment of disorders of neuromuscular function based upon the interrelationships between sensory and motor function of the central nervous system has developed in the last thirty-five to forty years. The methods are used by several disciplines for principal or contiguous treatment. Temple Fay (1954) was among the first to develop a method of "neuromuscular reflex therapy" which required repetition of phylogenetic motor patterns to restore functional movement. To elicit basic movements such as walking, reflex responses or a series of reflex responses were used as first steps to the successive forms of creeping, crawling, and climbing.

At about the same time in England, the Bobaths (1955, 1964, 1966) developed an approach based upon normal ontogenetic development. Their primary treatment principle is the inhibition of exaggerated phasic and tonic reflex activity, followed immediately or simultaneously by the facilitation of righting and equilibrium reflex responses.

Treatment is focused upon the inhibition of primitive tonic neck and tonic labyrinthine patterns which interfere with voluntary motor activity. The objective is to suppress reflexes in order to enable a later stage of maturation to take place. To inhibit these abnormal patterns a child must be positioned to contract muscles antagonistic to those activated by the primitive reflex. For example, the head-righting and extensor responses might be facilitated at the same time that the primitive tonic reflexes are inhibited by placing a child in the prone position. Hyperextension or hypertonia could be inhibited and functional use of the hands and arms facilitated by seating the child in the therapist's lap with the child's hips flexed, head slightly forward, and legs abducted and outwardly rotated.

In addition to these methods for normalizing postural mechanisms, the Bobaths use a technique called "tapping" to increase postural tone. Tapping is a technique providing proprioceptive and tactile stimulation. It is used with children whose postural control is dominated by hypertonia and impaired reciprocal innervation.

About 1946, Herman Kabat began a system of treatment providing proprioceptive stimulation to increase motor activity. He focused on muscle groups rather than isolated muscles, and called upon the patient for active participation in treatment. His techniques have been expanded by Margaret Knott and Dorothy Boss (1968), who are physical therapists.

Emphasis is placed on the use of stress or resistance for learning motor behavior. Beginning treatment is approached developmentally and follows normal functional patterns. Movement of each joint or body segment is facilitated by using the strongest and most coordinated movements first. The activity creates a pattern of "irradiation" of neural impulses which promotes strengthening of the weaker parts. In addition to techniques using resistance, positioning, and postural and righting reflexes, Voss (1972) uses tones of voice to control the degree of stress and to arouse motor neuron activity. Loud tones of voice are used to promote movement, softer tones are used to encourage stability. General activities used for the development of strength and balance include mat, gait, and self-care program.

Margaret Rood (1954) has introduced principles for treatment based upon the theory that sensory stimuli can be utilized to facilitate or inhibit motor expression. With reference to the developmental sequence of motor activity, the nature of the activating sensory stimuli is determined by the child's stage of development. Some of the early developmental tasks to be accommodated include head control, rolling over, on elbows in the prone position, maintaining the all-fours position, sucking, and rooting. Providing planned and controlled sensory input to influence motor behavior requires selection of stimuli in the form of body movement and positioning, tactile stimulation, and pressure on muscles and tendons. When inhibition or stimulation has resulted in the desired motor responses, the child's attention should be directed to play or self-care activities which will utilize the responses which have been elicited.

Sensory Integration

The difficulties in sensory and perceptual motor dysfunction in children with cerebral palsy are multiple. It seems likely that the quality of exteroceptive and proprioceptive input and feedback in children with cerebral palsy affects perceptual skills. Although the degree of involvement does not usually correlate with the degree of accuracy of perception, it can be assumed that the child who cannot make an appropriate response to the environment lacks sensory experience on which to organize complex adaptive motor behavior. For the reason of this interdependence of function, occupational therapists, in general, have chosen to treat difficulties in perceptual skills as a part of the integrated therapeutic program.

Ayres (1972b) has based a theory for treating disorders of sensory integration on neuromuscular therapy:

> The central principle in sensory integrative therapy is providing planned and controlled sensory input with usually—but not invariably—the eliciting of an adaptive response in order to enhance the organization of brain mechanisms. The plan includes utilization of neurophysiological mechanisms in a manner that reflects some aspect of the developmental sequence. The objective is progressive organization of the brain in a method as similar to the developmental process as possible.

Treatment emphasizes sensory input followed by a motor response that has functional significance to the child. The stimuli are essentially the same as those employed in neuromuscular therapy. The objective of treatment is toward more normal sensory organization as opposed to the improvement of motor skill. The motor response has meaning in that it provides sensory input and reflects neuronal integration:

> Sensory integration through motion is not limited to cortical function. It occurs at all levels of the nervous system. Therapeutic

results have led to the proposal that motor actions designed to elicit reflexes or automatic reactions organized primarily at one level of the brain tend to organize sensory integration at that level. Thus the goal of sensory integration at the brain stem level is hypothesized to be facilitated by utilization of motor patterns which may have integrating centers in the brain stem. (Ayres 1972*b*)

Sensory integrative therapy focuses primarily upon the subcortical structures of the brain. The lower brain structures tend to emphasize sensory integration. The response to stimuli at this level is not conscious and quickly becomes semi-automatic, a permanent part of the behavior repertoire. The cortex has more to do with sensory analysis and requires a voluntary response which is slower, more difficult, and time-consuming. It demands greater repetition and sometimes places stress that inhibits behavior. However, each part of the brain is integrally associated with other parts and sensory input is likely to have widespread influence over the rest of the brain (Moore 1973).

Sensory integrative dysfunction has been the basis for six different types of disorder of neural systems. Ayres (1972*b*) has referred to them as (1) disorders in postural, ocular, and bilateral integration; (2) apraxia, or disorders in motor planning; (3) disorders in form and space perception; (4) auditory and language problems; (5) tactile defensiveness; and (6) unilateral disregard. Treatment methods have been developed to alleviate these disorders through stimulation of the tactile, vestibular, proprioceptive, visual, and auditory systems.

Normally, the integration of the tactile system takes place early in life. Tactile stimulation elicits rooting and sucking responses in the newborn infant. The baby gets information about the environment as well as nurture through his or her mouth. The baby places objects in the mouth for tasting and testing. For the child with cerebral palsy who cannot put the hands to the mouth, it may be important to provide tactile stimulation to the mouth prior to and at feeding time. This can take the form of brushing, rubbing with a textured cloth, or touch pressure (Hope 1974). The hypotonic child can be aroused to activity through stimulation of face, hands, and feet. The hypertonic child may become overstimulated and disorganized unless stimulation is administered carefully in reflex inhibiting patterns, or with Rood's techniques of reciprocal innervation.

Because of its affect on the reticular system and postural responses, Ayres (1972*b*) considers vestibular stimulation one of the most effective means of treating sensory integrative dysfunction. The activation of the system makes the child aware of the pull of gravity and his or her relationship to the earth. It helps the child to feel motion and the speed of motion through increased muscle tone. Extraocular muscles are facilitated through vestibular stimulation. It seems likely that vestibular stimulation provides an integrating role in relation to all other sensory input. The vestibular system can function as both facilitator and inhibitor of activity depending upon the rate of stimulation.

Vestibular stimulation can be provided through a variety of means in a variety of positions. A hammock with both ends fastened to a single hood is commonly used to swing or spin a child. The best position for the child with cerebral palsy is seated as the hammock keeps the child's head forward and allows the hands to come together at the midline. Horizontal positions, whether prone, supine, or sidelying, are also used.

The use of resistance as a means of providing proprioceptive input has been described by the proponents of proprioceptive facilitation treatment techniques (Knott and Voss 1968; Rood 1954). Ayres (1972a) calls attention to the use of gravity as a major source of resistance and describes the use of the scooter board to achieve prolonged contraction of muscles and movement into a functional relationship to the environment. For example, extensor muscles of the trunk, hip, and shoulders must contract to hold the extremities off the floor as the child lies on the scooter board in the prone position.

Movement into a position in which the child may become oriented to the environment and objects in the environment is essential to the development of visual perception. Underlying experiences are, first, the perception and response to gravity and, second, the integration of postural reflexes and the development of righting and equilibrium responses. Treatment with emphasis on visual orientation follows this sequence. An effective means of achieving neck-righting and providing proprioceptive facilitation of the extraocular muscles is rolling in a tunnel made of a series of innertubes tied together. The child is encouraged to look toward the goal as he or she rolls. "The motor sequence is: (1) the eyes look to the side, (2) the head follows, rotating on the trunk, (3) the trunk follows the head" (Ayres 1972b). The child is encouraged toward the goal by the therapist's hands clapping appropriately to gain the child's visual attention.

Psychosocial Adaptation

The process of adaptation for the child with cerebral palsy is not only one of overcoming the effects of perceptual and motor dysfunction but it is also concerned with problems of limited social involvement and opportunity to identify life role relationships. Occupational therapy has much to offer to assist the child deal with these aspects of development and to prevent an eventual loss of self-esteem. At one developmental stage the child will have the opportunity to manipulate the environment. At another, the child must deal with the behavior of others, singly or in groups. Within a different context, the child must identify him or herself as a member of the family group, yet a distinct individual. The child must be able to establish a collaborative relationship with peers. The child's self-image must be as a contributing part of the family and community (Lorens 1974).

PARENTAL INVOLVEMENT IN TREATMENT

The therapist who works with children is aware of the necessity for ongoing communication with parents and their need to understand the goals of treatment. Therapists endeavor, whenever possible, to involve parents and siblings in the treatment program. Banus (1971) points out that early treatment in the form of home care by parents under the supervision of the therapist helps prevent dysfunctional compensating behavior at a time when the child is most responsive to treatment intervention. The early home program may help parents establish a positive attitude toward their handicapped child and develop realistic expectancies for the child's future. When a child receives therapeutic care administered in an agency or institution, "parents carry out treatment at home following the same principles of therapy as are being used by the therapist. They are taught the techniques by the therapist and practice them under her [sic] supervision." In supporting the therapeutic program, parents need to understand the dysfunction, the treatment program, and the purpose of the treatment they are performing. "They need to know the present level of functioning of the child and the next developmental step sought. The parents, with their intimate knowledge of how their child responds, often can find means of initiating therapeutic activities and can provide opportunities for practice of recently learned skills. The parents are in an optimal position to judge when a child is ready to move forward and to support the child's natural impetus (Sukiennicki 1971).

SUMMARY

In occupational therapy, methods of evaluating and treating a child with cerebral palsy will be both identical to and complementary to those used by other members of the professional team rendering service to the child. The overall goals of treatment will be identical with those of every other member of the treatment team and, ideally, those held by the child and the parents. If the underlying principles of treatment are based upon developmental theory, they are likely to be held in common by the occupational therapist, the physical therapist, the speech therapist, and the educator. At times, the modalities may be the same. The occupational therapist will place emphasis on those experiences and activities that best subserve programs for daily living appropriate to the developmental status, the capacities, and the inclination of the client. Johnson (1971) has said: "The therapist enters the life space of the patient in order (1) to help the patient develop skills he needs to influence his environment and fulfill his essentially personal role and (2) to act as a change agent in those instances in which it is the environment, or the family, or the agency, rather than the patient, that needs to change."

12

Educational Planning

WILLIAM M. CRUICKSHANK

IN THIS FIELD few bona fide research studies have been completed which have been accurate in terms of experimental design, careful in terms of statistical methodology, or of sufficient duration to allow observation of the long-term effects of educational methodology on achievement and adjustment. The status of educational research with cerebral palsied children is easy to understand, however, when one considers that while legally the door has been open for a long time, it is only since the mid-1950s that cerebral palsied children have in any large number been accepted as a public education responsibility. Certain school systems prior to 1920 have included such children to a greater or lesser extent within their provisions for crippled children. In effect it was about 1945, in response to many demands, that public education began the long, slow march to a full acceptance of the cerebral palsied child. Even yet this statement does not mean that completely adequate educational provisions are available for all cerebral palsied children. Evidence is abundant that many cerebral palsied and other types of handicapped children are discriminated against by school systems. Exclusion is still too often an administrative solution.

Furthermore, the isolated cerebral palsied child in rural areas still constitutes an educational challenge. The differentiation of educational methodology in terms of the intellectual capacities and characteristics of the child is not observed in any universal fashion as yet. The availability of adequately prepared teachers and administrators who understand the inherent problems of educating cerebral palsied children while improving, still leaves much to be desired. The complete acceptance of the cerebral palsied child, intellectually and emotionally, by general educators is still much needed. The small number of cerebral palsied children in a given locality, the still smaller numbers available in even large centers when one considers subtypes, and the lack of personnel trained in research are factors which have further deterred educational experimentation. Many things, alone or in combination, have thus functioned to keep research and good programs in the education of cerebral palsied children at a minimum.

While in earlier writings we excused the situation because of the newness of programs for cerebral palsied children, this situation cannot now be accepted. Clinics and treatment centers have been established and have operated in a stabilized manner, often as a part of a public school program. Still, little research has been undertaken. This must be a priority item in foundation and federal funding programs.

Crothers has stated in an informal communication to the writer that education for the cerebral palsied has been a "tutorial system without any particular philosophy." This is quite true. Its history has been one of overprotectiveness. It has often resulted in the creation of passivity and dependency. It has permitted feelings of inadequacy as a result of overstress on normalcy. The cerebral palsied child, not achieving normal development and movement, feels inadequate. The corollary is also often true, i.e., one overevaluates the abilities of the cerebral palsied child, and again thus permits a discrepancy to exist between reality and inadequate estimations.

An emphasis by this writer and others has frequently been on the fact that the handicapped child is like the normal child. Certainly there are more likenesses than differences, but *it is the differences with which the child has to work.* To state that the cerebral palsied child is first and foremost a child is certainly true. The child is still cerebral palsied, however, and that fact in and of itself cannot be denied. As a cerebral palsied child, the child has different personal needs and may have different educational needs and different educational goals and outcomes. This is not undemocratic; it is honest realism. Indeed, one must ask, what effect is the distortion of development going to have on educational development? Herein are the differences. The unavoidable implication is that the distortion does and will have some dynamic effect. An assessment and evaluation of the degree of the effect of abnormal development must be made before educational philosophy, methodology, placement, or other facet of the problem is contemplated. Differences exist in many exceptional children, and educators of such children must be the first to recognize them. To do other than this is to approach the problem ostrich fashion.

Much is being written and spoken at this time about the importance of integrating handicapped children into the regular educational programs of the schools. In large measure this is a reaction to poor special educational programs, inadequate policies of assessment and placement, and unsatisfactory instruments of psychological assessment. Little valid research exists on either side of the argument to support one's point of view. However, beginning in the early 1970s, a wholesale program of assignment of exceptional children to regular grades was begun. We have in the past written about the importance of integrating certain children, but the wave which has swept exceptional children, including many cerebral palsied children, into the regular grades has generally not been selective. Only time will indicate the validity of this rather thoughtless rush which has been spearheaded by both general and special educators. The program has been undertaken without adequately prepared general educators, either administrators or classroom personnel; without necessary support personnel; and without clear definition to the parents or to the handicapped children themselves as to what their expectancies realistically should be.

Parents and children, via the medium of class action suits in federal courts, have been stating that placement in special classes was often a violation of basic and constitutionally protected civil rights. In many cases the arbitrary assignment of handicapped children into regular classes without the supports which are necessitated by their differences is equally a violation of the Due Process Clause of the Fourteenth Amendment of the United States Constitution. It remains for this to be tested. Placement *per se* is not the crucial problem. The quality of the educational program wherever the child is placed is the issue. Educators, both special and general, have avoided and still continue to avoid coming to grips with the quality of education which children must have and do require.

TYPES OF EDUCATIONAL PROGRAMS

The plan for education of cerebral palsied individuals must be complete and inclusive in nature. Communities cannot afford to undertake the education of these children in a piecemeal fashion. If an educational program is going to be developed, it must be developed or at least viewed in its entirety. The cerebral palsied child is going to need educational facilities at all levels and of all types. To plan nursery school facilities without at the same time envisioning programs of education at other levels is only partially to meet the needs of the cerebral palsied child. In advance, then, of an actual educational program there must be full discussion and consideration of the scope of the educational problem. Suffice at this point to state that many groups and many different people must engage in the preliminary planning. Too often local groups undertake, for example, a preschool program for cerebral palsied children, but fail to realize that within a year or two these same children will reach a legal school age and will become the responsibility of another community agency which to date has been little considered. Thus, a community group that is farsighted in its planning will early involve public and parochial school administrators and teachers of all levels in both immediate and long-term plans. Only in this way can there be achieved continuity of program, solution to problems of legality regarding transportation and school district responsibility, or the creation of a program which is developmental in nature and geared to the peculiar needs of the cerebral palsied group.

The educational program for cerebral palsied children must encompass the total educational process. Thus, programs of early intervention and others at the nursery school level, at the elementary and secondary levels, and at the college or university level must be envisioned. Vocational, technical, or trade school programs must also be considered for those cerebral palsied children who are capable of deriving benefit from such experiences and who will not continue into liberal arts or professional collegiate programs of education. Furthermore, it is necessary to plan an educational program to meet several distinct needs of the cerebral palsied children. By this is meant that educational programs must be planned to meet the differing intellectual, physical, and learning problems of the cerebral palsied group. Fouracre and his associates have stated that a wide scope of educational programs must be available for the cerebral palsied child depending upon the child's needs as his potential classification becomes apparent. The several types of programs which are recommended at one age level include those for (1) the cerebral palsied child needing custodial care; (2) the cerebral palsied child with mental retardation; (3) the intelligent cerebral palsied with moderate or severe physical handicap; (4) the cerebral palsied child with minor physical handicap; and (5) the non-motor handicapped child with brain damage. The present writer feels that the latter group would perhaps be more inclusive if it were divided into two groups of children all of whom are characterized by perceptual-motor dysfunction. One group would include the non-motor handicapped child with perceptual problems as suggested by Fouracre and his colleagues; the other, cerebral palsied children with some degree of physical disability who also have psychological problems inherent in neurological dysfunction which are basic to learning and achievement.

Included in the first group mentioned above, i.e., cerebral palsied children needing custodial care, are also three subgroups. These include cerebral palsied children (a) with severe mental deficiency, (b) with both severe mental deficiency and severe physical disability, and (c) with severe physical disability but with little or no mental impairment. It is easily apparent from this breakdown that the education of the cerebral palsied child is a complicated one if it is fully and realistically contemplated and undertaken.

THE PSYCHOLOGICAL EVALUATION

Since a full discussion of the evaluation of intelligence and other psychological characteristics has been given in earlier chapters, no further elaboration is warranted here. However, lest the intimate relationship between such evaluations and the educational program be overlooked, its importance is reiterated at this point. Serial psychological evaluations which include current status and suggestions of a potential classification must be continued until such time as an accurate classification can be achieved. The serial nature of the psychological evaluations, however, will provide more than the base for classification. In the likely event that the child is characterized by perceptual-motor disabilities which result in specific learning problems, the teacher must have a continuous assessment of their status. Educational programs cannot be adequately conceived if the teacher is ignorant of such matters as change in status of the attention span, the figure-ground pathology, dissociative tendencies, and other perceptual-motor characteristics basic to successful achievement.

SELECTION OF CEREBRAL PALSIED CHILDREN FOR PROGRAMS OF EDUCATION

One of the most important elements in an educational program for cerebral palsied children is a *policy of selection and admission*. It is unrealistic to believe that all cerebral palsied children can profit from the same educational experiences. On the other hand, if a differentiated educational program here discussed is planned, then it follows that a policy of evaluation, selection, and admission will also be adopted which will direct children into the appropriate program in accordance with the child's need and abilities. Where educational programs have been established without adequate consideration of admission policies, dissatisfaction has frequently resulted on the part of both the parents of the children and the professional personnel involved. The admission policy should be realistic to the goals of education. It should provide for individual differences through the proper routing to differentiated programs. It should be reasonably flexible to avoid errors. It should include a policy of *continuous selection,* that is, a policy of re-evaluation and reappraisal of the child at intervals of six months or a year to ascertain the adequacy of earlier decisions and readjustment of the child, if necessary, in terms of accumulating data. Finally, the admissions policy should include the guidance of parents of the children not eligible for an educational program to the goal of healthy parental acceptance of the child's limitations and placement in day care centers, treatment centers, adult activity programs, community living centers, or in the appropriate child-care institution.

Dunsdon (1952) has formulated an excellent nine-point series of considerations in the development of an adequate selection policy.

1. *The criteria for selecting children for educational schemes designed for those with a cerebral palsy handicap are necessarily complex.*

The selection policy must not be dependent upon intellectual ability alone, although this is an important factor. The policy must include considerations of chronological age, maturational age, extent and degree of secondary physical disabilities, personality and adjustment of the child, level of development of self-help toilet skills (dressing, eating, bladder and bowel control, and self-help toilet skills, buttoning, walking, talking, etc.), distance between home and the educational facility, and other perhaps less important matters.

2. *No basis of education can be established without first considering the meaning of education in relation to these children.* The broader problem of education as social adjustment of any level or degree must be considered. Some cerebral palsied children can be admitted to an educational program geared only to self-help activities who cannot be admitted to a program which primarily emphasizes the more traditional academic skills and abilities. Selection policy must include both types of educational opportunities.

3. *The essential problem of selection in this field concerns the child who, because of the degree or extent of his motor handicap, requires a special type of provision either within a school for physically handicapped children, or in a center exclusively for children with cerebral palsy, where facilities for both education and physical therapy exist.* Uppermost in the minds of those who administer the selection program must be the fact that cerebral palsied children are, because of the limitations of their disability, essentially isolated. Placement in an educational program should be made not only on the basis of the child's physical needs, but also on the basis of the type of educational plan which will bring him most fully into contact with a variety of rich experiences and opportunities for social relations with as many other children and adults as possible.

4. *Where this dual approach, educational and physical, is planned, care must be taken that purely medical criteria are not allowed to determine selection or rejection.* Dunsdon points out that if this is not agreed upon *there is always a temptation for those concerned primarily with the physical aspects of the handicap to urge the admission of children who may present interesting physical problems, but in whom any likelihood of response to education, even in the broadest interpretation of that term, may be very slight or even minimal.* In this connection it should be pointed out that, while the selection committee should be composed of personnel from a number of disciplines related to cerebral palsy, the final decision regarding placement of a child in an educational facility is reserved to the professional educational personnel.

5. *Although mental ability cannot be the sole criterion, it is nevertheless a very important and, in some cases, a limiting one. It has been shown*

that, among children with cerebral palsy, [intellectual] *limitation and physical handicap are definitely and positively related, i.e., they are apt to go hand in hand, although this will not happen in every single case.* Although there are, of course, instances wherein mental capacity and the degree of physical involvement vary, there is evidence to indicate a high degree of relationship between the two factors. In general it has been observed that cerebral palsied children unable to attend schools or clinics by reason of the severity of their physical disability are of lower intelligence than those who are able to participate in school and clinic programs.

6. *Available evidence suggests that an IQ of about 85 may be taken as a fairly reliable guide to the minimum level of mental ability required to allow cerebral palsied children to profit from special education. It does not follow, of course, that all children who show this level of ability or better, will necessarily profit from special education. There should . . . be no automatic selection on grounds of . . . intelligence level alone. Much depends on the emotional and physical capacities of the child, particularly its capacity to go on trying.* Dunsdon's suggestion that an intelligence level of 85 be adhered to will not be universally accepted by educators or others interested in the education of cerebral palsied children. One must understand Dunsdon's point of view herein and then greater acceptance of her statement will be possible. Table 12.1 includes data on which she makes her generalization. It will be seen that nineteen of the twenty children included in this phase of her study who had intelligence quotients below 85 showed no progress. In speaking of progress she is not referring specifically to educational achievement alone, but to social independence and adjustment, the outcomes of educational programs. On the basis of the fifty-seven children included in Table 12.1, it would appear that Dunsdon's recommendation is appropriate.

TABLE 12.1

PERCENTAGE INCIDENCE OF GENERAL PROGRESS AND INTELLIGENCE LEVEL

Intelligence Range	No Progress	Slight Progress	Fair Progress	Total	Percentage Incidence
115 and above	—	4	1	5⎫	33
110-114	3	11	—	14⎭	
85-99	5	12	1	18	32
84 and below	10	—	1	20	35
Total	27	27	3	57	100
Percentage incidence	47.4	47.4	5.2	100	

Adapted with permission from Dunsdon, *The Educability of Cerebral Palsied Children,* p. 119.

This is not a new concept in educational practice. Numerous schools and school systems in the United States have for a long time had local regulations to the effect that physically handicapped children would be accepted into special educational programs only if they showed intellectual capacities at or above a measured IQ of 80. In this recommendation, an educational program geared ultimately to the acquisition by the children of abstract concepts involved in language arts, number concepts, and in social skills is meant. For educational programs geared to the self-help skills, intellectual levels lower than 80 or 85, as has been suggested, may be effectively utilized.

The whole issue of intelligence level which Dunsdon appropriately raises here is dependent on the adequacy of instrumentation. This point has been stressed earlier. The IQ *per se* is relatively unimportant. Educationally, the characteristics of the child which go to make up an intelligence quotient are the significant considerations for education.

7. *Even among those children of average intelligence, there is evidence, on the part of such children, of a too ready satisfaction with very small progress.*

8. *There is evidence to suggest a lower degree of resistance to illness, and of lower physical stamina, among children with cerebral palsy than among those who are normal.* This is a very important consideration to selection and is a fact which has often bee commented upon by educators of physically handicapped children. A careful evaluation of the general medical history must be taken into consideration when selection is in progress. The findings will often dictate the type of educational situation in which the cerebral palsied child can be placed, i.e., a regular school program where frequent absences would complicate instruction and retard achievement or a special school or clinic program where with smaller number of children and smaller classes greater individualization of instruction could compensate for absence due to illness.

9. *Age is . . . an important factor in selection for special* [education]. *. . . On the whole, younger children are less able to withstand the strain of the dual approach* [education and therapy]. Where cerebral palsied children, because of their physical disabilities, require extensive therapeutic programs, it may be better to delay the beginning of an educational program until somewhat later than the customary school age for kindergarten or first-grade registration.

When we write of delay, we focus specifically on the school-oriented program, i.e., writing, reading, spelling, number concepts. We do not want to minimize the significance of early intervention programs—the development of readiness concepts, perceptual training, and other related matters which are significant in the lives not only of cerebral palsied children but all children. If care is taken to develop an integrated program of therapy and the elements just mentioned, cerebral palsied children will be significantly assisted.

WHAT EDUCATORS NEED TO KNOW ABOUT CEREBRAL PALSIED CHILDREN

Decisions concerning selection of cerebral palsied children for educational programs and action regarding the appropriate placement in an educational program are essential steps in total planning. A further important element is the adequacy of the information about a given child with which the teacher is provided. Too often the teacher receives only the information that the child is of a given age, has a certain estimated intelligence level, and that he is of a such-and-such medical classification. A record recently brought to the attention of this writer by a teacher included the following information in the referral to a school program from a clinic: "John is 11-2 years of age; his birthday is March 11, 1965. We have had psychological examinations completed and it is estimated that he has a mental level of approximately nine years. His is diagnosed as cerebral palsy, spastic, right hemiplegia. Speech, fair." While this referral does not represent that coming from the thoughtful clinical director, it nevertheless is typical of many received by teachers. It provides little or no useful information through which a teacher could adequately develop a meaningful teaching situation.

The following letter addressed to the principal of a school system is a useful referral regarding a cerebral palsied child. This information is typical of that provided to schools and agencies by the personnel of an excellent cerebral palsy clinic and contains data which can immediately be incorporated into an educational plan for the child concerned.

June 1, 1975

Mrs. John Brown, Principal
Mulberry Central School
Mulberry, New York

Dear Mrs. Brown:

We examined Mary Doe on May 19, 1975. On the basis of our study we were able to arrive at some conclusions and recommendations which will be of significance for the educational situation. We will summarize for you only the information which seems pertinent to your purpose.

The medical examination revealed little motor handicap and there was no evidence of any gross sensory impairment. The neurological examination suggested a developmental defect and indicated that Rh incompatibility was probably not causal.

Psychological screening included an investigation of mental functioning, social development, and adjustment and included an interview with the mother, as well as direct examination of the child. At a chronological age of 5-6 the child's mental age was 3-11 (Binet IQ 71). The social age was comparable and approximated that of a child of 3-10 (Vineland Social Quotient 60). The qualitative aspects of the test situation and the behavioral observations made during examination were indicative of organic pathology and would lead us to suspect that the retardation seen here is on the basis of brain damage, rather than being endogenous in origin. This is particularly significant to the educational situation since it will necessitate special methods of instruction even within a special class for the retarded.

The qualitative disturbances to which we refer include hyperactivity and motor disinhibition which are related to her distractibility and forced responsiveness to irrelevant stimuli. That is, she is easily distracted by any and all stimuli in a room and is compelled to handle and explore things to which she is thus forced to attend. Thus, her hyperactivity is related to the distractibility, and the latter in turn is considered directly related to the possible brain damage. Similarly, there are temper tantrums and tendencies toward emotional hyper-reaction, emotional disinhibition—behavior which we also contend is related to the brain injury and is not to be considered as having an emotional basis, or to be related to inadequate handling by the parents.

There is a fairly wide range of abilities; the child showed some inadequacies at a 3-year level and some successes at a 5-year level in particular intellectual functions. Poorest abilities will be found in vocabulary and immediate span for relatively meaningless material (digits), while best abilities are seen in comprehension of wholepart relationships pictorially presented and in abstraction of similarities in simple pictorially presented designs and drawings. Visual perception would also appear to be more adequate than auditory perception, and this may be partially explanatory of the greater delay in language development as compared with other functions. Speech is marked by sound substitutions and omissions, but is understandable. Short sentences are used for expression of needs in the manner of a child of 2 to 3 years of age. Vocabulary level approximates $2\frac{1}{2}$ years.

It is interesting to note that examinations done elsewhere have previously revealed IQs of 56, 58, and 66. We consider our findings as being a particularly reliable indication of potential because they are higher, that is, we feel that successes are more indicative of ability than failures are of inability. We also learned from this examination that when the effort is made at rapid presentation of items, when distractions are cut to a minimum, when special devices to secure attention are used, the child is able to respond more successfully.

In summary, we reach the diagnostic conclusion that there is present a moderate degree of mental retardation with comparable social immaturity which we consider to be most probably on an exogenous basis (brain injury). Though medical confirmation of the latter would be required, the behavior is an almost classic illustration of this type of child, and we therefore feel that Mary may best be treated educationally from this point of view. Thus, we would recommend the special teaching methods set forth by Cruickshank (1967, 1975) and Marshall (1975). The educational situation recommended by these authors is an individualized program in which external and background stimuli are cut down, while the educational materials are accented by color and various other cues and the whole learning process is concretized. We would recommend that this specialized approach be used with Mary whenever she enters a school situation.

Mary would be best placed at this time in a pre-academic readiness program at her level. Though all recommend downward revision of the age for acceptance of these children in special classes, we realize that the regulations set up by the school system do not usually permit a child to enter a special class for the retarded until a mental age of at least 4 years, 6 months has been reached. If this is true of the program which will be set up in your community, Mary of course does not qualify at this time in terms of mental age, though her IQ is well above the lower limit. She will in all probability qualify for placement at age $6\frac{1}{2}$ or 7. We would consider a socially-occupationally oriented program to be the most appropriate for Mary with respect to curriculum content, but again we realize that the actual facilities available are not always the ideal.

We trust that the information provided above will be useful to you in your counseling with Mrs. Doe regarding proper placement of the child within your present educational framework. You are no doubt aware that this family is very much in need of such help, particularly with respect to their own attitudes regarding special individualized placement and training rather than the advancement through the regular grades which they had hoped for.

Very truly yours,

John B. Smith, *Clinic Director*

It will be noted from the above that there are relatively few medical data provided. Such is not necessary in an educational referral. Medical diagnosis of cerebral palsy per se does not define any child's educational problem. Only such medical data as are meaningful to the educational process need be transmitted. Educators need to have descriptive information regarding the child's (1) communicative abilities, (2) emotional behavior, (3) intellectual functions, (4) specific motor functions, (5) specific sensory functions, (6) conceptual or perceptual impairments involving the sensorymotor functions, and (7) information regarding other neurological problems which have a bearing on the educational process—epilepsy, for example. In each of the above categories the information should be descriptive in nature, indicating what the child can do and in general what he cannot yet adequately accomplish. If such information is not provided to the educator or if merely a copy of the medical diagnostic examination is forwarded to the school, much time is wasted on the part of the educators and the child, since no educational program can be developed until the type of information suggested above is accumulated.

THE EDUCATIONAL PROGRAM

As has been suggested in the above paragraphs, a wide variety of educational programs must be considered and provided in order adequately to encompass the diverse needs of the total cerebral palsied group. From nursery school to college, from simple self-help and childcare programs to complicated technical training and vocational programs—these must be appropriately available to cerebral palsied children. One group of educators in considering the various levels of educational programs has spoken of "pre-elementary, elementary, and post-elementary," instead of the usual nursery, elementary, and secondary levels. This terminology is meaningful in view of the fact that cerebral palsied children frequently have not reached the mental, social, emotional, or educational levels equivalent to those usually attained by physically normal children of similar chronological ages who are enrolled in the regular grades of the school system. A physically normal child of twelve would, other things being equal, typically be placed in the seventh grade of a junior high school. A cerebral palsied child of the same chronological age characterized by any one or a number of the factors considered in this text might be found to function at an achievement level typical of the elementary school. A cerebral palsied child of six years of age might be so handicapped physically and intellectually that she would need "pre-elementary" experiences of an educational nature for many years. Finally, it might be possible for an adolescent cerebral palsied child to be educated in a high school setting, but, because of problems inherent in the disease, he would be functioning educationally on a "post-elementary" level.

The Pre-Elementary Level

Reference is herein made to the excellent statement by Fouracre (1952) and his associates commented upon above. This statement is timeless, and continues to be relevant. Since it is difficult to make positive criticisms of their statement which would improve upon it, with permission it is included herein with comments. In considering the various educational programs listed below, the reader must keep in mind that these are different types of programs needed by cerebral palsied children with different physical and mental characteristics.

1. *The cerebral palsied child needing custodial care*

   (a) with severe mental deficiency

   The early years should be utilized to give this child the physical care and emotional security every child needs, by providing the parents with guidance in his management. He should be trained in self-help functions and physical independence to the degree to which he is able to profit from such training. The preparation of the parents in regard to the future recognition and acceptance of the child's severe limitation should be started during the pre-elementary period.

   (b) with severe mental deficiency and severe physical disability

   This child should be considered as in (a) except that training in self-help functions will probably not be possible and plans for the future will depend on the existence of facilities prepared to care for children with the degree of helplessness caused by the double handicap.

   (c) with severe physical disability but little or no mental impairment

   This child should be given educational benefits to enable him to participate in the cultural life of his contemporaries. Whether he will receive custodial care in his own home, a community living center, or in an institution, the life he must live out with his handicap will be more bearable for him and more tolerable for his environment if he is given opportunity to develop to his maximum capacity.

It can readily be ascertained that the educational problems of this group of children are not those typically assumed by public or parochial educational systems. The decision as to whether or not they should be the responsibility of an established educational system is, in the minds of many, controversial. Some would say that an equal educational opportunity must be provided for all, and that as such the state and local school systems in cooperation must assume responsibility for housing, personnel, and appropriate instruction of this group of children. Others would say that it is the function of the public schools of the nation to provide an educational experience which will make it possible for its graduates in varying degrees of effectiveness to make a positive contribution to the nation which provided the educational opportunity. Education, they say, is a function reserved to the state for its own betterment.

Since children as are described in the above paragraphs are unable and will remain unable to make a contribution to the state during the period of their lives, it is neither the responsibility nor the obligation of the states to provide educational facilities in the sense that the term "education" is usually used. Most educators and parents accept this latter position. Parents recognize that, while some school systems provide space for such child-care programs, the legal responsibility for this type of program does not reside solely in the department of education.

On the other hand, if education is defined as synonymous with adjustment, then there is no question but what some state or local agency must assume an interest in the problem. Certainly it is too great a financial problem for the parent alone. With such a point of view accepted, various plans have been adopted. In most instances the plan has generally resulted in a joint undertaking of state agencies or local organizations. Education has been represented, but the burden of administrative and financial responsibility has been reserved to departments of health, welfare, social welfare, mental hygiene, or a combination of two or more such administrative units. The state residential schools for the retarded have frequently played an important role in the education of this group of children and are destined to play an even greater role in the future.

Regardless of the personal position which one may take on this matter, many states are taking a positive action in establishing mandatory legislation for handicapped children. The stimulus for this has essentially come from parent organizations. The State of Michigan has recently mandated that public schools will provide educational services as appropriate to the chronological age of the child for all exceptional children between the date of birth and twenty-five years. The legislation makes no reference to the degree of severity of the disability, the intellectual level, or other limiting circumstances. Unfortunately it will take more legislation, more court actions, and continuous vigilance on the part of sponsoring groups to insure that finances are available to support mandated programs and that public school administrators and members of boards of education carry out the mandate in the exact spirit of the legislation.

2. The cerebral palsied child with mental retardation

Exploration of the specific area or areas involved in the limitations of the child's learning potentials begins at the pre-elementary level and educational approaches are worked out to meet his needs. The placement in the suitable educational facility for his needs is tentatively planned at this time. Parents are given a prognosis of his maximum potential for physical habilitation. Parental guidance in recognition and acceptance of the mental retardation could ideally be planned by exposing the child to a prolonged trial period in nursery and kindergarten groups and by permitting the parents to learn to understand the nature and the implications of their child's retardation. To the untrained observer the physical handicap often camouflages the mental retardation; clinical findings fail to convince parents, who cannot be expected to understand the ultimate implications of a slow rate of development; untold mental anguish and feelings of guilt of parents can be alleviated if the parents themselves have the opportunity, at the pre-elementary level, to convince themselves of the failure of their child to respond to educational opportunities which serve the child with similar physical impairment who has normal mentality.

The location of the educational facility for this group of children is not so nearly as much in question as for the first group discussed above. Most states have legal provisions in their state education laws which provide for the education of children with retarded mental development within the framework of the public education system. Other states have also made legal provisions for the public educational sponsorship of school programs for the so-called trainable or severely retarded child.

There is general acceptance that the mentally handicapped group (IQ generally above 50 and below 85) is the responsibility of the school. Whether or not this group at the *pre-elementary level* is the responsibility of the public school remains debatable in some states. Many local school systems have an educational regulation which provides that children may be accepted into the public school program provided they have reached a given chronological age, usually from four years and six months to six years of age. Some systems go further and specify that a mental age level of four and a half is also required for admission. This means that cerebral palsied mentally retarded children below the chronological age of five are definitely excluded and some for an even much longer period. Several states like Michigan, mentioned earlier, have lowered the legal age for school admission to below four years and six months. For the most part, the educational facilities about which we have been writing to this point are still and will remain for sometime in the future outside the scope of the public educational system in many communities. Nursery school or pre-elementary facilities are not yet the province of universal public education.

3. *The intelligent cerebral palsied child with moderate or severe physical handicap*

Without question this group of children should be provided the opportunity for a rich nursery school experience. The actual decision as to whether or not the child will participate in such an educational program is, of course, left to the selection and admission committee. The committee's decision will be made on the basis of the criteria mentioned above, namely, in terms of the extent of the therapeutic program needed by the child and the physical energy and stamina of the child. It is a matter in large degree of determining the most important factors in the life span of the child. If the therapeutic program can insure greater physical independence for the child and if this program demands a large portion of the child's time and energy, then the formal educational program may be delayed until a later time. If the young child comes to the nursery school experience tired as the result of an extended therapy session, he will be unable to profit from the nursery school program no matter how excellent it may be. It is far better to ascertain what first things must come firsts and then be patient in starting other facets of the total program which logically can be temporarily or permanently delayed.

On the other hand, if it is determined that the cerebral palsied child can profit from the pre-elementary program, independent of or in addition to the therapeutic schedule, then a rich educational experience should be provided which is in keeping both with best practice in nursery school kindergarten education and with the special considerations of the cerebral palsied child.

4. *The cerebral palsied child with minor physical handicap*

At the pre-elementary level this child may get along with physical habilitation services without requiring special adjustment in the school situation. Careful observance of his emotional adjustment and guidance toward wholesome mental attitudes may be necessary for a child with a minor handicap, who feels his difference from the norm more deeply because he is so near the fringe of normalcy himself. The possibility of deviations in the mental organization and the effect of the child's frustrations must constantly be kept in mind in the evaluation of any child with cerebral palsy.

5. *The non-motor handicapped child with brain damage*

At the pre-elementary level, the child who has personality deviations on the basis of organic pathology will frequently go undetected or misinterpreted, unless careful psychological study, educational evaluation and, when indicated, neurological examination of children, who deviate from the norm, become the rule rather than the exception. . . . [The child with perceptual-motor problems needs] a carefully planned educational environment, whether in the home or in a school situation, if he is to become able to utilize his potentialities in the face of his behavior difficulties and his learning difficulties.

In addition, one or two comments should be made regarding this problem, although a more detailed discussion will follow in sections below. If psychological and neurological diagnoses indicate the exogenous factors described in the preceding paragraph, then a decision will have to be made whether the child (1) will need a highly structured learning environment at the pre-elementary level apart from other nursery school facilities, (2) will be able to participate in a regular nursery school program with occasional periods of each day devoted to specific types of learning in a structured situation, or (3) will, because of demands of the therapeutic program and/ or because of the degree of behavior disturbance, profit more from home instruction than group experience at this early level. The latter can be carried on in the home in a relatively nonstimulating environment.

Education and the Parent at the Pre-elementary Level

From the above quotations and discussion the frequency with which references have been made to parents will be noted. Without question, the major responsibility of educators of pre-elementary cerebral palsied children pertains to parent education. The role of the parent cannot be too greatly stressed at this level, or for that matter at any age level. To assume that lay people without planned programs and with little or no experience in rearing children will have insight into normal growth and development patterns is naive. To assume that parents involved in the emotional problems of accepting a physical disability will be able to gain insight independently into the relationship between normal growth and development and the impact of cerebral palsy on such growth is to be more than naive. Some parents will be able to effect such an understanding independent of professional assistance. These parents are in the minority, however. A carefully planned program of parent education must be developed.

The importance of both formal and informal education programs for parents of cerebral palsied children cannot be overstressed. Such programs must be geared to the level of understanding of the parents. Frequently, parents of cerebral palsied children are exposed to highly technical materials of a neurological, orthopedic, pediatric, psychological, or therapeutic nature which they are emotionally unable to accept. The typical procedure of arranging a series of talks by the medical staff, the therapy staff, and clinic consultants may be interesting and is undoubtedly helpful to the ego of the staff members, but it accomplishes very little in terms of the kind of parent understanding that is really needed. The approach which we are criticising is perhaps important. Its importance will be more readily realized and accepted if the technical material can be made available to parents *after* they have come to the point at which they can freely express feelings about their child and after they have been given insight into the many practical but simple things which can be done for their child both in the home and in the neighborhood.

The Elementary Level

At this level of educational planning, as with the previous one, differentiated programs are necessary in order adequately to meet the needs of different cerebral palsied children. Included in the elementary level are cerebral palsied children comparable in chronological and/or mental age to physically normal children customarily found between the first and sixth grades of a school system. These children will normally be from six to eleven or twelve years of age. Four different types of educational programs will typically be required, namely, (1) for cerebral palsied children with severe mental deficiency and/or severe physical disability, (2) for cerebral palsied children with mental retardation, (3) for cerebral palsied children with moderate or severe physical impairment, and (4) for cerebral palsied children with minor physical impairment. Much of what has been said regarding educational programs for children at the pre-elementary level is also applicable at this level. Other factors, of course, need also to be stressed.

1. *Program for cerebral palsied children with severe mental and/or severe physical disability*

This program like that of the previously discussed level for a similar group of children will most generally be located in treatment centers, day-care centers, activity centers, or residential child-care facilities, even though in some states the responsibility for these children is legally that of some aspect of the public school system (in Michigan it is assigned by legislative enactment to the intermediate school district which usually is co-terminus with county geographical boundaries).

If the residential child-care facilities or a community living facility is utilized as being the most appropriate, certain essentials need to be understood. The facility may be used because of a very small local population, and under these circumstances only infrequently can the facilities of the public schools be of such a nature as to provide the complex transportation, attendant care, and other facilities which are basic to even a minimally effective program of this type. Furthermore, more and more residential schools are effectively reorganizing their educational and care programs to include this very disabled group of cerebral palsied children. Few parents are able to provide adequately for the life-span problems which these children present, and thus every effort should be made to develop good community living and institutional programs for the early acceptance and long-term adjustment of a very small percentage of such children.

The problem of initial placement and of parent-child separation is a major one. This is true more from the point of view of the parents than of the child. The separation is not always viewed by the parent solely from the point of view of reality, but in terms of parental guilt feelings, attitudes of the community toward parental responsibility for children, and from other ethical, social, and religious points of view. This being true, the importance of adequate counseling regarding residential school placement of cerebral palsied children is immediately apparent.

Of equal importance to care in placement, is the fact that a continuous effort must be made with the parents to keep them in touch with the residential facility, to visit the child, and to maintain a long-term relationship with the child. If at a later time, it is determined that the child can be returned to the home, the importance of continuous parent-child contacts and involvement of the parents in the treatment program of the facility becomes obvious. Many residential care facilities maintain a staff of field representatives who help to keep the relationship between the family and the individual child vital.

2. Program for cerebral palsied children with mental retardation

Fouracre and Thiel (1953) have described educational programs for children with cerebral palsy and mental retardation and Shotick has treated the problem here. Since their discussions are in greater detail than can be permitted here, no further elaboration will be given. Suffice to state that educational programs for multiple-handicapped cerebral palsied children are frequently found as separate classes or groups within both a clinic situation or public school program. Likewise, since in this instance mental retardation is considered the primary and controlling disability, these children, providing their physical disability is not excessive, are frequently included on the registers of classes for children with retarded mental development. While frequent adjustments in the special educational program for retarded children are necessary for the cerebral palsied pupil, the curriculum for the former group of children, if it has been conceived realistically and in terms of the different developmental patterns of retarded children, will often be suitable for the cerebral palsied child.

3. Program for cerebral palsied children with moderate or severe physical impairment

The educational program for children with normal intelligence who have moderate or severe physical impairments demands serious consideration by educators. This group of children, because of the *potential* of valuable contributions to society, must receive during the elementary period an educational experience which permits the individual to develop if he is actually capable of progress. A complete educational offering must be available, because at this stage of physical development the validity of the prognosis versus actual outcome of treatment is at best uncertain. This group together with that discussed next below, being intellectually normal, has the possibility of profiting from habilitation programs to the point at which they can in varying degree live relatively normal adult lives. This being true, educational programs are an essential and important element in the total planning.

The locus of this program is important. Without any question the responsibility for this educational program lies in public education. Few states or large communities fail to provide some school experience but quality programs of excellence are not the rule. There are no unsolved philosophical questions with this group regarding responsibility. Many boards of education, particularly in small communities and in rural areas, however, have been unable to provide school experiences for these children because of limited numbers, the high cost of such education, or because of the lack of medical and therapeutic services which must also be available. That it is a public school problem, however, is not a disputed question.

The responsibility established, the actual location of the school program demands consideration. The closer the educational work for cerebral palsied children is to the general elementary or secondary school program for physically normal children, the better. This means that a therapeutic facility should be added to a regular elementary school building. This will also include the classrooms and other spaces required for the school program for cerebral palsied children. To have the cerebral palsied program within a regular school means that the former can be a much richer experience for both children and teachers. Sharing of materials, benefitting from auxiliary programs of music, art, and homemaking, participating in auditorium programs and the recreational programs of patriotic and religious holidays are all possible to a greater extent for cerebral palsied children if their school program is thus logically placed. Administrative costs can be lessened in this respect also.

Typically, the program for cerebral palsied children has developed in a community as the result of parent encouragement. As such it has been started wherever space could be found. The board of education has frequently come into the picture as an active participant after the program was already under way. Both education and therapeutic programs thus have developed separate and apart from regular education. Often, even though the school board actively participates in providing teachers and equipment, such isolated programs are barren and restrictive. Little supervision is provided. Teachers are isolated and are treated as different. Little recognition is given to the fact that these teachers and the children frequently have the same educational problems and needs as the majority of the community's teachers and children. The setting of the educational program for cerebral palsied children is an important consideration. The goal should be to bring it under the same roof as that of a good elementary school for physically normal children.

The educational program for cerebral palsied children will itself be dictated by the children who are enrolled. This will include class size, educational materials, and method. Class size will be determined by the degree of physical disability presented by the various children, the chronological age spread, and the mental age variations within the final group. One teacher can certainly not handle more than approximately ten children. This number is too many in certain instances. Chronological age range within one group should not exceed four years for optimal programing. Similarly, mental age spread should be kept to a minimum in order to permit the children to function as a group insofar as possible. Although one speaks of educating cerebral palsied children as a group, the problem in the majority of instances is an individual one, or one of working with two or possibly three children together at a single time. Individual differences are so marked within this clinical group of children that grouping is nearly impossible.

Often there will be included in the elementary program children of chronological ages above twelve. This results from a number of reasons, i.e., prolonged hospitalization and therefore absence from school experiences, slow achievement rate as the result of borderline normal mentality, or inadequate educational experiences because of the greater need for therapy programs. The presence of such children in a school program requires careful adjustment of learning materials. Few well-adapted educational materials are at hand which at one and the same time have a high interest level to appeal to older children and a low vocabularly level to meet the actual educational age. However, some commercial firms have produced some excellent materials which should have real value to the teacher of this group of cerebral palsied children. Care in the selection of these materials must be exerted, for catalogues are full of over-priced and non-productive gadgetry.

Herein it has been suggested that the location of the elementary program for cerebral palsied children should be in a regular elementary school. For the child who is older than twelve years, educational placement in a building utilized by much younger children presents psychological hazards. Insofar as possible, the group of moderate or severely handicapped cerebral palsied children over twelve years of age should be located for educational purposes in a junior or senior high school building, although, of course, the educational program will be geared to their actual need. The importance of adequate peer relationships cannot be overstressed.

4. *Program for cerebral palsied children with minor physical impairment*

As the severity of the physical handicap decreases, the child can be more and more considered in the same light as the physically normal child. Integration of the cerebral palsied child into the regular school program is, of course, the desired goal. Educational planning for this group of children may take several forms.

Some children will have degrees of physical impairment so slight as to permit them to participate in their own school with infrequent or no contact during school hours with therapeutic facilities. Other children with somewhat more marked degrees of disability may participate in the regular grades of the school building in which the clinical services for cerebral palsied children are located. This permits easy access to therapy programs as needed by the child. He is, however, carried on the registers of the regular classroom teachers and uses the teachers of cerebral palsied children and the clinical facilities only as resources when necessary or when prescribed. Finally, there may be some children with still greater degrees of physical impairment who may be on the registers of the special class for cerebral palsied children, but who move from that class to groups of normal children for some of their educational experiences.

We mentioned earlier that there was a paucity of research in all aspects of the education of cerebral palsied children. Rafael (1973) has described a modest program for multihandicapped cerebral palsied children such as are being discussed here. Unfortunately no quantitative data are provided by the author. Rafael describes an early education program for children who are multihandicapped. Three objectives are cited:

    a. development of the child's potential so that as much independence as possible may be achieved;

    b. amelioration of the "developmental lag created by slow neuromotor development";

    c. preparation of the child for academic achievement in as "normal" a program as possible.

In Rafael's program goals are set and procedures outlined for each child by a team including a pediatrician, psychologist, psychiatrist, therapists, social workers, teachers, and others. Activities are provided which enable the student to use whichever means of learning (visual, tactile, auditory) appears to be most appropriate. A major sub-goal of the general program is teaching the child to deal with the environment, while at the same time adjusting the environment to respond to the needs of the child. This is evidenced by the physical environment of the school which is modified to the needs of handicapped children, but designed as similar as possible to a "typical preschool setting." Also, the children are taken regularly on tours through New York City, where the school is located. The value of standard instrument testing of these children is questioned appropriately by the author, and emphasis is therefore placed on measuring the child's progress over time, taking into account the child's particular strengths and weaknesses.

Parents take an active role in the program Rafael describes. Meetings are arranged and staff members participate with parents at least once a month. At these times parents observe their child in the classroom (each room is equipped with an observation facility) and, when appropriate, take part in classroom activities. Once a year there is a five-day family conference designed to facilitate a better understanding of cerebral palsy and means of caring for the handicapped. While it is argued that a program such as this requires a number of supportive services and a fewer-than-normal number of children in each classroom, it is argued logically that the expense incurred is less than that of long-term institutional care. Furthermore, although the author does not mention it, such a program serves a vital function of keeping the family intact and supporting the family members in a logical and appropriate manner.

The final type of elementary program, i.e., that for cerebral palsied children with psychomotor problems, will be discussed fully in later sections of this chapter.

The Post-elementary Level

As with the elementary level, a variety of types of educational programs will be required for preadolescent and adolescent cerebral palsied children. A self-help type of program will have to be provided for those children who present severe physical disabilities and marked mental deficiency. The sheltered educational program, quite separate in location and different in curriculum materials, will need to be provided for the cerebral palsied child whose intelligence level is higher but still within the range of mental retardation. The severely handicapped, but intellectually normal cerebral palsied child will need at a higher educational level and, appropriate to his more advanced achievement level, the type of program discussed in the previous section of this chapter. Finally, there will be those adolescent cerebral palsied children who will be able to participate in varying degrees in the regular school program of the junior and senior high school.

The social and emotional problems of cerebral palsied children must be kept uppermost in the minds of the educators and others who plan for this group of adolescent children. Inherent in the program of education for the adolescent must be a clear understanding of realistic goals for the post-elementary educational program. Fouracre (1953) states:

1. The adolescent should be physically efficient. He should understand the fundamental facts concerning physical and mental health and disease; should work to improve his own health and the health of his community.

2. The adolescent should understand the importance of the family to himself and society. In this respect we would add to Fouracre's statements the need of the cerebral palsied person for life fulfillment in the areas of human sexuality, and the necessity of families of the disabled person and of society itself to respect and accept the human and civil rights of the individual who possesses long term physical limitations.

3. The adolescent should be guided toward growth in the ability to think logically, to express his thoughts effectively, and to comprehend what he reads.

4. The adolescent should learn through experience the ethical values and principles which are basic to effective life in a democracy.

5. The adolescent should assume his civic, social, and moral responsibilities. He should have learned the basic skills necessary to assume these responsibilities. He should respect the law, accept his civic duties, understand social processes, and enjoy a social life as rich and varied as possible.

6. The adolescent should understand the contributions of science to human welfare.

7. The adolescent should aim to be economically efficient.

8. The adolescent should have resources for the use of leisure time, whether alone or with others.

Fouracre has discussed the nature of the educational program for adolescent cerebral palsied children in greater detail than can be included here. At this point, however, the importance of selective placement and realistic guidance for cerebral palsied children must be emphasized. Education for the cerebral palsied child in the post-elementary level is often terminal education. Disillusionment, frustration, and heartbreak can be avoided frequently if adequate guidance of both the adolescent and his family can be made available during this developmental period. *Guidance personnel who know cerebral palsy and who also know the vocational possibilities for the cerebral palsied within the community must be available.* Guidance personnel without insight into both facets of the problem are more than likely to be ineffective. Guidance of handicapped children is a much more definitive problem than guidance of high school children who are going on to college or of children going directly into the business world upon high school graduation. Guidance of the cerebral palsied child is always an individual matter involving individual assessment and often specific referral to a specific job or type of job. Large numbers of cerebral palsied children will not go on to college. College programs are purposeless for many such youth. Post-elementary school educational programs should be considered terminal for this group of children. Thus, early in the adolescent years, continuous assessment of the child and his potential must be begun in order to prepare for some type of vocational placement at approximately the sixteenth to eighteenth chronological year. Such educational and vocational planning requires that parents be continuously informed and be integral members of the planning group. Often the guidance personnel will spend as much or more time with the parent in seeking a realistic appraisal of the child and subsequent realistic vocational goals as with the child himself. Neither the parent nor the child can be forgotten in this important process.

For the severely handicapped, intellectually normal child, sheltered workshops may of necessity be considered. One of the real challenges in our culture is the intellectually normal or superior disabled child who cannot profit from therapeutic programs and who during his or her entire life span must function on occupational or vocational levels considerably below the mental ability. Realistic guidance with this child and the family early in the life of the child will avoid much tension later.

Some cerebral palsied children, but probably fewer than generally admitted, may be capable of moving into higher educational programs. At the post elementary level, however, great caution must be exercised in this phase of guidance.

Care must be taken to differentiate in the minds of the child and the parents the difference between a liberal arts enrichment experience and college training preparatory to professional pursuits.

STUDIES OF THE EDUCATION OF CEREBRAL PALSIED CHILDREN

Although the sequence of educational provisions for cerebral palsied children is incomplete, we will pause at this point to examine a few studies which have been undertaken in this field. Attention is called to the important study of Dunsdon, which while completed a number of years ago, provides excellent theoretical and quantitative data pertinent to the educability of cerebral palsied children.

Marlow (1968) published a very small survey concerned with the success of spastic children in ordinary school placements after participation in a nursery school program for cerebral palsied children. Ten spastic hemiplegics were studied over a six-year period. Material was collected concerning (a) physical progress, (b) educational progress, (c) social-emotional adjustment, and (d) parental opinions on their child's general adjustment.

The children's physical progress was generally good. Fifty percent of the children evidenced improvement in manual skills in the affected hand. Their physical conditions had not deteriorated despite the discontinuance of the physiotherapy program upon transfer to the ordinary classroom. This is most likely due to the fact that the parents continued therapy at home after the transfer. While only two children showed normal EEGs, five children made good social and emotional adjustment to their placements. The significance of any reference to the EEG is not understood, for its relation to education, social, or emotional adjustment, especially in a population as small as this, is questionable. Marlow concluded that an abnormal EEG is not necessarily linked to poor progress, but this is a tenuous conclusion under any circumstance with this miniscule population. In terms of educational adjustment, five of the ten children made satisfactory progress. One child made satisfactory educational growth, but unsatisfactory socioemotional progress. Another child performed poorly educationally, but satisfactory in the social and emotional realms. Only three parents expressed satisfaction with their children's situations!

Marlow makes some exceedingly equivocal statements in conclusion. In general, his results, he states, were not as positive as had been hoped. Early special education did not appear to him to be supportive of his initial thesis. The ordinary school environments, he feels, are not conducive to the education of persons with special needs. He, therefore, suggests that any child "who shows signs of future possible difficulties in learning to read or write should not be transferred to ordinary schools until a good grasp of these subjects has been obtained" (p. 12). There would be many who would question some of these conclusions in terms of the quantitative data presented and the educational position which the author has taken. This writer would be one of them.

Whittaker (1971), in rather optimistic terms, described an experimental program at the Ontario Crippled Children's Center in Toronto. The Integrated Treatment Unit of the Center combines physical, occupational, and speech therapy with classroom education in order to develop a well-rounded perspective concerning the needs of students with cerebral palsy. This enables the students, according to Whittaker, to see more clearly the connection between therapeutic and academic education. Also, staff persons begin to see the "whole child," not just the aspect of the child which manifests a particular disability.

The program, Whittaker reports, began in 1969 at the nursery class level, and continued in modified forms to higher class levels the next year.

While physical, occupational, and speech therapists simultaneously attended the half-day nursery class sessions, they attended the whole-day upper-level sessions separately. In general, classes became less structured so that therapists could intervene when necessary. This, of course, Whittaker points out, requires much coordination as well as innovation on the parts of teachers and therapists.

The overall reaction has been enthusiastic, Whittaker reported at the time of his publication. Some concern was expressed over the "danger of having too many adults and children in the same room at the same time" (p. 65), and the possibility of disruptive effects of classroom therapy. Still, the author is confident of the beneficial affects of this approach. He notes that, despite the difficulties of quantifying improvements and changes in the children, "there is continuous documentation on the Milani-Comparetti chart" (p. 66) to support his opinion. (The Milani-Comparetti Chart is described in *Developmental Medicine and Child Neurology*, 9 [1967]: 625–30, as an attempt to establish a "routine for studying the motor development of an infant or young child." Subjective observation of activity is the means of investigation employed in utilizing the chart.)

Unfortunately Whittaker mentions neither the ages of the students included in the program, nor the staff-student ratios. While methodologically Whittaker's article presents interesting concepts, statistically and quantitatively, there is much to be desired. One hopes that follow-up data will be presented.

Haskell (1973), in book form, presents a modest article concerned with programmed instruction for cerebral palsied children. The focus of his investigation is on the development of arithmetic skills in England. The study was designed to test the following hypotheses:

1. a. Cerebral palsied children can be taught by programmed instruction.
   b. Programmed instruction will prove more effective than teaching by conventional methods, especially in relation to
      (1) Time taken to learn
      (2) Level of computational achievement
      (3) Degree of pupil satisfaction
2. Children suffering from multiple handicaps will benefit more obviously from programmed instruction than children with single disabilities, because the pace of learning is directly monitored by the child.

Experimental and control groups, according to Haskell, each had five 30-minute sessions per week. Teachers shared time between the different groups in the hope that the influence of teaching styles would be minimized.

Tests were given at the end of each instructional set and at the end of the total program. The results of these tests showed no significant differences in level of attainment, but much more variance within the group taught by conventional methods is reported.

Learning time was somewhat less for the experimental group, but the "mean difference of 152.4 minutes" (p. 65) cited in the discussion is not consistent with figures presented in the results (p. 56). This, in addition to several extraordinarily inaccurate statements by the author in his review of supporting literature, makes one pause in assessing the validity of this writing. Better evidence of the value of using teaching machines is presented by Haskell in the wide range of individual times within the experimental (teaching machine) group for completion of the entire program.

The attempt to assess pupil satisfaction is meager in that teacher reports, rather than student reports, are used. "The neutral climate offered by work with a machine" (p. 66) is cited by the author as particularly advantageous for offsetting the discouraging experiences of failure inherent in the normal classroom situation.

Hypothesis 1a, abovementioned, is supported; empiric support for hypothesis 1b and 2 is not statistically significant. Haskell discussed possible causes for the lower-than-expected impact of the teaching machine. Lack of student familiarity with the new method and inadequate adaptive devices are his particular citations. He fails completely to note the possibility of visual-motor perceptive disabilities in his population of cerebral palsied children which indeed might well account for all of the results he obtained.

Much space is devoted by Haskell to a discussion of the high correlation between good Bender-Gestalt performance and arithmetic efficiency. Haskell's own data, however, show quite a low correlation. Good correlation is shown between the Morrisby Compound Series Test scores and performance on the Southerland and Schonnel arithmetic achievement tests. Consideration is given to the fact that tests which rely on motor as well as intellectual and perceptual abilities are not always accurate measurements of intelligence for individuals with cerebral palsy, is not necessarily an original observation by the author. Also, Haskell cites studies which assess the importance of perceptual and spatial ability for arithmetic achievement. He says that a test should be designed that measures the "(a) perceptual, (b) reasoning, and (c) motor" stages separately (p. 74). "Cerebral palsied children," he states, "may be as good as normals in recognizing and perceiving shapes, but slightly weaker at analyzing the shapes into their constituent parts, but find it quite impossible to reason out how the forms can be synthesized or assembled from separate elements" (p. 74). Much of the literature which Haskell cites in the early pages of his book illustrates this series of statements, but Haskell makes little attempt to relate his findings or opinions to earlier published data. "Combinations of the effects of brain injury and lack of visuomotor and perceptual experiences or an inability to assimilate them . . ." (p. 75) are seen as the best explanation for the correlations he reports between Bender Gestalt, CST scores, and arithmetic success. We could counter that it is not a lack of visuomotor and perceptual experiences, but the basic and absolute presence of visuomotor, auditory-motor, and tactile-motor disorders which have been demonstrated in extremely high percentages of children with cerebral palsy and which serve as barriers to achievement in new learning situations.

A study which might have been helpful in Haskell's analysis of his data is that of a Japanese psychologist and educator, Katsuto Shochi (1971). He studied the relation between cerebral palsied children's abilities to recognize and to reconstruct visual patterns. Three experiments using a block design test were conducted and performances of normal and cerebral palsied children were compared.

The first experiment tested recognition and reconstruction of figures against a plain white background. In the second, patterned backgrounds were substituted. The third experiment tested the ability of Shochi's subjects to reconstruct figures after presentation either of part of a figure or of a figure divided vertically or horizontally. This study is interesting, because Shochi, in his literature review, indicates his awareness of the significant English and United States research in this same field and himself possesses a command of English language so as to be able to extend his study from what has been done into some unexamined areas.

No significant differences between the recognition functions of normal and cerebral palsied children were obtained, although asymmetrical designs were notably more difficult for cerebral palsied children than were symmetrical patterns. Significant differences between the reconstruction functions of the two groups were obtained in the first and third experiments.

In the second experiment, the rate of improvement in reconstruction showed the same trends for both groups, "though the cerebral palsied children's level was greatly lower" (p. 9). Also, reconstruction was made easier for the cerebral palsied children when background consisted of color and lines or only of color. This finding is consistent with those of this writer and his associates, as Shochi notes.

The third experiment showed that reconstruction for cerebral palsied children was significantly more difficult when the design was divided vertically or when one-half or less of the design was perceived. The latter finding can be understood, but the issue of vertical function needs more emphasis, particularly when much of the emphasis educationally with all children is from "top to bottom", then left to right, in teaching the fundamentals of number concepts, handwriting and reading.

No interrelation between motor handicap and recognition function was found. Reconstruction, however, was influenced by the degree of severity of the child's handicap, according to Shochi.

Shochi states that it is "very necessary to (consider) the effect of color in (education) for cerebral palsied children" (p. 10). This statement reflects the opinion of the present writer and his colleagues who pointed out the significance of color in differentiating figure and background, an essential skill in reading and arithmetic functions. Shochi's second major conclusion is that it is important to distinguish tests of recognition ability from tests of reconstruction ability. The relationship between laterality and perceptual motor functioning is seen by the author to be the next subject for his study.

In examining the adequacy of a method of visual examination, Jones (1966) and his associates have provided a preliminary study of reading problems in cerebral palsied adults. Nine years have passed since the "pilot study" was published, and subsequent data implied has apparently not been published. So little data are available in the literature with respect to adult achievement that this study is included here even though the reading problems appear to be the lesser of two aims of the work. This study reports the reading deficits of twenty-eight cerebral palsied adults, all of average intelligence and all reading at the third grade level or better. Eye movements were examined by means of an *electro-oculogram*. The Gates Reading Test was used to measure reading performance (speed, vocabulary, and comprehension). The Gray Oral Reading Test constituted the experimental material employed.

The subjects were divided into two groups, i.e., those who read at the sixth grade level of comprehension or above (Group I), and those whose comprehension was below the sixth grade level (Group II). The data are analyzed in two ways: (a) comparison of the performance of spastics with the performance of athetoids, and (b) comparison of data for those with reading comprehension above or below the sixth grade level. Six subjects had electro-oculogram records which could not be scored for fixations. For the twenty-two subjects who could be adequately scored, no difference existed between spastics and athetoids. The proportion of athetoids was greater in Group I (ten of sixteen subjects) than in Group II (four of twelve subjects).

Reading speed was at least one level below comprehension level in thirteen of the sixteen subjects in Group I. "Disordered eye movements" were evidenced in ten of these thirteen subjects (p. 422). In Group II only four of the twelve subjects displayed disordered eye movements. As measured by the EOG for twenty-two of the subjects (eleven in each group), the frequency of return fixations and regressions increased in those with a reading speed lower than comprehension level. The mean number of fixations was similar for all subjects, except for those in Group II whose levels of speed and comprehension were equally low" (p. 422). These subjects "made an increased number of fixations, as might be expected because of their lower reading level." This finding is little different than those reported for many years in eye movement and reading studies.

Seventy-six percent of those subjects with speed level below comprehension level evidenced disordered eye movements, compared with 36 percent of those whose speed and comprehension were similar.

The authors conclude that, despite the difficulties encountered in attaining accurate measurements for the six subjects with severe cerebral palsy, the results of the study support the use of EOG's in providing information about reading problems in the cerebral palsied, "which is not obtainable by usual ophthalmologic examination" (p. 425).

EDUCATIONAL PLANNING AND PERCEPTUAL-MOTOR IMPAIRMENTS

Chapter 5 of this text is devoted to consideration of the personality characteristics of the cerebral palsied child. Therein several perceptual-motor problems involving visual-motor perception, tactual-motor perception, the figure-background relationship, and others were stressed. Psychologically, many cerebral palsied children, as it was therein discussed, present some or all of the characteristics which are frequently observed in other groups of children and adults with central nervous system disorders. Included are such factors as distractibility, perseveration, dissociation, and disinhibition. These characteristics, based as they are on the specific perceptual difficulties mentioned above and in Chapter 5, have direct meaning for educational planning. The fact that these characteristics exist in a child means that they must be considered with respect to the educational environment, the school program or curriculum, and the specific teaching materials themselves.

Strauss and Lehtinen (1949), Cruickshank, Bentzen, Ratzeburg, and Tannhauser (1961), Kephart (1960), and more recently Cruickshank (1975), among others, have treated this problem. In effect, a highly structured educational program is advocated and has been found beneficial. While the careful reader will be aware of the writer's intent, it must be emphasized that the method which is herein suggested, and which has been referred to in the writings of the authors mentioned above, is not required or appropriate for all cerebral palsied children. It is appropriate for those cerebral palsied children who on psychological tests and through careful clinical observation demonstrate the characteristics being considered.

The Learning Environment

Psychological distractibility dictates that the learning environment for this group of cerebral palsied children (or for other non-motor handicapped, brain-injured children who present similar psychological problems) be as free from stimulation as possible. Under discussion now is the educational setting, i.e., the schoolroom in which learning takes place. This group of children, research has demonstrated, are unable to withstand the impact of external stimuli. This being true, a nonstimulating learning environment must be provided.

Paper may be placed over windows to prevent the child from being distracted by visual stimuli outside the room or building. The room may be built without windows entirely. Some have removed transparent window lights and have substituted translucent or opaque lights. The room itself may be painted a single soft color, including ceiling, walls, floor, and permanent furniture. Pictures and other stimulating materials should be removed from the walls. In certain instances walls next to hallways and ceilings have been sound-treated to prevent extraneous auditory stimuli from penetrating the learning situation. A small room has been found to be more satisfactory than a large room. This means that a room which can be adapted as herein suggested can be more easily located. The goal throughout is not to make an uninteresting room, but to provide a learning environment for the child during those periods when his attention is demanded upon teaching materials.

Upon occasion this writer has used a room intended for other purposes, but which could be completely darkened. A light has been suspended from the ceiling over a desk, the shade of the light permitting a spread of illumination only over the area of the top of the desk. With this single light turned on, the area of the desk has been lighted; the remaining areas of the room stay completely dark. Thus, with this simple mechanism, extraneous visual stimuli have been removed from the perceptive area for the child, and he is able to focus on or attend to only those learning or teaching materials which are placed on the lighted desk in front of him.

In many educational programs, small cubicles advocated by the writer and described fully elsewhere are provided for the child and in these he works with materials which require his undivided attention. Often a single child may be provided for within a group of children by placing a desk and chair facing the corner of a room or in a similar position but behind a screen which temporarily separates him from the activities of the remainder of the group. The teacher will, of course, be cognizant of the importance of a mental-hygiene approach with the child prior to such educational adjustments. This can be treated for the most part in the same way as are adjustments within a school group involving other types of individual differences, i.e., glasses, hearing aids, special rest periods, or special feeding arrangements.

The author is hesitant to make generalizations regarding the learning environment and the adjustments which should be made. The problem is one which must be individually determined in the light of the findings of psychological examinations. An obvious generalization can be made, namely, that when hyperdistractibility is found, attempts to provide the child with a nonstimulating learning environment must follow as a logical corollary.

The Teaching Materials

If the reader will recall from Chapter 5, the characteristics of perceptual disturbances noted in some cerebral palsied children involve four major problems. Adjustment in the teaching materials will be briefly discussed in the light of each of these four factors. A much fuller discussion of the teaching method with brain-injured children which is applicable to cerebral palsy children who also have perceptual-motor disabilities is to be found in Cruickshank *et al.* (1961) and Marshall (1975).

Distractibility

The adjustments in the physical environment of the school have been suggested because, as has been stated, certain children are unable psychologically to refrain from reacting to external and extraneous stimuli. Merely to reduce the number and intensity of external stimuli is in itself not sufficient. If the child reacts in the fashion just described, cannot this tendency nevertheless be exploited to his benefit? Such can be done by reducing external stimuli and increasing the stimulus value of the teaching materials toward which the child's attention is directed. Educational materials of this type are for the most part unavailable commercially. They are therefore teacher-prepared materials. It is doubtful if commercial materials developed specifically for this problem would be feasible, since there are such marked individual differences present and since a given teaching technique needs to be developed for a given child and his problem.

Teaching materials which utilize increased stimulus value are relatively easy for the teacher to develop. If a child is having difficulty writing on a straight line, the difficulty may be alleviated in part by increasing the stimulus value of the paper on which his writing is placed. A colored piece of construction paper on which the teacher has drawn from ten to fifteen straight lines each of a different color may assist the child in attending to the writing activity initially and in continuing his attention for a sufficient period of time to permit positive learning to take place. The writer has found this technique appropriate with a number of children who, when using the commonly employed writing paper, were not sufficiently attracted to the line on which they were to write because the line itself was such a faint color (stimulus) or because there was too much uniformity of color (stimuli) on the entire page. When the lines were of numerous colors and when spacing on the horizontal plane was somewhat irregular, greater stimulation was provided, attention was gained, and visuo-motor learning took place.

The same concept can be carried into the preparation of reading and arithmetic materials (Cruickshank *et al.* 1961). Letters and numbers of different colors, sizes, and shapes can be arranged on a chart or large piece of paper. The multiplicity of stimuli thus presented frequently facilitates attention for a period long enough to assure that understanding and learning have taken place. When learning has taken place and such is demonstrated, the teacher can then move from the highly stimulating teaching materials to more uniform materials. Ultimately, experience has shown that transfer can be made to customary elementary school materials. Frequently, the teacher will find that he will have to use the stimulating teaching materials again after he has moved away from them. This is particularly true in situations involving new learning or a task involving a higher level of difficulty.

Perseveration

Cerebral palsied children who are found to have perseverative tendencies are characterized by the persistent repetition or continuation of a word or sentence or action after it has been begun or has recently been completed. The individuals are characterized by the tendency of any mental formation, once it is initiated, to remain and complete its temporal course. Thus, the visual pattern of a word or letter may have an influence on the recognition of a succeeding word or letter which is somewhat similar or even in some cases quite different from that on which attention has first rested. Ideas embodied in words may in some instances be carried over into subsequent words or sentences by a cerebral palsied child.

Strauss and Lehtinen have suggested the simple technique of placing brightly colored strips of paper between the words of a reading lesson which has been prepared by the teacher (Cruickshank 1975). This technique is employed to disrupt the perseverative tendencies in a child. A child with whom the writer worked benefited by having each word "boxed-in" in a square with a bright crayon. While such a technique will not be effective in every instance, in this situation it assisted the child, aged ten, to be aware of the independence in sound and content of each word to which he was reacting. The technique, often used by teachers for other purposes, of placing a cardboard in which a small hole has been cut over the reading material is effective in connection with the present topic. Only one word at a time is

thus exposed to the child. The influence of other stimuli and visual forma-
tions on the printed page do not then seem to have as important an influence
on subsequent words. Such a technique is also important with some children
in controlling distractibility noted in the preceding section.

Dissociation

Dissociation, as it was discussed in Chapter 5, involves a tendency on the
part of certain cerebral palsied children to break up a combination or a
configuration into parts. From the opposite point of view, such an individual
finds it difficult to conceptualize entities in terms of a whole or a *gestalt*. On
the Rorschach test, for example, there is a tendency to respond to D or Dd
type responses instead of W or whole responses which involve the total ink
blot. Such a tendency has important implications for educational programs
and teaching materials. Whether or not this is a psychological phenomenon
which can be completely overcome through training is unknown. Whether
or not maturation plays a role in this and other factors needs extensive research. It is recognized, of course, that specific or diffuse central nervous
system injury or impairment does not correct itself on a neural basis. It is,
however, the observation frequently encountered that a point is reached in
the development of some brain-injured children at which the psychological
characteristics earlier noted do not demonstrate themselves or do so in
lesser degree quantitatively on psychological tests. Whether this is a
function of learning, some neurophysiological changes, maturation and development, or possibly a combination, is not known. Research of a longitudinal nature involving psychologists and neurologists is needed to ascertain the exact status of this observed trend. This comment is made because it has been observed that specific teaching materials developed with
dissociative tendencies in mind do not lend themselves to progression
toward commonly used materials in the same fashion as suggested in connection with comments regarding distractibility. We do not know whether
one can teach a child not to be dissociative in the same manner as one can
teach a distractible child to attend through the use of appropriate materials
in the appropriate setting. Undoubtedly, a teacher or a psychologist can develop teaching aids which will assist the child during the specific instructional period. This, of course, is important. A further comment should be
made: It is to a certain degree artificial to speak of distractibility, dissociation, and other characteristics as specific entities in and of themselves.
Without question, there is a close interrelation between them. It probably
would be more correct to speak of a syndrome of psychological characteristics and then describe such a syndrome. The figure-background pathology is
undoubtedly in part a function of both distractibility and dissociation.
Dissociation, itself, may be a function of distractibility. Disinhibition may

be a function of distractibility. Thus, to isolate a single characteristic as we are herein doing is artificial and tends to oversimplify a complicated psychological problem.

With the above in mind, comment will be made on teaching materials and dissociative tendencies. In the experience of this writer some children have been assisted in attending to a single concept and perceiving it as a whole if the word, number, picture, sentence, or arithmetic problem is enclosed within a heavy black border. Again, the "peep-hole" technique has been employed effectively. A single problem, word, or sentence is exposed by placing a cardboard cover over the page, with the former having a hole cut the appropriate size to permit exposure of the desired learning material. At the readiness stage, the use of puzzles seems to be helpful. Through these the child learns to conceptualize a whole after actually constructing one out of its many parts. The puzzle technique was utilized with one child in helping him conceptualize arithmetic problems. Each number in a simple arithmetic problem involving addition or subtraction was placed on a separate small piece of cardboard. These he put together following the instructions of the teacher in the correct form, and then proceeded with the arithmetical process required. He had been unable to understand the relationship between the several numbers in the arithmetic problem. Putting the pieces to the problem together one-by-one assisted him in conceptualizing the "whole" problem.

Film strips, single slides, and motion pictures are exceedingly effective. They serve a number of functions. A child who is distractible has all the interfering environmental stimuli removed through the darkness of the room, and he thus attends to the stimulus presented on the screen. A child who is characterized by figure-background disturbances is presented a figure on the screen with no background to present interference. The blackness of the space surrounding the screen and the exposed picture or reading material is so intense that the child's adjustment to the stimulus is facilitated. Similarly, the use of such materials inhibits dissociative tendencies, since the black-white comparison between the projected figure and the darkened room is so dramatic.

Disinhibition

Motor disinhibition, as the term is here used, is the inability of the individual to refrain from reacting to stimuli which elicit motor response. That this is closely related to distractibility and forced responsiveness to extraneous stimuli is immediately apparent. Teaching materials, however, can be developed which exploit the child's disinhibition to his benefit and which reinforce the learning experience.

Practically any motor task appropriate to a given teaching situation is important in this connection. At the readiness level, for example, counting objects, sorting colors, completing puzzles, and other such motor activities tend to reinforce the abstract learning which the teacher desires. Puzzle boxes, in which the child places differently shaped wooden pieces corresponding to various-shaped holes, assists the child in form recognition and utilizes a motor activity in relation to the learning.

Arithmetic problems can be solved by having a single number painted on a small block. The child places the appropriately numbered blocks into a form board and then seeks other blocks which have numbers corresponding to the correct answer and places these in their proper place. Here again, a purposeful motor activity is utilized to reinforce the learning situation. Strauss and Lehtinen refer to boards in which nails or screws have been fixed. The child, in counting experiences or in the solution of simple addition or subtraction problems, places on these screws or nails the appropriate number of wooden blocks. Another situation involves a board into which rows of holes have been drilled. Into these the child fixes screws corresponding to numbers or groups of numbers. In each of these the child employs motor activity in completing a purposeful arithmetical experience. Motor movement is exploited by the teacher to the benefit of the child. Involved in purposeful motor activity, the child does not tend to become distracted through unrelated motor movement.

The learning situation itself should be free of stimuli eliciting motor activities. Unnecessary pencils, paper clips, books, and other materials which can be handled, twisted, moved, or rolled should be removed from the learning situation during periods when the child's attention is required. Here again reference is made to the extremely nonstimulating learning environment discussed in earlier pages of this section. Motor movement inhibits learning if it is not purposeful; motor movement which can be related to the learning reinforces learning.

CONCLUSION

In this chapter we have attempted to outline the variety of programs which are required in every state and local educational district desirous of serving cerebral palsied children and youth. It is a complicated problem, but one which must be dealt with if the human and civil rights of the handicapped are to be recognized and met. The essence of the concept of individual differences is immediately apparent to all who work with these children and young people. To ignore these fundamental psychological, perceptual, and educational differences is to deny an important segment of the individual's birthright.

13

Mental Retardation

ANDREW L. SHOTICK

UNTIL PERHAPS MORE THAN A DECADE AGO, the phrase "education of the mentally retarded" was used in a rather narrow context. It referred to planned programs of learning activities for the educable mentally retarded, i.e., those with IQs within an approximate range of 50–75 and whose prognoses for adult life functions were independent existence. Those programs, emphasizing developmental growth with literacy, were implemented in public schools and schools within institutions for the mentally retarded.

Inherent in the identification of individuals within the mild and borderline ranges of mental retardation as educable was the implication that those individuals within the moderate, severe, or profound ranges of mental retardation were not educable, i.e., could not profit from an education. Lack of educability in this context referred to the inability (because of level of measured intellect) to achieve in the programs as they existed in the schools, rather than to an incapability to learn. Education was specific as to content and the degree to which that content could be attained.

Even for the educable mentally retarded, however, educational provisions throughout the United States were not sufficiently accepted and implemented. Numbers of states in recent years have found it necessary to require through legislative enactment the mandatory provision of educational services.

Comprehensive programming for the trainable or moderately mentally retarded was being developed during these years. In-depth provisions including content, methods, and instructional organization to foster the development of these children and youth were being recommended. Major emphases were in the areas of self-help, communication, and personal and social development. There were few localities, however, where these programs were under the direction and supervision of and supported by public education. The major issue of the time was not really the need for service, but rather responsibility for such service, i.e., health, education, or welfare.

Currently, through mandatory services for exceptional children, public education for the trainable mentally retarded is being extended.

Developmental activities for the severely and profoundly mentally retarded were restricted mainly to scattered efforts of interested individuals in institutions and day-care services. They included attempts at toilet training, feeding, communication, mobility, extinguishing of self-abusive behaviors, and some general stimulation. Many of these activities were of a research or trial nature, rather than a continuation of systematic program efforts. Primary goals remained relief for the family and humane care.

Today, education of the mentally retarded is developing a new perspective. Two issues seem primarily responsible: (a) changing criteria for identification of the mentally retarded and (b) inclusion of mentally retarded children and youth in education.

First, within (a) above is the deletion or elimination by the American Association on Mental Deficiency (1973) of the former borderline level as an identifiable level of mental retardation. Should this action become generally accepted as a basis for placement in special services, a large number of those previously included in special education will be excluded (i.e., those between one and two standard deviations below the mean of measured intelligence).

A second aspect of this issue related to processes involved is diagnosis. In a comprehensive discussion by Cain (1971, p. 21) of this issue at a conference on the placement of children in special education programs for the mentally retarded, it was stated: "Cease labeling children as mentally retarded unless a comprehensive assessment of mental ability, physical health, and adaptive behavior demonstrates a handicap severe enough to justify the designation." Included in such an assessment are factors such as home, out-of-school behavior, social and cultural characteristics, and the individual's primary language. This diagnostic process has the positive effects of providing much information necessary for effective programming and eliminating from special classrooms those who are not retarded—thus reducing the range of necessary educational experiences to be provided.

The second basic issue, that of providing education for all mentally retarded, will have its greatest impact system-wide, rather than within the classroom. In several states, court actions have been initiated to compel public school systems to provide educational programs for all mentally retarded children and youth, including those profoundly and severely mentally retarded. Friedman (1973) reports a case involving the State of Pennsylvania in which the essential ruling prohibited the use of the school code to deny any mentally retarded child access to free public education. The nature, content, and place of provision of this education are not specified, but it is explicit that such a program be provided. Thus, responsibility for the education of all mentally retarded children and youth has been clearly established to be that of the public schools.

Involved with this ruling is an expansion of the conceptualization of education. Reference is made to acquiring a degree of self-care and achievement within the capacity of the child, without reference to previously accepted educational content and organizational pattern and structures. This ruling has, in effect, broadened the definition of education to include all areas of development in which the individual has the capacity to achieve. Thus, education of the mentally retarded now means, or is coming to mean, provision by public education of systematic learning experiences within all areas of human development. As Crosby (1974, p. 3) defined the guiding principle of the Accreditation Council for Facilities for the Mentally Retarded, the basic philosophy of the council's program is that services can and must be provided to meet the developmental needs of the disabled person throughout his life span, "so as to *maximize his human qualities, increase the complexity of his behavior, enhance his ability to cope with his environment, and enable him to live as normal a life as possible*" (italics added).

The above discussion is especially pertinent to the mentally retarded person with cerebral palsy. As is obvious, the more severe the handicapping condition, the less likelihood the provisions of educational experiences. Thus, in the past, with the exception of the so-called cerebral palsy schools, those with severe sensory and motor impairment who were also mildly mentally retarded, and those with mild sensory and motor involvement who were more severely mentally retarded, received little or no formal educational experience. Fortunately, through emphases and actions previously described, these children and youth are also beginning to receive the education they deserve.

IDENTIFYING MENTALLY RETARDED PERSONS

The use of diagnostic or identifying terminology, particularly in reference to behavioral conditions, often results in judgments about and reactions to persons so classified far beyond the real meaning and intent of such designations. In particular, attitudes are often formed which have significant ramifications on the function of that individual in society. Attitudes have been negatively generated toward mentally retarded persons to such an extent that the International League of Societies for the Mentally Handicapped (1968) has declared "The mentally retarded person has the same basic rights as other citizens of the same country and same age." Furthermore, the mentally retarded individual has the right to provision of proper medical care, physical habilitation, education and/or training, guidance, and economic security; participation in all aspects of community life; protection from abuse, exploitation, and degrading treatment; and to fair legal treatment. Thus, the mentally retarded are, first of all, people.

Through the years many definitions have been used to describe various conditions existing in many social, economic, educational and intellectual contexts. The American Association on Mental Deficiency (AAMD) (1973, p. 11) proposed the following definition as most meaningful at that time: "Mental Retardation refers to significantly subaverage general intellectual functioning existing concurrently with deficits in adaptive behavior, and manifested during the developmental period." "Significantly subaverage intellectual functioning" refers to performance which is two or more standard deviations below the mean as measured by a standardized intelligence test, while "adaptive behavior" refers to the degree to which an individual is capable of personal independence and of meeting the social expectations or responsibilities appropriate to a person of his cultural and age groups.

Within the above diagnostic description there are four levels of mental retardation based upon measured intellect *and* behavioral performance: mild, moderate, severe, and profound. On the basis of measured intellect an IQ score which falls two to three deviations below the mean (52–68) would indicate mild mental retardation, three to four standard deviations below the mean (36–51) moderate mental retardation, four to five standard deviations below the mean (20–35) severe mental retardation, and below five standard deviations (less than 20) profound mental retardation.

With the above definitions consideration must be given to activities in daily living and performance pertinent to developmental levels. The nature of activities includes self-help skills, physical performance, communication skills, economic activity, occupational tasks, and self-direction. Achievement levels are related to the degree of complexity and competency level of performance in these areas. Familiarity with the AAMD definitions is a necessity for those involved in evaluations and diagnosis of mentally retarded persons.

It is apparent that optimum performance on intelligence tests or in adaptive-behavior tasks requires a full range of sensory, motor, and communication skills and past experimental opportunity to develop competencies. Great caution must be experienced when making judgments about those individuals with cerebral palsy suspected of also being mentally retarded. Such evaluation should include comprehensive and exhaustive efforts to develop behavior repertoires before a diagnosis is made.

In addition to the above accepted criteria for diagnosis of mental retardation there are areas in the learning process about which questions have been raised concerning the performance of those identified as mentally retarded. Three of these areas are attention, motivation, and memory.

Attention

Many mentally retarded individuals do exhibit attentional deficits, which may be caused by any number of physiological, social, academic, and motivational factors. Careful thought and attention to the nature and origins of the attentional difficulties will assist in devising a number of strategies for acquiring and holding the student's attention.

Both research and common sense indicate that the attention value of a stimulus is dependent upon such factors as its size, intensity, complexity, novelty, color, loudness, and the like; that is, the bigger, brighter, louder a stimulus is, the more likely it is to attract and hold a student's attention. The implications of this concept for the learning situation are obvious; the relevant learning stimuli should be as attractive as possible, with all extraneous stimulation kept to a minimum. This last point has raised some controversy, primarily among distractibility versus non-distractibility theorists. However, Gorton (1972) has studied the effects of various types of distraction upon performance of both intellectually normal and mentally retarded children and found that seclusion from extraneous visual or auditory stimulation of the type normally found in the classroom served to improve performance on simple arithmetic problems. Thus, it seems that reduction of irrelevant stimulation in the classroom should have beneficial effects on attention and performance.

Similarly, in order to learn a specific mode of responding, the mentally retarded child must be confronted with a minimum of competing or irrelevant responses to avoid distraction and learning of incorrect responses. Denny (1966) suggests a number of techniques such as prompting, fading, guidance, and matching-to-sample for the evocation of responses to be learned. He further notes that when the learning context permits, it may be helpful to use barriers initially to inhibit incorrect responses. The use of immediate knowledge of results and differential feedback may also be helpful in minimizing errors in learning.

The use of incentives may also facilitate learning and maintenance of attention. A number of studies have shown incentive motivation to be an effective means of improving the performance of the mentally retarded. It is interesting to note that reinforcement need be neither direct nor continuous. Brown and Foshee (1971), while studying methods for increasing attending behavior among retarded children, discovered that modeling served as effectively as did direct reinforcement in increasing attention to stimuli within the classroom. A word of caution is in order, however, concerning the use of incentives for maintaining attention. The reward may function in the same way as any other extraneous stimulus; that is, preoccupation with reinforcers could serve to decrease rather than increase attention to relevant stimuli. This phenomenon may extend to the realm of social reinforcement, where the child's positive reaction tendencies may be so great as to make social interaction the most salient feature of the learning situation. Nonetheless, with planning and thought, the use of incentives may be a good tool for increasing retardate attention.

Finally, steps must be taken to ensure that the child simply does not become bored with the learning task. Here again, novelty and variety of stimuli presented will help to maintain interest; frequent changes in visual, auditory, tactile, and other stimulus modalities may aid in preventing boredom. Random presentation of different sorts of learning tasks may help minimize fatigue and maintain attentiveness. However, as Denny points out, presentation of too many new concepts may be confusing to the student. It is therefore perhaps best to use simple concepts, at least in initial sessions with a new task, and later increase the duration of sessions and difficulty of the task. It is imperative, if the child shows signs of boredom, that the task at hand be set aside; continued presentation could lead to conditioning of an avoidance reaction to the situation, thus hindering subsequent learning.

Motivation

There is substantial body of literature concerned with motivation of the mentally retarded. It is beyond the scope of this chapter to include a comprehensive in-depth review of the topic. However, some areas of concern should be identified. One such variable is reaction to success-failure as described by Gardner (1958). He obtained data to indicate that intellectually normal individuals exhibited significantly greater increments in performance than did mentally retarded individuals following both success and failure experiences. He further noted that mentally retarded children had a tendency to quit or give up under conditions of failure, whereas their normal counterparts continued to strive for achievement. Gardner interpreted his results to indicate that the intellectually normal child, having experienced failure less frequently, tends to perceive it as unacceptable and as a result strives to improve his performance; whereas the mentally retarded individual, having frequently failed, simply accepts his fate and quits trying.

It appears, then, that the mentally retarded person has a lower generalized expectancy for success than does his intellectually normal counterpart, and is motivated to avoid further failure rather than to achieve success.

Several explanations for this phenomenon have been posed. One is that the mentally retarded students, because of their reduced abilities, experience failure more often during their early years and thus come to expect failure. Another is that, because of the lack of programs appropriate to their intellectual growth rate and level, they experience a greater amount and frequency of failure and thus come to expect failure. For whatever reason, the teacher should be alert to the possibility of this expectation and be prepared to provide appropriate opportunities for success.

A second aspect of motivation pertains to identified and real interests. This concern is particularly evident with those mentally retarded youth whose out-of-school peer group is non-retarded. If they identify school tasks, whether the content or process, as significantly below that of the peer group, a negative motivation may ensue. Similarly, as meaningfulness creates positive motivation for all individuals, the teacher must be aware of the personal, intellectual, and cultural components which in totality comprise the individual mentally retarded pupil.

Memory

The question of deficits on learning and memory tasks by mentally retarded persons has received considerable attention both from classroom and laboratory personnel. The point of concern of today's investigators and educators is not the existence of deficits, but rather, when they are evident, what processes are involved. For example, does the problem involve an inability to store or encode information or a deficient retrieval mechanism? To answer such questions, researchers in the area of mental retardation have had to turn to the contemporary learning theories developed from data obtained on normal individuals.

A short review of the learning literature will reveal that there are in fact many seemingly unrelated learning theories which have been proposed by researchers working in both the areas of cognitive and biological learning. Though there are significant differences between the various theories, by in large the majority have one thing in common; that learning and/or memory is a multiprocess system. Furthermore, through the use of a correlative approach additional similarities may be obtained. For example, Shotick and Ray (1974), by means of a temporal analysis, concluded that the two seemingly dissimilar theories of Ellis (1970) and John (1967) do in fact have marked similarities. Their analysis revealed that learning may involve as many as five separate mechanisms or processes, each of which is operative at a different time after the presentation of information. Considering then that learning and/or memory is multiprocess in nature, which process or processes are involved in the learning deficits observed in the mentally retarded?

Ellis (1970) has developed a three-phase memory model and presented evidence that indicates that the memory deficits observed in the mentally retarded exist in the initial processing phases of memory. Specifically Ellis' model consists of an "attention mechanism," "primary memory," "secondary" and "tertiary memory" mechanisms. He proposes that the transfer of information from one memory mechanism or phase to another, and the recycling of information back through the system (i.e., through the attention process and primary memory) is achieved via "rehearsal strategies." The rehearsal strategy mechanism can be viewed as the "processor" by which information is either transferred from primary to secondary to tertiary memory, or is fed back through the entire system via a feedback loop. Additionally, information to be recycled via the feedback loop may be obtained from either primary, secondary, or tertiary memory. Ellis has proposed that the rehearsal strategy consists of several processes such as attention upon information which is being lost from the different stages of memory; thinking strategies or grouping and organizing devices; and encoding or the transduction of information, e.g., from a visual code to an auditory code. Furthermore, it is as though that "set" or "instructions" may alter the rehearsal strategy in such a way as to alter the transfer of information from one memory stage or mechanism to another. Other factors such as meaningfulness of the experiential input may also alter the rehearsal strategy system.

At this point it should be emphasized that Ellis has interpreted his data to indicate that the short-term recall deficits observed in the mentally retarded are due to deficits in the rehearsal strategy mechanisms. The fact that the retarded either fail to or cannot utilize rehearsal strategies would suggest that experiential input is neither effectively transferred to the secondary and tertiary mechanisms or recycled back through the system for reprocessing. This then would result in the immediate forgetting that has so commonly been observed.

By contrast, the literature on long-term memory in mentally retarded individuals does not reveal the existence of significant deficits.

To further illustrate this position, Robinson and Robinson stated:

> Workers who have studied long-term retention have generally failed to find significant deficits in retarded persons as compared with normal subjects. Contrary to popular opinion, once a retarded subject has learned a response he is about as likely to remember it as is a normal subject, provided, of course, that he has an equal opportunity to utilize the skills and information he has acquired. These findings, even though they have come mostly from laboratory studies, tend to suggest that when retardates do forget what they

have been taught in school, they may not have had an opportu
put their school work to use. A fourth-grade child of average intelligence ordinarily spends a significant part of his school day and
additional time after school in reading book after book; the retarded
child is much less likely to have such extensive exposure to the world
of words. It is not surprising then, if the retarded child forgets more
quickly how to use the words he has mastered in school.*

Such findings are responsible for the emphasis which contemporary researchers have placed upon short-term memory (STM) investigations.
Specifically, if the STM deficit of mentally retarded individuals can be alleviated or at least attenuated, then the overall performance of these individuals may be facilitated to a point nearer to the normal range.

The information presented above, in consideration with information
previously presented pertinent to those with cerebral palsy, identifies an individual not only with all human needs, motivations, and capabilities, but
also one who has a combination of conditions to challenge the best of a
number of therapy-treatment-education competencies. Those who would
serve such individuals must strive to determine attending, to ascertain motivation, and to insure reception, learning, and expression.

EDUCATION FOR THE MILDLY MENTALLY RETARDED

Educational planning and programming require a thorough understanding
of the learner in relation to the learning process. Basically involved in this
process are knowledges of (1) the motivation of the learner to participate,
(2) readiness (developmental capability and experiential background) for
achievement of the particular competency to be learned, (3) a series of
planned experiences through which learning can become a part of the individual's continuing performance. Through research and observation of patterns of development and performance of children and youth for many
years, excellent bases for education have been established.

These programs do not meet the needs for all children and youth,
however. As Cruickshank has stated in defining the exceptional child:

Essentially, an exceptional child is one who deviates intellectually,
physically, socially, or emotionally so markedly from what is
considered to be normal growth and development that he cannot

*From *The Mentally Retarded Child, A Psychological Approach,* by H. B. Robinson and
N. M. Robinson. Copyright © 1965, McGraw-Hill Book Co. Used with permission of
McGraw-Hill Book Co., p. 330.

receive maximum benefit from a regular school program and requires a special class or supplementary instruction and services.*

Although this description identifies a need for program modification, there
is nothing explicit or implicit in the above statement to denote only the existence of differences between "normal" and "exceptional" children or that
basic learning processes differ. Neither is there any implication in the statement of inability to achieve *per se* in a regular program or that goals should
differ. The critical term is *achieve maximum benefit.*

Special education is, therefore, the same process as for the nonexcep-
tional with modifications based on particular conditions in the learner which
have an impact on the learning process. Efforts must be made to provide for
specific behavioral or developmental conditions which exist which require
an educational modification in order to provide a program of greater benefit
to the learner. Certainly, for those students with both mental retardation
and cerebral palsy, the total range of human development (intellectual,
physical, social, and emotional) performance and growth potential must be
identified as clearly and precisely as possible. For the student is a complete
individual, functioning as a result of his or her interrelated capabilities.

Mildly mentally retarded persons are those generally identified as
having capability for independent function in society. Goals for education of
those with cerebral palsy also emphasize independence to a degree limited
only by constraints of the physical impairments of the individual in the environment. It is evident that multi-handicapping conditions reduce the
capability for functioning independently. The concomitant existence of intellectual and physical-sensory impairments requires far greater educational efforts to bring about independence. With individual capabilities as
guides, educational programs should reflect basic goals essential to the purpose of independent function. Implementation of the program, i.e., specific
curriculum content and instructional organization, will require attention to
the slower rate of intellectual growth and the lower maximal intellectual attainment that mentally retarded individuals demonstrate, and the motor
and sensory impairments associated with cerebral palsy.

In order to attend to basic humanism, to similarities of behaviors to
normative patterns, to manifest deficits which exist at the present, to present levels of intellectual growth, and to present rates of intellectual growth
while concurrently being alert for changes in any of the above, a developmental model using the competencies of persons from several different disciplines is recommended by Shotick and Rhoden (1973). Such an approach
includes a comprehensive status description of both developmental level and

---

*William M. Cruickshank and G. Orville Johnson, eds., *Education of Exceptional
Children and Youth,* 1958, Prentice-Hall, Inc., Englewood Cliffs, N.J., p. 3.

process functioning of the individual, based on results of standardized tests and other observations, by individuals from several competency disciplines in areas of intellectual, social, emotional, physical, and language development and from process areas of academic achievement, self-help skills, and vocational performance. Each individual making observations should note performance in all developmental areas. In this manner a comparison of similarities and differences in behavioral performance can be made with reference to type of situation, environment, time of day, persons in the environment, and other factors. Information generated in such evaluations and in discussions during a staff meeting to establish a differential diagnosis provides bases for establishment of the education program.

On the basis of the above, specific objectives for accomplishment by the student should be identified. As a part of this initial program specific instructional and other therapeutic procedures should be outlined with criteria for observation of the student's reaction to the processes detailed. This program is then, in effect, an extension of the evaluation for reasons of checking the validity and reliability of previous information and the efficacy of recommended program activities. Again, all personnel observing (special class and other teachers, psychologist, nurse, counsellor, speech therapist, and/or others) should note the performance in the environment.

After approximately a month, a second staffing should be held to compare initial evaluation data with that developed under the controlled conditions of special services. This discussion should lead to a comprehensive description of the development and performance of the student, the establishment of priorities for treatment, recommendations for processes in providing treatments, and criteria and processes for evaluation.

Language Development

Language performs a major function in the lives of all individuals. Oral communication is necessarily a viable process in which the speaker volitionally attempts to facilitate the reception by the listener and the listener volitionally attempts to understand the speaker, while aiding him by providing feedback relative to his understanding. Effective communication involves a sufficient knowledge of content (or personal awareness of the extent of one's knowledge of the content), competence in the use of linguistic structures, and the capability to appropriately use both in specific situations. All of these requirements can be learned.

There is no research evident to the writer which indicates that language acquisition and use by the mildly mentally retarded varies according to structure, developmental sequence, manner, or purpose from that by the intellectually normal. However, it is accepted that language development parallels intellectual development to some extent and is, therefore, delayed in mentally retarded persons. Possible difficulty with abstractions and lack of intellectual capability involved in concept development and under-standing of connotative meanings are aspects of delayed intellectual de-velopment which have some impact on content in communication. Also affecting language development is the difficulty of mentally retarded in understanding areas of grammar, which are primarily learned incidentally in an imitative rote manner by intellectually normal children.

There are other factors which may have impact on the language perfor-mance of some mentally retarded. Those children from culturally deprived backgrounds may have poorer backgrounds of experience and language models and less motivation to participate in language activities at school, particularly if these activities are of the traditional nature. Failure or other negative experience in school may likewise have a discouraging effect on oral language participation.

With the person who is mildly retarded but who also has cerebral palsy, oral language acquisition may present additional problems. Pro-grams of oral or written language development must be designed around the capabilities of each individual student. For a comprehensive discussion of speech and language problems in cerebral palsy, refer to the chapter by Ruth M. Lencione.

Reading

Reading as a process of acquiring information visually from printed ma-terial is a benefit which most mentally retarded have the capability to achieve. Reading essentially includes word recognition (whether in early stages where children read orally and actually say each word or in later stages where attention is given to broader passages), recalling or deter-mining various meanings of words, understanding the relationships of the words to provide meaning to the present passage, and reacting to the in-formation.

Reading Readiness

The first element in learning to read is development of those processes requisite for the task. These include speech and language, auditory and visual discrimination and memory, perceptual motor skills, and attainment of a sufficient intellectual maturity. Adequate language is of particular im-portance in the beginning stages of reading, especially if the chart story method of teaching reading is used. Use of this method requires students to express their thoughts and dictate stories and read them. If adequate lan-guage is not present, they will fail to read what is written. Language is also an important consideration in later stages of reading involving structural analysis and use of context clues in determination of meaning. Activities should be given special attention with reference to vocabulary development and appropriate sequential use of words to facilitate learning to read. The teacher of the mentally retarded must be especially alert to cultural differences in experiences and language patterns, status of intellectual development including level and possible specific deficits, and personal motivation for participation in language experiences. There is available to the teacher a wide variety of reading readiness tests to measure achievement of the various skills previously enumerated. These, with results of measures of intellectual attainment, and observation of performance on specific tasks, will provide indications for instruction. Readiness exists at all levels of achievement. Therefore, in all areas of instruction, whether it be use of phonics or selecting a central idea, the performance of the student in the sequence leading to ultimate independent function should be explicitly described. This is particularly critical in instruction for the mentally retarded who may demonstrate, because of etiological conditions or a past experience, wide differences in performance abilities.

Motivation

Motivation for those entering a primary program at the beginning or early in school life should present no particular concerns in the early stages of reading. A program planned and implemented in a manner which provides for a successful progression through the various competencies and levels of competencies will maintain sufficient motivation. Special attention may be required for those students who are placed in special classes after some years of experience in regular classes where they have failed in reading; for those students who identify reading materials as appropriate for younger children; and for those in classes for adolescents who see no apparent value of interest in the materials used. These conditions may be obviated through a wise selection of a variety of reading materials; personal counselling in the value of reading and the necessary gradual expansion of difficulty in the process of learning to read; and provision of opportunity to read from meaningful life materials.

Presentation

In the initial stages of learning to read students should first develop a sight vocabulary and the process of reading, i.e., that the words have relationships to each other to form meanings and the left to right orientation of the placement of words. The chart story method has been found to be quite effective for the mentally retarded. It is based on the use of personal experiences and thus provides a teacher with the control of vocabulary. It further provides the teacher with a greater flexibility in phrasing and length of sentences and story. The teacher should have plans for moving to some reading series so that the beginning vocabulary is included in these initial chart stories.

Following this initial procedure, and after the development of a basic sight vocabulary, instruction in word attack skills, fluency, and comprehension should receive stress. As always, the specific objective for each student must be explicit. During oral reading, for example, the teacher may be teaching or checking fluency, vocabulary, or word attack usage. When fluency is the objective, interrupting for sounding out words would interfere with the smooth flow being encouraged; and, at this time it is more appropriate to merely tell some word. With both teacher and student aware of the objective—fluency—the student is not confused when a word attack skill must later be used to identify and say a word.

The appropriate use of several word attack skills should be included in the instructional program to meet the wide range of literacy capability ranging from minimal to near normal in mildly mentally retarded students. In this context word attack includes skills both to recognize and to determine meanings. There are no such skills developed particularly for use with the mentally retarded. The teacher must approach instruction in skills selectively on the basis of success which students demonstrate.

There are those who do not progress beyond recognition of words by sight. Vocabulary may be developed through a number of labeling activities including bulletin board pictures, notebooks containing pictures relating to experiential activities, and items and locations in the classroom; identifying the variety of words used in everyday signs. This process is, of course, restrictive by the very nature of the effort needed both by the teacher and the student to learn a limited vocabulary and provides no means to expand this store once the school program is completed. It is recommended as a maintenance program during a time when efforts within the frustration level of the student are being attempted to develop a systematic method of word determination.

Fernald recommends the use of a training technique for those with severe difficulty in word recognition. The student traces, with finger in contact with the paper, a word written for him. While tracing the word and saying the component parts, the student has tactual and kinesthetic sensory experiences, perceives visually, and has auditory perception. Four senses are concomitantly in use.

Phonetic analysis, if used widely and in a modified form, is a process Kirk reports effective for the mentally retarded. He suggests an approach based on knowledge of a basic sight vocabulary, avoidance of use of rules, systematic instruction, with attention to a special time instructional period, limited introduction of phonic elements, and comprehension and use. If students can develop the use of syllabification, stress marks, and keys to pronunciation, a greater stride toward independence has been derived. Similarly, consideration should be given to instruction in the use of words, root, suffixes, and prefixes. It is critical for the teacher to plan well and include in evaluation not only success and failure, but also the rationale for this particular instructional methodology.

Comprehension skills must be taught as a continuing process in reading. Furthermore, the students must be aware that reading is comprehension and not merely fluent word-calling. They should know when the objective of reading instruction is emphasis on understanding. They should know the elements that comprise the skills: identifying and recalling factual information, relating these facts to each other, and drawing conclusions.

Basically this aspect of the reading process includes competencies such as locating factual information, using context clues, classifying and indexing ideas, sequential ordering, selecting main ideas, and interpreting figurative language. The end result desired is independence in reading a variety of materials. Each of the above are complex response patterns requiring a series of specific singular skills such as identification, memory, comparison, and number.

Instruction involves establishment of a level of comprehension relative to the level of word recognition. This may be accomplished through a combination of commercial reading tests, tests to accompany basal reading series, and informal reading inventories. It is not unusual to find mentally retarded students "word-calling" above comprehension level. At this point specific objectives should be established with the students for particular comprehension skills and instructional procedures for achievement outlined. This should involve attention to the use of these tasks in oral language both to demonstrate the task and to help overcome reaction to the task itself. People do things in sequential order; they relate why they had a good time (central idea); they use exaggeration ("I've told you a jillion times"—figurative language); and they remember what they have seen and heard. As the students realize this, the teacher then demonstrates and relates it to reading materials, selecting those with which the students can have success. It is important in the instructional process for the teacher to be alert to success-failure and to pace instruction at the rate of acquisition. It is the performance of the student and not the format of commercial materials that determines next steps. A further aspect of instruction should take cognizance of the increasing length and complexity of reading passages. The teacher should check continued competence and, if necessary, provide additional direction.

Practice

Opportunity should be provided to read a wide variety of materials in the different formats encountered in daily living: newspapers, magazines, forms, catalogs, and other advertisements. These materials have their own purposes and styles, both of which should be called to the attention of the student.

It has often been the procedure in school settings to provide seatwork or practice following each instructional session. At times students encountered difficulty to varying degrees in independently attempting to cope with these tasks. Practice, to be effective, requires the capability to perform tasks correctly, otherwise incorrect response patterns are reinforced. Therefore, students *should not* be assigned practice tasks unless (1) direct supervision or feedback is available or (2) it is known that the student can perform and with independent practice can develop greater ease, speed, etc. The purpose of practice is to facilitate performance after learning has taken place.

Assignment of practice in the use of reading skills should provide for use of the skills previously identified. In a special class for the mentally retarded this may include special times for practice in which the teacher is available for direct assistance (may mean no practice after each presentation if the teacher is involved with teaching another group); planned use of other students as monitor assistants; and accepted omissions of items where students are not sure. Finally the teacher must be aware of the nature of practice. If the students are practicing word attack skills, it is those skills which are being taught which must be used. If it is comprehension skills, they are the prime emphasis. If it is independence, then understanding is the ultimate criterion. Both the teacher and the student must realize the objective of the specific reading activity, how it is to be carried out, and the criteria for successful performance.

Arithmetic

Arithmetic, as a concept, comprises several elements. Herrick, Goodlad, Estran, and Eberman (1956) described it as quantitative thought, a language, and a system for use of quantitative information. As thought, people raise questions: Who won? Can I afford it? Is it big enough? How much time do I have? As a language there are symbols and words: $+ - \times \div =$, space, time, and measurement. And as a system for handling quantitative thought there are a number system and computation processes for determining comparative relationships. In order to derive maximum benefit from use of this concept all components must be developed to the capability of the learner. Thought must be precise in identification of problems to be solved or considerations given; language must give expression to such ideation; and the system must be understood and applied correctly to provide resolution for situations faced by the individual.

It is obvious that the mildly mentally retarded, because they live independently in society, perform at least at some minimal level of quantitative performance. Similarly, the individual with cerebral palsy and mental retardation will require these competencies. They must get to work on time, give sufficient money to pay for purchases, and drive within speed limits. This does not mean, however, that they live at a level which would be possible provided an optimum level of quantitative performance were developed. Teachers have consistently reported that the educable mentally retarded demonstrate far greater competency in arithmetic computation than in problem-solving. This is comparable to previously reported information in reading, where word-calling or identification is superior to comprehension. For some reason areas of achievement particularly responsive to rote means of attainment seem to be facilitated. The discussion that follows will depart from the format in previous sections on language and reading (readiness, motivation, presentation, and practice) to emphasize attention to concept in the instructional process.

Quantitative thought, in the context used here, refers to the consideration of arithmetic content areas such as time, measurement, money, quantity, and space in relation to meaningful life activities within a framework emphasizing the specificity of quantity usage and the necessity for adequate planning and evaluation for its appropriate use. Using time as an example one must realize it is a *specific;* time for school to begin, to punch in on a time clock, to take a cake out of the oven, and eight hours in a day. The use of time also requires *planning* in relation to values of the individual with regard to time availability and utilization such as amount of time necessary to get to work or to a bus station. *Evaluation* is then necessary. This may include questions not only relating to: Do I get to work on time? but, Should I look for another job that doesn't require so much time to get to work?

Providing expanded concrete experiences with discussion emphasizing each of the above elements, particularly with regard to their relationship to each other and the desired results in activities relating to present performance will help to establish the existence of singular quantitative referent points, the existence of relative values, and the necessity for comparing quantitative similarities and differences. This applies both concreteness and meaningfulness to an area (thought-problem identification and consideration) identified as a specific used for the mentally retarded. Use of this approach is recommended for the various areas of measurement (distance, weight, volume, liquid, and speed); money; and quantity (generic concepts of enough, too much, not enough in reference to specific value). It should be initiated as a directed activity (planned with reference to readiness, motivation, presentation, and practice) as soon as students begin to express awareness of such conceptualization and continued throughout the school experience. Much of this instruction should be carried out through planned participation experiences with little so-called seatwork.

The second element as originally included, language, is a necessary component of both the above, and the third element (system) to be considered later. Actually, all three are integral and concomitant components. It is through language, however, that expression is given to thought. Efforts should be made to teach the mentally retarded to express, to state problems as precisely as possible. Given the task of getting to a bus station on time involves getting oneself ready, packing, traveling to the station, buying a ticket, and boarding. There are included in this task specific clock times, i.e., to start getting ready, to begin packing, to leave home, to arrive at the bus station, and to board the bus. These are times to determine and identify. There is planning or judgment regarding elapsed time, i.e., how long to get ready, how long to pack, how long to be in transit to the bus station, how long to buy a ticket. Though these may be appropriately designated as thought they must also be expressed, even though only to oneself. Therefore such language use as early, on-time, late, delayed, extra time, clock time, time to start, time to leave, amount of time, specific numbers, and processes of accumulations of periods of time toward a future time or in reverse from a future time will contribute toward a more optimum function. Some of the difficulties that mentally retarded have with story problems undoubtedly arise because of reading insufficiency, but story problem and comprehension difficulties are also related to lack of facility with the language of arithmetic. Emphasis on the development of the use of arithmetic language should be reflected in the specific instructional objectives prepared by the teacher, in the instructional program presented, and in the evaluation used.

Finally, the arithmetic or number system provides the process or means to resolve quantitative matters in living needs. Ultimately this means an understanding of the number system and competency in the use of the computational processes. Certainly, in the development of the above a rich use of concrete, meaningful experience is desirable. But, just as it is inappropriate to teach numeration without reference to meaning, it is inappropriate to expect to teach all specific applications in the use of quantity. It is the guarded opinion of the writer that the seeming difficulties some mentally retarded have had in learning arithmetic have resulted from delayed placement in special services with the negative concomitants of instruction too early for success in ideation but some limited success in computation.

The going back later to teach some material then elicits a negative attitude toward such instruction resulting again in lack of success.

Instruction in arithmetic begins, as with all pre-academic readiness, with development of comparison discrimination. Students should learn to see similarities and differences in real objects: leaves, sticks, animals, etc.; they then progress to classes and properties of objects. With this capability established, efforts are made to compare and differentiate groups of objects on the basis of mass or number without reference to numeration. Number identification, rational counting, and computation (adding, subtracting, multiplying, and dividing) follow as a natural course. Teaching of arithmetic, quantitative understanding and use, must begin with the understanding of relationships. Instruction is specific. As Tisdall (1962) has related, if productive thinking receives emphasis, it can be developed in the mentally retarded; and as Richmond and Dalton (1973) have concluded, teachers' perceptions give direction to their emphases. Teachers should, therefore, emphasize the complete spectrum of quantitative thought, language, and number system.

Social Adjustment

Social behavior, defined essentially as interaction between individuals, might be characterized as existing on two different continua:

Depth of relationship	Nature of relationship
familial	legal
personal (positive or negative)	responsibility
occupational	moral (ethics-religion)
casual	personal need

These continua are developed and manifested through learning and adjustment. A major element involved in learning and development involves such maturational stages as ego-centrism, parallel play, cooperative play, heterosexual, and adult adjustment. Over these maturational factors, cultural determinants such as attitudes, values, and particular dynamics of the home, peer group, schools, and other institutions function to develop particular behavioral expectations and manifestations. Finally, the factor of the personal adjustment of the student bears a major impact on his acceptance or rejection selection (whether volitional or nonvolitional) of particular social interactions.

A description of specific patterns and individual social behaviors presently within the interaction repertoire of the student should be prepared. This should include both those behaviors present and appropriate and inappropriate and those which developmentally might be expected but are absent. Notation should be made relating to their appearance in group or one-to-one situations, with peers, with adults, in the several different kinds of social situations, and particular conditions in the situation which had reference to the student.

Further, efforts should be made to identify the range of knowledge regarding social behaviors including the variety of possibilities across situations and within particular situations and knowledge of how to select activities for these particular situations. This should include his knowledge of acceptability and non-acceptability and the values he places on the meaning of acceptability and non-acceptability. All of the above should be considered in reference to efforts to initiate interaction or to react to such efforts by others. Finally, it is of value to understand which particular behaviors have been taught (by whatever source); which arise because of efforts to imitate others; and which are the result of personal adjustment.

Discussion should be of behavior development rather than maladjustment. Initially the teacher should specify the particular behavior desired in reference to the situation with notation pertaining to necessity for concurrent reduction or elimination of a present behavior. Plans should then be implemented to teach the behavioral skill including practice in situations where it should occur. Too often the teaching of social behavior is approached through observation and discussion rather than participation. The same dynamics of instruction (motivation, readiness presentation, and practice) should apply. For example, is the student developmentally ready for cooperative or heterosexual activities? Has the student developed an awareness that appropriate social behavior reduces embarrassment, avoids conflict, puts others at ease, or shows respect for values and actions of others? What have been the past opportunities of the student to interact socially, under direction or independently? What has been the nature of past efforts to teach or develop social interactive behaviors?

Situations may be arranged in the classroom to role play riding on a school bus, talking to sales clerks, or being interviewed for jobs. This may then be extended to real situations with community members coming to the class or class members visiting and participating in actual situations. Field trips may be arranged specifically to observe reactions of people on the street, in public buildings, in a variety of work or recreational settings. Students may be video-taped in their actions and interactions and later view, evaluate, and discuss their performances. It is of paramount importance, as with all learning, that the end result is utilization. As teachers provide reading material, arithmetic problem solving, and use of spelling and language outside the specific instructional period, so should provisions be made in social behavior. Instruction, including discussion, may begin in the classroom but should expand to involve participation in the community where independent living takes place.

Finally a caution should be expressed regarding development of over-dependency or over-protection for the mentally retarded. In efforts to obviate one form of negativism toward the mentally retarded (unrealistic high levels of expectancy for achievement and behavior) another form has been engendered (an unrealistically low level of expectancy). Attention must be given to the development of appropriate independence in action including means of questioning authority rather than total dependence on authority. In effect, if the mentally retarded are to function socially in society, they require the total range of knowledge, attitudes, and competencies necessary.

Personal Adjustment

Personal adjustment refers to the individual's self-perception, particularly of his or her integrity and value, and his or her relationships with individuals and events in the environment. Integrity includes the physical self and preservation of life, safety, and comfort, while value includes areas such as respect, affection, and merit. As the individual strives to meet these conditions, either consciously or sub-consciously, he or she meets varying degrees of success or frustration and also perceives his or her performance and the acceptance of that performance in comparison to that of others. It is on the basis, then, of the person's perception of these events that personal adjustment develops. It is important to emphasize *the person's perception,* for whether a condition actually exists or is only perceived to exist, the individual acts as if it exists. Through these perceptions of interpersonal dynamics behavioral manifestations of fear, anger, aggression, withdrawal, jealousy, anxiety, frustration, self-worth, affection, approach, and love develop.

There is no evidence to indicate that greater numbers of the mentally retarded manifest personal maladjustment. They do face conditions because of their mental retardation which may lead to non-adjustment: failure in school, lack of acceptance by parents, being identified as mentally retarded, too high expectancies, or too low expectancies. Though in-depth therapy is more appropriately the responsibility of school psychologist, social worker, counsellor, and crisis intervention teacher, there is much that these same personnel can do in assisting the teacher to recognize symptoms and developing patterns of non-adjustment; to identify behaviors, which though negative, are of a casual or situational nature; and to learn to intervene with counselling or behavioral control reactions. Additionally, and of equal merit, the educational setting can be used to foster positive adjustment through direct teaching.

First, the teacher must know the personal adjustment of each of the students with reference to specifying in activity planning whether the objectives are maintenance and expansion of positive development or ameliorating negative development while concomitantly redeveloping positive adjustment patterns. The environment and activities are then ordered to provide support to facilitate attainment of the goals. This will require of the teacher basic respect and trust for the students; sufficient preciseness in instructions to reduce ambiguity; instruction for the students when situations arise in which they are not certain (completion of task, tasks which appear to be or are too difficult, new situations); and providing activities which are purposive for the students.

Initially, then, students should learn that all individuals have the same basic needs; that they may be met differently in different people and in different situations; that the means of meeting them are learned. Safety, for example, is an area where much information has been generated and laws enacted for its preservation. Yet performance in such behavior ranges from those who fail to meet even minimal recommendations in their living pattern to those who are overly cautious. A variety of foods are eaten to maintain health. To develop respect or self-worth, particular occupations are selected, activities participated in, companions or associates chosen, or numbers of activities or quality of participation valued. The means selected are done so because of learning experiences in families, schools or other institutions, peer groups, etc.

Efforts to meet human needs are often met with frustration which must be overcome. A variety of coping mechanisms may be used to reduce the effects of the difficulty including other methods of approach, selecting substitute goals, or use of withdrawal or aggressive behavior to reduce tension. The mentally retarded may face frustration of meeting self-worth through failure in school, being identified as mentally retarded, and placed in special services where these are not accepted by students, faculty, and administration. They may accept the identification and placement and under guidance strive to achieve. They may not accept the placement and through indirect behavior such as cursory efforts in achievement attempt to withdraw. Or, they may manifest aggression through acting-out behavior toward others in class or school.

Other sources of conflict in goal striving include situations where goals of individuals are in apparent opposition and the use of striving mechanisms which are incompatible or non-acceptable. Several want to be first, different activities are desired; or the teacher wants it quiet and a student wants tension release. Choice of words to express feelings vary in different cultures; expressions of happiness range from a suppressed smile to loud vocalisms and back slapping; and anger may be expressed with sarcasm, verbal thrust, or physical actions.

Studying the behavior of others and themselves in an atmosphere that in itself is positive will provide support for the development of security and self-respect. The following is suggested for planning and implementing program efforts in personal adjustment:

1. The teacher should know not only the adjustment of the student but also his or her capability for observing and discussing personal adjustment.

2. Situations within the capability of the students to note and react to personal interactions across the spectrum of the adjustment process should be prepared for presentation. These will include information from single pictures and pictures in sequence from magazines, newspapers, and commercial educational material; films; videotapes; stories; and personal observations of life situations.

3. From the discussions draw relationships of behavior shown to impact on those involved. As appropriate in a classroom situation (to teach and not open up possible negative personal reactions) relate these to activities of students in the class, school, and community.

4. These discussions may be expanded into participating activities such as puppetry, dramatization, and role playing.

Much of the above requires verbalizing concepts and drawing inferences from verbal expressions, areas where the mentally retarded may have difficulty. It is therefore well to plan, implement, and evaluate carefully and critically the participation of the students particularly for possible negative impact on adjustment.

Occupational Adequacy

Occupational adequacy may be defined as having those skills or competencies which provide the individual with the capability for independent support and those for whom he or she may be responsible, through earning capacity and efficient use of those earnings. These tasks include getting a job, holding a job, and meeting one's financial responsibilities. Inherent in these tasks are certain academic performance capabilities, personal and social adjustment, physical well-being, and all other factors which have impact on performance. This program is carried out in the public schools as the joint education-rehabilitation efforts of the cooperative work-study program. Though it may be implemented in various locales and states in a somewhat modified format, it entails establishment within a secondary school (for students beginning at ages either 14 or 16 CA), the cooperative efforts of a vocational rehabilitation evaluator, vocational rehabilitation counselor, and special class teacher. Three essential elements comprise the program: evaluation, education, and counselling.

The evaluation aspect is comprehensive in nature including status, and in some instances process, in psychological, medical, educational, and work-related areas. Assessment of intellectual and adjustive behavior are both part of the psychological evaluation; intellect to verify a diagnosis of mental retardation if not previously established and to indicate possible areas of relative strength; and adjustment to identify latent factors and to help understand the presence or absence of behaviors. The medical evaluation provides information pertinent to general well-being, physical conditions which may need and can be ameliorated, and conditions which may facilitate or be restrictive in mobility and employment functions. Evaluation of educational competency provides for general academic proficiency but more specifically emphasizes performance in reference to use in daily living and work-related areas. Both the special class teacher and vocational rehabilitation evaluator will participate in this phase of the process. Personnel from all three areas—education, evaluations, and counselling—provide input into evaluation of work-related areas which includes both status and process. Present level of performance in coordination, dexterity, speed, and stamina; use of tools, machines, devices, and materials; following directions; and making self-judgments regarding quality and acceptability of performance are necessary. However, of at least equal value is the capability of the student to improve under direction. This latter aspect becomes a part, then, of the instructional program which identifies conditions under which the individual can and will learn those tasks which will permit him to develop occupational independence.

A comprehensive education program in this service includes education and rehabilitation personnel through academic work in special education, work-related skills in shops and classroom, and work experience in the school and in the community. Some activities (locating and applying for a job) may involve all personnel identified earlier. Instruction in academic areas should emphasize reading, language, and arithmetic. Reading of various kinds of forms an individual must complete in adult living such as job applications, social security, health and insurance; meaningful information sources such as news media, traffic regulations, shopping guides; and recreational matter comprise essential elements. Stress in language programming has reference to demonstration and participation in job interviews, understanding directions, asking questions, and reporting progress on job tasks. Arithmetic instruction should focus upon such factors as payroll, how to spend money wisely, and application of concepts of time and measurement to daily function. As the student progresses through planned activities of observation and participation in meaningful young adult experiences, the use of quantitative expression will be reinforced. Work-related aspects of the program are specific to activities involved in (1) knowing oneself in relationship to particular occupations; what task and competencies are necessary and which ones does the individual have; (2) knowing how to locate jobs; what sources are available and how are they used; (3) knowing how to apply for a job; use of telephone, letters, personal interview; and (4) knowing how to keep a job; expectancies of employers and how to handle contingencies which arise.

The counselling phase begins upon entrance of the student into the program and continues through eventual placement in the competitive world of work to provide support in independent functioning. It may take the form of individual or group counselling to foster more effective personal and social adjustment; in applying to specific situations those competencies learned generally; or providing assistance in developing an integrated life style based on the elements as taught in the program.

The educational program for those with mild mental retardation is, then, one to develop competency for essentially independent living. The goal should remain so for those with cerebral palsy to the extent possible. The intellectual capability for learning competency development and judgment-making mandate this; with the participating of professionals from occupational therapy, physical therapy, nursing, rehabilitation, and others as indicated, a meaningful therapeutic program can be developed. Severity of additional impairments may eventually indicate somewhat less than independent living. This is a decision that should be accepted only after extended and exhaustive education and rehabilitative efforts.

EDUCATION FOR THE MODERATELY MENTALLY RETARDED

The moderate or trainable mentally retarded (TMR) child is generally characterized as the school-aged whose IQ falls within the moderate range of mental retardation, approximately 35 to 50. His mental development proceeds at a rate of about one-third to one-half of that of the intellectually normal child, and as an adult he may be expected to have attained a mental age of 3.5 to 7.5 years. Retarded intellectual development is typically the result of some organic defect—mongolism, phenylketonuria, microcephaly, cretinism, and other prenatally determined factors, brain injury or dysfunction, and the like—rather than of an endogenous deficit, although exceptions do exist. Characteristically deficits are manifest in all areas of adaptive behavior: motor coordination is impaired at both gross and fine levels; communication abilities are severely limited; and social skills are immature and inadequate. Mastery of, or self-sufficiency in, basic academic skills cannot be expected. Nonetheless, the trainable mentally retarded child can, with training, acquire many of the skills basic to daily adult functioning, and can learn to perform a variety of tasks which will be both socially and economically useful to the person, the family, and the community.

Until the 1950s few formal programs existed for the TMR-level child outside the residential institution. The early part of that decade, however, witnessed a growing interest among professionals in the utility, feasibility, and development of school programs for the trainable pupil. This interest, coupled with public and parental concern for maintaining the mentally retarded individual within the community, has led to a significant increase in the number of such programs, as well as growth in quality. The trainable mentally retarded child is no longer invariably dubbed "uneducable" and warehoused accordingly; the child's needs are now being considered and met; the potentialities explored and developed.

The majority of existing school programs for TMR-level children has grown from what was once the case, simply "watered down" versions of standard classroom curricula and from efforts to duplicate the format of classes for the educable mentally retarded. The trainable pupil, because of his or her moderately limited abilities, can profit little from exposure to traditional academic subject matter, and most educators and parents feel that it is far more important to concentrate on those skills which should aid the child in becoming more socially adept and economically useful. More precisely, in training the TMR child, emphasis is placed primarily on developing those skills which are essential to his or her adjustment to, participation in, and acceptance by society as a whole. For example, a typical curriculum for the trainable mentally retarded might include communication skills, including speaking, listening, word recognition, and perceptual skills; self-help skills such as eating, dressing, personal hygiene, grooming, and self-awareness, social skills such as respect for others, cooperation, obedience, courtesy, etc.; and vocational skills, including household chores, specific skills, and personal economics.

Just as the subject matter suitable for the moderately retarded student differs from that used with intellectually normal and mildly mentally retarded students, the instructional program also requires adaptation for the trainable child. Traditional classroom methods emphasizing the development and application of generic and abstract principles are of little use to the child whose mental abilities and communication skills are limited; they are therefore replaced to a great degree by demonstration and specific competency reinforcement. The child is taught to function efficiently rather than to attempt to comprehend the subtleties of his functioning; although it is desirable to have the child understand the importance of a particular task, and the need for his mastering it to the degree that he can, this insight may often be best attained through the child's application of a newly learned skill. Behavior modification or operant conditioning principles find direct application in the training of the TMR-level child; extensive use is made not only of the principles of reinforcement and extinction but also of such techniques as prompting and fading, shaping, and chaining. The trainable child profits little from solely verbal instruction, but learns most easily by being shown and assisted with verbal mediation. Similarly, the child seldom "picks up" a skill which others may have performed in his or her presence; tasks must be directly demonstrated, guided, and repeatedly practiced before they can become an integral part of the child's behavioral repertoire.

Planning for the child's school day must take into consideration needs and handicaps, whether educational, social, or emotional. Many potential classroom problems can be remedied through a well-planned, structured day, a well-equipped classroom and an able, well-trained teacher. Problems created by the prevalence of short attention spans, hyperactivity and distractibility may be minimized via a variety of activities, none prolonged in time, with proper alternation of active and quiet periods; effective use of attention-getting classroom aids, along with reduction of other possible distractors; active efforts to draw each child into the group activity and to maintain his or her attention; and a variety of other techniques. Proper application of behavior modification techniques, along with close attention to each child and his or her reactions, can go far toward maintaining an orderly classroom from which the child can derive greatest benefit. Similarly, careful observation by the classroom teacher, coupled with the assistance of other specialists and close parent-teacher communication, is invaluable in identifying and rectifying individual problems of adjustment.

In sum, then, we see that school programs for the TMR child involve a variety of objectives and activities, each designed to facilitate the child's adjustment to and efficient functioning in society to the best of his abilities. It may be helpful at this point, in terms of developing a more thorough understanding of the goals and methods of training for the moderately retarded individual, to examine some particular objectives of training programs, the skills required of the child attempting to meet these goals, and techniques by which those skills may be taught.

Language and Communication

The trainable mentally retarded child may enter the school program with severely limited communication abilities. One of the primary objectives in any TMR classroom is, then, the development of adequate communication skills. Communication training is an integral part of every comprehensive curriculum for the moderately retarded, and includes such skills as receptive language, oral communication, object recognition and perceptual training, and functional reading and writing.

Receptive Language

This area is vitally important, for without the ability to listen, comprehend, and react no child could function in the classroom or in social situations. Although most, if not all, trainable children have learned through their home experiences to respond to commands or requests and to pay at least minimal attention when addressed, it is of value to extend these kinds of learning experiences to the classroom. Daily classroom routine, with the delegation of responsibility for distributing and collecting materials and cleaning up, the teacher's direction of classroom activities, the children's interactions, and participation in games and songs requiring student reaction provide ample practice in following instructions. Listening to stories and songs and engaging in show-and-tell and group discussions provide additional practice in listening and responding. In terms of long range goals, these activities should help the individual, not only in terms of ability to follow instructions and to respond appropriately to commands in his later educational and occupational environments, but also to converse with others and to enjoy music and other forms of entertainment.

Expressive Language

Ability of the child to express him or herself is also of vital importance to the child's adjustment in home, school, and community. Baumgartner (1960) stressed this need by pointing out the frustration often faced by those unable to make themselves understood by others. Children differ considerably in their expressive ability upon admission to the TMR classroom. It is the teacher's responsibility to encourage them to speak and to reinforce every effort at communication, whether it be an appropriate response, imitation of others' vocalizations, or, in the case of the severely language-deficient child, mere babbling. Language development should have emphasis over speech correction. It is more desirable that the moderately mentally retarded individual be able to express him or herself (with some minimum of understandability) in a variety of situations, than that the child's speech be perfectly articulated but severely limited in terms of its applicability.

Almost every classroom situation offers opportunities for language development. Perhaps the most effective stimulus for pupils' vocalization is the language of the teacher; to elicit responses most effectively, the teacher's speech should be clearly articulated, short and simple in structure, and concrete in terms of vocabulary. A number of classroom activities may serve more specifically to develop speaking skills: simple word games, singing, recitation, show-and-tell, and other class discussions are only a few.

Object Recognition and Perceptual Training

These tasks are included in the language curriculum for the trainable mentally retarded for a number of purposes, including increase of functional vocabulary, development of awareness and understanding of the physical environment, and preparation for learning word recognition and writing skills. Ultimately such training should help the child function efficiently at home and in the classroom. Activities which contribute to the realization of these goals are as diverse as the goals themselves: simple word games such as "Simon Says" or "I Spy," artwork, music activities, show-and-tell, field trips and consequent class discussions, as well as more formal instruction with materials specifically developed for these programs. A number of techniques and methods have been suggested for ensuring success with the latter. For example, presentation of only one object or concept at a time is imperative to avoid confusion; motor activities may be paired with verbal responses to ensure that the child grasps the meaning of his or her verbalization (motor responses later being faded); presentation of a variety of stimuli possessing the salient property both prevents discrimination based on irrelevant characteristics and promotes generalization of learning.

Reading and Writing

The value and feasibility of regular programs in reading and writing for the trainable mentally retarded has been a subject of much debate. While some maintain that the moderately retarded child can and should attain a second or perhaps third-grade level in these skills, others argue that such achievements, if they are indeed possible, would require so great an amount of time and effort in terms of their relative usefulness as to be prohibitive. There is general agreement, however, that at least some word recognition and reproduction skills must be taught if safe and efficient function in the community is to be attained. Competencies generally considered essential are the ability to recognize signs and directions related to safety and social functioning (e.g., "danger," "poison," "men," "women," "stop," "exit," "hot," "cold," "slow"), to recognize and reproduce his or her own name and address and the names and addresses of other people and places which he or she might need to know, and to recognize words which would facilitate independent functioning (such as those related to the pupil's particular vocational skill, labels, and the like). It might also be desirable to develop a simple reading and writing vocabulary of familiar words or phrases, so that the individual can read simple instructions and write short letters. A number of classroom activities may facilitate such acquisition: games and songs using visual aids, filmstrips, "field" experiences, books, charts, dramatizations, and a number of other techniques may be utilized in conjunction with more traditional approaches. As in teaching other skills, however, it is best to present only one concept at a time to avoid confusion; to break the learning task down into component parts (e.g., the child attempts reproducing his or her full name only after mastering writing only his or her first name); to guide the child as much as is necessary during early learning experiences with later fading of assistance; and to present short, frequently repeated learning opportunities to avoid frustration and maintain motivation.

To summarize, communication is a vital part of every individual's daily life, and deficits in the areas of oral and written language are severely limiting. Language curricula in school programs for the trainable mentally retarded are therefore designed to anticipate difficulties which the student may face and to prepare him or her to cope with a variety of social situations efficiently and with confidence.

Self-Help Skills

Intellectual limitations and poor motor coordination restrict or delay development of these tasks. While intellectually average children simply "pick up" or "figure out" the process of putting on a coat, brushing their teeth properly, or using a napkin, the trainable mentally retarded child usually requires specific, detailed instruction. Although parents may make strides toward accomplishing such instruction, they often lack the time and knowledge to have fully trained their children by the time the child is enrolled in special classes. This situation has led to the incorporation of self-help training into school programs. Mastery of self-care habits not only makes the child more pleasant to be near and more independent of those who care for him, but also imparts to him a sense of accomplishment, maturity, and personal worth.

Skills subsumed under the general term "self-help" are numerous and diverse. Most programs stress: personal hygiene skills, such as washing, toileting, brushing teeth; dressing and grooming (including putting on and removing clothing, shoes, and wraps, and combing and arranging the hair); care of personal belongings; eating habits, encompassing diet, food preferences, proper rate of ingestion, table manners, and preparing and cleaning the dining table. This is, of course, only illustrative; other skills may be included according to the needs and abilities of the pupils.

The primary method of teaching self-help skills is simple habit formation; the child learns that in certain situations he or she carries out a particular set of operations. This is the area in which principles of operant learning are most directly applied; techniques of guidance, prompting, shaping, and chaining, along with the use of incentives and positive and negative reinforcement, are the most popular and effective teaching methods. Skills to be learned are generally broken down into their smallest component parts. Each step is learned separately and sequentially; the components are chained together as new ones are mastered, until the entire sequence can be performed. Demonstration and guidance are usually necessary as new tasks are being introduced, but are faded as the pupil develops the ability to perform the task unassisted. Verbal instruction should be minimal and used primarily as a stimulus for the child to perform a specific duty. When used in conjunction with demonstration, they should be task relevant (e.g., "button coat," rather than "do this"). Motivation is an important consideration, and it may be helpful occasionally to make some reward contingent on the child's performance; for example, the child might be required to button a jacket before going outside to play, or to wipe the mouth before being given dessert. However, every effort must be made to make learning experiences pleasant and to avoid undue pressure on the child.

Within the sub-area of personal hygiene, the establishment of daily routines is perhaps the most significant additive to the above procedure. Within the limits of individual differences, specific times of the day should be set aside for toileting, with handwashing becoming habitual following a visit to the bathroom. Similarly, washing hands before meals, brushing teeth afterward, and other routines become habitual with time. Trainable mentally retarded children can learn with prompting and practice to use a handkerchief, bathe regularly, care for menstrual needs, and perform other regular or periodic activities.

Skills involved in dressing and grooming, however, may be slightly more complicated and therefore require more practice. Practice boards or models aid in the development of motor skills necessary for fastening and unfastening clothing and lacing and tying shoes; oversize clothing may facilitate initial learning of dressing skills. Color codes attached to clothing may be useful in introducing the concepts of inside and outside, back and front, left and right, and top and bottom, as well as in reducing shoe-lacing confusion. Individual lockers and hangers promote pride in learning to care for clothing properly. In addition to these skills, older children may be interested in learning make-up skills, shoe care, nail care, and more extensive clothing care.

Eating skills, because of limited opportunities for practice, may be somewhat more slowly and laboriously developed. Nonetheless, through the teacher's demonstration of, insistence upon, and reinforcement of such behaviors as proper food ingestion, diet regulation, manipulation of utensils, and use of napkins, these skills can be mastered by most trainable children.

Other activities—preparation and clearing of the table, nutrition studies, dishwashing—may be desirable for older trainable children.

In sum, then, the TMR-level child enters the classroom with only minimal skills in caring for his personal needs. With detailed instruction and practice, however, he can become quite self-sufficient in many respects. This accomplishment is quite desirable not only in terms of social and health concerns, but also as a means of imparting to the child a sense of accomplishment, self-direction, and personal worth.

Social Skills

With the recent trend among parents toward maintenance of the moderately mentally retarded child in the home and community, rather than institutionalization, it has come necessary to teach the trainable child to function acceptably in social situations. Many TMR individuals in the past have failed to develop competency in social behavior primarily because of programmatic efforts which have not taken into account their levels of intellectual development and capabilities for learning. Because of this failure, the average TMR individual has been sheltered and excused from adequate social performance because of retardation. It has now become the task of the school program to teach the social skills which will be necessary for him or her to function easily at home, in the community, and on the job. Included in this category is a wide range of "other-directed" behaviors: courtesy, cooperation, giving and receiving assistance, obeying rules, sharing, and other social interactions. It is also desirable that the child obtain as thorough a functional understanding of our social system (i.e., home, family, community, public servants such as policemen, doctors, bus drivers) as is possible.

In teaching these skills, the influence of the teacher's model is invaluable; many habits, such as following "yes" with "please" or "no" with "thank you," may be acquired through imitation and modeling. Prompting and insistence on proper social behavior are essential and are especially effective when combined with formal recognition of the child's achievements in these areas. Songs, games, bulletin board displays, and structured experiences (including planning and evaluation with the student during and after the experience) within the class, the school, and the community are useful means of helping the child learn to conduct himself or herself properly as well as teaching the child the basic dynamics of social structure.

Vocational Skills

As the moderately mentally retarded child grows and develops, he or she becomes ready to assume responsibility within the home and community. Although the expectation is not full economic independence, contributing to home maintenance and community economic growth through the performance of a variety of simple chores is realistic. Many participate in the responsibilities of routine housekeeping and hold down part or even full-time jobs. These accomplishments are not only beneficial to the community and the individual's family, but also a source of pride to the individual—a demonstration to himself or herself and others that he or she is a contributing member of society. Furthermore, Gold (1973b) has seriously questioned acceptance of the position that the TMR are capable of only the most mundane, simple (one operation), repetitive tasks. He reported results of a training production study indicating TMR capability for production far beyond that presently found regarding both quantity and quality.

Training for vocational employment requires attention to two phases: (1) the generic area of work, and (2) specific occupational task performance; both, in turn, require sequence development in task-specific competency. In the general area of work, there are many opportunities within the school to teach understanding of tasks, task performance in a prescribed temporal order, and correct task completion without attending to distractions. This training begins with the teacher's first expectation of the student wherein a mutually known response is successfully elicited. As the child learns, develops, and participates through responsibilities within the classroom and school (e.g., room maintenance, errands, homemaking, shop), his or her knowledge of and capability for work responsibility matures.

Training for specific occupational tasks remains within the domain of sheltered workshops, special programs under the direction of education or rehabilitation, and the employing agency. Gold (1973a) has cited research to support the value of such training. He discussed, for example, activities which not only elevated performance level but also had a positive impact on quality. It was further noted that verbal directions are variables which facilitate competency in task performance.

Along with learning skills required for vocational or home tasks, trainable youth must be prepared to function with some degree of autonomy at home and in the neighborhood. Training in use of public transportation facilities, traffic safety, and community resources aids the pupil in moving about in and enjoying his community. Functional use of quantitative concepts expands to include identification of time, money, house numbers, etc. Preparation for the use of leisure time to foster more positive personal and social adjustment facilitates their assumption of vocational responsibility. In short, as education draws to a close for the trainable mentally retarded, they must be prepared for the new life experiences which are available to them.

Preparation for semi-independent living for the moderate mentally retarded generally means to live in their own homes in their own communities. Competencies are sufficiently developed to facilitate performance in as full a range of activities as possible. Just as with the mildly mentally retarded, additional developmental disabilities as in cerebral palsy with moderate retardation have impact on the range of human performance. Learning must come through participation. Learning programs must include task analysis to reduce performance objectives to all the necessary sequential tasks and pre-tasks. Then, making use of all competencies available, a total developmental plan can be specified and implemented.

EDUCATIONAL PROGRAMMING FOR THE SEVERELY AND PROFOUNDLY MENTALLY RETARDED

Typically the severely (IQ 25–40) and profoundly (IQ < 25) mentally retarded have been viewed as unproductive and nonparticipating members of society. This is particularly evident by the fact that in the past custodial services were the sole means of providing for the SMR and PMR. Fortunately, a different trend is developing as a result of a new awareness of their capability for performance achievement. Through research and clinical program development of behaviors in self-feeding, self-dressing, proper toilet and hygiene behaviors, work skills, communication, and social skills are being successfully attained.

Various approaches have been used to facilitate the development of desired or appropriate behaviors. One means involves the encouragement of behaviors that compete with undesirable or inappropriate behaviors (Johnson and Werner 1975). This procedure entails the use of positive reinforcement of appropriate behaviors which already exist in the individual's repertoire, or the creation of new behaviors or behavior patterns through "shaping" techniques when the appropriate behavior does not already exist. Specifically, shaping techniques involve positive reinforcement by successive approximations, i.e., positive reinforcement of only those behaviors which more and more closely resemble the desired behavior. Success with the above approach and acceptance of the statement on human rights are being effective factors in elimination or severe restriction in the use of punishment (aversive reinforcement).

Educational goals, phrased in the terms of adult life prognosis, are not presently stated for persons with severe and profound mental retardation. Programming efforts are too new to even speculate on probable ultimate performance achievement. Present organization and delivery of services can be defined as a new beginning.

Self-Care

Traditionally, little effort has been expended with SMR and PMR individuals in the development of self-help or self-care skills (i.e., self-feeding, dressing, toilet training). Using operant conditioning techniques, attempts have been made to improve self-dressing behaviors. Prior to training, the individuals are evaluated, projections are made concerning expected capabilities, including determination of particular skills that would be emphasized for each individual. Results indicate that such a procedure is successful in promoting new dressing skills with a reduction of total time spent on the task. Minze and Ball (1967) reported that positive improvements in dressing were achieved following a similar training program for PMR female individuals. In addition to improved dressing behavior, Minze and Ball reported that the PMR individuals showed increased attentiveness and amenability to verbal commands, reduced self-aggression, and decreased tantrum behavior following training.

Martin, McDonald, and Omichinski (1971) proposed that the use of social reinforcement alone is not sufficient to train or condition behaviors in SMR individuals. To test their proposition they used social disapproval and "time out" procedures separately to negatively reinforce sloppy eating behaviors. Results indicated that social reinforcement had little or no effect on eating habits, whereas "time out" procedures significantly reduced undesirable eating practices. However, Henriksen and Doughtry (1969) reported that when operant conditioning is paired with social reinforcement, the latter can acquire response-eliciting qualities. When a PMR male exhibited undesirable feeding behavior, the trainer would show facial displeasure and say "that is a bad boy"; if the behavior continued, the training situation was terminated, and the subject's arms were restrained. At the end of the thirteen-week training period, the occurrence of disruptive behavior was reported to be significantly reduced. Additional support for successful operant conditioning of desirable self-feeding behaviors in SMR and PMR individuals has been reported by Groves and Carroccio (1971). Their training procedure was designed to develop the proper use of a spoon and to reduce hand feeding and food stealing. Whenever one of the negative behaviors was observed, the individual's tray was removed and returned only after the subject picked up his spoon. Removal of the tray was coupled with a "use your spoon" command. After ninety-five days of training, all individuals were successfully using a spoon. Additionally, the number of individuals removed from their meal because of disruptive behavior and/or hand-feeding occurrences was significantly reduced.

By far, the most basic and important of the self-care skills is that of proper toilet habits. Baumeister and Klosowski (1965) have stressed the importance of toilet training for SMR and PMR individuals: "Probably nothing among those with severe and profound mental deficiency is quite so degrading as the lack of adequate toilet habits. A degree of success in mastery of these is essential to human dignity and a prerequisite for more advanced forms of training and rehabilitation."

There have been several approaches suggested in this particular area, but one proposed by Ellis (1963) seems most comprehensive for SMR and PMR individuals. Considering toilet training as a stimulus-response problem, Ellis presented a model program using operant conditioning procedures. He proposed that tension in the bladder or rectum may be considered as a stimulus or drive stimulus, and that urination or defecation releases or attenuates these tensions, thus forming a goal stimulus. Ellis further proposed that an operant chain of appropriate behaviors (i.e., going to the bathroom, removing one's pants, sitting on the toilet, eliminating) may be developed if strict control and appropriate reinforcers are employed. His program (designed specifically for use in an institution) basically involves: (a) careful selection and training of attendants; (b) subjects who are ambulatory and have intact sensory systems; (c) maintenance of subjects on a fixed diet; (d) carefully recorded data regarding frequency and time of occurrences of toilet behavior; (e) development of a schedule of training (based on each individual's data); (f) immediate reinforcement with an item desirable to the individual when an appropriate response occurs while the person is seated on the toilet; (g) an interval of time (delay) between inappropriate behavior and the removal of the aversive stimulus (i.e., wet clothing) to insure that inappropriate behaviors are not mistakenly positively reinforced; (h) directing of subjects (shaping) toward target responses by successive approximation techniques; (i) maintaining the program on a full-time basis; (j) maintenance of accurate records. Ellis admits that such a program would require intensive and long-term efforts, but further points out that the benefits over the life span of a SMR or PMR individual would more than make the effort worthwhile. Dayan (1964) reported that when a program similar to Ellis' was instituted in a cottage of six PMR boys, the laundry load dropped from an average of 1200 lbs. to 600 lbs. per week, apparently significantly adding to the self-help skills of these individuals.

Work Skills

The traditional approach to the development of work skills by the severely mentally retarded has been to place the individuals in positions of employment that are well within their behavioral capabilities. Such an approach frequently and severely limited the types of tasks made available to the SMR. Fortunately, the contemporary approach is to train the SMR to perform complex tasks that in the past were thought to be too difficult for them. Behavior modification, imitation training, and token economy systems have all been successfully used to teach work skills to the SMR.

Crosson (1969) initiated a thorough training program which revealed the previously unknown or untapped potential which the SMR individual has for acquiring complex work skills. The program involved training SMRs for work that was available, rather than attempting to locate available work suited to the SMR's natural capabilities. He designed his program to teach seven SMR males ($\overline{X}$ IQ = 27, CA range 16–34) to construct wooden pencil holders and flower boxes. Each of these complex tasks required approximately 100 separate behavioral components. The procedure involved specifying the functional units of behavior that would be included in each individual's training according to his discrete level and his present repertoire. The cues or stimuli associated with each behavioral component (e.g., vibration of an electric drill) had to be specified; in cases where the stimuli were not strong enough, stronger substitute stimuli replaced them. The most difficult behavioral components were shaped prior to task programming; the responses that were not in the subject's repertoire were either shaped by approximation or by physical guidance, each behavioral component was demonstrated to the subject several times before proceeding to the next segment of the chain, and all correct responses were immediately reinforced. The program was so successful that none of the individuals required more than three hours to acquire the desired skills. Additionally, retention measures made two and twelve months after the training session revealed that all of the subjects correctly performed over 95 percent of the behavioral components contained in the overall sequence.

Bender (1972) developed a program involving visual instruction followed by imitation by the subjects to train twenty-five SMR males to perform industrial tasks. His procedure involved demonstrating the task for the subject while instructing him to watch what was being done; then the subject was instructed to imitate the demonstrator's behavior. Results subsequent to training revealed that the subjects acquired the ability to perform the tasks and furthermore retained the ability over a period of time.

Musick and Luckey (1970) reported data obtained from a token economy system which indicated that not only could work productivity in SMR individuals be effectively increased, but also the frequency of undesirable behaviors could be simultaneously decreased. Specifically, individuals were rewarded with social and/or recreational privileges for participation in productive activities. Different token values were associated with each activity: (a) voluntary participation in group recreation was rewarded by one token; (b) voluntary participation in training sessions (word recognition and number games) was rewarded by one token; (c) full-time work outside the dormitory was rewarded by four tokens; (d) half-time work outside the dormitory was rewarded by two tokens; (e) courtesy toward the staff was rewarded by one token; (f) personal grooming was rewarded by one token. Two months after the program was initiated, there was an 80 percent decrease in illness complaints, and significant increases in participation in all of the above mentioned activities, excluding half-time work, were exhibited.

Delivery of services is expanding broadly in both the range of services provided and in the nature of the delivery systems themselves. Within communities, for example, there are day care centers striving to foster development in mental retardation from early childhood to young adulthood; sheltered workshops in which work competencies can be learned and used; group homes which provide a home-like atmosphere for those who have no homes or live in homes unable to provide for their needs; placement in nursing homes; recreation programs; and direct assistance to families who have an infant in the home.

Similarly states are developing small regional hospitals and expanding evaluation and diagnostic services to make them more nearly available to the individual's home community. As new information is generated, as personnel develop and refine competencies needed, as individuals in communities see the positive results of these efforts, the developmentally disabled will assume their rightful role in society.

14

Family Process

BERNARD FARBER

THE PLIGHT OF PARENTS of cerebral-palsied children stems in part from the necessity to handle various kinds of offensive situations associated with their offspring. The parents must face numerous situations which are an affront to them—the stares, the furtive glances, the feigned disregard, the curiosity, the strained conversations, the pity expressed or implied, the rejections, the avoidances, the pain of observing other children, the strains of child care, the enjoyments that must be foregone, the siblings whose needs must be minimized, the guilt. Even routine activities require infractions of ordinary rules of conduct (through no one's "fault" perhaps, but nevertheless infractions); special allowances must be made for the child's playing with other children, for teaching the child simple self-care tasks, for the child's going to school, for visiting or shopping, for leaving the child with babysitters, for explaining the child's abnormality to others, or for just imagining the future. In violating the parents' sense of propriety, justice, or dignity, these situations evoke such reactions as shame, humiliation, outrage, grief, frustration, or a general sadness. It is the potential of these situations to foster this misery that qualifies them as offensive.

By focusing on the mobilization of the family to handle the continuing *offensive* situations and *offensive* behavior, we can observe the dynamics of family interaction in trying to live with unpleasantness. Not all families or family members find living with a severely handicapped child equally offensive. There are variations in the sense of stigma, in the amount of time and energy required in childcare, in community attitudes, in the extent of family resources, in prior loyalties and commitments, and so on. These variations require more extreme adaptations on the part of some families (and some family members) than others. The presence of such differences in adapting to a cerebral palsied child evokes the question: How do families decide on how much they must change their mode of existence in order to permit their lives to be bearable?

This chapter discusses the extent of adaptation which families with severely handicapped children are prepared to undergo. The first section is concerned with the assumptions about the adaptational process, the second section with a putative description of this process, and the third with the effect of the social context on the process of adaptation. The term "adaptation," incidentally, is not to be confused with "adjustment" or "acceptance." It is used rather in the traditional sense in which social scientists have applied the term—that of creating means for dealing with functional problems.

ASSUMPTIONS REGARDING THE ADAPTATIONAL PROCESS

This section will suggest some basic assumptions underlying the process of adaptation to problematic family situations (see Farber 1974, for fuller discussion of these assumptions). Following the lead of theories on social exchange it will relate a principle of minimal adaptation to questions pertaining to role renegotiation and will then outline a tentative progression of successive minimal adaptations.

The Principle of Minimal Adaptation

In the analysis of change in family interaction, one can make various assumptions about the choice of adaptations by family members. The assumption explored here is that of minimal adaptation. This assumption implies that families will make as minimal adaptations as possible to solve problems involving family relationships (or to create a situation making it possible to live with these problems). The term "family problem" as used here is any event or chronic situation which the family members collectively perceive as interfering with the successful attainment of their goals in family life. Ideally, before the onset of the offensive situation, family relationships had been sufficiently gratifying that family members are reluctant to change their mode of living. An "adaptation" is any sustained change in roles, norms, or family interaction which family members make individually or collectively with the intention of effectively handling (either solving or living with) the offensive situation. The minimal adaptation assumption implies a *temporal* progression of adaptations from the simple to the complex, from the least disruptive to the potentially fully disruptive. Since these adaptations represent means for counteracting a threat to the integrity of the family, members are not likely to resort to more extreme measures until less risky ones have been tried. Especially as adaptations become more extreme, differences in the opinions of family members as to the propriety of adaptations may themselves generate additional family problems.

Role Renegotiation and Adaptation

As people marry and have children, their roles as spouses and parents emerge through the give-and-take of daily interaction. Although young couples may use a variety of sources as models for family roles, the differences in background of husband and wife and the unique problems they face force them to modify their conduct in ways which are mutually agreeable. The resulting family roles can thus be regarded as informal contracts which the husband and wife have negotiated in achieving a *modus vivendi*. As conditions change, a need arises to renegotiate family roles.

The principle of successive minimal adaptations involves a series of renegotiations of family relationships. At any given time participants in a social relationship have a negotiated set of understandings. A potentially new allocation of time, funds, or responsibility requires a renegotiation. At each phase of the adaptation process, the parents and siblings are likely to test their role arrangements on each other and on outsiders. Apparently, so long as the parents feel that they can manage the child's disability, they can regard themselves as capable of handling offensive situations. Only as they come to regard themselves as powerless does their role bargaining ability deteriorate (Voysey 1972).

If household interaction were uniformly intensive among all family members, one might anticipate that the whole family would progress as a unit through successive adaptations. However, because of variation in intensity of interaction, these phases refer more to family dyads—husband-wife, parent-and-normal-child, parent-and-handicapped-child, and sibling-sibling. The necessity of living with a handicapped sibling or child may stimulate a variety of family problems. As secondary issues arise within these dyads, other adaptations are apparently generated. Whereas in the initial series of adaptations the cerebral palsied child may be seen as a problem, in later phases the focus may be on difficulties between parents or on a disturbed sibling. Eventually, the issue of divorce as a possible adaptation may overshadow that of permanent hospitalization of the handicapped child.

Successive Minimal Adaptations

The previous paragraphs have suggested that families start out with the most minimal adaptations to their problems and proceed to successively more extensive and drastic ones only when the simpler adaptations are not satisfactory. This characterization of family adaptation to crisis suggests the need to identify adaptations along a continuum from the most minimal to the most extensive and then to determine the extent to which families follow this sequence in reacting to critical events. One would anticipate, as a general principle, that the families would stabilize their mode of adaptation when the solutions developed shield them from situations they find unbearable. Otherwise, the adaptational process would continue until the family units dissolved. What follows below is an ideal progression of adaptations to crisis and cannot apply to all empirical situations; the manner in which various conditions may affect this process will be discussed later.

Assuming a principle of successive minimal adaptations, one can postulate a process in terms of the phases outlined below. At any stage, if the kind of adaptation is effective the family would cease to seek further adaptations to their problems and would stabilize its organization, and the crisis-meeting would cease. The successive adaptations include the following:

1. In the *labeling phase* bases for existing role arrangements are removed, and there is a realization that major understandings underpinning family relationships may have to be renegotiated.

2. In the *normalization phase* the family tries to maintain its normal set of roles, all the while being considerate of each other for role lapses in an attempt to make family life as normal as possible. The family presents a face of normality to the outside world and seeks to maintain liaisons with normal families.

3. In the *mobilization phase* family members increase the time and effort given to family demands, without, however, giving up their claim to normality as a family.

4. In the *revisionist phase* the family, isolating itself from community involvements, can no longer maintain an identity of normality, and it revises age and sex standards in its organization of family roles. This revision represents an attempt to maintain cohesiveness in an uncaring and misunderstanding world.

5. In the *polarization phase* the family, finding itself unable to maintain its coherence in an alienated or perhaps hostile world, turns its attention inward to seek the sources of this alienation or hostility within the family.

6. In the *elimination phase* polarization results in arrangements to preclude contact with the offending person himself. In this phase, the family seeks to renegotiate (with whatever resources remain) to regain those roles regarded as normal.

PHASES IN THE ADAPTATIONAL PROCESS

The previous section outlined a series of putative phases in the adaptation process. It is difficult to determine from that outline the special features of each phase and the ways which these phases are related to recent research on families with deviant children. This section presents a more detailed discussion of these phases.

The continued presence of a severely handicapped child in the home represents a dynamic set of problems rather than a static problem which the term "stigma" might imply. Even in so-called normal families, relationships are under continual pressure to change. This inherent instability derives from the fact that age-sex roles vary with the family life-cycle. As both children and their parents age, role expectations are modified.

The presence of a severely handicapped child in the family can be regarded as a factor in the arrest of the family cycle. This assumption is made on the following basis:

1. In interaction with their children, parents tend to assign a status to each child commensurate with the capabilities they impute to him. (a) The roles embodied in the status are classified on the basis of age grading. By definition, capability age is approximately equal to chronological age. (b) Age grading in a culture is regarded more as a psychological and social activity than as a chronological variable, e.g., the chronologically middle-aged severely handicapped individual is generally regarded as a "boy" or "girl" by those with whom he or she interacts.

2. As the child proceeds in his or her life career, the parents normally tend to revise their self-concepts and roles. With respect to their normal children, ideally, parents continually redefine their roles, obligations, and values to adjust to the changing role of the child. With respect to their cerebral palsied child, the parental role is fairly constant. Regardless of his or her birth order in the family, the severely handicapped child eventually becomes the youngest child socially. A very severely handicapped child at home would not engage in dating and courtship, belong to organizations, seek part-time employment, or take part in other activities characteristic of adolescents. In the progressive movement to the youngest-child status, the severely handicapped child would not merely slow the family cycle but also prevent the development of the later stages in the cycle. Birenbaum (1970) describes an increasing severity of family problems as the handicapped child reaches adolescence.

Even when there are no age differences between a cerebral palsied child and his or her siblings, there will likely be a social revision in their birth-order. Shere (1955) investigated thirty pairs of twins. Within each pair, one child was cerebral palsied. The behavior of the parents toward the twins differed in certain respects: (1) the parents generally expected the non-cerebral palsied child to assume more responsibilities and to act older than the age or capabilities would warrant; (2) the parents tended to be more responsive to the problems of the cerebral palsied child and oblivious to those of the twin; (3) the parents overprotected the cerebral palsied twin, permitting little discretion in his or her activities. The non-cerebral palsied twin was more curious and adventurous, less patient, more excitable, less cheerful, more resistant to authority, and more prone to emotional outbursts than the cerebral palsied twin.

The Farber (1960a) study of 240 Chicago-area families with severely retarded children, some of whom were cerebral palsied, investigated characteristics of those normal siblings who were closest in age to the retarded child. Farber found that the retarded child's siblings were affected by the child's high degree of dependency, which adversely affected the siblings' relationships with their mother. When the children were young, interaction between the normal and the retarded brothers and sisters tended to be on an equalitarian basis. As they grew older, the normal siblings frequently assumed a superordinate position in the relationship. However, siblings who did not interact frequently with their retarded brother or sister generally were affected less than those who interacted frequently.

Factors related to the family life cycle provide an impetus for revising adaptations. What may be merely an impropriety at one phase of the family life cycle becomes offensive in another. The minimal amount of adaptation at one stage of the family life cycle is insufficient to handle offensive behavior that may emerge at a later stage.

1. *Labeling Phase: Improprieties and Offensive Behavior*

When a child fails to develop at a normal rate, we ordinarily try to explain this failure by choosing the less offensive labels first, dreading the more stigmatizing ones.

What makes behavior offensive? The consequences of the behavior are important. For example, suppose a child does not walk when it normally might be expected to or does not start using language at the appropriate developmental time. While the parents might not consider this proper, they would not, however, view it as offensive. They could merely regard the child as a late walker, a late talker, or late in muscular coordination. They might regard the same behavior as extremely offensive to them, though, if they believed it to be symptomatic of a severe handicap. Having a personal diagnosis validated by a physician or psychologist infuses a dreadful significance into the behavior.

As the parents redefine the child's behavior as symptomatic of a permanent disabling condition, they are faced with its shocking implications. Parents almost always report this realization as constituting a major tragedy in their lives. Sometimes, one parent may take this occasion to turn against his or her spouse, regarding him or her as offensive for having some sort of role in this event. Occasionally, it is the physician who is regarded as offensive. To regard another person as offensive is not to discredit him or her personally, as in denying the validity of a diagnosis, but instead blaming the other for offending oneself. Unlike stigmatization, which in effect implies that the defective individual has no right to continued interaction, offensiveness constitutes a transgression which does not damage an individual's right to interaction, but does make continued interaction disagreeable. Having reached the point of defining the child's failure to develop normally as offensive to them, the parents must now decide how to handle this offensiveness.

2. Normalization Phase

The parents must either eliminate their child's offensiveness or learn to live with it. When asked to participate in a study of families with severely retarded children, parents have responded: "But we don't have any special problems; we are a normal family, everything about us is normal. The fact that one of our children has a special problem makes us no different. In most families some children have problems of one kind or another." The minimal family adaptation, following the acceptance of the deviance label, is to try to handle the offending child within the existing arrangements of family roles and norms. The maintenance of deviance within the normal scheme of things, despite the family consensus that something is amiss, can occur in several ways: (a) some family members may suppress their perceptions about the existence of a problem, (b) some family members may convince others to change their perceptions (i.e., their labels), or (c) as in "pseudo-mutuality," the family members may all pretend that all is well. Although pseudo-mutuality has been discussed mainly in connection with mental illness (Wynne et al. 1969), the fiction of normality in family relationships occurs in numerous offensive situations: deviance disavowal in interaction with physically disabled persons; the pretense of uncertainty of prognosis in polio and leukemia; shopping around for a favorable diagnosis for severely mentally retarded children; the family's denial of a parent's compulsion to drink or to take drugs; or the denial of bizarre behavior of a psychotic parent. As long as the deviant person and his family can carry off the fiction of normality, there is no need for further adaptations in family roles or norms. It is only when the fiction of normality cannot be sustained (or interferes with the attainment of family goals) that more complex adaptations must be sought.

In his discussion of courtesy stigma (i.e., someone who has a spoiled identity because he is affiliated with a stigmatized person). Birenbaum (1970) writes that "to the extent that mothers of retardates are able to perform roles similar to those performed by mothers of normal children, the consequences of the courtesy stigma they bear are manageable" (p. 198). These are manageable when (a) under conditions of role nonconformity, others are "considerate" in accepting "the plight of the family with a disabled child," or (b) situations can be avoided in which the risk of exposing the nonconformity is high. As long as others with whom one interacts "forgive" failures in role performance, there is no need to renegotiate the basis for continuing the relationship. The failures are seen as improper but not offensive.

When do people stop forgiving failures in role performance? Presumably, there are several kinds of situations in which outsiders regard interaction with the family as offensive: (a) when role failures are no longer seen as unavoidable lapses, (b) when the outsiders themselves suffer disappointments of their own as a result of interacting with the family, (c) when their own resources are tapped excessively, and (d) when they believe that the family is taking advantage of them.

The presence of extrafamilial resources may be a crucial factor in sustaining a normal role arrangement in the family. A supportive grandmother (usually the mother's mother), community centers for the handicapped, and specialized professions (e.g., teachers, social workers, and pediatricians) may provide necessary resources to permit the continuation of normal family routines. Yet, there is evidence that many families lack these resources, particularly outside middle-class neighborhoods or large metropolitan areas. Even where community facilities are present, parents are often reluctant to use them. Without these resources, chances of failure in role performances apparently increase. There then comes a time when existing role resources have been expended. Finding the situation offensive, the parent calls for renegotiation of the allocation of family roles, either directly or through an intermediary (such as a professional or relative).

3. Mobilization Phase

When the family cannot resolve the offensiveness within existing arrangements, it must make minor adaptations or exert greater efforts to fulfill existing roles. This extension of responsibilities requires a change in expectations of all the family members in a systematic reapportionment of duties. The family members then retain many of their previous privileges and obligations, but are faced with a change (probably minor) in the authority structure and division of labor. Thus, the wife may encroach upon the husband's household domain, or the husband on the wife's, or perhaps the child on the mother's. Yet, the original person retains primary responsibility for that domain.

In "normal" family life, participation in organizations with friends outside the family ordinarily supports the norms and values associated with everyday life. For the family in crisis, these ordinary community relationships do not support norms and values pertinent to handling the problem.

On the other hand, other extrafamily coalitions do assist family members in handling the crisis. Women with husbands in the military service shift reliance to grandparents and relatives; the wife of the mental patient withdraws from family and friends and forms coalitions with the mental hospital staff; parenthood ordinarily involves a curtailment of social activities (especially activities with friends who have no children); attempts are made to decrease the social visibility of drinking, and eventually coalitions are formed with doctors, social workers, psychologists, and the like, and with nondrinking alcoholics; and the family of the unemployed tends to withdraw from friends at the old social level and to find new friends at the lower socioeconomic level.

There is widespread evidence that parents of severely handicapped children tend to isolate themselves socially. Describing mothers of retarded children, Birenbaum (1970) further suggests that while reciprocal visiting may decrease significantly, parents "found it more comfortable to receive guests in their home than to visit other people's houses"; perhaps there was less awkwardness and embarrassment. This isolation does not seem to extend so much to relatives. Either relationships with kinsmen do not change or they may even be intensified as the relatives show "consideration" for lapses in role performance.

The diminution of normal socializing behavior by parents of handicapped children is accompanied by sundry modifications in parent-child interaction. Generally, parents with severely handicapped children, including cerebral palsied sons and daughters, exhibit more controlling or authoritarian behaviors and attitudes than do mothers with nonhandicapped children. The extent of authoritarian control seems to increase as the handicapped children grow older, but at the same time, mothers of severely handicapped children also tend to exhibit much warmth in their interaction with these children. Heightened intensity of interaction characterized by continual controlling behavior and strong emotional involvement tends to isolate the mother-and-handicapped-child dyad from the outside community and, to a lesser extent, from other family members. Given the central role of the mother in coordinating the activities of the other family members, this situation may create much tension in the family. The normal siblings may resent the additional attention that the parents give to the handicapped child (sometimes without the parents even becoming aware of this resentment) or the marital relationship may suffer (Farber 1960b).

The principle of minimal adaptation suggests an uneven kind of transformation of the family in handling offensive behavior. The less important inconveniences and more threatening actions are given up in role trade-offs, and the more significant aspects of existence are clung to. It is in this context that the ability of the family to formulate its priorities in order to provide coherence to its efforts is especially important. In an earlier study (Farber 1960a), it was feasible to identify families as home-oriented, parent-oriented, or child-oriented in decision-making and to classify other families as relying upon residual strategies. These residual category families had apparently not been able to retain or to agree on these more significant elements in their family life, and the parents were evidencing some difficulty in their marital relationship. Bermann's (1973) more recent analysis of family interaction patterns also indicates strongly that, in the process of eventual polarization, diverse preferences of the individual members become highlighted above common concerns.

The potential care required by the severely handicapped child highlights the *kinds* of alleviation needed by parents and siblings. The introduction of housekeepers to assist the mother, of babysitting services for the handicapped, and of daycare facilities for the handicapped may seem prosaic, but they appear almost essential if the family is to retain its self-concept of normality. The school or parent group by minimizing the "anxious concern for the future" of severely handicapped children may further increase the effectiveness of parent education programs. Perhaps even more important may be the presence of empathic, helpful relatives (particularly grandparents) who can provide emotional support as well as personal service (and attention to neglected siblings). Similarly the ability of parents to counsel other parents with handicapped children may in some ways be far more effective than that of professionals. While none of these resources can remove the stigma and problems associated with severe handicap, they can at least permit a semblance of normality of family life for the parents, siblings, and the handicapped child himself.

4. *Revisionist Phase*

At some point, family members may begin to regard themselves as having "special problems." The minor revision made in family roles may not resolve the offensiveness in family relationships satisfactorily. In fact, there may be a diffusion of offensive behavior throughout the family. When everyone is offended by what is required (for example, the large investment of time, energy, and/or personal trauma), there is a general demand for changing the basic role structure of the family. Family life in a crisis situation may be sustained eventually only through a drastic rearrangement of age, sex, and generation roles in the family. The duty and power structure of the family is rearranged. In the case of the chronic alcoholic, the drinking husband is demoted in generation to the role of recalcitrant child, and the mother assumes her husband's responsibilities, while sharing some of her own with the children. Similarly, the unreliable behavior of the mentally ill husband causes a comparable demotion. The unemployed husband withdraws from planning and management; children assume adultlike roles, contribute financially, and demand a change in power structure in the family. In these instances, the family members have departed from conventional age, sex, and generation roles. The family organization itself becomes deviant.

One of the organizational problems that occurs with extensive revision of family roles is how to maintain a coherent set of social relationships in the face of high tension. Since there is a cultural conception that handicapped children do generate family problems, the parents can feel free to blame the state of the family upon the presence of the cerebral palsied child. The child is in a powerless position; he cannot effectively counteract the parents' efforts to regard him as a scapegoat; and he obviously represents a symbol of failure to them. Moreover, the handicapped child can carry out the role of a problem child without any special effort—he has seriously violated social norms, but he is rewarded for his offensiveness by being exempt from any responsibilities and obligations. Thus, the child has earned his role by drawing off aggression and thereby permitting the family to maintain its integrity.

In the extensive revision of family roles, the mother, faced with a daily life she finds impossible to endure, may become sick. This situation tends to occur more often in lower socioeconomic level families (Farber 1960b). However, like any other role, a "sick role" in the family must be negotiated with other family members. The absence of a parent, for example, would eliminate the possibility of negotiating such a role. Roghmann, Hecht, and Haggerty (1973, p. 58) find that persons in incomplete families tend to report more chronic conditions and more difficulty in coping with illness and other family problems than is the case of people in complete families.

The tendency of mothers in stress to negotiate a sick role is suggested in several studies. In his analysis regarding mothers of severely retarded children, Farber (1960b) found that mothers who report that they are not in good health (as compared with those who regard their health as good) generally have a lower degree of marital integration. Schaefer (1949, 1974) also reported an association between poor physical health of mothers and the presence of marital conflict. It is difficult to determine which came first, the marital problems or the poor health. If the poor health came first, one can then regard the marital problems as emerging from the unwillingness of the husband to acquiece to the wife's assuming a sick role. If the marital problems preceded the self-conception of being in poor health, one can then consider the attempt to negotiate a sick role as a means from withdrawing from the unpleasantness of the marriage. In either case, the mother's stress is generalized so that she apparently resents her maternal obligations as well as her wifely activities. In Farber's study, the mothers in poor health also saw their retarded children as making greater demands on them than did mothers in good health, and the mothers reporting poor health were, in addition, more willing to place their retarded child in an institution. In Schaefer's analysis, high marital conflict and poor physical health of mothers were related to ratings of maternal hostility and rejection of children. Hence, feeling inadequate to the tasks of being wife and mother, the mothers reporting poor health show considerable resentment of husband and handicapped child, both of whom apparently (a) place additional burdens on them and (b) refuse to regard the mother as too sick to carry out her duties to them.

The extensive revision of roles in the family may be negotiated at a high cost. Farber (1959) and others have noted how daughters (when the retarded child lives at home) are called upon to provide much household and childcare assistance. They have also noted the tension which exists between the retarded child's mother and sister in this situation. This tension extends beyond the household. Gath (1973) has found that sisters of children with Down's Syndrome show a high amount of anti-social behavior in school. At the same time, however, Farber and Jenne (1963) have also found that the siblings who interact a good deal with their retarded brothers and sisters tend to be more serious in outlook on life and less concerned with acceptance by peers. They tend more to place a high value on devotion to a cause or to helping mankind. This priority of altruistic values leads them frequently to select a career in special education, nursing, or medicine. Indeed, as a consequence of a program in which adolescent siblings were trained as behavior modifiers, Weinrott (1974) found a concomitant increase in the amount of general interaction between the adolescent and retarded brothers and sisters, greater participation and interest by the sibling in educational and familial matters related to retardation, and (in a few instances) shifts in career plans. Thus, although frequent interaction with a handicapped sibling may provoke some tension, it may also accelerate maturity and may help to shape life goals of the handicapped child's brothers and sisters.

5. *Polarization Phase: Identities in Danger*

At a minimum, family members would regard extensive revision of family roles to meet the exigencies of the situation as departing from the ordinary norms of propriety. One would expect such families to carefully manage information about themselves to the outside world. As family members encounter situations within the home (as well as outside) which they see becoming offensive to themselves and to each other, their careful information management extends into the household itself.

Eventually, family members may participate in pseudo-negotiation with each other whereby superficial "offers" of services are made and accepted, but actually the contracted roles are never played out. Nor is there overt redress over failure to comply with contracted roles. In describing interaction process analysis in a troubled family, Bermann (1973) writes that as the crisis continues, the family members "pointedly behave in ways that seem calculated to abort extensive interaction, that appear designed to attentuate continuing exchange between family members." Whereas in the earlier phases of the crisis family members had been placed in a position where they were encouraged to sustain interaction, in later stages their behavior is polarized. Interaction is either extremely non-controversial and superficial or highly antagonistic and disruptive. In the face of potential conflict, family members are either ready to withdraw and meekly acquiesce or to lash out and terrorize each other.

Although family members may remain under the same roof, they establish a tacit agreement to interact as briefly as possible in order to permit coexistence with as little sense of abuse as possible. In this manner, some sense of cohesion as a family can be maintained.

Wynne *et al.* (1958) emphasize the large role that secrecy and privacy play in families which are pseudo-mutual in their interaction: "Each family member may be expected to conceal large areas of his experience and not open to communication with others" (p. 638). The norm for the family is based on a perhaps exaggerated right of privacy, with the amount of sharing intimate, personal things the prerogative of each family member. In an effort to maintain an appearance of cohesion, there may be sweeping approval of any kind of behavior, with departures from acceptable standards explained away by some rationalization. In this manner, all semblance of the family as an interacting group which socializes its members and guides their conduct is lost. One finds that in families with a severely retarded child, normal brothers may be given free reign as long as they do not get in the way at home. Similarly, in those families in which the parents' marriage shows signs of low integration, there is a tendency (where there is a retarded child in the home) for the parents to seek escape outside the home.

There is ample evidence that marital tension and polarized behavior in the family are related to emotional and antisocial problems in children. One can readily understand how tension in family interaction and socialization problems in children feed upon one another. It is not merely that parents may allocate a scapegoat role to the child. Rather, the general demeanor of the parent may carry over from one situation to another, so that the child imputes parental dissatisfaction with his behavior where in fact no such dissatisfaction exists. The child increasingly expects parental disapproval and harshness, with perhaps a corresponding growth of a sense of confusion and/or hostility gnawing at the child. This reaction by the child might indeed stimulate behavior which the parent finds offensive. The relationship between family tensions and emotional problems in children is thus a highly complex one and not simply a matter of parental mismanagement or abuse.

6. Elimination Phase: The Formation of New Identities

Ordinarily when we think about eliminating the offending person in families with severely handicapped children, we have in mind institutionalization of the children themselves. Indeed, in most families when the offense of the handicapped child is sufficiently grave (e.g., interfering with the parents' and/or siblings' mental health or social mobility), institutionalization seems an appropriate solution.

Yet in some families the progression of adaptations may have generated so much offensive behavior in the family that "transgressions" of a spouse or normal child may be considered as more serious than those of the retarded child. As a consequence, the parents may divorce or a sibling may be sent to live with a relative.

One might review conceptions of institutionalization to determine how families with retarded children handle the elimination phase. Some parents, particularly those of middle-class background, prefer to regard the institutionalized child as dead or "depersoned." Their contact with him or her is minimal. Those of lower socioeconomic background, however, more often regard institutionalization as living-away-from-home, and their contact and readiness to reincorporate the child may be strong. Perhaps lower-class families are less inclined to avoid crises, regarding them as part of normal family life.

THE CONTEXT OF ADAPTATION

The progression of successive minimal adaptations described in the previous paragraphs requires the qualification that all other things are equal. Empirically, however, numerous factors impinge upon family interaction and affect the course of events, and given different conditions, the succession of adaptations may be modified. Families may skip some phases of the process, or complex adaptations may precede simpler ones. It thus seems advisable to suggest conditions under which modifications of the adaptation process occur. Some of these conditions are sketched briefly below.

Priorities in Family Values

If the offensive person has been regarded by other family members as essential to fulfilling dreams and goals, then the family would be more reluctant to make changes which might reduce the status and participation of this person. For example, in an earlier study, I found it useful to distinguish among families with a strong parent-orientation, child-orientation, general home-orientation, and mixed or vague orientations (Farber 1960a). These families differed by age of parents, social-mobility orientation, handling of their retarded and normal children, and in adaptations to family problems. Especially among parent-oriented, upwardly mobile families, there was a tendency to institutionalize the retarded child as soon as possible (Culver 1967; Farber 1968). Many of them skipped any attempt to live with the retarded child and immediately eliminated him from their lives (Downey 1965). Not so with the child-oriented families wherein jobs, social life, and home life were all organized around the children. In any case, an offending member, whose presence otherwise promotes familial goals about which there is consensus, would be more likely to generate successive minimal adaptations than one whose presence contributes less to the overall family goals.

The Strength of Family Bonds

In some families, marital or filial ties may have been fragile even prior to the handicapped child's presence. In these cases, we would anticipate a willingness to accentuate activities outside the nuclear family or to dissolve family relationships altogether. Williams (1974) suggests a growing tendency for some young mothers to be only marginally attached to their children. Although young, unwed mothers are keeping their babies at birth, there is a growing tendency "to give them up two or three years later" (p. 74). The movement by women toward increased participation in the labor force (especially in professional and managerial positions) is leading to a growing ambivalence toward maternal roles. One would expect women in traditional homemaking roles to have a strong investment in their children's behavior. To be sure, in a study in Westchester County, New York, concern over possible deviance in child's behavior was greatest in the more traditional groups. As one might expect, given the "Jewish Mother" stereotype, "more Jewish than non-Jewish mothers reported worrying, though their children were no more impaired than those of other religious groups" (Lurie 1974, p. 113). In line with the current trend in women's work commitment, one would anticipate a lesser proclivity to proceed with the early phases of a series of successive minimal adaptations and a greater willingness to institutionalize handicapped children.

Reliance on Experiential Guides

The family may not build up a succession of minimal adaptations itself but may rely instead upon previous experiences of others (or its own prior adaptations to crisis). Influences here may include (a) professional therapy or advice, (b) the experiences of relatives or friends facing similar crises, (c) the family's previous experiences with problem situations, (d) mental experiments which anticipate probable consequences of different adaptations, or (e) cultural prescriptions. In any of these situations, the family members may discard lesser adaptations as unworkable and go on to ostensibly more complicated, more drastic ones. However, knowledge that these adaptations do work precludes the necessity of having to renegotiate roles from scratch.

The Relative Attractiveness of Alternative Adaptations

Excluding the handicapped child from the home is a drastic decision. One is seldom certain whether the reasons given for this exclusion are actually factors influencing the decision or merely rationalizations justifying it. For example, hospitalizing a child in a residential installation because of his harmful effect on the mental health and development of siblings (Grossman 1972) may be considered as acceptable (if one is weighing the possibility of having two damaged children against keeping the number of damaged children at one); but hospitalizing the child because one is ambitious and desirous of upward social mobility might be considered as selfish and therefore unacceptable. Yet parents who are upwardly socially mobile do tend to institutionalize their severely retarded children earlier and at a higher rate than do other parents (Culver 1967). However, the blocking of upward mobility may actually provoke a disturbance in family relationships which in turn does affect the mental health of the siblings. One is thus never sure if the reasons given are merely a reconstruction of reality after the fact. In a similar vein, institutionalizing a handicapped child because of superior facilities for care, companionship, education, or recreation may be a derived or secondary factor rather than a primary motive for institutionalization.

DISCUSSION

What are the mechanisms by which a family adapts to a handicapped child? This chapter has presented a set of assumptions which appear to justify the formulation of a progression of phases in the adaptation of families to crisis. Briefly, the argument is that families try to make as few changes as possible in roles, norms, and values to the problems they perceive. Only as the simplest adaptations fail to produce an acceptable accommodation to the offending problem do they seek a more complex solution; as a more complex solution fails, they go on to a still more complex solution; and so on. This principle of minimal adaptation to crisis seems to account for a predictable progression of phases of adaptation.

While the empirical test of the principle of minimal adaptations (and the progression of successive changes derived from it) would undoubtedly reveal shortcomings of the scheme, it should also suggest directions for revision of sociological analysis of family crisis (for example, the development of crisis fugues, in which stresses are multiplied). Such an analysis might suggest, for example, how adaptations to an offensive situation may be functional up to a certain point in terms of continuity of general values or mental health; yet as the family continues to introduce further adaptations in an effort to handle the offense, these later efforts are destructive of the basic conditions for the family's integrity.

15

Social Work

ROBERT M. SEGAL

THE DEVELOPMENT OF SOCIAL WORK AS A PROFESSION

HISTORICALLY, the profession of social work has been primarily concerned with assisting individuals and families in their efforts to resolve their social problems. Initially social work practice found its support through charitable church-supported organizations. Its major thrust was to help the troubled person by providing spiritual guidance. The individual was expected to resolve his or her own problem through inner strength and increased spirituality aided by the support and intervention of the social worker. The need for an organized structure to carry out these "good works" led to the development of social agencies with a "charitable" perspective. With the recognition that there was a need for a theoretical base for social work practice, social agencies seconded the need for the development of professional training. These agencies had a great influence on the development of the curriculum for professional training. Thus the education provided by professional schools of social work was seen as a preparation for functioning within an agency setting.

The primary methods taught by the schools of social work to assist individuals and families with their problems are: (1) casework; (2) group work; and (3) community organization practice.

Casework is a problem-solving process that enables the individual to understand the nature and causes of the problem and to find, within him or herself or within the environment, resources to resolve the problem. Group work utilizes the group interactional process to resolve social conflicts. Community organization practices recognize the impact that social institutions have upon individuals and their families and attempt to modify those institutions to better meet the needs of individuals suffering from social problems.

Social workers, providing services to the cerebral palsied and their families, are usually trained with a major focus in medical social casework and function primarily in a hospital or an outpatient clinic setting. The social worker, working with the cerebral palsied client, tends to focus on the following concerns: (1) understanding and treating the impact of illness; (2) helping patients make better use of health and medical care facilities; (3) participating in the prevention of those factors that tended to create or exacerbate illness.

In addition to these traditional approaches, the social worker has more recently incorporated the "advocate" role as an effective procedure to assist the cerebral palsied client and the family. As an advocate, the social worker is especially concerned in instances where service delivery systems may be involved in the violation of the client's human and legal rights. As an advocate, the social worker also attempts to effect change in the service delivery system on behalf of the client. Wherever the social worker functions (hospital or clinical setting) and whichever process (casework, group work, or community organization) is utilized, professional commitment is toward problem resolution; and the social worker's ultimate objective is to enable the client to achieve self-actualization through the utilization and enhancement of the client's potential for improved functioning.

SPECIAL SKILLS AND KNOWLEDGE

In working with the family and the cerebral palsied individual, one of the most important skills that the social worker must possess is the capacity to develop a meaningful interpersonal relationship. It is through the social worker's interviewing skills that a sense of trust and confidence on the part of the client can be established.

The worker must be fully aware of the specific aspects of the disease and its potential effects on the ability of the client to function as normally as possible. The worker must also be aware of the prognosis of the client's particular situation and what actual treatment interventions are required.

The social worker, by training and experience and with knowledge of human behavior, family relationships, and community resources, is uniquely equipped to offer the cerebral palsied client and the family help with problems in daily living.

THE INTAKE ROLE

When parents apply for help from a social agency or a clinic serving the cerebral palsied child, they are often seen first by a social worker, who will attempt to obtain a psycho-social evaluation of the child and the family. The psycho-social diagnosis is extremely important because it tells us who the child and the parents are. We need to know the child's milieu and how the environment is affecting him or her as well as how the child is affecting the environment.

When the parents embark on an effort to obtain help, they may feel overwhelmed and lost when they arrive at the agency. The parents will need much support in these efforts. They will need to know what to expect from the agency, the nature of its services, and the procedures that they will be involved in. The social worker plays a crucial role during this initial phase. It is the social worker who can set the tone of the course of treatment. How the social worker represents the agency and the worker's skill in making the parents comfortable in their initial contacts does much to set the stage for a cooperative relationship between the clients and the agency.

During the initial contacts with the agency or clinic, the family will naturally be concerned about fees and costs for services. The social worker can assist in the clarification of the fee schedules and how to utilize existing health-medical coverage programs. If the parents do not have medical coverage and have some problems regarding fees, the social worker can often assist them in considering the utilization of appropriate community financial resources.

The clinical social worker may also serve as a liaison to public or private agencies that may supplement needed help to the client such as financial assistance, orthopedic braces, recreational programs, or dental care.

SOCIAL WORK AND THE FAMILY

How well the child with cerebral palsy adjusts to his or her handicap may be related to the manner in which the parents, siblings, and relatives have dealt with the situation. In the past it was usually advocated that if the child was markedly mentally retarded and had extensive physical involvement in relation to cerebral palsy, it would be best for the child to be institutionalized. The trend toward institutionalization of the handicapped person has decreased and the emphasis is presently on making every effort toward keeping the child in the community. Because of this the involvement of the parents and siblings becomes even more important in the management planning for the cerebral palsied individual. The social worker plays a key role in involving the family in such planning.

We know that life styles vary considerably from one family to the next. Cultural influences, educational background, finances, religion, and other social factors play an important part in determining life style. We know there is no one way to raise children or a best way to interact, nor can we guarantee an atmosphere that is conducive to growth and development.

Each family finds its own way in developing meaningful interactional patterns related to its own emotional and physiological needs, customs, and value system. However, even within these diverse patterns some guidelines can be proposed which may positively influence the family relationship and improve the adjustment of the individual attempting to cope with the condition of cerebral palsy. It is important to recognize that family attitudes and behavioral patterns can have an impact on the cerebral palsied person, for better or worse. As Towle (1971) pointed out, the effect these attitudes have had "will depend largely on the meaning which the handicap has had for parents and other family members responsible for the care of the individual during childhood."

It is necessary to ascertain the parents' attitude so as to determine whether they are fairly objective, too pessimistic, too optimistic, or defensive. By understanding the parents' perception of the child, we can better develop a meaningful management plan.

PARENTAL REACTIONS

It is not surprising that, initially, many parents may feel a sense of shock when they learn their child is cerebral palsied. If their awareness about the condition occurs at the child's birth, the parents may become extremely upset. The mother and father may go through a period of depression which may immobilize them. Rather than face the reality of the situation, some parents may deny the occurrence and refuse to recognize the many symptoms that are ever present. The depression may cast a shadow over the family for an extended period of time unless they are helped to move through this phase. Medical social workers in the hospitals are often helpful to the family at this time.

Many professionals are aware that the most traumatic period in the lives of parents of handicapped children is the period between the moment they learn that their child is handicapped and the time they discover what they can do about it. Confusion and anxiety result often from lack of information about the condition.

Following the initial shock, parents may begin to feel sorry for themselves and the baby. They may continually wonder and ask, "Why did this happen to us?" As they begin to live with the pain and as the shock begins to ebb, they can be helped to move toward focusing on the needs of the baby. Pulling themselves together, they begin to ask, "What can I do for my baby?" It is usually at this point that the family is referred to an agency for help to deal with the need for a clearer understanding of what they can expect and what specifically can be done to help this child.

Parents of handicapped children need to recognize that there may be times they do not love or like their children and that these are appropriate feelings. Parents of normal children have these feelings, but they are not plagued by guilt. The ever presence of the handicap tends to stir up feelings of guilt and tension on the part of parents, and they often find it hard to discharge these feelings. Some parents find it hard to accept these momentary feelings of rejection, and they tend to deny them. This only leads to further conflict.

SIBLING REACTION

The impact on other children in the family is also examined by the social worker. Crothers and Paine (1959) point out that the impact, regarding the anxiety that the siblings often experience, is often overestimated and that "normal children are not disturbed much by it." Children seem more able to tolerate traumatic situations than we give them credit for. Often they are forced to learn how to live more easily with stress and strain and become more aware of the difficulties and adjustments that life poses. Consequently, siblings of handicapped children may become more sensitive to the needs of others and, in the process, become fuller human beings. When siblings cannot cope with the situation they may need counseling help to deal with the conflict situation.

PARENT COUNSELING

Little progress can be made in implementing a therapeutic management plan for children without the involvement of parents. The child must be viewed within the context of the family. While clinical perceptions of the child are important, one must view the child within the framework of his total environment. It is crucial, therefore, to be aware of the patient's home environment and how the parents and siblings interact with the cerebral palsied person. Counseling with the family becomes a vital ingredient in the management plan.

One of the primary functions of the social worker in agencies or clinics serving the cerebral palsied child is the provision of counseling to the parents.

Parent counseling can start at the birth of their cerebral palsied child or continue throughout the lifetime of the cerebral palsied person, depending upon the strains and stresses that arise. The focus of counseling is primarily to assist the family to resolve a problem that they may temporarily be unable to deal with.

Parents of handicapped children, like parents of normal children, can withstand a moderate amount of stress and strain. If this stress becomes too great, serious problems in their general social adjustment may develop. In the course of this stress, parents may express various behavior patterns which the social worker is trained to perceive. Parents may feel so overwhelmed, at first, that they may throw their hands up and claim, "I just can't care for a cerebral palsied child." Sometimes, relatives or grandparents are forced to provide assistance with child care. Other parents may simply deny the reality of the situation and claim the child is improving even when there is no basis for this perception. Other parents may take a reverse stand and see the situation as getting hopelessly worse and view the future in a most pessimistic light. Still others may project on to others their anger and frustration by being unduly critical of how professionals attempt to help them. There are some who may even withdraw from the situation and seldom talk about the child as an individual. They relate to the child in a mechanistic robot-like fashion, hardly seeing the uniqueness or individuality of the child.

In handling these various responses, the social worker must first accept these reactions with understanding and empathy. With proper support and guidance, parents can be moved out of these temporary defensive states toward a more positive and appropriate use of their emotional energies.

The primary focus here is on assisting the family and the cerebral palsied individual in developing a realistic approach to the problems that they are attempting to resolve. The family may need help to recognize that they have placed inappropriate expectations upon themselves and the patient. They can be helped to view their situation and the patient's potential in more realistic terms.

Practitioners have highlighted some of the desirable objectives of social casework with parents of handicapped children. These objectives can be enumerated as follows:

(1) *Parents need to know the degree of the child's handicap and the implications for further management.* Specific knowledge about cerebral palsy from a neurological, physiological, psychological, and social perspective can often allay fears and anxieties that have developed due to misinformation. This information must be presented in terms that can be understood. Too often medical information is shared in such abstract ways or couched in such confusing clinical terms that parents often feel overwhelmed. Rather than exhibit their ignorance, they remain silent just at the point they should be asking questions to clarify their confusion. Open and realistic communication between the family and the professional, particularly the physician, regarding the complexities of cerebral palsy is a necessity if the family is to be given the help they need.

(2) *Parents need to recognize that their child has a unique personality.* Too often parents think of their child as a cerebral palsied child

with the emphasis on the condition rather than a child who happens to have a cerebral palsied condition. The parents must learn to identify the child's assets and limitations and to discover the child's special talents and interests. Each child is special, and we must enable the parent to discover and rejoice in this uniqueness.

(3) *Parents need help in recognizing the impact that the child's physical and emotional difficulties have upon the family.* Sometimes, new family patterns and roles have to be developed in order to accomodate the chronic problems that the family is continually forced to cope with. Siblings will often need special help with their fears and anxieties relative to the condition of cerebral palsy.

(4) *Recognition of the attitudes of family, friends, and neighbors regarding the child's disabilities is important.* Parents need to be prepared that relatives and friends may feel uncomfortable in the presence of their child. There are effective ways to deal with these social pressures that will reduce these tension-producing situations.

(5) *Parents need assistance to cope with the practical problems which have to be solved if the child is to function as independently as possible.* The parents need to learn where they can obtain transportation, orthopedic appliances, medication, education, recreation, and other support programs that will enable the child to fulfill his potential. It is the responsibility of the social worker to help the family develop a pattern of community resource utilization.

(6) *Parents need help to recognize that their own attitudes may be preventing or interfering with their child's treatment plans.* Parents may need to examine how their fears and anxieties may actually be sabotaging the management plan that has been developed for their child.

(7) *Parents need to be educated to the fact that they, as consumers, can effect positive change in the service delivery system.* Parents of handicapped children can be encouraged to band together to form coalition groups to help initiate, develop, expand, or improve resources in the community that are so essential to meet the needs of the cerebral palsied individual. They need to become advocates for their own child and for all individuals with cerebral palsy.

PARENTAL ATTITUDES

A review of the literature related to the attitudes of parents of handicapped children indicates that professionals have tended to view many parents as having pathological feelings regarding their child's condition. Kozier (1957) has focused on the great emotional and material investment parents have in the preparation for their newborn and the consequent trauma that follows should the baby be born handicapped. Goodman and Rothman (1961) concluded that when the baby was found to be defective, the parents felt themselves to be defective as well. Mandelbaum (1960) comments that the birth of a handicapped child may often cause the parents to suffer chronic grief. Towle (1971) considers the birth of a handicapped child as posing a threat to parental pride and that it often instilled in the parents a sense of inferiority leading to the possibility of rejection of the child. Freeman (1971) described this potential for rejection when he wrote, "If the handicap is obvious at birth, maternal depression and working through grief over the loss of the anticipated normal child make appropriate stimulation by the mother less likely."

Cummings and Stock (1962) referred to the expression of "overprotectiveness as symptomatic of the parents' sense of dissatisfaction with the child's condition as evidenced in the behavior of parents of mentally retarded children." Overprotectiveness may be a means of compensating for the child's handicap. A case example of overprotectiveness on the part of the parents is illustrated by this social work contact:

> Bill was referred to the clinic for a comprehensive evaluation. Current problems include: under weight, sleeping difficulties, daytime and nighttime wetting. Parents also are interested in getting more information about the severity of his hearing loss. There are also questions about the feasibility of placing him in a day-training program. The parents are very anxious about placing Bill in the care of anyone outside the family. The parents want some indication as to the degree of beneficial influence provided by a school program.
>
> Bill is a very small, endearing seven year old, cerebral palsied child with severe spastic athetoid quadriplegic involvement. His arms and legs are very thin and tiny in comparison to his torso. He has difficulty breathing and usually keeps his mouth open. Bill is not ambulatory and is always carried around by a member of the family; at home he has a relaxation chair.
>
> Mrs. B is an RH-negative mother, who has successfully delivered and reared five other children in addition to Bill. Because of the RH-factor incompatibility, all of the other children had to undergo transfusions immediately after birth. Because of previous complications, the parents made elaborate arrangements for Bill's care and delivery. However, because of unforeseen circumstances (the doctor was involved in an accident on the way to the hospital), his blood transfusion was delayed three and one-half hours after birth. This delay resulted in severe brain damage. The parents took Bill home after three weeks in the hospital; they were unaware of his condition at that time. There had been a break in communications between the

doctors involved in the case. Within a week, the parents became aware that something was wrong with Bill and they sought an explanation. When Bill was six months of age, the family doctor recommended institutionalization. This was not a tenable solution to the parents because at that time they did not accept Bill's problems. He seemed like a normal healthy baby in so many ways. Thereafter, the parents began to "make the round of doctors to get answers."

The parents later did seriously consider institutionalizing him and concentrating their energies on their five healthy children. However, Mr. and Mrs. B see Bill as part of themselves and feel they couldn't separate from him. Mrs. B stated that she feels, somehow, that everything has worked out all right. Through Bill's infancy she didn't put him down for a year and a half. Her husband had decided that since he might possibly be blind and deaf, he needed some comfort and constantly holding him would provide it. The parents took turns holding him.

Mr. and Mrs. B tended to think of Bill as a baby and they would like to keep him as a baby. Of course, Mrs. B and the family would give "anything" to have him healthy; but even as helpless as he is, they "do not know what they would do without him."

Mrs. B is very apprehensive about sending Bill to school, although she has been contacted by the School District to enroll him in the day-training program. In fact, the whole family is very reluctant to send him to school. Mrs. B says she thinks of many excuses why she could not send him to school but that, at bottom, she feels that she probably could not separate from him. Furthermore, she wonders what school could possibly do better for him than his family does.

Mrs. B is able to talk about her complete devotion and commitment to Bill. Presently, his growth and growth potential "worries her sick," she says. Over the years, he has grown larger and, therefore, more difficult to handle. She "blanks out" any concern over not being able to handle him for the moment. Other concerns are: (1) if he should go to school, he would not be loved as he is at home; (2) he might cry, and (3) he might contract pneumonia or other fatal infections.

Mrs. B does not reflect too much on the future and has not made any particular plans about it. She likes to take one day at a time and tackle problems as they arise. When asked what would happen to Bill if something happened to his parents, Mrs. B says that she prays that she will live one day longer than Bill.

Gardner (1971) questioned the classical Freudian theory regarding parental guilt. He studied twenty-three parents of children with a severe physical disease to determine if there were other factors besides the classical psychoanalytic concept that might account for the inappropriate sense of guilt that parents tend to carry. His findings indicated the following: (1) some of the parents experienced guilt for reasons which supported the classical theory (i.e., related to unconscious hostility toward the child); (2) some parents experienced guilt explained by an alternative behavioral hypothesis: that it represented an attempt to control the uncontrollable; and (3) with some parents neither mechanism seemed to be operating. Gardner concluded that guilt may be used as a defense mechanism to handle anxiety.

Most parents, at the birth of their child, have great expectations for its future. They tend to live vicariously through the present and future experiences of their children. For some parents it can be catastrophic when their dreams are cut off with the recognition that their cerebral palsied child may face a rather limited life. The limitations are real but not total. However, for the parents whose fantasies for their child's future may have been somewhat grandiose, it is indeed traumatic to deal with the reality. Parents experience a sense of loss when they finally realize that their child cannot fulfill their dreams and hopes. Some parents may experience guilt feelings for producing this handicapped child and for feeling, at times, that they do not love him. While these reactions are understandable, given the stress of the situation, the feelings may not always be chronic. Many parents of handicapped children are able to recognize and understand these feelings and come to grips with them. Despite the many claims that these feelings of anxiety or hostility are neurotic in nature, these feelings are normal and are often based not on a neurotic reaction to stress, but rather may be expressions of frustration due to society's failure to provide meaningful community services that could help in alleviating the problem.

The following is an example of a family that had to disrupt their lives because of a lack of community resources. This excerpt from a social work interview illustrates how the lack of community resources can disrupt a family's life:

> Mary, a 9-year-old cerebral palsied child, was referred to the clinic for comprehensive evaluations by the Intermediate School District. Her present placement at the Educational Center is in a Day Training classroom, where she has been for the past two years. Mary was enrolled in a kindergarten program for the physically handicapped which was sponsored by the Society for Crippled Children. According to school records, her progress there was noted to be slow in both academic skills and social development.
>
> The parents spoke freely about Mary and how she functions in the home. During the winter months Mary's activities are mostly in-

doors due to her limited mobility. However, when it is warm enough, she loves being outdoors and she is allowed to crawl around and play with supervision. Her self-care skills are minimal and the parents take care of all her needs. In describing Mary, the P's tended to focus predominantly on her physical disabilities, and how they, in turn, limit the whole family and their activities as a family unit. The P's spoke of the difficulty of finding a responsible babysitter for Mary and of the need to leave her at home when they do take vacations so that they can be relieved of her care for a short time. They talked about the need for respite care facilities but none presently exist. The respective families of the P's do not assist with Mary's care. Mrs. P's parents are both deceased; although her mother was helpful with Mary when she was an infant. Mrs. P stated that her husband's mother tends to avoid Mary as the child seems to make her uncomfortable. The few times she cared for Mary proved to be disastrous.

Mrs. P explained that she feels Mary has not been as much of a problem to them as have other people and their lack of understanding. The P's feel that they have been able to adjust their lives satisfactorily to having a physically disabled child. However, they resent the general lack of concern shown for the extra problems associated with physical disabilities and the lack of community resources that would make Mary's care easier.

Mr. P stated that they plan to keep Mary with them for as long as they can care for her. He sees institutionalization for her in the future because presently he feels that there are few community facilities adequate for the needs of a "complete care case" such as Mary. They would in the future consider a group home placement for Mary if such facilities become available. Again, they expressed anger at the lack of services for the physically disabled.

Mrs. P states she had the hard measles early in her pregnancy with Mary, which was otherwise normal. They gradually became aware of her problems because all of Mary's developmental milestones were delayed. They sought testing for her at the hospital where she was first diagnosed as mentally retarded and having cerebral palsy. The P's described their shock and feelings of helplessness when they were told of her diagnosis by the doctors. After Mary's diagnosis her grandfather, who had an executive position in the school system arranged special services for her, such as a physical therapy program. However, with his death the P's feared that programs for Mary in town would deteriorate. At that time they were sending her to a preschool for the physically handicapped in a nearby city. As Mary neared school age, they learned of a special facility for her and moved the family to a nearby state because of the residency requirement. However, when Mary was tested for placement there, her intellectual functioning proved too low and she was not eligible for placement in the school. The program that was available to her then proved unsatisfactory to the parents because it was not equipped for children with physical problems. They then returned to their home town and their current residence because they were unhappy living in the neighboring state, and the school system there could not offer them more than what had been originally available at home.

It is important, then, to determine whether the problems of coping are being exacerbated by a paucity of community services or are primarily related to an emotional disequilibrium. Treatment intervention will be based on this diagnostic assessment. If it is the former, the social worker has the responsibility to mobilize whatever resources exist on behalf of the client. If resources are limited, the social worker's goal is to assist in the development of these needed services.

If services exist but parents are unable to utilize them effectively because of emotional blocks, the social worker provides counseling help to deal with these feelings.

Through counseling, parents can learn to accept these feelings and consequently learn to accept their handicapped child. Laycock (1952) concluded that, "It is not their handicap that matters, but how the individual feels about the handicap." The handicapped child can only be helped if he is accepted as he is, without embarrassment or resentment, without shame or guilt. It is imperative that the counselor has dealt with his own feelings about handicapping conditions. Neisser (1973) saw the counselor's positive attitude influencing the attitude of the parents toward a more constructive approach.

MANAGEMENT PLANNING AND INDIVIDUAL COUNSELING

There are various steps in devising a management plan for parents as they begin to face the task of habilitating their handicapped child. The social worker, while providing emotional support to the clients, must also assist them with the realities of the situation by undertaking the following steps: (1) encouraging the parents to have the cerebral palsied child evaluated completely by professional specialists who can make a clear determination of the extent of the neurological and physiological disability; (2) providing the parents with information and literature regarding the patterns of growth and development of children; (3) broadening the parent's perceptions of the problems by encouraging them to become members of an association of parents of the cerebral palsied. (There are local chapters of the United Cerebral Palsy Association in most major cities.) Through this contact they can learn about the scope of the problem on a state and national level. They can also learn about the various treatment facilities within their community or state. Most important, they can come in contact with other parents of cerebral palsied children and learn from their experiences in a shared way.

A positive action program needs to be implemented as soon as possible. The social worker should assist the parents in obtaining the appropriate medical care and the various recommended therapies (e.g., physical therapy, occupational therapy). The social worker may advise the parents exactly what part home training should play in the child's program after the social worker, with the parents' involvement, confers with the helping team. The social worker should try to provide a follow up at home to monitor the implementation of the home management plan.

In developing a management plan for the cerebral palsied child, it is not infrequent that the treatability of the physical handicap is made on the basis of a mental evaluation. This is an incorrect procedure since there is no correlation between the two. What must be known about the cerebral palsied child or adult in planning for his future is his general capabilities and, most specifically, the type of cerebral palsy for which the individual needs treatment.

There is interdependence between the physical and social development of the cerebral palsied person. Every cerebral palsied person needs help to maximize his growth potential. He should be helped to develop physically to the highest level of his ability. Because of the multiple problems encountered, unless physical development is forthcoming, the emotional and social aspects of the personality may be thwarted. The cerebral palsied person must learn to be as self-sufficient as possible within the limits posed by his physical handicap.

One important point, which social workers often try to help families recognize, is that the physically handicapped have emotions, drives, and desires that are very similar to those of normal individuals. However, the physically handicapped person often learns to mask these drives, expecially when he learns from those in his environment that certain behaviors are not socially acceptable coming from a physically handicapped person. Shearer (1972) reported that many people found it disgusting to think that physically handicapped persons had sexual feelings. Consequently they treated the handicapped person as if he were a non-sexual being. One can understand how the handicapped person would soon learn to conform to these expectations and, indeed, present himself as a non-sexual person due to social pressures.

If the handicapped person has experienced prolonged periods of hospitalization or convalescence he begins to learn to play the role of the patient and, consequently, may develop a more passive way of interacting with others.

The social worker provides counseling to the handicapped person in order to examine and acknowledge some of these personality stresses which may have created an over-sensitivity to his situation. The cerebral palsied person may develop a resentment toward sympathy despite his need for understanding. He may become unduly self-conscious and feel he doesn't belong in the normal world. He may place excessive restrictions upon himself and perceive himself as more limited than he really is, thus emphasizing his sense of failure.

In addition to the psychological aspects of his condition, the cerebral palsied person may feel a keen sense of stigma. Goffman (1963) pointed out that the physical "blemish" or stigmata has great impact on the handicapped person. Feeling stigmatized often forces the handicapped person to develop defensive patterns of behavior. He may therefore anticipate rejection from those around him even when it is not warranted.

From a sociological perspective, society perceives the cerebral palsied person as belonging to a marginal group. In a sense he can be considered part of a minority group many of whose rights have been disenfranchised. As his many human and even legal rights are violated, the cerebral palsied person may perceive himself as a nonperson.

To restore his ego strengths, the social worker must deal with the reality of the situation. He cannot deny society's attitudes or the client's limitations. He can, however, assist the client in learning how to overcome feelings of worthlessness and despair. This is achieved by offering concrete assistance so that he can more adequately deal with his problems of daily living, such as financial aid, education, employment, housing, recreational, and social activities. Enabling the client to live as normally as possible within the mainstream of society is crucial to sound management planning.

GROUP WORK WITH THE CEREBRAL PALSIED AND THEIR FAMILIES

The group work process is extensively utilized by social workers as a method to assist parents and the cerebral palsied individual to deal with some of their social and personal problems. The focus of the group experience can be either educational or therapeutic.

Educational Group Work Programs

Educational groups may be informational in nature. Some agencies may provide the group with a series of guest lecturers who present specific expert knowledge in their areas of speciality. The social worker may coordinate or lead these groups and serve as the moderator of these educational sessions. Speech therapists, physical therapists, dentists, and pediatricians may be called upon to present their disciplinary perspectives. The focus of the educational group may be: (1) the causes of cerebral palsy; (2) discussion of symptomatology; (3) clarification of the role of the therapists and the objectives of their management plans; (4) clarification of the joint responsibility of parents and professionals in carrying out the management plan; and (5) delineation of available community resources which can assist the parents in their child's management and care.

The educational group process can be viewed as a teaching device that affords parents an opportunity to decrease their anxiety and tension by learning more about their child's condition and behavior as well as learning techniques for handling specific problems. Agencies serving the cerebral palsied individual, particularly those providing services to children, have found the educational group very effective in assisting the parents to work more cooperatively with the agency on behalf of the child.

Educational groups for cerebral palsied individuals can be extremely helpful as a means of providing clarification and information about the condition. The group member can utilize the group experience to ask questions that may have concerned him and to learn new techniques about management so that he can deal more effectively with his activities of daily living.

Armstrong (1957), in writing about his three years of experience with adult cerebral palsied groups at the Erie Neighborhood House in Chicago, cited the following factors as pertinent issues to consider in implementing group counseling programs for cerebral palsied adults:

1. Support the idea of acceptance of the handicap and the sharing of feelings.
2. Understand the background and past experiences of the members.
3. Provide transportation to meetings.
4. Provide group leadership and clarity of leader's role.
5. Encourage the members to join other groups.
6. Provide clarity of group objectives so that there is agreement as to the group focus on social or therapeutic needs or both.
7. Determine the spectrum of group activities: i.e., social dancing, crafts, trips, camping, picnics, speakers, rap sessions.
8. Move toward having the members assume various leadership roles within the group.

Armstrong concluded that the group experience had many positive therapeutic results for the members. It provided them with the opportunity to interact socially with their peers and to understand and discover various facets of their personalities. They began to learn the rudiments of testing relationships and developing a sense of trust in themselves and in their peers. It also provided them with the awareness that other cerebral palsied persons shared their concerns around employment, dating, and their relationship with their parents and siblings. The group discussions provided them with an opportunity to learn from each other appropriate methods of dealing with these problems.

Some of the problems engendered by the group experience were (1) inability of some members to communicate with one another due to speech disorders; (2) the expression of dependence and independence in relationship to the other group members; (3) the ambivalence of dependence and independence on the group leader; and (4) the fear of new experiences whenever the group attempted to undertake new activities.

Evaluation of the group program indicated that there was a similarity in the needs of adult group members and the needs of parents and professionals, particularly in the following areas: (1) ability to comfortably communicate feelings and ideas; (2) conflicts regarding feelings of independence and dependence; and (3) ability to appropriately and constructively offer criticism.

Therapeutic Group Counseling Programs

Group counseling with a therapeutic focus is a very important social work method of helping parents and cerebral palsied individuals understand and resolve their conflicting feelings related to the handicapping condition.

The purpose of the group process is to provide the opportunity for each member to bring forth concerns, to ventilate anger, and to integrate his confused thoughts so that he ultimately can gain more knowledge about himself and others in the group.

At times the process may be painful and the procedure may be slow. Usually, there is a repetitive discharge of these intense feelings. However, through these emotional reactions and intellectual endeavors, the group member begins to adapt to the reality of his situation.

Many group leaders noted the intense quality of the hostility expressed by group members. The bitter feelings of parents are not limited in their expression only to professional people who have failed to provide all the help the parents expected or who have reported a condition which the parents prefer to believe does not exist. Often they are directed at neighbors or even strangers. With careful guidance, the group leader can enable the group members to recognize the basis for the hostility and to determine when it is realistic and when it is distorted. The group member then moves toward dealing with the anger in a more appropriate fashion, thus freeing his psychic energies to deal with the ongoing problems related to the handicapped condition.

Milman (1971) reported that in a group therapy program for parents of children with physical handicaps, the following parental attitudes were continuously elicited: (a) shame; (b) painful self-consciousness; (c) personal distaste for their child's appearance; (d) dread of being pitied or ridiculed; and (e) feelings of inadequacy. Milman saw the therapeutic aims of group counseling as being "to minimize individual feelings of isolation and difference, the hypothesis being that the parent derives a feeling of strength and solace from discovering that he is not unique in his tragedy."

The primary objective of group therapy, then, appears to be a resolution of unresolved feelings leading to the development of a more appropriate method of dealing with conflict. The catalytic agent may be the guidance given by therapists as well as by the patients in the group.

Selection of members for groups may be done on the basis of similarity of problems, sex, age, or socio-economic status, in order to develop a sense of unity. In other instances, no effort is made to order such similarities. Beck (1973) states that it may not be found "particularly necessary to strive toward homogeneity of social strata, intellectual capacity, personality makeup or degree of defect in the member's child. Groups soon develop a homogeneity of their own, the members become quite supportive of one another."

Group counseling with a therapeutic focus has been a very effective mode of social work intervention. It can be even more effective when used in conjunction with social casework, which provides the individual group member the opportunity to examine his problems from an additional perspective.

THE SOCIAL WORKER AS AN ADVOCATE AND COMMUNITY ORGANIZER

Responsibility to Advocate

Intellectually, most professionals accept the responsibility for advocating on behalf of their clients. Social workers, for example, are aware that the National Association of Social Workers supports advocacy, which is inherent in its code of ethics, which states, "I regard as my primary obligation the welfare of the individual or group served, which includes action to improve social conditions." Implied in this statement is that the social worker's obligation to the client comes before his obligation to his employer—even when these two interests compete with one another.

Professionals who believe in the dignity and the worth of human beings must commit themselves to defending the rights of their clients and to taking issue when these human and legal rights are violated. This commitment, however, is not always forthcoming; for it takes courage and wisdom to deal with the anxieties and threats that are posed to the professional who assumes the advocate role.

Definition of Advocacy

In discussing advocacy with various professionals, it has been noted that the term "advocacy" is often used somewhat loosely. Some professionals feel that whatever they do for a client is a form of advocacy. Simply providing basic services, they feel, is serving as an advocate for clients. The term "advocacy," however, has come to take on a more specialized meaning. To advocate denotes an aggressive form of action. Webster defines an *advocate* as "one who pleads the cause of another," also, "one who argues for, defends, maintains or recommends a cause or proposal." An advocate usually acts on behalf of the interest of a particular group or class. Wineman and James (1969), therefore, find him speaking out when the situation gets pretty "crunchy"—when he and the client are pushed up against the wall. He's there when the going gets tough. The advocate, then, is the client's advisor or champion in his dealings with the court, the police, social agencies, the school or other organizations that have direct bearing on the client's well-being. The advocate plays the ombudsman role.

Social workers, practicing in the area of community organization, recognize that advocacy is a pertinent strategy to use in their efforts to effect change in the service delivery system. The role of "change agent" has become a vital component of community planning and is being assumed more and more by social workers concerned with the need for social change.

The Social Worker as an Advocate for the Cerebral Palsied Client

A recent development in the social worker's role in the field of cerebral palsy is his assumption of advocate responsibility on behalf of the cerebral palsied client. An example of this endeavor is the Child Advocacy Project, initiated, developed, and implemented by the United Cerebral Palsy Association, Inc., a national organization located in New York City.

The IHF Plan

In 1968, the United Cerebral Palsy Association developed a broad plan for improving services called The Individual with Cerebral Palsy and His Family (the IHF Plan). The core of this plan essentially related to the concern that the needs of children and adults with cerebral palsy change through the course of their growth and development. It was recommended that the United Cerebral Palsy Association should serve in the role of a lifetime partner to these individuals and their families in helping them to obtain and utilize the right service at the right time.

Recognizing its need to play the advocate role, the United Cerebral Palsy Association began to consider strategies that would enable persons with cerebral palsy and other developmental disabilities to more quickly obtain services and resources. A logical procedure to implement this goal was to undertake a demonstration project, funded by the Department of Health, Education, and Welfare, that would enable the Association to carry out its commitment to improving the service delivery system on behalf of its clients. In July 1972, the Association launched the Child Advocacy Project under the direction of Ernest Weinrich, a social worker, who also served as the Coordinator of Planning for Long Term Services of the Professional Services Program of the Association.

National Child Advocacy Project

The United Cerebral Palsy Association implemented a very unique and challenging advocacy project, which it hoped would deal with many service delivery issues that the Association was experiencing on a nationwide level. The title of the project was "A Demonstration of Three Models of Advocacy Programs for Developmentally Disabled Children."

The uniqueness of the project was the stress it placed on the utilization of consumer's input, which, it is hoped, would lead to the formation of a coordinated pressure group that would advocate on behalf of the developmentally disabled throughout the country.

Three affiliates of the United Cerebral Palsy Association, Inc., were selected as participants in the project; and they contributed funds on a matching basis. UCP of New York State, UCP of Southeastern Wisconsin (Milwaukee), and UCP of San Mateo–Santa Clara County (California) were selected to develop demonstration advocacy models on the criteria that they represented (1) diverse geographic and population differences, (2) areas with varying patterns of service delivery and availability, and (3) a unique style of program development within the affiliate.

That there was a need for such a project was unquestionable. Ernest Weinrich (1972) stated: "The advocate role of our Association is essential. It assures that someone takes responsibility for seeing that the legal and human rights of the person with a developmental disability and his family are met. These include the rights to education, property, community services, employment, social involvement, and other necessities of life as well as medical and therapeutic care." The project's goals and objectives were described as follows (Weinrich 1973): "The goals, objectives, and strategies for the three models of advocacy have evolved from a number of specific problems which include: (1) getting services at the time they are needed; (2) being discriminated against in receiving generic community services; (3) lack of service and resource development; (4) terrible living conditions in state institutions; and (5) problems associated with poverty and racism." It was recognized that attempts should be made "to change the status quo in many areas of decision-making by involving individuals who are historically powerless." He felt the project would provide a level of increased visibility and power for these people. By utilizing fact-finding and systems analysis, which would examine (1) attitudinal barriers, (2) lack of accountability to consumers within the service delivery systems, and (3) other factors that place people into positions of unequal opportunities, social systems change could be effected.

Each of the three models within the Project attempted to demonstrate a different approach to advocacy. The Milwaukee model could be described as the "Agency Advocate—Ombudsman Model." This model offers a consumer information program and direct assistance to clients in utilizing community resources. It is also involved in legislative and governmental activities, fact-finding, and community organization services. The San Mateo–Santa Clara (California) Model follows the "Consumer Advocate—Community Planning Model," which provides a system analysis of service, planning for case funding, and development of forums for consumer interaction with service delivery and planning units. The New York State model has been described as the "Agent Advocate—Program Developer Model." It has attempted to implement legislative activities and has devised mechanisms for the planning and expansion of services among unserved and underserved populations in rural areas and state institutions. It has also attempted to utilize local consumer advocacy councils.

The Milwaukee Model: The Ombudsman Role

The advocacy coordinator of the Milwaukee Model utilizes the advocate and community organizer role undertaken by many social workers today. As advocate and community organizer, the coordinator, among his many community "change agent" roles, serves as an ombudsman to those consumers who have unmet needs and have difficulty in finding solutions to their complex problems. For example:

> The Kiwanis Children's Center called the Coordinator to inform him that Billy's parents were having trouble getting him admitted to school. It was reported that there was considerable difficulty in obtaining the required testing for Billy, who was physically handicapped. Without such testing, the principal was putting off consideration of admitting Billy to school since the school had been thinking of a special placement for him. The Coordinator (ombudsman) called the principal on behalf of Billy, and his parents,

and learned that the testing had taken place and the school was now waiting for the results to be forwarded to the central office so a decision could be made regarding Billy's placement. The coordinator placed pressure on the principal, not only for clarification of the ultimate special education placement, but also urged for Billy's immediate admission to the school program on the basis of Billy's right to be in school. The next day the principal called the coordinator to inform him that Billy was going to be admitted to the school within the week.

Another case example that occurred in the Milwaukee Model that typifies the advocate role taken by many social workers and other rehabilitation workers is as follows:

Psychological testing had been arranged through the Division of Vocational Rehabilitation for George, a young handicapped adult. He was very eager to begin some type of employment training program. He recognized that future employment planning was dependent upon the test scores. He was, therefore, quite anxious when a number of weeks went by without any notification of the test results. He had hoped he would receive a follow-up appointment with the psychologist or the Division of Vocational Rehabilitation worker to discuss the test scores, but none was forthcoming. As the delay lengthened, the Coordinator (ombudsman) was notified of George's dilemma. The Coordinator immediately contacted the testing service and learned that "a period of 6 weeks or longer was normal between testing and reporting. It was not considered uncommon nor out of line." The Coordinator immediately contacted the Director of the Technical College responsible for the testing and stated his objections to the rather casual attitude voiced about the delay. He pointed out the importance of quick feedback so that employment planning for the handicapped person could commence without unnecessary delay. The Coordinator challenged the system's cavalier treatment of the client and requested a written statement of what constituted a "reasonable period" for completion of testing and follow-up reporting of test scores. Such confrontation made the College re-examine its organizational procedures as well as evaluate its attitudes toward the handicapped person.

A third example describes the ombudsman's efforts to obtain residential care for his client:

The coordinator learned that Donald, age 4, a mentally retarded youngster with cerebral palsy, was not enrolled in any educational program. The coordinator, at the request of Donald's parents, contacted the Superintendent of a nearby State Residential Center to request consideration for Donald's placement in the program. The coordinator pointed out that Donald was unable to utilize the existing community nursery school because he could not tolerate riding in a car for more than ten to thirty minutes. The nearest appropriate nursery school was located one hour to an hour and a half (each way) from Donald's home. At the present time, there is no physical therapy program available to Donald in his home. He has little, if any, peer contacts. It appeared that he would receive only minimal benefit from enrollment in the nursery school program. The coordinator urged the superintendent that while Donald was on the Center's waiting list for future placement, immediate attention needed to be given to Donald's situation because of the dire impact his condition was having on his family. The stress on the family was mounting because the mother had no one to care for Donald if she wanted to go out. She was forced to spend almost all of her time with Donald, and, in consequence, has experienced many feelings of depression. Not only was it harming her own self-concept, but the marriage seemed to be suffering adversely.

Thus, the coordinator acted as an advocate in all three instances for individuals who had legitimate grievances. The coordinator investigated the circumstances of the situation and then initiated action to resolve the problem by presenting the facts to those who were on a policy-making level.

As an advocate the community organizer, the coordinator in the Milwaukee Model undertakes these additional activities to assist the consumer: (1) He provides a consumer-information program, which utilizes a newsletter that includes information on pending legislation of concern to the developmentally disabled. How this legislation can be utilized to benefit the consumer is clarified. The television media is also utilized to educate the community. A series of spot announcements and half-hour public service programs are effective ways of describing and highlighting the needs and problems of the developmentally disabled. (2) He participates in legislative and governmental activities, such as: (a) attending state level hearings concerning the developmentally disabled; (b) providing testimony to assemblymen and legislators; (c) corresponding with governmental officials concerning the needs of the developmentally disabled; and (d) communicating with the attorney general's office and other governmental agencies concerning the legal status of the developmentally disabled in relation to policies, procedures, and practices of the general spectrum of services designed to meet the needs of these people.

As a community organizer, the coordinator is considerably involved in the following activities on behalf of the developmentally disabled: (1) fact-finding concerning the unmet needs and problems faced by the developmentally disabled. For example, the following kinds of projects are being undertaken: (a) a project to determine the need for a comprehensive follow-up program for infants treated and released from high-risk infant nurseries and neonatal intensive care units of area hospitals; (b) a project to determine the availability of appropriate opportunities for social interaction and recreation among the severely developmentally disabled in the community; and (c) a project to determine the need for special community residential facilities for the developmentally disabled. (2) Involvement in community interagency functions through participation in (a) interorganization planning activities related to the needs of the developmentally disabled; and (b) involvement in coalition units of consumer oriented organizations that monitor existing programs serving the developmentally disabled. (3) Development of Grant Applications to be submitted to the State for developmental disabilities funding. For example, a grant concerning the development of a Neighborhood Advocate Program in the central city, which has predominantly a black population, has been drafted, as well as a proposal concerning the development of a legal advocacy program.

The National Child Advocacy Project is continually being evaluated regarding its effectiveness. During the initial years it has encountered some difficulties, specifically in its abilities to involve more consumers who have not previously been involved in such activities, particularly parents from ethnic-minority or low socioeconomic groups. There have been a very limited number of Chicanos involved in the San Mateo–Santa Clara Project and blacks in the Milwaukee project. New strategies and techniques must be devised that will encourage these ethnic groups to participate more fully. Segal (1970) noted in his study that the Associations for Retarded Children encountered similar obstacles in their efforts to involve blacks in their membership activities. However, many exciting results have been achieved by the three models in the projects, namely: (1) Coalitions have been formed in all programs. (2) Data gathering is well underway. (3) Demonstrations have successfully been implemented to indicate how existing resources can be more effectively utilized and expanded. (4) A greater awareness has been developed by the National United Cerebral Palsy Association regarding its future priorities and how it might more effectively carry out its current policies and procedures so as to meet its organizational objectives. Consequently, the national organization is making an increased effort to give priority to the following concerns: (a) early identification and referral; (b) legal advocacy; (c) legislative actions; and (d) increased consumer involvement at various levels in its decision-making process.

The procedures utilized by the staff of the National Child Advocacy

Project within its three distinct models clearly illustrates the vital and exciting new directions that are taking place within the areas of advocacy and community organization. While these methods are generic and are being used by various professionals, whether they are rehabilitation workers or special educators, they are becoming an important technique that social workers are utilizing more often on behalf of their clients.

Marie Moore (1974) the National Advocacy Coordinator for the Child Advocacy Project, clearly described the changing role and responsibility of the professional who attempts to help the developmentally disabled. She points out that it is no longer sufficient to primarily meet the needs of the individual, but it is incumbent upon all professionals to develop methods to effect positive change in service delivery systems that are designed to meet the needs of the developmentally disabled. Miss Moore comments: "Because we are attempting to change the status quo in many areas of decision-making, we are attempting to create dynamic social change . . . We have involved ourselves in the business of adjusting systems to meet the needs of people—not adjusting people to fit into the systems. Hopefully, we are about to establish a new system within a voluntary health agency that cannot be institutionalized but is in a state of everchanging to meet the needs and insure the rights of people with developmental disabilities. The system must become a constant change agent to make the rights of citizens into the realities of life for all people."

Wayne County Referral Center, Detroit, Michigan

Another example of an advocacy program involving social workers is an agency called the Wayne County Referral Center located in Detroit, Michigan. The Center was organized in May 1973 to act as a case management agency for developmentally disabled children and young adults. While the Center's major concern is with mentally retarded individuals, a large number of their clients have multiple disabilities, frequently including cerebral palsy.

The Center was established because the traditional patterns of providing services through state and local agencies has been fractionalized and administratively compartmentalized. Families and individuals with health and social problems have a difficult time obtaining multiple services for their complex problems within an uncoordinated service delivery system. The cerebral palsied client, attempting to obtain needed assistance within the spectrum of community services finds that the various agencies providing these services have different eligibility criteria and the facilities are often too far apart geographically (and sometimes philosophically) to insure adequate referral and follow-up. Owen (1974) contends that most agencies serving the handicapped person are unable to provide an effective case management system (a system that insures that individuals or families are receiving all of the services required to assist in the resolution of their health and welfare problems) because: (1) they have eligibility criteria which limits the scope of their clientele; (2) being responsible for the provision of direct services potentially conflicts with the responsibility of total advocacy; and (3) case management functions are not traditionally seen as high priority responsibilities of the agency.

When the concept of the Wayne County Referral Center was presented to the Wayne County Board of Commissioners for its approval, County Commissioner Paul Silver presented a resolution, on May 17, 1973, which stated that the basis for the implementation of such an agency was due to the fact that community resources for developmentally disabled children were not coordinated and easily accessible to their families. Silver called for the establishment of this new agency to coordinate these services and proposed "that the Center provide an advocacy component and that the Center be primarily responsible for advocating the rights of its clients to adequate and needed services." Silver further described the Center's function as follows:

> The new center shall receive referrals from all appropriate sources, including state and local agencies, physicians, schools and parents. Upon receipt of the referral, the staff from the Center shall determine a treatment plan to meet the child's needs based on a collection of data. This collection phase shall include a home visit. If specialized diagnostic services are needed they shall be acquired through the Center. After a determination of the treatment plan is made, referral shall be made to an agency for service. The Center staff shall monitor the service agency to insure that the prescribed care is being given. In addition, this agency shall have available funds to purchase needed services not available in the existing delivery system.

Thus, the Wayne County Referral Center was established to provide a much needed case management program. In September 1973, the Detroit Wayne County Community Mental Health Services Board signed a contractual agreement with the Wayne County Associations for the Retarded to establish the Center with a budget of $524,050 through June 30, 1974, and a full year funding of $1,000,000. The County appropriated 25 percent of the funds and the Michigan Department of Mental Health allocated 75 percent of the funds (Owen 1974).

While the Center does not provide services directly to clients, its mission is to insure that clients receive appropriate services within the health and welfare delivery system.

In essence, then, the Center serves as an advocate for the client by (1) identifying clients' needs; (2) involving the child and family in the decision making process around obtaining services; (3) monitoring the process to determine if the client is receiving appropriate services; (4) attempting to have an input into planning and policy development for services within the region served by the Center; (5) attempting to seek out new or innovative approaches in programming when the existing agencies are not responsive to the needs of the client; and (6) attempting to remain independent from the providers of services so that its advocacy stance can be maintained.

As an example of the social worker playing the advocate role in the Center, the following illustration is presented:

At age 3, Bill White was diagnosed as having cerebral palsy. Bill, now 25, suffers from severe spastic triplegia secondary to cerebral palsy. His main means of locomotion is through a wheelchair. He handles stairs by crawling. He has no voluntary motion in his legs and is able to transfer into and out of an automobile. Bill is also mildly retarded. His speech is slowed as he occasionally "searches" for a word. He also must work to articulate his speech.

Bill was committed by the Probate Court to the Department of Mental Health for institutional care in 1962. He was admitted to a State Home at age 10 where he remained for 10 years. In 1972, he was placed in a family care program out of the State Home under the supervision and planning of a Family and Children Services Agency. He attended the Multi-Handicap School in the local Intermediate School District. A year later, Bill began prevocational training, and he also attended an Art Center for a drawing class for one semester but had to quit due to transportation problems.

Bill also attended a local church with the help of members of the church who picked him up each Sunday. He learned to ride the bus to Detroit (about 2 hours away) so that he could visit his mother.

Problems between Bill and his foster mother arose as he matured and as he increasingly wanted his independence. Both Bill and his mother requested that he return to Detroit to live with her. His original goal was to be able to return home and build a life for himself. Now he felt he was ready to achieve his goal.

In April, 1974, a Training and Treatment Program Evaluation Planning Conference was held with representatives from 5 agencies: Youth Opportunities Unlimited; Vocational Rehabilitation Services; Department of Social Services Adult Foster Care Program; Family and Children Services; and Multi-Handicap School Staff. Bill and his Mother and older sister also attended.

After reviewing all of the information each agency provided, it was decided that Bill would return to Detroit and live with his mother,

Mrs. White. It was recognized that Bill needed vocational guidance, medical assistance, physical therapy, and social contacts if he were to become more independent.

It was decided that Vocational Rehabilitation Services in Detroit would be contacted for vocational training and for assistance in remodeling Mrs. White's home so that a first floor bathroom, adequate first floor sleeping arrangements, and front door ramp could be constructed. Department of Social Services would arrange for the change in Bill's Supplemental Security Income checks. Bill needed to improve his reading and math skills since his present level was that of approximately the third grade. Bill wanted to enter a job training program so that he could learn a trade and become financially able to support himself. He also wanted to learn to drive a car so he could become more independent. It was recognized that it was imperative that "Bill must not be allowed to sit home."

The target date for his return home was set for June 1, 1974.

On May 31, 1974, the Coordinator of Mental Retardation Services of the Children and Family Services sent referral letters with background data to: a rehabilitation clinic, Vocational Rehabilitation Services and a cerebral palsy agency. The coordinator also wrote to Bill and his mother telling them of the referrals she had made. She enclosed a folder of the Wayne County Referral Center, stating she felt that agency might be helpful in following up on Bill's program if any problems developed.

In July, 1974, Bill's mother called Wayne County Referral Center, stating she was receiving service from Vocational Rehabilitation Services but that they were very slow and wondered if Wayne County Referral Center could help.

A social worker was then assigned to serve as Bill's advocate and to follow up on the management plans that were proposed for Bill prior to his return to his mother's home.

The social worker contacted the various community agencies who were to be involved in Bill's "rehabilitation plan" and was dismayed to find that little was being done for Bill. Either the agency personnel were resistive toward assuming responsibility for developing a program for Bill or they simply were unaware of the referral to them by the agencies in the community Bill left.

It was almost as if the social worker had to start from the beginning in order to involve the agencies in implementing a meaningful rehabilitation program for Bill. Sometimes, the bureaucratic procedures regarding eligibility requirements or the fact that there were specific agency procedures that had to be adhered to almost made the task of getting Bill the help he needed seem insurmountable.

In her advocate role, the social worker had to educate, persuade, and, at times, cajole the various agencies so that they would move ahead to begin planning for Bill. She made arrangements for a doctor at a rehabilitation clinic to verify Bill's physical needs and to write a letter of recommendation to Vocational Rehabilitation Services regarding the need for remodeling Mrs. White's home. He agreed that Bill should not have to continue to crawl upstairs to use the bathroom. However, the doctor would not recommend driver's training or physical therapy, which was in contrast to the previous proposed recommendations made for Bill.

The social worker attempted to enroll Bill in a vocational evaluation and training program. He was excited about this plan, but the transportation required to reach the program was not available. The social worker expended a considerable amount of time trying to arrange for this transportation but with no success.

In addition, she expended considerable time in trying to get community recreation programs to serve Bill. The summer camp program was full and efforts were made to recruit volunteers to help get Bill to sporting events. Church groups and agencies geared to provide transportation to the handicapped were contacted with no positive results because their services were not available on an extended daily basis or Bill was not in their geographic service area. Numerous other agencies whose mandates are service provision for cerebral palsied or otherwise physically impaired individuals were called on to involve them in developing a coordinated rehabilitation program for Bill. While each of these agencies expressed interest and concern with Bill's needs, they were unable to assist in any substantial way because their programs were already filled to capacity and/ or their services did not include the needed transportation component.

At the time of this writing, only minor victories have been recorded in the fight to provide Bill with a meaningful and comprehensive service plan. However, the social worker, in her role as an advocate, has been successful in finding resources outside of the traditional service delivery system; and she continues to exert persuasion and pressure to enlist the cooperation of all agencies so that the picture of Bill White's future is brighter currently than at the point of referral to the Center a few months ago. The fact that an interested "outsider" has competently and diligently shouldered the responsibility in the fight to obtain quality services has been a major contribution to the well being of Bill and his family.

This illustration clearly shows the need for the coordination of community-based services so that the cerebral palsied client and the family can be better served. The social worker in the advocate role can do much to assure the achievement of this objective.

16

Vocational Guidance and Employment

JULIUS S. COHEN

*If a man does not keep pace with his companions, perhaps it is
because he hears a different drummer. Let him step to the music
which he hears, however measured or far away.**

IN 1918, Congress dealt with a national concern about the inability of handicapped veterans to engage fully in the work world by passing the first legislation providing services for this group. The Vocational Rehabilitation Act
of 1920 set up the federal-state rehabilitation programs and was the next
step in the effort to develop rehabilitation services and expanded eligibility
to handicapped civilians.

The Vocational Rehabilitation Act of 1943 provided great stimulus to
the rehabilitation movement, and extended services to the mentally
disabled. The 1954 Amendments provided funds for training personnel for
the field, and it supported the expansion of rehabilitation facilities and
workshops. The next major legislation passed in 1965 provided additional
funds and opportunities for program expansion. A commission was established to insure that architectural barriers be considered and that buildings would be made more accessible to handicapped persons.

The Rehabilitation Act of 1973 (Public Law 93-112, 87 STAT. 394)
represents the most recent step in the process of meeting the needs of
disabled citizens in this society. This new law requires that employers
operating under federal contracts must undertake affirmative action to employ and advance in employment qualified handicapped individuals. As a
safeguard against discrimination, Section 504 states: "No otherwise
qualified handicapped individual in the United States, as defined in section 7

---

*Acknowledgment is made to Random House, Inc., for permission to quote from *Walden
and Other Writings of Henry David Thoreau* (New York: Modern Library, 1937), p. 290.

(6), shall, solely by reason of his handicap, be excluded from the participation in, be denied the benefits of, or be subjected to discrimination under
any program or activity receiving Federal financial assistance."

It is against this background of growing services and rights that vocational programming for individuals with cerebral palsy must be considered.
Professionals in rehabilitation have had to work with fears, superstitions,
and folklore in their efforts to assist clients. These problems are especially
acute when the problems of the cerebral palsied are considered.

Rehabilitation of individuals with cerebral palsy may suggest a wide variety of images to the reader, as wide as the range of problems that are
subsumed under the condition known as cerebral palsy. Does rehabilitation
mean the employment of the college graduate who, although somewhat
handicapped by a slight limp and an awkward speech pattern, was able to
complete his course work successfully? Does it mean placement of the individual who has rather severe speech problems (making communication extremely difficult), but who is quite capable of performing the wide variety of
movements required on the job? Does it suggest the individual who has
spontaneous and uncontrolled movements and whose mobility and em-
ployability are severely limited? Does the term "rehabilitation" refer to the
individual who, while quite able and otherwise acceptable to employers in
many ways, possesses uncontrolled facial grimaces? Is competitive employment the goal for a person who, in addition to physical involvement, has
demonstrated somewhat limited mental abilities? Does rehabilitation include the consideration of the person who, with optimal services, will be able
to be partially self-supporting in a sheltered working environment; the individual who as a result of intensive care and treatment is better able to maintain himself and take care of activities of daily living? Does it mean the
person who is handicapped only while standing, but in a seated job is a
person with abilities?

The rehabilitation of the cerebral palsied individual can be any of these
or many more. Basic to the understanding of the services necessary for this
group is a clear understanding of the differences between the disability "cerebral palsy" and the handicaps that result to the individual and impinge
upon the effectiveness of rehabilitation programming.

Because of the single label, "cerebral palsy," it is easy and program-
matically dangerous to see individuals so labeled as part of a homogeneous
group with similar vocational potentials and goals. Muthard and
Hutchinson (1968) studied cerebral palsied college students and found great
individual differences among them. While their schooling developed somewhat slower than other college students, and while they required special
techniques and assistance, they are able to use the college experience to
move toward a variety of vocational goals.

Robinault and Denhoff (1973) discuss the variety of strengths and problems that are found in individuals with cerebral palsy. They consider the personal and environmental factors which impinge on adjustment and cite rehabilitation as "concerned with the multiply handicapped individual's evolution from the total dependency of infancy to the independence of maturity."

Thus, problems of realistic vocational guidance and employment are similar no matter what the specific disability. The frequency of multiple handicaps within this population requires adaptations in the provision of professional services. In addition, general factors relating to rehabilitation will be considered and their implications to this group will be discussed. These general characteristics may be subsumed under problems in a number of areas: personality, communications, mobility, evaluation, and education and training for the selection of realistic goals.

PROBLEMS IN THE REHABILITATION PROCESS

Personality

Contrary to popular belief, there appears to be little relationship between the type or degree of disability and personality. Wright (1960) concludes that there is no evidence that there are certain personality factors related to particular disabilities, nor is there a correlation between the level of adjustment and the severity of the condition.

In terms of developmental experiences, the individual with cerebral palsy might be expected to exhibit a greater degree of problems than might be found in a normal population. For example, individuals who have been the center of a wide variety of services and activities may continue to expect to be the focus of continuing relationships even in adult situations. It is necessary to help individuals with these and related problems to recognize the limitations that such expectations may have, but also the strengths that they bring to the adult life situation and, it is hoped, to aid them in making any necessary adjustments.

Communications

A second major area focuses on the problems of communication, both oral and written. Among individuals who are cerebral palsied, there is a relatively high incidence of communication problems. These problems may stem from a variety of handicaps. Mental retardation, speech and hearing defects, seizures, perceptual problems, and other difficulties all add to the communication problem. In the home or school, with parents and teachers accustomed to this pattern, there may not be too great a handicap.

However, these communication problems may become increasingly severe with adulthood when relationships change and higher standards of performance may be applied.

Unintelligible speech may lead the listener to conclude inaccurately that the speaker is mentally retarded. Extensive blocks in the speech pattern, often accompanied by facial grimaces, often cause great discomfort in the listener. These problems may interpose in the conseling situation, create difficulties with employers and fellow workers, and may interfere with the development and implementation of a vocational plan and vocational goals.

Mobility

It is expected that adults who are participating fully in society are able to move with few problems throughout their environment. Unfortunately, poor architecture and poor planning preclude the utilization of many buildings, services, and facilities by the individual who is mobile only with braces, crutches, or wheelchair. This problem may exceed the ability of the individual to deal with it. Of what value is a rehabilitation program if the individual, upon completing it, is unable to apply his training because a flight of stairs has been built between him and employment?

In many states, public buildings are required by law to have entrances accessible to physically disabled individuals. How unfortunate it is that this thinking is not applied to all construction. How many persons are denied the best possible education because private schools and universities do not follow these practices? How frequently do churches, built with impressive flights of stairs to raise them above street level, also rise above the ability of the disabled person to utilize them?

The National Society for Crippled Children and Adults (2023 West Ogden Avenue, Chicago, Illinois 60612), in assuming a leadership role in this problem with other interested organizations, has made available a kit on architectural barriers. Of special interest would be "American Standard Specifications for Making Buildings and Facilities Accessible to, and usable by, the Physically Handicapped," a statement of standards which was sponsored by the National Society for Crippled Children and Adults and the President's Committee on Employment of the Handicapped and approved by the American Standards Association, Inc. These documents collectively reflect the current status of concern for the limitations imposed by the man-made environment on the rehabilitation of the physically handicapped.

This concern has been incorporated as an important aspect of the Vocational Rehabilitation Act of 1973 which requires the establishment of an Architectural and Transportation Barriers Compliance Board. The Board is to consider architectural, transportation, and attitudinal barriers confronting handicapped individuals and to recommend on the elimination of such barriers. A careful review of the housing needs of handicapped persons and the elimination of barriers to mass transportation should be important factors in the incorporation of these individuals into full, productive adult lives.

Evaluation

Determining the true level of intellectual functioning of persons with motor and communicative problems is exceedingly difficult and may require special instruments, techniques, and training in this type of evaluation. Interpretation of test scores may be made more difficult by the lack of suitable norms and by problems in determining the extent to which the test results reflect the interaction of the disability and the instrument while not showing the ability of the person. This problem is made even more acute by the shortage of professionals sufficiently trained and experienced to meet these problems in assessing the potential of cerebral palsied individuals.

As rehabilitation programs expanded and as services often are based on a vocational assessment of the handicapped individual, the workshop increasingly has become the site for such evaluations. Clients may be served on a long- or a short-term basis in a workshop. Long-term placement is equivalent to an employment status; short-term for evaluation, work adjustment, and preparation for employment. Nelson (1971) lists as the short-term objectives of workshops:

1. assessment of work potential,
2. demonstration to industry and workshops,
3. preparation for employment,
4. development of work readiness,
5. development of work adjustment,
6. competence in vocational skills,
7. improvement of the handicapping condition,
8. provision of related services.

The workshop provides a unique arena for the conduct of assessments. Usually staffed by an interdisciplinary team, vocational, psychological, physical, and social evaluations and services can be provided within a work-like milieu. Such efforts in a "real" situation may provide better and more useful data than reliance on standard instruments which may have more limited value with this population.

Education

Problems in the educational area present certain specific challenges to the educator and to the rehabilitation worker. Accurate interpretation of school records may be hampered by an inability to judge the degree to which the student received special help, privileges, or other considerations in doing the work required. Frequently, it is extremely difficult if not impossible to determine the extent to which some of the work represented in these reports is truly indicative of the individual's ability to function in various vocational areas. Also, a rehabilitation program may involve educational experiences which might not be directly related to the client's ultimate vocational goals.

Relatively early in the school career, planning should be initiated for the full development of the individual. Planning for high school and post high school experiences must consider the degree and variety of the handicap, but should not automatically exclude a consideration of vocational or trade schools or of college. Secondary school experiences should emphasize social development and a sense of responsibility. Exposure to vocational opportunities is especially important at this time.

When the child enters school, prevocational activities should start. The earliest steps are to select broad areas that are vocationally possible considering the intellectual and physical limitations; work with the individual and the family regarding realistic goals; minimize negative aspects of appearance and to initiate techniques and behaviors which will lead to optimal adult self-sufficiency. Early counseling and guidance and prevocational experiences can prepare individuals for the problems of entry-level jobs, the demands and responsibilities of work and for the attitudes that are required to obtain and maintain employment.

The college experience may be a poor one for many cerebral palsied persons. Students must be directed to campuses which can accommodate their physical limitations (see Hall and Lehman 1967). College placement may be an effort to delay adequate vocational programming for the bright student who is otherwise handicapped. The result of this is a college graduate who is unable to find employment commensurate with the college education. Unfortunately, the decision at this point may be continuation into graduate school, thus exacerbating the problem.

Developing Vocational Goals

In much of the literature available to the professional rehabilitation worker in the past, the problem of cerebral palsy is usually considered from a rather limited point of view. That is, most of these materials focus on the infant or the child and approach the individual through the traditional channels of medicine, physical therapy, occupational therapy, or education. Rehabilitation too frequently has been limited to and equated with medical rehabilitation. While many of these materials and the programs they describe consider the assessment and improvement of the current functioning of the individual, sufficient attention does not appear to be paid to the ultimate adult role.

Although some of this material considers the broad areas of suitable leisure time and vocational activities, there is a paucity of materials focused primarily on specific vocational areas. Success in an area appears to be related to basic success experiences on which to build future experiences. Through the planned development of such successful experiences, an individual might be expected to participate and cooperate most fully in his own rehabilitation program. Wright (1960) indicates: "The effectiveness of rehabilitation whether it involves physical, vocational, or emotional adjustment, depends largely upon the degree to which the client has made the plan his own. Barring special circumstances, this support on the part of the client in the long run is enhanced when he takes an active part in decision making; it is often weakened when he feels that his life is being manipulated behind the scenes, even when it is by the experts who know best where he is to go and how to get there" (p. 345).

Basic problems within the vocational sphere include those found with many other individuals. The individual disabled from early childhood frequently does not have a clear set of vocational goals, has acquired few if any previous work experiences, may be extremely unrealistic in terms of aspirations, and may be comparatively unmotivated and uninterested in being involved fully in a vocational rehabilitation program.

The differences between disability and handicap must be viewed with considerable care to understand the implications of these problems, and the development and implementation of a specific rehabilitative program in the current American culture. Hamilton (1950) presents a helpful frame of reference for this: "A disability is a condition or impairment, physical or mental, having an objective aspect that can usually be measured ... a handicap is the cumulative result of the obstacles which disability interposes between the individual and his maximum functional level" (p. 17).

While the greater emphasis of medical and educational interest in programming for the cerebral palsied to date has been on the handicaps, with a changing emphasis to vocational rehabilitation services, the focus of attention must emphasize the individual's abilities and view his potentials in terms of whatever handicap may exist. Thus, by insuring selected success experiences and by providing opportunities for self-involvement in the rehabilitation program, the probability of successful rehabilitation is greater.

Goals are in large measure set by the experiences and models available to the individual. Elementary school programs which encourage outreach into community settings can initiate work on goals. Part-time employment, school-work programs, and workshop activities all provide desirable experiences. Realistic information regarding the vocational ladder and an understanding of the relationship of jobs through the top positions are required, as are models of handicapped workers functioning successfully in the work world. An integrated program, held together with the necessary counseling services will help insure the development of positive attitudes, necessary skills and optimal performance.

For any disabled individual, the total life program must be geared to bring the person to an optimal level of performance as an adult. This level will be dependent upon the extent of the disability, the handicap which results from the individual's and society's perception of that disability and their reaction to it, and the extent to which the person and society are able and willing to utilize and capitalize on the individual's abilities.

FACTORS OF EMPLOYABILITY

The response of employers to handicapped applicants has been increasingly favorable when viewed in historical perspective of forty or fifty years. The President's Committee on Employment of the Handicapped, the various governors' committees, and the efforts of individual citizens have demonstrated that handicapped workers are capable and competitive workers when selectively placed in appropriate settings. The Rehabilitation Services Administration reported that in 1921, 523 individuals were rehabilitated through the federal-state rehabilitation programs. It was not until 1962 that more than 100,000 persons were rehabilitated in a single year. The 200,000 level was reached in 1968 and the 300,000 level in 1972. A more positive picture of the handicapped worker is developing, and may overcome the stereotyped image that the general public may have of a disabled individual not capable of productive effort; an image which may be reinforced by the type of "Poster Child" frequently utilized for fund-raising efforts by volunteer groups serving the cerebral palsied.

It is impossible to generalize whether, as a group, there are limited or extensive opportunities for employment of persons with cerebral palsy in competitive industry. The kind and extent of employment opportunities are determined by the degree of disability that the individual suffers and by the attitudes of prospective employers. With appropriate programming and help, the client may be able to achieve his optimal level of vocational functioning. However, serious barriers to the efforts to obtain and hold a job may include a lack of social maturity, suitable experiences,and self-confidence. The client and the family may have some unrealistic attitudes about the individual's abilities, excessive fears regarding acceptance, and fears of the unknown work situation. Experiences within real vocational settings and help in developing independence and maturation within an appropriate educational and vocational programs will assist the individual in finding a suitable role as an adult.

Increased efforts at rehabilitation of the cerebral palsied are reflected in the many services being made available to this group. A report by the New York State Division of Vocational Rehabilitation can be used to illustrate this (Newman 1963). An analysis of their figures for fiscal year 1963 helps highlight the efforts and some of the typical problems faced in serving persons with cerebral palsy. During that year, the State Division of Vocational Rehabilitation rehabilitated a total of 7,163 persons representing all disability groups. Of this number, 153 or 2.1 percent were afflicted with cerebral palsy. Generally, they were much younger at point of acceptance than the total group of rehabilitants; the data indicated a median age of nineteen years for this group as compared to thirty-three for the total group. The median of education for the cerebral palsy group was eleven years of schooling completed while the total group had ten years as a median. More than 56 percent of the cerebral palsy clients accepted were under nineteen years of age, twice the percentage for the total group. The ratio of males to females in this group, 58.8 to 41.2, approximates the ratio within the total group, 62.0 to 37.1.

It should be noted that, because of the type of reporting employed in New York State, it would be very difficult to identify the number of persons who had some other major disabilities with a secondary disability of cerebral palsy. However, of the 153 individuals in whom cerebral palsy was the primary disability, 73 or 74.7 percent had an additional disability. These secondary conditions most frequently included mental or emotional disorders (twenty-six cases), speech defects (twenty-three), and mental retardation (eighteen).

While 15.3 percent of the total group rehabilitated during this year were gainfully employed at the time of their acceptance for rehabilitation services, only 6.5 percent of the cerebral palsied individuals were so employed. Almost 87 percent of the subgroup had no dependents while only 55 percent of the total group had no dependents. For both groups, the primary source of support and acceptance was the family or friends, with 81 percent of the cerebral palsied and 50 percent of the total group receiving such support.

In terms of the sources of referral, almost 37 percent of the cerebral palsy group, over twice the percentage of the total group, were referred from educational institutions. Referrals from physicians, hospitals, health agencies, and organizations for the handicapped for each group included approximately one-third of the total referrals.

The report further notes, in terms of costs and benefits to the total economy, that there was a reduction of approximately 30 percent in the public assistance necessary for the 153 cerebral palsied clients served. Furthermore, annual earnings went from somewhat more than $19,000 to over $326,000. In the first year after rehabilitation, this group paid almost $45,000 in state and federal income taxes. Thus, in their first year, they returned an amount exceeding 41 percent of the case costs for their rehabilitation. It is estimated that during an average working life, these 153 rehabilitated persons will return, in total income taxes paid, more than fifteen times the cost of case services for them. Thus, in terms of costs alone, it would seem that rehabilitation services could be justified for all of the disabled to help convert them from a drain on society to supporters of the economy.

In reviewing these materials from a participating agency of the federal-state rehabilitation program, there are some notable characteristics of the cerebral palsied group which are highlighted. First, it appears as if a reasonably representative proportion of the total number of clients rehabilitated during the year were cerebral palsied. As a group, these clients were much younger than the other rehabilitants and almost twice as many received services prior to nineteen years of age. This would suggest that cerebral palsied clients tend to be referred to or apply for services at a point in life when they have had limited vocational experiences and knowledge.

While this group has approximately the same number of years and schooling and the same ratio between males and females as the total population reported, almost half of the cerebral palsied individuals have other disabilities which would complicate a rehabilitation plan and which would further limit the extent to which successful completion of such a plan might be anticipated. As additional support of the picture of a young and inexperienced population, it is noted that very few of the cerebral palsied individuals were employed at the time of their acceptance for services. The vast majority of these persons were without dependents and were receiving support from their families or friends.

It is noteworthy that the educational facilities are taking such a strong role in making referrals of the disabled cerebral palsied individual to the state rehabilitation agency. However, such referrals might be made when the school had completed its efforts and had terminated services for the individual and was looking for some suitable place to pass on the responsibility for this person.

Professionals espouse the cause of the individual—the need to develop and selectively to apply services designed for the client. Thus, it is unfortunate that the justification of many rehabilitation efforts is made in terms of the numbers of the clients served or the amount of money returned to the economy. The extent to which this group, during the first after year rehabilitation, "paid back" the cost of their case services is impressive and in all probability is helpful in securing additional funds from legislatures for support of rehabilitation programs. Is there a maximum value that can be placed on a rehabilitation; an amount each case should cost? There should be a shifting from this emphasis on numbers of clients and costs of services to a focus on quality of services to the person, and the responsibility of this society to improve the quality of the life of its citizens.

It might be desirable to compare this report with a report from a private agency. In a summary of the follow-up activities of vocational placement of two hundred cerebral palsied adults, Curtis (1954) indicated that as soon as a guidance and placement program was established, there was a constant flow of clients representing varying degrees of severity of cerebral palsy. It was reported that, as a group, the clients were greatly overdependent on their parents and it was not infrequent that adult individuals capable of coming by themselves were accompanied by a parent. The clients presented many indications of having been sheltered and not having been allowed to attempt various activities, or to learn and profit from their own mistakes.

Often, they had not learned how to conduct themselves with others and they did not know how to respond to questions put to them. They were ill at ease and often terrified in the presence of strangers; they did not know how to dress or groom themselves properly. Not recognizing how essential it is to be on time for interviews, clients frequently appeared minutes, hours, or days late for appointments. Above all they frequently deferred to their parents before making any final decisions.

In terms of the services which were rendered, approximately 20 percent were provided with diagnostic counseling and guidance and placement services only, and 57 percent were provided with training. The total cost for services provided for the 153 rehabilitants with cerebral palsy was $109,203. The average period from referral to closure was slightly more than two years.

Of the 202 applicants reported in the study, 54 were placed; and of these, 11 were placed in skilled jobs, 34 in semiskilled, sales, and industrial positions, and 11 in unskilled jobs. For the clients with cerebral palsy, the placements included: clerical and similar, 38 percent; professional, semiprofessional, and managerial, 8 percent; sales and services, 12 percent; skilled, 3 percent; semiskilled, 21 percent; and unskilled, 7 percent.

Curtis' findings on the individuals included in his follow-up study closely parallel those of the state rehabilitation agency's report. Emphasized again were the problems of immaturity, the value of specialized services, and the need for positive experiences to help overcome the dependency apparent in so many of these clients.

It is somewhat more difficult to determine the number of cerebral palsied individuals served nationwide, as this condition often is combined with other orthopedic impairments. However, a consideration of the characteristics of clients rehabilitated through the federal-state program in fiscal year 1972 may help provide a broader picture. A total of 326,138 individuals were rehabilitated that year. Of these, 17 percent or 52,778 had orthopedic impairments as their major disabling conditions. Those diagnosed as cerebral palsied were 3.4 percent of this group; a total of 1,771. The report does not indicate cases in which cerebral palsy is a secondary condition, nor are demographic data provided on the cases. Over the five years ending in 1972, the number of cerebral palsied persons served each year stayed quite stable, averaging 1,730 per year.

VOCATIONAL REHABILITATION SERVICES

A community must mobilize its facilities and personnel into a meaningful spectrum of experiences for the client, utilizing special programs and techniques to overcome the barriers to rehabilitation. An integral aspect of the rehabilitation approach is the development and application of the team concept in the services for the cerebral palsied. Team members ideally might be expected to include, but not be limited to, such areas as special education, rehabilitation counseling, psychology, medicine, physical therapy, occupational therapy, speech therapy, dentistry, nursing, recreational therapy, and social work. The team approach has many advantages, but it is difficult to assemble a total professional team, knowledgeable and experienced in the rehabilitation of the cerebral palsied. However, with the combined effort of these specialists, each client may have available the best possible services. While each team member represents a specific professional area, team interaction in evolving a management plan has been demonstrated as one of the more positive factors in successful rehabilitation.

In addition, the adult cerebral palsied individual needs a wide range of support services in order to achieve an optimum level of vocational performance. These services should be provided through a logical, step-by-step process which permits the professional and the client to evaluate the progress of the individual at every stage of his program. Services within a community must be established to provide a broad spectrum of the help necessary to rehabilitate this group. These services should include vocational information and guidance services, prevocational evaluation, training, sheltered employment, home employment, residential facilities, placement services, follow-up, social programs, and psychological counseling.

Vocational Information

Information concerning many job levels should be made available to the individual. Some cerebral palsied persons will be able to achieve the highest vocational level; for others, the vocational goals may be geared to a variety of service, unskilled or semiskilled entry-level jobs. There is little material available for these levels which can be utilized in a meaningful way to help the individual in the early stages of career planning. A compounding problem is that vocational information materials often have to be modified in terms of the individual's disability, his potential, and his interests.

Of major concern is the appropriate application of vocational information materials for the cerebral palsied population. Considering the wide range of intellectual and physical abilities within the group, it is difficult to provide any simple guidelines. However, for the severely physically limited individual or the person who is functionally mentally retarded, job opportunities are usually limited to the lower skill levels. Occupational information for these levels is limited, and much of this material is based on the assumption that the reader has the ability to read, interpret, and apply. Much of the occupational information material is geared for the physically and intellectually normal person and is aimed at the higher skill levels. Individualized interpretations and new materials developed for the more limited clients are required.

Counseling and Guidance

Supplementing the basic information available in various career areas, clients frequently need extra services or support. The rehabilitation counselor might be expected to meet and serve their need most adequately through counseling. A focus of rehabilitation counseling services with adult clients is developing an appropriate interaction between the disabled individual and the world of work. The integration of the principles and techniques of vocational counseling and guidance with the available facts and knowledge of the disability, and with anticipated work conditions helps the individual in making appropriate plans and decisions concerning the future.

The counseling relationship is a continuous one throughout the vocational rehabilitation process, and its success may be measured by the extent the client understands personal strengths, aptitudes, interests, abilities, and limitations, and can relate these to the demands and potentials of the adult work world. While counseling and guidance services can be provided by a variety of team members, it is the vocational rehabilitation counselor who usually has this responsibility in programs serving handicapped persons. Ayers (1969) claims that one of the barriers to the team approach is when the vocational rehabilitation counselor is not represented. The counselor not only provides direct services, but he also is informed about and able to use the network of available rehabilitation services. An extensive annotated listing of the role of the rehabilitation counselor is presented in Wright and Butler (1968).

Vocational counseling and guidance for the cerebral palsied person must recognize that the adult world makes certain specific demands on each disabled individual. While many persons are able to adapt to the adult environment with minimal help, some persons require a wide variety of support in order to make this adjustment. The principles of counseling the cerebral palsied are essentially the same as the principles which govern the counseling of any individual; human personality and the techniques of working with it are not changed by the presence of a physical disability. The cerebral palsied individual may have many problems, but only some of them will concern his disabilities.

As with any person, the cerebral palsied individual may require psychological counseling to aid in his total adjustment. While problems of communication may create difficulties in establishing a counseling relationship and in effecting the kinds of change that might be desired as a result thereof, such services are a necessary component of the total program. The cerebral palsied person often has had fewer opportunities for reality-testing and may develop a self-concept which is not consistent with those others have of him. Counseling helps to provide an understanding of the dynamics of new situations and an orientation to the reality of current experiences.

Prevocational Evaluation

For the client with limited experiences, an intensive prevocational evaluation may be required. This may be considered as part of a personal development program where the client has opportunities to perform in a worklike setting. This is especially important for individuals with arrested developmental patterns. This evaluation may range from the use of standardized psychological tests, through a standardized work-sample system, such as the TOWER system developed and utilized at the Institute for Crippled and Disabled (1967) in New York City, to a comparatively long-term evaluation in a sheltered or actual working situation.

Many standardized tests may have limited value because they are designed primarily for a normal population and the norms do not have the same meaning when applied to a person with cerebral palsy. Other techniques may be adopted which introduce a bias, even while attempting to provide an adequate evaluation. For example, the test may be read to the subject or there may be other modifications in administration. While these procedures may not invalidate the results totally, the data must be viewed in terms of the changes from normal test administration.

Psychological tests, particularly those of vocational aptitudes and abilities, may present these limitations when applied to the severely disabled. Simulated work tasks are a useful supplement to the available standardized tests, and effective evaluations can be made whenever these work-sample tasks are standardized and used objectively. Not all clients are interested in, suited for, or limited to the kinds of mechanical or craft tasks for which most samples are designed. Too often there is no objective or standardized use for work samples, and certain kinds of selected work tasks sometimes are not pertinent or appropriate for the cerebral palsy client. Rosenberg (1972) discusses the use of this technique with cerebral palsied clients. The five major areas for which the work samples were developed included manual dexterity, clerical ability, basic hand-tool evaluation, basic vocational equipment, and academic skills.

It would seem appropriate to consider some other techniques that can be used to evaluate vocational performance. These procedures may range from a gross evaluation of the ability to use the hands through measuring performance with tools or other basic hand implements to ability to perform complex tasks. These ratings reflect the utilization of one hand or both hands on combination, as well as the ability to maintain normal working schedules on an actual job.

Work samples approach the reality of actual job tryouts in working situations. The sheltered workshop is a setting in which work samples are used in supplementing evaluation of work abilities and capacities. At times, this may be the only setting where there is a means of encouraging and motivating some clients toward work. The sheltered workshop is particularly useful in determining work tolerance, skills, and related factors of the client's performance. Since the workshop involves groups of workers, it is also a source for evaluating the clients functioning in the area of personal relationships. It is necessary to recognize the importance of experience and productivity for the individual, and individuals should begin productive work for pay as early as possible in their rehabilitation program.

While work samples may be used for these ratings, the evaluation process also can be accomplished by an on-the-job evaluation. Here, the individual is evaluated or rated on an actual job assignment, based upon the industrial norms prevalent. A client could be placed in an actual working situation and the foreman would, in effect, evaluate his performance. This evaluation might be reflected in a decision to continue the person in employment, to recommend some type of training, or to terminate the relationship.

This utilization of job tryouts is important as the client can experience reality-testing in a situation in which maximum learning can occur and which permits the individual to adjust to the work situation over a comparatively long period of time. The job tryout also provides the client with a *real* situation, rather than the *realistic* work-sample setting. It is in these settings that the individual is best able to compare his functioning with that of other workers and is able to experience reality-testing concerning his own performance, hopes, and goals. The professional evaluator should consider the client's total performance in a broad spectrum of real, realistic, and clinical testing conditions.

Vocational Training

Job training experiences may be programmed within two broad approaches. The first is training represented by vocational high schools, special trade schools, or programs of higher education designed to prepare an individual for employment. Subsumed under this type of training would be training experiences provided within sheltered working settings. Included also would be development of suitable work habits, motivation, work tolerance, and the interpersonal relationships required for any and all types of employment. These would include relationships with co-workers as well as relationships with supervisors.

The other approach to a vocational training program would provide specific job training in the vocational area in which the individual has demonstrated the greatest potential and in which he has the greatest possible opportunity for ultimate employment in the community. The technique which is utilized frequently in this type of job training is training "on the job." In these situations, the client is placed in an actual work situation where the employer serves as the trainer. Occupational information concerning these situations is required to provide the client with knowledge of suitable work available in the local community and exactly how the work is done.

The vocational guidance and counseling provided during this experience enable the individual realistically to measure his or her own abilities against the requirements of the job and show related jobs in the same work area. The client then is better able to understand what movement is possible and available in the work world, both horizontally to closely related kinds of jobs and vertically in terms of promotion to higher skill levels.

No matter which approach toward training is utilized, it is important that vocational activities be provided for the client as early as possible, keeping the individual active and occupied in the rehabilitation program. At first, these activities will be directed toward physical rehabilitation including physical therapy and occupational therapy, and educational programming. The early focus in cerebral palsy is on habilitation, activities of daily living, work experience and activities and independent living skills. However, as soon as possible, job-training activities should be selected in terms of the individual's developing vocational interest and should be graded to intellectual and physical capacities.

The rehabilitation counselor must have available complete medical, neurological, and psychological evaluations. These services usually are provided within a comprehensive program including a large staff of specialists. Basic to the selection of any training program must be a consideration of all aspects of the client's functioning: neurological, sensory, motor, language, cognitive, emotional, and personality areas. Program decisions should not be made by one discipline, but should be developed in a process of interaction between the various specialists working in cooperation and pooling their findings through team conferences and discussions.

Definite decisions and long-term vocational choices should be avoided until the individual has an opportunity to experience as many vocational areas as possible; tentative vocational decisions and initial steps in occupational preparation should and can be made early. However, care must be exercised to insure that the individual does not get bound into a single track too quickly. For maximum benefit, the client must be active in something the client sees as interesting and meaningful. Activities should have a positive stimulus value and should be presented in light of their vocational significance in order to capitalize on the client's motivation. While decisions concerning ultimate vocational goals should not be delayed for too long, every effort should be made to stimulate and measure the broadest possible variety of vocational experiences, until those decisions can be made most appropriately.

Sheltered Employment

Many sheltered-workshop programs provide long-term employment for disabled individuals. While these programs are generally thought of when sheltered employment is being considered, it is also possible to obtain sheltered employment for clients in a much wider variety of settings. Positions may be obtained in institutions, family businesses, nursing homes, and other settings where employment can be, in fact, of a protective nature. Of considerable importance is the use of the sheltered-work setting as a transitional experience for those individuals whose ultimate potential is competitive employment. Family employment often provides a form of a sheltered employment that is used extensively.

While short-term placement in a sheltered workshop may be for evaluation or training, long-term placement provides opportunities to work with an individual over an extended period and to pursue objectives which otherwise might not be obtainable. Nelson (1971) cites as the principal purposes of long-term placement the provision of long-term employment (both for wages and for supplementary income), sustaining or maintaining physical and mental health and social adjustment, and the reduction of personal dependence. Workshop and other sheltered employment opportunities have been especially important for the individuals who could not compete in the regular workforce. Although limited producers, sheltered employment provides them with opportunities to perceive themselves as wage earners, to develop adult social relationships, to move toward greater self-sufficiency and generally to lead more full lives.

Home Employment

As an aspect of the total rehabilitation services for persons with cerebral palsy, it is necessary to recognize that certain individuals may not be able to avail themselves of even those employment opportunities afforded in sheltered situations outside the home. Frequently, homeboundedness is the result of architectural barriers which prevent the person from going in and out of his home freely; public transportation which either is not available at all or is not adapted to the handicapped person's needs; or the lack of another person whose help would enable the individual to leave his home for work, recreation or other purposes.

To the extent to which homebound persons are able to perform meaningful work, it should be made available to them in their communities and wherever necessary within their homes. This "homework" often is provided as an extension of the basic program of the sheltered workshops in the community. When on home employment, the individual has the raw materials brought to his home and the completed products picked up on some regular schedule.

While performing the work at home, the client knows that he is involved in meaningful tasks and is remunerated at the level of his productivity. It is not infrequent that the home-employment program, when properly designed and implemented, leads to higher levels of employment— working within a sheltered work setting or eventually in a competitive work environment. Support services should be made available to the homebound worker as needed. These might include the services of a visiting social worker, teacher, rehabilitation counselor, therapist, nurse or other team member.

Residential Facilities

On occasion, individuals are able to compete on a vocational level but because of problems in some sphere of the person's life, require a supervised living experience. This supervised situation may be within a residential facility, or it may be within a community-based residential house where a number of people requiring such services can be housed. It is important that the community-based program be established to augment the more usual residential facilities so as to provide maximum opportunity for each client to remain in his or her home community rather than be transposed to a somewhat more distant residence.

In recent years there has been a rapid growth of community residences for special groups. Halfway houses are provided for ex-residents of institutions for the retarded, mental hospitals, and prisons. There are community homes for drug addicts and for the elderly. Many groups have seen the value of such community placements.

Some advantages of the community-based facility include: (1) continuing contacts with the family; (2) continuing service from professionals

TABLE 16.1
SUMMARY OF THE *SINGLE MOST* PRODUCTIVE AND *SINGLE LEAST* PRODUCTIVE
PLACEMENT PROCEDURES LISTED BY EACH OF SEVENTEEN MEDIUM
STATE VR AGENCIES FOR THE NONBLIND

Single Most Productive Placement Procedure	No. of Agencies
1. Counselor contact with employers.	5
2. Contacting employers personally (not stated by whom).	1
3. Client locates own job	3
4. Client locates own job or returns to former employment.	1
5. Counselor-client cooperate for client self-placement.	1
6. State employment service	
a. Referral to	
b. Referral to, and cooperation with counselor, handicapped placement specialist, training agency, and client	
c. Close liaison with	3
7. Client placed by or with assistance of training agency	1
8. Placement of college-trained graduates	1
9. No response	1
Total	17

Single Least Productive Placement Procedure	No. of Agencies
1. Client locates job without counselor participation.	3
2. State employment service.	3
3. State employment service, without VR agency involved in employer contact	1
4. Counselor takes total responsibility for placement	1
5. Selective placement.	1
6. Placement conference among counselors only.	1
7. Placement by schools and training institutions	1
8. Placement by labor unions.	1
9. Radio spot announcements of available clients.	1
10. No response	4
Total	17

From Dishart (1964), pp. 121–22.

involved with the case prior to placement; (3) the availability of familiar set-tings into which the individual may return on a trial basis; and (4) extended opportunities for a variety of integrated residential and community services. Community residences should provide a more realistic experience and give the client opportunities to assess developing skills in the community. A real danger has been the development in some cities of "community institu-tions" comprised of a great many of these homes in a single, poor or run-down neighborhood. This practice must be guarded against so that the potential of these homes can be realized.

Placement Services

The terminal phase of a total program of rehabilitation services usually is a fully developed placement program. This phase should have two major components: selective job placement and follow-up activities. Selective job placement is based on the premise that ideally, a disabled individual and a job can be so matched that the individual is either literally not handicapped or is only minimally handicapped in terms of that particular job. Matching of the requirements of the total working situation and the abilities of the client so that a successful rehabilitation can be accomplished is the skill on which the success of the rehabilitation process is measured.

This ultimate criterion (a successful vocational placement) which is usually utilized in determining the effectiveness of a rehabilitation program has been the focus of much rehabilitation activity. Dr. Martin Dishart (1964) of the National Rehabilitation Association has reported this aspect of rehabilitation services. The data for state vocational rehabilitation (VR) agencies for serving nonblind clients were reported for both medium and large agencies (see Tables 16.1 and 16.2). The size was determined by the number of applicants for service during the first quarter of the year.

Considering the data from the medium agencies, it is to be noted that the selective-placement process with direct counselor involvement seems to be the most effective one in achieving productive placements. The data pre-sented for the large agencies agree in general with the above. It is to be noted that the same items are listed occasionally as single most and least productive process. This suggests the importance of the individual pro-fessional in selecting the technique personally most effective. Other factors may include the relationship with the employer, the employer's awareness of the problems presented by the client, and the employer's responsibilities toward the client, including the role in client training and rehabilitation. The family and other professional workers have a responsibility in this process and the roles of other agencies must be fully integrated.

It is indeed unfortunate when the professional worker leaves the responsibilities for placement totally in the hands of a client or simply refers

TABLE 16.2
SUMMARY OF THE *SINGLE MOST* PRODUCTIVE AND *SINGLE LEAST* PRODUCTIVE
PLACEMENT PROCEDURES LISTED BY EACH OF NINETEEN LARGE STATE VR
AGENCIES FOR THE NONBLIND

Single Most Productive Placement Procedure	No. of Agencies
1. Counselor contact with employers.	3
2. Counselor's personal contact with employers	3
3. Counselor contact with known employers	1
4. Counselor contact with employer where good working relationships have been developed.	1
5. Counselor motivates client to find own job	2
6. Counselor motivates client to find own job by developing client strengths in acceptable interview and job behavior	1
7. Prepared client locates own job	1
8. Counselor prepared clients for specific occupation by training and job counseling.	1
9. Counselor cooperates with vocational schools and rehabilitation facilities, does preplacement counseling, direct placement, staffs old cases, uses placement bulletin	1
10. Use of placement supervisor in each district office who is consultant to the staff in all phases of employment, makes job analyses, locates job openings and does liaison work	1
11. Training facility makes placement.	1
12. On-the-job training.	1
13. Provide services to client for return to former job	1
14. Counselor locates job; client alone contacts employer	1
Total	19

Single Least Productive Placement Procedure	No. of Agencies
1. State employment service	5
2. State employment service, mass referrals to, especially of marginal clients	1
3. Client canvasses for jobs.	2
4. Difficult-placement client seeks job on own	1
5. Want ads	1
6. Want ads or posted job recruiting	1
7. General publicity about hiring the handicapped.	1
8. Unplanned placement efforts	1
9. Passive placement attitude	1
10. No response	5
Total	19

From Dishart (1964), p. 118.

him to another agency to be responsible for placement. The need for intensive selective-placement activities becomes even more acute for many of the multiply disabled who require special assistance.

Follow-Up

Follow-up is important not only, in providing whatever support may be necessary to the client while he is on the job, but also in providing a basis for evaluating the appropriateness of the various segments of the total program. Without intensive follow-up, it is difficult if not impossible to ascertain the extent to which the various aspects of the program actually met the needs of the client and of the industrial community.

To find the job best suited to the capability of the handicapped individual, considerable skill, patience, and knowledge of the client, the job, and the community are necessary. In order to provide the client with the skills necessary to keep the job, a full determination should be made of the specific abilities required to maintain employment. Effective utilization of follow-up activities introduces the need to consider a broad spectrum of abilities. It has become almost axiomatic that most individuals (not just the disabled) lose their jobs not because of an inability to perform the vocational skills required by that job, but rather because of a variety of personal and/or interpersonal factors.

For example, reporting to work late, inability to adjust to supervision, poor interpersonal relationships with the co-workers, inappropriate social behavior on the job, and inappropriate use of supplies or equipment are all factors which would result in the loss of a job for any individual. These factors represent problem areas, not only for the individual with cerebral palsy, but for all workers. Steps to minimize these problems must be initiated as early as possible so as to be a part of the life experiences of the individual, and should be a focus of the program from the client's earliest years.

Extensive program follow-up provides the feedback loop to help insure a flexible program which will continue to prepare clients for changing work demands. The follow-up process also permits the counselor to evaluate the suitability of the employer and the work situation for the client; the client's overall adjustment; the need for new services; when services should be terminated; and the possibility of job promotions.

Social Adjustment

A total rehabilitation program must, as an aspect of its total scope, provide a meaningful series of experiences which will insure the social adjustment and desirable personality development of the client. Frequently, this aspect of the program is left as the least structured, and assumptions are made that some other segment of the service area will meet the client's social adjustment needs. As a result, the client may not become integrated into post-school educational programs or suitable recreational and other social programs, and may become somewhat of an isolate. It is through meaningful programming that the individual is enabled to achieve maximum benefits from social situations. These activities permit the evaluation of the effectiveness of the program parts, relating to social adjustment.

The counselor must understand social factors in the vocational development of the individual. Six areas that the counselor must consider are: social class membership, home influences, school, community, pressure groups, and role perception (Lipsett 1966). It is interesting that there is not a consideration of handicapping conditions or the general view of such problems by society and the impact of these on the social adjustment of the individual. Goffman (1963) provides an excellent overview on the impact of stigma and deviance on the interaction of the individual and society. The concept of child variance has been dealt with extensively by the Conceptual Project in Emotional Disturbance, and Volume One of their reports presents six fields of thought within the field: psycho-dynamic theory, learning theory, ecological theory, biophysical theory, sociological theory and counter theory (Rhodes and Trace 1972). It provides the counselor with a systematized view of behavior, its etiology, and basic ameliorating approaches.

The Disadvantaged Disabled

Any consideration of disability would be incomplete if it did not reflect on the dual handicaps of disability and poverty. With the passage of Public Law 88-452, the Economic Opportunity Act of 1965, there was a concerted effort to attack the problems of poverty in this country. Many new programs were developed and the hope was high that with adequate training and services, the poor could make their way up the work ladder to middle class status. Many poor people were drawn into these programs, both as staff and as clients. However, there was little initial input from practitioners in the vocational rehabilitation field.

In an effort to draw together staffs from the Vocational Rehabilitation Administration, the Office of Economic Opportunity and other federal agencies involved with developing poverty programs, the Rehabilitation Counselor Training Program at Syracuse University conducted an invitational conference on rehabilitation counseling and the poverty field. This was one of the earliest efforts to bring the skills, training and orientation of rehabilitation counselors to this developing area, and to provide guidelines for federal, state, and local planners. The report of that conference (Cohen *et al.* 1966) explores the impact of poverty on disability and considers the high rates of related problems which are found with chronic poverty: delinquency, academic underachievement, a high incidence of health problems and physical disability and mental illness. It was noted that while rehabilitation programs had served some clients with poverty backgrounds, those served were somewhat more mobile than their peers, came to the attention of rehabilitation agencies, and were able to participate in the program. Moreover, program services may not have been provided as adequately as in other cases because of the biases of the professional workers.

A review by the Department of Health, Education, and Welfare (1967) of the delivery of health services to the poor demonstrates many problems in this system. The maldistribution and inefficient organization of personnel, as well as their treatment of low-income people, has a negative effect on those individuals. This is complicated by the attitudes and experiences of the service recipient and by the much higher incidence of health problems among this population. For example, about 29 percent of people with annual family incomes below $2,000 (fiscal years 1964–65) had chronic conditions limiting their activity. Limited persons with incomes over $7,000 were less than 7.5 percent of their group. Both maternal and infant mortality were greatly higher for poor and non-white families than for families who were white or had a higher income. That report indicates that for the income group under $2,000, there are 54 people per thousand population with orthopedic impairments, while there are only 15 per thousand with family incomes over $7,000.

It should be expected that even with the greater infant mortality rate, a large portion of cerebral palsied clients should come from poverty areas. Because of the pervasiveness of their problems, such clients probably require more time, money, and effort on the part of the counselor. The client brings a spectrum of problems including educational deficits, reduced economic capability, cultural deprivation, mental illness, physical disability, a variant family structure and function, poor housing, poor nutrition, and discrimination.

There has been an increasing concern over the inability of service delivery systems, designed mainly for the middle class, to meet the needs of low-income disabled people. The Vocational Rehabilitation Administration funded a number of research and demonstration projects which were designed to rehabilitate disabled public assistance clients. The analysis of data from fourteen such projects reflects on the potential of such concerted efforts (Grigg et al. 1970). Chances of rehabilitation were improved with the number of contracts between counselor and client. Chances also were better for the individual who did not have a secondary disability than one who did. The report has considerable value for personnel interested in vocational programs for the poor.

The philosophy and procedures used by the Texas Rehabilitation Commission in providing vocational rehabilitation services to the disabled—disadvantaged client has been reported (Place 1974). Program emphasis must be on early identification, referral and team action directed to a specific vocational goal. The relationships between cooperating social welfare and rehabilitation agencies must be monitored carefully to insure that these particular difficult-to-work-with clients are not dropped. Guidance personnel must play advocacy roles, especially for individuals who do not traditionally receive adequate services. It is an error to focus on change within the disabled individual when often that person is a victim of society. The person must be viewed in the context of an environment which also may be changed to help in the rehabilitation process.

It might be anticipated that individuals from a poor environment, multiply handicapped, unable to communicate well or to move freely through the environment would be difficult to locate as clients. Such individuals may not have been served by the schools and, even when school programs are available, may not be referred to the rehabilitation program at an appropriate time. Parent organizations which tend to be middle class oriented are not very helpful in this process either. Case finding and outreach by the counselor is a critical variable in the identification of potential clients.

Considering the problems of serving this population in the inner city, Feinberg and English (1969) cite as especially important: (1) public attitudes toward the poor and the inner city community; (2) national priorities and program support; (3) fragmentation of services; and (4) racism in the helping professions. Unless these are dealt with in a forceful way, guidance and placement programs for the disadvantaged disabled, especially for individuals with multiple problems like cerebral palsy, will not meet the needs of a major portion of this population.

SUMMARY

Although the focus has been on rehabilitation problems for the more severely disabled client and the problems of the disadvantaged disabled person, the upper potential for persons with cerebral palsy would be the same as for anyone in society. It must be recognized that cerebral palsied individuals can and do attend college, graduate, and secure appropriate jobs. In analyzing the reasons for such college attendance, Rusalem (1962) indicates that the patterns of motivation are individual and varied. The dominant interest may be self-realization, an affection for learning, status, parental pressure, vocational plans, and expectations for youth in that particular class, the influence of a key person, improvement in social levels or other factors. Some specialized services, approaches, or understanding may be required on the part of those involved in the education of the cerebral palsied. With a minimal consideration of the handicapping conditions, individual students can benefit fully from programs of higher education and can apply their college training in the work world provided there was a good match between the individual's strengths, interests, and limitations and the college program. It is necessary to recognize that the experience of higher education must be a stepping stone to some vocational goal. It avails a man not at all if he has absorbed a lifetime of learning and cannot put it to work in some way.

This chapter has considered the problems in vocational programming for a group which offers special challenges to the providers of service. As an integral aspect of rehabilitation, individual limitations must be recognized and accepted; and furthermore, assets must be recognized and capitalized on. For the severely limited client a simple task, done well, may be better for his general adjustment than performing inadequately at a higher level. On the other hand, clients should not be routinely regulated to simple, routine, low-level, unskilled work. Each person must be studied as an individual to uncover particular assets and abilities which may not be apparent. The individual who is highly motivated toward something which may appear to be beyond him should not be discouraged or prevented from attempting it. The client should, of course, be made aware of the requirements of the job, and the extent it appears plausible, especially in terms of the person's own limitations. If recognizing these, the client who wants to attempt it generally should be encouraged to do so to the edge of individual tolerance and abilities, and should be helped in every possible way to increase both. Moreover, the environment must be perceived as a potential "client" also and must be studied as carefully as the individual so that changes can be affected to minimize the handicapping impact of that environment on the individual.

In work with persons with cerebral palsy, a basic principle of vocational rehabilitation must be highlighted in attempting to provide services: that is, the treatment of the client as an *individual*. The nature, variety, and multiplicity of expressions of this particular disability can result in many different vocational, educational, and social handicaps ranging in degree from mild to severe. With the presence of general physical and intellectual limitations, communication problems, and motor deficiencies, broad career opportunities may not be appropriate or possible. Nevertheless, each person must be judged on individual abilities, not on the label which is used.

Complications of the order seen in individuals with cerebral palsy often make evaluation, vocational training and placement extremely difficult and time-consuming. However, various public and private vocational rehabilitation agencies have been providing expanding services for this group. Special projects have demonstrated what can be done. This is especially true in programs for the disadvantaged disabled. When problems of cerebral palsy, poverty and perhaps racial minority background are viewed from a biased racial-class conscious orientation, the likelihood of adequate services and a successful rehabilitation is minimal.

Counselors working closely with the client, training facilities, and agencies must fit each person into a suitable job situation. Some individuals are capable of performing in a competitive job environment; for others, there is an ever-increasing obligation of providing sheltered work settings. Within these sheltered programs, some clients progress until they are able to move into a competitive job. For them, the workshop is a transitional experience. For others, it may serve as long-term employment, by means of which they can remain in the community and function as adults—working adults.

It should not be surprising to find handicapped workers holding responsible positions at all levels of business, industry, and government, functioning in both competitive and sheltered environments. There are over 200,000 individuals of working age who have cerebral palsy. Relatively few of them are working. This results from a mix of the limitations of the individual, the service provider, and the society. It is the responsibility and the goal of vocational rehabilitation to help each individual, as an individual, to achieve an optimal functioning level in the adult world.

17

Collaborative Approaches to Professional Intervention

RICHARD E. DARNELL

THE PURPOSE OF THIS CHAPTER is to enhance the effectiveness of professional intervention in cerebral palsy. The necessity for such an enterprise is based on the view that technical disciplinary advances in the understanding and treatment of cerebral palsy have greatly surpassed the ability of professional practitioners to coordinate and integrate their contributions in an efficient manner. This problem is by no means unique to the field of cerebral palsy. However, the particular characteristics of cerebral palsy demand increasing attention to this issue. Its occurrence early in life and its persistence throughout life make constant professional monitoring and/or intervention necessary. Since cerebral palsy is far more than a motor problem, effective intervention requires the knowledge and skills of many health-care professions. Furthermore, effective intervention in cerebral palsy is a responsibility of many societal institutions in addition to the health-care establishment. Educational, social, vocational, legal, and religious support services are required. Each of these vital resources expands the necessity for examining the collaborative relationships which mediate the efforts of professional interveners.

Any approach to this issue must be based upon specific fundamental, philosophical, and ethical assumptions. The following are offered as those upon which the contents of this chapter will be developed:

1. Society defines itself by the resources it provides to the cerebral palsied and others in need. To the degree that these resources are both made available and utilized efficiently and effectively, a society gains strength, stability, and purpose. Current professional intervention in cerebral palsy is a manifestation of societal interest in self-maintenance and growth.

2. There are numerous categories of interveners necessary for productive intervention in cerebral palsy. Emphasis on the intervention of professionals and/or their surrogates cannot be misconstrued as representing a higher order of intervention than the contributions of the cerebral palsied,

their parents and/or surrogates, community resource persons, and the lay public.

3. The goal of professional involvement in cerebral palsy is to assist the cerebral palsied in establishing and utilizing their capacities to the point where professional intervention is no longer necessary. Even though the pace of this reduction in professional dominance is slow measured, the ethical tenents of all professions and formidable forces within society itself are providing increasing impetus in this direction.

It is quite possible for the seasoned practitioner to take exception to these assumptions. Arguments may be made for the use of societal resources for the cerebral palsied as a barrier imposed in order to shelter society from deviance, for professional primacy and autonomy based upon an exclusive body of knowledge, and for professional attention to a specific category of disability such as cerebral palsy as a necessity for professional opportunity. Indeed, specific examples of shortsighted public policy, professional self-seeking, and the reinforcement of primary and superimposed disability by organizational fiat are easily found today. However valid these objections may be, they cannot be permitted to become central organizing concepts around which professional role development occurs and professional practice patterns are established. To do so is to impugn the concept of productive service to the cerebral palsied and in the process to demean both the recipient and the provider of professional intervention.

The reduction of the incongruence between what practitioners know from their experience to be optimally effective factors in intervention with the cerebral palsied and present practice patterns, given the constraints under which they operate, is the central focus of this chapter. The development of what "can be" from "what is" is not an exercise in wishful thinking, futility, or a phoenix-like caricature in which new modes of professional function can arise only from the ashes of the old. Productive intervention in cerebral palsy can be facilitated by an appreciation of:

1. The historical development of interest in cerebral palsy and events which have influenced the development of professional practice patterns.

2. Barriers to collaborative professional enterprise and methods of analysis to reduce these barriers.

3. Societal factors specifically modifying current and future professional intervention in cerebral palsy.

HISTORICAL UNFOLDING OF COLLABORATIVE PROFESSIONAL EFFORT IN CEREBRAL PALSY

Initial Efforts

Evidences of cerebral palsied persons have been reported in early Egyptian, Hebrew, Greek, and Roman culture. As stated earlier in this volume, although scattered reports of cerebral palsy appeared in the literature as early as the mid-eighteenth century, William J. Little, an English surgeon, managed, in the short time from 1843 to 1861, through his teaching and publications, to raise the problem of cerebral palsy to a legitimate focus for medical attention. In doing so, he established intervention in cerebral palsy within the medical domain which became the model the developing health professions would seek to emulate.

There is today little agreement among students of occupational sociology on professions. There are generally two views: the normative approach in which the role of the physician is a model for complete professional development and a non-normative or alternative approach. "This alternative approach avoids the complicated problems of establishing a definition of a profession, handling the component elements of a concept, developing indices for arranging occupations along a continuum and measuring their professionalism . . . it considers the mechanisms through which an occupational group obtains power, pay off and independent control over the activities of its members. It permits a fuller examination of the internal workings of an occupation, and it provides descriptions of occupational behavior which are many faceted rather than dichotomous" (Sussman 1965, p. 182).

The force of Little's accomplishments, combined with increasing medical interest within the next forty years, consolidated the normative approach for professional development within the field of cerebral palsy. With increasing identification of professional development also came increasing allegiance by developing health professions to medical practice patterns emphasizing diagnosis and treatment. Although many of these practitioners legitimated their function by medical prescription, the search for the autonomy and control characteristic of medical practice at that time gave increasing impetus for these professions to refine their skills and gain recognition for their contributions. Thus began a conflict which could potentially impair the progress of collaborative professional intervention in cerebral palsy. Internal conflict within members of the health care establishment over power, research, and status became a characteristic problem surrounding the provision of services for the cerebral palsied. Comparison to the profession of medicine rather than attention to the development of individual professional assets became a part of the milieu in which further developments in cerebral palsy were to occur.

At the turn of the twentieth century, major interest in cerebral palsy developed at the neurological division of the Children's Hospital in Boston. Through the pioneering efforts of Jennie Colby, a revered founder of the profession of physical therapy, a member of the allied health professions demonstrated the benefits which could be reaped by the cerebral palsied through productive collaboration among practitioners representing different professional backgrounds. Furthermore, it was at the neurological division that many predominant medical figures in the habilitation of the cerebral palsied established the necessity for productive collaboration. Dr. Bronson Crothers, Dr. Elizabeth Lord, and their student, Dr. Winthrop M. Phelps, contributed greatly to increasing the scope of professional intervention in cerebral palsy. The period between 1900 and 1935 represented the efforts of a small, but growing, group of professionals.

They demonstrated two principles which undergird modern collaborative relationships among professionals:

1. The boundaries of interest, capacity and concern of professionals dealing with cerebral palsy were not fixed, but were constantly evolving.

2. Professional prerogatives, however valid, deferred to the interest of those who were served.

It was the unswerving dedication of early workers in cerebral palsy which provided sustenance for those who followed. Such sustenance was necessary to overcome the barriers to productive professional collaboration which were concomitant with developments in the period 1935–60.

The Formative Years

Establishment of the Contribution of the Health Care Professions

The rise and legitimation of health care professions in cerebral palsy was seen in the period 1935–60. Given impetus by the rise of health care technology made necessary by the Second World War, these professions soon encountered the problem of competing interests. Special education, nutrition, social work, speech and language, occupational therapy, nursing, psychology, and physical therapy were noteworthy for their growth during this period. In addition, new professional roles, arising out of specific patient need, developed as an expansion of more traditional professional role identifications. The profession of rehabilitation counseling took its impetus from the need for specialized skills with regard to vocational development as well as the concern for lack of coordination and integration of rehabilitation efforts between health care agencies, vocational preparation, education and placement and social integration into community life. From this sudden proliferation of professional resources, competition began for the development of professional prerogatives, for the establishment and expansion of members of one particular discipline rather than another in treatment settings, and for the principle of professional autonomy for individual professional practitioners. This territoriality was based on the "scarcity principle." In an arena of limited resources in which status and reward could occur to one profession only at the expense of another, professional entrepreneurship was fostered. Chauvinism was also fostered by the patterns of professional role development characteristic of health care education. Practitioners were indoctrinated with the concept that they were the future of the profession, that they had a historical obligation to its founders, as well as to the recipient of their services, to insure that their profession was respected, rewarded, and popularized. Procedures in health care education also emphasized the isolation of one profession from another by insuring that students were not contaminated by contact with students and faculty from other disciplines. Thus, practitioners were ill-equipped to mount a coordinated, unified attack upon the problems of the cerebral palsied.

The Development of Different Philosophies and Techniques of Professional Intervention

This period also gave rise to the development and popularization of different philosophies and techniques in the treatment of cerebral palsy. Approaches associated with Fay, Deaver, Phelps, Schwartz, Pohl, Collis, Kabot and Knott, Rood, Bobath, Doman, and Delacato became part of the therapeutic resources of many professional interveners. Although the development of these approaches provided a necessary balance for an over-reliance on the use of orthopedic surgery, they were the source of considerable discussion and debate. Issues such as the relative merits of an ontogenetic as compared to a phylogenetic approach, a neurological as compared to a functional approach, and the validity of competing claims regarding the utilization of one school of thought as compared to another became a central focus of professional attention. In addition, movement in education and psychology was producing an increasing base of knowledge which required professional attention and consideration. The contribution of Werner, Strauss, and Cruickshank added further insights, but further challenges as well in terms of selection of intervention strategies.

The development of multiple systems of treatment in cerebral palsy had major consequences for productive professional collaboration. No single profession could any longer consider cerebral palsy in a proprietory way. The "ownership" of cerebral palsy had passed to a consortium of professions represented by those who had developed unique system models leading to different intervention strategies. These multiple systems served as a heuristic for further theoretical and empirical endeavors. They also served as a vehicle for vertical mobility of individuals associated with these systems and for the development of leaders not only within the field of cerebral palsy, but within the professions with which these persons identified. It has long been recognized by students of occupational sociology that various elements within professions move at different rates. This incongruence leads to dissonance within professions and alters patterns of diffusion of innovation. Although attempts toward reduction of such incongruence by empirical means can be a stimulus for professional development, it can also be a major source of intradisciplinary controversy and diffusion of professional energies. Thus, the developers of systems of intervention had to contend with strong resistance from members of other professions, but more formidable obstacles were presented by those in their own disciplines.

Attempts at diffusion of innovation introduced by those at the cutting edge of progress had multiple effects. The basis of the foundation of an "elite" or establishment within the field of cerebral palsy had been established and with it a second source of dissonance had to be resolved. Professional controversy became a strong force as advocates of one system sought to influence others through exhaltation, clinical demonstration and empirical research. This controversy has by no means abated. For example, in recent years the contributions and the relative merits of the Doman-Delacato system have been a source of major contention.

Supporters of given systems could also be found widely dispersed among a host of professions. In some cases, these professionals chose to be primarily identified with that system rather than their professional background, e.g., Bobath Therapists or Rood Therapists. Thus, the practicing professional had to contend with a battleground of conceptual perspectives and intervention strategies in which disciplinary perspectives might become more or less significant. Each had a series of choices for which he was responsible. Vital dimensions had been added with the potential of impeding collaboration: the advocacy of a particular system of intervention and the development of therapeutic eclecticism. These issues were compounded by other factors related to the rise and legitimation of the health care professions in cerebral palsy. As previously mentioned, professional development had become associated with two processes: autonomy and control of the work group. These factors exerted a strong influence upon professional practitioners, often contributing to a negative view of productive collaborative effort. It thus becomes possible to identify three critical factors which developed during this period, each of which can be conceptualized along a continuum in which end points can be specified. Each of these continua represents the perception of individual practitioners as they considered their role development within their profession, their choice of therapeutic orientation, and the importance attached to collaborative professional effort (see Figure 17.1). It is important to stress that individual practitioners did not adopt a stationary orientation along any of the continua. Positions upon each of the continua were constantly changing depending upon a large number of factors such as experience, work setting, and personality variables.

The major significance of the three continua is that they assist in defining crucial historical elements of professional development within the

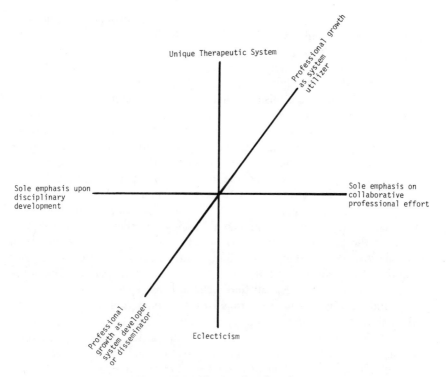

Figure 17.1.   Therapeutic orientation.

field of cerebral palsy which are not dependent solely upon the specific ascribed roles of a given profession. As we shall explore later in this chapter,
this particular issue becomes of extreme importance in assisting in the development of collaborative professional functioning in current practice.
They are also of assistance in understanding the current pressures operating
upon professionals within the field of cerebral palsy. No specific value
judgment is implied with regard to end points on any of the continua. Emphasis on disciplinary development in terms of developing technical
expertise and incorporation of the ethical tenets of a profession are extremely important functions which must precede any emphasis on
collaborative professional effort. Furthermore, there is much to say for
unique therapeutic systems as well as for an eclectic orientation. Advocates
of a singular therapeutic orientation have had outstanding clinical efforts,
often leading to significant research undertaking. Strong support or equally
strong opposition to a singular approach often has great influence upon a
practitioner's position in reference to vertical mobility within his profession.
The different schools of thought also described in explicit fashion specific

approaches which then became a basis upon which productive communication could eventually occur. This dialogue did not necessarily support the contention that individual strengths of specific theoretical orientations could be combined together to create a single, unified, uniquely strong approach. Indeed, it often became apparent that different schools of practice had not sufficiently established their exact parameters or that certain differences seemed irreconcilable no matter how fervent a search was made for common elements. The lack of empirical evidence for the support of individual approaches also added to the complexity of the issue. The different therapeutic systems did not all arise simultaneously.

Clinical experience showed the inadequacies of some approaches for providing a consistent framework to explain clinical reality. This led to expansion of other conceptual models. Practitioners who adopted a single therapeutic orientation often missed a significant portion of the reality surrounding the patient. As seasoned practitioners saw the inadequacies in clinical practice based upon deduction rather than induction, a greater tolerance for pragmatic approaches to treatment occurred. Even more significantly, it became evident that a clinical approach must be able to explain and deal with the wide range of behaviors and symptomatology exhibited by the cerebral palsied. The eclectic approach with its dependence on operational procedures taken from a wide variety of different schools, demonstrated that the selection and combination of elements, even taken from conflicting theoretical positions, produced a stronger product than any single given approach. Although it remained evident that a single theoretical orientation was a necessary central organizing concept, it could most effectively serve as a point of departure for such seasoned practitioners. From these roots arose the basis of modern collaborative efforts among professions. The accommodations which occurred between a single theoretical orientation and theoretical multiplicity associated with eclecticism were a precursor of the accommodations which would occur between members of different professions in their search for principles and procedures for collaborative function. A singular position serving as a point of departure for further understanding, the inadequacies of an isolated individual contribution to address the total needs of patients, and the professional growth achieved by "therapeutic openness" formed the cornerstone of the development of collaborative professional function.

Establishment of Public and Professional Organizations Interested in Cerebral Palsy

The unfolding of professional and public organizations dealing with the cerebral palsied also provided a historical foundation for collaboration among professionals. The American Academy for Cerebral Palsy was founded in

1947 by a group of six physicians, representing five different medical specialties. From its initial conception, a major objective of the Academy was to assist different specialists in developing a unified attack on the problems of cerebral palsy. According to Hillman (1970), when the American Academy of Cerebral Palsy was formed representing the specialties of neurology, pediatrics, physical medicine, neurological surgery, and orthopedic surgery, it was committed to providing an opportunity for the merging of resources from medical and related fields into an ecumenical congress. Meeting this challenge was to place considerable stress on the establishment in the field of cerebral palsy.

> Over the ensuing years, there were many new developments in medical, paramedical, and governmental agency programs which all carried implications for the future of cerebral palsy. Cerebral palsy treatment centers were developed in countless locations. Rehabilitation medicine emerged as a new discipline with unprecedented funds and the capability of developing services for the disabled, education of personnel, and research in problems of disability. In a somewhat disorganized pattern, reflecting suboptimal planning at both the community and institutional level, there also developed a new spectrum of special services and disciplines. . . .
>
> Each of these new spheres of interest brought along its own liability or hazard for duplication of services, rivalries for funds, dramatization of relevance and elbowing for status. Each one needed a patient treatment arena as a laboratory for its own group of professional and technical trainees. Those who were self-characterized as research-based eschewed any long term commitment to the patient once the study was completed, and few who had arrived on the scene without previous clinical experience were enthusiastic about the long term implications of management of neuromuscular dysfunction.

To this complicated picture was added another major consideration: the growth of United Cerebral Palsy Association, Incorporated. Beginning with a small group of parents in New York City in 1945, the establishment of the "Committee for a Cerebral Palsy Foundation" led to the New York Association of Cerebral Palsy. Through its initiative, a charter was developed which was to lead to the National Organization for Cerebral Palsy in 1949. Among the objectives of their organization were to mount a unified, over-all, long-range attack on the entire problem of cerebral palsy, including not only provision of necessary treatment, care, and education but also a dedication to intervening in societal factors affecting the cerebral palsied. Public understanding, legislative intervention, vocational adjustment, research into etiology, education, and training of specialists in the field, parental support and guidance, and information exchange were among the goals to which this organization was committed. The dedication and intensity with which they sought to accomplish these objectives are well known to workers in the field. Directly attributable to the development of United Cerebral Palsy are several principles which undergird current collaborative efforts among professionals:

1. Recognition of the effectiveness of special interest groups in influencing the resources made available to the cerebral palsied.

2. Acceptance of the parents as equal partners in the evaluation and intervention process.

3. Appreciation of the contribution of the cerebral palsied themselves, not as passive recipients of services, but as organizers, synthesizers, and legitimators of professional effort.

The integration of professional, public, and private efforts on behalf of the cerebral palsied was not accomplished without considerable dissonance. Attempts at collaborative professional effort continued, but it soon became apparent that a host of significant variables could determine the direction of that effort.

Funding came from many developing voluntary agencies and from large grant programs whose goals were often in conflict between provision of services and research. Lay groups, such as United Cerebral Palsy, often took initiative in program development.

In 1954, the Academy, recognizing the significance of the events which had occurred, opened membership to all qualified physicians who were involved in cerebral palsy. But even more significantly, associate membership was extended to all related disciplines and a major emphasis was placed upon cross-fertilization among disciplines through continuing education and training. The experience of the Academy in the following years in merging workers from medical and related disciplines provided legitimation of collaborative professional effort on a prestigious level.

Recent Influences Upon Collaborative Professional Effort

The Paraprofessional Explosion

The period of 1960–74 saw a movement toward the development of aides and assistants. This occurred as a result of unrelenting societal pressures with regard to the entire health care delivery system (Darnell 1971). These include:

1. The nature of the population seeking service had changed. People were living longer and with the conquest of many acute

diseases, those living longer were developing long-term chronic illnesses.

2. The standards of living had increased dramatically with an accompanying increase in expectations regarding the provision of health care.

3. The general understanding of the population regarding disease, its prevention, and amelioration had increased.

4. Popular attention had been called to the spectacular nature of advances in medicine and other fields leading to increased demand for higher levels of intervention for a broader segment of the population.

5. Costs associated with the health care delivery system had risen extensively, leading to a search for methods of increasing the efficiency of health care delivery.

6. The knowledge of professional excesses often associated with total disregard for the needs and desires of recipients of services became widespread as the public media expanded their influence in society.

7. The rise of awareness of racial inequities and the demand of racial minorities for equal opportunity gave rise to entry into the health care establishment through routes other than professional training.

8. Governmental policy made funding available for the encouragement of the training and introduction of paraprofessionals.

9. Analysis of professional function had revealed that what had been components of practice which did not require the use of technical expertise or judgment could reasonably be delegated to others.

Changes in society and patterns of illness necessitate alterations in established methods of delivery of health care (Cherkasky *et al.* 1961). The arrival of the concept of paraprofessional utility leads to many intense intraprofessional debates. What would these persons actually do? To whom would they be responsible? For what kind of patient problem in what kinds of settings could or should they be employed? How should they be trained? How would they be legitimated? What effect would they have on the welfare of both the professional establishment and the public? As might be anticipated, the introduction of supportive personnel initially produced a degree of professional withdrawal and entrenchment. Rather than emphasizing collaborative efforts among members of different professions, the introduction of supportive personnel forced each profession to reexamine its basic philosophical, ethical, and societal nature.

It is somewhat paradoxical that the final outcome of this process was to contribute substantially to enhanced relationships among representatives of different professions. The process by which this occurred is founded upon the historical nature of the evolution of professions. Professionalization is a product of Western culture. As Western Europe emerged from the Middle Ages, several trends developed which were to lay the foundations of man's formalized helping relationship to his fellow man: (1) the division of labor; (2) the rise of technology; (3) necessity for transmitting technological advances to learners; and (4) increasing demand for control over the physical environment.

The rise of the guild structure and the large Western university legitimated the pursuits of theology, medicine, and law. This division of areas of knowledge was in keeping with the view held at that time that man was best viewed as a spiritual being contained within a corporal body whose relationships with others were mediated by a set of divinely inspired prescriptions for acceptable behaviors. Along with medicine, the rise of nursing and social work as vocational pursuits following the social welfare movement in England helped to evolve a concept of the meaning of a profession which has survived to the present day. An essential element of this concept relates to control of the work group through what this author describes as the "barrier concept." The barrier concept is characterized by those structures which maintain the closed nature of professions. Two elements of this concept are pertinent to the present discussion: (1) a single route of entry into a profession through formal training legitimated by the work group; (2) a definition of function which makes categorical distinctions among different professional work groups. These categorical distinctions serve both to maintain professional role identification and to bar representatives of other professions from membership within that particular discipline.

The barrier concept was seriously challenged by the evolution of supportive personnel upon the health care scene. Health care education of many disciplines preparing practitioners for many speciality areas, such as cerebral palsy, turned to career mobility models to assist in providing a conceptual overview of the place of supportive personnel. Two of these have been reviewed in the literature previously (Darnell 1973). The model developed by Perry (1969) represents career mobility occurring in two dimensions: (1) the "career ladder" or vertical dimension; and (2) the "career lattice" or horizontal dimension. The concept of career ladder implies a career pattern which would make it possible for qualified individuals in health care delivery to move with relative ease from the level of aide, to the assistant, to the fully qualified professional practitioner, to more responsible professional roles in a given health profession. Career development in the health professions followed a similar vertical mobility pattern. Those who had made contributions to patient care, teaching, administration, research, and professional organizational functions enjoyed the rewards associated with intraprofessional vertical mobility. Another form of vertical mobility had been demonstrated by those who had left health professions for other careers which they perceived as offering greater rewards, beginning their preparation for those careers without having benefited formally from their previous educational or clinical experience. The theoretical implications of such movement between these levels in an upward direction have been dealt with extensively in the career-development literature (Holland 1959; Roe 1957).

The concept of the "career lattice" or horizontal dimension of career mobility implies a career pattern which would provide a possibility for the lateral transfer between health professions. With recognition of educational and clinical components common to several health fields, entry to a new health career would be readily achievable by such lateral movement. The mobility model developed by Perry for health care professions differs markedly from the mobility model which has been developed by occupational sociologists. This latter model may offer greater promise for understanding the enhancement of the development of collaborative professional effort in response to the introduction of supportive personnel.

The concepts of vertical and horizontal mobility first appeared in the occupational sociology literature about thirty years ago (Sorokin 1947). Vertical mobility was used by Sorokin to indicate a change in rank, and horizontal mobility was defined as a change in function. A few years later, a spatial model to describe the relationship between vertical and horizontal mobility was developed: "The position of an individual in any social system may be described by his rank in a hierarchical scheme of relationships, his functions as a participant in group life and his location in time and space . . . visualized as a three dimensional graph of which one horizontal axis represents function, the intersecting horizontal axis represents distance, and the vertical axis is a status scale" (Caplow 1954). In this model, horizontal mobility is defined as a change of function, including both the technical and social functions which arise from group membership.

If one can estimate the position of a supportive or professional person in the three-dimensional space, it is then possible to determine a mobility position for that individual. It is evident from this model that rarely, if ever, can career mobility be considered exclusively vertical or exclusively horizontal, in nature. The health care mobility model thus differs from the sociological mobility model in one significant way: while the health care model permits movement to be either horizontal or vertical, the sociological model permits any interactional combination of horizontal and vertical mobility as a function of the work setting. The sociological mobility model thus effectively diminishes the inordinate effect of professional role identification in the health care model by focusing upon settings as a significant variable, and can assist in the provision of an adequate conceptual basis for understanding the development of collaborative effort among both supportive and professional personnel in the field of cerebral palsy. Its potential weakness lies in its emphasis on status considerations, a deficiency which could be overcome by redefining the basis upon which status is rewarded.

The costs of adaptation of the health care model as a central organizing concept for supportive personnel was far too great to achieve widespread professional support for it threatened to undermine the "barrier" concept. Complete vertical mobility for supportive personnel implied an erosion of a single route of entry into the profession. Horizontal mobility threatened professional role identity. Infiltration by persons whose philosophical and ethical patterns might be different and whose professional loyalties might be diffused mediated against horizontal mobility. Therefore, the primacy of the work setting for the development of collaborative effort was enhanced among supportive personnel as well as professionals. Its acceptance was not based perhaps on a recognition of the advantages of such a position, but rather upon the disastrous consequences to professional role identity perceived in fully implemented horizontal and vertical mobility.

Acceptance of paraprofessionals as full partners in habilitative efforts within the field of cerebral palsy has been a gradual but steadily increasing phenomenon. Many cerebral palsy clinics utilize their services extensively. As the principles and practices of collaborative effort become internalized within professional workers, the degree of acceptance of the contribution of paraprofessionals, as well as parents and the cerebral palsied themselves, can be expected to increase. Further support for the role of paraprofessionals can be expected as professional workers recognize the skills that paraprofessional workers bring in establishing meaningful relationships with the cerebral palsied and their families, and as professional workers are provided greater opportunities for creative research and continuing education due to more efficient approaches to delivery of services. The introduction of paraprofessionals will require alteration of the armamentum of most professionals. Technical clinical skills will be necessary, but not sufficient. Emphasis on gaining professional competency in teaching, consultation, supervision, and administration is required in settings where paraprofessionals are utilized extensively. In addition, in order to attract more competent paraprofessionals, attention must be given not only to their occupational mobility, but also to geographic mobility, competitive wages and distinctly visible membership in the health team.

Development of Joint Training Experiences

A second major development in the 1960s was the establishment of collaborative efforts in training both professionals and paraprofessionals. Within the field of cerebral palsy, the historical foundation for these joint training programs could be found in the efforts of major clinical training programs which introduced in a single setting learners from a multitude of settings.

Within university settings, the development of core curriculi were undertaken. Although many of these efforts were really nothing more than administrative realignments of separate professional schools within schools of allied health professions, the concept of integrated training experiences gained increasing popularity. The full utilization of joint collaborative training efforts is to be found in University Affiliated Facilities, a series of approximately forty training centers established upon university campuses for the purpose of providing students collaborative learning experiences with students of other disciplines, preparing for career with the cerebral palsied, developmentally disabled, and the mentally retarded. This is of major significance in introducing the concept of joint effort early in the professional role development of future practitioners so that it becomes part of both their affective and cognitive armamentum.

Expansion of the Parameters of the Field of Cerebral Palsy

The history of cerebral palsy is resplendent with efforts both to define its basic parameters and to characterize its symptomatology. Freud, Fay, Phelps, Perlstein, Minear, Denhoff, and Robinault were among noteworthy contributors to this effort to establish a common set of understandings around which practitioners of all disciplines could relate. In the last decade, there has been a general effort to widen the scope of concern of those interested in cerebral palsy to include such descriptions as "minimally brain damaged," "perceptually motor impaired," and the "learning disabilities." The change from the view that cerebral palsy is a problem of cortical motor control associated with birth trauma to the view of it as a functional syndrome in which psychological function and social parameters were also present was a major contribution of Denhoff and Robinault (1960). The effect of this expansion was twofold: (1) broadening of the professional concerns of practitioners in the field of cerebral palsy; (2) development of interest in cerebral palsy by professionals who had not previously identified with it.

This cross-fertilization served to provide further impetus for the development of collaborative effort as well as to crystallize the need to define more specifically the principles and practices of mounting a unified effort on behalf of the cerebral palsied.

CURRENT PATTERNS OF COLLABORATIVE EFFORT IN CEREBRAL PALSY

The history of the development of professional interest and capacity in the field of cerebral palsy clearly demonstrates increasing awareness of the importance of collaborative effort. However, attempts to introduce collaborative effort in settings providing services to the cerebral palsied are often fraught with difficulty. These difficulties are partially dependent upon the particular environment in which such efforts occur. In the university setting, collaborative relationships often become tenuous because academic freedom may be interpreted as a freedom to withdraw from contacts with other disciplines. In the clinical setting, collaborative efforts are often submerged by the frustration of dealing with specific needs of an individual patient. In research endeavors, different philosophical and theoretical orientations present formidable barriers. However, some barriers have a peculiar commonality which exists independent of the therapeutic environment. An examination of such central factors may help professionals toward collaborative effort.

Barriers to Collaborative Enterprise

Threat to Personal and Professional Identity

Most collaborative relationships are limited by perceived threats to individuals rather than by a threat to the disciplinary identification of that individual. It is not uncommon to find individuals who use the cloak of their profession to hide their insecurities. Many are not willing to expose and risk the human part of themselves. A concomitant factor is the fear of obliteration of professional roles. Professional health care workers often fear, unrealistically, that the goals of cooperative professional enterprise are consistent with the evolution of a work setting in which all professionals relinquish their traditional roles and all therapeutic personnel blend into a single, new, disciplinary identification with common goals, skills, and perspectives. This concern is heightened because all health care professions are experiencing a change in the nature of their work in relation to their past, each other, and the public. A growing array of new specialized diagnostic and therapeutic techniques has resulted in an increasing interdependence of health care professions. This has resulted in procedures and problems of judgment in health care today which cannot be clearly designated as being solely the province of a single profession. Although different health care professions exercise different means to obtain the goals they share, their collaboration in the process of arriving at a therapeutic program and the activities in which they both engage serve to blur the distinctive features of each role. In the field of cerebral palsy, this tendency has been highlighted by the development of particular approaches to treatment in which technical competency rather than disciplinary identification is a primary focus. Excessive focus upon solely disciplinary identication or technical competency can create a formidable barrier to the internalization of principles of collaborative effort by professionals.

Exclusive Focus on Normative Approaches to Professionalization

At first examination, there is nothing within the normative approach itself to cause barriers to collaborative effort. Indeed, many of the attributes of the normative approach are desired. For example, major characteristics inherent in this approach include the following items also mentioned in the Preamble to Ethical Standards issued by the American Personnel and Guidance Association:

a. a body of specialized knowledge, skills, and attitudes which is derived and tested through constant scientific inquiry and scholarly learning. Members of a profession acquire this body of specialized knowledge, skills, and attitudes through academic preparation, usually on the graduate level, in a college or university, as well as through continuous inservice training and personal growth after completion of formal education.

b. a philosophy and a code of ethics which emphasizes service to the individual and society above personal gain.

c. constant examination and improvement of the quality of professional preparation and services to the individual and society.

d. membership based on compliance with stated standards of preparation and competence.

e. public recognition, confidence in, and compensation for the services of its members.

f. development of a body of knowledge and a literature for dissemination.

However, in the process of achieving these objectives, the lack of collaborative effort among workers representing different disciplines results in almost an opposite effect. These are often described as consequences of professionalization and are generally considered negative characteristics. Among these are:

a. professional isolation through identification with a specific occupation;

b. selection of a "hidden audience" for which the professional role is played;

c. the constant state of flux of the "typical professional role" in reaction to conservative and progressive intraprofessional forces as well as societal demands;

d. territorial disputes arising among professions whose roles overlap, engendering suspicion and hostility.

e. deterrence of innovative applications of professional function as a result of legal standards for professional practices;

f. careful regulation of minimal competence in role definition of one's own profession while endorsing role expansions;

g. unilateral control by professional associations of membership standards, desired or requisite preparation and practice and sometimes of individual, social, legal, and ethical matters.

h. occasional degeneration to flagrant self-interest rather than dedication to the interests of others;

i. censure of professionals who utilize the skills and perspectives of other disciplines.

The constant competition for the individual worker's loyalties between a normative approach to professional growth and his responsibilities to joint effort has been a major impediment in addressing the issues of productive collaborative effort.

Professional Uncertainty Regarding the Validity of Principles of Collaborative Effort

Many professional workers in cerebral palsy have serious reservation about the sagacity of enumerating and clarifying principles of collaborative effort. Often, it is felt that it is sufficient to have "a good working relationship" with one's colleagues. Furthermore, when and if strains appear in collaborative relationships, it is often considered far less "dangerous" to deal with the specific aspects of that single situation which produces stress, rather than to deal with underlying mechanisms. There is, however, an increasing number of workers who take the position that there must be clarification of important directional elements, namely, central organizing concepts which influence the decisions made and the values attributed to them which are independent of a given situation. Most professionals are familiar with this approach to achieve a given objective for it serves as the foundation for the practice of every health profession. Advocates of this position contend it is equally applicable for building the theory and practice of joint effort utilizing the contribution of members from a wide variety of health care disciplines. Polarization of professional views regarding this issue often presents significant dissonance when attempts are made to address the principles of collaborative effort.

Inefficiency of Collaborative Processes

Resistance to the study of collaborative processes is often associated with negative valuations of the time and cost efficiency of such efforts. While professionals are focused primarily upon the product of their efforts in terms of immediate or long-term benefit to the cerebral palsied, it is sometimes considered by professionals to be poor personal and professional judgment to pause in these efforts to consider the processes which support these efforts. This attitude is often supported by the difficulty encountered in bringing groups to consensus about defining critical collaborative process variables and appropriate strategies to resolve them.

Lack of Acceptable Terminology

A major obstacle in the development of collaborative efforts in the field of cerebral palsy lies not in the identification of such processes, but rather in communicating them in a consistent fashion. At present, there is mass confusion regarding the use of particular terminology both within and between professions. Of particular difficulty is the term "interdisciplinary." Difficulty in developing a common set of operational definitions has contributed greatly to a lessening of efficiency of collaborative effort. Although a label by itself does not insure productive collaborative effort, the inability of professional workers in a given setting to develop a consistent terminology regarding the central organizing concepts often makes communication impossible and attempts at improved collaborative effort futile. Attempts to seek assistance from the literature often is not fruitful. There has been a profusion of publications in the area of collaborative effort with little agreement among authors with regard to uniformly acceptable terminology. A recent MEDLINE search indicated over 300 articles identified from this source alone (Ingersoll 1974).

Differing Value Orientations

Different professionals at any time have different degrees of commitment to and expectation from collaborative effort. Often, individual concerns become paramount and self-preservation becomes a single overriding objective. Because of the high individual investment necessary to support collaborative efforts, specific professional workers become drained and diffused of commitment to it. This "collaborative unevenness" can lead to feelings of failure by those sincerely committed to joint effort and cast suspicion on the integrity of their previous efforts, impeding further group development.

Excessive Focus on Administrative Factors

Current administrative philosophy is highly varied in environments which emphasize collaborative efforts on the part of professionals serving the cerebral palsied. Enlightened administrative philosophy generally purports to provide resources and support systems to facilitate collaborative effort. It has become evident in such settings that the persistence of mutual effort depends increasingly upon two conditions: its effectiveness as measured by the accomplishment of a common purpose, and its efficiency as measured by the satisfaction of individual needs (Barnard 1962). There are two interwoven elements of collaborative effort: human components and organization. Both of these elements are affected by two unremitting consequences of technical advance: (1) a division of labor in which complex professional role components are reduced into less demanding components; (2) the synthesis of the resulting components into a functioning whole—the organization (McGraw 1968).

In such settings, arbitrary and capricious administrative decisions can completely undermine collaborative effort. However, even when administrative practices are enlightened, rational, and consistent, they are often seen as the cause of disruption of collaborative effort. Indeed, it is not uncommon to find that the major expressed deterrent to collaborative professional effort in clinical settings are lack of resources, and lack of appropriate administrative procedures.

The relative merits of particular administrative practices and procedures is not within the scope of this discussion. However, it is increasingly clear that a major barrier to collaborative effort lies not so much in the nature and extent of administrative practices as in the degree to which professionals attribute dissonance to them. Any administrative system, regardless of its degree of perfection, can be made less adequate by those whom it seeks to serve. Likewise, any administrative system, no matter how inept, can be made to function more efficiently by those committed to collaborative effort. To the degree that administration and collaborating health care professionals are perceived dichotomously by members of the organization, barriers to consideration of the principles of collaborative effort are imposed.

ANALYSIS OF CURRENT APPROACHES TO COLLABORATIVE EFFORT IN CEREBRAL PALSY

There have been three distinct, but related, streams of development in the field of cerebral palsy. Each of these represents a different view of the collaborative process; however, all three share the common focus in assisting professionals to coordinate and integrate their activities more efficiently and effectively on behalf of recipients of service.

The evolutionary concept emphasizes the relationship between the ability and willingness of the individual practitioner to participate in collaborative effort based upon the historical development of his individual profession and a series of specific accommodations among professions in current practice patterns. A second approach, the structural approach, attempts to clarify the basis of collaborative function by analysis of role components and specific attributes of the work setting. A third major avenue, the interactive approach, sees collaborative effort as a function of interpersonal relationships.

Evolutionary Approach

The evolutionary approach is based upon the premise that each professional worker in the field of cerebral palsy undergoes certain specific changes in the nature and extent of his professional role identification as a result of response within his profession to the need for collaborative effort. These changes are compatible with changes that have occurred within his given profession in terms of collaborative efforts with other disciplines. The evolutionary approach is founded upon the differential development of professions with regard to collaborative effort based upon inter-professional communication and problem solving. Occupational sociologists have ascertained that although differences among professions have been very great, the more established the profession, the more likely the professional was to emphasize self-regulation, and a sense of autonomy and to view the professional organization rather than the client as the significant reference group. Furthermore, the more established the profession, the less the professional was likely to emphasize a belief in service to the public and to other professional workers, and a sense of calling to the profession. Members of less established professions within cerebral palsy should thus have somewhat greater freedom in developing productive collaborative relationships utilizing this approach. However, as discussed below, this distinction is not generally valid.

For purposes of description, it is best to divide into two distinct phases the dynamic process by which successful joint professional enterprise occurs within the evolutionary approach. Each of these phases has constantly changing parameters. The present state of one given profession may be best described as an amalgamation of these phases, while others appear to be suitably described by a single phase. In addition, professions in movement are often cyclic in nature, having achieved one phase, internal and external forces often impede increasing innovation and force a return to a previous level of development. Such forces are often the result of the particular demands of a given work setting and the community in which that setting is found. These phases are presented as a convenience to the reader in order to provide him or her with a point of departure from which suitable estimates can be made regarding personal and professional orientation. They will be found to be most helpful when applied to specific issues and procedures which are of concern to the reader rather than the more global area of professional development.

Striving Phase

The striving phase is marked by a great deal of ambivalence toward the concept of collaborative effort. Its major characteristic is resistance to correctives for the debilitative consequences of previous professional practices.

With the emergence of a large number of new professional roles, some members of established professions see as their responsibility the coordination and integration of all professions to provide the highest level of patient care. Enlightened leadership in these established professions encourages collaborative effort, but practitioners in evolving professions are often educated within a chauvinistic ideology and they strive for professional status. They follow professional leaders who espouse professional isolation as a way to achieve the professional autonomy and control enjoyed by more established professions. As a result, these practitioners are not equipped to meet the challenges of collaborative functions. Voices raised in favor of collaborative effort are ignored by powerful, entrenched professional forces.

The striving phase of professional collaboration in health care professions is often marked by the assertive dominance and authority of one profession in determining the nature and extent of professional collaboration with another profession. Examples of this attempt to dictate the conditions of joint professional effort can be found in the literature of almost every health care profession. As an illustration of this tendency, one can call upon the relationship of medicine to other helping professions: "In a hospital or a center, the head of the team . . . must inevitably be a physician. He may, and often does, delegate certain of his duties to a nonmedical member of the team, but, by force of training and of law and licensure, the final responsibility for what may or may not be done lies firmly upon the physician" (Pattison 1957). Supporters of this view often feel that "the physician has been delegated by our unwritten moral and ethical code as responsible for each and any one of us . . . this is not to say that others than physicians may not have usable skills which the physicians themselves have not cultivated. It is to say that those skills are paramedical when they reach out to an individual who is or has been under medical care" (Rathbone and Lucas 1959).

Attempts to alter the physician's role are often seen as a mark of professional and personal incompetence, or rank insubordination. As Pattison notes, "some men and women, not too few in number, who are trained in various specialties . . . do not subordinate positions gracefully." "A controversial point has been the question of authority in the management of the patient. Only training, knowledge, and experience in his special field can qualify a team member as an authority on the expressions of each team member. However, the authority for ultimate decisions rests with the physician, for his alone is the ultimate responsibility for the patient's welfare. Perhaps another reason for the confusion in understanding the team concept stems from the inability, or refusal of members of the allied professions to subordinate their personal prominence and personal bias. In their anxiety to establish personal stature, or to obtain professional recognition for reasons of sustaining independent, private practices, they have lost sight of their proper roles as members of a coordinated team functioning in the interest of a disabled patient" (Delagi *et al.* 1955).

It is important to note that the profession of medicine is often inappropriately seen as the chief culprit of the striving phase. None of the professions which has had and continues to have active input in the field of cerebral palsy is immune to such dynamics, and each must share equal responsibility for its presence. Dissonance is often expressed between social work and psychology, between physical therapy and occupational therapy, between nursing and administration, between special education and school psychology.

Attempts to resolve the failures of collaborative effort in the striving phase often result in a slow and painful realization that interaction variables are responsible for the inhibition of personal and professional fulfillment.

Multidisciplinary Phase

In the multidisciplinary phase, a series of accommodations occur which redefine the roles of professionals with respect to each other. These accommodations occur in three major areas: (a) authority, (b) leadership, and (c) status differentials.

Authority—The right to command and enforce obedience has been a significant barrier to joint professional enterprise. Each profession brings with it unique skills and insights necessary to provide viable approach to a common problem. In a multidisciplinary environment, it becomes clear that the legal authority of one profession over another does not promote effective joint problem solving. In spite of the fact that newer helping professions have grown out of successive refinement and increasing specialization of other more traditional professions, authority cannot be claimed merely on the basis of seniority. Furthermore, the increasing level of postgraduate education of health care workers in all major disciplines has further eroded any meaningful differentiation. It becomes evident that the supposed formal authority of any one profession serves only to hinder the attempts of professionals to work together. Real authority is derived not from the definition of stereotypic professional roles, but rather from the nature of a common task which confronts professional workers. The complexities of the habilitation process in cerebral palsy and the differential input of professions at various stages in that process lead to greater acceptance of Barnard's view that authority depends upon a personal attitude of individuals on the one hand, and the system of communication on the other. Thus, in the multidisciplinary phase, the concept of authority vested in one profession or one individual is progressively viewed as antithetical to joint professional effort.

Leadership—To health care workers, it has long been a maxim that legal authority and leadership are inseparable. During the multidisciplinary phase, health care personnel begin to distinguish between nominal command and leadership variables. According to Jane Warters (1960) there is a difference between leadership and headship. A leader is someone who achieves leadership status through some special attainment or personal ability, and the head is someone formally appointed to the leadership position. "Headship can develop into domination, and at the other extreme, need not preclude leadership . . . however, being a head makes it difficult . . . to achieve the status of leader" (p. 71). Furthermore, leadership functions include task functions (helping the group to work on its task and problems) and social-emotional functions (helping the group to maintain itself as a group), and the two functions are rarely fulfilled by the same person.

An important concept consistent with the multidisciplinary phase is that any health care professional or other significant person in the patient environment can fulfill a leadership function while headship is maintained by another.

Status Differentials—There has been much small-group research which has pointed to the fact that status differentials are often deleterious for the development of group productivity. Moreover, the effect of status differentials among health care professionals joining together in a collaborative effort has been seen to be dehumanizing and undemocratic. During the multidisciplinary phase an opposite and more productive trend often develops in reaction to the use of status differentials, and equal importance is assigned to all health care workers regardless of disciplinary identification. Differential status becomes more and more dependent upon the contributions of the individual health care worker to the solution of common group problems. Focus upon the evolutionary approach thus allows the professional to internalize an appreciation of his profession's historical passage through the striving phase and his own professional obligation to adopt current professional attitudes consistent with the multidisciplinary phase. It commits the professional to recognize and modify his practices in keeping with the principles supporting common effort. Analysis and modifications of practice patterns in the multidisciplinary phase can best be understood by conceptualizing the relationship within and among professions (Figure 17.2).

It is important to note that professional interaction in the multidisciplinary phase is also characterized by forces which tend to hamper the implementation of joint professional effort. Health care professionals often find collaborating with each other in a team effort a task for which they have not been prepared, either by training or experience. While unproductive function in the striving phase occurs as a result of the inability to accept the concept of joint professional endeavor, serious debilitation of the productive aspects of the multidisciplinary phase may occur mainly as a re-

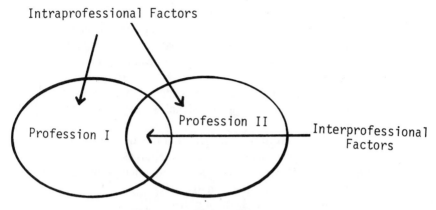

Figure 17.2. Multidisciplinary stage.

sult of professional practices which unknowingly and unintentionally inhibit the development of productive effort toward a common goal. Such practices can be conveniently categorized as intraprofessional factors and interprofessional factors (Darnell 1972).

Intraprofessional Factors—

1. Stress on professional jargon.

2. Emphasis on specialization and expertness to the exclusion of group process.

3. Covert manipulation of situational variables for professional self-aggrandizement.

4. Acquisition of professional prerogatives without skills to assume additional professional responsibilities.

5. Promoting self-confidence on the part of professional team members by unknowingly encouraging insufficiency on the part of the recipient of service.

6. Lack of innovativeness and resistance to planned change.

7. Exclusion of persons having other than professional training.

8. Understanding the workings of a given system, exclusive of understanding self.

Interprofessional Factors—

1. A mechanistic view of life and man, engendered by rigidly splitting up the patients' needs into categories which correspond to standard professional roles.

2. Irreconcilable conflicts over group goals and solutions to patient problems.

3. Excessively formalized procedures.

4. Reluctance to share resources.

5. Intergroup competition.

6.   Artificial dichotomies between the medical and non-medical service professions, education and technology, basic and applied science.

7.   Excessive conformity to established patterns of group functioning.

8.   Characterization as a member on one side of a conflict.

9.   Conflict between personal, professional, and group loyalties.

10.   Suppression of self-direction and leadership capacities.

11.   Lack of personal and professional security for the "outside worker" coming in.

12.   Lack of collaboration between therapeutic and administrative staff with regard to the control of therapeutic resources.

13.   Overt or covert censorship in communication patterns.

14.   Over-emphasis upon time constraints.

15.   Controversy over the rights of patients.

The experiences of the multidisciplinary phase present the professional with two major questions. How can each team member integrate his specific skills into an efficient group effort to attack a common problem? How can the identification of areas of professional responsibility be established most productively? One's strategies for resolution of these issues are taken from the present position of one's profession toward collaborative effort and internal agreements within the work group regarding authority, leadership, and status variables.

The cornerstone of the evolutionary approach is the concept of profession. The weakness of the evolutionary approach lies in its assumption that collaborative effort is characterized by a number of different professions directed toward the accomplishment of a common goal. It does not take into account the persons within the professions attempting to interact with each other. The science of productive collaboration between persons also requires addressing the special combination of talents and perspectives which characterizes each professional worker as an individual different from other workers within the same discipline, as well as specific role accommodations based upon factors indigenous to the work setting.

Structural Approach

While the evolutionary approach places its emphasis on the development of disciplinary perspectives, the structural approach focuses upon the roles of individual practitioners within a given setting. For example, in a cerebral palsy center or a special education classroom, the evolutionary approach would address the contribution of physical therapy to collaborative effort, while the structural approach emphasizes the contribution of a specific physical therapist serving in that setting. Primary consideration is given to the specific characteristics of that setting in determining the nature and extent of collaborative effort. Analysis of the nature of such roles explains why and how individuals in collaborative effort perform as they do and demonstrates the dependency of such roles upon broader social structures such as the work setting and the organizations and institutions of the community. Expectations regarding normative functions, sensitization regarding dynamic changes in key aspects of behavior, and inferences as to why certain aspects of collaborative functions are more or less effective and satisfying can be assessed by utilization of the structural approach.

Incongruence Between Roles of Professional Practitioners in Cerebral Palsy

The concept of role is a method of characterizing the behavior of persons involved in collaborative effort. However, any professional so engaged has at one particular time not one, but three, different orientations to that behavior. The first of these is an ascribed role. An ascribed role is a given set of responsibilities for a person in a given position. Examples of ascribed roles are definitions of functions of professionals promulgated by professional associations, state and federal regulatory agencies, guidelines for acceptable programs, and in specific job descriptions utilized to recruit professionals into specific settings. A second is a perceived role in which the individual interacts with his ascribed role in keeping with his own orientation, values, strength and weakness, and redefines for himself the set of expectations he has for his function within a given setting. A third is an enacted role of the professional practitioner: the actual set of behaviors that the professional demonstrates in the work setting. A basic foundation of the structural approach is the dissonance caused within the individual practitioner by incongruence between ascribed, perceived, and enacted roles and the response to that incongruence by both that practitioner and his colleagues in their individual and group relationship with him. This incongruence is more or less resolved by analysis of expectations and behavior patterns based upon two central organizing concepts: (1) complementary and substitutionary role relationships, and (2) full and partial delegation of responsibility.

Complementary and Substitutionary Function

Complementary and substitutionary function is based upon the utilization of the concept of enacted roles. The incongruence between perceived roles is reduced by role negotiation and alteration among professional collaborators. A common set of understandings regarding what function is to be performed by whom under what circumstances is worked out among professionals within the work setting.

Members of different disciplines have specific technical skills developed through education and experience. These skills can be divided into four categories of task contributions which determine the relationship between what a specific practitioner undertakes in reference to the roles of others (see

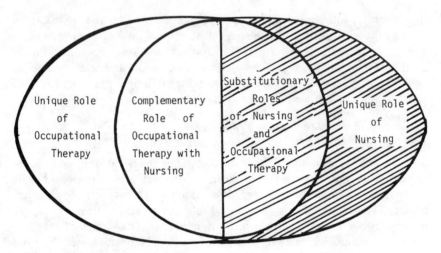

Figure 17.3.   Complementary and substitutionary relationships.

Substitutionary Areas-partial Delegation
of Responsibility

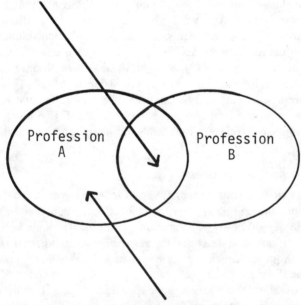

Complementary Areas-full Delegation of Responsibility

Figure 17.4.   Partial and full delegation of responsibility.

Figure 17.4). They are (1) unique contribution, (2) complementary contribution, (3) substitutionary contribution, and (4) no contribution.

Let us take the role of an occupational therapist as he or she interacts with other disciplines in a clinical institutional setting for the cerebral palsied. For a given patient, this therapist might have no contributions to make toward the treatment of a congenital heart defect, a unique contribution in enhancing the quality of motor performance during feeding, a complementary contribution with nursing in structuring the institutional environment to promote independent self-care (both the occupational therapist and the nurse have the competence, but the occupational therapist executes this task), and a substitutionary relationship with nursing in terms of training this patient in transfer activities associated with toileting (the occupational therapist and the nurse work interchangeably).

A complementary role is, thus, an enacted role which, by mutual agreement, a specific professional practitioner representing a disciplinary area of expertise holds to his own. A substitutionary role is an enacted role which members of different disciplines feel free to assume within a given setting (see Figure 17.3). The role relationships among two or more professionals within a given setting thus determine the nature and extent of collaborative practice. Capacity for successful negotiations regarding responsibility of individual practitioners for specific substitutionary and/or complementary functions is dependent upon recognition of a dual pattern of delegation of responsibility.

Delegation of Responsibility

The concept that tasks can be delegated, but responsibility may not, has been an enduring principle in the health care professions as with most other professions. The structural approach differentiates two patterns of delegation of responsibility: full and partial. This differentiation became necessary with the increasing recognition that one debilitating consequence of legal ascription of formal responsibility to one profession for the activities of another can be erosion of productive joint effort between representatives of these professions. Allen R. Solem has skillfully articulated the concepts of limited and full delegation of responsibility. He describes limited delegation as delegation in which the "superior must retain the authority to modify or reject ideas of decisions which do not merit his approval" and full delegation as delegation in which "the superior reserves the right to decide (for himself) the decisions he must make himself, and those to be delegated. However, once the responsibility for making a decision or developing a solution has been placed on one's subordinates, the assumption is that the superior will accept or support the action regardless of whether he personally agrees with it or not. This means that subordinates are held responsible for results, not for developing solutions

designed to obtain the approval of the superior" (Solem 1958). Full delegation has a crucial advantage in patient care in that as Solem says, a "superior who reserves to himself the authority to make final decisions may not
always expect as satisfactory results as when full responsibility for solving
certain problems is delegated to one's subordinates . . . and an important
contribution of the full delegation attitude of the superior is that it
influences subordinates toward constructive solutions of a problem on its
own merits. In doing so, it helps to avoid any tendencies toward merely
giving lip service to a superior's solutions, of arguing with him, or doing as
directed with reduced motivation." Although Solem articulates his position
in terms of persons whose roles are superior or subordinate, it is possible to
translate his approach into the area of collaborative efforts where superior
and subordinate interest and capacity in specific task functions exist. Thus,
delegation of responsibility must be limited when a practitioner sees the
task in question to be part of his substitutionary function. Practitioners
performing the same task are jointly responsible to each other. Delegation
of responsibility must be full when the task is seen as part of complementary function (see Figure 17.4).

Primacy of the Work Setting

The location and purpose of work settings are determinants in role
definition. Furthermore, the specific characteristics of such work settings
are of critical importance in determining the nature and extent of role release and role retention. The work situation and the institution itself are not
simply places where people of various occupations and professions come
together and enact standard occupational roles. These locales constitute the
arenas wherein such roles are forged and developed. The setting in which a
professional practices not only determines the nature of both his or her ascribed and enacted roles but also in part determines his or her skill level.

Work settings in which professionals provide services to the cerebral
palsied vary widely in both the objective of intervention and the role alterations required by internal factors. These include hospitals, state residential
facilities, community living facilities, day care centers, early intervention
programs, home training programs, special education classrooms, vocational preparation and educational facilities, community social and recreational facilities, and a host of other environments. To enhance the utility of
the structural approach, there must be recognition of the uniqueness of
each agency, no matter which type. Workers must negotiate roles based
upon the specific characteristics of their own agency, clientele, and staff.

Individual Attributes of Professionals to Role Retention and Role Release

The position of a given professional worker with regard to what specifically
is to be considered complementary function and what is to be considered

substitutionary function is dependent upon a large number of factors. These constitute the critical dynamics upon which perceived and enacted roles are based. Taken together, these factors determine the relative position of each professional worker to every other worker in efforts toward collaborative relationships. They are:

1. Need of recipient of service.
2. Availability to perform task.
3. Interest in performing task.
4. Capacity as judged by self to perform task.
5. Credibility to others in performance of the task.
6. Flexibility and comfort in role negotiation.
7. Characteristics of pertinent co-workers.

The major contribution of the structural approach is in the avoidance of role conflict. Conflict may be experienced in a variety of ways. For example, the enacted roles of two or more professionals may overlap and tend to exclude one another. Differing expectations may create a series of perceived roles which are conflicting and inefficient in nature. Generally speaking, the structural approach provides the professional practitioner with two conceptual tools to analyze and remove barriers to collaborative effort: negotiation of role retention and role release and types of delegation of responsibility. It is found wanting in addressing those aspects of collaborative effort which are based upon the failure of interpersonal relationships rather than the concept of role. The interactional model assumes collaborative effort occurs on the basis of personal interaction rather than a system of role defined relationships. Rather than addressing collaborative effort within the work groups, it focuses upon individualistic or psychological explanations for phenomena which either facilitate or detract from group process.

The Interactive Approach

Major deterrents to the development of collaborative effort are found not only in a lack of explicit definition of roles or in differences in knowledge or reciprocation of theory and practice among disciplines. More often such deterrents are found in lack of dedication to a common cause, lack of trust in the capacity or ethical armamentum of one's colleagues, unwillingness to share oneself, and the inability to give or receive help from professional colleagues when necessary or appropriate. Such deterrents clearly mark the boundary between what has previously been described as attributes of the multidisciplinary stage in the evolutionary approach and interdisciplinary functioning characteristic of the interactive approach. In the literature, the terms "multidisciplinary" and "interdisciplinary" have been utilized synonymously. The characteristic pattern of interdisciplinary performance is one which "requires individuals willing to submerge themselves into the greater effort of the group" (Cruickshank 1970), and requires a mentality which can focus upon the goal of collaborative effort. In the interactive approach, face-to-face interaction and decision-making is accompanied by a transaction in which joint commitment and accountability accrues in each of the following areas: (1) the nature and implications of data base obtained, (2) the goals to be achieved, (3) the transactional strategies of intervention to be employed, (4) the means by which they are to be accomplished, and (5) the assignment and assumption of responsibilities for which each individual practitioner is accountable to the group.

The product of successful implementation of the interactive approach is unitary programming (Shotick and Rhoden 1973), in which individual professional activities are meaningful and valued only as long as they contribute to group intermediate or long-range objectives. It is extremely important to recognize that the product of the interactive stage, i.e., unitary programming, is not the process by which it is achieved. That process, interdisciplinary perspective, is a dynamic force operating within the professional and personal orientation of collaborating professionals. Interdisciplinary perspective is the *internalization* of a commitment by each member of the staff of a given work setting to moderate the principles and practices of one's personal and professional objectives and prerogatives in order to enhance the ability of members of associated disciplines to contribute to productive joint effort and to take actions consistent with that commitment. Interdisciplinary perspective is the means by which unitary programming is accomplished in the interactive approach.

The dyadal relationship is a key concept of the interdisciplinary perspective. The dyad and its multiple projections encompass professional collaborators through a series of one-to-one relationships. The foundation for the primacy of the dyad in the interactive approach lies in the skills and experiences of each professional practitioner to formulate a therapeutic dyadal relationship with a recipient of service. The ability to formulate productive dyadal interprofessional relationships is founded upon each practitioner's full awareness of a significant social-emotional dimension which permeates relationships between providers and recipients of services. The characteristics of multiple dyads provides a completeness of perspective to patterns of collaborative effort associated with the interactive approach which appears to be lacking within both the evolutionary and structural approachs.

Analysis of Dyadal Patterns

A psychological frame of reference provides different means and criteria for the analysis of collaborative effort on behalf of the cerebral palsied than does a mechanistic group model approach. The professional worker in cerebral palsy attempting to utilize a dyadal approach in facilitating collaborative effort immediately finds himself faced with a substantial problem: only one half of the dyad is clearly under his control and available to introspection. Although his objective is to decrease the interpersonal distance and reduce interpersonal barriers between himself and his colleagues, he must operate somewhat in a vacuum as to the meaning of his actions and perspectives as perceived by another. The avenues of inquiry open to him are limited often because review and analysis of interpersonal relationships directly by mutual sharing occurs only after a concerted and prolonged effort to establish a meaningful relationship and is often accompanied by a high level of threat. Furthermore, since different members of the work group have different levels of commitment to and appreciation of the interactive approach, analysis of function is usually limited to addressing two major questions:

1.   How can I know if I am functioning in a manner which implies that an interdisciplinary perspective is present?

2.   How can my colleagues and I know if we are functioning together in a manner which implies that an interdisciplinary perspective is present?

To address the first question, the individual worker must reflect upon the following:

1.   Do I consider both my own capacities and those of the group as potential resources for problem solving?

2.   Do I accept, recognize, respect, and encourage the expressing of attitudes and opinions from others? Am I willing to adopt flexible commitment to my own views toward problem identification and resolution?

3.   Do I believe that in most cases the best solution for group task is an approach which grows out of the combined resources of its members?

4.   Am I willing to accept a leadership role assumed by any member of the group?

5.   Do I consider every person in the team a potential resource person including not only professional colleagues, but paraprofessions, recipients of services, and their families?

6.   Within legal and ethical limits, am I willing to be responsible for the collective wisdom and action of the group? If I do not, am I willing to state my position without fear of personal rejection?

7.   Do I trust the overwhelming majority of my colleagues to develop an enacted role which will be supportive of group goals?

8.   Do I consistently refrain from manipulating the behavior of others?

9.   Do I feel that team maintenance functions are as important as, if not more important than, fulfilling responsibility for specific task outcomes at a given time?

10.   Am I secure in the quality of my own enacted role?

To address the second large question, one must examine critically the activities and functions of his work setting to ascertain whether they are operating with characteristics which imply that an interdisciplinary perspective is present. The reader is cautioned to consider that the question is not "are we functioning with an interdisciplinary perspective or not?", but "to *what degree* have we put into operation a viable way of working with each other which will provide a continuingly elevating level of support simultaneously for ourselves and our colleagues?" Interdisciplinary perspective is enhanced to the degree that the policies and practices of the work setting encourage and accept the following by its staff members. These policies and practices are simultaneously the cause and effect of the internalization of the interdisciplinary perspective.

Administrative Procedures—

1.   Dedication to a set of common goals is present and their rank order of importance clarified.

2.   Group goals are guides for exploration rather than prescriptions for action. Philosophical considerations, administrative responsibilities, and the output of services are not seen as incompatible with each other.

3.   Descriptions of the goals of the team effort and the method by which they are to be achieved are identified with the group rather than with the individual practitioner in the professional discipline he represents.

4.   Senior personnel reflect a sense of trust and colleagueship in both their statements and actions.

5.   Status is not based on educational attainment.

6.   Personal and professional freedom is not surrendered for security and stability.

7.   Communication is valued above rules which constrain productive function.

8.   Competition is fostered only to the extent that it results in the highest quality of support for colleagues.

9.   Each team member sees other team members as persons possessing different skills rather than more or less valuable skills.

10.   There is acceptance of the concept of a team as a collection of persons rather than a collection of professionals enacting standard roles.

11.   There is demonstrated ability to utilize more than one reference group in evolving standards for a constellation of task performances.

12.   Emphasis is placed on ability to see one's interaction in professional collaboration as a growth experience for one's self. "Task performance by the interdisciplinary team reflects the outlooks and beliefs of individuals, but the team, in turn, influences individual values" (Horwitz 1970).

13.   Members of the team may represent many different career vantage points; e.g.,

　　　a. a first work experience,

   b. a seasoned worker broadening the base of his professional activities,

   c. the culmination of a health care career.

14. Each team member maximizes the proportion of his time devoted to his highest level of skill.

15. Leadership is shared and is seen as a function rather than a status or position.

16. Strategies for resolving disputes and controversy involving a professional collaborator do not apply one stereotypical approach for all situations, but rather include a large variety of approaches, as Horwitz notes:

   "a. an incumbent of a focal position may define what most of his rights and obligations are and an incumbent of a counter position accept his definitions.

   b. incumbents of a counter position may define most expectations and an incumbent of the focal position may accept them.

   c. an incumbent of the focal position may define his obligations (or their own rights) and both may accept each other's definitions of these role segments.

   d. Neither the incumbent of the focal or the counter position may have well-defined expectations for each other's behavior in their initial interaction, and they may be eventually worked out through a trial and error process.

   e. some expectations may be learned prior to, and others during, position incumbency" (Horwitz 1970, pp. 48–49).

17. There is discussion and general agreement on what types of decisions will be accomplished by consensus, by administrative fiat, by rule of majority, by small groups, and by committees of the whole. However, there is a propensity to accept decisions made by consensus rather than majority or authority decisions.

18. Criticism of a particular disciplinary intervention is not misconstrued as an attack on the individual or the discipline he represents.

19. Dissent is not just tolerated, but valued.

20. Control of undesirable deviance is seen to rest with one's self, influenced by normative structures generated by colleagues.

21. The development of new professional manpower categories is encouraged.

Educational Activities—
1. Professional jargon is clarified and reduced.
2. Students are given an awareness and appreciation of disciplines besides those in which they are being trained.

3. Techniques, theories, and ideologies distinctive to a given professional discipline undergo a degree of interpenetration and subsequent amalgamation with parallel ones in other disciplines.

4. Emphasis is placed upon an appreciation of the common historical humanistic base from which all health care professions take their origins.

5. Teaching of interdisciplinary concepts occurs by modeling as well as the formulation of specific objectives, content, and instructional methodologies.

6. Students engage in a degree of risk-taking and are encouraged to demonstrate ingenuity in the solution of problems related to professional cooperation and collaboration.

7. Instructional settings provide students with practice in each of the following activities: defining group goals; identifying the positive contributions of other disciplines; defining their own professional role in a large variety of settings; utilizing the input of other professional collaborators to define their own professional role; and defining, operationalizing, and evaluating alternative modes of team practice.

8. Students make choices based on a value system which cultivates advocacy on behalf of the recipient of service in contrast to professional accommodation.

9. Responsibility to students from other disciplines is equally valued with responsibility to students from one's own discipline. With regard to this equal responsibility, each team member is willing to risk intraprofessional criticism due to the implication of the weakening of professional loyalties.

10. Colleagues from different disciplines feel free to offer uninvited suggestions and comments.

11. Educational problems are not seen as the exclusive concern of one member of the team or a single disciplinary identification.

12. Cross-professional cooperation is popularized by the team member in his or her relationship with the university community as a whole team.

Clinical Activities—

1. The expertise of professional persons as resources in their area of professional competency is assumed. Initial distrust or skepticism provides an unproductive advance attitudinal organizer.

2. Evaluation and treatment relationships are the most valued when crossing disciplinary boundries to provide more effective care.

3. There is willingness to share responsibility to the recipient of services.

4. There is willingness to take responsibility for problem-solving and decision-making.

5. Professional judgment is seen as an attribute contributing to, rather than detracting from, team functioning.

6. There is ability to recognize and tolerate value differences and deviations from typical work patterns.

7. There is willingness to negotiate roles and to view one's role as both complementing and substituting for the roles of others.

8. Role expectations are clarified by continuing discussion and the evolution of novel and unique roles is welcomed.

9. Primary identification is with the team rather than with the profession of which the person is a member.

10. Ability is demonstrated in recognizing, as Horwitz writes, "the importance of coordinating assessment, treatment, and evaluation along physical, psychological, and vocational lines; at different stages, as a case develops, greater stress is laid upon one or another of these. Workers, to survive in this setting, must, therefore, be adaptable enough to accommodate to shifting work demands. Medical skills, for example, which may be most important at the outset, come to be essentially secondary at a point where vocational assessment, training, and placement are the order of the day."

11. Team members value self-evaluation and feedback from colleagues as well as external sources of evaluation.

12. Each member of the team is willing to accept senior therapeutic responsibility for a given case, and responsibility for coordinating and integrating patient care when appropriate.

13. Consultations between professional colleagues are informal and frequent.

14. Communication methods are unfettered and information-sharing is maximized.

15. Gaps in role performance are willingly filled by assistance from other related professions.

16. Error and failure do not deter significantly from the group's ability to carry out its work.

Research Activities—

1. Research covering broad areas of concern is engaged in by the team of collaborating professionals.

2. Each practitioner takes steps to facilitate the research achievement of his colleagues.

3. Academic disciplines stressing theoretical research and professional orientation stressing goal-directed clinical practice are not seen as conflicting.

The interactive approach thus provides the individual practitioner the opportunity to examine his own perspectives with regard to collaborative effort, as well as the capacity to identify specific aspects of the work-setting which are associated with the interdisciplinary perspective.

Relationship Between Current Patterns of Collaborative Effort in Cerebral Palsy

It is obvious to seasoned practitioners that the evolutionary, structural, and interactive approaches are not mutually exclusive. Indeed, each can be utilized to analyze the clinical situation which confronts the practitioner. Furthermore, each is in need of considerable improvement before it can be considered even minimally acceptable in examining the collaborative relationships among professional interveners. A significant problem also arises when different professional workers may choose to view collaborative phenomena utilizing different approaches to address problems in collaborative function. In addition, the same practitioner may utilize different approaches depending upon the circumstances in which it is applied. However, each approach can be valuable both singularly and in combination with others. Each of the approaches has central or unifying characteristics which can be of distinct value:

1. They provide the practitioner with a method of reorganizing the critical aspects of collaborative function in the operational reality which confronts him.

2. They provide a foundation for communication through which greater understanding of professional practices and values may occur.

3. They each describe the effort toward more effective patterns of collaborative function in terms which can be quantified.

4. Although they are founded upon different assumptions regarding human behavior, the set of conventions inherent in each allows predictions of alterations in professional practice patterns and each may be useful in the determination of specific testable propositions which can lead to new knowledge.

5. They all provide a variable alternative to the dire consequences of the exercise of spontaneous and idiosyncratic approaches to conflict resolution which often undermine further efforts toward collaborative function.

6. They legitimate the effort which professions may expend in searching for more effective patterns of collaborative function.

7. Each of the approaches appears to be broad enough to offer general explanations of collaborative behavior and specific enough to be of particular value in defined circumstances. For example, the evolutionary approach may be preferred in understanding the contribution of professional input recently introduced within the work setting. The practice patterns of sex education might serve as an example here. The structural approach may be more useful in determining the enacted roles of two or more professionals whose ascribed roles are almost analogous. A time

honored reference to this problem may be found in the relationship between psychiatry, psychology, social work and vocational counseling. Similarly, differences which arise between professionals on the basis of personality conflicts may best be understood and resolved through the utilization of the interactive approach. However, the true value of all of these approaches lies not in their specific attributes, but rather in their appeal to the professional practitioner and his willingness to utilize them.

FLEXIDISCIPLINARY METHODS OF SERVICE DELIVERY

Collaborative patterns of professional function must be clearly differentiated from flexidisciplinary methods of service delivery. Evolutionary, structural, or interactive patterns are methods which individual professionals utilize to understand and positively influence joint function. They are strategies which are applied to mediating their function and are related to the processes which are employed in seeking common ground for effective effort.

In sharp contrast are flexidisciplinary methods of service delivery. These methods are related to specific organizational staffing patterns and are defined by (1) the number and disciplinary designation of professional personnel available, and (2) administrative decision-making with regard to the operational model of service delivery to be employed. Methods of service delivery are usually expressed in schematic form in which the relationship of providers of service and the recipient of services are portrayed (see Figure 17.5). These methods vary both between organizations which have different goals and objectives and within organizations as changes in philosophy, resources, and commitments occur.

A major misinterpretation which impedes collaborative relationships among professionals working in the field of cerebral palsy results from the confusion between the array of professional services available in a particular setting and the collaborative processes which mediate their efficiency and effectiveness. Although it is true that some collaborative processes may be more or less associated with specific methods of service delivery, they are separate and distinct from them. Failure to recognize this distinction often results in the assumption that because a particular service method is employed, specific collaborative patterns of function are present. An outstanding example of this occurs when cerebral palsy clinics are represented as being "interdisciplinary" in nature solely because they have a large number of practitioners representing different disciplines within their staff.

Attention must be given to both collaborative processes and flexidiscipline patterns. The relationship between the two is somewhat analogous to

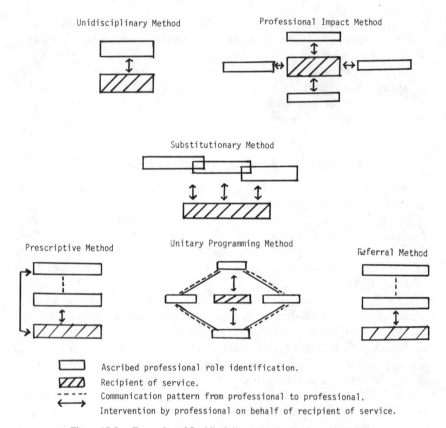

Figure 17.5.   Examples of flexidisciplinary methods of service delivery.

the building of a house: the bricks, mortar, and architecture which form the house, only partially determine how the house is lived in, not the quality of life within.

It is a characteristic of collaborative patterns of professional function that they are constantly evolving despite the fact that they can be conveniently categorized as being either evolutionary, structural, or interactive in nature. On the other hand, flexidisciplinary methods of service delivery are static at any given point in organizational history, but respond dramatically to changing organizational objectives. Understanding of the distinction between collaborative patterns of professional effort and flexidisciplinary methods of service delivery is essential to the meaningful examination of societal factors specifically modifying the nature and extent of current and future professional intervention in cerebral palsy.

CURRENT SOCIETAL FACTORS INFLUENCING COLLABORATIVE
PROFESSIONAL EFFORT

Professions serving the cerebral palsied are now vigorously involved in preparing for a future which promises to alter dramatically both disciplinary professional role identification and relationships among professions. Dramatic sociological changes in expectations concerning the contribution of professionals serving the cerebral palsied have provided impetus and direction for the introduction of these developments. Many of these current trends have occurred as a result of increasing attention to the needs of those cerebral palsied who have mental retardation, in addition to neuromotor and neurosensory handicaps.

Presently Emerging Factors Influencing Collaborative Professional Effort

Normalization

The normalization principle has been described as making available patterns and conditions of everyday life which are as close as possible to the norms and patterns of the mainstream of society (Nirje 1969). This concept implies increasing attention to the development of a normal routine of life in which the choices, wishes, and desires of the cerebral palsied are guides for professional intervention as much as possible. To the degree that professional intervention isolates the cerebral palsied from full participation in life experiences, the legitimacy of that intervention becomes questionable.

Deinstitutionalization

One of the most damaging practices for the cerebral palsied with mental retardation has been the widespread use of institutional placement in state residential facilities. The location of these facilities in rural areas, their chronic underfinancing, "institutional serfdom" associated with the work performed by residents necessary to keep institutions operating, overcrowding, lack of professional and community resources, and the deterioration of residents because of the lack of both environmental demands and therapeutic supports, have led to a concerted effort to return residents of such institutions to the community. This has precipitated several new demands influencing collaborative professional functioning within residential settings.

    1.   Those residents whose physical or psychological condition make community placement impossible require greater care and more efficient methods of intervention.

    2.   Professional practice patterns must include community practi-

tioners in the development of long-term management plans for residents being prepared for community placement.

Debureaucratization

The practice of professions in current society is closely associated with the major institutions of society, such as, government, religion, education, law, and health care. As such, professions provide leadership for the development of policies and procedures which define the relationship of these institutions to the needs of the members of the society they serve. Many of these institutions in the past have been less than responsive to these needs. At the present time, there is hard societal press for the ascendancy of individual caring relationships over the centralization and authoritarianism often associated with bureaucratic structures. To the degree that collaborative professional relationships are seen as supporting such bureaucratic structures to the exclusion of reaching out to persons in need, considerable resistance to joint professional effort can be expected by professional practitioners in the field of cerebral palsy.

Antiprofessionalism

Closely associated with debureaucratization is a sociological movement which questions the value of professional contribution with regard to the recipient of service. In an outstanding treatment of this issue, Rhodes and Tracy (1972) suggest that professional intervention can be conceptualized as a barrier imposed by society in order to protect it and isolate it from deviance. The radicalization of society is interpreted by Rhodes as a means of eradicating this barrier and manifests itself in a wide variety of forms such as: criticism of the care-giving function; revolt against care-giving metaphors such as diagnostic classification and etiological distinctions; revolt against the social dominance of care-givers over care receivers; revolt against economics and politics of care; underclass revolt by those who see themselves as involuntary care receivers.

Rhodes sees antiprofessionalism as a function of a new consciousness of caring as "credentialized care takers themselves are being questioned with respect to their qualifications and capacity to intervene in the lives to whom they give care." The impact of these changes upon professional function in cerebral palsy is unclear at present. Most certainly, however, there is reflected within Rhodes's view a prima facia case against current professional practices in cerebral palsy with the burden of responsibility cast upon professional workers to justify the legitimacy of their current practices to the individual recipient of service, his family, and society at large.

There are significant efforts presently under way by professionals to reduce the intensity of antiprofessionalism. Clear recognition of this problem is found in statements of the goals and objectives of such indigenous community health care facilities as the Free Peoples Clinic, Ann Arbor, Michigan: "In delivery of health care the clinic has tried to live up to its ideals which include the belief that health care is a human right, not a privilege based on income or anything else; that health care means caring about *people,* not just treating their diseases; that an emphasis on health education, preventive medicine, demystification and deprofessionalization of medicine must underlie all interactions between staff and patients; and that no hierarchical structures can exist among clinic staff and between staff and patients."

Legalization

A major movement has occurred in defining the nature and extent of professional services required for the cerebral palsy through legal means. Although professional practice is internally regulated by state practice acts or certification at the national level, a large number of court cases dealing with the rights of the developmentally disabled have established two basic trends: certain current professional practices be discontinued, and professional resources not previously provided be made available. Up to this point, much of the legal constraints on professional practice were related to malpractice considerations in medicine. Today, every professional must be concerned about the impact of the law in the lives of the cerebral palsied and current and future trends in legal rights. Efforts to secure the legal rights of the developmentally disabled presently center around the right to be born, the right to life after birth, the right to physical access to buildings, the right to education, the right to work, the right to marry, the right to have sex, the right to procreate, the right to raise children, the right to vote, the right to contract, the right of access to the courts, the right to be free unless proven dangerous and the rights of persons in institutions (Burgdorf 1973).

This trend exerts great influence upon professional practice patterns in cerebral palsy. As Gettings (1973) points out, "From the vantage point of the profession, the possibility of court intervention poses both a promise and a threat. It is, therefore, incumbent upon the training institution to prepare future professionals to deal with law suits in a constructive manner and to recognize when loyalty to a service system ends and adherence to one's own personal and professional ethics begins."

A productive utilization of legal constraints is the dynamic incorporation of those constraints within the ethical context of professional practice. For example, the following elements of informed consent for experimentation on human subjects are becoming part of the standard practice patterns of many professionals working with the cerebral palsied

and their families (Guidelines of the Committee on the Protection of the
Rights of Human Subjects, School of Medicine, University of Michigan):

  a. a fair explanation of the procedures to be followed, including an
     identification of those which are experimental;
  b. a description of the attendant discomforts and risks;
  c. a description of the benefits to be expected;
  d. a disclosure of the appropriate alternative procedures that would
     be advantageous for the subject;
  e. an offer to answer any inquiries concerning the procedures;
  f. an instruction that the subject is free to withdraw his consent and
     to discontinue participation in the project or activity at any time.

Standardization through Accreditation

There is a strong current trend to limit the degrees to which professional
workers may exercise certain prerogatives which formerly accrued to their
position. This effort takes its impetus from three related factors: (1) the
influence of governmental standards for care related to Aid to Dependent
Children, Maternal and Child Health Care, Developmental Disability,
Medicare, and Medicaid; (2) the efforts of third-party payers such as Blue
Cross, Blue Shield, and private insurance carriers; and (3) the efforts
toward maintaining standards of service associated with accreditation by
special interest groups.

   A noticeable trend is occurring in which such agencies band together
in an area of common concern to develop criteria and mechanisms for
certification. A noteworthy example of this phenomenon is the recently
published standards for residential facilities for the retarded in which the
United Cerebral Palsy Association collaborated with the American
Association on Mental Deficiency, the National Association for Retarded
Citizens, the Council for Exceptional Children, and the American Psychiatric Association in joint development and legitimation of those standards. Such efforts are often advantageous for professional practice because they raise the levels of professional resources and programs which
must be available in order to qualify for certification. However, these efforts
also restrict the options available administratively with regard to the organization, distribution, and utilization of professional services.

Educationalization

In the past decade, there has been a shift in central focus in the treatment of
cerebral palsy from the medical environment to the educational environment. This shift has occurred through the passage of mandatory special
education legislation in six states. As this trend continues, professional
workers in the field of cerebral palsy will find greater practice opportunities

in educational settings, such as early intervention programs, day training centers, and special educational classrooms. Their practice will be greatly influenced by the concept of zero reject education and the requirement for an individualized educational plan appropriate to the child's physical, social, psychological, and vocational needs, as well as those related to basic learning skills. The normalization concept known as mainstreaming will require that the educational program in all its aspects occur in as integrated a setting as possible. The presence of parents in educational planning and placement conferences and their influence in local and state task forces to plan, oversee, and monitor the educational facilities made available to the developmentally disabled will provide new challenges and opportunities for professional practice.

Influence Upon Professional Practice Patterns

There is little question that the influence of the preceding factors signify a historical turning point in the nature and extent of professional involvement in cerebral palsy. A reduction of professional prerogative appears certain as the focus of power moves away from credentialized care givers. This does, and will continue to, place great demands upon professional adaptability as professional knowledge and position become clearly secondary to adequate performance. Each professional worker can expect that management by objectives will be applied to professional practice to insure professional accountability. Management by objectives is not an unfamiliar procedure for professional practitioners. It is an extension of the systematic approach by which professionals have historically developed intervention strategies for recipients of services (see Figure 17.6). To insure accountability in the management by objective approach, professional contributions can be ex-

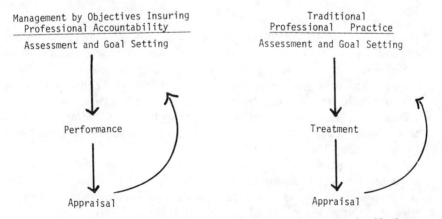

Figure 17.6.   Relationship of traditional practice patterns to management by objectives.

Standardized Clinical Operating Procedure	Problem Oriented Approach
Team pre-appraisal conference	Problem recognition and development of strategy for data gathering
Utilization of standardized or non-standardized evaluation format	Establishment of a data base:
Team conference to determine management plan including specification of:	1. Objective 2. Subjective
1. Person responsible for intervention.	Problem definition
2. Setting in which intervention will take place.	Problem differentiation and synthesis (problem grouping)
3. Time when intervention is to be initiated.	Problem group ordering in terms of therapeutic importance
4. Time when intervention is to be examined for effectiveness.	Hypothesis generation regarding therapeutic approach to resolve problem or problem group.
	Rank ordering of plausibility of hypotheses.
	Selection of highest ranked hypothesis regarding plan for problem or problem group resolution.
Treatment	Implementation of highest ranked plan
Follow-up	Evaluation of effectiveness of plan in resolving problem or problem group.
	Should need require, institution of next highest ranked plan, redefinition of problem or problem group, and/or establishment of increased data base.

Figure 17.7.   Example of a programmatic model for a clinical setting.

pected to be monitored at specific review points at which time performance objectives previously established will be utilized to assess the efficiency and effectiveness of professional performance. This approach, rapidly being adopted in many facilities for the cerebral palsied, can be expected to have several significant productive effects upon resolution of conflicts between ascribed, perceived, and enacted roles, and, thus, it supports a high level of collaborative function among professionals. It also facilitates administrative support and the provision of resources to accomplish task functions (Schemerhorn 1974).

The influence of management by objectives has been reflected in patterns of service delivery by the introduction of the program model. The program model has as its foundation professional accountability to a set of objectives individually defined for each recipient of service through the process of collaborative effort among care-givers.

The Program Model

The program model is best described as a set of standardized procedures for a specific therapeutic environment based upon scientific principles. Hence, although each professional will still make contributions based upon his individualized professional judgment, clear constraints are present which limit the nature, extent, and appropriateness of such judgments.

There are three elements which define a program for a specific therapeutic environment:

1.   The resolution of the needs of the individual recipient of services by central foci defined in terms of therapeutic tasks to be accomplished by specific intervention strategies.

2.   The insuring of professional accountability by identifying the service deliverer, and the time and location of initial and subsequent interventions.

3.   The establishment of an evaluation methodology for each central focus and contingencies should a specific intervention strategy prove unsuccessful.

The programmatic model can be expressed most clearly in terms of parallel processes which integrate a problem-oriented approach to clinical intervention with standardized clinical operating procedures. An example of such a model is found in Figure 17.7.

The Effect of the Program Model on Professional Organization in Facilities for the Cerebral Palsied

Since 1970, facilities for the cerebral palsied have undergone a dramatic change in both their function and structure. A major focus for such settings has become a deemphasis upon traditional professional practice patterns and an affirmation of their role in preparing the cerebral palsied for productive community living. Concurrently, such facilities have been transformed from administrative structures, based upon disciplinary departments into goal-directed program units composed of professional teams.

A major effect of movement toward the program model has been the utilization of allied health professions in far broader practice patterns. Rather than a traditional emphasis on singular approaches to management, health professionals are now regularly called upon to play a major role in the development and implementation of joint management plans utilizing a synthesis of orthopedic, developmental, neurophysiological, and psychoeducational factors based upon biophysical, behavioral, psychodynamic, or ecological theory. This approach also has often resulted in a significant realignment of the traditional relationship between junior/ senior personnel within specific health care disciplines.

Administrative and Supervisory Considerations

The most striking effect of the development of a program model has been the influence upon the administrative and supervisory responsibilities of senior personnel in specific health professions in most facilities. Each program is usually operated as a unit independent of other programs within the facility and is headed by a professional person who is chosen on the basis of his experience and capacities. This person may come from any of the health professional disciplines. As a result, junior health professionals find themselves in one of two situations:

1.   They may serve in a program in which the administrative head is not a representative of their discipline, and who may or may not have an appreciation for the administrative support and therapeutic methods necessary for effective intervention in that discipline, or,

2.   They may serve in a program in which the administrative head is a member of that discipline. However, the disciplinary identification of such an administrative head is secondary to his responsibilities for coordinating and integrating the activities of the program staff.

Senior personnel in allied health care professions have responded to the development of the program model in a variety of ways. Generally, senior personnel have: (1) been appointed program directors, or (2) drastically redefined their relationship to staff personnel in their disciplines. Such staff health professionals are often jointly responsible to the director of the program in which they are practicing for administrative areas, such as a job description and conditions of employment, and to the senior person in their discipline for the exercise of professional judgment and appropriate levels of therapeutic skills in case management. The total effect of these alterations has been to separate the administrative and supervisory functions typically performed by senior disciplinary personnel and to remove those administrative functions and prerogatives. The stated purpose of this approach has been to make more available the experience and expertise of senior disciplinary personnel to staff personnel representing all professional disciplines and to facilitate efficient problem-solving.

The dislocation of the traditional role of the senior professional personnel in settings for the cerebral palsied has in some cases brought about fears of professional role erosion, loss of status, and an identity crisis. However, most senior professional personnel have seized upon the opportunity in order to expand their professional skills and their potential impact on the facility as well as the community. Free from administrative responsibilities they have expanded their capacities in disciplinary endeavors through raising the standards of practice. In addition, increasing capabilities are being developed in consultation and teaching in order to translate the theory and practice of their discipline in terms which are meaningful to representatives of other disciplines, other supportive personnel including aides and attendants, as well as families, community caretakers and lay persons. In those cases where professional personnel have become program directors, they have benefitted from their previous administrative experience in their disciplines.

Several issues which have not yet been uniformly resolved are (1) determination of staff allocation to individual program units; (2) effective allocation and utilization of disciplinary therapeutic equipment without unnecessary duplication of facilities within each program unit; (3) securing uniform procedures for the acquisition and utilization of adaptive equipment for specific residents; (4) securing the support of individual program directors for making available resources to enhance continuing disciplinary education of personnel in such programs; and (5) ascertainment of which responsibilities are supervisory, which are administrative, and which must be jointly adjudicated by senior disciplinary personnel and the program director.

A major implication of these developments is that professionals preparing for careers in cerebral palsy should have specialized disciplinary competencies in developmental disability as well as specific training opportunities in supervision, teaching, and consultation. In addition, those preparing for careers in administration in cerebral palsy and related disabilities should emphasize in their training broad based administrative skills in health care administration which includes an understanding and appreciation of the contribution of other disciplines to joint professional effort.

Implications of the Program Model for Health Care Professionals

The recognition of the special clinical contribution of the allied health professions to the habilitation of the cerebral palsied and the realignment of the traditional relationship between disciplines are welcome developments. However, they also involve special responsibilities for the health care practitioner. Not only must he maintain and expand his knowledge and skill base in his own discipline, but he must be able to translate them to members of other health professions. To facilitate this process a close working relationship with representatives of other disciplines must be developed early in his professional role development. Such relationships are a large determinant of the ability of a program to reach its stated objectives effectively. To operate with equal effectiveness in the pre-appraisal, appraisal, management plan development, implementation, evaluation and revision phases which often constitute the operational components of the program employed in such facilities, and to allow both creativity and accountability in individualized management of the cerebral palsied, didactic opportunities to develop understanding, appreciation, and utilization of the contribution of

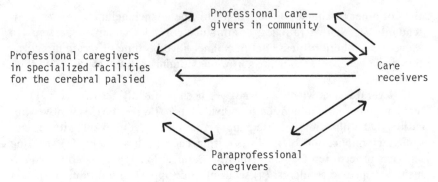

Figure 17.8.   Alternatives to direct caregiving by professional interveners.

other disciplines must be part of basic health care education for all health care personnel. Furthermore, practitioners in the field have a responsibility to model such processes in clinical education.

With increasing emphasis upon community resources for the cerebral palsied, professional care givers must consider a redefinition of their traditional provider of care–recipient-of-care relationship. Instead of direct personal contact with the recipient of services, alternative strategies must be explored which will best meet the needs of recipients of services. Every professional has the responsibility to determine if replacement of direct personal service is a more efficient and effective mode of intervention. Distinct alternatives are available to direct intervention in which the professional practitioner has the responsibility of coordinating and integrating his professional contribution with other care-givers who have complementary or substitutionary capacities (see Figure 17.8). Specialists in dealing with the problems of cerebral palsy may often most efficiently use their skills in collaborative function with professionals and/or paraprofessionals from their own or related disciplines within the community.

The Cross Modality or Transdisciplinary Approach

Of increasing importance is the cross-modality or transdisciplinary approach specifically developed through the auspices of the United Cerebral Palsy Association for the cerebral palsied whose neuromotor and neurosensory handicaps are accompanied by mental retardation. Its purpose is to minimize the number of significant adult figures coming into contact with a care receiver who requires the input of many disciplines because of the magnitude of his problems. It differs fundamentally from the disciplinary pattern in that a single primary deliverer of service, usually a paraprofessional, program aide, or attendant, has the benefit of continuing consultation with practitioners of many disciplines in order to assist him with the development of an effective intervention plan and therapeutic techniques to accomplish it. A singular advantage of the cross modality approach is that it mandates the alteration of fixed therapeutic roles and places a premium on the responsibility of health care practitioners to delegate fully basic evaluation and intervention functions. It also maximizes the accountability of individual health care practitioners for translating the theory and practice of their discipline into methods and procedures which are meaningful to the primary deliverer of services. This approach provides a potential vehicle for the alleviation of shortages in the technical inputs of scarce disciplines by making their contributions more efficient through the provision of continuous consultation to others with less training (Darnell 1973).

The importance of this approach has been underscored by the Community Alternative and Institutional Reform Program sponsored by developmental disabilities legislation in which a concerted effort has been made to disseminate the concept on a national basis, and by others who see in the transdisciplinary approach an amalgamation of an efficient pattern of collaborative effort with an optimal method of service delivery.

SUMMARY

Examination of the development of professional interest in cerebral palsy has demonstrated historical precedent for collaborative professional effort. Approaches to collaborative effort have been identified and have been differentiated from patterns of service delivery. Recent societal changes have been shown to require increasing professional attention to accountability and participation in program based rather than disciplinary oriented patterns of service delivery.

The challenge to professional adaptability is clear. In an ethical climate that demands advocacy on behalf of the estimated 750,000 persons with cerebral palsy, with 25,000 babies born each year with this problem, professional workers find themselves in the midst of concerted political and social forces which are dramatically reducing the centralization of the power of the health care professions and demanding reduction of barriers among them.

Professional prerogative is being replaced by cost-effectiveness analysis. The traditional status orientations reserved for health care professionals are being redefined by the active participation of the paraprofessional and members of racial and ethnic minorities. Public intervention is eroding the large institutional structures associated with professional practice and is developing smaller community based facilities more responsive to indigeneous needs and control. Human and legal rights of recipients of service are clearly outweighing professional autonomy and privilege.

Professional responsibility to the cerebral palsied—the elimination of handicaps, assistance in the development of competency and integration into community life—can only occur today in an atmosphere where collaborative professional effort is fostered. In this sense, professionals serving the cerebral palsied can be likened to species near extinction, only one course remains open—adapt to the changing environment or perish in their present form.

BIBLIOGRAPHY

Abercrombie, M. L. J., and Tyson, M. C. "Body Image and Draw-a-Man Test in Cerebral Palsy." *Developmental Medicine and Child Neurology* 8 (1966):9–15.

Achilles, R. "Communicative Anomalies of Individuals with Cerebral Palsy." *Cerebral Palsy Review* Part I, 16 (1955):15–24.

———. "Communicative Anomalies of Individuals with Cerebral Palsy." *Cerebral Palsy Review* Part II, 17 (1956):19–26.

Adler, E. "Familial Cerebral Palsy." *Journal of Chronic Diseases* 13 (1961):207.

Ainsworth, M.; Bell, S.; Blehar, M.; and Main, M. "Physical Contact: A Study of Infant Responsiveness and Its Relation to Maternal Handling." Paper presented at Society for Research in Child Development, Minneapolis, 1971.

American Association on Mental Deficiency. *Manual on Terminology and Classification in Mental Retardation,* edited by H. J. Grossman. Washington, D.C., 1973.

American National Standards Institute. "Specifications for Audiometers." ANSI S3.6–1969. New York, 1970.

American Occupational Therapy Association. "Occupational Therapy: Its Definition and Functions." *American Journal of Occupational Therapy* 26 (1972):204–205.

Ando, K. "A Comparative Study of Peabody Picture Vocabulary Test and Wechsler Intelligence Scale for Children with a Group of Cerebral Palsied Children." *Cerebral Palsy Journal* 29 (1968):7–9.

André-Thomas, P.; Chesni, P.; and Saint-Anne Dargassies, S. *The Neurological Examination of the Infant.* London: Heinemann, 1960.

Armstrong, Robert. "Group Work with Cerebral Palsied Adults." *Cerebral Palsy Review* 18 (July–August 1957):20–21.

Asher, P., and Schonell, F. E. "A Survey of 400 Cases of Cerebral Palsy." *Archives of Disease of Children* 25 (December 1950):360–79.

Avery, M. E. *The Lung and Its Disorders in the Newborn Infant,* 2nd ed. Philadelphia: Saunders, 1972.

Ayres, A. J. *Southern California Sensory Integration Tests.* Los Angeles: Western Psychological Services, 1972a.

———. *Sensory Integration and Learning Disorders.* Los Angeles: Western Psychological Services, 1972b.

Ayres, C. E. "Vocational Rehabilitation Counseling." In *Expanding Dimensions in Rehabilitation*, edited by L. S. Zamir. Springfield, Ill.: Thomas, 1969.

Bailey, D. M. "Vocational Theories and Work Habits related to Childhood Development." *American Journal of Occupational Therapy* 25 (1971):289–302.

Balf, C. "Neonatal Behavior of Infants Born by Spontaneous and by Forceps Delivery." *Archives of Diseases of Childhood* 23 (1948):142.

Banks, C., and Sinha, U. "An Item Analysis of the Progressive Matrices Test." *British Journal of Psychology, Statistical Section* 4 (1951): Part II.

Banus, B. S. *The Developmental Therapist.* Thorofare, N.J.: C.B. Slack, 1971.

Barraga, N. C. *Increased Visual Behavior in Low Vision Children.* Research Series No. 13. New York: American Foundation for the Blind, 1964.

Barrett, M., and Jones, M. "The Sensory Story: A Multi-Sensory Training Procedure for Toddlers." *Developmental Medicine and Child Neurology* 9 (1967):448–56.

Bateman, B. *Reading and Psycholinguistic Processes of Partially Seeing Children.* Washington, D.C.: Council for Exceptional Children, 1962.

_____. *The Illinois Test of Psycholinguistic Abilities in Current Research, Summaries of Studies.* Urbana: Illinois Institute for Research on Exceptional Children, 1964.

Bauer, C. H. "An Overview of Low Birth Weight Babies." *Pediatric Annals, the Low Birth Weight Baby 1 (1972):10–27.*

Baumeister, A., and Klosowski, R. "An Attempt to Group Toilet Train Severely Retarded Patients." *Mental Retardation* 3 (6) (1965):24–26.

Baumgartner, B. B. *Helping the Trainable Mentally Retarded Child.* New York: Teachers College Press, 1960.

Beck, H. "Group Treatment for Parents of Handicapped Children." Washington, D.C.: U.S. Department of Health, Education and Welfare, Public Health Services, 1973.

Beckwith, L. "Relationships Between Infant's Vocalizations and Their Mother's Behaviors." *Merrill-Palmer Quarterly* 17 (1971):211–26.

Beery, K., and Butenka, N. *Developmental Test of Visual-Motor Integration.* Chicago: Follett, 1967.

Bell, R. "Stimulus Control of Parent or Caretaker Behavior by Offspring." *Developmental Psychology* 4 (1971):63–72.

Benda, C. E. *Developmental Disorders of Mentation and Cerebral Palsies.* New York: Grune and Stratton, 1952.

Bender, M. "An Experiment Using a Visual Method of Instruction Followed by Imitation to Teach Selected Psychomotor Tasks to Severely Mentally Retarded Males." *International Dissertation Abstracts* 1972 (March) 32 (9-A):5004–5005.

Bercel, N. A. "Diagnosis and Treatment of Epileptic and Epileptoid Disorders." *Journal of the American Medical Association* 149 (1952):1,361–65.

Berenberg, W.; Byers, R.; and Meyer, E. "Cerebral Palsy Symposium: Cerebral Palsy Nursery Schools." *Quarterly Review Pediatrics* 7 (1952):27–33.

Berko, F. "Amelioration of Athetoid Speech by Manipulation of Auditory Feedback." Unpublished doctoral dissertation, Cornell University, 1965.

_____. *The Special Children's Center's Infant and Toddler Program.* Ithaca, N.Y., 1974: special material prepared for chapter.

Bermann, E. "Regrouping for Survival: Approaching Dread and Three Phases of Family Interaction." *Journal of Comparative and Family Studies* 4 (1973): 63–87.

Berry, M., and Eisenson, J. *Speech Disorders.* New York: Appleton-Century-Crofts, 1956.

Bharucha, P. E.; Patel, S.; Bharucha, E. P.; and Mulla-Frioze, P. K. "Intelligence in Cerebral Palsy." *Proceedings of the Australian Association of Neurology* 5 (1968):171–75.

Bice, H. V., and Cruickshank, W. M. "Evaluation of Intelligence." In Cruickshank, W. M., ed. *Cerebral Palsy: Its Individual and Community Problems,* 2nd ed. Syracuse: Syracuse University Press, 1966.

Bick, E. M. *Source Book of Orthopaedics.* New York: Hafner, 1968, 2nd ed.

Birch, H., ed. *Brain Damage in Children.* Baltimore, Md.: Williams and Wilkins, 1964.

———, and Belmont, L. "Auditory-Visual Integration in Normal and Retarded Readers." *American Journal of Orthopsychiatry* 34 (1964):852–61.

———, and Belmont, L. "Auditory-Visual Integration in Brain Damaged and Normal Children." *Developmental Medicine and Child Neurology* 7 (1965): 135–44.

———, and Bortner, M. "Stimulus Competition and Category Usage in Normal Children." *Journal of Genetic Psychology* 109 (1966):195.

———, and Bortner, M. "Stimulus Competition and Concept Utilization in Brain Damaged Children." *Developmental Medicine and Child Neurology* 9 (4) (1967):402–10.

———, and Lefford, A. "Intersensory Development in Children." *Monographs Society in Research in Child Development* 28 (5) (1963).

———, and Lefford, A. "Visual Differentation, Intersensory Integration and Voluntary Motor Control." *Monographs Society for Research in Child Development* 32 (2) (1967):1–87.

Birenbaum, A. "Non-Institutionalized Roles and Role Formation: A Study of Mothers of Mentally Retarded Children." Unpublished doctoral dissertation, Columbia University, 1968.

———. "On Managing Courtesy Stigma." *Journal of Health and Social Behavior* 11 (1970):196–206.

Birns, B.; Blank, M.; Bridger, W.; and Escalona, S. "Behavioral Inhibition in Neonates Produced by Auditory Stimuli." *Child Development* 36 (1965): 249–56.

Bloom, L. *One Word at a Time.* The Hague: Mouton, 1973.

Blumberg, M. "Respiration and Speech in the Cerebral Palsied Child." *American Journal of Diseases of Children* 89 (1955a):48–53.

———. "Vital Capacity and Related Therapies in Cerebral Palsy." *Cerebral Palsy Review* 16 (1955b):23–26.

Blumel, J.; Evans, E. B.; Eggers, G. W. N. "Hereditary Cerebral Palsy: A Preliminary Report." *Journal of Pediatrics* 50 (1957):454.

Bobath, B. "The Treatment of Motor Disorders of Pyramidal Extrapyramidal Origin by Reflex Inhibition and by Facilitation of Movement." *Physiotherapy* 41 (1955):146–53.

Bobath, K. *The Motor Deficit in Patients with Cerebral Palsy.* Clinics in Developmental Medicine #23. London: Heinemann, 1966.

————, and Bobath, B. "Tonic Reflexes and Righting Reflexes in Diagnosis and Assessment of Cerebral Palsy." *Cerebral Palsy Review* 5 (1955):310–26.

————, and Bobath, B. "The Facilitation of Normal Postural Reactions and Movements in the Treatment of Cerebral Palsy." *Physiotherapy* 50 (August 1964):246–62.

————, and Bobath, B. "The Neuro-Developmental Treatment of Cerebral Palsy." *Physical Therapy* 47 (11) (1967):1039–41.

Boök, J. A. "Agentie and Neuropsychiatric Investigation of a North Swedish Population." *Acta Genetica* (separate vol.) 4 (1953):370.

Bower, T. "The Visual World of Infants." *Scientific American* 215 (6) (1966):80.

Broen, P. *The Verbal Environment of the Language-Learning Child,* ASHA Monograph No. 17. Washington, D.C.: American Speech and Hearing Association, 1972.

Brown, L., and Foshee, J. G. "Comparative Techniques for Increasing Attending Behavior of Retarded Children." *Education and Training of the Mentally Retarded* 6 (1) (1971):4–10.

Buchwald, J. S. "A Functional Concept of Motor Control." *American Journal of Physical Medicine* 46 (1967):141.

Bull, B. "Assessment of Intelligence of Cerebral Palsied Children in Windsor and Essex County, Ontario." *Canadian Medical Association Journal* 95 (1966):241.

Burgdorf, M.P. "Growing Influence of the Law in the Lives of Handicapped Citizens: Current Future Trends." In *Manpower Projections for Developmental Disabilities in the 1980's.* Developmental Disabilities Center, Temple University, Philadelphia, Pennsylvania, June, 1973.

Burgemeister, B. B.; Blum, L. H.; and Lorge, I. *Manual, Columbia Test of Mental Maturity.* Yonkers-on-Hudson, N.Y.: World Book, 1954.

Byrne, M. "Speech and Language Development of Athetoid and Spastic Children." *Journal of Speech and Hearing Research* 24 (1959):231–40.

Cain, L. F., Conference Director. *A Very Special Child.* Report of a conference on placement of children in special education programs for the mentally retarded sponsored by the President's Committee on Mental Retardation, Bureau for Education of the Handicapped, the Council for Exceptional Children, Lake Arrowhead, Ca., March 7–10, 1971.

Caplow, T. *The Sociology of Work.* New York: McGraw-Hill, 1954.

Carhart, R. "Clinical Application of Bone Conduction Audiometry." *Archives of Otolaryngology* 51 (1950):798–808.

Cazden, C. "Some Implications of Research on Language Development for Pre-School Education." in *Early Education,* edited by R. Hess and R. Bear. Chicago: Aldine, 1968.

Chomsky, N. *Syntatic Structures.* The Hague: Mouton, 1957.

————. *Aspects of the Theary Syntax.* Cambridge, Mass.: MIT Press, 1966.

Churchill, J. "On the Etiology of Cerebral Palsy in Premature Infants." Note in neurology program abstracts, *American Academy of Neurology Program* 20 (April 1970):405.

Clark-Stewart, K. "Interactions Between Mothers and Their Young Children:

Characteristics and Consequences." *Monograph of the Society for Research in Child Development* (1973):38.

Cohen, H., and Diner, H. "The Significance of Developmental Dental Enamel Defects in Neurological Diagnosis." *Pediatrics* 46 (5) (1970):735–47.

Cohen, J. S.; Gregory, R. J.; and Pelosi, J. W. *Vocational Rehabilitation and the Socially Disabled.* Syracuse: Syracuse University, 1966.

Collard, R. "Exploratory and Play Behaviors of Infants Reared in Institutions and in Lower and Middle Class Homes." *Child Development* 42 (1971):1003–16.

Connolly, K. "Sensory Motor Coordination: Mechanisms and Plans." In *Planning for Better Learning,* edited by P. Wolff and R. Mac Keith. Clinics in Developmental Medicine No. 33. London: Heinmann, 1969.

———. "Learning and the Concept of Critical Periods in Infancy." *Developmental Medicine and Child Neurology* 14 (6) (1972):705–14.

Cotton, E. "The Institute of Movement Therapy and School for Conductors: A Report on a Study Visit." *Developmental Medicine and Child Neurology* 7 (4) (1965):437–46.

———, and Parnwell, M. "From Hungary, the Peto Method." *Special Education* 54 (4) (1967):7–12.

———, and Parnwell, M. "Conductive Education with Special Reference to Severe Athetoids in a Non-Residential Centre." *Journal of Mental Sub-Normal* 14 (1968):50–56.

Cravioto, J.; DeLicardie, E. R.; and Birch, H. G. "Nutrition, Growth, and Neurointegrative Development: An Experimental and Ecologic Study." *Pediatrics* 38 (Supplement 2) (1966):319.

Crickmay, M. *Speech Therapy and the Bobath Approach to Cerebral Palsy.* Springfield, Ill.: Thomas, 1966.

Cronholm, B., and Schalling, D. "Cognitive Test Performance in Cerebrally Palsied Adults with Mental Retardation." *Acta Psychiatrica Scandinavica* 44 (1968): 37–50.

Crosby, K. G. "Accreditation Council for Facilities for the Mentally Retarded." *Perspectives,* February 1974, p. 3.

Crosson, J. E. "A Technique for Programming Sheltered Workshop Environments for Training Severely Retarded Workers." *American Journal of Mental Deficiency* 73 (1969): 814–18.

Crothers, B., and Paine, R. S. *The Natural History of Cerebral Palsy.* Cambridge, Mass.: Harvard University Press, 1959.

Cruickshank, W. M. "The Multiply Handicapped Cerebral Palsied Child." *Exceptional Children* 20 (October 1953):16–22.

———. "The Development of Education of Exceptional Children." *Education of Exceptional Children and Youth,* edited by W. M. Cruickshank and G. O. Johnson. Englewood Cliffs, N.J.: Prentice-Hall, 1958.

———. "The Multiply Handicapped Child and Courageous Action." *The International Journal for the Education of the Blind* 13 (March 1964):65–75.

———. "An Interdisciplinary Model for Manpower Development for Mental Retardation." In *The Challenge of Mental Retardation in the Community,* edited by Julius Cohen. Institute for the Study of Mental Retardation and Related Disabilities, University of Michigan, Ann Arbor, Michigan, 1970.

———. "The Psychoeducational Match," In *Perceptual and Learning Disabilities in Children.* Vol. 1, *Psychoeducational Practices,* edited by W. M. Cruickshank and D. P. Hallahan. Syracuse: Syracuse University Press, 1975.

_____; Bentzen, F. A.; Ratzeburg, F. H.; and Tannhauser, M. T. *A Teaching Method for Brain-Injured and Hyperactive Children.* Syracuse: Syracuse University Press, 1961.

_____; Bice, H. V.; Wallen, N. E.; and Lynch, K. A. *Perception and Cerebral Palsy.* 2nd ed. Syracuse: Syracuse University Press, 1957.

_____, and Hallahan, D. P. *Perceptual and Learning Disabilities in Children.* Syracuse: Syracuse University Press, 1975.

_____, and Trippe, M. J. *Services to Blind Children in New York State.* Syracuse: Syracuse University Press, 1959.

Cruttenden, A. "A Phonetic Study of Babbling." *British Journal of Disorders of Communication* 5 (1970):110–17.

Crystal, D. "The Case of Linguistics: A Prognosis." *British Journal of Disorders of Communication* 7 (1972):3–16.

_____. "Linguistic Methology and the First Year of Life." *British Journal of Disorders of Communication* 8 (1973):29–36.

Culver, M. "Intergenerational Social Mobility Among Families with a Severely Mentally Retarded Child." Unpublished Ph.D. dissertation, University of Illinois, Urbana, 1967.

Cummings, T., and Stock, D. "Brief Group Therapy of Mothers of Retarded Children." *American Journal of Mental Deficiency* 66 (1962).

Curtis, L. W. *Vocational Placement of the Cerebral Palsied.* New York: New York City Cerebral Palsy Association, Inc., 1954.

Cypreanson, L. "An Investigation of the Breathing and Speech Coordinations and Speech Intelligibility of Normal Speaking Children and of Cerebral Palsied Children with Speech Defects." Unpublished doctoral dissertation, Syracuse University, 1953.

Cyrulik-Jacobs, A.; Shapira, Y.; and Jones, M. "Automatic Operant Response Procedure (Play Test) for the Study of Auditory Perception of Neurologically Impaired Infants." *Developmental Medicine and Child Neurology* 17 (2) (1975):186–97.

Darnell, R.E. "Concepts and Patterns of Interaction Among Professions Working with the Mentally Retarded—A Position Paper." *First Edition.* Institute for the Study of Mental Retardation and Related Disabilities, University of Michigan, Ann Arbor, Michigan, September, 1972.

_____. "The Promotion of Interest of the Physician Associate as a Potential Career Opportunity for Nurses—An Alternative Strategy." *Social Science and Medicine* 7 (1973):495–505.

Davies, H., and Kirman, B. H. "Microcephaly." *Archives of Diseases of Childhood* 37 (1962):623.

Davies, P. A.; Robinson, R. J.; Scopes, J. W.; Tizard, J. P. M.; and Wigglesworth, J. S. *Medical Care of Newborn Babies.* Philadelphia: Lippincott, 1972.

Davis, H. "Biophysics and Physiology of the Inner Ear." *Physiological Review* 37 (1957):1–49.

_____. "Guide for the Classification and Evaluation of Hearing Handicap in

Relation to the International Audiometric Zero." *Transcriptions of the American Academy of Ophthalmology and Otolaryngology* 69 (1965):740.

———, and Silverman, S. R. *Hearing and Deafness.* 3rd ed. New York: Holt, Rinehart, and Winston, 1970.

Dayan, M. "Toilet Training Retarded Children in a State Residential Institution." *Mental Retardation* 2 (2) (1964):116–17.

de Hirsh, K. "A Review of Early Language Development." *Developmental Medicine and Child Neurology* 12 (1) (1970):87–97.

de Hoop, W. "Listening Comprehension of Cerebral Palsied and Other Crippled Children as a Function of Two Speaking Rates." *Exceptional Children* 31 (1965):233–40.

Delagi, Edward F.; Abramson, Arthur S.; Ebel, Alfred; and Brent, Sidney Z. "Teamwork in Medicine." *American Archives of Rehabilitation Therapy* (March 1955).

Denhoff, E. "Cerebral Palsy." *New England Journal of Medicine* 245 (November 8 and 15, 1951):728–35; 770–77.

———. "Cerebral Palsy: Medical Aspects." In *Cerebral Palsy,* 2nd ed., edited by W. M. Cruickshank. Syracuse: Syracuse University Press, 1966.

———; D'Wolf, N.; and Komich, P. "The Meeting Street School Home Developmental Guidance Program: A Beacon for Future Early Educational Methods." In *Interdisciplinary Programming for Infants with Known or Suspected Cerebral Dysfunction,* edited by G. Hensley and W. Patterson. Boulder, Colo.: Western Interstate Commission for Higher Education, 1970.

———, and Holden, R. H. "Pediatric Aspects of Cerebral Palsy." *Journal of Pediatrics* 39 (1951):363–73.

———, and Holden, R. "Family Influence on Successful School Adjustment of Cerebral Palsied Children." *Journal of International Council of Exceptional Children* 21 (1954):5–7.

———, and Holden, R. H. "Relaxant Drugs in Cerebral Palsy, 1949–1960." *New England Journal of Medicine* 204 (1961):475–80.

———, and Robinault, I. P. *Cerebral Palsy and Related Disorders.* New York: McGraw-Hill, 1960.

———; Silver, M.; and Holden, R. H. "Prognostic Studies in Children with Cerebral Palsy." *Journal of the American Medical Association* 161 (1956):781–84.

———; Siqueland, M.; Komich, M.; and Hainsworth, P. "Development and Predictive Characteristics of Items from the Meeting Street School Screening Test." *Developmental Medicine and Child Neurology* 10 (2) (1968):220–32.

Denny, M. R. "A Theoretical Analysis and Its Application to Training the Mentally Retarded." In *International Review of Research in Mental Retardation,* edited by N. R. Ellis. Vol. 2. New York: Academic Press, 1966.

Deutsch, C. P. and Schumer, F. "Brain-damaged Children: A Modality Oriented Exploration of Performance." Final Report to Vocational Rehabilitation Administration. Washington, D.C.: U.S. Department of HEW, 1967.

Dishart, M. *Patterns of Rehabilitation Services Provided by the 90 State Vocational Rehabilitation Agencies of the United States.* Washington, D.C.: National Rehabilitation Association, 1964.

Dodd, B. "Effects of Social and Vocal Stimulation on Infant Babbling." *Developmental Psychology* 7 (1) (1972):80–83.

Dolphin, J., and Cruickshank, W. "Pathology of Concept Formation in Children with Cerebral Palsy." *American Journal of Mental Deficiency* 56 (1951).

———, and Cruickshank, W. M. "The Figure Background Relationship . . ." *Journal of Clinical Psychology* 7 (1951):228–31.

———, and Cruickshank, W. M. "Visuo-Motor Perception in Children with Cerebral Palsy." *Quarterly Journal of Child Behavior* 3 (1951).

———, and Cruickshank, W. M. "Tactual Motor Performance of Children with Cerebral Palsy." *Journal of Personality* 20 (1952):466–71.

Donlon, E.T. "Identification and Categorization of Descriptive Terms Used in the Evaluation of Deaf-Blind Children." Unpublished doctoral dissertation, Syracuse University, 1969.

———, and Burton, L.F. *An Introduction to the Severely and Multiply Handicapped.* New York: Grune and Stratton, 1976.

———, and Curtis, W. Scott. *The Development and Evaluation of A Video-Tape Protocol for the Examination of Multihandicapped Deaf-Blind Children.* Multiple Disability Project, Syracuse University, 1972.

Downey, K. "Parents' Reasons for Institutionalizing Severely Mentally Retarded Children." *Journal of Health and Human Behavior* 6 (1965):163–69.

Dunn, L. M., and Harley, R. K. "Comparability of Peabody, Ammons, Van Alstyne, and Columbia Test Scores with Cerebral Palsied Children." *Exceptional Children* 16 (1959):70–74.

Dunsdon, M. I. *The Educability of Cerebral Palsied Children.* London: Newnes, 1952.

Eimas, P.; Siqueland, F.; Jusczyk, P.; and Vigorito, J. "Speech Perception in Infants." *Science* 171 (1971):303–306.

Eisenberg, R. "Auditory Behavior in the Human Neonate: Functional Properties of Sound and Their Ontogenetic Implications." *International Audiology* (1969): 34–45.

———. "The Development of Hearing in Man." *American Speech and Hearing Association* 12 (1970):119–23.

———; Griffin, E.; Coursin, D.; and Hunter, A. "Auditory Behavior in the Human Neonate: A Preliminary Report." *Journal of Speech and Hearing Research* 7 (1964):245–69.

Ellis, N. R. "Toilet Training the Severely Defective Patient: An S-R Reinforcement Analysis." *American Journal of Mental Deficiency* 68 (1963):98–103.

———. "Memory Processes in Retardates and Normals." In *International Review of Research in Mental Retardation,* edited by N. R. Ellis. Vol. 4. New York: Academic Press, 1970.

Erikson, E. H. *Childhood and Society.* New York: Norton, 1963.

Evans, A. "Meet the Magne-Typer." *Journal of Rehabilitation* 26 (1960):32–33.

Farber, B. "Effects of a Severely Mentally Retarded Child on Family Integration." *Monographs of the Society for Research in Child Development* 75 (1960a).

———. "Perception of Crisis and Related Variables in the Impact of a Retarded Child on the Mother." *Journal of Health and Human Behavior* 1 (1960b): 108–18.

———. *Family: Organization and Interaction.* San Francisco: Chandler, 1964.

———. *Mental Retardation: Its Social Context and Social Consequences.* Boston: Houghton-Mifflin, 1968.

———. "Family Adaptations to Severely Mentally Retarded Children." Conference on Mentally Retarded in Society: A Social Science Perspective. Niles, Michigan, sponsored by NICHD and Albert Einstein Mental Retardation Center, Yeshiva University, 1974.

———, and Jenne, W. C. "Interaction with Retarded Siblings and Life Goals of Children." *Marriage and Family Living* 25 (1963):96–98.

Farmer, A. "A Phonetic and spectrographic Analysis of a Pre-Vocalization Phenomenon in Three Adult Cerebral Palsied Individuals Imitating Specifically Designed Sentences with Varied Phonetic Contexts." Unpublished doctoral dissertation, Syracuse University, 1972.

Fassler, J. "Performance of Cerebral Palsied Children Under Conditions of Reduced Auditory Input." *Exceptional Children* 37 (1970):201–209.

Fay, T. "The Use of Pathological and Unlocking Reflexes in the Rehabilitation of Spastics." *American Journal of Physical Medicine* 33 (1954):347–52.

Feallock, B. "Communication for the Non-Verbal Individual." *American Journal of Occupational Therapy* 12 (2) (1958):60–63.

Finnie, N. *Handling the Young Cerebral Palsied Child at Home.* New York: Dutton, 1970.

Fishman, S. R., et al. "The Status of Oral Health in Cerebral Palsy Children and Their Siblings." *Journal of Dentistry for Children* 34 (July 1967):219–27.

Fouracre, M. H., ed. *Realistic Educational Planning for Children with Cerebral Palsy: Pre-Elementary School Level,* Pamphlet No. 2. New York: United Cerebral Palsy Associations, 1952.

———, ed. *Realistic Educational Planning for Children with Cerebral Palsy: Post-Elementary Level,* Pamphlet No. 4. New York: United Cerebral Palsy Associations, 1953.

———, ed. *Realistic Educational Planning for Children with Cerebral Palsy: Psychological Evaluation,* Pamphlet No. 5. New York: United Cerebral Palsy Associations, 1953.

———, and Theil, E. A. "Education of Children with Mental Retardation Accompanying Cerebral Palsy." *American Journal of Mental Deficiency* 57 (1953):401–14.

Fox, L. A. "Preventive Dentistry for the Handicapped Child." *Pediatric Clinics of North America* 20 (1) (February 1973):245–58.

Free Peoples Clinic Informational Brochure. Ann Arbor, Michigan, 1972.

Freeman, R. D. "Controversy over 'Patterning' as a Treatment for Brain Damage in Children." *Journal of American Medical Association* 202 (1967):385–88.

Freeman, R. "Emotional Reactions of Handicapped Children." In *Social Work and Mental Retardation,* edited by Meyer Schreiber. New York: John Day, 1971.

Friedlander, B. "The Effects of Speech Identity, Voice Inflection, Vocabulary, Message Redundancy on Infants' Selection of Vocal Reinforcement." *Journal of Experimental Child Psychology* 6 (1968):443–59.

———. "Receptive Language Development in Infancy: Issues and Problems." *Merrill-Palmer Quarterly* 7 (1970):16.

_____. "Listening, Language, and the Auditory Environment: Automated Evaluation and Intervention." In *Exceptional Infant,* edited by J. Hellnauth. Vol. 2. New York: Brunner/Mazel, 1971.

_____, and Cyrulik-Jacobs, A. "Automated Home Measurement of Infants Preferential Discrimination of Loudness Level." Paper presented at annual meeting of the American Speech and Hearing Association, New York, 1970.

Friedman, P., ed. "A Report on Status of Current Court Cases." *Mental Retardation and the Law.* Washington: Office of Mental Retardation Coordination, April 1973.

Frostig, M. A. *Developmental Test of Visual Perception.* Palo Alto: Consulting Psychologists Press, 1964.

Fry, D. B. "The Development of the Phonological System in the Normal and Deaf Child." In *Genesis of Language,* edited by F. Smith and G. Miller. Cambridge, Mass.: MIT Press, 1966.

Gardner, R. "The Guilt Reaction of Parents of Children with Severe Physical Disease." In *Counseling Parents of the Ill and the Handicapped,* edited by Robert Noland. Springfield, Ill.: Thomas, 1971.

Gardner, W. I. "Effects of Interpolated Success and Failure on Motor Task Performance in Mental Defectives." Paper presented at the Southeast Psychological Association, Nashville, 1957.

_____. *Reactions of Intellectually Normal and Retarded Boys After Experimentally Induced Failure—A Social Learning Theory Interpretation.* Ann Arbor, Mich.: University Microfilms, 1958.

Gath, A. "The Mental Health of Siblings of a Congenitally Abnormal Child." *Journal of Child Psychology and Psychiatry* 13 (1972):211–18.

Gesell, A. L. *The First Five Years of Life.* New York: Harper and Row, 1940.

_____, and Amatruda, C. S. *Developmental Diagnosis.* New York: Hoeber, 1947.

Gettings, R.M. "The Impact of Politics in the Next Decade." In *Manpower Projections for Developmental Disabilities in the 1980's.* Developmental Disabilities Center, Temple University, Philadelphia, Pennsylvania, June, 1973.

Gillette, H. E. *Systems of Therapy in Cerebral Palsy.* Springfield, Illinois: Thomas, 1969.

Gilroy, J., and Meyer, J. S. *Medical Neurology.* Toronto: Macmillan, 1969.

Girardeau, F., and Spradlin, J. *A Functional Analysis Approach to Speech and Language.* ASHA Monographs No. 14. Washington, D.C.: American Speech and Hearing Association, 1970.

Goffman, E. *Stigma: Notes on Management of Spoiled Identity.* Englewood Cliffs, N.J.: Prentice-Hall, 1963.

Gold, M. W. "Research on the Vocational Habilitation of the Retarded: The Present, the Future." In *International Review of Research in Mental Retardation,* edited by N. R. Ellis. Vol. 6. New York: Academic Press, 1973*a.*

_____. "Factors Affecting Production." *Mental Retardation* 11 (6) (1973*b*):41–45.

Goldberg, H., and Fenton, J., eds. *Aphonic Communication for Those with Cerebral Palsy: Guide for the Development and Use of a Conversation Board.* New York: United Cerebral Palsy Association of New York State, 1961.

Goldberg, S., and Lewis, M. "Play Behavior in the Year Old Infant: Early Sex Differences." *Child Development* 40 (1969):21–31.

Goldstein, M. A. "The Acoustic Method for the Training of the Deaf and the Hard of Hearing Child." *Laryngoscope Press,* 1939.

Goldstein, R., and Kendall, A. "Electroencephalic Audiometry in Young Children." *Journal of Speech and Hearing Disorders* 28 (1963):331–54.

Goodman, L., and Rothman, R. "The Development of a Group Counseling Program in a Clinic for Retarded Children." *American Journal of Mental Deficiency* 65 (1961):789–95.

Gorton, C. E. "The Effects of Various Classroom Environments on Performance of a Mental Task by Mentally Retarded and Normal Children." *Education and Training of the Mentally Retarded* 7 (1) (1972):32–38.

Gray, B., and Ryan, B. *A Language Program for the Nonlanguage Child.* Champaign, Ill.: Research Press 1973.

Griffin, K. "Certain Auditory Perceptual Abilities in Selected Cerebral Palsied Children." Unpublished doctoral dissertation, University of Oregon, 1971.

Griffiths, M. I. "Cerebral Palsy in Multiple Pregnancy." *Developmental Medicine and Child Neurology* 9 (1967):713–31.

———, and Bassett, N. M. "Cerebral Palsy in Birmingham." *Developmental Medicine and Child Neurology* 9 (1967):33–46.

Grigg, C. M.; Holtmann, A. G.; and Martin, P. Y. *Vocational Rehabilitation for the Disadvantaged.* Lexington, Mass.: Heath, 1970.

Grossman, F.K. *Brothers and Sisters of Retarded Children.* Syracuse: Syracuse University Press, 1972.

Groves, I. D., and Carroccio, D. F. "A Selve-Feeding Program for the Severely and Profoundly Retarded." *Mental Retardation* 9 (3) (1971):10–12.

Guberina, P. "The Verbotonal Method: Questions and Answers." *Volta Review* 71 (1969):213–24.

Gudmondsson, K. R. "Cerebral Palsy in Iceland." *Acta Neurologica Scandinavica* 43 (1967): supplement 34.

Guidelines of the Committee on the Protection of the Rights of Human Subjects. School of Medicine, University of Michigan, Ann Arbor, Michigan.

Gustavson, K. H.; Hagberg, B.; and Sanner, G. "Identical Syndromes of Cerebral Palsy in the Same Family." *Acta Paediatrica Scandinavica* 58 (1969):330–40.

Hagberg, B.; Sonner, G.; and Steen, M. "The Dysequilibrium Syndrome in Cerebral Palsy." *Acta Paediatrica Scandinavica* Suppl. 226 (1972).

Hagen, C.; Porter, W.; and Brink, J. "Nonverbal Communication: An Alternate Mode of Communication for the Child with Severe Cerebral Palsy." *Journal of Speech and Hearing Disorders* 38 (4) (1973):448–55.

Hagen, J. W. "The Effect of Distraction on Selective Attention." *Child Development* 38 (1967):685–94.

———, and Huntsman, N. J. "Selective Attention in Mental Retardates." *Developmental Psychology* 5 (1971):151–60.

Hainsworth, P., and Siqueland, M. *Early Identification of Children with Learning Disabilities: The Meeting Street School Screening Test.* Providence, R.I.: Crippled Children and Adults of Rhode Island, 1969.

Hall, R. E., and Lehman, E. F. *Some Colleges and Universities with Special Facilities to Accommodate Handicapped Students.* Washington, D.C.: Office of Education, 1967.

Hallahan, D. P. "Distractibility in the Learning Disabled Child." In *Perceptual and Learning Disabilities in Children.* Vol. 2, *Research and Theory,* edited by W. M. Cruickshank and D. P. Hallahan. Syracuse: Syracuse University Press, 1975.

————, and Cruickshank, W. M. *Psychoeducational Foundations of Learning Disabilities.* Englewood Cliffs, N.J.: Prentice-Hall, 1973.

————; Kauffman, J. M.; and Ball, D. W. "Selective Attention and Cognitive Tempo of Low Achieving and High Achieving Sixth Grade Males." *Perceptual and Motor Skills* 36 (1973):579–83.

————; Stainback, S.; Ball, D. W.; and Kauffman, J. M. "Selective Attention in Cerebral Palsied and Normal Children." *Journal of Abnormal Child Psychology* 1 (1973):280–91.

Hamilton, K. W. *Counseling the Handicapped in the Rehabilitation Process.* New York: Ronald, 1950.

Handelbaum, Arthur, and Wheeler, Marry Ella. "The Meaning of a Defective Child to Parents." *Social Casework* (July 1960).

Hardy, J. "Intraoral Breath Pressure." *Journal of Speech and Hearing Disorders* 26 (4) (1961):309–19.

————, and Rembolt, R. "A Study of Breathing Patterns of Children with Cerebral Palsy." Unpublished paper presented at 1959 Convention of the American Academy for Cerebral Palsy.

Harford, E., and Dodds, E. "The Clinical Application of CROS." *Archives of Otolaryngology* 83 (1966):455–64.

Harper, L. "The Young as a Source of Stimuli Controlling Caretaker Behavior." *Developmental Psychology* 4 (1971):73–88.

Harrison, L. M. "Dentistry for Handicapped Children." *Journal of the Michigan State Dental Association* 45 (October 1964):277–85.

Haskell, P. H., and Anderson, E. M. "Some Aspects of the Psychological Assessment of Young Cerebral-Palsied and Brain-Damaged Children in Uganda." *Developmental Medicine and Child Neurology* 12 (1970):198–201.

Haskell, S. *Arithmetical Disabilities in Cerebral Palsied Children.* Springfield, Ill.: Thomas, 1973.

Hatten, J.; Goman, T.; and Lent, C. *Emerging Language.* Thousand Oaks, Calif.: The Learning Business, 1973.

Havighurst, R. J. *Developmental Tasks and Education.* New York: McKay, 1967.

Hayes, M., and Komick, M. P. "Development of Visual-Perceptual-Motor Function." In Banus, *The Developmental Therapist.* Thorofare, N.J.: Slack, 1971.

Heber, R. F. *Expectancy and Expectancy Changes in Normal and Mentally Retarded Boys.* Ann Arbor, Mich.: University Microfilms, 1957.

Henderson, J. L. *Cerebral Palsy in Childhood and Adolescence.* Edinburgh: Livingston, 1961.

Henriksen, K., and Doughtry, R. "Decelerating Undesirable Meal-time Behavior in a Group of Profoundly Retarded Boys." *American Journal of Mental Deficiency* 72 (1969): 40–44.

Herman, S. C., and McDonald, R. E. "Enamel Hypoplasia in Cerebral Palsied Children." *Journal of Dentistry for Children* 30 (1st quar., 1963):46–49.

Herrick, V. E.; Goodlad, J. I.; Estran, F. J.; and Eberman, P. W. *The Elementary School.* Englewood Cliffs, N.J.: Prentice-Hall, 1956.

Hillman, J. William. "Presidential Address to the American Academy for Cerebral Palsy, 1969." *Developmental Medicine and Child Neurology* 12 (1970):555–64.

Hirschenfang, S., and Benton, J. G. "Delayed Intellectual Development in CP Children." *The Journal of Psychology* 60 (1965):235–38.

Hirsh, I. J.; Davis, H.; Silverman, S. R.; Reynolds, E. G.; Eldert, E.; and Benson, R. "Development of Materials for Speech Audiometry." *Journal of Speech and Hearing Disorders* 17 (1952):321–37.

Hood, P., and Perlstein, M. "Infantile Spastic Hemiplegia V. Oral Language and Motor Development." *Pediatrics* 17 (1956):58–62.

Hope, M. J. "Program and Rationale for the Intervention of Sensory-Motor Dysfunction in the Young Infant." In Publication #1 *Studies in Sensory Integrative Dysfunction*. Center for Study of Sensory Integrative Dysfunction, 201 South Lake Avenue, Pasadena, California 91101 (1974).

Hopkins, T.; Bice, H. V.; and Colton, K. C. *Evaluation and Education of the Cerebral Palsied Child—New Jersey Study*. Washington, D.C.: International Council for Exceptional Children, 1954.

Horwitz, J. J., ed. *Team Practice and the Specialist: An Introduction to Interdisciplinary Team Work*. Springfield, Ill.: Thomas, 1970.

Hull, H. "A Study of the Respiration of Fourteen Spastic Paralysis Cases During Silence and Speech." *Journal of Speech and Hearing Disorders* 5 (1940): 275–76.

Institute for Crippled and Disabled. *Tower: Testing, Organization, and Work Evaluation*. New York: The Institute, 1967.

Irwin, O. "Acceleration of Infant Speech by Story Reading." In *Behavior in Infancy and Early Childhood*, edited by Y. Brackbill and G. Thompson. New York: The Free Press, 1967.

_____. *Communication Variables of Cerebral Palsied and Mentally Retarded Children*. Springfield, Ill.: Thomas, 1972.

_____, and Hammill, D. A. "A Second Comparison of Sound Discrimination of Cerebral Palsied and Mentally Retarded Children." Form B. *Cerebral Palsy Review* 26 (1965):3–6.

_____, and Jensen, P. J. "A Test of Sound Discrimination for Use with Cerebral Palsied Children." *Cerebral Palsy Review* 24 (1963a):5–11.

_____, and Jensen, P. J. "A Parallel Test for Sound Discrimination for Use with Cerebral Palsied Children." *Cerebral Palsy Review* 24 (1963b):3–10.

_____, and Jensen, P. J. "A Third Study of a Sound Discrimination Test for Use with Cerebral Palsied Children." *Cerebral Palsy Review* 25 (1964):3–7.

_____, and Korst, J. W. "Correlations among Five Speech Tests and the WISC Verbal Scale." *Cerebral Palsy Journal* 28 (1967):9–11.

Jenkin, R. "Possum: A New Communication Aid." *Special Education* 51 (1) (1967):9–11.

Jerger, J. "Bekesy Audiometry in Analysis of Auditory Disorders." *Journal of Speech and Hearing Research* 3 (1960):275–87.

_____, ed. *Modern Developments in Audiology*. 2nd ed. New York: Academic Press, 1973.

_____; Shedd, J.; and Harford, E. "On the Detection of Extremely Small Changes in Sound Intensity." *Archives of Otolaryngology* 69 (1959):200–11.

John, E. R. *Mechanisms of Memory.* New York: Academic Press, 1967.

Johnson, J. A. "Consideration of Work as Therapy in the Rehabilitation Process." *American Journal of Occupational Therapy* 25 (1971):303–304.

Johnson, V. M., and Werner, R. A. *A Step-by-Step Learning Guide for Retarded Infants and Children.* Syracuse: Syracuse University Press, 1975.

Joint Committee to Study the Problem of Cerebral Palsy. *Report to the Legislature of the State of New York.* Document No. 55 (1949) and Document No. 61 (1953), Albany, New York.

Jones, B., and Alexander, R. "Cross-Modal Matching by Spastic Children." *Developmental Medicine and Child Neurology* 16 (1974):40–46.

Jones, J. W. *The Visually Handicapped Child: At Home and School.* Washington: U.S. Dept. of Health Education and Welfare, 1963.

Jones, M.; Barrett, M.; Olonoff,. C.; and Andersen, E. "Two Experiments in Training Handicapped Children at Nursery School." In *Planning for Better Learning,* edited by P. Wolff and R. Mac Keith. Clinics in Developmental Medicine No. 33. London: Heinemann, 1969.

——; Wenner, W.; Toczek, A.; and Barrett, M. "Prenursery School Program for Children with Cerebral Palsy." *Journal of the American Medical Women's Association* 17 (9) (1962):713–19.

——, et al. "Pilot Study of Reading Problems in Cerebral Palsied Adults." *Developmental Medicine and Child Neurology* 8 (1966):417–27.

Jones, M. V. "Electrical Communication Devices." *American Journal of Occupational Therapy* 15 (3) (1961):11–111.

Josephy, J. "Brain in Cerebral Palsy: Neuropathologic Review." *Nervous Child* 8 (1949):152–60.

Kafafian, H. *Study of Man-Machine Communications Systems for the Handicapped.* Vols. I and II. Vol. III. Washington, D.C.: Cybernetics Research Institute, 1970, 1971.

Kagan, J. *Change and Continuity in Infancy.* New York, Wiley, 1971.

——. "Do Infants Think." *Scientific American* 266 (1972):74–82.

Kapur, R. N.; Girgis, S.; and Little, T. M. "Diphenylhydantoin Induced Gingival Hyperplasia: Its Relationship to Dose and Serum Level." *Developmental Medicine and Child Neurology* 15 (1973): 483–87.

Katz, J. "The Use of Staggered Spondaic Words for Assessing the Integrity of the Central Auditory Nervous System." *Journal of Audiology Research* 2 (1962):327.

——. "The SSW Test: An Interim Report." *Journal of Speech and Hearing Disorders* 33 (1968):132.

——; Myrick, D. W.; and Winn, B. "Central Auditory Dysfunction in Cerebral Palsy." Paper presented at ASHA convention, Washington, D.C., 1966.

Keith, R. A., and Markie, G. S. "Parental and Professional Assessment of Functioning in CP." *Developmental Medicine and Child Neurology* 11 (1969): 735–42.

Kenney, W. "Certain Sensory Defects in Cerebral Palsy." *Clinical Orthopaedics Related Research* 21 (1963):193–95.

Kephart, N. C. *The Slow Learner in the Classroom.* Columbus: Merrill, 1960.

_____. "The Perceptual-Motor Match." In *Perceptual and Learning Disabilities in Children,* Vol. 1, *Psychoeducational Practices,* edited by W. Cruickshank and D. Hallahan. Syracuse: Syracuse University Press, 1975.

Kessen, W., and Nelson, K. Paper presented at Piaget Society Symposium, Temple University, 1974.

Kilbane, E. "Pioneering in Dentistry for Those with Cerebral Palsy." *Cerebral Palsy Review* 18 (March–April 1972).

Kirk, S. A., and McCarthy, J. J. "The Illinois Test of Psycholinguistic Abilities— An Approach to Differential Diagnosis." *American Journal of Mental Deficiency* 66 (November 1961):399–412.

Klapper, Z. A., and Birch, H. G. "A Fourteen-Year Follow-up Study of Cerebral Palsy: Intellectual Change and Stability." *American Journal of Orthopsychiatry* 37 (1967):540–47.

_____, and Werner H. "Developmental Deviations in Brain-Injured (Cerebral Palsied) Members of Pairs of Identical Twins." *The Quarterly Journal of Child Behavior* 2 (1950):288–313.

Knott, M., and Voss, D. *Proprioceptive Neuromuscular Facilitation.* New York: Harper Bros., 1956; 2nd ed. 1968.

Kogan, K.; Tyler, N.; and Turner, P. "The Process of Interpersonal Adaptation Between Mothers and Their Cerebral Palsied Children." *Developmental Medicine and Child Neurology* 16 (4) (1974):518–27.

Köng, E. "Very Early Treatment of Cerebral Palsy." *Developmental Medicine and Child Neurology* 8 (2) (1966):198–02.

Koster, S. "The Diagnosis of Disorders of Occlusion in Children with Cerebral Palsy." *Journal of Dentistry for Children* 23 (2nd quar., 1956):81–83.

Kozier, A. "Casework with Parents of Children Born with Severe Birth Defects." *Social Casework* 38 (1957):183–89.

Krieger, D. "Attitudes Toward Physically Deviant Behavior and Social Class Membership of Significant Persons, and Social Responsibility in the Cerebral Palsied Adult." Unpublished doctoral dissertation, New York University, 1967.

Kroll, R. "The Effect of Premedication on Handicapped Children." *Journal of Dentistry for Children* 36 (March–April 1969):103–14.

Lagergren, J. "Motor Handicapped Children: A Study From a Swedish County." *Developmental Medicine and Child Neurology* 12 (1970):56–63.

Langworthy, O. R. *The Sensory Control of Posture and Movement: A Review of the Studies of Derek Denny-Brown.* Baltimore, Md.: Williams and Wilkins, 1970.

Lappin, C. W. "The Instructional Materials Reference Center for the Visually Handicapped." *Education for the Visually Handicapped* 4 (3 and 4) (October and December 1972):65–70, 101–107.

La Voy, R. "Risks Communicator." *Exceptional Children* 23 (1957):338–40.

Laycock, S. R. "Helping Parents to Accept Their Exceptional Children." *Cerebral Palsy Review* 13 (August 1952).

Lehman, H. E., and Hanrahan, G. E. "Chlorpromazine: New Inhibiting Agent for Psychomotor Excitement and Manic States." *Archives of Neurology and Psychiatry* 71 (1954):227–37.

Lencione, R. "A Study of the Speech Sound Ability and Intelligibility Status of a Group of Educable Cerebral Palsied Children." Unpublished doctoral dissertation, Northwestern University, 1953.

Lenneberg, E. *The Biological Foundations of Language.* New York: Willey, 1967.

Lennox, W. G. "Control of Seizures with Drugs." *Modern Medicine* 19 (1951):57–65, 95–126.

Levine, E. S. "Studies in Psychological Evaluation of the Deaf." *Volta Review* 65 (1963):496–510.

Lewis, M., and Spaulding, S. "Differential Cardiac Response to Visual and Auditory Stimulation in the Young Child." *Psychophysiology* 3 (3) (1967):229–37.

Lipsett, L. "Social Factors in Vocational Development." In *Vocational Guidance and Career Development,* edited by H. J. Peters and J. C. Hansen. New York: Macmillan, 1966.

Lipsitt, L. "Learning in the Human Infant." In *Early Behavior: Comparative and Developmental Approaches,* edited by H. Stevenson, E. Tess, and H. Rheingold. New York: Wiley, 1967.

Little, W. J. "Nature and Treatment of Deformities." *Lancet* 1 (1844):318.

_____. *Deformities of the Human Frame.* London: Longman, Brown, Green and Longmans, 1853.

_____. "On the Influence of Abnormal Parturition, Difficult Labor, Premature Birth, Asphyxia Neonatorum, on the Mental and Physical Condition of the Child, Especially in Relation to Deformities." *Trans. Obstetrical Society* (London) 3 (1862):293.

Livingston, E.; Kajda, L.; and Budge, E. M. "The Use of Benzedrine and Dexedrine Sulfate in the Treatment of Epilepsy." *Journal of Pediatrics* 32 (1949):490–94.

Llorens, L. A. "Facilitating Growth and Development: the Promise of Occupational Therapy." *American Journal of Occupational Therapy* 24 (1970):93–101.

_____. "Occupational Therapy in Community Child Health." *American Journal of Occupational Therapy* 25 (1971):335–39.

_____. "The Effects of Stress on Growth and Development." *American Journal of Occupational Therapy* 28 (1974):82–86.

Logue, R. D. "Visual Distractibility in Cerebral Palsy." *Cerebral Palsy Review* 26 (1965):9–11.

Love, N. "The Relative Occurrence of Secondary Disabilities in Children with Cerebral Palsy and Other Primary Physical Handicaps." *Exceptional Children* 37 (1970):301–302.

Love, R. "Oral Language Behavior of Cerebral Palsied Children." *Journal of Speech and Hearing Research* 7 (1964):349–59.

Lowenfeld, B. "Physchological Problems of Children with Impaired Vision." *Psychology of Exceptional Children and Youth,* edited by W. M. Cruickshank. Englewood Cliffs, N.J.: Prentice-Hall, 1963.

Luchsinger, R., and Arnold, G. *Voice, Speech and Language.* London: Constable, 1965.

Lurie, O. R. "Parents' Attitudes toward use of Mental Health Services." *American Journal of Orthopsychiatry* 44 (1974):109–20.

Luster, M. J. Cerebral Palsy Communication Group, University of Wisconsin, 922

ERB, 1500 Jackson Drive, Madison, Wisconsin, Personal Communication, 1974.

McConnell, B. "Survey of Undergraduate and Graduate Educational Exposure of Treating Handicapped Children in Dental Schools." *Proceedings of Curriculum Workshop on Undergraduates and Graduate Dental Education Concerning Dental Treatment of Handicapped People,* edited by J. Grewe. Minneapolis, 1967, pp. 40–48.

McDonald, E., and Chance, B. *Cerebral Palsy.* Englewood Cliffs, N.J.: Prentice-Hall, 1964.

_____, and Schultz, A. "Communication Boards for Cerebral Palsied Children." *Journal of Speech and Hearing Disorders* 38 (1) (1973):73–88.

McGraw, R. H. "Interdisciplinary Teamwork for Medical Care and Health Services." *Annals of Internal Medicine* 69 (4) (1968):812–35.

McNaughton, S. "Preliminary Survey of Ontario Crippled Children's Centre Symbol Communication Programme Users." Ontario Crippled Children's Centre, Canada, 1974.

McNeill, D. "The Development of Language." In Carmichael's *Manual of Child Psychology,* edited by P. Mussen. Vol. I. New York: Wiley, 1970.

Manual for Children's Dental Care Programs. Prepared by the Joint Committee on Dental Care Programs of the American Academy of Pedodontics and the American Society of Dentistry for Children. B. Johnson and W. Young, editors.

Marlow, M. E. "Spastics in Ordinary Schools." *Special Education* 57 (1968):8–13.

Marshall, E. D. "Teaching Materials." In *Perceptual and Learning Disabilities in Children.* Vol. 1, *Psychoeducational Practices,* edited by W. M. Cruickshank and D. P. Hallahan. Syracuse: Syracuse University Press, 1975.

Martin, G. L.; McDonald, S.; and Omichinski, M. "An Operant Analysis of Response Interactions During Meals with Severely Retarded Girls." *American Journal of Mental Deficiency* (76) (1971):68–75.

Massler, M., and Perlstein, M. A. "Neonatal and Prenatal Enamel Hypoplasia in Children with Cerebral Palsy." Workshop on Dentistry for the Handicapped Patient. University of Pennsylvania, School of Dentistry, September 1958.

Matsutsuyu, J. "Occupational Behavior: A Perspective on Work and Play." *American Journal of Occupational Therapy* 25 (1971):291–94.

Maurer, P. "Antecedents of Work Behavior." *American Journal of Occupational Therapy* 25 (1971):295–97.

Melcer, J. D. "Sensory-Motor Experience and Concept Formation in Early Childhood." Unpublished doctoral dissertation, University of Texas, 1966.

Menyuk, P. *The Development of Speech.* Indianapolis: Bobbs-Merrill, 1972.

Meyer, P. "A Comparison of Language Disabilities of Young Spastic and Athetoid Children." Unpublished doctoral dissertation, University of Texas, 1963.

Miller, A. S. "An Evaluation Method for Cerebral Palsy." *American Journal of Occupational Therapy* 9 (1955):105–11.

Miller, E., and Rosenfeld, G. "The Psychological Evaluation of Children with Cerebral Palsy and Its Implications in Treatment." *Journal of Pediatrics* 61 (1952):613–21.

Miller, H. C., and Hassinein, K. "Fetal Malnutrition: Maternal Factors." *Pediatrics* 52 (1973):504–12.

Miller, J., and Carpenter, C. "Electronics for Communication." *American Journal of Occupational Therapy* 18 (1) (1964):20–23.

Miller, J. B., and Taylor, P. P. "A Survey of the Oral Health of a Group of Orthopedically Handicapped Children." *Journal of Dentistry for Children* 37 (July–August 1970):331–43.

Milman, D. "Group Therapy with Parents: An Approach to the Rehabilitation of Physically Disabled Children." In *Counseling Parents of the Ill and the Handicapped,* edited by Robert Noland. Springfield, Ill.: Thomas, 1971.

Minear, W. C. "A Classification of Cerebral Palsy." *Pediatrics* 18 (1956):841–52.

Minze, M. R., and Ball, T. S. "Teaching Self-Help Skills to Profoundly Retarded Patients." *American Journal of Mental Deficiency* 71 (1967):864–68.

Moffitt, A. "Consonant Cue Perception by Twenty to Twenty-Four-Week-Old Infants." *Child Development* 42 (1971):717–31.

Monsees, E. *Structured Language for Children with Special Language Learning Problems.* Washington, D.C.: Children's Hospital of the District of Columbia, 1972.

Moore, J. C. Unpublished lecture notes, Workshop for Rehabilitation Personnel in Sensorimotor Treatment Techniques, University of Missouri, St. Louis, June 12–16, 1973.

Moore, M. "A Demonstration of Three Models of Advocacy for Developmentally Disabled Children." New York: United Cerebral Palsy Association, 1974.

Mosey, A. *Occupational Therapy: Theory and Practice.* Medford: Pothier Brothers, 1968.

Mowrer, O. *Learning Theory and the Symbolic Process.* New York: Wiley, 1960.

Mueller, H. "Facilitating Feeding and Pre-Speech." In *Physical Therapy Services in the Developmental Disabilities,* edited by P. Pearson and C. Williams. Springfield, Ill.: Thomas, 1972.

Muller, H. "Feeding" and "Speech." In *Handling the Young Cerebral Palsied Child,* 2nd ed. London: Heinemann, 1974.

Musick, J. K., and Luckey, R. E. "A Token Economy for Moderately and Severely Retarded." *Mental Retardation* 8 (1970):35–36.

Muthard, J., and Hutchinson, J. *Cerebral Palsied College Students—Their Education and Employment.* Gainesville: University of Florida Press, 1968.

Myers, P. "A Study of Language Disabilities in Cerebral Palsied Children." *Journal of Speech and Hearing Research* 8 (1965):129–36.

Myklebust, H. R. *The Psychology of Deafness,* 2nd ed. New York: Grune and Stratton, 1964.

Mysak, E. "Cerebral Palsy Speech Syndromes." In *Handbook of Speech Pathology and Audiology,* edited by L. Travis. New York: Appleton-Century-Crofts, 1971*a*.

Nakano, T. "Research on Hearing Impairment in Cerebral Infantile Palsied School Children." *International Audiology* 5 (1966):159–61.

Neisser, M. "The Sense of Self Expressed Through Giving and Receiving." *Social Casework* 54 (5) (1973):294–301.

Nelson, N. *Workshops for the Handicapped in the United States.* Springfield, Ill.: Thomas, 1971.

Netzell, R. "Evaluation of Velopharyngeal Function in Dysarthia." *Journal of Speech and Hearing Disorders* 34 (2) (1969a):113–22.

_____. "Changes in Oropharyngeal Cavity Size of Dysarthric Children." *Journal of Speech and Hearing Disorders* 2 (3) (1969b):646–49.

Newland, T. E. "Psychological Assessment of Exceptional Children and Youth." In *Psychology of Exceptional Children and Youth,* 3rd ed., edited by W. M. Cruickshank. Englewood Cliffs, N.J.: Prentice-Hall 1971.

Newman, G. S. *Facts in Brief—No. 4—Persons with Cerebral Palsy.* Albany: Division of Vocational Rehabilitation, 1963.

Neye, R. L.; Blanc, W.; and Paul, C. "Maternal Nutrition and the Fetus." *Pediatrics* 52 (1973):494–503.

Nicholson, C. L. "Correlations among CMMS, PPVT, and RCPM for Cerebral Palsy Children." *Perceptual and Motor Skills* 30 (1970):715–18.

Nielsen, H. H. *A Psychological Study of Cerebral Palsied Children.* Copenhagen: Munksgaard, 1966.

_____. "Psychological Appraisal of Children with Cerebral Palsy: A Survey of 128 Reassessed Cases." *Developmental Medicine and Child Neurology* 13 (1971):707–20.

Nober, E. H. "GSR Magnitudes for Different Intensities of Shock, Conditional Tone, and Extinction Tone." *Journal of Speech and Hearing Research* 1 (1958):316–24.

_____. "Pure Tone Air Conduction Thresholds of Deaf Children." *Volta Review* 65 (1963):229–41.

_____. "Pseudoauditory Bone-Conduction Thresholds." *Journal of Speech and Hearing Disorders* 29 (1964):469–76.

_____. "Physiogenic Auditory Problems in Adults." In *Speech Pathology,* edited by R. Rieber and R. Brubaker. North Holland Publishing Co., 1966.

_____. "Vibrotactile Sensitivity of Deaf Children to High Intensity Sound." *Laryngoscope* 12 (1967):2128–46.

_____. "Cutile Air and Bone Conduction Thresholds of the Deaf." *Exceptional Children* (April 1970):571–79.

_____. "Nonauditory Effects of Noise." *Maico Audiological Series* 12 (6) (1974a):1–6.

_____. "Noise Doesn't Just Harm Hearing." *International Journal of Occupational Health and Safety* 43 (1974b):13–18.

Nober, L. W., ed. "The HI-FI Program (Hearing Impaired Formal In-Service Program)." Amherst, Mass.: Northeast Regional Media Center for the Deaf. 1974.

Nolan, C. Y., and Bott, Joan E. "Relationship Between Visual Acuity and Reading Medium for Blind Children." *New Outlook for the Blind* 65 (March 1971):31, 90–96.

Northern, J., and Downs, M. *Hearing in Children.* Baltimore: Williams and Wilkins, 1974.

Nussbaum, J. "Self-Concept of Adolescent with Cerebral Palsy." *Cerebral Palsy Journal* 27 (1966):5–7.

Olson, J. L.; Hahn, H. R.; and Hermann, A. L. "Psycholinguistic Curriculum." *Mental Retardation* 3 (April 1965):14–19.

Osgood, C. E. "A Behavioristic Analysis." In *Contemporary Approaches to Cognition.* Cambridge, Mass.: Harvard University Press, 1957.

———. "Motivational Dynamics of Language Behavior." *Nebraska Symposium on Motivation.* Lincoln: University of Nebraska Press, 1957.

———, and Sebeok, T. *Psycholinguistics: A Survey of Theory and Research Problems.* Bloomington, Ind.: Indiana University Press, 1965.

Owen, G. "Case Management vs. Direct Delivery of Services: A Policy Position." Wayne County Referral Center, Detroit, Mich., May 1974.

———. "Wayne County Regional Referral Center: Goals and Objectives." Detroit, Mich., November 1974.

Paine, R. S. "On the Treatment of Cerebral Palsy." *Pediatrics* 29 (1962):605–16.

———; Brazelton, T. B.; Donovan, D. E.; Drosbaugh, J. E.; Hubbell, J. P.; and Sears, E. M. "Evolution of Postural Reflexes in Normal Infants and in the Presence of Chronic Brain Syndromes." *Neurology* 14 (1964):1036.

Papousek, H. "Conditioning During Early Postnatal Development." In *Behavior in Infancy and Early Childhood,* edited by Y. Brackbill and G. Thompson. New York: The Free Press, 1967.

Patel, S., and Bharucha, E. P. "The Bender Gestalt Test as a Measure of Perceptual and Visuo-Motor Defects in Cerebral Palsied Children." *Developmental Medicine and Child Neurology* 14 (1972):156–60.

Pattison, H. A. *The Handicapped and Their Rehabilitation.* Springfield, Ill.: Thomas, 1957; Chapter 17, "The Rehabilitation Team."

Pearson, P. H., and Williams, C. E., eds., *Physical Therapy Services in the Developmental Disabilities.* Springfield, Illinois: Thomas, 1972.

Peiper, A. *Cerebral Function in Infancy and Childhood.* New York: Consultant's Bureau, 1963.

Perlstein, M. A. "Medical Aspects of Cerebral Palsy." *Nervous Child* 8 (1949): 125–51.

———. "Infantile Cerebral Palsy: Classification and Clinical Correlations." *Journal of the American Medical Association* 149 (1952):30–34.

———, and Barnett, H. E. "Nature and Recognition of Cerebral Palsy in Infancy." *Journal of the American Medical Association* 148 (April 1952):1389–97.

———; Gibbs, E. L.; and Gibbs, F. A. "The Electroencephalogram in Infantile Cerebral Palsy." *Proceedings of Research in Nervous and Mental Diseases* 26 (1947):377–84.

———, and Shere, M. "Speech Therapy for Children with Cerebral Palsy." *American Journal of Diseases of Children* 72 (1946):389–98.

Perry, W. J. "Career Mobility in Allied Health Education." *Journal of the American Medical Association* 210 (1) (1969):107–10.

Phelps, W. M. "Let's Define Cerebral Palsy." *Crippled Children* 26 (1948):3–5.

———. "Cerebral Palsy." *Nervous Child* 8 (1949):107–27.

———. "The Cerebral Palsies." In *Textbook of Pediatrics,* edited by Mitchell-Nelson, 5th ed. New York: Saunders, 1950.

Piaget, J. *The Origins of Intelligence in the Child.* New York: International University Press, 1952.

Pigasson-Albany, R., and Fleming, A. "Amblyopia and Strabismus in Patients with Cerebral Palsy." *Annals of Ophthalmology* 7 (2) (March 1975):382–87.

Place, D.H. "Vocational Rehabilitation of the Disabled Disadvantaged." In *Special Problems in Rehabilitation,* edited by A. B. Cobb. Springfield, Ill.: Thomas, 1974.

Prechtl, H., and Bientema, D. *The Neurological Examination of the Full Term Newborn Infant.* London: Heinemann, 1964.

Rafael, B. "Early Education for Multihandicapped Children." *Children Today* 2 (1973):22–27.

Rathbone, J. L., and Lucas, C. *Recreation in Total Rehabilitation.* Springfield, Ill.: Thomas, 1959.

Rehabilitation Services Administration. *Characteristics of Clients Rehabilitated in Fiscal Years 1968-1972.* Washington, D.C.: U.S. Dept. of HEW, undated.

Reilly, M. "The Educational Process." *American Journal of Occupational Therapy* 23 (1969):299–307.

Rheingold, H.; Gewirtz, J.; and Ross, H. "Social Conditioning of Vocalizations in the Infant." *Journal of Comparative Physiology* 52 (1959):68–73.

Rhodes, W. C., and Tracy, M. L. "A Study of Child Variance." Institute for the Study of Mental Retardation and Related Disabilities, University of Michigan, Ann Arbor, Michigan, 1972.

Richmond, R. O., and Dalton, J. L. "Teacher Ratings and Self-Concept Reports of Retarded Pupils." *Exceptional Children* 40 (1973):178–83.

Riviere, M. *Rehabilitation Codes: Classification of Impairment of Visual Functioning.* Final Report. New York: Rehabilitation-Codes, 1970.

Roach, E. G., and Kephart, N.C. *The Purdue Perceptual-Motor Survey.* Columbus, Ohio: Merrill, 1966.

Robinault, I. P., and Denhoff, E. "The Multiple Dysfunctions called Cerebral Palsy." In *Medical and Psychological Aspects of Disability,* edited by A. B. Cobb. Springfield, Ill.: Thomas, 1973.

Robinson, H. "Research in Cognition: Implications for Early Care." In *Interdisciplinary Programming for Infants with Known or Suspected Cerebral Dysfunction,* edited by G. Hensley and V. Patterson. Boulder, Colo.: Western Interstate Commission for Higher Education, 1970.

――――, and Robinson, N. M. *The Mentally Retarded Child: A Psychological Approach.* New York: McGraw-Hill, 1965.

Roghmann, K. J.; Hecht, P. K.; and Haggerty, R. J. "Family Coping with Everyday Illness: Self Reports from a Household Survey." *Journal of Comparative Family Studies* 4 (1973):49–62.

Rood, M. S. "Neurophysiologic Reaction as a Basis for Physical Therapy." *Physical Therapy Review* 34 (1954):444–49.

Rosenberg, B. "The Use of Work Samples for the Cerebral Palsied." *Vocational Evaluation and Work Adjustment Bulletin* 5 (1) (1972):18–21.

Rosso, P., and Winick, M. "Relation of Nutrition to Physical and Mental Development." *Pediatric Annals, Malnutrition, Growth, and Development* 2 (1973):10–17.

Routh, D. "The Conditioning of Vocal Response Differential in Infants." Unpublished doctoral dissertation, University of Pittsburgh, 1967.

Rusalem, H. *Guiding the Physically Handicapped College Student.* New York: Teachers College Publications, 1962.

Ruszczynska; Sulestrowska; Jankowicz; and Szelozynska. "Difficulties in the Assessment of Mental Development in Children With the Extra-pyramidal Form of Infantile Cerebral Palsy." *Polish Medical Journal* 2 (1972):208–12.

Schaefer, E. S. "A Circumplex Model for Maternal Behavior." *Journal of Abnormal and Social Psychology* 59 (1959):226–35.

————. "Factors that Impede the Process of Socialization." Conference on Mentally Retarded in Society: A Social Science Perspective. Niles, Michigan, sponsored by NICHD and Albert Einstein Mental Retardation Center, Yeshiva University, 1974.

Schaltenbrand, G. "The Development of Human Mobility and Motor Disturbances." *Archives of Neurology and Psychiatry* 20 (1928):720–30.

Schermann, A. "Cognitive Goals in the Nursery Schools." *Child Study* 28 (2) (1966):15.

Schlesinger, H., and Meadow, K. *Sound and Sign.* Berkeley: University of California Press, 1972.

Sedlackova, P. "Acoustic Composition of Infant Vocal Manifestations During the Period of Lallation." *Folia Phoniatrica* 19 (1967):351.

Segal, R. *Mental Retardation and Social Action.* Springfield, Ill.: Thomas, 1970.

Selwyn, D., Director, National Institute for Rehabilitation Engineering, Pompton Lakes, New Jersey. Personal Correspondence, 1974.

Shane, H. "A Device and a Program for Aphonic Communication." Unpublished Master's thesis, University of Massachusetts, 1972.

Shapira, Y.; Jacobs, A.; Bisno, A.; and Jones, M. "Objective Evaluation of Receptive Language in Infants with Motor and/or Sensory Deficits." Paper presented at the 27th Annual Meeting of the American Academy for Cerebral Palsy, Washington, D.C., 1973.

Shaw, M. C. "A Study of Certain Aspects of Perception and Conception Thinking in Idiopathic Epileptic Children." Unpublished doctoral dissertation, Syracuse University, 1955.

Shere, M. O. "An Evaluation of the Social and Emotional Development of the Cerebral Palsied Twin." Unpublished doctoral dissertation, College of Education, University of Illinois, 1954.

————. "Socio-emotional Factors in Families of the Twin with Cerebral Palsy." *Exceptional Children* 22 (1955).

Shere, E., and Kastenbaum, R. "Mother-Child Interaction in Cerebral Palsy: Environmental and Psychosocial Obstacles to Cognitive Development." *Genetic Psychology Monographs* 73 (1966):255–335.

Shearer, Ann. "A Right to Live." London: Spastic Society and National Association for Mental Health, May 1972.

Sherrington, C. S. *The Integrative Action of the Nervous System.* New Haven: Yale University Press, 1947.

Shochi, K. "An Analytical Study of Visual-Motor Function in Cerebral Palsied Children." *Japanese Journal of Psychology* 42 (1971):55–66.

Shotick, A. L., and Ray, A. B., Jr. "Speculations on Behavioral and Biological Processes Involved in Learning and Memory." Paper presented at the Seventh Annual Gatlinburg Conference on Research and Theory in Mental Retardation, Gatlinburg, Tenn., 1974.

Shotick, A. L., and Rhoden, J. O. "A Unitary Approach: Programming for the Mentally Retarded." *Mental Retardation* 11 (1) (1973):35–38.

Shurtleff, D. B. "Transillumination of the Skull in Infants." *American Journal of Diseases of Children* 107 (1964):14–24.

Siege, M. "Congenital Malformations Following Chickenpox, Measles, Mumps, and Hepatitis." *Journal of the American Medical Association* 226 (1973):1, 521–24.

Siegel, G. "Vocal Conditioning in Infants." *Journal of Speech and Hearing Disorders* 34 (1) (1969):3–19.

Simpson, S. A. "Perceptual Functions in Cerebral-Palsied Children." Unpublished doctoral dissertation, Yeshiva University, 1967.

Siqueland, E. "Basic Learning Process." In *Experimental Child Psychology: The Scientific Study of Child Behavior and Development,* edited by H. Reese and L. Lipsitt. New York: Academic Press, 1970.

Skinner, B. *Verbal Behavior.* New York: Appleton-Century-Crofts, 1957.

Smith, V. H. "A Survey of Strabismus in Cerebral Palsy." *Visual Disorders and Cerebral Palsy,* edited by V. H. Smith. London: Medical Books, 1963.

Solem, A. R. "An Evaluation of Two Attitudinal Approaches to Delegation." *Journal of Applied Psychology* 42 (1) (1958):36–39.

Steinberg, A. D., and Bramer, M. L. "A New Concept in Extra and Intra-Oral Radiographs." *Journal of Dentistry for Children* 21 (1st quar., 1964):34–37.

Sterritt, G. M. and Rudnick, M. "Reply to Birch and Belmont." *Perceptual and Motor Skills* 22 (1966):662.

Strauss, A. A., and Lehtinen, L. *Psychopathology and Education of the Brain-Injured Child.* New York: Grune and Stratton, 1949.

———, and Werner, H. "Disorders of Conceptual Thinking in the Brain-Injured Child." *Journal of Nervous and Mental Disease* 96 (1942):153–72.

———, and Werner, H. "Impairment in Thought Processes of Brain-Injured Children." *American Journal of Mental Deficiency* 47 (1943):291–95.

Strother, C. "The Role of the Psychologist in Programming for Infants with Known or Suspected Cerebral Dysfunction." In *Interdisciplinary Programming for Infants with Known or Suspected Cerebral Dysfunction,* edited by G. Hensley and V. Patterson. Boulder, Colo.: Western Interstate Commission for Higher Education, 1970.

Sukiennicki, D. A. "Neuromotor Development." In *Developmental Therapist,* edited by B. S. Banus. Thorofare, N.J.: Slack, 1971.

Sussman, M. B. "Occupational Sociology and Rehabilitation." In *Sociology and Rehabilitation,* edited by M. B. Sussman. American Sociological Association, 1965.

Swallow, J. N. "Dental Disease in Cerebral Palsied Children." *Developmental Medicine and Child Neurology* 10 (2) (April 1968):180–89.

Swartz, R. P., *et al.* "Motivation of Children with Multiple Functional Disabilities." *Journal of the American Medical Association* 145 (1951):951–55.

Swinyard, C. "Developmental Aspects of Neurological Structure Relevant to Cerebral Palsy." *Developmental Medicine and Child Neurology* 9 (2) (1967):216–21.

Tabary, J. C., and Faillot, M. F. "Evolution du quotient intellectuel chez les enfants infirmes moteurs cerebraus an cours de la re-education." *Revue de Neuropsychiatrie it d'Hygiene Mentale de l'Enfant* 15 (1967):725–36.

Tachdjian, M., and Minear, W. "Sensory Disturbances in the Hands of Children with Cerebral Palsy." *Journal of Bone Joint Surgery* 40A (1958):85–90.

Taft, L. T. "Early Recognition of Cerebral Palsy." *Pediatric Annals* 2 (1973):30.

Taibl, R. M. "An Investigation of Raven's 'Progressive Matrices' as a Tool for the Psychological Evaluation of Cerebral Palsied Children." Unpublished doctoral dissertation, University of Nebraska, 1951.

Terman, L. M., and Merrill, M. A. *Measuring Intelligence.* Boston: Houghton Mifflin, 1937.

Thelander, H. "A Preschool Cerebral Palsy Program." *Journal of American Medical Women's Association* 9 (1954):157–59.

―――, and Phelps, J. "Programming for Children with Neurological Deficits." *Journal of Pediatrics* 58 (1961):389–91.

Tisdall, W. J. "Productive Thinking in Retarded Children." *Exceptional Children* 29 (1962):36–41.

Tizard, T.; Paine, R.; and Crothers, B. "Disturbances of Sensation in Children with Hemiplegia." *Journal of the American Medical Association* 155 (1954):628–32.

Todd, G., and Palmer, B. "Social Reinforcement of Infant Babbling." *Child Development* 39 (1968):591–96.

Towbin, A. "Organic Causes of Minimal Brain Dysfunction." *Journal of the American Medical Association* 217 (1971):1201–13.

Towle, Charlotte. "The Handicapped Also Are People." In *Social Work and Mental Retardation,* edited by M. Schrieber. New York: John Day, 1971.

Una, R. K. "The Role of Pharmacotherapy in Abnormal Muscular States and Abnormal Movements in Patients with Cerebral Palsy." *Quarterly Review of Pediatrics* 2 (1953):149–56.

United States Department of Health, Education, and Welfare. *Human Investment Programs: Delivery of Health Services for the Poor.* Washington, D.C.: US GPO, 1967.

Vanderheiden, G., Director, Cerebral Palsy Communication Group, University of Wisconsin, 922 ERB, 1500 Jackson Drive, Madison, Wisconsin, 1974.

Van Riper, C. *Speech Correction Principles and Methods,* 3rd ed. Englewood Cliffs, N.J.: Prentice-Hall, 1954.

Vassella, F. "Organization of Measures for Early Detection and Treatment of Cerebral Palsy in Berne." *Developmental Medicine and Child Neurology* 8 (2) (1966):195–202.

―――, and Karlsson, B. "Asymmetrical Tonic Neck Reflex." *Developmental Medicine and Child Neurology* 4 (1963):363–69.

Vicker, B., ed. *Nonoral Communication System Project.* Iowa City: Campus Stores, Publishers, 1974.

Voysey, M. "Impression Management by Parents with Disabled Children." *Journal of Health and Social Behavior* 13 (1972):80–89.

Warters, J. *Group Guidance.* New York: McGraw-Hill, 1960.

Watson, A. O. "Infantile Cerebral Palsy." *Dental Journal of Australia* 27 (1):6–14; 27 (2):72–83; 27 (3):93–102.

Weaver, E., and Lawrence, M. *Physiological Acoustics.* Princeton, N.J.: Princeton University Press, 1954.

Webster, R. "Selective Suppression of Infant Vocal Response by Classes of Phonemic Stimulation." *Developmental Psychology* 4 (1969):410–14.

———; Steinhardt, M.; and Senter, M. "Changes in Infants' Vocalizations as a Function of Differential Acoustic Stimulation." *Developmental Psychology* 7 (1) (1972):39–43.

Wedell, K.; Newman, C.; Reid, P.; and Bradbury, I. "An Exploratory Study of the Relationship Between Size Constancy and Experiences of Mobility in Cerebral Palsied Children." *Developmental Medicine and Child Neurology* 14 (5) (1972):615–20.

Wedenberg, E., and Wedenberg, M. "The Advantage of Auditory Training: A Case Report." In *The Hard of Hearing Child,* edited by Berg and Fletcher.

Weinrich, E. Grant Proposal: "A Demonstration of Three Models of Advocacy for Developmentally Disabled Children." New York: United Cerebral Palsy Association, 1972.

———. "State of the Project: A Progress Report of the Child Advocacy Project— A Demonstration of Three Models of Advocacy Programs for Developmentally Disabled Children." New York: United Cerebral Palsy Association, September 1973.

Weinrott, M. R. "A Training Program in Behavior Modification for Siblings of the Retarded." *American Journal of Orthopsychiatry* 44 (1974):362–75.

Weir, R. "Some Questions on the Child's Learning of Phonology." In *The Genesis of Language,* edited by F. Smith and G. Miller. Cambridge, Mass.: MIT Press, 1966.

Wepman, J. M.; Jones, L. V.; Bock, R. D.; and Pelt, D. V. "Studies in Aphasia: Background and Theoretical Formulations." *Journal of Speech and Hearing Disorders* 25 (November 1960):323–32.

West, R.; Ansberry, M.; and Carr, A. *The Rehabilitation of Speech,* 3rd ed. New York: Harper and Brothers, 1957.

Westlake, H., and Rutherford, D. *Speech Therapy for the Cerebral Palsied.* Chicago: National Society for Crippled Children and Adults, 1961.

White, B. *Human Infants.* Englewood Cliffs, N.J.: Prentice-Hall, 1971.

White, R. E. "Motivation Reconsidered: The Concept of Competence." *Psychological Review* 66 (1959):297–333.

———. "The Urge Towards Competence." *American Journal of Occupational Therapy* 25 (1971):271–74.

Whittaker, J. S. "Therapy Integrated with Teaching in the Treatment of Cerebral Palsy." *Scandinavian Journal of Rehabilitation Medicine* 3 (1971):64–66.

Williams, T. M. "Childrearing Practices of Young Mothers." *American Journal of Orthopsychiatry* 44 (1974):70–75.

Wineman, D., and James, A. "The Advocacy Challenge to Schools of Social Work." *Social Work* 14 (April 1969):23–32.

Winitz, H. *Articulatory Acquisition and Behavior.* New York: Appleton-Century-Crofts, 1960.

Wohlwill, J. "Developmental Studies of Perception." *Psychology Bulletin* 57 (1960):60.

Wolfe, W. "A Comprehensive Evaluation of Fifty Cases of Cerebral Palsy." *Journal of Speech and Hearing Disorders* 15 (1950):234–51.

Wright, B. A. *Physical Disability—A Psychological Approach.* New York: Harper and Row, 1960.

Wright, G. N., and Butler, A. J. *Rehabilitation Counselor Functions: Annotated References.* Madison: University of Wisconsin, 1968.

Wynne, L. C.; Ryckoff, I. M.; Day, J.; and Hirsch, S. I. "Pseudo-Mutuality in the Family Relations of Schizophrenics." *Psychiatry* 21 (1958):205–20.

Yannet, H. "Infantile Cerebral Palsy Cases with Severe Mental Deficiency." *Pediatrics* 6 (1949):820–23.

Yarrow, L.; Rubenstein, J.; Pedersen, F.; and Jankowski, J. "Dimensions of Early Stimulation and Their Differential Effects on Infant Development." *Merrill-Palmer Quarterly* 18 (1972):205–18.

Yeni-Komshian, G.; Chase, R.; and Mobley, R. "The Development of Auditory Feedback Monitoring" II. Delayed Auditory Feedback Studies of the Speech of Children Between Two and Three Years of Age." *Journal of Speech and Hearing Research* 2 (2) (1968):307–15.

Zivkovic, M.; Glogorijevic, B.; and Racic, R. "Methodological Approach to the Study of Cerebral Palsy in Belgrade." *Italian Archives of Pediatrics* 25 (1967):13–16.

Index

CEREBRAL PALSY

A Developmental Disability

Third Revised Edition

was composed in 10-point Datapoint Times Roman, leaded two points,
with display type in Photon Univers and Times New Roman,
and printed offset on 50-pound Maxopaque by Science Press;
cover printed on Columbia's Apollo by
Vicks Lithograph and Printing Corporation;
Smyth-sewn and bound
over boards by Vail-Ballou Press;
and published by

SYRACUSE UNIVERSITY PRESS

Syracuse, New York 13210